R. Gupta's®

POPULAR MASTER GUIDE

HTET

HARYANA TEACHER ELIGIBILITY TEST

LEVEL–III

Post Graduate Teacher (PGT)

COMMON SUBJECTS

- Child Development & Pedagogy • Hindi • English • Quantitative Aptitude
- Reasoning Ability • Haryana GK & Awareness

by

RPH Editorial Board

2026 EDITION

RAMESH PUBLISHING HOUSE, NEW DELHI

Published by
O.P. Gupta *for* Ramesh Publishing House

Admin. Office
12-H, New Daryaganj Road, Opp. Officers' Mess,
New Delhi-110002 ✆ 23275224, 23245124

E-mail: info@rameshpublishinghouse.com
For Online Shopping: www.rameshpublishinghouse.com

Showroom
• Balaji Market, Nai Sarak, Delhi-110006 ✆ 23282525 📱 9354373464
• 4457, Nai Sarak, Delhi-110006

Book Code: R-1593

ISBN: 978-93-5477-798-1

Price: ₹ 340

Printed at: B.K. Offset, Delhi

CONTENTS

Scheme of Exam

Level-3: Post Graduate Teacher (PGT)

S.No.	Subjects	No. of Questions	Marks
1.	Child Development and Pedagogy	30	30
2.	**Languages** (Hindi 15 MCQs and English 15 MCQs)	30	30
3.	**General Studies** (Quantitative Aptitude 10 MCQs, Reasoning Ability 10 MCQs and Haryana G.K. and Awareness 10 MCQs)	30	30
4.	Subject Specific	60	60
	Total	**150**	**150**

NATURE AND STANDARD OF QUESTIONS

- The test items on Child Development and Pedagogy will focus on educational psychology of teaching and learning, relevant to the age group of 14-17 years. They will focus on understanding the characteristics, needs and psychology of diverse learners, interaction with learners and the attributes and qualities of a good facilitator of learning.
- The test items for Languages (Hindi & English) will focus on the proficiencies related to the medium of instruction relevant to the age group of 14-17 years.
- The test items for Quantitative Aptitude, Reasoning Ability and Haryana G.K. and Awareness Language will focus on the elements of Mental and Reasoning ability and General Knowledge regarding Haryana State.
- The test items in subject specific will focus on the concepts, problem solving abilities and pedagogical understanding of these subjects.

NEGATIVE MARKING

- There shall be no negative marking.

LANGUAGE OF QUESTION PAPERS

- All questions except those concerning language subjects, will be bilingual *i.e.* Hindi and English.

Previous Years' Paper

Haryana Teacher Eligibility Test (HTET)

PGT (Level-3), Common Subjects, Exam–2024

(Exam held on 30-07-2025)

PART-I

Child Development and Pedagogy

1. Which statement is **incorrect** about the development and its relationship with learning?
1. Deprivation of learning opportunities limits development.
2. Children can not learn until they are developmentally ready to learn.
3. Development is the product of maturation and learning.
4. Despite the limits of maturation the development can go beyond a certain point, when learning is encouraged.

2. Which one of the following is **not** a component of progressive education?
1. Discussion 2. Memorization
3. Experimentation 4. Interaction

3. Which of the following types of questions is **not** suitable for testing student's expression of feelings and logical thinking?
1. Analytical type 2. Critical type
3. Discussion type 4. Multiple option type

4. 'A disorder of writing ability in which a learner has difficulty with letter formation, spelling, fine motor co-ordination etc.' This disorder is called as:
1. Dyslexia 2. Dysgraphia
3. Dyspraxia 4. Dyscalculia

5. Which option is **correct** regarding emotions in early adolescence?
1. Intense and rational
2. Uncontrolled and rational
3. Uncontrolled and irrational
4. Controlled and intense

6. Select the **correct** sequence (top to bottom) of hierarchical intelligence theory of Vernon:
1. General factor → Specific factor → Major factor → Minor factor
2. Specific factor → General factor → Minor factor → Major factor
3. General factor → Major factor → Minor factor → Specific factor
4. Major factor → General factor → Specific factor → Minor factor

7. Arrange the steps of Bandura's social learning theory in sequence:
(*a*) Perception of behaviour
(*b*) Reinforcement of behaviour
(*c*) Remember of behaviour
(*d*) Convert the memory into action
Choose the **correct** code:
1. (*a*), (*c*), (*d*), (*b*) 2. (*b*), (*a*), (*c*), (*d*)
3. (*c*), (*d*), (*a*), (*b*) 4. (*b*), (*c*), (*d*), (*a*)

8. Which of the following is **not** an environmental factor affecting teaching-learning?
1. Learning material 2. Physical conditions
3. Recreational facilities 4. Maturation

9. Which of the following is **not** influenced by heredity?
1. Aptitude 2. Attitude
3. Emotions 4. Interest

10. When the assessment is designed to evaluate student's overall achievements and proficiency at the end of a learning period is known as:
1. Assessment of learning
2. Assessment for diagnosing
3. Assessment for learning
4. Assessment for remedy

11. According to McDougall, the emotion of 'disgust' is associated with which basic instinct?
1. Repulsion 2. Escape
3. Combat 4. Curiosity

12. Which of the following should **not** be a need of children with impairment from the point of view of inclusive education?
1. Need for coping with own's impairment
2. Need for proper guidance & counselling
3. Need for being dependent on others
4. Need for assistive equipments

13. Which constitutional right of children with special needs does inclusive education protect?
1. Right to Education 2. Right to Respect
3. Right to Acceptance 4. Right to Integration

14. Which of the following is **not** an acquired motive?
1. Affiliation 2. Achievement
3. Approval 4. Pain avoidance

15. Which of the following ways of instruction is suitable for hearing impaired children?
(*a*) Sign language (*b*) Finger spelling
(*c*) Lip reading (*d*) Cued speech

Choose the **correct** code:
1. (*a*) and (*c*) 2. (*a*), (*b*) and (*c*)
3. (*a*), (*c*) and (*d*) 4. (*a*), (*b*), (*c*) and (*d*)

16. According to Freud's psycho-sexual development theory, the stage in which adolescent attracts towards opposite sex, is known as:
1. Phallic stage 2. Anal stage
3. Genital stage 4. Latency stage

17. According to Piaget's cognitive development theory, when the learner maintaining a proper balance between himself/herself and his/her environment, this mechanism is called as:
1. Accommodation 2. Assimilation
3. Equilibration 4. Integration

18. Which of the following is **not** a characteristic of inclusive education?
1. It supports special educational needs
2. It says to celebrate diversity
3. This ensures the participation of teacher, parents, child and society
4. It is limited to the special education of disabled children

19. Which tests can be administered by the teacher to identify creative children?
(*a*) Figure construction test
(*b*) Product improvement test
(*c*) Usual uses test
(*d*) Picture completion test

Choose the **correct** code:
1. (*a*) & (*d*) 2. (*b*) & (*c*)
3. (*a*), (*b*) & (*d*) 4. (*a*), (*b*), (*c*) & (*d*)

20. Which of the following is **not** a helpful action of teacher in promoting socialization among children?
1. Giving the individual project work
2. Assigning social responsibilities
3. Organizing co-curricular activities
4. Motivating for social participation

21. Which of the following is **not** a child centered method of learning?
1. Demonstration
2. Field Trip
3. Programmed Instruction
4. Project

22. Which strategies of learning is **not** appropriate for the learner of senior secondary level?
1. Learning tasks at memory level
2. Allowing self-discovery of knowledge
3. Giving appropriate space to classroom interaction
4. Student centered teaching-learning

23. Which of the following statements regarding intelligence are **not** true?
(*a*) Intellectual development is influenced by genetics, not environment.
(*b*) Gender differences do not causes intellectual differences.
(*c*) Sharp intelligence is a sign of sharp memory.
(*d*) Intelligence gives the ability to adjust in new situations.

Choose the **correct** code:
1. (*a*) and (*b*) 2. (*a*) and (*c*)
3. (*b*) and (*d*) 4. (*c*) and (*d*)

24. Which of the following is **not** a feature of continuous and comprehensive evaluation?
1. Regularity of assessment
2. Frequency of unit tests
3. Diagnosis of learning gaps
4. Measuring only scholastic achievement

25. Which of the following is **not** an example of developmental changes under acquisition of new features?
1. Permanent teeth
2. Primary sex characteristics
3. Secondary sex characteristics
4. Thymus gland

26. Match the following stages of Kohlberg's moral development theory with their characteristics:

Moral Stages	**Characteristics**
(*a*) Conforming to obtain reward	(*i*) Getting the approval of others
(*b*) Maintaining social order	(*ii*) State based on self-interest
(*c*) Good interpersonal relationships	(*iii*) Eternal value accepted by conscience
(*d*) Universal ethical principles	(*iv*) Importance of justice and law

Choose the **correct** code:

	(a)	(b)	(c)	(d)
1.	(ii)	(iv)	(i)	(iii)
2.	(iii)	(i)	(ii)	(iv)
3.	(iv)	(iii)	(i)	(ii)
4.	(i)	(ii)	(iv)	(iii)

27. Which of the following statements is **not** correct regarding individual differences?
1. Individual differences exists in both cognitive and psychomotor domain.
2. Species characteristics influence individual differences.
3. The cause of individual differences is the social environment, not the physical environment.
4. Age also has an effect on individual differences.

28. In a learning situation presenting relevant facts separately from non-relevant facts, is indicative of which principle of learning?
1. Principle of multiple response
2. Principle of analogy
3. Principle of prepotency of elements
4. Principle of associative shifting

29. Which of the following is **not** a common characteristics of deprived children?
1. They look physically challenged
2. They are socially disadvantaged
3. They are economically deprived
4. They feel emotionally inferior

30. Which of the following gender biased actions are **not** to be involved in educational practices?
(*a*) Homogeneous grouping
(*b*) Gender neutral content
(*c*) Stereotyped occupation guidance
(*d*) Teacher's prejudiced attitude

Choose the **correct** code:
1. (*a*) and (*b*)
2. (*a*), (*c*) and (*d*)
3. (*c*) and (*d*)
4. (*a*), (*b*) and (*c*)

PART-II

भाषा-I : हिन्दी

निर्देश (प्रश्न संख्या 31-34) : *निम्नलिखित गद्यांश को ध्यानपूर्वक पढ़कर नीचे दिये गये प्रश्नों के उत्तर दीजिए :*

नया निश्चय ही एक मूल्य है। पर निरंतरता भी एक मूल्य है। साहित्य दोनों में से एक को चुनने की हिमाकत सौभाग्य से नहीं करता है, क्योंकि वह जानता है कि एक के बिना दूसरा संभव नहीं है। परंपरा अपने को पुनर्नवा किए बिना सजीव नहीं रह सकती। मनुष्य दोनों आयामों में रहता है : इतिहास में और अनन्त में। वह बदलता है और फिर भी बना रहता है। दोनों आयाम मनुष्य के यहाँ अंतर्भुक्त हैं - वे अलग-थलग या विविक्ति नहीं होते। बहुत कुछ बदलता है : समाज, परिस्थितियाँ, आर्थिक व्यापार, मानव संबंध और उनके संगुंफन आदि पर प्रेम, ईर्ष्या, मोह-मत्सर, रोग-विराग, हर्ष-विषाद आदि वही बने रहते हैं। नयी दृष्टि होती है, तो अपने लिए अनवार्यतः नया शिल्प भी खोजती है। विश्लेषण के लिए भले हम कथ्य और शिल्प को अलग-थलग कर लेते हैं, पर रचना में वे अद्वैत हैं। नया अंततः निरंतरता में समाहित होकर अपनी वैधता पता है, पर वह निरंतरता को कहीं न कहीं बदल भी देता है। निरंतरता नए के हस्तक्षेप और उसके समाहार के बाद वही नहीं रह जाती, जो पहले थी। हम यह भूल जाते हैं कि आज जो पुराना लगता है, वह कभी नया था। बिना समाकालीनता के कालातीत नहीं हुआ जा सकता, लेकिन सिर्फ समाकालीनता के बाड़े में बँधे रहकर भी कालातीत नहीं हुआ जा सकता। नया समय को सीधे और उसके बदले हुए ब्योरों में पकड़ने के साहस से उपजता है, पर अगर वह समय के पार में देख पाये, तो टिकाऊ नहीं हो सकता। जो कालातीत है, वही हर समय नया होता चलता है।

31. साहित्य का अभीष्ट है :
1. मात्र नए को चुनना
2. मात्र निरंतरता को चुनना
3. नयेपन एवं निरंतरता दोनों को चुनना
4. मात्र समकालीन को चुनना

32. निम्नलिखित में से कौन-सा कथन **सत्य** है?
1. मनुष्य की मूल प्रवृत्तियाँ समय के साथ परिवर्तनशील हैं।
2. मनुष्य का समाज समय के साथ परिवर्तनशील है।
3. मनुष्य मात्र इतिहास में जीता है।
4. निरंतरता सदैव अपरिवर्तनीय होती है।

33. कौन-सा कथन **असत्य** है?
1. साहित्य में दृष्टि का अवबोधन कथ्य से होता है।
2. नवीन कथ्य अपने लिए नवीन शिल्प भी लाता है।
3. कथ्य और शिल्प दोनों एक-दूसरे से स्वायत्त होते हैं।
4. साहित्यिक रचना में कथ्य और शिल्प परस्पर अनुस्यूत होते हैं।

34. नयापन टिकाऊ होता है :
1. जब वह समकालीन हो।
2. जब वह समकालीन भी हो और कालातीत भी।
3. जब उसमें चमत्कार हो।
4. जब वह परंपरा को बदलता हो।

35. समास की दृष्टि से **संगत** विकल्प चुनिए :
1. चक्षुश्रवा - इतरेतर द्वन्द्व
2. आपादमस्तक - बहुव्रीहि
3. जातिगत - अधिकरण तत्पुरुष
4. श्रमसाध्य - करण तत्पुरुष

36. वाक्य में प्रयुक्त क्रिया की दृष्टि से **असंगत** विकल्प का चयन कीजिए :
1. अध्यापिका छात्राओं को भूगोल पढ़ा रही है - द्विकर्मकक्रिया
2. निशीथ जोर-जोर-से हँस रहा है - अकर्मक क्रिया
3. मदारी अनेक करतब दिखलाकर बच्चों को ललचाता है - अकर्मक क्रिया
4. लड़-झगड़कर वह अपना हिस्सा ले ही मरा - रंजक क्रिया

37. निम्नलिखित में से **अशुद्ध** शब्द समूह का चयन कीजिए :
1. सीधा साधा, अठोतर, उहापोह
2. दाशरथि, स्थायित्य, विद्यार्थिपरिषद्
3. सुधीजन, प्रेयसी, निजीकरण
4. वेश्या, शशिभूषण, शक्तीकरण

38. संधि की दृष्टि से **अनुपयुक्त** विकल्प चुनिए :
1. दैत्यारि, गत्यानुसार, अगन्याशय - यण् संधि
2. मिताहार, विकलांग, भूर्ध्व - दीर्घ संधि
3. दिग्विजय, अब्ज, वृहन्नेत्र - व्यंजन संधि
4. वयोवृद्ध, पुरोधा, प्रादुर्भूत - विसर्ग संधि

39. विलोम की दृष्टि से **असंगत** विकल्प चुनिए :
1. आकृष्ट - विकृष्ट
2. आह्वान - अनाह्वान
3. कलंकित - निष्कलंक
4. ऐहिक - पारलौकिक

40. वर्णों की ध्वनिगत विशेषताओं के संदर्भ में **असंगत** चुनिए :
1. उ - पश्च, संवृत, वृत्तमुखी
2. ऋ - अग्र, संवृत, वृत्तमुखी
3. अ - मध्य, ह्रस्व, उदासीन
4. आ - पश्च, विवृत, अवृत्तमुखी

41. प्रत्यय की दृष्टि से **संगत** विभाजन चुनिए :
1. मैथुन, शौच, राघव - 'अ' प्रत्यय
2. फिकैत, डकैत, लड़ैत - 'एत' प्रत्यय
3. नारदीय, स्थानीय, मानवीय - 'अनीय' प्रत्यय
4. कौशेय, सौजन्य, कौमार्य - 'एय' प्रत्यय

42. हिंदी अध्यापक की विशिष्ट विशेषताओं में सम्मिलित **नहीं** है :
1. साहित्य का ज्ञान
2. भाषा शिक्षण की विधियों का ज्ञान
3. हिंदी भाषा पर विशिष्ट अधिकार
4. शिक्षा तथा उपाधियाँ

43. किस विकल्प में उपसर्ग - विभाजन नियामानुसार है?
1. अपरिग्रह, अपरोक्ष, अपर्ण - 'अप' उपसर्ग
2. आरण्यक, आवश्यक, आधुनिक - 'आ' उपसर्ग
3. निःशुल्क, निष्पक्ष, निस्स्वार्थ - 'निस्' उपसर्ग
4. व्याधि, वीक्षण, व्यतिरेक - 'वी' उपसर्ग

44. किस विकल्प में सार्वनामिक विशेषण का प्रयोग **नहीं** हुआ है?
1. जिसने परिश्रम किया, वह सफल हो गया।
2. यह पुस्तक किससे मँगवाऊँ।
3. ऐसे व्यक्ति पर कभी विश्वास मत करो।
4. आपके घर से कल कोई नौकर आया था।

45. निम्नलिखित में से मौन वाचन का उद्देश्य **नहीं** है :
1. उचित लय और गति प्रदान करना।
2. स्वाध्याय की आदत विकसित करना।
3. तीव्र गति से पढ़ने का अभ्यास करना।
4. अर्थ ग्रहण कर उसका केन्द्रीय भाव समझना।

Language-II : English

46. Choose the **correct** option:

Assertion A: The disadvantage of print material is that it lacks interaction and the use of audio-visual elements.

Assertion B: Print materials are not portable, not easily available and are not cost effective.
1. A is true; B is false
2. B is true; A is false
3. Both A & B are true
4. Both A & B are false

Direction: (Q. 47 to 56): *Read the following poem and answer the questions that follow :*

Mother, I am the one
you sent away
when the doctor told you
I would be
a girl – In the end they had to
give me an injection to kill me.
Before I died I heard
the traffic rushing outside, the monsoon
slush, the wind sulking through
your beloved Mumbai –
I could have clutched the neon blue
no one wanted –
No one wanted
To touch me – except later in the autopsy room
when they knew my mouth would not search
for anything – and my head could be measured
and bent cut apart.
I looked like a sliced pomegranate.
The fruit you never touched.
Mother, I am the one you sent away
When the doctor told you
I would be a girl – your second girl.
Afterwards, as soon as you could
you put on your grass – green sari –
the orange stems of the parijatak blossoms
glistened in your hair –
Afterwards
everyone smiled.
But now I ask you

to look for me, mother,
look for me because
I won't come to you in your dreams,
Look for me, mother, look
because I won't become a flower
I won't turn into a butterfly
And I am not a part of anyone's song.
Look, mother,
look for the place where you have sent me.
Look for the unspeakable.
for the place that can never be described.
Look for me, mother, because
this is what you have done.
Look for me, mother, because
this is not 'God's will'.
Look for me, mother
because I smell of formaldehyde –
I smell of formaldehyde
and stili, I wish you would look
for me, mother.

47. Who does the girl address?
1. the doctor 2. the society
3. the father 4. the mother

48. In which city does the foeticide take place?
1. Delhi 2. Chennai
3. Mumbai 4. Pune

49. What does the killed infant smell of?
1. formaldehyde 2. parijatak
3. chlorine 4. slush

50. Who is "I" in the opening line?
1. the poet 2. the killed infant girl
3. mother 4. the doctor

51. Fill in the blank with the **correct** option:
According to the speaker the mother disliked .....
1. oranges 2. parijatak blossoms
3. pomegranates 4. the grass-green sari

52. Find a word from the poem which means "post mortem":
1. formaldehyde 2. injection to kill
3. neon blue 4. autopsy

53. Why was the infant in the womb killed?
1. because it was defective
2. because the mother didn't want a second girl child
3. doctor's mistake
4. it was ugly

54. Which one of the following is used as a literary device in the poem for effectiveness?
1. repetition 2. climax
3. irony 4. metaphor

55. Fill in the blank with the **correct** option:
"I looked like a sliced pomegranate" is an example of _______.
1. metaphor 2. an implied simile
3. irony 4. simile

56. Find the word in the poem which means "shone due to being wet".
1. glistened 2. sulking
3. clutched 4. blossom

57. Fill in the blank with the **correct** option:
Nesfield's grammar is an instance of _____ grammar.
1. universal 2. cognitive
3. descriptive 4. prescriptive

58. Fill in the blank with the **correct** option:
_______ skill involves training the learner to listen for the English speech sounds including stress and intonation patterns.
1. listening 2. aural-oral
3. reading 4. writing

59. Fill in the blank with the **correct** option:
Teaching learners to discuss a poem in English in their native language is an instance of the use of _______.
1. evaluative comprehension
2. multilingual resources
3. pre-reading skills
4. first language acquisition

60. Fill in the blank with the **correct** option:
The two kinds of listening are _____.
1. active and passive
2. skimming and scanning
3. intensive and extensive
4. referential and inferential

PART-III

General Studies : Quantitative Aptitude, Reasoning Ability and GK & Awareness

61. A square and an equilateral triangle are inscribed in a cricle. If a and b denote the lengths of their sides respectively, then which of the following is **true**?
1. $2a^2 = 3b^2$ 2. $3a^2 = 2b^2$
3. $a^2 = 3b^2$ 4. $b^2 = 2a^2$

62. The surface areas of the two spheres are in the ratio 1 : 2. The ratio of their volumes is:
1. 1 : 2 2. $1 : \sqrt{2}$
3. $1 : 2\sqrt{2}$ 4. 1 : 4

63. Find the missing term in the following number series:
2, 9, 28, ?, 126, 217, 344
1. 37
2. 65
3. 91
4. 115

64. The volume of the metallic cylindrical pipe is 748 cm^3. Its length is 14 cm and its external radius is 9 cm. The thickness of pipe is equal to:
1. 0.25 cm
2. 0.5 cm
3. 1.0 cm
4. 1.5 cm

65. Line : Square : : Arc : ?
1. Ring
2. Sphere
3. Circle
4. Ball

66. Rekha walks 10 km straight and then turns right and walks 10 km. Then every time turning to her left, she walks 5, 15 and 15 km respectively. How far is she now from her starting point?
1. 20 km
2. 15 km
3. 10 km
4. 5 km

67. Next term of the following series is:

$$\left(\frac{AG}{d}\right)^{6}, \left(\frac{CK}{g}\right)^{21}, \left(\frac{EO}{j}\right)^{45}, \left(\frac{GS}{m}\right)^{78}, ?$$

1. $\left(\frac{IX}{p}\right)^{127}$
2. $\left(\frac{IV}{q}\right)^{133}$
3. $\left(\frac{IW}{p}\right)^{120}$
4. $\left(\frac{IX}{q}\right)^{127}$

68. A is father of C and D is son of B. E is brother of A. C is sister of D. How is B related to E?
1. Daughter
2. Sister-in-law
3. Mother
4. Husband

69. Five men P, Q, R, S and T read a newspaper. The one who reads first, gives it to R. The one who reads last, had taken from P. T was not the first or last to read. There were two readers between P and Q. Who reads the newspaper last?
1. Q
2. R
3. S
4. T

70. A, P, R, X, Y and Z are sitting in a row. Y and Z are in the centre and A and P are at the ends. R is sitting on the immediate left of A. Who is sitting on the immediate right of P?
1. X
2. Y
3. Z
4. R

71. If it was Saturday on 10th December, 2022, what will be the day on 8th December, 2024?
1. Saturday
2. Sunday
3. Monday
4. Tuesday

72. Find the next term of the following letter series:
MONRO, JSKTL, GUHVI, DWEXF, ?
1. AYBZC
2. AZCYC
3. BYBYD
4. BZCZD

73. If $\tan\theta + \sec\theta = 4$, then the value of $\cos\theta$ is equal to:
1. $\frac{17}{8}$
2. $\frac{8}{17}$
3. $\frac{15}{17}$
4. $\frac{17}{15}$

74. What is the smallest number by which 2880 must be divided in order to make it a perfect square?
1. 2
2. 3
3. 4
4. 5

75. P began a business with ₹ 45,000 and Q joined with ₹ 30,000 after some time. If the profit at the end of the year were divided among them in the ratio 2 : 1, when did Q join?
1. after 3 months
2. after 4 months
3. after 5 months
4. after 6 months

76. If three numbers are in the ratio 3 : 2 : 5 such that the sum of their squares is equal to 1862, the middle number is equal to:
1. 7
2. 14
3. 21
4. 35

77. A, B and C together completed a work for ₹ 5,290. A and B together did $\frac{19}{23}$ of the whole work. Amount received by C in ₹ is equal to:
1. 920
2. 900
3. 880
4. 850

78. The difference between the compound interest and simple interest on a certain amount at 5% per annum for 2 years is ₹ 15. The principal amount is equal to:
1. 2,000
2. 4,000
3. 6,000
4. 8,000

79. The radius of a circular field, whose areas is equal to the sum of the area of the three circular fields having radii 8 m, 9 m and 12 m respectively, is equal to:
1. 16 m
2. 17 m
3. 18 m
4. 19 m

80. In a certain code language "sun shines brightly" is written as "ba lo sul", "houses are brightly lit" as "kado ula ari ba" and "light comes from sun" as "dopi kup lo nro". What code words are written for "sun" and "brightly" respectively?
1. sul, ba
2. sul, lo
3. ba, lo
4. lo, ba

81. Which of the following wild life sanctuaries is located in Shivalik hights?
1. Khaparwas Sanctuary
2. Bhindawas Sanctuary
3. Khol Hi-Raitan Sanctuary
4. Nahar Sanctuary

82. Which of the following was the theme State for the 37th Surajkund International Crafts Fair?
1. Madhya Pradesh 2. Rajasthan
3. Manipur 4. Gujarat

83. Who was the First Chairman of Haryana Public Service Commission?
1. Dalbir Singh 2. Darbari Lal Gupta
3. Bhim Singh 4. Manoj Pandey

84. Where the Indian Institute of Information Technology is being set-up?
1. Kilohad 2. Baraut
3. Pipali Khera 4. Rasulpura

85. Which of the following districts is **not** part of Rohtak division?
1. Jhajjar 2. Sonipat
3. Bhiwani 4. Rewari

86. The woman wrestler of Haryana who received the Arjuna Award of 2023?
1. Antim Panghal 2. Anshu Malik
3. Geetika Jakhar 4. Sakshi Malik

87. Read the following statements about Pehowa Inscription:
(*i*) The inscription was issued by a ruler of Gurjar Pratihar dynasty.
(*ii*) As per the inscription, Pehowa was a famous market of horse dealers.

Choose the **correct** code:
1. Only statement (*i*) is true.
2. Only statement (*ii*) is true.
3. Neither statement (*i*) nor statement (*ii*) is true.
4. Both the statements are true.

88. Who among the following did **not** serve as the Chief Secretary during the Chief Ministership of Manohar Lal Khattar?
1. S.C. Chaudhary 2. P.K. Gupta
3. Shakuntala Jakhu 4. Vijay Vardhan

89. Which of the following statements about Sir Chhotu Ram are **correct**?
(*a*) He began his career as a Congress man.
(*b*) Later be joined Unionist Party.
(*c*) He was a Minister in the government of Undivided Punjab.

Choose the **correct** code:
1. Only statement (*b*) & (*c*) are correct.
2. Only statement (*a*) & (*c*) are correct.
3. Only statement (*a*) is correct.
4. Statement (*a*), (*b*) & (*c*) are correct.

90. Which of the following are **correctly** matched?
(*a*) Gujari Mahal – Hisar
(*b*) Aram-e-Kausar – Narnaul
(*c*) Tomb of Sheikh Tayyab – Jind

Choose the **correct** code:
1. (*a*) and (*c*) 2. (*a*) and (*b*)
3. (*b*) and (*c*) 4. (*a*), (*b*) and (*c*)

ANSWERS

1	**2**	**3**	**4**	**5**	**6**	**7**	**8**	**9**	**10**
4	2	4	2	3	3	1	4	2	1
11	**12**	**13**	**14**	**15**	**16**	**17**	**18**	**19**	**20**
1	3	1	4	4	3	3	4	4	1
21	**22**	**23**	**24**	**25**	**26**	**27**	**28**	**29**	**30**
1	1	2	4	4	1	3	3	1	2
31	**32**	**33**	**34**	**35**	**36**	**37**	**38**	**39**	**40**
3	2	3	2	4	3	1	1	2	2
41	**42**	**43**	**44**	**45**	**46**	**47**	**48**	**49**	**50**
1	4	3	1	1	1	4	3	1	2
51	**52**	**53**	**54**	**55**	**56**	**57**	**58**	**59**	**60**
3	4	2	1	4	1	4	2	2	3
61	**62**	**63**	**64**	**65**	**66**	**67**	**68**	**69**	**70**
2	3	2	3	3	4	3	2	3	1
71	**72**	**73**	**74**	**75**	**76**	**77**	**78**	**79**	**80**
2	1	2	4	1	2	1	3	2	4
81	**82**	**83**	**84**	**85**	**86**	**87**	**88**	**89**	**90**
3	4	2	1	4	1	4	1	4	2

EXPLANATORY ANSWERS

1. **Despite the limits of maturation the development can go beyond a certain point, when learning is encouraged:** Development is always shaped by both maturation (biological readiness) and learning. While learning enriches and optimizes development, it cannot surpass the natural limits of maturation. For example, a child cannot learn abstract reasoning before the brain reaches the necessary stage of maturity. The statement suggests that learning can push development beyond these limits, which is incorrect. Maturation sets the boundaries, and learning works within those boundaries to actualize potential.

2. **Memorization:** Progressive education, inspired by thinkers such as John Dewey, stresses experiential learning, problem-solving, interaction, and active participation. It values creativity, exploration, and critical thinking rather than passive recall. Memorization, which depends on rote learning, directly contradicts the spirit of progressive education because it focuses on repetition rather than true understanding.

3. **Multiple option type:** Multiple option type questions (such as MCQs) are limited to recognition and recall of fixed choices. They do not allow students to freely express feelings, present complex reasoning, or construct arguments. In contrast, analytical, critical, and discussion-type questions give space for creativity, logical thinking, and personal expression. Therefore, multiple option type questions are unsuitable for testing these higher-order abilities.

4. **Dysgraphia:** Dysgraphia is a specific learning disorder related to writing ability. Learners with dysgraphia face problems in letter formation, poor spelling, and fine motor coordination. It is different from dyslexia (difficulty in reading), dyspraxia (difficulty in motor planning and coordination), and dyscalculia (difficulty in mathematical abilities).

5. **Uncontrolled and irrational:** In early adolescence, emotions are typically intense, unstable, and often expressed without rational control. Due to hormonal changes and ongoing brain development, adolescents may struggle with regulating emotions, leading to emotional volatility and irrational responses.

6. **General factor → Major factor → Minor factor → Specific factor:** In Vernon's hierarchical theory of intelligence, at the top is the general factor (g), followed by two broad major group factors (verbal-educational and practical-mechanical), then narrower minor group factors, and finally specific factors at the bottom. This hierarchy shows the structured nature of intelligence from broadest to most specific.

7. **(a), (c), (d), (b):** According to Bandura's social learning theory, the correct order is—first, the learner perceives or observes the behaviour (a), then retains or remembers it (c), later converts this memory into action through imitation (d), and finally the behaviour is reinforced through rewards or consequences (b). This sequence shows how observation, memory, action, and reinforcement together shape learning.

8. **Maturation:** Environmental factors influencing teaching-learning include learning materials, classroom conditions, and recreational facilities. Maturation, however, is a biological and hereditary factor, not an environmental one. It refers to the natural growth and readiness of the learner, independent of external surroundings.

9. **Attitude:** Heredity strongly influences aptitude, emotional tendencies, and even certain interests through genetic predispositions. Attitude, however, is shaped by environment, culture, social interactions, and experiences rather than heredity. It reflects personal outlooks and values, which develop primarily through learning and socialization.

10. **Assessment of learning:** This type of assessment is carried out at the end of a course or learning period to evaluate the learner's overall achievement, mastery of skills, and proficiency. It is summative in nature, aiming to measure learning outcomes against predefined standards or objectives.

11. **Repulsion:** According to William McDougall's theory of instincts and emotions, the emotion of disgust is directly linked to the instinct of repulsion. This instinct drives avoidance of harmful, unpleasant, or undesirable stimuli, ensuring protection and survival.

12. **Need for being dependent on others:** Inclusive education emphasizes empowering children with impairments by providing coping strategies, counselling, and assistive devices to support independence. Promoting dependency on others is contrary to inclusive principles, as the goal is to build self-reliance and equal participation in learning.

13. **Right to Education:** Inclusive education ensures that children with special needs enjoy the same constitutional right to education as other children. It guarantees access to schooling, equal opportunities, and participation in mainstream classrooms, thereby protecting their fundamental educational rights.

14. **Pain avoidance:** Acquired motives are learned through social interaction and experience, such as affiliation, achievement, and approval. Pain avoidance, however, is an innate or primary motive, biologically rooted in survival instincts, not acquired through learning.

15. **(a), (b), (c) and (d):** For hearing-impaired children, multiple instructional methods are effective. These include sign language for full communication, finger spelling for letters and words, lip reading to interpret spoken language, and cued speech to clarify sounds. Using all these methods together best supports comprehensive learning and communication.

16. **Genital stage:** In Freud's psycho-sexual stages, the genital stage begins from adolescence onwards. At this stage, sexual interests are directed toward others, and adolescents experience attraction to the opposite sex. It signifies maturity of sexual instincts and development of adult relationships.

17. **Equilibration:** According to Piaget, equilibration is the process of maintaining balance between assimilation (fitting new information into existing schemas) and accommodation (modifying schemas to incorporate new information). It helps the learner achieve harmony between self and environment, driving cognitive growth.

18. It is limited to the special education of disabled children: Inclusive education is not confined only to children with disabilities. Instead, it embraces all learners by celebrating diversity, supporting special educational needs, and ensuring active participation of teachers, parents, peers, and the community. Limiting it to disability alone misrepresents its true scope.

19. (a), (b), (c) and (d): All four tests—figure construction, product improvement, unusual uses, and picture completion—are widely recognized as effective measures of creativity. They form part of creative thinking assessments like the Torrance Tests of Creative Thinking (TTCT). These tests evaluate fluency of ideas, flexibility in thinking, originality in responses, and elaboration of concepts, making them suitable for teachers to identify creative children.

20. Giving the individual project work: Socialization thrives on group interaction, cooperation, and shared responsibilities. Assigning individual project work emphasizes independence and self-reliance, which reduces opportunities for collaboration. By contrast, assigning social responsibilities, organizing co-curricular activities, and motivating children for social participation directly enhance peer bonding and group problem-solving, thus fostering socialization.

21. Demonstration: Demonstration is largely teacher-centered, as students watch while the teacher performs an activity. This restricts active engagement and exploration by learners. In contrast, child-centered methods like field trips, programmed instruction (which supports self-paced exploration), and project work actively involve learners, allowing them to construct knowledge through participation and experience.

22. Learning tasks at memory level: At the senior secondary stage, learners are expected to engage in higher-order thinking, such as analysis, synthesis, critical evaluation, and application of concepts. Pure memory-level tasks are inadequate at this stage, as they do not challenge intellectual abilities or promote deeper understanding. Therefore, strategies focusing solely on rote memorization are not appropriate.

23. (a) and (c): Statement (a) is not true because intellectual development is influenced by both genetics and environment; environment plays a significant role in shaping intellectual growth. Statement (c) is also incorrect since sharp intelligence does not necessarily indicate sharp memory—intelligence relates to reasoning, problem-solving, and adaptability, while memory is only one aspect of cognitive functioning. Statements (b) and (d) are true: gender does not create intellectual differences, and intelligence indeed helps in adjustment to new situations.

24. Measuring only scholastic achievement: Continuous and Comprehensive Evaluation (CCE) emphasizes both scholastic (academic) and co-scholastic (skills, attitudes, values, creativity, participation) aspects. It involves regular and diagnostic assessment of overall growth. Limiting it only to scholastic achievement contradicts its comprehensive nature, making this option not a feature of CCE.

25. Thymus gland: Developmental changes under acquisition of new features include permanent teeth (physical maturity), primary sex characteristics (organs directly related to reproduction), and secondary sex characteristics (features like facial hair, voice change, breast development). The thymus gland, however, does not represent acquisition of a new feature; it is an existing gland that gradually diminishes with age (involution), so it does not fall under this category.

26. (a) (ii), (b) (iv), (c) (i), (d) (iii):
- (a) Conforming to obtain reward → (ii) State based on self-interest: At this stage, children obey rules mainly for personal benefit or to gain rewards.
- (b) Maintaining social order → (iv) Importance of justice and law: At this stage, morality is guided by law, duty, and maintaining social system.
- (c) Good interpersonal relationships → (i) Getting the approval of others: Individuals seek acceptance and approval from peers and authority figures.
- (d) Universal ethical principles → (iii) Eternal value accepted by conscience: Moral reasoning is guided by universal principles of justice, equality, and human rights.

27. The cause of individual differences is the social environmental, not the physical environment: This is incorrect because individual differences arise due to both social and physical environments along with hereditary factors. Climate, nutrition, living conditions (physical environment), as well as family, culture, and peer influences (social environment), all contribute. Limiting it to only social environment is therefore wrong.

28. Principle of prepotency of elements: This principle states that learners can focus on the significant elements of a task or situation while ignoring irrelevant details. Presenting relevant facts separately from non-relevant ones helps students concentrate on essential aspects, thereby improving understanding and learning efficiency.

29. They look physically challenged: Deprived children typically suffer from social disadvantage, economic deprivation, and emotional inferiority due to lack of resources, opportunities, or support. However, being physically challenged is not a common characteristic of deprivation—it relates to disability, not deprivation.

30. (a), (c) and (d): Gender-biased actions in education include homogeneous grouping (separating by gender), stereotyped occupational guidance (directing boys and girls into traditional roles), and teacher's prejudiced attitude. These practices reinforce inequality. On the other hand, gender-neutral content promotes equality, so it should be included in educational practices, not avoided.

31. नयेपन एवं निरंतरता दोनों को चुनना : गद्यांश में कहा गया है कि साहित्य केवल नया या केवल निरंतरता नहीं चुनता, बल्कि दोनों को साथ लेकर चलता है। परंपरा बिना नवीनता के जीवित नहीं रह सकती और नवीनता निरंतरता में समाहित होकर ही वैधता पाती है। अतः साहित्य का अभीट नयेपन और निरंतरता दोनों का चयन करना है।

32. मनुष्य का समाज समय के साथ परिवर्तनशील है : गद्यांश में स्पष्ट कहा गया है कि समाज, परिस्थितियाँ, आर्थिक व्यापार और मानव संबंध समय के साथ बदलते रहते हैं। जबकि मनुष्य की मूल प्रवृत्तियाँ (जैसे प्रेम, ईर्ष्या, मोह आदि) स्थिर रहती हैं। इसलिए सही कथन यही है कि समाज समय के साथ परिवर्तनशील है।

33. कथ्य और शिल्प दोनों एक-दूसरे से स्वायत्त होते हैं : यह असत्य है क्योंकि गद्यांश में कहा गया है कि विश्लेषण के लिए कथ्य और शिल्प को अलग किया जा सकता है, लेकिन साहित्यिक रचना में वे अद्वैत और परस्पर अनूस्यूत रहते हैं। इसलिए कथ्य और शिल्प का स्वायत्त होना असत्य है।

34. जब वह समकालीन भी हो और कालातीत भी : गद्यांश में कहा गया है कि बिना समकालीनता के कालातीत नहीं हुआ जा सकता और केवल समकालीनता तक सीमित रहकर भी कालातीत नहीं हुआ जा सकता। नयापन तभी टिकाऊ होता है जब वह समय की वास्तविकता से जुड़ते हुए कालातीत दृष्टि भी प्रदान करे।

35. श्रमसाध्य - करण तत्पुरुष : 'श्रमसाध्य' का विग्रह है - *श्रम से साध्य* (मेहनत से प्राप्त होने वाला)। यहाँ 'से' करण कारक है जिसका लोप हुआ है। यह करण तत्पुरुष समास की स्पष्ट पहचान है। अन्य विकल्पों में त्रुटि है - 'चक्षुश्रवा' करण तत्पुरुष/बहुव्रीहि है, 'आपादमस्तक' अव्ययीभाव है, और 'जातिगत' करण तत्पुरुष अधिक उपयुक्त है।

36. मदारी अनेक करतब दिखलाकर बच्चों को ललचाता है - अकर्मक क्रिया : यह असंगत है क्योंकि 'ललचाता है' क्रिया सकर्मक है। इसका प्रभाव कर्म 'बच्चों को' पर पड़ता है। अन्य वाक्य संगत हैं - 'पढ़ा रही है' द्विकर्मक है, 'हँस रहा है' अकर्मक है, और 'मरना' रंजक क्रिया है।

37. सीधा साधा, अठोतर, उहापोह : 1. सीधा साधा, अठोतर, उहापोह : यहाँ "अठोतर" अशुद्ध है। सही शब्द "अठहत्तर" (78) या "अठहत्तरवाँ" होता है। बाकी शब्द "सीधा साधा" और "उहापोह" (दुविधा) शुद्ध हैं।

38. दैत्यारि, गत्यानुसार, अगन्याशय - यण् संधि : यह विकल्प अनुपयुक्त है। 'दैत्यारि' में *दीर्घ संधि* है (अ + अ = आ), 'गत्यानुसार' और 'अगन्याशय' में *यण संधि* है। इसलिए पूरे समूह को 'य संधि' मानना गलत है। अन्य विकल्प सही हैं - 2 में दीर्घ संधि, 3 में व्यंजन संधि, और 4 में विसर्ग संधि है।

39. आह्वान - अनाह्वान : यह असंगत है क्योंकि 'आह्वान' (बुलाना) का मानक विलोम 'प्रत्याह्वान' या 'विसर्जन' माना जाता है। 'अनाह्वान' का अर्थ है 'न बुलाया गया', जो विरोधार्थी न होकर केवल निषेधार्थी है। अन्य युग्म -'आकृष्ट-विकृष्ट', 'कलंकित-निष्कलंक', और 'ऐहिक-पारलौकिक' - सही विलोम हैं।

40. ऋ - अग्र, संवृत, वृत्तमुखी : यह असंगत है क्योंकि 'ऋ' स्वर *अग्र* और *संवृत* तो है, पर यह वृत्तमुखी (गोल होंठों से) नहीं है। गोल होंठों वाले स्वर केवल 'उ', 'ऊ', 'ओ', 'औ' आदि हैं। इसलिए 'ऋ' को वृत्तमुखी बताना गलत है। शेष विवरण - 'उ' (पश्च, संवृत, वृत्तमुखी), 'अ' (मध्य, ह्रस्व, उदासीन), 'आ' (पश्च, विवृत, अवृत्तमुखी)-सही हैं।

41. मैथुन, शौच, राघव - 'अ' प्रत्यय : यह संगत है क्योंकि इन शब्दों में 'अ' (या मूल 'अण्') प्रत्यय का प्रयोग है। 'मैथुन' = मिथुना + अ, 'शौच' = शुचि + अ, 'राघव' = रघु + अ। ये भाववाचक या अपत्यवाचक संज्ञाएँ बनाते हैं। अन्य विभाजन गलत हैं - 'फिकैत, डकैत, लड़ैत' में 'ऐत' नहीं; 'नारदीय, स्थानीय, मानवीय' में 'ईय' प्रत्यय है, 'अनीय' नहीं; 'कौशेय, सौजन्य, कौमार्य' में 'य' प्रत्यय है, 'एय' नहीं।

42. शिक्षा तथा उपाधियाँ : एक हिंदी अध्यापक की विशिष्ट विशेषताओं में साहित्य का गहरा ज्ञान, भाषा-शिक्षण की विधियों की समझ, और हिंदी भाषा पर विशेष अधिकार आते हैं। शिक्षा और उपाधियाँ केवल योग्यता का प्रमाण हैं, पर ये अध्यापक की विशिष्ट पेशेवर विशेषताओं में नहीं गिनी जातीं।

43. निःशुल्क, निष्पक्ष, निस्स्वार्थ - 'निस्' उपसर्ग : यहाँ उपसर्ग 'निस्' का प्रयोग नियमानुसार है। 'निः' + शुल्क = निःशुल्क, 'निः'+ पक्ष = निष्पक्ष, 'निस्' + स्वार्थ = निस्स्वार्थ। ध्वन्यात्मक नियमों के अनुसार 'निस्' उपसर्ग 'श' के पहले 'निः', 'प' के पहले 'नि', और 'स' के पहले 'निस' रूप लेता है। अतः यह विकल्प सही है।

44. जिसने परिश्रम किया, वह सफल हो गया : इस वाक्य में सार्वनामिक विशेषण का प्रयोग नहीं हुआ है। यहाँ 'जिसने' संबंधवाचक सर्वनाम और 'वह' निश्चयवाचक सर्वनाम हैं, जो संज्ञा के स्थान पर प्रयुक्त हुए हैं। वे किसी संज्ञा की विशेषता नहीं बता रहे।

सार्वनामिक विशेषण तब होता है जब कोई सर्वनाम संज्ञा के पहले आकर उसे विशेषित करता है -

- *यह पुस्तक* - 'यह' पुस्तक की ओर संकेत करता है।
- *ऐसे व्यक्ति* - 'ऐसे' व्यक्ति की विशेषता बताता है।
- *कोई नौकर* - 'कोई' अनिश्चयवाचक सार्वनामिक विशेषण है।

अतः सही उत्तर विकल्प 1 है।

45. उचित लय और गति प्रदान करना : मौन वाचन का उद्देश्य अर्थ ग्रहण करना, केंद्रीय भाव समझना, और स्वाध्याय की आदत डालना है। परंतु इसमें उच्च स्वर से पढ़ने जैसी लय और गति प्रदान करना उद्देश्य नहीं होता। यह उद्देश्य मुखर वाचन का होता है।

46. A is true; B is false: Assertion A is correct because the limitation of print material is indeed that it lacks interactivity and cannot incorporate audio-visual elements, making it less engaging compared to digital resources. Assertion B is false because print materials *are* portable, widely available, and generally cost-effective compared to other instructional media. Therefore, only A is true.

47. the mother: The speaker directly addresses her mother throughout the poem, repeatedly saying "Look for me, mother."

48. Mumbai: The poem mentions "your beloved Mumbai," showing the foeticide occurs in Mumbai.

49. formaldehyde: The infant explicitly says "I smell of formaldehyde," referring to the chemical used for preserving dead bodies.

50. the killed infant girl: The "I" is the unborn female child, who narrates her own killing through female foeticide.

51. pomegranates: The line "I looked like a sliced pomegranate. The fruit you never touched" shows the mother disliked pomegranates.

52. autopsy: The word "autopsy room" in the poem directly refers to post-mortem examination.

53. because the mother didn't want a second girl child: The doctor told the mother it would be a girl, and since she was already the second girl child, the foetus was killed.

54. repetition: The poem repeatedly uses phrases like "Look for me, mother" for emphasis and emotional impact.

55. simile: The line *"I looked like a sliced pomegranate"* is a simile because it directly compares the killed infant's body to a pomegranate using the word "like," which is the clear marker of a simile.

56. glistened: The line "the orange stems of the parijatak blossoms glistened in your hair" shows "glistened" means "shone due to being wet."

57. prescriptive: Nesfield's grammar belongs to the traditional prescriptive school, which sets rules of correctness and dictates how language should be used rather than how it is actually used.

58. aural-oral: The aural-oral skill trains learners to recognize English sounds, stress, rhythm, and intonation, forming the foundation for correct pronunciation and speech.

59. multilingual resources: Allowing learners to discuss a poem in English using their native language utilizes multilingual resources, making comprehension easier and supporting language learning.

60. intensive and extensive: In language teaching, listening is mainly classified into intensive and extensive types. Intensive listening focuses on close, detailed listening for accuracy, pronunciation, or specific information, often in classroom practice. Extensive listening involves listening to longer or larger amounts of material, such as stories, songs, or lectures, to develop overall comprehension and fluency, usually outside the classroom or for enjoyment.

61. Square: $a=\sqrt{2}R \Rightarrow a^2=2R^2$
Equilateral triangle: $b=\sqrt{3}R \Rightarrow b^2=3R^2$
Thus, $3a^2=2b^2$.

62. Surface area ratio = 1 : 2 $\Rightarrow r_1 : r_2 = 1 : \sqrt{2}$

Volume ratio $= r_1^3 : r_2^3 = 1 : (\sqrt{2})^3 = 1 : 2\sqrt{2}$.

63. Series follows $n^3 + 1$:
$1^3 + 1 = 2$, $2^3 + 1 = 9$, $3^3 + 1 = 28$, $4^3 + 1 = 65$, $5^3 + 1 = 126$.
Missing term = 65.

64. Volume $V = \pi(R^2 - r^2)L$, $R = 9$, $r = 9 - t$, $L=14$
$\pi.14(81-(9-t)^2) = 748 \Rightarrow \pi.14(18t-t^2) = 748$
Using $\pi=22/7$: $44(18t-t^2)=748 \Rightarrow 18t-t^2 = 17$

$$t^2 - 18t + 17 = 0 \Rightarrow t = \frac{18 \pm 16}{2} = 17,\ \mathbf{1} \Rightarrow t=1 \text{ cm}.$$

65. Line : Square (completed form) :: Arc : **Circle** (completed curve).

66. Path (take North as + y) :

$$(0,0) \xrightarrow{10N} (0, 10) \xrightarrow{\text{right } 10E} (10,10)$$

Left turns : +5N → (10, 15), +15W → (-5, 15), +15S → (-5, 0)

Distance from start : $\sqrt{(-5)^2 + 0^2} = 5\text{km}$.

67. Second letter: G(7), K(11), O(15), S(19), **W(23)** ⇒ +4 each → needs **W**.
First letter: A(1), G(7), E(5), G(7), **I(9)** → fits option IW.
Middle letter: d, g, j, m, **p** ⇒ +3 each.
Numbers: 6, 21, 45, 78, **120** (diffs +15, +24, +33, +42).

68. A is father of C; C is sister of D ⇒ A and B are parents of C & D.
E is A's brother ⇒ **B is E's sister-in-law.**

69. Order: First → gives to R ⇒ R is 2nd. Last took from P ⇒ P is 4th.
Two between P and Q ⇒ Q is 1st. Remaining {S,T} at {3,5}; T not first/last ⇒ T=3, **S = 5 (last).**

70. Seats: Y, Z in centers (3, 4); A, P at ends → A at 6 (since R is left of A) ⇒ R at 5, P at 1, remaining X at 2 ⇒ right of P is X.

71. 10-Dec-2022 (Sat) → +365 days = 10-Dec-2023 (Sun) → +364 days = 8-Dec-2024 (Sun).

72. AYBZC : By position:
1st: M→ J → G → D (−3) ⇒ A; 2nd: O → S(+4) → U(+2) → W(+2) → Y(+2);
3rd: N → K → H → E (−3) ⇒ B; 4th: R→T→V→X (+2) ⇒ Z; 5th: O → L → I → F (−3) ⇒ C.

73. Given $\tan\theta+\sec\theta=4$. Then $\sec\theta-\tan\theta=1/4$.
Add: $2\sec\theta = 4 + 1/4 = 17/4 \Rightarrow \sec\theta = 17/8 \Rightarrow \cos\theta = 8/17$.

74. $2880 = 2^6.3^2.5$. For a perfect square, exponents must be even ⇒ remove the lone 5.
Smallest divisor = 5.

75. P : 45000×12, Q : $30000\times t$, ratio 2 : 1.

$$\frac{45000.12}{30000.t} = \frac{2}{1} \Rightarrow \frac{18}{t} = 2 \Rightarrow t = 9 \text{ months invested}$$

⇒ joined after 12 − 9 = 3 months.

76. Let numbers = $3k$, $2k$, $5k$.
$(3k)^2+(2k)^2+(5k)^2 = 1862 \Rightarrow 9k^2+4k^2+25k^2 = 38k^2 = 1862$

$$\Rightarrow k^2 = \frac{1862}{38} = 49 \Rightarrow k = 7$$

Middle number = $2k$ = 14.

77. A+B = 19/23 of work ⇒ C = 4/23.
Share of C = 4/23 × 5290 = 4 × 230 = **920**.

78. For 2 years, $CI - SI = P\left(\frac{r}{100}\right)^2$.

$$\text{Given } 15 = P\left(\frac{5}{100}\right)^2 = P.\frac{25}{10000} = \frac{P}{400}$$

⇒ P = 15 × 400 = 6000.

79. **17 m :** We need the radius of a circular field whose area equals the combined areas of three smaller circular fields (radii 8 m, 9 m, and 12 m).

Formula: $\pi R^2 = \pi(r_1^2 + r_2^2 + r_3^2)$

Cancelling π: $R^2 = r_1^2 + r_2^2 + r_3^2$

Substitute values: $R^2 = 8^2 + 9^2 + 12^2$

$= 64 + 81 + 144 = 289$

$R = \sqrt{289} = 17\,m$

☞ So, the radius of the larger field is **17 m.**

80. **lo, ba**

We must decode the words from the code language:

1. *sun shines brightly* → **ba lo sul**
2. *houses are brightly lit* → **kado ula ari ba**
3. *light comes from sun* → **dopi kup lo nro**

Step 1: Find *brightly*

- Common word in (1) & (2) = **brightly**
- Common code in (1) & (2) = **ba**

☞ *brightly* = ba

Step 2: Find *sun*

- Common word in (1) & (3) = **sun**
- Common code in (1) & (3) = **lo**

☞ *sun* = lo

Thus, the code for **sun** = **lo** and **brightly** = **ba**.

81. **Khol Hi-Raitan Sanctuary :** The question asks which sanctuary is in the Shivalik hills (outer Himalayas).

- **Khol Hi-Raitan Sanctuary** → Panchkula district, Haryana; located in the Shivalik range ✓
- **Khaparwas Sanctuary** → Jhajjar district, Haryana; a wetland, not in Shivaliks ×
- **Bhindawas Sanctuary** → Jhajjar district, Haryana; a bird sanctuary in plains ×
- **Nahar Sanctuary** → Rewari district, Haryana plains ×

☞Therefore, the correct answer is Khol Hi-Raitan Sanctuary.

82. **Gujarat :** The theme state for the **37th Surajkund International Crafts Fair (February 2024)** was Gujarat. The state displayed its handicrafts, folk music, tribal art, and rich heritage. Such fairs give artisans a platform to present regional culture at an international level. Gujarat's stalls attracted wide attention for their embroidery, beadwork, and traditional dance forms.

83. **Darbari Lal Gupta :** After Haryana was carved out from Punjab on 1st November 1966, the Haryana Public Service Commission (HPSC) was established. The very first chairman of the HPSC was Darbari Lal Gupta. He played a key role in setting up the administrative structure for recruitment in the new state. His appointment ensured smooth functioning of the state's selection process.

84. **Kilohad :** The **Indian Institute of Information Technology (IIIT), Sonepat** is being set up at Kilohad village in the Sonepat district of Haryana. This institution is established under the Public-Private Partnership (PPP) model. It has been declared an Institute of National Importance by the Government of India. Its aim is to promote excellence in information technology and allied studies.

85. **Rewari :** The **Rohtak Division** of Haryana comprises five districts: Rohtak, Jhajjar, Sonipat, Charkhi Dadri, and Bhiwani. These districts are grouped for better administrative management. Rewari, however, is not included in Rohtak Division. Instead, **Rewari** falls under the Gurugram Division of Haryana.

86. **Antim Panghal :** The woman wrestler from Haryana who received the **Arjuna Award for 2023** is Antim Panghal. She was honoured in January 2024 for her historic sporting achievements. Antim became the first Indian woman to win two consecutive U-20 World Wrestling Championship gold medals. Her award highlights Haryana's dominance in the field of wrestling.

87. **Both the statements are true :** The **Pehowa Inscription** belongs to the reign of the Gurjar-Pratihara king Mahendrapala I (c. 885–910 CE). It clearly confirms that it was issued under the Gurjar-Pratihar dynasty, making statement (i) true. The inscription also mentions Prithudaka (ancient Pehowa) as a bustling horse market, where dealers from different places gathered and made donations to the temple. Hence, statement (ii) is also true.

88. **S.C. Chaudhary :** Manohar Lal Khattar became CM of Haryana in October 2014. At that time, Shakuntala Jakhu was Chief Secretary (July–Nov 2014), followed by P.K. Gupta (Nov–Dec 2014) and later Vijay Vardhan (2020–2021). S.C. Chaudhary's tenure (2013–July 2014) ended before Khattar assumed office, so he never served as Chief Secretary under Khattar.

89. **Statement (a), (b) & (c) are correct :** Sir Chhotu Ram began his career in the Congress Party in 1916, later resigning in 1920. He co-founded and joined the Unionist Party in 1923–24, which became his primary political base. He also served as a minister in the Government of Undivided Punjab, handling Agriculture, Education, and Development portfolios. Therefore, all three statements are correct.

90.
- **Gujari Mahal – Hisar:** Built by Firoz Shah Tughlaq in Hisar for his beloved Gujari, this is correct.
- **Aram-e-Kausar – Narnaul:** A Mughal-era garden palace complex in Narnaul, also correct.
- **Tomb of Sheikh Tayyab – Jind:** Incorrect, since it is located in Kaithal, not Jind.

Thus, only (a) and (b) are correctly matched.

Previous Years' Paper

Haryana Teacher Eligibility Test (HTET)

PGT (Level-3), Common Subjects, Exam 2023

(Exam held on 02-12-2023)

PART-I : CHILD DEVELOPMENT AND PEDAGOGY

1. Which type of education would be appropriate for socially deprived children?

A. Informal education B. Special education
C. Inclusive education D. Religious education

2. Which of the following statement is **correct** regarding adolescence, under Erikson's Psycho-social development theory?

A. Ego-identity is a positive psycho-social aspect.
B. Ego-identity is a negative psycho-social aspect.
C. Ego-identity is a neutral psycho-social aspect.
D. Ego-identity is not just a psycho-social aspect.

3. Which of the following characteristic is **not** seen in a creative child?

A. Divergent thinking B. Extreme curiosity
C. High imaginations D. Conventional thoughts

4. Which of the following characteristics does **not** have a positive effect on the process of socialisation?

A. Socially approved behaviour
B. Playing approved social roles
C. Development of social attitude
D. Development of social prejudices

5. Vygotsky's 'Zone of Proximal Development' refers to:

A. What the child can do independently
B. What the child can't do independently
C. What the child can do with guidance of knowledgeable person
D. What the child can't do even under guidance of knowledgeable person

6. If a learner does **not** achieved the expected performance, what type of testing is done to find out the reason?

A. Formative B. Diagnostic
C. Remedial D. Summative

7. "Inclusion is not confined to the disabled but it also mean no exclusion of any child".
This meaning of inclusion in education has been clarified by:

A. NCF 2005 B. NCERT
C. UNESCO D. UNICEF

8. Which type of changes occur in growth and development?

(*a*) Change in body size
(*b*) Change in body proportion
(*c*) Disappearance of old features
(*d*) Acquisition of new features

Choose the **correct** code:

A. (*a*), (*b*) & (*c*) B. (*a*), (*b*) & (*d*)
C. (*a*), (*c*) & (*d*) D. (*a*), (*b*), (*c*) & (*d*)

9. Which of the following statements does **not** explain the positive impact of motivation on learning?

A. Motivation impairs learning behaviour
B. Motivation provide definite direction to learning behaviour
C. Motivation energizes learning behaviour
D. Motivation makes learning

10. Match the stages of morality with their level, under the Moral Development theory of Kohlberg:

Stages of Morality	Level of Morality
(*a*) Good interpersonal relations	I
(*b*) Individualism and exchange	II
(*c*) Social contracts and individual rights	III
(*d*) Universal principles	

Code:

	(*a*)	(*b*)	(*c*)	(*d*)
A.	I	III	II	I
B.	III	II	III	I
C.	II	III	I	II
D.	II	I	III	III

1. C	2. A	3. D	4. D	5. C	6. B	7. A	8. D	9. A	10. D

11. When the learner learns a task automatically, without any desire or purpose, then it is called:
A. Massed learning B. Whole learning
C. Part learning D. Incidental learning

12. Which of the following statement is **not** true regarding biological motives?
A. They are universal
B. They are inborn
C. They are essential to survival
D. They are not related to the homeostasis of the individual

13. Which of the following examinations are the basis of continuous and comprehensive evaluation?
(*a*) Written (*b*) Oral
(*c*) Behavioural (*d*) Practical
Choose the **correct** code:
Code:
A. (*a*), (*b*) & (*d*) B. (*a*), (*b*) & (*c*)
C. (*a*), (*c*) & (*d*) D. (*a*), (*b*), (*c*) & (*d*)

14. Which of the following statement is **not** correct in reference to intelligence tests?
A. Alexander's Pass along test is a performance test.
B. Verbal test can be either individual or group.
C. Illiterate people cannot do performance test.
D. In non-verbal tests intelligence is measured through pictures and figures.

15. Which of the following pair is not correct regarding elements of intelligence and their dimensional under the Three Dimensional Intelligence theory of Guilford?

	Elements of Intelligence	Dimension
A.	Unit	Product
B.	Cognition	Operation
C.	Evaluation	Operation
D.	Relations	Content

16. Which one of the following is **not** a key feature of child centred learning approach?
A. Meaningful learning opportunities
B. Single learning pathway
C. Continuous assessment
D. Accessible learning settings

17. According to Bandura, which is **not** the interrelated processes of observational learning?
A. Attentional Processes
B. Retentional Processes
C. Motivational Processes
D. Combinational Processes

18. According to Bandura's Social Learning theory, what is it called when a person learns the same behaviour by observing and repeating the behaviour of others?
A. Adaptation B. Self-observation
C. Modeling D. Efficacy expectation

19. Which sub-component is **not** included in componential intelligence under the Sternberg Triarchic Theory?
A. Meta component
B. Experimental component
C. Performance component
D. Knowledge acquisition component

20. A learning disability that affects the acquisition of arithmetical skill is:
A. Dyscalculia B. Dysgraphia
C. Dyslexia D. Dysmagnisia

21. Choose the **correct** sequence of the five stages of Freud's Psychosexual development theory:
A. Oral stage → Phallic stage → Latency stage → Anal stage → Genital stage
B. Anal stage → Latency stage → Phallic stage → Genital stage → Oral stage
C. Oral stage → Anal stage → Phallic stage → Latency stage → Genital stage
D. Latency stage → Anal stage → Oral stage → Genital stage → Phallic stage

22. According to Pavlov's Classical Conditioning theory of learning, which temporal sequence presentation of natural and conditioned stimuli will most affect learning?
A. Simultaneous B. Delay
C. Trace D. Backward

23. In which stage of Piaget's Cognitive Development theory does the ability of abstract thinking and generalization develop?
A. Sensory motor B. Pre-operational
C. Concrete-operational D. Formal operational

24. Which of the following educational arrangements shouldn't be made for talented students?
A. Opportunities for independent project work
B. Acceleration
C. Remedial teaching
D. Enrichment program

25. Which one of the following is **not** a principle of inclusive education?
A. Principle of segregation
B. Principle of cooperation
C. Principle of celebrating diversity
D. Principle of right to education

11. D	**12.** D	**13.** D	**14.** C	**15.** D	**16.** B	**17.** D	**18.** C	**19.** B	**20.** A
21. C	**22.** B	**23.** D	**24.** C	**25.** A					

26. Which of the following way does **not** support the teaching according to individual differences?
A. Large group of students
B. Individualized instruction
C. Curriculum adaptation
D. Knowledge of student's abilities

27. Which is **not** a role of educational institutions in addressing the needs of children with special need?
A. Admission to school without discrimination
B. Provide accessible infrastructural facilities
C. Identify their special needs and exclude them from mainstreaming
D. Provide necessary support services

28. Which of the following statement is **not** correct in context of development?
A. Development is the product of maturation and learning.
B. Later development is more critical than early development.
C. Development proceeds from head to foot.
D. Development proceeds from central axis to extremities.

29. The three dimensional model of the inclusive education propounded by whom?
A. Griffith, Cooper and Ringlaben
B. Gartuer and Lipsky
C. Kauffman and Hallahan
D. Levenski, Davis and Hooper

30. "Socialization means attaining of maturity in social relationships". This definition of socialization is given by whom?
A. John Dewey B. Garret
C. Sorenson D. Hurlock

PART-II : भाषा – हिन्दी

31. विशेषण के संबंध में कौन-सा सही सुमेलित **नहीं** है?
A. भारतीय - संज्ञा से निर्मित विशेषण
B. पवित्रतम - विशेषण की उत्तरावस्था
C. परिश्रमी - गुणवाचक विशेषण
D. आलस्य - विशेषण से निर्मित भाववाचक संज्ञा

32. किस विकल्प में शब्द-युग्म का सही अर्थ भेद **नहीं** है?
A. बाजी - दाव, वाजी - घोड़ा
B. मेध - हवन, मेघ - बादल
C. माणिक्य - चर्बी, माणिक्या - मछली
D. मुक्ता - मोती, मुक्ति - मोक्ष

33. कौन-सा युग्म संगत **नहीं** है?
A. भिक्षुक - तत्सम शब्द B. मस्तक - तद्भव शब्द
C. खिचड़ी - देशज शब्द D. अमानत - विदेशज शब्द

34. निम्नलिखित में से किस विकल्प का शब्द संधि-विच्छेद की दृष्टि से **संगत** है?
A. कुशासन = कुश + असन B. वार्तालाप = वार्ता + अलाप
C. जानकीश = जनक + ईश D. लघूर्मि = लघु + ऊर्मि

35. किस विकल्प के समस्त पद में बहुव्रीहि समास का उदाहरण **नहीं** है?
A. शेषशायी, क्षपानाथ B. दीर्घश्वास, पाषाणहृदय
C. आशुतोष, मंदोदरी D. पंचशर, पशुपति

36. किस विकल्प का शब्द 'अन्' उपसर्ग से निर्मित **नहीं** है?
A. अनंतर B. अनीति
C. अनिष्ट D. अनाचार

37. निम्न में से किस विकल्प के शब्द विदेशज प्रत्ययों से निर्मित हैं?
A. पल्लवित, नीलिमा B. अड़ियल, कसावट
C. रिश्वतखोर, रोजगार D. झगड़ालू, हठीला

38. पर्यायवाची शब्दों के संबंध में कौन-सा विकल्प **अनुचित** है?
A. चन्द्रमा - हिमकर, अमृतांशु, महताब
B. गरुड़ - खगनाथ, वृषभी, भद्रा
C. चन्दन - गोरोचन, मलयज, सर्पावास
D. गंगा - अमरतटिनी, अद्रिजा, सुरसरि

39. वार्तनिक दृष्टि से किस विकल्प के सभी शब्द **शुद्ध** हैं?
A. अभ्यार्थी, त्यौहार B. याज्ञवल्क्य, हस्तक्षेप
C. मैथली, अहिल्या D. वैदेहि, वापिस

40. '<u>महात्मा</u> गाँधी ने <u>भारत</u> को आजाद कराया।' उक्त वाक्य में रेखांकित शब्द क्रमशः हैं :
A. व्यक्तिवाचक संज्ञा तथा जातिवाचक संज्ञा
B. जातिवाचक संज्ञा तथा भाववाचक संज्ञा
C. व्यक्तिवाचक संज्ञा तथा व्यक्तिवाचक संज्ञा
D. भाववाचक संज्ञा तथा व्यक्तिवाचक संज्ञा

26. A	**27.** C	**28.** B	**29.** A	**30.** D	**31.** B	**32.** C	**33.** B	**34.** D	**35.** B
36. B	**37.** C	**38.** B	**39.** B	**40.** C					

41. निम्न में से किस मुहावरे का अर्थ संगत **नहीं** है?
A. अपने पैरों पर खड़ा होना - आत्मनिर्भर होना।
B. अंधे के हाथ बटेर लगना - बिना प्रयास के कोई चीज प्राप्त कर लेना।
C. एक घाट पानी पीना - एकता और सहिष्णुता होना।
D. कमान से तीर निकल जाना - किसी का भेद खुलना।

42. क्रिया के संबंध में **अनुचित** विकल्प चुनिए :
A. कर्म के आधार पर क्रिया के 'सकर्मक' एवं 'अकर्मक' दो भेद माने जाते हैं।
B. सभी प्रेरणार्थक क्रियाएँ अकर्मक होती हैं।
C. 'पिता पुत्र से पत्र लिखवाता है।' उक्त वाक्य में प्रेरणार्थक क्रिया प्रयुक्त हुई है।
D. 'बतियांना', 'लठियाना' एवं 'अपनाना' नामधातु क्रिया के उदाहरण हैं।

43. सर्वनाम के संबंध में कौन-सा कथन **असत्य** है?
A. प्रयोग के आधार पर सर्वनाम के छह भेद हैं।
B. 'कोई' तथा 'कुछ' अनिश्चयवाचक सर्वनाम शब्द हैं।
C. 'पुरुषवाचक' सर्वनाम के चार भेद माने जाते हैं।
D. जिस सर्वनाम से वक्ता के पास अथवा दूर की किसी वस्तु का बोध होता है, उसे निश्चयवाचक सर्वनाम कहते हैं।

44. किस विकल्प में विपरीतार्थक युग्म **असंगत** है?
A. नूतन - पुरातन B. दुराशय - सदाशय
C. दनुज - दानव D. जंगम - स्थावर

45. वाक्यांश के लिए एकल शब्द के संबंध में अनुचित युग्म है :
A. जो कानून की दृष्टि से उचित न हो - अवैध
B. जिसमें कोई छिद्र न हो - नीरन्ध्र
C. समुद्र में लगने वाली आग - दावानल
D. जो भोजन रोगी के लिए उचित है : पथ्य

PART-II : LANGUAGE – ENGLISH

46. Fill in the blank with the **correct** option:
Note it down ______ you should forget it.
A. that B. because of
C. till D. lest

47. Choose the **correct** option that gives the meaning of the given idiom:
Spill the beans
A. increase work B. face a great loss
C. to leak a secret D. segregate

48. Fill in the blank with the **correct** option:
The Pak army turned hostile _______ ISIS.
A. to B. for
C. at D. with

49. Choose the **correct** passive of the given sentence:
Please give me some more time.
A. Some more time might please be given to me.
B. Some more time may please be given to me.
C. Some more time could please be given to him.
D. Some more time should please be given to him.

50. Which of the following options express the **correct** meaning of the sentence given below?
No sooner did I reach the college than the bell rang.
A. The sooner I reached the college the earlier the bell rings.
B. I reached the college and the bell was rang after.
C. Although I reached the college the bell began to ring.
D. As soon as I reached the college, the bell rang.

51. Change the narration:
He said, "What a charming sight!"
A. He exclaimed with joy that it was a very charming sight.
B. He exclaimed with joy that what a charming sight it is!
C. He told with joy that is a charming sight.
D. He said to me what a charming sight it is!

52. Fill in the blank with the **correct** form of the verb:
I _______ a lot of calls today.
A. had have B. has had
C. have had D. had had

53. Which of the following sentences is the **correct** option to express a probable condition?
A. If I were a bird, I would fly to you.
B. If you touch a live wire, you will get a shock.
C. If you will read this book, you will learn grammar.
D. If I had reached in time, I could have saved her.

54. Choose the part of the sentence that is grammatically **incorrect**:
He thought (*a*) / he will be able to do (*b*) / whatever he wanted (*c*) / with his job. (*d*)
A. (*a*) B. (*b*)
C. (*c*) D. (*d*)

41. D	**42.** B	**43.** C	**44.** C	**45.** C	**46.** D	**47.** C	**48.** A	**49.** B	**50.** D
51. A	**52.** C	**53.** B	**54.** B						

55. Choose the part of the sentence that is grammatically **incorrect**:

The Jews were *(a)* / most reluctant *(b)* / to contribute *(c)* / in the Palestinian cause. *(d)*

A. *(a)* B. *(b)*
C. *(c)* D. *(d)*

56. The word 'slither' means:

A. lick B. venomous
C. hinder D. slide

57. Fill in the blank with the **correct** form of the verb:

When I last ______ her, she was deeply involved in debt.

A. have met B. met
C. has met D. did met

58. Fill in the blank with the **correct** option:

How did the thief _____ the padlock.

A. open B. opened
C. had opened D. had been opening

59. Fill in the blank with the **correct** 'Modal Auxiliary':

_______ you mind lending me your pen? (Request)

A. Should B. Ought
C. Would D. Must

60. Arrange the following jumbled options in the correct order and then choose the **correct** option:

(a) is heartening *(b)* is going abroad
(c) the news *(d)* that she

A. *(c)*, *(d)*, *(b)*, *(a)* B. *(d)*, *(a)*, *(c)*, *(b)*
C. *(d)*, *(c)*, *(b)*, *(a)* D. *(d)*, *(c)*, *(a)*, *(b)*

PART-III : GENERAL STUDIES

Quantitative Aptitude, Reasoning Ability and GK & Awareness

61. If A stands on his head with his face towards North, in which direction will his left hand point?

A. North-East B. West
C. East D. North-West

62. A boat goes 20 km downstream in one hour and the same distance upstream in two hours. The speed of the boat in still water is:

A. 10 km/h B. 12 km/h
C. 13 km/h D. 15 km/h

63. In a group of 15 people, 7 read Hindi, 8 read English, while 3 of them read none of these two. How many of them read Hindi and English both?

A. 0 B. 3
C. 4 D. 5

64. In a class of 35 students, A is placed 7th from the bottom whereas B is placed 9th from the top and C is placed exactly between these two. What is A's position from C?

A. 9th B. 10th
C. 11th D. 12th

65. In a certain code language 'CEG' is written as 'TSR' and 'FHJ' is written as 'QPO', then in the same code language 'IKM' is written as:

A. NOP B. NOL
C. NMK D. NML

66. How many meaningful words can be formed with the letter EAML?

A. 1 B. 2
C. 3 D. 4

67. The ratio of an interior angle to the exterior angle of a regular polygon is 7 : 2. The number of sides of the polygon is:

A. 7 B. 8
C. 9 D. 11

68. Find the next term of the following number series:

2, 3, 10, 15, 26, ?

A. 33 B. 34
C. 35 D. 36

69. Pipe A alone can fill a tank in 8 hours. Pipe B alone can fill it in 6 hours. If both the pipes are opened and after 2 hours pipe A is closed, then pipe B will fill the tank in:

A. 2 hours B. 2½ hours
C. 3 hours D. 3½ hours

70. In a certain pattern, if 38 * 15 = 32, 62 * 91 = 7 and 74 * 81 = 29, then in the same pattern the value of 47 * 33 is:

A. 40 B. 41
C. 38 D. 53

71. If it was Saturday on 17th December, 2002, what was the day on 22nd December, 2004?

A. Sunday B. Saturday
C. Monday D. Tuesday

55. D	**56.** D	**57.** B	**58.** A	**59.** C	**60.** A	**61.** C	**62.** D	**63.** B	**64.** B
65. D	**66.** C	**67.** C	**68.** C	**69.** B	**70.** B	**71.** A			

72. The next of the series is:
Z1A, X2D, V6G, T21J, ?
A. R87M B. R87N
C. R88P D. R88M

73. In English alphabet, the number of letters skipped in between adjacent letters in the series is decreased by one. Which of the following series observes the rule?
A. DJOTV B. DJOSV
C. DJOSW D. DIOSU

74. The radius of the circumcircle of the triangle made by x-axis, y-axis and $4x + 3y = 12$ is:
A. 2 unit B. 2.5 unit
C. 3 unit D. 4 unit

75. Find the least number which must be added to 15463 so that the resulting number is exactly divisible by 107:
A. 52 B. 55
C. 71 D. 76

76. What proportion of water must be added to milk to gain 20% by selling it at the cost price?
A. 1 : 5 B. 2 : 5
C. 3 : 5 D. 4 : 5

77. The ratio of compound interest and simple interest on a certain sum at the rate of 4% per annum for 2 years is:
A. 52 : 51 B. 52 : 50
C. 51 : 50 D. 53 : 50

78. If A, B and C enter into a partnership with shares in the ratio $\frac{7}{2}:\frac{4}{3}:\frac{6}{5}$. After 4 months, A increase his share by 50%. If the total profit at the end of one year be ₹ 21,600, then B's share in the profit is:
A. ₹ 2,400 B. ₹ 3,600
C. ₹ 4,000 D. ₹ 4,200

79. A man sold an article at a loss of 20%. If he sells the article for ₹ 12 more, he would have gained 10%. The cost price of an article is:
A. ₹ 22 B. ₹ 30
C. ₹ 36 D. ₹ 40

80. $\frac{a^{1/2}+a^{-1/2}}{1-a}+\frac{1-a^{-1/2}}{1+\sqrt{a}}$ is equal to:
A. $\frac{a}{a-1}$ B. $\frac{a-1}{2}$
C. $\frac{2}{a-1}$ D. $\frac{2}{1-a}$

81. Historical village Sugh is located in:
A. Ambala district B. Kurukshetra district
C. Yamunanagar district D. Panchkula district

82. Which Haryanvi conquered Mount Elbrus in August, 2023?
A. Sandeep Bishnoi B. Rohtash Bishnoi
C. Ajay Khichad D. Mohit

83. Who among the following Governors of Haryana was an ICS officer?
A. Shri Dharma Vir
B. Shri Muzaffar Hussain Burney
C. Shri Hari Anand Barari
D. Shri Surjit Singh Sandhawalia

84. The evidence of Stupa of Mauryan period is found at:
A. Topara B. Bhiwani
C. Thanesar D. Rohtak

85. Geeta Jayanti Samaroh is celebrated in the month of:
A. Kartik B. Margshirsh
C. Ashvin D. Shravana

86. Who is the Chief Commissioner of Haryana Right to Service Commission?
A. Shri T.C. Gupta B. Shri Vijay Vardhan
C. Shri Rajesh Khullar D. Shri Vikas Gupta

87. Read the following statements about Sadhu Nischal Das:
(*i*) He was a Dadu's disciple.
(*ii*) He compiled a book 'Vichar Sagar' which is in form of dialogue.

Choose the **correct** code:
A. Only statement (*i*) is correct.
B. Only statement (*ii*) is correct.
C. Neither statement (*i*) nor statement (*ii*) are correct.
D. Both the statements (*i*) and (*ii*) are correct

88. In Haryana, where the Chinkara Breeding Centre is located?
A. Pinjore B. Panipat
C. Jhajjar D. Bhiwani

89. When the Haryana State Cooperative Agriculture and Rural Development Board Ltd. was established?
A. January, 1967 B. November, 1966
C. March, 1980 D. January, 1996

90. Where in Haryana, the Indian Institute of Information Technology is located?
A. Sonipat B. Panipat
C. Ambala D. Kurukshetra

72. D	**73.** B	**74.** B	**75.** A	**76.** A	**77.** C	**78.** C	**79.** D	**80.** D	**81.** C
82. B	**83.** A	**84.** A, C	**85.** B	**86.** A	**87.** B	**88.** D	**89.** *	**90.** A	

EXPLANATORY ANSWERS

1. **(C):** Inclusive education is the most suitable type for socially deprived children as it ensures they learn alongside their peers from different backgrounds. This approach promotes equality, diversity, and respect, fostering a sense of belonging and reducing social barriers.

2. **(A):** According to Erik Erikson's theory, adolescence involves the crisis of identity vs. role confusion. Ego-identity, a sense of self and personal identity, is a positive psycho-social aspect of adolescence as it leads to stronger self-awareness and independence.

3. **(D):** Creative children typically exhibit qualities like divergent thinking, extreme curiosity, and high imagination. Conventional thoughts, which involve adherence to traditional or standard ways of thinking, are generally not characteristic of a creative child.

4. **(D):** Development of social prejudices does not have a positive effect on the process of socialization. Such prejudices can lead to discrimination and social conflict, which are detrimental to societal harmony and individual development.

5. **(C):** Vygotsky's 'Zone of Proximal Development' (ZPD) describes the difference between what a child can achieve independently and what they can achieve with guidance from a more knowledgeable individual. This concept underscores the importance of supportive learning environments.

6. **(B):** Diagnostic testing is used to identify the reasons why a learner has not achieved the expected performance. This type of testing analyzes specific areas of difficulty and identifies underlying causes, such as gaps in knowledge or misconceptions, allowing for targeted interventions and support.

7. **(A):** The National Curriculum Framework (NCF) 2005 in India emphasizes that inclusion in education should not be confined to children with disabilities but should ensure that no child is excluded. This broader perspective on inclusion aims to create a learning environment that is accessible and equitable for all students.

8. **(D):** Growth and development involve multiple types of changes: changes in body size (height and weight), changes in body proportions (such as limb length), disappearance of old features (like baby fat), and acquisition of new features (such as secondary sexual characteristics during puberty). All these aspects are integral to the physical and developmental changes that occur over time.

9. **(A):** Motivation impairs learning behaviour is incorrect as motivation generally has a positive impact on learning. It provides definite direction to learning behaviour, energizes learning behaviour, and makes learning more engaging and purposeful. Motivated learners are more likely to set goals, persist through challenges, and achieve higher levels of success.

10. **(D):** Under Kohlberg's Moral Development theory, the stages of morality match their levels as follows:
    (*a*) Good interpersonal relations (Stage 3) correspond to Level II (Conventional)
    (*b*) Individualism and exchange (Stage 2) correspond to Level I (Pre-conventional)
    (*c*) Social contracts and individual rights (Stage 5) correspond to Level III (Post-conventional)
    (*d*) Universal principles (Stage 6) correspond to Level III (Post-conventional)

    This classification reflects the progression from self-interest to adherence to social norms and finally to abstract principles of justice.

11. **(D):** Incidental learning occurs when a learner acquires knowledge or skills unintentionally and without a specific desire or purpose. It often happens through exposure to different environments or activities, where learning is a byproduct of the experience rather than a focused effort.

12. **(D):** Biological motives, such as hunger, thirst, and sleep, are universal, inborn, and essential for survival. They are directly related to homeostasis, which is the body's ability to maintain a stable internal environment. Therefore, the statement that they are not related to homeostasis is incorrect.

13. **(D):** Continuous and comprehensive evaluation (CCE) uses various methods to assess students, including written exams, oral tests, behavioural assessments, and practical examinations. CCE aims to provide a holistic evaluation of a student's performance across different domains, ensuring a more rounded understanding of their abilities and progress.

14. **(C):** The statement that illiterate people cannot do performance tests is incorrect. Performance tests are designed to assess intelligence through tasks that do not rely on verbal skills, making them accessible to individuals regardless of their literacy level. These tests often involve problem-solving with objects, patterns, or figures.

15. **(D):** In Guilford's Three-Dimensional Structure of Intellect, the elements of intelligence are categorized into operations, contents, and products. "Relations"

refers to the operation dimension rather than the content dimension. Operations involve the mental processes used, such as cognition and evaluation, while contents and products describe the material and outcomes of these processes.

16. **(B):** Single learning pathway is not a key feature of child-centered learning. Child-centered learning emphasizes providing meaningful learning opportunities, continuous assessment, and accessible learning settings. It involves multiple learning pathways to cater to individual differences, interests, and needs, ensuring that each child can learn in a way that suits them best.

17. **(D):** Combinational processes are not one of the interrelated processes of observational learning according to Bandura. The key processes are attentional processes (focusing on the model's behaviour), retentional processes (remembering the behaviour), motor reproduction processes (ability to reproduce the behaviour), and motivational processes (having the desire to perform the behaviour).

18. **(C):** According to Bandura's Social Learning Theory, when a person learns the same behaviour by observing and repeating the behaviour of others, it is called modeling. This process involves observing the actions of a model, retaining the information, and then imitating the observed behaviour.

19. **(B):** The experimental component is not included in componential intelligence under Sternberg's Triarchic Theory. The three sub-components of componential intelligence are the meta component (executive processes for planning and decision-making), the performance component (processes for executing tasks), and the knowledge acquisition component (processes for learning and acquiring new information).

20. **(A):** Dyscalculia is a learning disability that affects the acquisition of arithmetic skills. It involves difficulties in understanding numbers, learning how to manipulate numbers, and performing mathematical calculations. This condition impacts a person's ability to perform basic arithmetic operations and understand mathematical concepts.

21. **(C):** Freud's Psychosexual Development Theory outlines five stages in the following sequence: Oral stage → Anal stage → Phallic stage → Latency stage → Genital stage. Each stage represents the focus of the libido on different areas of the body and significant psychological developments.

22. **(B):** According to Pavlov's Classical Conditioning theory, the delay conditioning, where the conditioned stimulus (CS) precedes and overlaps with the unconditioned stimulus (US), is the most effective for learning. This sequence allows the subject to associate the CS with the US strongly.

23. **(D):** The formal operational stage, which occurs from approximately age 12 onwards in Piaget's Cognitive Development theory, is when the ability for abstract thinking and generalization develops. Children can think logically about abstract propositions and test hypotheses systematically.

24. **(C):** Remedial teaching is not suitable for talented students as it is designed to help students who are struggling with their studies. Talented students benefit more from opportunities for independent project work, acceleration, and enrichment programs that challenge and extend their abilities.

25. **(A):** The principle of segregation is not a principle of inclusive education. Inclusive education is based on principles such as cooperation, celebrating diversity, and ensuring the right to education for all children. Segregation, on the other hand, isolates children with disabilities or differences, which is contrary to the inclusive education approach.

26. **(A):** Large groups of students do not support teaching according to individual differences. To address individual needs effectively, smaller groups or individualized instruction, curriculum adaptation, and understanding each student's abilities are essential. Large groups make it difficult to cater to the unique learning styles and needs of each student.

27. **(C):** Identifying special needs and excluding children from mainstreaming is not a role of educational institutions in addressing the needs of children with special needs. Schools should aim for inclusive education by admitting students without discrimination, providing accessible facilities, and offering necessary support services.

28. **(B):** The statement that later development is more critical than early development is incorrect. Early development is often considered more critical because it lays the foundation for future growth and development. Early experiences and learning are crucial in shaping a child's cognitive, social, and emotional development.

29. **(A):** The three-dimensional model of inclusive education was propounded by Griffith, Cooper, and Ringlaben. This model emphasizes the inclusion of all students in the educational process, considering multiple dimensions such as physical, instructional, and social inclusion.

30. (D): "Socialization means attaining of maturity in social relationships". This definition of socialization is given by Hurlock. Socialization is the process by which individuals learn and adopt the norms, values, behaviours, and social skills necessary to function effectively in society.

31. (B): 'पवित्रतम - विशेषण की उत्तरावस्था' सही सुमेलित नहीं है। सही उदाहरण 'पवित्रतम' है, जो विशेषण की उच्चतम अवस्था को दर्शाता है।

32. (C): 'माणिक्य - चर्बी, माणिक्या - मछली' सही अर्थ भेद नहीं है। 'माणिक्य' का अर्थ होता है रत्न (माणिक), जबकि 'माणिक्या' शब्द का उपयोग सामान्यतः नहीं होता है। सही युग्म 'माणिक्य - रत्न, मणिका - मछली' होता है।

33. (B): 'मस्तक - तद्भव शब्द' संगत नहीं है। 'मस्तक' तत्सम शब्द है, जो संस्कृत से सीधे लिया गया है। तद्भव शब्द वे होते हैं जो संस्कृत के शब्दों से परिवर्तित होकर हिंदी में आए हैं, जैसे 'सिर' तद्भव शब्द है।

34. (D): 'लघूर्मि = लघु + ऊर्मि' संगत है। यह सही संधि विच्छेद है जिसमें 'लघु' और 'ऊर्मि' शब्दों के मिलकर बनने वाला शब्द 'लघूर्मि' है।

35. (B): 'दीर्घश्वास, पाषाणहृदय' में बहुव्रीहि समास का उदाहरण नहीं है। बहुव्रीहि समास वह समास होता है जिसमें दोनों पद मिलकर किसी तीसरे पद का बोध कराते हैं, जैसे 'शेषशायी' (विष्णु जो शेषनाग पर शयन करते हैं)। 'दीर्घश्वास' और 'पाषाणहृदय' तत्पुरुष समास के उदाहरण हैं।

36. (B): 'अनीति' शब्द 'अन' उपसर्ग से निर्मित नहीं है। 'अनीति' का निर्माण 'अ-' उपसर्ग से हुआ है जो 'न' का समानार्थी है। 'अंतर', 'अनिष्ट', और 'अनाचार' सभी में 'अन' उपसर्ग का प्रयोग हुआ है।

37. (C): 'रिश्वतखोर, रोजगार' विदेशज प्रत्ययों से निर्मित शब्द हैं। 'खोर' और 'गार' प्रत्यय उर्दू और फारसी भाषा से आए हैं और हिंदी में इस्तेमाल होते हैं। अन्य विकल्पों में देशज और तद्भव प्रत्ययों का प्रयोग है।

38. (B): 'गरुड़ - खगनाथ, वृषभी, भद्रा' अनुचित है। गरुड़ के पर्यायवाची 'खगनाथ' और 'भद्र' हैं, लेकिन 'वृषभी' (वृषभ) और 'भद्रा' अन्य शब्दों के पर्यायवाची हैं। गरुड़ के अन्य पर्यायवाची शब्द जैसे 'वैनतेय' और 'पक्षिराज' हैं।

39. (B): 'याज्ञवल्क्य, हस्तक्षेप' वार्तनिक दृष्टि से शुद्ध शब्द हैं। याज्ञवल्क्य (एक ऋषि) और हस्तक्षेप (intervention) दोनों ही शब्द शुद्ध हैं। अन्य विकल्पों में त्रुटियाँ हैं, जैसे 'मैथली' की बजाय 'मैथिली' और 'वापिस' की बजाय 'वापस'।

40. (C): 'महात्मा गाँधी ने भारत को आजाद कराया।' इस वाक्य में 'महात्मा गाँधी' व्यक्तिवाचक संज्ञा हैं, जबकि 'भारत' भी व्यक्तिवाचक संज्ञा है। व्यक्तिवाचक संज्ञा विशेष व्यक्तियों या स्थानों के नाम होते हैं।

41. (D): 'कमान से तीर निकल जाना - किसी का भेद खुलना' का अर्थ संगत नहीं है। सही अर्थ 'घटना घट जाना या अवसर हाथ से निकल जाना' है।

42. (B): 'सभी प्रेरणार्थक क्रियाएं अकर्मक होती हैं' असत्य है। प्रेरणार्थक क्रियाएं सकर्मक भी हो सकती हैं, जैसे 'लिखवाना' और 'पढ़वाना'। उदाहरण के लिए, 'पिता पुत्र से पत्र लिखवाता है' वाक्य में प्रेरणार्थक सकर्मक क्रिया 'लिखवाता' प्रयुक्त हुई है।

43. (C): 'पुरुषवाचक सर्वनाम के चार भेद माने जाते हैं' असत्य है। पुरुषवाचक सर्वनाम के केवल तीन भेद होते हैं : उत्तम पुरुष, मध्यम पुरुष, और अन्यतमा पुरुष।

44. (C): 'दनुज - दानव' विपरीतार्थक युग्म असंगत है। दोनों शब्दों का अर्थ 'राक्षस' है और ये पर्यायवाची शब्द हैं। सही विपरीतार्थक युग्म 'दनुज - देवता' होता है।

45. (C): 'समुद्र में लगने वाली आग - दावानल' अनुचित युग्म है। दावानल का अर्थ 'जंगल की आग' होता है। 'बड़वानल' समुद्र में लगने वाली आग के लिए एक शब्द होगा।

46. (D): "Note it down lest you should forget it". The word "lest" means 'for fear that' and is used to introduce a clause expressing the reason for the prevention of something undesirable.

47. (C): Spill the beans means to leak a secret. This idiom is used when someone reveals confidential or sensitive information, often unexpectedly or prematurely.

48. (A): "The Pak army turned hostile to ISIS". The correct preposition to use here is "to", which indicates direction or orientation toward something.

49. (B): "Some more time may please be given to me". This is the correct passive form of the sentence. It retains the polite request structure and appropriately places the focus on the time being given.

50. (D): "As soon as I reached the college, the bell rang". This option correctly conveys the meaning of the sentence, indicating that the bell rang immediately after reaching the college.

51. (A): "He exclaimed with joy that it was a very charming sight". This option correctly changes the narration from direct to indirect speech and retains the exclamatory nature and joy expressed.

52. (C): "I have had a lot of calls today". The present perfect tense ("have had") is appropriate here because it refers to actions that occurred at an unspecified time before now, relevant to the present context.

53. (B): "If you touch a live wire, you will get a shock". This sentence expresses a probable condition in the present or future and follows the correct structure for a first conditional sentence, which is used to express real and possible situations.

54. (B): The error is in part (*b*). The correct tense should be "would be able to" instead of "will be able to" because the sentence is in past tense. The corrected sentence is: "He thought he would be able to do whatever he wanted with his job".

55. (D): The error is in part (*d*). The correct preposition should be "to" instead of "in". The corrected sentence is: "The Jews were most reluctant to contribute to the Palestinian cause".

56. (D): The word 'slither' means: "slide". "Slither" means to move smoothly over a surface with a twisting or oscillating motion, typically like a snake. It does not mean "lick", "venomous", or "hinder".

57. (B): "When I last met her, she was deeply involved in debt". The correct form of the verb is "met" because it is the simple past tense, which is used to indicate an action completed in the past. "Have met", "has met", and "did met" are incorrect forms in this context.

58. (A): "How did the thief open the padlock". The correct option is "open" because the sentence is in past tense, and "open" is the base form of the verb used after "did" in questions. "Opened", "had opened", and "had been opening" are incorrect forms in this context.

59. (C): "Would you mind lending me your pen? (Request)" The correct modal auxiliary for making a polite request is "would". "Should", "ought", and "must" are not typically used for making polite requests in this context.

60. (A): "The news that she is going abroad is heartening". The correct order of the jumbled options is (*c*), (*d*), (*b*), (*a*).

61. (C): A stand with his face towards North

$\Rightarrow$ His left hand will point in West direction.

Similarly, A stand on his head with his face towards North

$\Rightarrow$ His left hand will point in East direction.

62. (D): Let the speed of boat in still water be x km/h and the speed of current be y km/h

Then, Speed downstream $= x + y = \dfrac{20}{1}$

$\Rightarrow \quad x + y = 20$ km/h $\quad \ldots(i)$

and speed upstream $= x - y = \dfrac{20}{2}$

$\Rightarrow \quad x - y = 10$ km/h $\quad \ldots(ii)$

From adding (*i*) and (*ii*), we get,

$$2x = 30 \Rightarrow x = 15$$

Hence, The speed of the boat in still water is 15 km/h.

63. (B): In group of 15 people, 7 read Hindi, 8 read English and 3 read none of these languages.

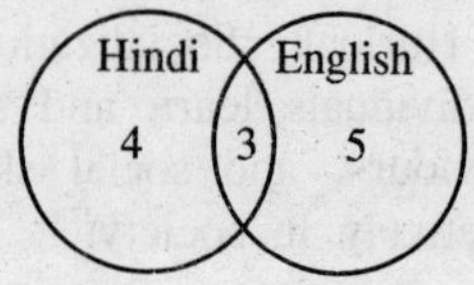

Number of people who speak at least one language $= (15 - 3) = 12$

Number of people who can speak both Hindi and English $= (7 + 8) - 12 = 15 - 12 = 3.$

64. (B):

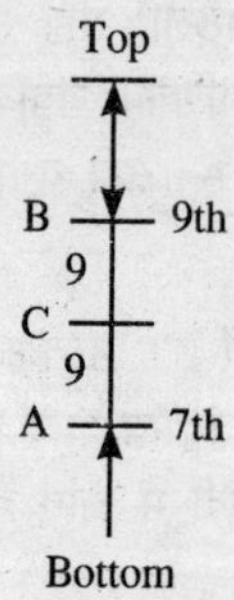

Given, the number of students in a class = 35

A = 7th from bottom, B = 9th from top

$\therefore$ The number of students between A and B

$= 35 - (7 + 9) = 19$

Given, C is placed exactly between A and B

$\therefore$ The number of students between A and C

= B and C = 9

Hence, A's position from C = 9 + 1 = 10th.

66. (C): Given, EAML

Meaningful words: MALE, LAME, MEAL.

Hence, 3 meaningful words can be formed with the letter EAML.

67. (C): An interior angle of a regular polygon

$$= \left(\frac{n-2}{n}\right)\pi$$

and an exterior angle of a regular polygon $= \dfrac{2\pi}{n}$

Therefore, $\left(\dfrac{n-2}{n}\right)\pi : \dfrac{2\pi}{n} = 7 : 2$

$\Rightarrow \quad \left(\dfrac{n-2}{n}\right)\pi \times 2 = \dfrac{2\pi}{n} \times 7$

$\Rightarrow \quad n - 2 = 7$

$\Rightarrow \quad n = 2 + 7 \Rightarrow n = 9$

Hence, the number of sides of the polygon is 9.

68. (C): 2, 3, 10, 15, 26, $\boxed{35}$

Here, $1^2 + 1 = 2 \qquad 2^2 - 1 = 3$

$3^2 + 1 = 10 \qquad 4^2 - 1 = 15$

$5^2 + 1 = 26 \qquad 6^2 - 1 = 35$

Hence, ? = the next term of the number series = 35.

69. (B): Part filled by pipe A in 1 hour $= \frac{1}{8}$,

and part filled by pipe B in 1 hour $= \frac{1}{6}$

$\because$ After 2 hours pipe A is closed

$\therefore$ Part filled by pipe (A + B) in 2 hours

$$= 2\left(\frac{1}{8}+\frac{1}{6}\right) = 2\left(\frac{3+4}{24}\right) = \frac{7}{12}$$

$\therefore$ Remaining part $= 1 - \frac{7}{12} = \frac{5}{12}$

Now, remaining part filled by pipe B in

$$\frac{\frac{5}{12}}{\frac{1}{6}} \text{ hours} = \frac{5}{12}\times\frac{6}{1} = \frac{5}{2}$$

Hence, remaining part of tank will be filled by pipe B in $2\frac{1}{2}$ hours.

70. (B): Given, 38 * 15 = 32

$\Rightarrow$ 83 – 51 = 32

62 * 91 = 7

$\Rightarrow$ 26 – 19 = 7

Reverse digit and subtract

Similarly, 47 * 33 = ?

$\Rightarrow$ 74 – 33 = $\boxed{41}$ which is required answer.

71. (A): The year 2004 is a leap year and hence there would be 29 days in February.

17th December 2002 to 16th December 2003
= 365 days

17th December 2003 to 16th December 2004
= 366 days (leap year)

17th December 2004 to 22nd December 2004
= 6 days

Total number of days = 365 + 366 + 5
= 737 days

737 ÷ 7 = 105 weeks 2 days

The 105th week would end on Friday. Thus, the next two days would be Saturday and Sunday. Hence, the day on 22nd December 2004 would be Sunday.

72. (D):

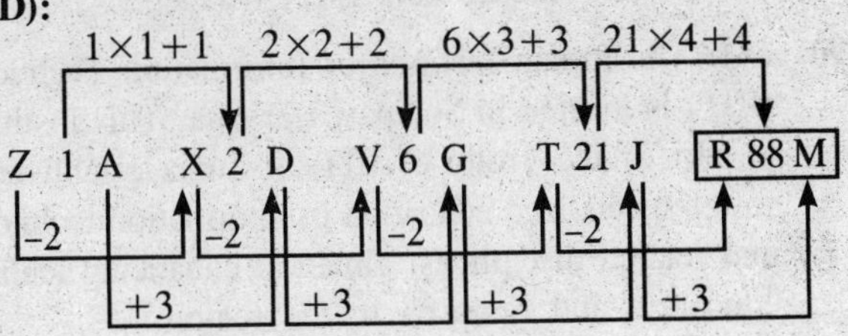

Hence, ? = the next term = R88M.

73. (B):

(A) D J O T V (+6 +5 +5 +2)

(B) D J O S V (+6 +5 +4 +3)

(C) D J O S W (+6 +5 +4 +4)

(D) D I O S U (+5 +6 +4 +2)

Here, option (B) observes the rule.

75. (A): $\because$ 15463 + x = 107 × 145

$\therefore$ 15463 + x = 15515

$\Rightarrow$ x = 15515 – 15463 $\Rightarrow x$ = 52

Hence, Required least number which must be added = 52.

76. (A): Let C.P. of 100 unit Milk = ₹ 100

Then, C.P. of 120 unit milk = ₹ 120

and C.P. of 20 unit water + 100 unit milk = ₹ 100

$\therefore$ S.P. of 20 unit water + 100 unit milk = ₹ 120

$\therefore$ Profit = ₹ 120 – 100 = ₹ 20
= 20%

Hence, proportion of water must be added to milk
= 20 : 100 = 1 : 5.

77. (C): Compound Interest

$$= P\left[\left(1+\frac{r}{100}\right)^n - 1\right] = P\left[\left(1+\frac{4}{100}\right)^2 - 1\right]$$

$$= P\left[\left(\frac{26}{25}\right)^2 - 1\right] = P\left[\frac{676}{625} - 1\right] = P\left[\frac{51}{625}\right]$$

And simple interest $= \frac{P\,r\,t}{100} = \frac{P\times4\times2}{100} = \frac{8P}{100}$

Hence, required ratio

$$= \frac{51P}{625} : \frac{8P}{100} = \frac{51}{25} : \frac{8}{4} = \frac{51}{25} : 2 = 51 : 50.$$

78. (C): Ratio of partnership

$$A : B : C = \frac{7}{2} : \frac{4}{3} : \frac{6}{5} = 105 : 40 : 36$$

After 4 months: Ratio of Share in the profit,

A : B : C

$$= 105\times4 + 105\times\frac{150}{100}\times8 : 40\times12 : 36\times12$$

$$= 420 + 105\times\frac{3}{2}\times8 : 480 : 432$$

= 420 + 105 × 12 : 480 : 432

= 420 + 1260 : 480 : 432

= 1680 : 480 : 432 = 35 : 10 : 9

Given, the total profit at the end of one year
= ₹ 21,600

Hence, B's share in the profit

$$= 21600\times\frac{10}{35+10+9} = 21600\times\frac{10}{54} = \frac{216000}{54}$$

= ₹ 4000.

79. (D): Let the C.P. of an article = ₹ x

Then, the S.P. of an article = ₹ $x \times \frac{100-20}{100} = \frac{4}{5}x$

Now, For profit 10%

The S.P. of the article = ₹ $\left(\frac{4}{5}x + 12\right)$

$$\therefore \quad \text{Profit} = \text{S.P.} - \text{C.P.}$$

$$= \frac{4}{5}x + 12 - x = \left(12 - \frac{1}{5}x\right)$$

$$\therefore \quad \text{Profit\%} = \frac{\text{Profit} \times 100}{\text{C.P.}}$$

$$\Rightarrow \quad 10 = \frac{\left(12 - \frac{1}{5}x\right) \times 100}{x}$$

$$\Rightarrow \quad 10x = \left(12 - \frac{1}{5}x\right) \times 100$$

$$\Rightarrow \quad x = 10\left(12 - \frac{1}{5}x\right)$$

$$\Rightarrow \quad x = 120 - 2x$$

$$\Rightarrow \quad x + 2x = 120$$

$$\Rightarrow \quad 3x = 120 \Rightarrow x = 40$$

Hence, the cost price of an article = ₹ 40.

80. (D): $\frac{a^{1/2} + a^{-1/2}}{1-a} + \frac{1 - a^{-1/2}}{1+\sqrt{a}}$

$$= \frac{a^{1/2} + \frac{1}{a^{1/2}}}{1-a} + \frac{1 - \frac{1}{a^{1/2}}}{1+\sqrt{a}}$$

$$= \frac{\frac{a+1}{a^{1/2}}}{1-a} + \frac{\frac{a^{1/2}-1}{a^{1/2}}}{1+\sqrt{a}} = \frac{1}{a^{1/2}}\left[\frac{a+1}{1-a} + \frac{a^{1/2}-1}{1+\sqrt{a}}\right]$$

$$= \frac{1}{\sqrt{a}}\left[\frac{a+1}{(1-\sqrt{a})(1+\sqrt{a})} + \frac{\sqrt{a}-1}{(1+\sqrt{a})}\right]$$

$$= \frac{1}{\sqrt{a}(1+\sqrt{a})}\left[\frac{a+1}{1-\sqrt{a}} + \sqrt{a} - 1\right]$$

$$= \frac{1}{\sqrt{a}(1+\sqrt{a})}\left[\frac{a+1}{1-\sqrt{a}} - (1-\sqrt{a})\right]$$

$$= \frac{1}{\sqrt{a}(1+\sqrt{a})}\left[\frac{a+1-(1-\sqrt{a})^2}{1-\sqrt{a}}\right]$$

$$= \frac{a+1-1-a+2\sqrt{a}}{\sqrt{a}(1+\sqrt{a})(1-\sqrt{a})} = \frac{2\sqrt{a}}{\sqrt{a}(1-a)} = \frac{2}{1-a}.$$

81. (C): Sugh is a historical village located in Yamunanagar district, Haryana. It is known for its ancient archaeological significance, with remains dating back to the Harappan civilization. This district encompasses the area where Sugh village is situated, contributing to its historical and cultural heritage.

82. (B): Rohtash Bishnoi, a Haryanvi mountaineer, successfully conquered Mount Elbrus in August 2023. Mount Elbrus is the highest peak in Europe, and conquering it is a significant achievement in mountaineering.

83. (A): Shri Dharma Vir, who served as the Governor of Haryana, was an Indian Civil Service (ICS) officer. The ICS was the administrative civil service of the British Empire in India, and being a part of it was considered prestigious.

84. (A, C): Topara and Thanesar in Haryana are known for their historical importance with evidence of Buddhist structures such as stupas from the Mauryan period.

85. (B): Geeta Jayanti Samaroh is celebrated in the month of Margshirsh according to the Hindu lunar calendar. This festival marks the anniversary of the Bhagavad Gita, which is believed to have been delivered by Lord Krishna to Arjuna on the battlefield of Kurukshetra on this day.

86. (A): Shri T.C. Gupta serves as the Chief Commissioner of the Haryana Right to Service Commission. This commission is tasked with ensuring that public services in Haryana are delivered in a timely, efficient, and transparent manner, with Gupta leading these efforts.

87. (B): Statement (*ii*) about Sadhu Nischal Das is correct; he compiled 'Vichar Sagar,' a book presented in the form of a dialogue, which delves into philosophical discussions. However, he was not a disciple of Dadu Dayal, making statement (*i*) incorrect.

88. (D): The Chinkara Breeding Centre in Haryana is located in Bhiwani. This center is crucial for the conservation of the Chinkara, focusing on breeding and caring for this species to support its population growth and ensure ecological balance.

90. (A): The Indian Institute of Information Technology (IIIT) is located in Sonipat, Haryana. This institution is part of the group of IIITs in India established to foster specialized education in information technology and related disciplines, aimed at enhancing technical education and research in the region.

Previous Paper (Solved)

Haryana Teacher Eligibility Test (HTET)

PGT (Level-3), Common Subjects, Exam 2022

(Exam held on 03 December, 2022)

PART-I

Child Development and Pedagogy

Directions: *Answer the following questions by selecting the **most appropriate** option.*

1. Which of the following is ***not*** a symptom of good mental health of students?
   A. Living in fantasy world
   B. Balance in Life
   C. Knowledge of our potentials and limitations
   D. Free from undesirable worries

2. Which of the following is ***not*** a level of teaching?
   A. Basic Level B. Memory Level
   C. Understanding Level D. Reflective Level

3. Which of the following task is ***not*** related to Baqer Mehdi's test of Creativity?
   A. Unusual uses related task
   B. New relation between pairs related task
   C. Product improvement related task
   D. Ask and guess related task

4. Which way is the most appropriate for social development of adolescents?
   A. Discussion on socialization
   B. Essay competition on social values
   C. Organizing group activities
   D. Documentary on social relations

5. Which pair is ***not*** correct with reference to emotions and basic instincts?

	Emotion		**Basic Instinct**
A.	Anger	–	Repulsion
B.	Ownership	–	Collection
C.	Wonder	–	Curiosity
D.	Fear	–	Escape

6. According to Triarchic Theory, which of the following is ***not*** a type of intelligence?
   A. Analytical B. Creative
   C. Theoretical D. Practical

7. Which of the following factors positively affects learning?
   A. Meaningless content B. Lack of maturation
   C. Lack of motivation D. Informational feedback

8. Rohit helps others to get praise. This is an example of:
   A. Intrinsic Motivation B. Extrinsic Motivation
   C. Innate Motivation D. None of these

9. What will be the intelligence quotient of a 15 year old boy, when his mental age is 12?
   A. 80 B. 90
   C. 100 D. 110

10. What type of reinforcement schedule is it, when reinforcement is provided to the learner only after a certain number of responses?
    A. Fixed ratio B. Variable ratio
    C. Fixed interval D. Variable interval

11. Who developed the Thematic Apperception Test for personality assessment?
    A. Murray and Morgan B. Bellack
    C. Eysenck D. Allport and Cattell

12. Spranger's classification of personality is related to which approach of personality assessment?
    A. Trait Approach B. Type Approach
    C. Instinct Approach D. Psychoanalytic Approach

13. Development which proceeds from 'centre to the periphery', is known as:
    A. Cephalic Caudal B. Proximodistal
    C. Spiral D. Circular

14. Who is called the father of Trait Theory for study of personality?
    A. Allport B. Woodworth
    C. McDougall D. Eysenck

15. Which of the following statement is ***not*** correct with reference to individual differences?
    A. No two persons can be exactly alike.
    B. Individual differences may belong to different areas.
    C. Individual differences affects different dimensions of development.
    D. Individual differences arises only due to heredity.

16. A type of intelligence test in which the difficulty level of questions gradually increases and the time factor is secondary:
A. Verbal Test B. Power Test
C. Speed Test D. Performance Test

17. According to Kohlberg's theory, what level of morality is it, when morality includes self-accepted moral principles?
A. Pre-conventional B. Conventional
C. Post-conventional D. None of these

18. Which one of the following is ***not*** a direct method for measurement of attitude?
A. Interview B. Projection
C. Questionnaire D. Observation

19. As a teacher which of the following work would ***not*** be done by you to develop the creativity of the students?
A. Encouragement of originality
B. Removal of fear
C. Freedom to respond
D. Avoidance of divergent thinking

20. According to Piaget's Cognitive Development Theory, 'The basic unit of the cognitive structure that helps in the implementation of cognitive behaviour', is termed as:
A. Reflexes B. Basic Instincts
C. Schema D. Conservation

21. Hunger and Thirst is which type of motive?
A. Extrinsic B. Acquired
C. Intrinsic D. Social

22. 'When an adolescent is unable to show anger to his parents, then he shows his anger to his younger brother.' This is an example of which type of defence mechanism?
A. Repression B. Regression
C. Projection D. Displacement

23. Which of the following is ***not*** a general characteristic of adolescence period?
A. It is a transitional period.
B. It is period of unrealism.
C. It is time for search of identity.
D. It is the threshold of puberty.

24. Which one of the following is ***not*** a part of Bronfenbrenner's Ecological System theory?
A. Micro system B. Macro system
C. Minor system D. Meso system

25. Which of the following pairs of communication skills is ***correct*** for receiving the information?
A. Listening and Writing
B. Speaking and Reading
C. Listening and Reading
D. Speaking and Writing

26. According to Maslow's Need Hierarchical theory, 'Esteem Needs' are which type of need?
A. Personal B. Social
C. Intellectual D. Emotional

27. According to the moral development theory of Piaget, adolescence period is:
A. Stage of moral realism
B. Stage of morality constraint
C. Stage of heteronomous morality
D. Stage of autonomous morality

28. 'A horse can be brought near water, but cannot be forced to drink'. This statement reveals the truth of Thorndike's which law of learning?
A. Law of Readiness B. Law of Exercise
C. Law of Effect D. Law of Multi Responses

29. "Emotional Intelligence may be defined as the capacity to reason with emotion in four areas–to perceive emotion, to integrate it in thought, to understand it and to manage it".
Who gave this definition of emotional intelligence?
A. Daniel Goleman
B. Mayer and Peter Salovey
C. Peter and Michael
D. Halverson

30. A teaching-learning strategy in which small groups of students with different level of ability use a variety of learning activities to improve their understanding of a subject:
A. Multi-sensory learning
B. Team teaching
C. Co-operative learning
D. Programmed learning

PART-II

भाषा : हिन्दी

निर्देश : *निम्नलिखित प्रश्नों के उत्तर देने के लिए **सबसे उचित** विकल्प चुनिए।*

31. विलोम की दृष्टि से **असंगत** विकल्प चुनिए :
A. उपत्यका — अधित्यका
B. उन्मुख — अभिमुख
C. कल्पना — यथार्थ
D. कुत्सा — प्रशंसा

32. इनमें से कौन-सा वाक्य **अशुद्ध** है?
A. तुम्हारा व्यवहार सर्वश्रेष्ठ है।
B. हम सभी में मनुष्यी दुर्बलताएँ हैं।

C. वह पाँव से जूता उतार रहा है।
D. शीला को अपनी योग्यता पर गर्व है।

33. किस विकल्प में निजवाचक सर्वनाम का प्रयोग हुआ है?
A. हमें अपना काम स्वयं करना चाहिए।
B. तेते पाँव पसारिये, जेती लाँबी सौर।
C. हम किसी का कुछ नहीं बिगाड़ सकते।
D. जैसा करोगे, वैसा ही भरोगे।

34. "आनन्दा चुपके-से चली गई।" वाक्य में किस प्रकार के क्रिया-विशेषण का प्रयोग हुआ है?
A. कालवाचक B. रीतिवाचक
C. परिमाणवाचक D. स्थानवाचक

35. शब्दकोश में वर्णानुक्रम की दृष्टि से 'श्रद्धा' शब्द इनमें से किस शब्द के पहले आएगा?
A. शौर्य B. श्याम
C. शृंगार D. श्रमिक

36. 'पशु' शब्द से निर्मित विशेषण है :
A. पाशविक B. पशुपति
C. पशुता D. पशुत्व

37. समास की दृष्टि से **असंगत** विकल्प चुनिए :
A. कनकलता – कर्मधारय
B. सचिवालय – तत्पुरुष
C. चौराहा – द्विगु
D. आकंठ – बहुव्रीहि

38. उसने मुझे सदैव धोखा दिया। वाक्य में प्रयुक्त 'धोखा' शब्द कौन-सी संज्ञा का उदाहरण होगा?
A. समुदायवाचक संज्ञा
B. जातिवाचक संज्ञा
C. भाववाचक संज्ञा
D. व्यक्तिवाचक संज्ञा

39. 'तत्सम-तद्भव' की दृष्टि से **असंगत** विकल्प चुनिए :
A. लोमशा – लोमड़ी
B. रज्जु – रस्सी
C. पाषाण – पत्थर
D. मस्तक – माथा

40. इनमें से किस शब्द में 'आवट' प्रत्यय का प्रयोग **नहीं** हुआ है?
A. गुर्राहट B. सजावट
C. बुनावट D. तरावट

41. किस शब्द में एक से अधिक उपसर्गों का प्रयोग हुआ है?
A. अध्यापक B. अन्वेषण
C. अनुष्ठान D. व्याधि

42. उच्चारण की दृष्टि से 'ल' वर्ण का उच्चारण स्थान होगा :
A. ओष्ठ B. मूर्धा
C. तालु D. दन्त

43. समश्रुत भिन्नार्थक शब्दों का अर्थ भेद की दृष्टि से **बेमेल** विकल्प है :
A. सदेह – देह सहित; सन्देह – संशय
B. सुअन – पुत्र; सुमन – फूल
C. सुकृती – सत्कर्म; सुकृति – पुण्यवान्
D. स्वजन – बन्धु; श्वजन – कुत्ता

44. किस विकल्प में विसर्ग सन्धि का प्रयोग हुआ है?
A. युधिष्ठिर
B. वयोवृद्ध
C. परोपदेश
D. निष्ठुर

45. पर्यायवाची की दृष्टि से **असंगत** विकल्प चुनिए :
A. गधा – लंबकर्ण, वैशाखनन्दन, गर्दभ
B. गरुड़ – वैनतेय, कामारि, काक
C. गणिका – सर्ववल्लभा, वारांगना, पतुरिया
D. ग्वाला – आभीर, अहीर, गोप

Language : English

Direction: *Answer the following questions by selecting the* ***most appropriate*** *option.*

46. Which of the following sentences is the ***correct*** option to express present perfect continuous tense?
A. Mr. Mehta has been waking for 2 O'clock in the morning.
B. Mr. Mehta has been waking since 2 O'clock in the morning.
C. Mr. Mehta has been waked since 2 O'clock in the morning.
D. Mr. Mehta has been waking from 2 O'clock in the morning.

47. Fill in the blank with the ***correct*** option that completes the idiom:
A rolling stone _______ .
A. carries rough winds B. kills no one
C. gathers no sauce D. gathers no moss

48. Choose the part of the sentence that is grammatically ***incorrect***:
The thief took towards/his heels/on seeing/the Police-van arrive.
A. The thief took towards B. his heels
C. on seeing D. the Police-van arrive.

49. Change the narration:

Kavin said to Mr. Cowper, "Please, be kind to me."

A. Kavin requested Mr. Cowper to be kind to him.
B. Kavin requested Mr. Cowper to be kind to me.
C. Kavin asked Mr. Cowper to be please kind to me.
D. Kavin asked Mr. Cowper that he must be kind to him.

50. Fill in the blank with the ***correct*** form of verb:

You had better ______ your hands before you eat.

A. been washing B. washing
C. washed D. wash

51. The word 'garrulous' means:

A. talkative B. abusive
C. violent D. abundant

52. Arrange the following jumbled options in the correct order and then choose the ***correct*** option:

(*i*) too many (*ii*) spoil
(*iii*) the broth (*iv*) cooks

A. (*i*), (*iv*), (*iii*), (*ii*) B. (*i*), (*iv*), (*ii*), (*iii*)
C. (*iii*), (*iv*), (*ii*), (*i*) D. (*iv*), (*ii*), (*i*), (*iii*)

53. Fill in the blank with the ***correct*** option:

When Monisha reached the bus stand, the bus _______.

A. was already left B. had already left
C. already left D. has been already left

54. Choose the part of the sentence that is grammatically ***incorrect***:

He has committed/a blunder/mistake/today morning.

A. He has committed B. a blunder
C. mistake D. today morning

55. Which of the following options express the ***correct*** meaning of the sentence given below?

He is too cute to overlook.

A. He is too cute and he can be overlooked.
B. He is too/ cute but he can be overlooked.
C. He is so cute that he cannot be overlooked.
D. Although he is not cute, but he cannot be overlooked.

56. Fill in the blank with the ***correct*** form of verb:

Neither you nor she ________ made the mistake.

A. have B. has
C. had D. did

57. Fill in the blank with ***correct*** 'Modal Auxiliary':

Passengers _______ not walk across the railway line. (Prohibition)

A. should B. can
C. need D. must

58. Fill in the blank with the ***correct*** option:

Mr. Sudhir Soni is _______ R.A.S. Officer.

A. an B. a
C. the D. ×

59. Choose the ***correct*** passive of the given sentence:

Did he kill a lion?

A. Did a lion killed by him?
B. Was a lion killed by you?
C. Was a lion killed by him?
D. Had a lion been killed by you?

60. Fill in the blank with the ***correct*** option:

Let us stay here, while it ______.

A. is raining B. was raining
C. has been raining D. had been raining

PART-III

General Studies : Quantitative Aptitude, Reasoning Ability and GK & Awareness

Direction: *Answer the following questions by selecting the **most appropriate** option.*

61. If the amount is $3\frac{3}{8}$ times the sum after 3 years at compound interest compounded annually, then the rate of interest per annum is:

A. $16\frac{2}{3}\%$ B. $33\frac{1}{3}\%$
C. 33% D. 50%

62. A reduction of 20% in the price of rice enables a customer to purchase 12.5 kg more for ₹ 800. The original price of rice per kg is:

A. ₹ 12 B. ₹ 14
C. ₹ 15 D. ₹ 16

63. In a division sum, the divisor is 12 times the quotient and 5 times the remainder. If the remainder is 36, then the dividend is:

A. 2726 B. 2736
C. 2796 D. 2826

64. Find the next term of the following series:

Z1A, X2D, V6G, T21J, R88M, P445P, ?

A. N2676T B. T2670N
C. N2676S D. M2670S

65. A number when divided by 5, 9, 13 leaves remainder 2, 6 and 10 respectively. The least such number is:

A. 602 B. 592
C. 572 D. 582

66. In a certain code language "PARTICLE" is written as "USBQFMDJ" and "GENERATE" is written as "FOFHFUBS", then in same code language "DOCUMENT" will be written as:
A. VDEPUOSF
B. VDPENFUQ
C. VDPEUOFN
D. VDPEUOSF

67. A tank is filled in 5 hours by three pipes P, Q and R. The pipe R is twice as fast as Q and Q is twice as fast as P. How much time will pipe P alone take to fill the tank?

A. 22 hours	B. 25 hours
C. 30 hours	D. 35 hours

68. If $x=\frac{\sqrt{3}+1}{\sqrt{3}-1}$ and $y=\frac{\sqrt{3}-1}{\sqrt{3}+1}$, then the value of $(x^2 + y^2)$ is:

A. 14	B. 12
C. 13	D. 16

69. In a row of girls, A is 10th from the left and B is 14th from the right. If they interchange their positions, A becomes 24th from the left. How many girls are there in a row?

A. 31	B. 33
C. 37	D. 39

70. Out of 1865 people, 660 can speak English and 1305 can speak Hindi, but 120 persons cannot speak either language, then how many persons can speak both languages?

A. 220	B. 440
C. 120	D. 1085

71. The population of a town is 9000. If the males increase by 5% and females by 8%, the population would be 9600 in a year. The number of males is:

A. 3000	B. 4000
C. 5000	D. 5600

72. D is taller than C and E. A is not as tall as E. C is taller than A. D is not as tall as B. Who is the tallest among of them?

A. A	B. B
C. C	D. D

73. Pointing to a girl in photograph, X said "She is the daughter of my grandfather's only son". How is the girl related to X?

A. Father	B. Brother
C. Sister	D. Mother

74. A steam engine train runs from East to West and wind is blowing from North to South, then the smoke from the train would blow in which direction?

A. N-W	B. N-E
C. S-E	D. S-W

75. The next term of the following number series is:

3, 13, 22, 32, 59, 69, 120, 130, ?

A. 201	B. 211
C. 227	D. 232

76. The average of nine consecutive numbers is n. If the next two numbers are also included, the new average is:

A. remain the same	B. increase by 1
C. increase by 1.5	D. increase by 2

77. A shopkeeper sells an article at 15% gain. Had he sold it for ₹ 18 more, he would have gained 18%. The cost price (in ₹) of the article is:

A. 360	B. 540
C. 600	D. 640

78. A boat covers a certain distance downstream in 3 hours, while it comes back in 4.5 hours. If the speed of the stream be 3 kmph, then the speed of the boat in still water is:

A. 10 kmph	B. 12 kmph
C. 13 kmph	D. 15 kmph

79. A metallic sphere of radius 10.5 cm is melted and then recast into small cones each of radius 3.5 cm and height 3 cm, then the number of cones thus formed is:

A. 112	B. 126
C. 132	D. 138

80. X and Y are facing each other at sunrise. The shadow of Y is falling towards right of X, then Y is facing in which direction?

A. North	B. South
C. East	D. West

81. Which of the following monuments of Haryana have the status of State protected monuments?
(*i*) Sheikh Tayyab's Tomb
(*ii*) Shobha Sagar Pond
(*iii*) Bhimadevi Temple Complex

Choose the ***correct*** code:

A. (*i*) and (*ii*)	B. (*ii*) and (*iii*)
C. (*i*) and (*iii*)	D. (*i*), (*ii*) and (*iii*)

82. Which of the following institute is responsible for the development of infrastructure facilities in industrial areas of Haryana?

A. HARTRON	B. HUDA
C. HSIIDC	D. District Industries Centre

83. Consider the following statements:
(*i*) The institution of Lokayukta was established in Haryana in the year 2002.
(*ii*) Justice Pritam Pal was the first Lokayukta in the State of Haryana.
A. Only (*i*) is correct.
B. Only (*ii*) is correct.
C. Both (*i*) and (*ii*) are correct
D. Both (*i*) and (*ii*) are incorrect

84. Who among the following is ***not*** appointed by the Governor of Haryana?
A. Chief Minister of Haryana
B. A Judge of Punjab and Haryana High Court
C. A Member of Haryana Public Service Commission
D. A Member of Haryana Human Rights Commission

85. Who among the following Governors of Haryana was a civil servant?
A. Muzaffar Hussain Burney
B. Jaisukh Lal Hathi
C. Dhanik Lal Mandal
D. Babu Parmanand

86. Read the following statements about 'Parivar Pehchan Patra Yojna':
(*i*) This scheme identifies family as a unit and is creating a reliable socio-economic database of all the families in Haryana.
(*ii*) An eight digit unique family ID is being issued for every family and the ID will be linked to birth, death and marriage records.
(*iii*) The data available in family ID database will be utilized to determine automatic verification for various welfare schemes and families will not be required to apply themselves for benefits.

Choose the ***correct*** code:
A. Only (*ii*) is correct.
B. (*i*) and (*ii*) are correct.
C. (*ii*) and (*iii*) are correct.
D. (*i*), (*ii*) and (*iii*) are correct.

87. Which places of Haryana have been notified as Ramsar site under Ramsar convention of UNESCO?
A. Sultanpur National Park & Bhindawas Wildlife Sanctuary
B. Kalesar National Park & Khaparwas Wildlife Sanctuary
C. Nahar Wildlife Sanctuary & Bir Shikargarh Wildlife Sanctuary
D. Abushahar Wildlife Sanctuary & Khol-Hi-Raitan Wildlife Sanctuary

88. The Lok Sabha and Rajya Sabha seats in Haryana are:
A. 7 and 4 B. 10 and 4
C. 10 and 5 D. 12 and 5

89. Which of the city of Haryana is known as the 'City of War Heroes'?
A. Gurugram B. Sonipat
C. Panipat D. Bhiwani

90. Consider the following statements regarding the Governor of Haryana:
(*i*) He is the Chancellor of Central University of Haryana.
(*ii*) He can hold any office of the profit in the State.
(*iii*) He is the President of Indian Red Cross Society, Haryana State Branch.
(*iv*) He does not have any discretionary power granted under the Constitution.

Which of the above statement(s) is/are ***correct***?
A. (*i*), (*ii*), (*iii*) and (*iv*) B. (*ii*), (*iii*) and (*iv*)
C. Only (*iii*) D. Both (*ii*) and (*iii*)

Answers

1. (A)	**2. (A)**	**3. (D)**
4. (C)	**5. (A)**	**6. (C)**
7. (D)	**8. (B)**	**9. (A)**
10. (A)	**11. (A)**	**12. (B)**
13. (B)	**14. (A)**	**15. (D)**
16. (B)	**17. (C)**	**18. (B)**
19. (D)	**20. (C)**	**21. (C)**
22. (D)	**23. (*)**	**24. (C)**
25. (C)	**26. (B)**	**27. (D)**
28. (A)	**29. (B)**	**30. (C)**
31. (B)	**32. (B)**	**33. (A)**
34. (B)	**35. (D)**	**36. (A)**
37. (D)	**38. (C)**	**39. (C)**
40. (A)	**41. (D)**	**42. (D)**
43. (C)	**44. (B)**	**45. (B)**
46. (*)	**47. (D)**	**48. (A)**
49. (A)	**50. (D)**	**51. (A)**
52. (B)	**53. (B)**	**54. (C)**
55. (C)	**56. (B)**	**57. (D)**
58. (A)	**59. (C)**	**60. (A)**

61. (D): At compound interest compounded annually

$$\therefore \quad A = P\left(1+\frac{r}{100}\right)^n$$

$$\Rightarrow \quad 3\frac{3}{8}P = P\left(1+\frac{r}{100}\right)^3$$

$$\Rightarrow \quad 3\frac{3}{8} = \left(1+\frac{r}{100}\right)^3$$

$$\Rightarrow \quad \frac{27}{8} = \left(1+\frac{r}{100}\right)^3$$

$$\Rightarrow \quad \left(\frac{3}{2}\right)^3 = \left(1+\frac{r}{100}\right)^3$$

$$\Rightarrow \quad \frac{3}{2} = 1+\frac{r}{100} \Rightarrow \frac{3}{2}-1 = \frac{r}{100}$$

$$\Rightarrow \quad \frac{1}{2} = \frac{r}{100} \Rightarrow r = 50$$

$\therefore$ The rate of interest per annum, $r = 50\%$.

62. (D): Let the original price of rice per kg is ₹ x

Then, new price per kg = $\dfrac{x \times 100 - 20}{100}$

$$= x \times \frac{80}{100} = ₹\ \frac{4}{5}x$$

According to question,

$$\therefore \quad \frac{800}{\frac{4}{5}x} - \frac{800}{x} = 12.5$$

$$\Rightarrow \quad \frac{1000}{x} - \frac{800}{x} = \frac{25}{2}$$

$$\Rightarrow \quad \frac{1}{x}(1000 - 800) = \frac{25}{2}$$

$$\Rightarrow \quad \frac{200}{x} = \frac{25}{2} \Rightarrow 25x = 400 \Rightarrow x = 16$$

∴ The original price of rice per kg is ₹ 16.

63. (B): Let quotient = x

then, Divisor = $12x = 5 \times 36$

$$\Rightarrow \quad x = \frac{5 \times 36}{12} = 15$$

$\because$ Dividend = Divisor × Quotient + Remainder

$\therefore$ Dividend = $12x \times x + 36$

$= 12 \times 15 \times 15 + 36$

$= 12 \times 225 + 36$

$= 2700 + 36 = 2736.$

64. (C)

65. (D): Here, $5 - 2 = 9 - 6 = 13 - 10 = 3$

the difference of all the divisors with their corresponding remainder in each case is same as 10

So, Required number = (LCM of 5, 9, 13) – 3

$= 585 - 3 = 582.$

66. (C): Given,

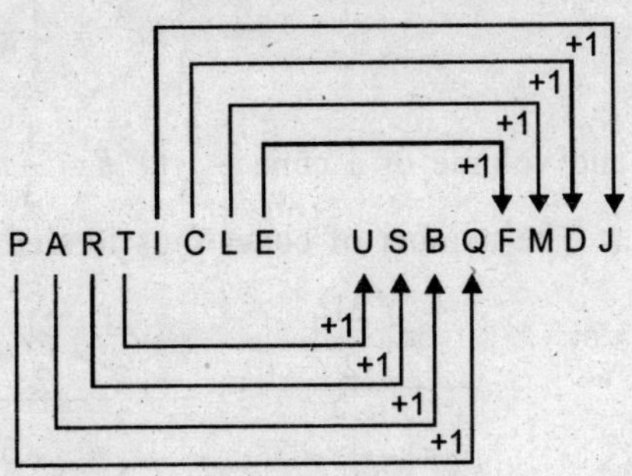

and

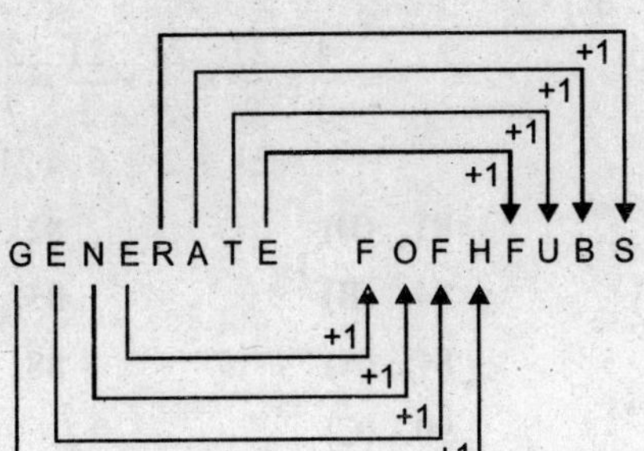

Similarly,

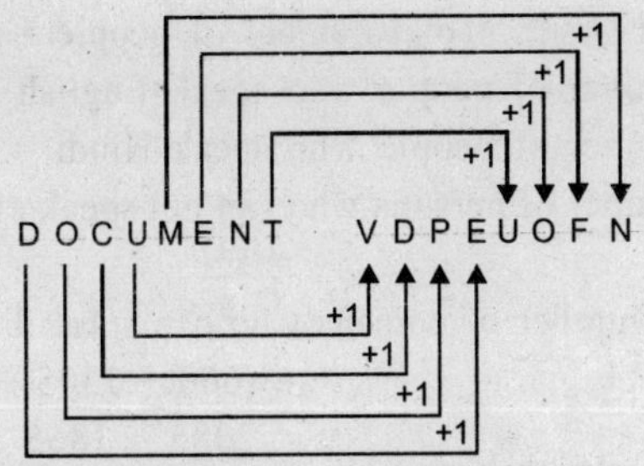

∴ In same code language 'DOCUMENT' will be written as 'VDPEUOFN'.

67. (D): Ratio of Efficiency of pipes

R : Q = 2 : 1, Q : P = 2 : 1

⇒ P : Q = 1 : 2

and Q : R = 1 : 2 ⇒ Q : R = 2 : 4

∴ P : Q : R = 1 : 2 : 4

Ratio of time,

$$P : Q : R = 1 : \frac{1}{2} : \frac{1}{4} = 4 : 2 : 1$$

By question, (P + Q + R)'s 1 hour's work:

$$\frac{1}{4x} + \frac{1}{2x} + \frac{1}{x} = \frac{1}{5} \Rightarrow \frac{1+2+4}{4x} = \frac{1}{5}$$

$$\Rightarrow \quad \frac{7}{4x} = \frac{1}{5} \Rightarrow x = \frac{35}{4}$$

$$\therefore \quad \text{P's 1 hour's work} = \frac{1}{4x} = \frac{1}{4 \times \frac{35}{4}} = \frac{1}{35}$$

∴ Pipe P alone will take 35 hours to fill the tank.

68. (A): Given, $x = \dfrac{\sqrt{3}+1}{\sqrt{3}-1} = \dfrac{\sqrt{3}+1}{\sqrt{3}-1} \times \dfrac{\sqrt{3}+1}{\sqrt{3}+1} = \dfrac{(\sqrt{3}+1)^2}{3-1}$

$$= \frac{3+1+2\sqrt{3}}{2} = \frac{4+2\sqrt{3}}{2} = 2+\sqrt{3}$$

and $y = \dfrac{\sqrt{3}-1}{\sqrt{3}+1} = \dfrac{\sqrt{3}-1}{\sqrt{3}+1} \times \dfrac{\sqrt{3}-1}{\sqrt{3}-1}$

$$= \frac{(\sqrt{3}-1)^2}{3-1} = \frac{3+1-2\sqrt{3}}{2} = 2-\sqrt{3}$$

$$\therefore \quad x^2 + y^2 = (2+\sqrt{3})^2 + (2-\sqrt{3})^2$$

$$= 4+3+4\sqrt{3}+(4+3-4\sqrt{3})$$

$$= 7+4\sqrt{3}+7-4\sqrt{3} = 7 + 7 = 14$$

$$\Rightarrow \quad x^2 + y^2 = 14.$$

69. (C):

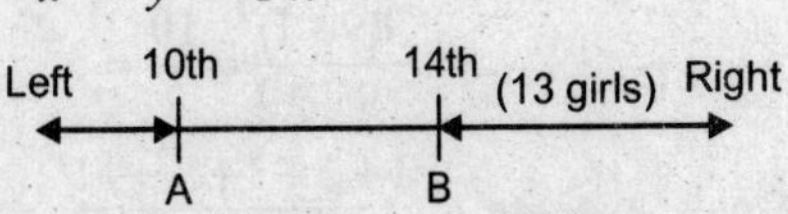

Again,

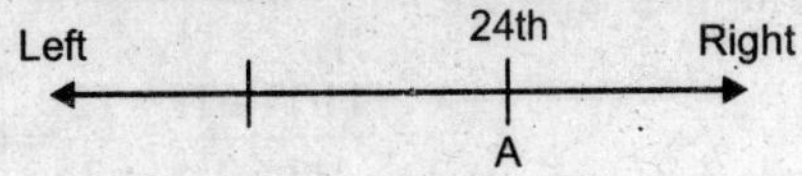

∴ The number of girls in this row

$= 24 + 13 = 37.$

70. (A): Given, Total number of people = 1865
Number of people who speak English = 660
Number of people who speak Hindi = 1305
Number of persons who can not speak either language = 120

$\therefore$ Number of persons who can speak both languages
$= (660 + 1305 + 120) - 1865$
$= 2085 - 1865 = 220.$

71. (B): Let the number of males is x
then, the number of females is $(9000 - x)$

$$\therefore \quad x \times \frac{105}{100} + (9000 - x) \times \frac{108}{100} = 9600$$

$$\Rightarrow \quad \frac{105x}{100} + \frac{972000}{100} - \frac{108x}{100} = 9600$$

$$\Rightarrow \quad \frac{972000}{100} - \frac{3x}{100} = 9600$$

$$\Rightarrow \quad 9720 - 9600 = \frac{3x}{100} \Rightarrow 120 = \frac{3x}{100}$$

$$\Rightarrow \quad 3x = 12000 \Rightarrow x = 4000$$

$\therefore$ The number of males $= x = 4000$.

72. (B): B > D > C > E > A
Here, B is the tallest among them.

73. (C): Here, the girl is the sister of X.

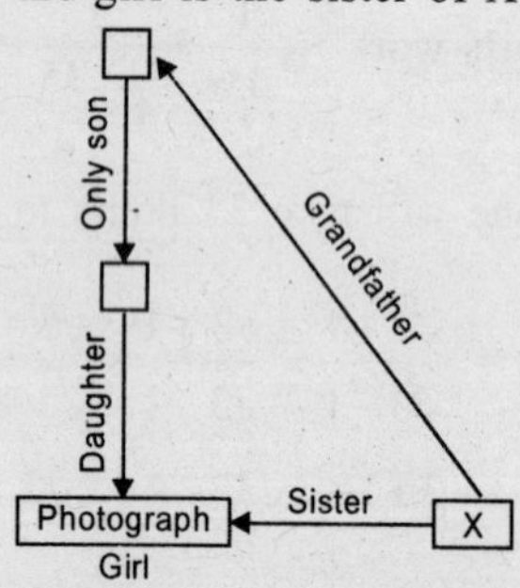

74. (C)

75. (B):

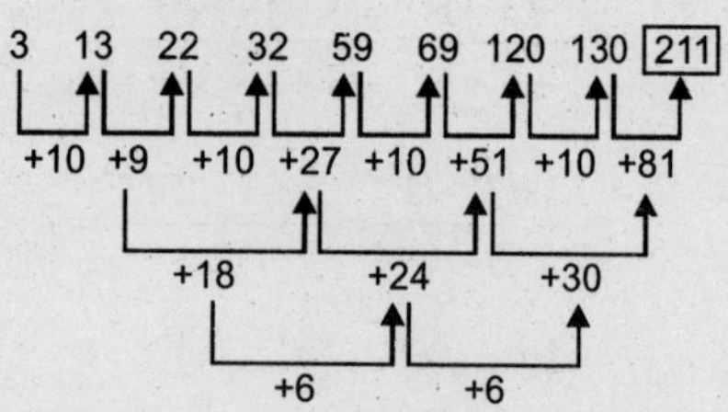

$\therefore$? = The next term = 211.

76. (B):

$$n = \frac{1+2+3+....+9}{9}$$

$$= \frac{9(9+1)}{9 \times 2} = \frac{10}{2} = 5$$

$$\text{The new average} = \frac{1+2+3+...+11}{11}$$

$$= \frac{11(11+1)}{11 \times 2} = \frac{12}{2} = 6$$

Hence, the new average is increased by 1.

77. (C): Let the cost price of the article is ₹ x

Then, $\quad \text{S.P.} = x \times \frac{115}{100} + 18 = x \times \frac{118}{100}$

$$\Rightarrow \quad \frac{115}{100}x + 18 = \frac{118}{100}x$$

$$\Rightarrow \quad \frac{118}{100}x - \frac{115}{100}x = 18$$

$$\Rightarrow \quad \frac{3x}{100} = 18 \Rightarrow \frac{x}{100} = 6$$

$$\Rightarrow \quad x = 600$$

$\therefore$ The cost price of the article = ₹ 600.

78. (D): Let the speed of a boat in still water is x kmph then, speed of boat in downstream $= (x + 3)$ kmph and speed of boat in upstream $= (x - 3)$ kmph
Let certain distance $= d$ km

Then, $\quad \frac{d}{x+3} = 3$

$$\Rightarrow \quad d = 3(x + 3) \quad ...(i)$$

and $\quad \frac{d}{x-3} = 4.5$

$$\Rightarrow \quad d = \frac{9}{2}(x-3) \quad ...(ii)$$

From (*i*) and (*ii*), $\quad 3(x + 3) = \frac{9}{2}(x-3)$

$$\Rightarrow \quad 6(x + 3) = 9(x - 3)$$

$$\Rightarrow \quad 6x + 18 = 9x - 27$$

$$\Rightarrow \quad 9x - 6x = 18 + 27$$

$$\Rightarrow \quad 3x = 45$$

$$\Rightarrow \quad x = 15$$

Hence, the speed of the boat in still water = 15 kmph.

79. (B): Volume of a metallic sphere

$$= \frac{4}{3}\pi r^3 = \frac{4}{3}\pi\left(\frac{21}{2}\right)^3 \text{ cm}^3$$

and volume of a cone $= \frac{1}{3}\pi r^2 h = \frac{1}{3}\pi\left(\frac{7}{2}\right)^2 \times 3 \text{ cm}^3$

$\therefore$ The number of cones thus formed is

$$\frac{\frac{4}{3}\pi\left(\frac{21}{2}\right)^3}{\frac{1}{3}\pi\left(\frac{7}{2}\right)^2 \times 3} = \frac{4 \times \frac{21}{2} \times \frac{21}{2} \times \frac{21}{2}}{\frac{7}{2} \times \frac{7}{2} \times 3}$$

$$= \frac{4}{3} \times \frac{21}{2} \times \frac{21}{2} \times \frac{21}{2} \times \frac{2}{7} \times \frac{2}{7}$$

$$= 3 \times 21 \times 2 = 6 \times 21 = 126.$$

80. (A)	**81. (D)**	**82. (C)**
83. (C)	**84. (B)**	**85. (A)**
86. (D)	**87. (A)**	**88. (C)**
89. (D)	**90. (C)**	

Previous Paper (Solved)

Haryana Teacher Eligibility Test (HTET)

PGT (Level-3), Common Subjects, Exam 2021

(Exam held on 18 December, 2021)

PART-I

Child Development and Pedagogy

Directions: *Answer the following questions by selecting the **most appropriate** option.*

1. Which of the following is ***not*** the type of dynamic trait of personality given by Cattell?
   A. Attitude B. Urge
   C. Sentiment D. Conservative

2. Which one of the following stage is ***not*** prescribed by James Draver in the context of development of character?
   A. The stage of crude emotion
   B. The stage of sentiment
   C. The self regard stage
   D. Conforming conventional stage

3. Which of the following is the ***false*** characteristic of motivation?
   A. In motivation, behaviour of person is goal oriented.
   B. Motivated behaviour does continuity
   C. Nature of motivated behaviour is rigid.
   D. Motivation does energy changes in human beings.

4. Which of the following theory is ***not*** related with the theories of transfer of learning?
   A. Theory of mental discipline
   B. Theory of rote memory
   C. Theory of identical elements
   D. Theory of generalisation

5. Which of the following is ***not*** the characteristic of good mental health?
   A. Emotional maturity
   B. Self confidence
   C. Intolerance
   D. Capacity of self evaluation

6. For which age group the Children Apperception Test (CAT) is applicable?
   A. 2 to 5 years B. 0 to 4 years
   C. 16 to 18 years D. 3 to 10 years

7. Out of the following which one is the ***wrong*** statement in context of characteristics of instincts?
   A. Intinct is innate.
   B. Instinct is very powerful
   C. Instinct is ephemeral.
   D. Instinct is psycho-physical disposition.

8. Which of the following is ***not*** the other name of Thorndike's theory of Connectionism?
   A. Stimulus response theory
   B. Bond theory of learning
   C. Theory of conditioned response
   D. Trial and Error theory

9. Who developed the first intelligence test?
   A. Lavator B. Sanguin
   C. Francis Galton D. Alfred Binet and Simon

10. Which of the following concept is ***not*** introduced by Jean Piaget in his Cognitive Development theory?
    A. Assimilation B. Accommodation
    C. Symbolic D. Equilibration

11. Which of the following is ***not*** the innate motive?
    A. Safety B. Hunger
    C. Thirst D. Rest

12. Who was the founder of socio-culture theory of cognitive development?
    A. Jean Piaget B. Jerom Bruner
    C. Lev Vygotsky D. Kohlberg

13. Which one of the following is ***not*** correct way of releasing pent up emotional energy?
    A. Substitute responses B. Displacement
    C. Regression D. Self pity

14. Which of the following structure of mind directed according to Hedonistic and pleasure principle?
    A. Id B. Ego
    C. Super Ego D. Choleric

15. Which of the following is the ***correct*** logical order of elements of memory?
    A. Learning → Recall → Retention → Recognition
    B. Recall → Learning → Retention → Recognition
    C. Learning → Recall → Recognition → Retention
    D. Learning → Retention → Recall → Recognition

16. Which of the following is ***not*** the type of one of the component content under three dimensional model of intellect given by J.P. Guilford?
A. Figural B. System
C. Symbolic D. Behavioural

17. The mental activities associated with thought, decision making, language and other higher mental processes is called:
A. Visual images B. Cognition
C. Concepts D. Propositions

18. Which of the following is behavioural perspective of modern psychology?
A. Focuses on overt behaviour.
B. Focuses on cognitive processes.
C. Focuses on the biological events.
D. Focuses on critique of male bias.

19. Who was the propounder of pyschoanalytical method?
A. J.B. Watson B. Wilhelm Wundt
C. Sigmund Freud D. J.M. Cattell

20. According to Stanford-Binet IQ scale, what is the IQ range of low mentally retarded children?
A. 52 to 67 B. 36 to 51
C. 20 to 35 D. below 20

21. A branch of psychology which studies how people change physically, cognitively and socially over the entire life span is known as:
A. Clinical psychology
B. Counselling psychology
C. Developmental psychology
D. Experimental psychology

22. Which of the following is the ***false*** statement?
A. Learning is a process not a product.
B. Learning process is always purposeful.
C. Area of learning is broader.
D. Behaviour changes through instincts and reflex actions are also considered as learning.

23. Which of the following is ***not*** the type of projective technique of personality measurement?
A. Word Association Test
B. Woodworth's Personal Data Sheet
C. Sentence Completion Test
D. Thematic Apperception Test

24. Who was the propounder of Anticipatory theory of play?
A. Karl Groos B. McDougall
C. Herbert Spencer D. G. Stanley Hall

25. Who stated that "Adolescence is a period of stress, strain, storm and strife"?
A. William H. Barton
B. Stanley Hall
C. J.A. Hadfield
D. Jean Piaget

26. Which of the following is ***not*** the characteristic of Adolescence?
A. Weight of muscles is 20% of total weight of body.
B. Tendency of day dreams increased.
C. Vocabulary too increases.
D. Mental abilities reach at their highest level.

27. Which of the following is the non-projective technique of personality measurement?
A. Association technique
B. Sociometric technique
C. Construction technique
D. Completion technique

28. Which of the following is the highest level in hierarchical theory of learning given Gange?
A. Problem solving learning
B. Principle learning
C. Concept learning
D. Multiple discrimination learning

29. Who propounded Brain storming method for fostering and boosting creativity?
A. Torrance B. Myres
C. Osborn D. Gordon

30. Out of the following which one is the ***wrong*** statement in context of characteristics of habits?
A. Habit is automatic response to specific situation.
B. Habit is acquired through heredity.
C. Habit is a well learned performance.
D. Habit is performed only under similar circumstances.

PART-II

भाषा : हिन्दी

निर्देश: *निम्नलिखित प्रश्नों के उत्तर देने के लिए* ***सबसे उचित*** *विकल्प चुनिए।*

31. ***अनुचित*** विलोम शब्द युग्म युक्त विकल्प पहचानिए :
A. विधि – निषेध B. खल – सज्जन
C. अमर – मर्त्य D. वैर – क्रोध

32. कौन-सा वाक्य संबंधसूचक अव्यय का उदाहरण है?
A. इतना खा लिया, इसे कैसे पचाओगे।
B. शीला के समान कोई आलसी नहीं है।
C. मैंने पर्याप्त पढ़ लिया है, अब थोड़ा आराम करूँगा।
D. जरा सोच-समझकर बोलिए।

33. वाक्य के संदर्भ में कौन-सा विकल्प सुमेलित ***नहीं*** है?
A. दुष्ट! तुझे धिक्कार है। – विस्मयादिबोधक वाक्य
B. मैनें माँ का कहना नहीं माना। – निषेधबोधक वाक्य
C. हो सकता है वह आज शाम को आए। – इच्छाबोधक वाक्य
D. समय पर भोजन करोगे तो स्वस्थ रहोगे। – संकेतार्थक वाक्य

34. अर्थ की दृष्टि से कौन-सा मुहावरा संगत ***नहीं*** है?
A. खयाली पुलाव पकाना – व्यर्थ की बातें करना
B. अपना-सा मुँह लेकर रह जाना – असफल होने पर लज्जित होना
C. अँधेरे घर का उजाला – एकमात्र सहारा
D. ऊँट का सूई की नोक से निकलना – शक्तिशाली का कमजोर होना

35. निम्न में से किस विकल्प की सभी क्रियाएँ 'अकर्मक' हैं?
A. चलना, मुस्कराना, खिलना B. दौड़ना, रूठना, लिखना
C. हँसना, खाना, सोना D. रोना, उठना, काटना

36. 'दादुर, भेक, शालुर' शब्द किसके पर्यायवाची हैं?
A. हाथी B. बंदर
C. मेंढ़क D. सिंह

37. प्रत्यय की दृष्टि से ***असुमेलित*** विकल्प का चयन कीजिए :
A. भागिनेय = भगिनी + य
B. वार्धक्य = वर्धक + य
C. ऐश्वर्य = ईश्वर + य
D. वैशिष्ट्य = विशिष्ट + य

38. निम्न में से ***असंगत*** विकल्प पहचानिए :
A. सातत्य – अव्यय से निर्मित भाववाचक संज्ञा
B. निजता – सर्वनाम से निर्मित भाववाचक संज्ञा
C. रोगिणी – भाववाचक संज्ञा से निर्मित विशेषण
D. शक्तिशाली – विशेषण से निर्मित भाववाचक संज्ञा

39. निम्न में से ***सही*** संधि युक्त शब्द कौन-सा है?
A. युधि + स्थिर = युधिष्ठिर
B. गुरु + उपदेश = गुरोपदेश
C. अभि + इप्सा = अभिप्सा
D. गति + अवरोध = गत्यावरोध

40. उपसर्ग से निर्मित शब्दों के संदर्भ में कौन-सा विकल्प ***असंगत*** है?
A. परि – पर्यंक, पारिभाषिक, पर्युषण
B. अति – अत्युक्ति, अतीत, अत्यावश्यक
C. अन – अनसूया, अनधिकार, अनशन
D. प्रति – प्रत्यर्पण, प्रतीक्षा, प्रतीक

41. 'चिकना मुँह पेट खाली' लोकोक्ति का सही अर्थ है :
A. अपने हाथ से दान देना
B. देखने में सुखी भीतर से दुःखी
C. अत्यधिक प्यारा होना
D. जबरदस्ती गले पड़ना

42. समास-विग्रह की दृष्टि से कौन-सा विकल्प ***असंगत*** है?
A. शुभंकर – शुभ को करने वाला
B. रसमलाई – रस में डूबी हुई मलाई
C. नवयुवक – नौ युवकों का समूह
D. शाखामृग – शाखाओं पर रहने/दौड़ने वाला मृग

43. निम्नलिखित वर्णों के संदर्भ में कौन-सा विकल्प ***असंगत*** है?
A. य – तालव्य, अल्पप्राण, घोष
B. इ – तालव्य, ह्रस्व, अवृत्तमुखी
C. ब – ओष्ठ्य, घोष, अल्पप्राण
D. ष – मूर्धन्य, अल्पप्राण, अघोष

44. 'सचिन क्रिकेट खेलता है।' उक्त वाक्य को कर्मवाच्य में बदलिए :
A. सचिन क्रिकेट खेलेगा।
B. सचिन क्रिकेट नहीं खेलता है।
C. सचिन से क्रिकेट खेला जाता था।
D. सचिन के द्वारा क्रिकेट खेला जाता है।

45. शब्द-प्रकृति की दृष्टि से ***असंगत*** युग्म चुनिए :
A. गोस्वामी – तत्सम शब्द B. मुकद्दमा – देशज शब्द
C. पंख – तद्भव शब्द D. तहसीलदार – संकर शब्द

Language : English

Directions: *Answer the following questions by selecting the **most appropriate** option.*

46. Choose the ***correct*** meaning of the underlined idiom:

He is friendly to the minister, he jumped the queue and got promotion.
A. replace something
B. hopping
C. blame somebody
D. get something out of turn

47. Change the voice from Active to Passive. Choose the ***right*** option:

We shall discuss the question tomorrow in the meeting.
A. The question will be discussed tomorrow in the meeting.
B. We will be discussing the question tomorrow in the meeting.
C. We shall be discussing tomorrow the question in the meeting.
D. The question shall discuss tomorrow in the meeting.

48. Select the ***correct*** tense form:

The car (belong) to my mother. She (use) it today to take Tom to the dentist.
A. belonged, is using
B. belonged, using
C. belong, used
D. belongs, is using

49. Select the ***correct*** meaning of the underlined phrasal verbs:

I cannot make out the meaning of this verse.

A. discovery B. understand
C. reading D. start

50. Choose the ***correct*** form of tense given in the option:

She (play) the sitar since 6 o'clock this morning. He just (stop).

A. playing, stops
B. was played, stopping
C. has been playing, has just stopped
D. have been playing, stopped

51. Choose the option which has ***error*** in it:

(*a*) You should (*b*) tell to me
(*c*) exactly what (*d*) happened there

A. (*a*) B. (*b*)
C. (*c*) D. (*d*)

52. Select the ***correct*** preposition to fill in the blank:

They live ______ the same roof.

A. in B. before
C. after D. under

53. Select the ***correct*** preposition to fill in the blank:

He broke the jug ______ a hundred pieces.

A. in B. into
C. over D. about

54. Choose the ***correct*** option:
Transformation from Simple sentence to Complex sentence:

A lost moment is lost forever.

A. A moment which is lost is lost forever.
B. A lost moment is forever lost.
C. Forever a lost moment is lost.
D. No moment is lost forever.

55. Choose the ***correct*** option:

Transformation of sentences: Simple to Compound.

He must work hard to make up for the lost time.

A. He must work hard, cover the lost time.
B. Making up for the lost time he must work hard.
C. He must work hard and make up for the lost time.
D. Working hard will make up for the lost time.

56. Choose one word substitution for the following:

A word spelt and pronounced similar but differing in meaning.

A. Antonym B. Homonym
C. Synonym D. Pseudonym

57. Select the ***correct*** conjunctions for the blanks:

We will come ______ it rains ______ not.

A. if, and B. even, but
C. whether, or D. either, and

58. Change the following sentences into Reported Speech by choosing the ***correct*** option:

"We're waiting for the school bus," said the children, "It's late again."

A. The children told they're waiting for the school bus and it is late.
B. The children said they were waiting for the school bus and it is late.
C. The children complained that they were waiting for the school bus and it was late again.
D. The children complained that they were waiting for the school bus and it is late.

59. Change the following sentences into Reported Speech by choosing the ***correct*** option.

"If you want to smoke you'll have to go upstairs." said the landlord.

A. The landlord told him that if he wants to smoke he'll have to go upstairs.
B. The landlord told him that if he wanted to smoke he would have to go upstairs.
C. The landlord said that if he would want to smoke he would go upstairs.
D. The landlord says if you wanted to smoke you would have to go upstairs.

60. Select the ***correct*** infinitive form of the given sentence:

Seeing is believing.

A. To see is to believe. B. Seen is to believe.
C. To see is believing D. Seeing is to believe.

PART-III

General Studies : Quantitative Aptitude, Reasoning Ability and GK & Awareness

61. If the Independence Day in 1988 was celebrated on Wednesday. On what day was it celebrated in the year 1989?

A. Monday
B. Tuesday
C. Thursday
D. Friday

62. Vijay walks 10 km towards North, from there, he walks 6 km towards South, then he walks 3 km towards East. How far and in which direction is he with reference to his starting point?

A. 5 km West B. 5 km North-East
C. 7 km East D. 7 km West

63. In a row of girls, Shilpa is 8th from the left and Reena is 17th from the right, if they interchange their positions, Shilpa becomes 14th from the left. How many girls are there in a row?

A. 27 B. 29
C. 32 D. 30

64. In a certain pattern, if 9 * 3 = 36, 10 * 6 = 64, 9 * 1 = 25, then in the same pattern what is the value of 23 * 3 = ?

A. 169 B. 52
C. 32 D. 576

65. In a certain code MONKEY is written as XDJMNL. How is TIGER written in that code?

A. SDFHS B. SHFDQ
C. QDFHS D. UJHFS

66. If A means 'plus', B means 'minus', C means 'divide by', D means 'multiply'. Then what will be simplified value of

18 A 12 C 6 D 2 B 5 = ?

A. 25 B. 27
C. 15 D. 17

67. If 7 carpenters can make 7 chairs in 8 hours, how many hours will 70 carpenters take to make 70 chairs?

A. 8 hours B. 560 hours
C. 56 hours D. 70 hours

68. Which number must be added to each term of the ratio 2 : 5, so that it may equal to 5 : 6?

A. 12 B. 11
C. 13 D. 14

69. A sum of ₹ 10,000 deposited at compound interest becomes double after 5 years. After 20 years the amount will be:

A. ₹ 40,000 B. ₹ 60,000
C. ₹ 80,000 D. ₹ 1,60,000

70. A sold a watch to B at a gain of 10% and B sold it to C at a loss of 10%. If C paid ₹ 990 for it, then how much amount paid by A?

A. ₹ 900 B. ₹ 1,000
C. ₹ 1,200 D. ₹ 950

71. The price of any item is increased by 20%. Find the reduction in the consumption of the item by a consumer so that there is no increase on his expenditure:

A. $16\frac{2}{3}\%$ B. $15\frac{2}{3}\%$
C. $17\frac{2}{3}\%$ D. $16\frac{1}{3}\%$

72. What is the value of $\sqrt{2\sqrt{2\sqrt{2\sqrt{2\sqrt{2}}}}}$?

A. 0 B. 2
C. 1 D. $2^{31/32}$

73. Two trains 132 meters and 108 meters long are running in opposite direction, one at the speed of 32 km/hr and another at the speed of 40 km/hr. In what time will they cross each other?

A. 8 sec. B. 10 sec.
C. 12 sec. D. 11 sec.

74. $0.34\overline{67}+0.13\overline{33}$ is equal to:

A. 0.48 B. $0.48\overline{01}$
C. $0.\overline{48}$ D. $0.4\overline{8}$

75. What is the HCF of 11, 11.11, 0.11, 0.011?

A. 0.011 B. 1.1
C. 0.11 D. 0.111

76. The ratio of the areas of the incircle and circumcircle of a square will be:

A. 1 : 4 B. 4 : 1
C. 1 : 2 D. 2 : 1

77. Find the missing letters in the given letter series:

a_cdaab_cc_daa_bbb_ccddd

A. *bdbda* B. *bddca*
C. *dbbca* D. *bbdac*

78. The number in the following question numbers are written according to certain pattern row-wise or column-wise. Identify the pattern and find the missing character accordingly.

6	11	25
8	6	16
12	5	?

A. 18 B. 16
C. 12 D. 10

79. Find the next term of the number series:

127, 128, 136, 163, 227, ______.

A. 352 B. 350
C. 357 D. 341

80. There are five different houses A to E in a row. A is to the right of B and E is to the left of C and right of A. B is to the right of D. Which of the house is exactly in the middle?

A. A B. B
C. D D. E

81. Who among the following is the recipient of 'Padma Bhushan' in 2021?

A. Jai Bhagwan Goyal B. Virendra Singh
C. Tarlochan Singh D. Mukesh Singh

82. 'Pran Vayu Devata Pension Scheme' is aimed to:

A. Conserve older trees in Haryana State
B. Provide financial assistance to the non-government doctors in their old age
C. Provide economic relief to the non-government paramedical staff in their old age
D. Encourage plantation of Tulsi and Giloya in urban households

83. Origin of the which of the following rivers is ***not*** correctly matched?

River		**Origin Site**
A. Saraswati	—	Dangushai
B. Indori	—	Mewat hills
C. Markanda	—	Sivalik hills
D. Tangdi	—	Morni hills

84. Who among the following Governors of Haryana died while in the office?

A. B.N. Chakraborty
B. Ranjit Singh Narula
C. J.L. Hathi
D. Sardar H.S. Brar

85. Which of the following is ***not*** true about the proposed investment region/industrial area under Delhi-Mumbai industrial corridor in Haryana?

A. Faridabad — Palwal industrial area
B. Rewari — Hisar investment region
C. Kundli — Sonipat investment region
D. Manesar — Bawal investment region

86. Who among the following did ***not*** serve as the Chief Justice of the Punjab and Haryana High Court?

A. Justice Mukund Mudgal
B. Justice A.K. Sikri
C. Justice M.S. Jain
D. Justice Sanjay Kishan Kaul

87. The total number of medals won by the athletes of Haryana in the Tokyo Paralympics 2021 are:

A. 04 B. 06
C. 08 D. 19

88. The Haryana Public Service Commission presents its annual report of the work done by the commission to the:

A. Governor
B. President
C. Parliament
D. State Legislative Assembly

89. Identify the text/texts, in which the reference of Thanesar is found:

(*i*) Harshcharit
(*ii*) Travelogue of Yuvan Chang
(*iii*) Kadambari
(*iv*) Karpur Manjari

Choose the ***correct*** code:

A. Only (*i*) B. (*i*) and (*ii*)
C. (*i*), (*ii*) and (*iii*) D. (*i*), (*ii*) (*iii*) and (*iv*)

90. Monthly magazine 'Hariprabha' is published by:

A. Information and Public Relations Department
B. Haryana Sahitya Academy
C. Haryana Sanskrit Academy
D. Haryana Hindi Granth Academy

Answers

1	2	3	4	5	6	7	8	9	10
D	D	C	B	C	D	C	C	D	C
11	**12**	**13**	**14**	**15**	**16**	**17**	**18**	**19**	**20**
A	C	D	A	D	B	B	A	C	A
21	**22**	**23**	**24**	**25**	**26**	**27**	**28**	**29**	**30**
C	D	B	A	B	A	B	A	C	B
31	**32**	**33**	**34**	**35**	**36**	**37**	**38**	**39**	**40**
D	B	C	D	A	C	A	D	A	C
41	**42**	**43**	**44**	**45**	**46**	**47**	**48**	**49**	**50**
B	C	D	D	B	D	A	D	B	C
51	**52**	**53**	**54**	**55**	**56**	**57**	**58**	**59**	**60**
B	D	B	A	C	B	C	C	B	A
61	**62**	**63**	**64**	**65**	**66**	**67**	**68**	**69**	**70**
C	B	D	A	C	D	A	C	D	B
71	**72**	**73**	**74**	**75**	**76**	**77**	**78**	**79**	**80**
A	D	C	B	A	C	D	B	A	A
81	**82**	**83**	**84**	**85**	**86**	**87**	**88**	**89**	**90**
C	A	A	A	B	C	B	A	B	C

Explanatory Answers

61. The number of day = from 15 August, 1988 to 15 August, 1989 = 365 days

$\because$ $365 = 7 \times 52 + 1$

$\therefore$ Odd day = 1.

Hence, the independence day in 1989 was celebrated on Thursday (Wednesday + 1).

62. Here, Starting point = A

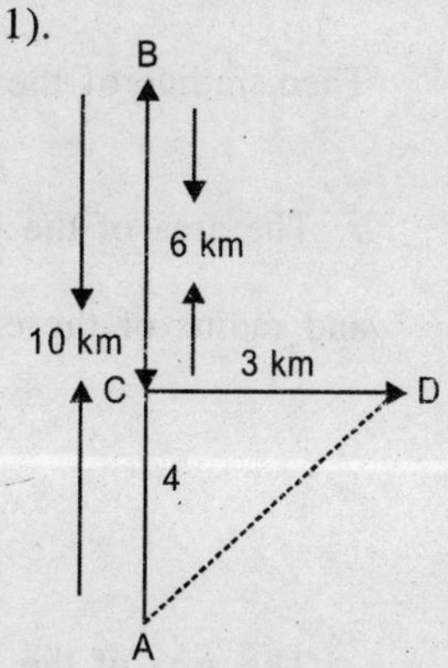

AB = 10 km

BC = 6 km

CD = 3 km

$$AD = \sqrt{AC^2 + CD^2}$$
$$= \sqrt{4^2 + 3^2}$$
$$= \sqrt{16+9} = \sqrt{25}$$
$$= 5 \text{ km}$$

Hence, Vijay is north-east direction and 5 km far from his starting point.

63.

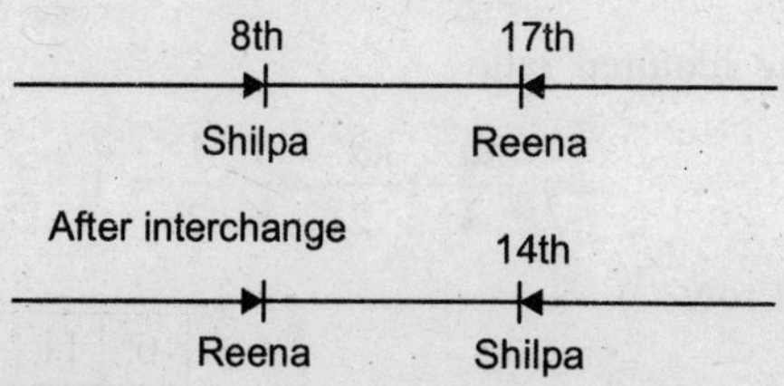

Hence, the number of girls in row = 14 + 16 = 30.

64. Given, $9 * 3 = 36$

$$\Rightarrow (9+3)\times\left(\frac{9+3}{4}\right) = 12 \times 3 = 36,$$

$$10 * 6 = 64$$

$$\Rightarrow (10+6)\times\left(\frac{10+6}{4}\right) = 16 \times 4 = 64,$$

$$9 * 1 = 25$$

$$\Rightarrow (9+1)\times\left(\frac{9+1}{4}\right) = 10\times\frac{5}{2} = 25$$

Similarly, $23 * 3 = (23+3)\times\left(\frac{23+3}{4}\right) = 26\times\frac{26}{4}$

$$= 13 \times 13 = 169.$$

65. Given,

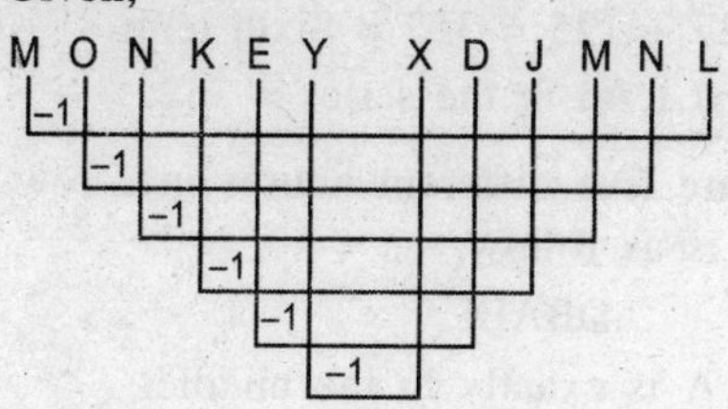

Similarly,

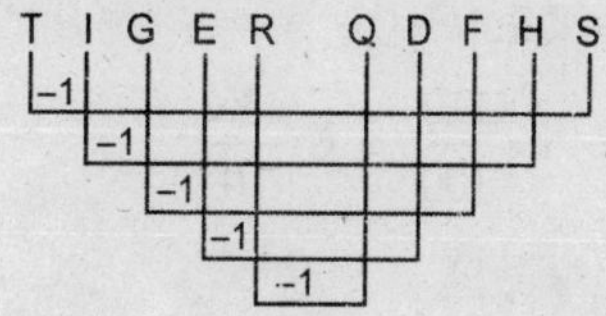

Hence, TIGER is written as QDFHS.

66. Given, A = +, B = –, C = ÷, D = ×

$\therefore$ 18 A 12 C 6 D 2 B 5

$$= 18 + 12 \div 6 \times 2 - 5$$
$$= 18 + 2 \times 2 - 5$$
$$= 18 + 4 - 5 = 22 - 5 = 17.$$

67. Here, M_1 = 7 carpenters,

w_1 = 7 chairs

h_1 = 8 hours

and M_2 = 70 carpenters,

w_2 = 70 chairs

$\therefore$ h_2 = ?

$$\frac{M_1 d h_1}{w_1} = \frac{M_2 d h_2}{w_2}$$

$$\Rightarrow \frac{7\times 8}{7} = \frac{70\times h_2}{70}$$

$$\Rightarrow h_2 = 8 \text{ hours.}$$

68. Let x number must be added to each term.

Then, $\frac{2+x}{5+x} = \frac{5}{6}$

$\Rightarrow$ $12 + 6x = 25 + 5x$

$\Rightarrow$ $6x - 5x = 25 - 12$

$\Rightarrow$ $x = 13$

Hence, the required number = x = 13.

69. Here, P = ₹ 10,000, A = ₹ 20,000, n = 5 years at compund interest

$$A = P\left(1+\frac{r}{100}\right)^n$$

$$\Rightarrow ₹\ 20{,}000 = 10{,}000\left(1+\frac{r}{100}\right)^5$$

$$\Rightarrow \left(1+\frac{r}{100}\right)^5 = 2$$

$$\Rightarrow \left(1+\frac{r}{100}\right)^{5\times 4} = 2^4$$

$$\Rightarrow \left(1+\frac{r}{100}\right)^{20} = 16$$

$$\Rightarrow 10{,}000\left(1+\frac{r}{100}\right)^{20} = 16 \times 10{,}000$$

$$\Rightarrow \quad 10{,}000\left(1+\frac{r}{100}\right)^{20} = 1{,}60{,}000$$

Hence, After 20 years the amount will be ₹ 1,60,000.

70. Let, C.P. for A = ₹ x,

then S.P. for A = $x \times \frac{110}{100}$ = ₹ $\frac{11x}{10}$

C.P. for B = ₹ $\frac{11x}{10}$,

S.P. for B = ₹ $\frac{11x}{10} \times \frac{90}{100}$ = ₹ $\frac{99}{100}x$

C.P. for C = ₹ $\frac{99}{100}x$

Therefore $\frac{99}{100}x$ = ₹ 990

$\Rightarrow$ x = ₹ 1000

Hence, Amount paid by A is ₹ 1000.

71. The required reduction $= \frac{20}{100+20} \times 100$

$$= \frac{20}{120} \times 100 = \frac{1}{6} \times 100 = \frac{50}{3} = 16\frac{2}{3}\%.$$

72. $\sqrt{2\sqrt{2\sqrt{2\sqrt{2\sqrt{2}}}}}$

$$= 2^{\frac{1}{2}} . 2^{\frac{1}{2}\times\frac{1}{2}} . 2^{\frac{1}{2}\times\frac{1}{2}\times\frac{1}{2}} . 2^{\frac{1}{2}\times\frac{1}{2}\times\frac{1}{2}\times\frac{1}{2}} . 2^{\frac{1}{2}\times\frac{1}{2}\times\frac{1}{2}\times\frac{1}{2}\times\frac{1}{2}}$$

$$= 2^{\frac{1}{2}} . 2^{\frac{1}{4}} . 2^{\frac{1}{8}} . 2^{\frac{1}{16}} . 2^{\frac{1}{32}}$$

$$= 2^{\frac{1}{2}+\frac{1}{4}+\frac{1}{8}+\frac{1}{16}+\frac{1}{32}} = 2^{\frac{16+8+4+2+1}{32}} = 2^{\frac{31}{32}}.$$

73. Here, Train to cover 132 + 108 = 240 m distance and trains are running in opposite direction

$\therefore$ relative speed = 32 + 40 = 72 km/hr

$$= 72 \times \frac{5}{18} \text{ m/s} = 4 \times 5 = 20 \text{ m/s}$$

Therefore, Time taken by the trains to cross each other

$$= \frac{\text{distance}}{\text{speed}} = \frac{240}{20} = 12 \text{ seconds.}$$

74. $0.34\overline{67} + 0.13\overline{33}$

$$= \frac{3467-34}{9900} + \frac{1333-13}{9900} = \frac{3433+1320}{9900}$$

$$= \frac{4753}{9900} = \frac{4753}{99\times100} = \frac{48.01010101}{100} = 0.48\overline{01}.$$

75. HCF of 11, 11.11, 0.11, 0.011

HCF of $11, \frac{1111}{100}, \frac{11}{100}, \frac{11}{1000}$

$$= \frac{\text{HCF of } 11, 1111, 11, 11}{\text{LCM of } 1, 100, 100, 1000} = \frac{11}{1000} = 0.011.$$

76. Let, Side of Square = a unit

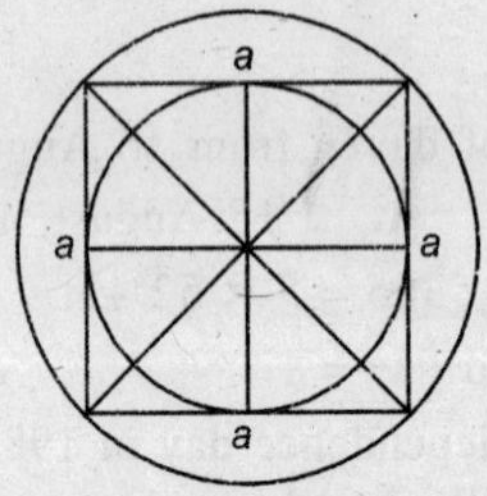

Then, radius of the incircle $= \frac{a}{2}$

$\therefore$ The area of the incircle $= \pi\left(\frac{a}{2}\right)^2 = \frac{\pi a^2}{4}$ sq. units

and radius of the circumcircle

$$= \frac{\text{diagonal of square}}{2}$$

$$= \frac{a\sqrt{2}}{2} = \frac{a}{\sqrt{2}} \text{ unit}$$

$\therefore$ The area of the circumcircle

$$= \frac{\pi a^2}{2} \text{ sq. units}$$

Hence, the required ratio

$$= \frac{\pi a^2}{4} : \frac{\pi a^2}{2} = \frac{1}{4} : \frac{1}{2} = 1 : 2.$$

78. From first row

6	11	25
8	6	16
12	5	?

$$\frac{6}{2} + (11\times2) = 3 + 22 = 25$$

From second row

$$\frac{8}{2} + (6\times2) = 4 + 12 = 16$$

From third row

$$\frac{12}{2} + (5\times2) = 6 + 10 = 16$$

Hence, the missing number = 16.

79. 127 —($+1^3$)→ 128 —($+2^3$)→ 136 —($+3^3$)→ 163 —($+4^3$)→ 227 —($+5^3$)→ **352**

$\because$ 127 = First term

$\therefore$ 127 + 1^3 = 127 + 1 = 128 = Second term

128 + 2^3 = 128 + 8 = 136 = Third term

136 + 3^3 = 136 + 27 = 163 = Fourth term

163 + 4^3 = 163 + 64 = 227 = Fifth term

227 + 5^3 = 227 + 125 = 352 = Sixth term

Hence, the next term in the series = 352.

80. Given, there are five different houses in a row and their position is as follow:

DBAEC

Hence, house A is exactly in the middle.

Previous Paper (Solved)

Haryana Teacher Eligibility Test (HTET)

PGT (Level-3), Common Subjects, Exam 2020

(Exam held on 2 January, 2021)

PART-I

Child Development and Pedagogy

Directions: *Answer the following questions by selecting the* ***most appropriate*** *option.*

1. Which of the following is ***not*** the true characteristic of Development?
A. Development involves changes
B. Early Development is more critical than later development
C. Development Patterns are unpredictable
D. There are individual differences in development

2. Which of the following is indirect method of measurement of motives?
A. Sentence completion technique
B. Questionnaire
C. Checklist
D. Interview

3. What are the basis of 'Self Concept'?
A. Social Roles B. The Body Image
C. Above (A) and (B) D. None of the above

4. Which of the following is ***not*** the characteristic of introverted thinking type personality as given by Jung?
A. Self Centered
B. Optimistic
C. Absorbed in his own intellectual pursuit
D. Support Theory with facts

5. What is the approximate weight of the Brain upto 16 year age?
A. 750 gm to 900 gm B. 1200 gm to 1400 gm
C. 1000 gm to 1200 gm D. 800 gm to 1000 gm

6. Which Psychologist presented scientific description of 'Individual differences' in his Book 'Hereditary Genius'?
A. Allport B. Biggi and Hunt
C. Jean Piaget D. Sir Fransis Galton

7. Which of the following is Direct Method of Adjustment?
A. Repression
B. Regression
C. Withdrawl and Submissiveness
D. Rationalization

8. Which of the following orientation falls under the post convention level of Moral Development Theory propounded by Kohlberg?
A. Punishment and Obedience
B. Social contract
C. Good boy/Nice girl
D. Law and Social order

9. Which of the following is ***not*** the characteristic of Adolescence?
A. Emotional Stability
B. Contrasting Mental Moods
C. Anxiety of Vocation
D. Feeling of Hero worship

10. A statement of knowledge or skills that student should master after instruction, is known as:
A. A content analysis
B. An individualized educational programme (IEP)
C. An instructional objective
D. General Aims

11. Which of the following is ***not*** the symptoms of Good Memory?
A. Rapidity
B. Average retention
C. Accuracy
D. Recall of right material at right time

12. Which of the following concept is ***not*** related with Bandura's Social Learning Theory?
A. Modelling B. Adaptation
C. Imitation D. Observational learning

13. What is the ranking ratio given by Sheldon for predominant endomorph person according to physique?
A. 7-1-1 B. 1-7-1
C. 1-1-7 D. 4-4-4

14. Which is the fifth stage of Personality development according to Erikson?
A. industry v/s inferiority
B. identity v/s role confusion
C. intimacy v/s isolation
D. generativity v/s stagnation

15. Which of the following is ***not*** the element of creativity as given by Guilford?

A. Fluency B. Incubation
C. Flexibility D. Originality

16. Which of the following is ***not*** the type of positive transfer of learning?

A. Lateral transfer B. Sequential transfer
C. Horizontal transfer D. Zero transfer

17. Which of the following is ***not*** the Freud's Psychosexual stage?

A. Phallic stage B. Autonomy stage
C. Anal stage D. Oral stage

18. Who stated that "Psychology is the Positive Science of conduct of living creatures"?

A. Sir William McDougall
B. Sir Francis Galton
C. Max Wertheimer
D. William James

19. Which of the following is ***not*** the type of "Psychophysical Method" of study of Educational Psychology?

A. The method of minimal changes or method of limits
B. The method of constant stimuli
C. The method of average or mean error
D. Modifying the individual attitude

20. 'Knowledge is constructed by transforming, organizing and re-organizing previous knowledge.' This best explains the idea of which of the following?

A. Piaget B. Vygotsky
C. Freud D. Bandura

21. According to the Cognitive Development Theory of Piaget, 'The basic building block of knowledge' is called:

A. Schema B. Assimilation
C. Accommodation D. Equilibration

22. An English teacher taught their students that plural of Cat is Cats, plural of House is Houses, plural of Pen is Pens, in this manner student by mistake made plural of Mouse as Mouses. This is the example of which type of transfer of learning?

A. Positive transfer B. Negative transfer
C. Zero transfer D. Vertical transfer

23. Which of the following is objective determinants of Attention?

A. Interest B. Habit
C. Curiosity D. Duration of stimulus

24. Murray's "Thematic Apperception Test" is related to which theory of personality?

A. Trait theory B. Trait and Type theory
C. Type theory D. Psychoanalytical theory

25. Which of the following is I.Q. Range of 'Moderate mental retarded' children?

A. 52 to 67 B. 36 to 51
C. 20 to 35 D. below 20

26. Which of the following is ***not*** the type of life styles for the development of personality given by Adler?

A. Lazy type B. Ruling type
C. Go-getting type D. Escaping type

27. How many cards are used in Rorschach Inkblot Test?

A. 10 B. 12
C. 15 D. 28

28. Which of the following is ***not*** a type of Personality given by Sprenger in values point of view?

A. Theoretical B. Economic
C. Asthetic D. Athletic

29. Which of the following is the subordinate law of learning given by Thorndike?

A. Law of readiness B. Law of exercise
C. Law of mental set D. Law of effect

30. Which of the following is ***not*** the true characteristic of Adolescence?

A. Adolescence is transitional stage between childhood and adulthood.
B. In adolescence there is a vague individual status.
C. Adolescence is the threshold of adulthood.
D. Adolescence is a time of realism.

PART-II

भाषा : हिन्दी

*निर्देशः निम्नलिखित प्रश्नों के उत्तर देने के लिए **सबसे उचित** विकल्प चुनिए।*

31. निजवाचक सर्वनाम युक्त वाक्य छाँटिए :

A. आप अत्यन्त आकर्षक व्यक्तित्व के स्वामी हैं।
B. लड़के आप ही चले जाएँगे।
C. आप लोग शान्त हो जाएँ।
D. आप हुजूर जरूर पधारें।

32. वार्तनिक दृष्टि से ***अशुद्ध*** विकल्प चुनिए :

A. मृत्योपरान्त B. योगिराज
C. प्रोज्ज्वल D. प्रज्वलित

33. विलोम की दृष्टि से ***असंगत*** जोड़े को छाँटिए :

A. लंबा-नाटा B. अभिज्ञ-अनभिज्ञ
C. अनुरक्ति-विराग D. सत्कार-तिरस्कार

34. किस विकल्प में 'इल' प्रत्यय का प्रयोग ***नहीं*** हुआ है?

A. उर्मिल B. मरियल

C. फेनिल D. जटिल

35. निम्न में से 'बकरी' का पर्याय ***नहीं*** है?

A. वर्धकी B. छागी

C. अजा D. छेरी

36. जातिवाचक संज्ञा युक्त वाक्य ***नहीं*** है :

A. आजकल की पढ़ाइयाँ बहुत महँगी हैं।

B. उँचाइयाँ नापनी हैं तो पर्वतों की सैर कीजिए।

C. कभी-कभी बुराइयाँ ही अच्छाइयाँ बन जाती हैं।

D. मैंने अनुभव किया है कि उसे ऊँचाई से डर लगता है।

37. किस विकल्प में व्यंजन संधि का प्रयोग ***नहीं*** हुआ है?

A. चिदाभास B. वागीश्वर

C. तदर्थ D. तिरोहित

38. शुद्ध वाक्य का चयन कीजिए :

A. मैंने काम कोई वकील से ही हो सकता है।

B. मैंने उनका धन्यवाद किया।

C. कृपया दरवाजा बंद करने की कृपा करें।

D. हम सभी में मानवीय दुर्बलताएँ हैं।

39. समास की दृष्टि से ***असंगत*** विकल्प छाँटिए :

A. भयभीत - करण तत्पुरुष

B. सेठ-साहूकार - समाहार द्वन्द्व

C. विद्याहीन - अपादान तत्पुरुष

D. स्वर्गगत - कर्म तत्पुरुष

40. वाक्यांश के लिए एक शब्द की दृष्टि से ***असंगत*** विकल्प चुनिए :

A. किसी कथा के अन्तर्गत आने वाली कोई दूसरी कथा–अन्तर्कथा

B. सर्वाधिकार सम्पन्न शासक या अधिकारी–अधिनायक

C. बिना किसी प्रयास के–आयास

D. जिसे शाप दिया गया है–अभिशप्त

41. अनिश्चित संख्यावाचक विशेषण चुनिए :

A. पिछले वर्ष की तुलना में इस बार अधिक वर्षा हुई।

B. सब्जी में थोड़ा-सा नमक डालिए।

C. सारा काम मुझे ही करना होगा।

D. सारे देश आतंकवाद के खिलाफ खड़े हैं।

42. सकर्मक क्रिया युक्त वाक्य चुनिए :

A. भिखारी मंदिर के बाहर चिल्ला रहे थे।

B. मछलियाँ तालाब में तैर रही हैं।

C. धावक सड़क पर दौड़ रहे हैं।

D. बहन ने भाई को मिठाई खिलाई।

43. किस विकल्प में अव्ययीभाव समास है?

A. विरोधजनक B. कृपापूर्वक

C. अवसरवंचित D. स्वाधीन

44. प्रत्यय की दृष्टि से असंगत विकल्प चुनिए :

A. गृहस्थ + इक = गार्हस्थिक B. दिष्ट + इक = दैष्टिक

C. अभिजात + त्य = आभिजात्य D. पाणिनि + ईय = पाणिनीय

45. किस विकल्प में 'आ' उपसर्ग का प्रयोग हुआ है?

A. आधिकारिक B. आधुनिक

C. आलम्बित D. आरण्यक

Language : English

Directions: *Answer the following questions by selecting the **most appropriate** option.*

46. Choose the part of sentence that is grammatically ***incorrect***:

That's twice I've been forgetting to bring my diary to work this week.

A. That's twice B. I've been forgetting

C. to bring my diary D. to work this week

47. Fill in the blank with the ***correct*** option:

Of the two Novels, this is ....

A. interesting B. more interesting

C. interested D. much interesting

48. Change the narration:

He said, "I've been spending a lot more time with my children."

A. He told me that he had been spending a lot more time with his children.

B. He told me that he is spending a lot more time with my children.

C. He told me that he had spent a lot more time with his children.

D. He said that he spends a lot more time with his children.

49. Fill in the blank with the ***correct*** present perfect continuous tense:

Who .... was coming to see me this morning?

A. you should say B. did you say

C. you did said D. did you say that

50. Fill in the blank with the ***correct*** present perfect continuous tense:

He .... for five hours.

A. been slept B. is sleeping

C. been sleeping D. has been sleeping

51. Fill in the blanks:

The growing number of visitors .... the footpaths.

A. are damaging B. is damaging

C. were damage D. was damaged

52. Fill in the blank with the ***correct*** present perfect continuous tense:

She is one of the few people ....

A. who I look up to B. whose I look up
C. I look up to D. Both (A) and (C)

53. Choose the option and arrange the following sentence in the *correct* order:

I. Resigned
II. To sack him
III. Had he not
IV. We would have been forced

A. IV, III, II, I B. III, II, I, IV
C. IV, II, I, III D. III, I, IV, II

54. Change the sentence into passive:
Someone has picked my pocket.
A. My pocket is picked.
B. Somebody picked my pocket.
C. My pocket pick by somebody.
D. My pocket has been picked.

55. Choose the grammatically *correct* sentence:
A. No sooner we reached the station and the train arrived.
B. No sooner did we reach the station than the train arrived.
C. No sooner did we reach the station then the train arrived.
D. No sooner did we reach the station the train arrived.

56. Fill in the blank with the *correct* option:
..........., they slept soundly.
A. Hot though was the night air
B. Hot though the night air was
C. Hot was the night air that
D. Hot although the night air was

57. Fill in the blank with the *correct* present perfect continuous tense:
.... thinks that Julie should be given the job.
A. neither of us B. practically everyone
C. A no. of people D. Both (A) and (B)

58. To have 'a bee in the bonnet' means:
A. to know perfectly
B. something you are obsessed with
C. not to take anything seriously
D. to deviate from the point

59. Choose the part of sentence that is grammatically *incorrect*:
The world's supply of oil is soon running out.
A. The world's
B. supply of oil
C. is soon running out
D. Both (A) and (B)

60. The word 'juncture' means:
A. in a joyous manner
B. to put in danger
C. to sound harshly
D. point rendered critical by circumstances

PART-III

General Studies : Quantitative Aptitude, Reasoning Ability and GK & Awareness

61. In a code language, 'DISTANCE' is written as 'IDTATOEC' and 'DOCUMENT' is written as 'ODDMUFTN', then in same code language, 'THURSDAY' will be written as :
A. HTRUDSYA B. HTVSREYA
C. UHVSTEYA D. VIRUDSZB

62. Kamal walks 10 m towards North. From there, he walks 6 m towards South. Then he walks 3 m towards East. In which direction is he with reference to his starting point?
A. West B. South-West
C. North-East D. South

63. In the first year, the population of a village increased by 5% and in the next year it decreased by 5%. If at the end of the second year, the population was 79,800, what was it at the beginning of the first year?
A. 79,800 B. 80,200
C. 80,000 D. 79,600

64. Find the ***wrong*** terms of the following series:
1CV, 5FU, 9IT, 15LS, 17OR
A. 5FU B. 9IT
C. 15LS D. 17OR

65. The radii of two cylinders are in the ratio 2 : 3 and their heights are in the ratio 5 : 3. The ratio of their volumes are:
A. 27 : 20 B. 20 : 27
C. 4 : 9 D. 9 : 4

66. Mr. X said about Mrs. Y, "Mrs. Y is the wife of the grandson of my mother." How is Mr. X is related to Mrs. Y?
A. Father B. Grandfather
C. Husband D. Father-in-law

67. How many independent meaningful words can 'HEARTLESS' be divided into without changing the order of the letters and using each letter only once?
A. 1 B. 2
C. 3 D. 4

68. In an examination, 27% students failed in English and 38% failed in Science. If 19% failed in both the subjects, then the percentage of passed in both the subjects is:
A. 46% B. 54%
C. 62% D. 81%

69. Next terms of the following number series are:

20, 20, 19, 16, 17, 13, 14, 11, ?, ?

A. 10, 10 B. 10, 11
C. 13, 14 D. 10, 9

70. A man rows upstream 13 km and downstream 28 km taking 5 hours each time. What is the speed of water?

A. 1½ km/hr B. 2 km/hr
C. 2½ km/hr D. 3 km/hr

71. If Shyam writes down all the integers from 1 to 100, then how many times does he write 3 ?

A. 19 B. 11
C. 20 D. 21

72. A is elder to B while C and D are elder to E. E lies between A and C and C is elder to B, then which of the following statements is necessarily ***true***?

A. A is elder to C. B. C is elder to D.
C. D is elder to C. D. E is elder to B.

73. Among M, T, R, K and D, each having a different height, M is shorter only from T and D is taller only from K. Who will be the third tallest person among them?

A. T B. D
C. M D. R

74. The square root of $\dfrac{\left(1\frac{3}{4}\right)^4 - \left(2\frac{1}{3}\right)^4}{\left(1\frac{3}{4}\right)^2 - \left(2\frac{1}{3}\right)^2}$ is equal to :

A. $2\frac{11}{12}$ B. $2\frac{1}{12}$
C. $3\frac{11}{12}$ D. $3\frac{1}{12}$

75. After 5 years, father's age will be three times of his son's age. 5 years ago, father's age was 7 times of his son's age. The present age of the father is:

A. 40 years B. 30 years
C. 50 years D. 45 years

76. A man is performing yoga with his head down and legs up. His face is towards the West. In which direction will his left hand be?

A. North B. South
C. West D. East

77. Two taps A and B would fill a tank completely in 30 and 36 minutes respectively. Both taps being opened, find when the tap A must be turned off so that the tank must be just filled in 18 minutes?

A. After 15 minutes B. After 12 minutes
C. After 14 minutes D. After 16 minutes

78. In how many years will a sum of ₹ 800 become ₹ 926.10 at 10% per annum interest compound half yearly?

A. 3 years B. 1½ years
C. 4½ years D. 2 years

79. The least square number, which is divisible by 8, 15 and 24 is equal to:

A. 120 B. 1800
C. 3600 D. 6400

80. If the selling price of 6 pens is equal to the cost price of 8 pens, then profit/loss in percentage is:

A. 25% profit B. 25% loss
C. $33\frac{1}{3}$% loss D. $33\frac{1}{3}$% profit

81. Who is the Chairman of the newly constituted 6th State Finance Commission of Haryana?

A. Vikas Gupta B. Rajesh Khullar
C. P. Raghvendra Rao D. T.V.S.N. Prasad

82. Who is the vice-chairman of Haryana Urdu Academy?

A. Gopichand Narang B. Kumud Bansal
C. Chander Trikha D. Suraj Bhan

83. Where is the palace of Begum Samru located in Haryana?

A. Faridabad B. Sonipat
C. Gurugram D. Rohtak

84. The award is given by the Haryana Government to the gold medal winner in the Commonwealth games:

A. Three crore B. Two crore
C. Seventy Five lakh D. One & half crore

85. Who was the Collector of Rohtak during the uprising of 1857?

A. Thomas Semton B. W. Eden
C. Adam Loch D. Hudson

86. Rivulet, which is one of the tributary of Ghaggar:

A. Chautang B. Sahibi
C. Dohan D. Indori

87. In which district of Haryana 'Tikkar lake' is located?

A. Rohtak B. Panchkula
C. Karnal D. Kaithal

88. The assembly of Haryana, which has been constituted after the election of October, 2019:

A. 12th B. 13th
C. 14th D. 15th

89. Vinesh Phogat is recently honoured with which National Award?

A. Dronacharya Award
B. Arjuna Award
C. Rajiv Gandhi Khel Ratna Award
D. Dhyanchand Award

90. Which city has its ancient name as Kanaud?

A. Mahendragarh B. Ambala
C. Kaithal D. Sonipat

Answers

1	2	3	4	5	6	7	8	9	10
C	A	C	B	B	D	C	B	A	C
11	**12**	**13**	**14**	**15**	**16**	**17**	**18**	**19**	**20**
B	B	A	B	B	D	B	A	D	A
21	**22**	**23**	**24**	**25**	**26**	**27**	**28**	**29**	**30**
A	B	D	D	B	A	A	D	C	D
31	**32**	**33**	**34**	**35**	**36**	**37**	**38**	**39**	**40**
B	A	C	B	A	D	D	D	A	C
41	**42**	**43**	**44**	**45**	**46**	**47**	**48**	**49**	**50**
D	D	B	C	C	B	B	A	*	D
51	**52**	**53**	**54**	**55**	**56**	**57**	**58**	**59**	**60**
B	*	D	D	B	B	*	B	C	D
61	**62**	**63**	**64**	**65**	**66**	**67**	**68**	**69**	**70**
B	C	C	C	B	D	*	B	A	A
71	**72**	**73**	**74**	**75**	**76**	**77**	**78**	**79**	**80**
C	D	D	A	A	A	A	B	C	D
81	**82**	**83**	**84**	**85**	**86**	**87**	**88**	**89**	**90**
C	C	C	D	C	A	B	C	C	A

Explanatory Answers

61. Given,

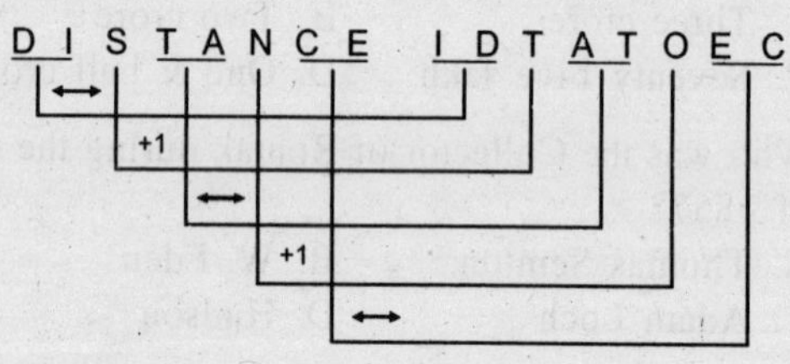

and

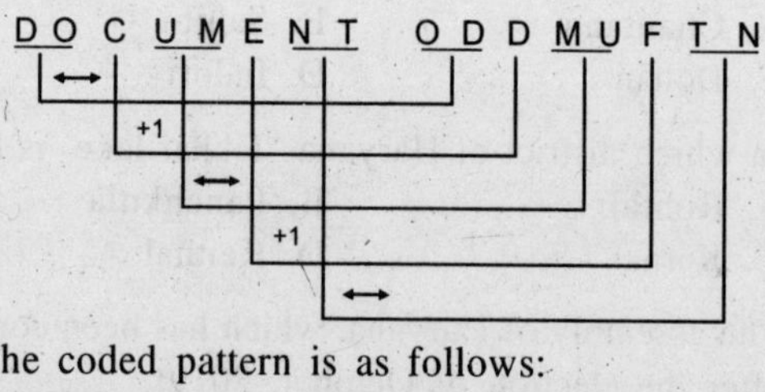

The coded pattern is as follows:
The first two and IV, V and VII, VIII letters of the word are written in the reverse order and each of the remaining letters is moved one step forward to get the code.

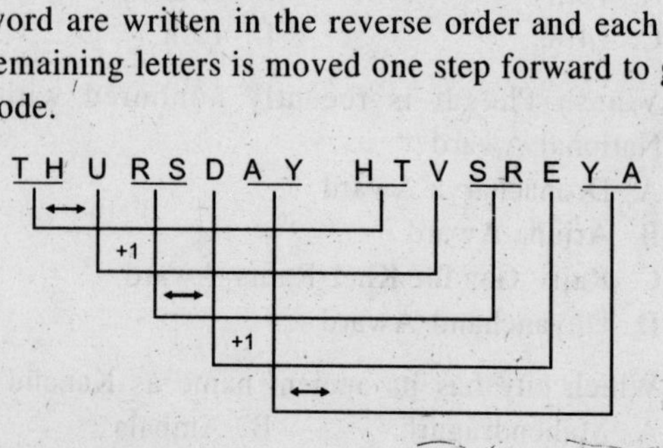

Hence, 'THURSDAY' will be written as 'HTVSREYA'.

62.

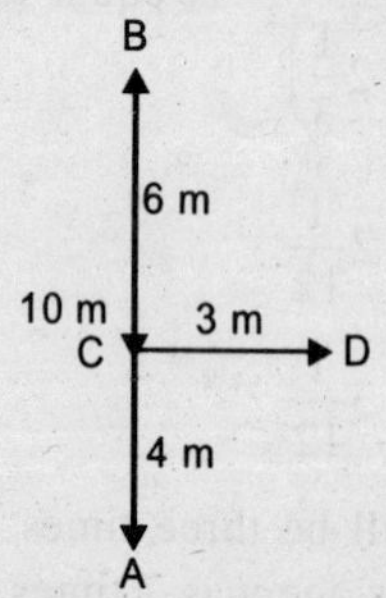

Here, starting point = A

AB = 10 m

BC = 6 m

CD = 3 m

He is in North-East direction from starting point (A).

63. Let x was the population in the beginning of the first year.

Then,

$$x\left(1+\frac{5}{100}\right)\left(1-\frac{5}{100}\right) = 79{,}800$$

$$\Rightarrow \quad x\left(1+\frac{1}{20}\right)\left(1-\frac{1}{20}\right) = 79{,}800$$

$$\Rightarrow \quad x\left(\frac{21}{20}\right)\left(\frac{19}{20}\right) = 79{,}800$$

$$\Rightarrow \quad x = 79800 \times \frac{20 \times 20}{21 \times 19} = 79800 \times \frac{400}{399}$$
$$= 200 \times 400 = 80000$$

Hence, $x = 80000$.

64. 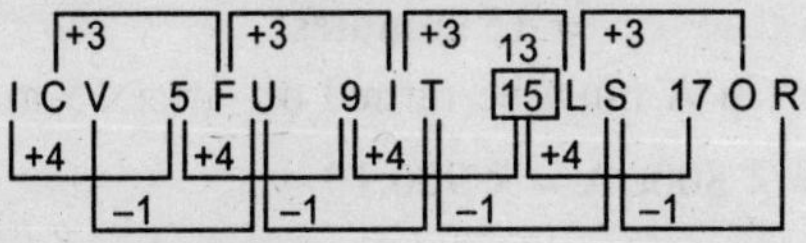

In given series,

Place of 15LS should be 13LS

$\therefore$ Wrong term = 15LS.

65. Let the radius of two cylinders are $2r$, $3r$ and their heights are $5h$, $3h$

Then, volume = $\pi r^2 h$

$$\therefore \quad V_1 = \pi(2r)^2 \times 5h = \pi \times 4r^2 \times 5h = 20\pi r^2 h$$

and
$$V_2 = \pi(3r)^2 \times 3h = \pi \times 9r^2 \times 3h = 27\pi r^2 h$$

Hence, the ratio of their volumes = $\frac{V_1}{V_2}$

$$= \frac{20\pi r^2 h}{27\pi r^2 h} = \frac{20}{27} = 20 : 27.$$

66. According to question,

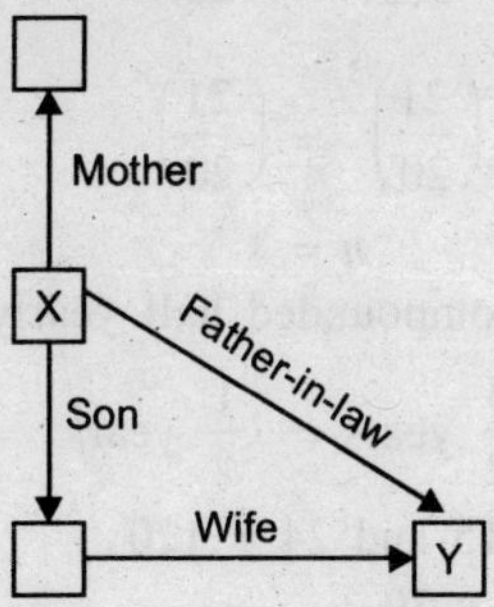

Hence, X is Father-in-law of Y.

68. $\because n(E \cup S) = n(E) + n(S) - n(E \cap S)$

$$\therefore \quad n(E \cup S) = 27 + 38 - 19 = 65 - 19 = 46\%$$

$\because$ The percentage of failed in English and Science is 46%

$\therefore$ The percentage of passed in both the subject
$$= 100 - 46 = 54\%.$$

69. Given, series,

20, 20, 19, 16, 17, 13, 14, 11, ?, ?

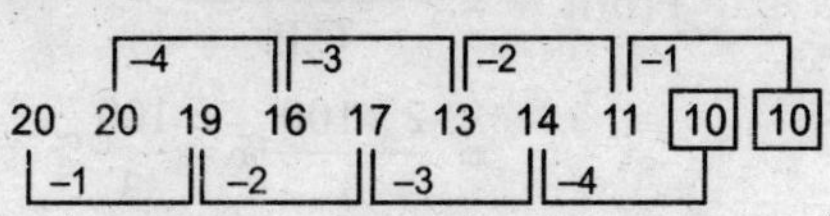

Here, the next term in the series are 10, 10.

70. Let the speed of a boat in still water is u km/hr and the speed of water is v km/hr

Then, upstream,

$$u - v = \frac{13}{5} \text{ km/hr} \quad \ldots(i)$$

$$\text{downstream, } u + v = \frac{28}{5} \text{ km/hr} \quad \ldots(ii)$$

From $(i) + (ii)$, we get

$$2u = \frac{13}{5} + \frac{28}{5} = \frac{41}{5}$$

$$\Rightarrow \quad u = \frac{41}{10} = 4.1 \text{ km/hr}$$

From (i),

$$v = u - \frac{13}{5} = \frac{41}{10} - \frac{13}{5} = \frac{41 - 26}{10} = \frac{15}{10} = \frac{3}{2} = 1\frac{1}{2} \text{ km/hr}$$

Hence, the speed of water is $1\frac{1}{2}$ km/hr.

71. Clearly, from 1 to 100, there are ten numbers with 3 as the unit's digit:

3, 13, 23, 33, 43, 53, 63, 73, 83, 93

and ten numbers with 3 as the ten's digit:

30, 31, 32, 33, 34, 35, 36, 37, 38, 39.

So, required number = 10 + 10 = 20.

72. Here,

A > B, C & D > E

E is between A & C

C > B

D & C > E > A > B

Hence, it is clear that E is elder to B.

73. Given, M is shorter only from T *i.e.*, T > M

and D is taller only from K *i.e.*, D > K

Hence, T > M > R > D > K

Hence, R be the third tallest person among them.

74. Given, $$\frac{\left(1\frac{3}{4}\right)^4 - \left(2\frac{1}{3}\right)^4}{\left(1\frac{3}{4}\right)^2 - \left(2\frac{1}{3}\right)^2} = \frac{\left(\frac{7}{4}\right)^4 - \left(\frac{7}{3}\right)^4}{\left(\frac{7}{4}\right)^2 - \left(\frac{7}{3}\right)^2}$$

$$[a^2 - b^2 = (a - b)(a + b)]$$

$$= \frac{\left[\left(\frac{7}{4}\right)^2 - \left(\frac{7}{3}\right)^2\right]\left[\left(\frac{7}{4}\right)^2 + \left(\frac{7}{3}\right)^2\right]}{\left(\frac{7}{4}\right)^2 - \left(\frac{7}{3}\right)^2}$$

$= \left(\frac{7}{4}\right)^2 + \left(\frac{7}{3}\right)^2 \qquad [a^2 + b^2 = (a+b)^2 - 2ab]$

$= \left(\frac{7}{4}+\frac{7}{3}\right)^2 - 2\times\frac{7}{4}\times\frac{7}{3} = \left(\frac{21+28}{12}\right)^2 - \frac{49}{6}$

$= \left(\frac{49}{12}\right)^2 - \frac{49}{6} = \frac{49}{6}\left[\frac{49}{12\times 2} - 1\right]$

$= \frac{49}{6}\left[\frac{49-24}{24}\right] = \frac{49}{6}\times\frac{25}{24} = \frac{49\times 25}{144}$

Hence, the required square root

$= \sqrt{\frac{49\times 25}{144}} = \frac{7\times 5}{12} = \frac{35}{12} = 2\frac{11}{12}.$

75. Let after 5 years, son's age = x years

then, father's age = $3x$ years

$\therefore$ son's present age = $(x - 5)$ years

and father's present age = $(3x - 5)$ years

5 years ago, son's age = $(x - 10)$ years

and father's age = $(3x - 10)$ years

According to question,

$7(x - 10) = (3x - 10)$

$\Rightarrow \quad 7x - 70 = 3x - 10$

$\Rightarrow \quad 7x - 3x = 70 - 10 = 60$

$\Rightarrow \quad 4x = 60 \Rightarrow x = 15$ years

Hence, the present age of father

$= (3x - 5)$ years

$= (3 \times 15 - 5)$ years

$= (45 - 5)$ years = 40 years.

76.

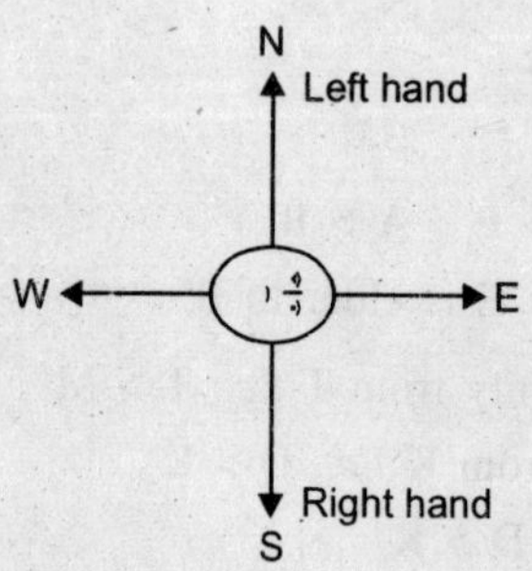

Here, his left hand is in North direction.

77. Part filled by tap A in 1 minute = $\frac{1}{30}$

and part filled by tap B in 1 minute = $\frac{1}{36}$

Let the tap A must be turned off after x minutes

Then, $\frac{x}{30}+\frac{18}{36}=1$

$\Rightarrow \quad \frac{x}{30}+\frac{1}{2} = 1$

$\Rightarrow \quad \frac{x}{30} = 1-\frac{1}{2}$

$\Rightarrow \quad \frac{x}{30} = \frac{1}{2}$

$\Rightarrow \quad x = 15$ minutes

Hence, the tap A must be turned off after 15 minues.

78. Given, P = ₹ 800, A = ₹ 926.10

$r = 10\%$ per annum

$\because$ Interest compounded half yearly

$\therefore \quad r = \frac{10}{2} = 5\%$

$\because \quad A = P\left(1+\frac{r}{100}\right)^n$

$\therefore \quad 926.10 = 800\left(1+\frac{5}{100}\right)^n$

$\frac{926.10}{800} = \left(1+\frac{1}{20}\right)^n$

$\frac{926.10}{800} = \left(\frac{21}{20}\right)^n$

$\frac{92610}{80000} = \left(\frac{21}{20}\right)^n$

$\frac{9261}{8000} = \left(\frac{21}{20}\right)^n$

$\left(\frac{21}{20}\right)^3 = \left(\frac{21}{20}\right)^n$

$n = 3$

$\because$ Interest compounded half yearly

$\therefore$ Time = $\frac{3}{2}$ years = $1\frac{1}{2}$ years.

79. LCM of 8, 15 and 24 = 120

$\because$ 120 = $2^2 \times 30$

$\therefore$ The least square number = $2^2 \times 30 \times 30$

$= 2^2 \times 30^2 = 4 \times 900 = 3600.$

80. Let the cost price of 1 pen = ₹ 1

Then, the cost price of 8 pens = ₹ 8

Given, The S.P. of 6 pens = the C.P. of 8 pens = ₹ 8

$\because$ The S.P. of 6 pens = ₹ 8

and the C.P. of 6 pens = ₹ 6

$\therefore$ Profit = S.P. – C.P.

= 8 – 6 = ₹ 2

$\therefore$ Profit % = $\frac{\text{Profit}\times 100}{\text{C.P.}}$

$= \frac{2\times 100}{6}\% = \frac{100}{3}\% = 33\frac{1}{3}\%.$

Previous Paper (Solved)

Haryana Teacher Eligibility Test (HTET)

PGT (Level-3), Common Subjects, Exam 2019

(Exam held on 16 November, 2019)

PART-I

Child Development and Pedagogy

Directions: *Answer the following questions by selecting the **most appropriate** option.*

1. According to Vygotsky, a range of task too difficult for the child to do alone but possible with the help of adults and more skilled peers is called:

A. Scaffolding
B. Inter subjectivity
C. Guided participation
D. Zone of proximal development

2. Which of the following psychologist defined adolescence as "Adolescence is that span of years during which boys and girls move from childhood to adulthood, mentally, emotionally, socially and physically"?

A. A.T. Jersild B. E.B. Hurlock
C. I.P. Davis D. H. Sorenson

3. Learner centered instructional strategy in which students are encouraged to construct their understanding with the assistance of teacher through questions and directions is:

A. Discovery learning
B. Guided discovery learning
C. Problem based learning
D. Project based learning

4. Positive facilitation of present learning through past learning, for example addition helps multiplication. This type of transfer of learning is called:

A. Vertical B. Sequential
C. Lateral D. Bilateral

5. Which of the following statement most appropriately defines the term inclusion?

A. Educating children with special needs in special school
B. Educating children with special needs in special classroom of school
C. Educating children with special needs most of the time in regular class
D. Educating children with special needs full time in the regular classroom

6. Which of the following programme is ***not*** suitable for gifted children?

A. Special classes
B. Remedial Teaching
C. Acceleration
D. Enrichment in regular classroom setting

7. According to Piaget, adolescents ability to evaluate the logic of verbal statement without referring to real-world circumstances is:

A. Propositional thought
B. Transitive inference
C. Cognitive mapping
D. Decentration

8. Parul's intelligence test indicate that she is average to above average intelligent. However, her grades in reading, spellings, social sciences and science are very low. Her maths grades are quite high & her writing skills are adequate. Parul most likely has:

A. Dyscalculia B. Dysgraphia
C. Dyslexia D. Dysphasis

9. According to Gardner, the ability to detect and respond appropriately to the moods, temperaments, motivations and intentions of others, is known as:

A. Linguistic intelligence
B. Bodily – kinesthetic intelligence
C. Interpersonal intelligence
D. Intrapersonal intelligence

10. The democratic organisation of school influence learning, this factor of learning is related to:

A. Methodological aspect
B. Social aspect
C. Physiological aspect
D. Psychological aspect

11. Which of the following type of learning style is used when students approach of learning material in a way that helps them understand the meaning of the materials?

A. Practical style B. Impulsive style
C. Surface style D. Deep style

12. Which of the following is a good assessment strategy to avoid cultural bias?
A. Assess students using a variety of methods
B. Use a single, good standardized test
C. Assume that ethnic differences are due to heredity
D. Avoid using portfolio for assessment purposes

13. Rohan is reading a latest Bahubali comic book because he cannot wait to see what happens to Bahubali and his family. This is best example of:
A. Only intrinsic motivation
B. Only extrinsic motivation
C. Both intrinsic and extrinsic motivation
D. Neither intrinsic nor extrinsic motivation

14. Learning situation in which multiple partners stimulate and encourage one another is called:
A. Team teaching B. Programmed instruction
C. Cooperative learning D. Discovery learning

15. Which of the following is ***not*** an appropriate strategy for improving students problem solving?
A. Functional fixedness of student
B. Give extensive opportunities to solve real-world problems
C. Involve parents in children's problem solving
D. Monitor students effective and ineffective problem solving strategies

16. According to Bronfenbrenner's Ecological Theory, student's family, peers and school etc. influence his/her development and they belong to the:
A. Chrono system B. Micro system
C. Macro system D. Exo system

17. ______ is to social cognitive theory as Vygotsky is to social constructivist theory.
A. Skinner B. Seigler
C. Piaget D. Bandura

18. Speaking or writing in such a way as to have an impact on others is known as the:
A. Grammar of language B. Phonemes of language
C. Pragmatics of language D. Morphemes of language

19. In Kohlberg's theory, at which level moral development is internalized and not based on external standards?
A. Preconventional level
B. Conventional level
C. Post conventional level
D. Mutual interpersonal level

20. According to Piaget, which of the following characteristics is not related to formal operational stage of children?
A. Hypothetico-deductive reasoning
B. Idealistic reasoning
C. Spatial reasoning
D. Abstract reasoning

21. Which of the following statement is ***correct*** about the nature of emotions?
A. Emotional expressions are modified by learning.
B. Emotions are permanent state of the organism.
C. Emotions are aroused by internal stimuli.
D. Certain facial expressions of emotions have different meanings.

22. Children considered as low vision who have a visual acuity between:
A. 20/70 to 20/200
B. 20/20 vision with corrective lenses
C. 6/6 vision with corrective lenses
D. 20/10 to 20/30

23. Most suitable strategy for a teacher, when he/she is working with adolescent students is to:
A. Ask students to make comparisons
B. Propose a problem and invite students to form hypothesis
C. Give children experience in ordering operations
D. Construct an inclined plane or a hill

24. Which of the following statement is ***incorrect*** about the principles of child development?
A. Development follows a definite and predictable pattern.
B. All individuals are similar in their development.
C. Development is product of hereditary and environment.
D. Development works on the principle of integration.

25. A child's diet affect how tall the child grows and even how effectively the child can think and solve problems. In this example development is primarily influenced by:
A. Heredity B. Environment
C. Early-later experience D. Continuity

26. Which teaching strategy is most likely to foster he development of critical thinking skill of students?
A. Giving a multiple choice test
B. Assignment for students to create timelines of important historical dates
C. Giving worksheets to students that require them to recall the facts presented in their text books
D. Presenting students with statements such as "Lal Bahadur Shastri was our greatest Prime Minister" to defend or refute

27. According to Erikson, in complex societies teenagers experience which of the following state?
A. Identity crisis B. Identity achievement
C. Identity moratorium D. Identity foreclosure

28. Which of the following question is most likely to get students to reflect on their purpose?
A. What is most important to you in your life?
B. How can you organise your life?
C. What can you do to get good grades?
D. How can you set better short term goal?

29. Child's symptoms when, he/she cannot stay focused on a task, act impulsively, ignoring social rules and lashing out with hostility when frustrated, is indication of:
A. Attention – deficit hyperactivity disorder
B. Slow learner
C. Mentally retardation
D. Amnesia

30. Young people mainly girls engage in strict dieting and excessive exercise. This eating disorder in adolescence is known as:
A. Anorexia Nervosa
B. Obsessive Compulsive Neurosis
C. Neuro-developmental Disorder
D. Bulimia Nervosa

PART-II

भाषा : हिन्दी

निर्देशः *निम्नलिखित प्रश्नों के उत्तर देने के लिए **सबसे उचित** विकल्प चुनिए।*

31. निम्न में 'पार्श्विक' वर्ण कौन-सा है?
A. य B. व
C. र D. ल

32. किस विकल्प में दो उपसर्गों का योग ***नहीं*** हुआ है?
A. व्युत्पत्ति B. व्याधि
C. व्यापादित D. वैनाशिक

33. किस विकल्प में 'अपादान तत्पुरुष' का प्रयोग ***नहीं*** हुआ है?
A. जन्मरोगी B. जलजात
C. राजद्रोह D. पदाक्रांत

34. वार्तनिक दृष्टि से ***शुद्ध*** शब्द का चयन कीजिए:
A. दृष्टव्य B. परिशिष्ठ
C. आदिष्ठ D. अन्त्येष्टि

35. किस विकल्प में 'भाववाचक कृत् प्रत्यय' का प्रयोग ***नहीं*** हुआ है?
A. परोसैया B. छिड़काव
C. पछतावा D. गड़गड़ाहट

36. संधि-विच्छेद एवं शब्द-निर्माण की दृष्टि से ***असंगत*** विकल्प चुनिए:
A. विश्व + एक्य = विश्वैक्य B. अधम + ऋण = अधमर्ण
C. परि + कृत = परिष्कृत D. तत् + अनन्तर = तदनन्तर

37. "मोनू सबसे घटिया विचारों वाला लड़का है"–
इस वाक्य में विशेषण की कौन-सी अवस्था का प्रयोग हुआ है?
A. स्वतन्त्रावस्था B. मूलावस्था
C. उत्तरावस्था D. उत्तमावस्था

38. संज्ञाओं की दृष्टि से ***असंगत*** विकल्प चुनिए:
A. व्यक्तिवाचक संज्ञाएँ सदैव एकवचन में प्रयुक्त होती हैं।
B. व्यक्तिवाचक संज्ञाएँ अनन्त होती हैं।
C. ईर्ष्या, रोग, जन्म, मृत्यु आदि यौगिक भाववाचक संज्ञाएँ हैं।
D. व्यक्तिवाचक एवं भाववाचक संज्ञाओं का जातिवाचक संज्ञाओं में रूपांतरण किया जा सकता है।

39. 'लिंग-विचार' की दृष्टि से ***असंगत*** कथन को छाँटिए:
A. फौज, भीड़, सरकार स्त्रीलिंग पद हैं।
B. 'लिंग' विकारक तत्त्वों की श्रेणी में आता है।
C. संज्ञा, सर्वनाम एवं विशेषणवाचक सभी शब्दों में लिंग की दृष्टि से विकार होता है।
D. कोयल, मैना, चील आदि शब्द नित्य स्त्रीलिंग शब्दों के वाचक पद हैं।

40. "आज का अधिकतम तापमान पैंतीस डिग्री सेन्टीग्रेड रहा" –इस वाक्य में प्रयुक्त विशेषण का भेद इंगित कीजिए:
A. निश्चित संख्यावाचक विशेषण
B. अनिश्चित संख्यावाचक विशेषण
C. निश्चित परिमाणवाचक विशेषण
D. पूर्णांक बोधक संख्यावाचक विशेषण

41. वार्तनिक दृष्टि से ***अशुद्ध*** शब्द का चयन कीजिए:
A. पड़ोसी B. सुधीजन
C. सरलतापूर्वक D. द्रवीभूत

42. इनमें कौन-सी भाववाचक संज्ञा का निर्माण विशेषणवाचक शब्द से ***नहीं*** हुआ है?
A. नकटापन B. सयानापन
C. अपनापन D. गोरापन

43. क्रिया के संबंध में ***असंगत*** कथन चुनिए:
A. गौणकर्म के साथ सदैव 'को' चिह्न जुड़ा रहता है तथा क्रिया से अपेक्षाकृत दूर रहता है।
B. यदि वाक्य में दो कर्म हों, तो क्रिया से 'किसे' या 'किसको' प्रश्न करने पर जो उत्तर मिलता है वह 'मुख्य कर्म' होता है।
C. जिन्हें कर्म के अतिरिक्त अन्य किसी पूरक शब्द की आवश्यकता नहीं पड़ती है उन्हें 'पूर्ण सकर्मक क्रिया' कहते हैं।
D. आना, उड़ना एवं तैरना गत्यर्थक पूर्ण अकर्मक क्रियाएँ होती हैं।

44. किस शब्द में 'अव' उपसर्ग का प्रयोग हुआ है?
A. अवाच्य B. अवधि
C. अवचन D. अविनष्ट

45. संधि की दृष्टि से ***असंगत*** विकल्प है:
A. उपनिषद् + मीमांसा = उपनिषन्मीमांसा
B. विद्वत् + मूर्ति = विद्वन्मूर्ति
C. षठ् + मास = षण्मास
D. शरद् + माला = शरन्माला

Language : English

Directions: *Answer the following questions by selecting the* ***most appropriate*** *option.*

46. Choose the ***correct*** set of articles from the given options in the following sentence against the blank space:

"The teacher wrote _______ outline of a story on _________ blackboard."

A. a, a B. an, the
C. the, a D. a, the

47. Choose the ***correct*** verb form in the following sentence against the blank space so as to complete the sentence:

"My father _______ for Delhi yesterday."

A. leave B. will leave
C. left D. will be leaving

48. Choose the ***correct*** option to fill in the blank space in the sentence which expresses the correct notion hinted in the bracket against the blank space:

"You _________ (command) apologise or face the consequences."

A. must B. shall
C. may D. could

49. Pick out the ***correct*** option to indicate the use of adjective in the following sentence:

"A Cool breeze blew from the sea."

A. breeze B. sea
C. cool D. blew

50. Identify the underlined word in the given sentence.

I see him passing my house every day.

A. Gerund B. Present Participle
C. Infinitive D. Object

51. Identify the compound word from the options given below:

A. Development B. Newspaper
C. Powerful D. Childhood

52. Fill in the blank with the ***correct*** preposition:

Do you usually go out _______ Saturday evenings?

A. in B. at
C. on D. within

53. Which one of the following sentence in the options given below illustrates the use of Intransitive verb?

A. Fire burns.
B. The principal hoisted the flag on Independence Day.
C. She is reading the newspaper.
D. Our team won the match.

54. Which one of the following words is ***not*** a noun?

A. advice B. rice
C. device D. nice

55. Choose the word which is spelt ***correctly***:

A. Beegning B. Biginning
C. Beginning D. Begining

56. Which of the options given below is the ***correct*** passive form of the following sentence?

"The Bhagvad Gita presents a balanced philosophy of life."

A. A balanced philosophy of life is presented by the Bhagvad Gita.
B. A balanced philosophy of life has been presented by the Bhagvad Gita.
C. The Bhagvad Gita has presented a balanced philosophy of life.
D. A balanced philosophy of life was presented by the Bhagvad Gita.

57. "Reading improves your knowledge."

Identify the gerund in the above sentence from the options given below:

A. knowledge B. improves
C. reading D. your

58. Select the ***correct*** option from the following that correctly transforms the following sentence from Direct speech to Indirect speech:

He said, 'Congratulations!'

A. He congratulated me.
B. He said to me congratulations.
C. He exclaimed congratulations.
D. He is saying congratulations.

59. Identify the ***correct*** meaning of the underlined idioms in the following sentence from the options given below:

"Climbing Mt. Everest is not a child's play for anyone."

A. very easy to do
B. very difficult to do
C. pleasant to do
D. boring to do

60. Which one of the following words underlined in the sentences given as options has been used as a verb?

A. The stage performances are called Raas Leela.
B. The performers enacted Raas Leela on the stage.
C. Each actor performed in a circular space on the stage in Raas Leela.
D. The performing artist moved in a circular space on the stage in Raas Leela.

PART-III

General Studies : Quantitative Aptitude, Reasoning Ability and GK & Awareness

61. If English alphabets are written in opposite order, then which is the 8th letter of the 19th letter from left side?
A. T B. P
C. Q D. R

62. Find the ***Odd*** one out from given options:
A. 171 B. 131
C. 161 D. 181

63. Write the following words in the order given in the dictionary:
1. Critical
2. Criterion
3. Crisis
4. Crisp

A. 3, 4, 2, 1 B. 1, 3, 4, 2
C. 3, 4, 1, 2 D. 4, 3, 1, 2

64. In the word 'PROPERTY' how many such pairs of letter exist, which has the same number of letters between them here as what they have between them in their order in English Alphabet?
A. 0 B. 1
C. 4 D. 3

65. Find the ***wrong*** term in the following series:

1CV, 5FU, 9IT, 15LS, 17OR
A. 5FU B. 9IT
C. 15LS D. 17OR

66. Two persons A and B stand in front of each other in morning. If A's shadow's lies in the left side of 'A', then in which direction B's facing?
A. South B. North
C. East D. West

67. A businessman gives 15% discount on the list price of his items. How much price he should mark on his items to the cost price to get 19% profit?
A. 34% B. 40%
C. 25% D. 30%

68. After 5 years, father's age will be three times of his son's age. 5 years ago, father's age was 7 times of his son's age. The present age of the father is:
A. 40 years B. 30 years
C. 50 years D. 45 years

69. If the selling price of 6 pens is equal to the cost price of 8 pens, then profit/loss in percentage is:
A. 25% profit B. 25% loss
C. $33\frac{1}{3}\%$ loss D. $33\frac{1}{3}\%$ profit

70. If $\frac{2x+7}{5} - \frac{3x+11}{2} = \frac{2x+8}{3} - 5$, then x = ?
A. 1 B. –1
C. 2 D. –2

71. The curved surface area of a cylinder is 264 m^2 and its volume is 924 m^3, then what is the ratio between its diameter and height?
A. 7 : 6 B. 6 : 7
C. 3 : 7 D. 7 : 3

72. What principal on compound interest has their amount ₹ 650 in one year and ₹ 676 in two years?
A. ₹ 520 B. ₹ 572
C. ₹ 600 D. ₹ 625

73. A principal lends on simple interest for two years. If rate of interest more than 1% the simple interest increased by ₹ 240. Find out the principal:
A. ₹ 5,000 B. ₹ 6000
C. ₹ 8,000 D. ₹ 12,000

74. At the speed of 60 km per hour, 125 meter long train crosses a bridge in 30 seconds. What is the length of bridge?
A. 375 meter B. 225 meter
C. 125 meter D. 250 meter

75. The average age of three boys is 16 years and the ratio of their ages is 4 : 5 : 7, find out the age of smallest boy.
A. 8 years B. 9 years
C. 12 years D. 16 years

76. In an examination 60% of students passed in English and 70% students passed in Maths, 20% students failed in both subjects, 2500 students passed in both subjects. Find out total number of students.
A. 3000 B. 3500
C. 4000 D. 5000

77. A is elder to B while C and D are elder to E. E lies between A and C and C is elder to B, then which of the following statements is necessarily ***true***?
A. A is elder to C
B. C is elder to D
C. D is elder to C
D. E is elder to B

78. Bottom surface of a cube is empty. X is marked between A and B. Y marked on the left of A. Then Z marked on which surface of cube?
A. bottom side B. up side
C. in front side D. in back side

79. A is the brother of B and C. D is the mother of C. E is the father of A. Then which statement is ***false***?

A. B is son of E B. E is father of B
C. E is husband of D D. A is son of D

80. In English alphabet, how many letters are unchanged in mirror image?

A. 8 B. 9
C. 12 D. 11

81. The Markanda river does ***not*** flow in which of the following district?

A. Kurushetra B. Sonipat
C. Karnal D. Ambala

82. The district, which is mainly irrigated by Jui Canal:

A. Hisar B. Jhajjar
C. Bhiwani D. Rohtak

83. Which of the following was the partner nation in Surajkund International Craft Fair-2018?

A. Egypt B. France
C. Kazakhstan D. Kyrgyzstan

84. The distinct, in which Gujari Mahal is situated:

A. Hansi B. Hisar
C. Panchkula D. Ambala

85. On the basis of extent of the period as Chief Minister, arrange the following Chief Minister of Haryana in descending order (longest serving first):

1. Bhajan Lal
2. Bansi Lal
3. Bhupinder Singh Hooda
4. Devi Lal

Choose the ***correct*** code:

A. 1, 2, 3, 4 B. 2, 1, 3, 4
C. 1, 2, 4, 3 D. 2, 4, 3, 1

86. Consider the following statements about Shanno Devi:

1. Shanno Devi was the Deputy Speaker of Punjab Legislative Assembly.
2. When Haryana was formed; she was elected as the Speaker of Haryana Legislative Assembly.

Which of the above statement/statements is/are ***true***?

A. Only 1 is true
B. Only 2 is true
C. Neither 1 nor 2 is true
D. Both 1 and 2 are true

87. Who was the editor of 'Khair Andesh' Newspaper?

A. Chandulal B. Murlidhar
C. Chhotu Ram D. Sham Lal

88. Consider the following statements about Eastern Peripheral Expressway:

1. It is also known as Kundli-Ghaziabad-Palwal Expressway.
2. The total length of this expressway is more than 200 km.

Which of the above statement is/are ***true***?

A. only 1 is true
B. only 2 is true
C. neither 1 nor 2 is true
D. both 1 and 2 are true

89. Which of the following districts has the lowest population density?

A. Karnal B. Sirsa
C. Jhajjar D. Mewat

90. The state tree of Haryana is:

A. Peepal B. Khejari
C. Banyan D. Neem

Answers

1	**2**	**3**	**4**	**5**	**6**	**7**	**8**	**9**	**10**
D	A	B	B	D	B	A	C	C	B
11	**12**	**13**	**14**	**15**	**16**	**17**	**18**	**19**	**20**
D	A	A	C	A	B	D	C	C	C
21	**22**	**23**	**24**	**25**	**26**	**27**	**28**	**29**	**30**
A	A	B	B	B	D	A	C	A	D
31	**32**	**33**	**34**	**35**	**36**	**37**	**38**	**39**	**40**
D	D	D	D	A	A	D	C	C	C
41	**42**	**43**	**44**	**45**	**46**	**47**	**48**	**49**	**50**
C	C	B	B	C	B	C	B	C	B
51	**52**	**53**	**54**	**55**	**56**	**57**	**58**	**59**	**60**
B	C	A	D	C	A	C	A	A	C
61	**62**	**63**	**64**	**65**	**66**	**67**	**68**	**69**	**70**
B	A	A	D	C	A	B	A	D	B
71	**72**	**73**	**74**	**75**	**76**	**77**	**78**	**79**	**80**
D	D	D	A	C	D	D	B	A	D
81	**82**	**83**	**84**	**85**	**86**	**87**	**88**	**89**	**90**
B	C	D	B	B	D	B	A	B	A

Explanatory Answers

61. ZYXWVUTSRQPONMLKJIHGFEDCBA

Here, 19th letter from left side = H

∴ The 8th letter of the 19th letter from left side = P.

63. The order in the dictionary:

Crisis → Crisp → Criterion → Critical.

64. PROPERTY

∵ Two pairs are same (PR = PR)

Hence,, such pair of letter exists = 3.

65. 1CV 5FU 9IT 15LS 17OR (+4, +4, +4, +4; 13 L S)

In given series,

Place of 15LS should be 13LS

∴ Wrong term = 15LS.

66.

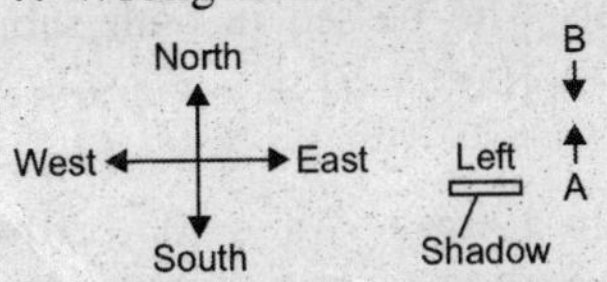

Here, A's facing in North direction and B's facing in South direction.

67. Let cost price of item = ₹ 100

and the list price = ₹ $(100 + x)$

Then, selling price = $(100+x)\times\frac{100-15}{100}=119$

$\Rightarrow \quad (100+x)\times\frac{85}{100} = 119$

$\Rightarrow \quad (100+x)\times\frac{17}{20} = 119$

$\Rightarrow \quad 100 + x = \frac{119\times 20}{17}$

$\Rightarrow \quad 100 + x = 7 \times 20$

$\Rightarrow \quad 100 + x = 140$

$\Rightarrow \quad x = 140 - 100 =$ ₹ 40

Hence, he should mark 40% price on his item to the cost price to get a profit of 19%.

68. Let after 5 years, son's age = x years

then, father's age = $3x$ years

∴ son's present age = $(x - 5)$ years

and father's present age = $(3x - 5)$ years

5 years ago, son's age = $(x - 10)$ years

and father's age = $(3x - 10)$ years

According to question,

$7(x - 10) = (3x - 10)$

$\Rightarrow \quad 7x - 70 = 3x - 10$

$\Rightarrow \quad 7x - 3x = 70 - 10 = 60$

$\Rightarrow \quad 4x = 60 \Rightarrow x = 15$ years

Hence, the present age of father

$= (3x - 5)$ years

$= (3 \times 15 - 5)$ years

$= (45 - 5)$ years = 40 years.

69. Let the cost price of 1 pen = ₹ 1

Then, the cost price of 8 pens = ₹ 8

Given, The S.P. of 6 pens = the C.P. of 8 pens = ₹ 8

∵ The S.P. of 6 pens = ₹ 8

and the C.P. of 6 pens = ₹ 6

∴ Profit = S.P. – C.P.

= 8 – 6 = ₹ 2

∴ $\text{Profit \%} = \frac{\text{Profit}\times 100}{\text{C.P.}}$

$= \frac{2\times 100}{6}\% = \frac{100}{3}\% = 33\frac{1}{3}\%.$

70. Given, $\frac{2x+7}{5}-\frac{3x+11}{2} = \frac{2x+8}{3}-5$

$\Rightarrow \quad \frac{2(2x+7)-5(3x+11)}{10} = \frac{2x+8-15}{3}$

$\Rightarrow \quad \frac{4x+14-15x-55}{10} = \frac{2x-7}{3}$

$\Rightarrow \quad \frac{-11x-41}{10} = \frac{2x-7}{3}$

$\Rightarrow \quad 3(-11x - 41) = 10(2x - 7)$

$\Rightarrow \quad -33x - 123 = 20x - 70$

$\Rightarrow \quad -33x - 20x = 123 - 70$

$\Rightarrow \quad -53x = 53$

$\Rightarrow \quad x = \frac{53}{-53} = -1$

Hence, $x = -1$.

71. Given, the curved surface area of a cylinder = 264 m^2

$\Rightarrow \quad 2\pi rh = 264\ m^2$ ...(*i*)

and, its volume = 924 m^3

$\Rightarrow \quad \pi r^2 h = 924\ m^3$ ...(*ii*)

On dividing (*i*) by (*ii*), we get,

$\frac{2\pi rh}{\pi r^2 h} = \frac{264}{924} \Rightarrow \frac{2}{r} = \frac{264}{924}$

$\Rightarrow \quad r = \frac{2\times 924}{264} = \frac{924}{132} = 7$ m

From (*i*), we get, $2\pi rh = 264$

$\Rightarrow \quad 2\times\frac{22}{7}\times 7\times h = 264$

$\Rightarrow \quad h = \frac{264}{44} = 6$ m

Hence, the ratio between its diameter and height

$= 2r : h = 2 \times 7 : 6$

$= 14 : 6 = 7 : 3.$

72. $\because$ $A = P\left(1+\frac{r}{100}\right)^n$

$\therefore$ $₹\ 650 = P\left(1+\frac{r}{100}\right)^1$ ...(*i*)

and $₹\ 676 = P\left(1+\frac{r}{100}\right)^2$ ...(*ii*)

On dividing (*ii*) by (*i*), we get,

$$\therefore \quad \frac{P\left(1+\frac{r}{100}\right)^2}{P\left(1+\frac{r}{100}\right)^1} = \frac{676}{650}$$

$$\Rightarrow \quad \left(1+\frac{r}{100}\right) = \frac{676}{650}$$

$$\Rightarrow \quad \frac{r}{100} = \frac{676}{650} - 1 = \frac{676-650}{650} = \frac{26}{650}$$

$$\Rightarrow \quad r = \frac{26}{650}\times 100 = \frac{26}{13}\times 2$$

$$= 2 \times 2 = 4\%$$

From (*i*), we get, $₹\ 650 = P\left(1+\frac{r}{100}\right)^1$

$$\Rightarrow \quad 650 = P\left(1+\frac{4}{100}\right)$$

$$\Rightarrow \quad 650 = P\left(1+\frac{1}{25}\right) = P\left(\frac{26}{25}\right)$$

$$\Rightarrow \quad P = \frac{650\times 25}{26} = \frac{50\times 25}{2}$$

$$= 25 \times 25 = 625$$

Hence, Principal = P = ₹ 625.

73. Let Principal = P, Rate = $r\%$
given, t = 2 years

$$\text{Then, } \frac{P\times(r+1)\times 2}{100} - \frac{P\times r\times 2}{100} = 240$$

$$\Rightarrow \quad \frac{2Pr}{100} + \frac{2P}{100} - \frac{2Pr}{100} = 240$$

$$\Rightarrow \quad \frac{2P}{100} = 240 \Rightarrow \frac{P}{50} = 240$$

$$\Rightarrow \quad P = ₹\ 240 \times 50 = ₹\ 1200$$

Hence, principal = P = ₹ 1200.

74. Here, speed of a train = 60 km/hr

$$= \frac{60\times 1000}{60\times 60} \text{ m/sec} = \frac{100}{6} \text{ m/sec} = \frac{50}{3} \text{ m/sec}$$

length of train = 125 m and time = 30 seconds

Let the length of bridge = x m

Then, distance covered in passing the bridge

$= (x + 125)$ m

$$\therefore \quad \frac{x+125}{30} = \frac{50}{3} \qquad \left[\frac{\text{Distance}}{\text{Time}} = \text{Speed}\right]$$

$$\Rightarrow \quad x + 125 = \frac{50}{3}\times 30 = 500 \text{ m}$$

$$\Rightarrow \quad x = 500 - 125 = 375 \text{ m}$$

Hence, the length of bridge = 375 m.

75. The total age of three boys = 3 × 16 = 48 years

$\because$ The ratio of their ages is 4 : 5 : 7

$\therefore$ The age of smallest boy

$$= 48\times\frac{4}{4+5+7} \text{ years} = 48\times\frac{4}{16} \text{ years}$$

$$= 48\times\frac{1}{4} = 12 \text{ years.}$$

76. Here, 60% of students passed in English = 60%

$\therefore$ Failed in English = 100 – 60 = 40% = $x\%$

and 70% of students passed in Maths = 70%

$\therefore$ Failed in Maths = 100 – 70 = 30% = $y\%$

and failed in both subjects = 20% = $z\%$

Hence, % of students who passed in both subjects

$= 100\% - (x + y - z)\%$

[We know that]

$= 100\% - (40 + 30 - 20)\%$

$= 100\% - 50\% = 50\%$

$$\text{Hence, Total students} \times \frac{50}{100} = 2500$$

$$\Rightarrow \quad \text{Total students} = 2500\times\frac{100}{50}$$

$$= 2500 \times 2 = 5000.$$

77. Given, A > B, C > E, D > E and C > B
and E lies between A and C

$\therefore$ D > C > E > A > B

Hence, E is elder to B.

78.

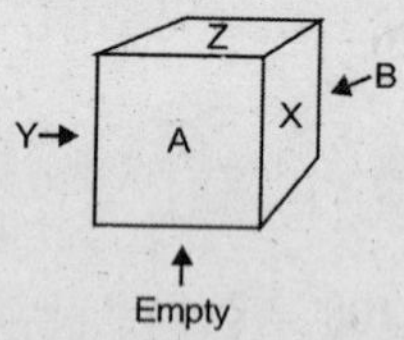

Here, Z marked on up side of cube.

79.

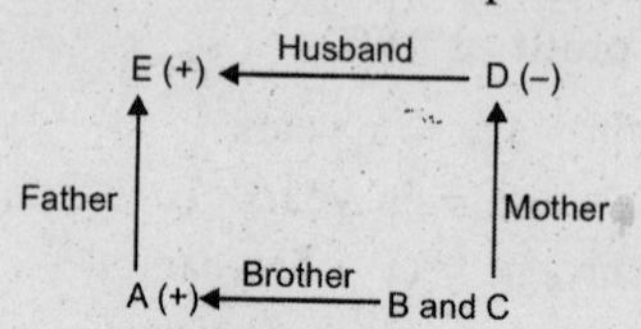

False Statement:

1. B is son of E.

80. In English Alphabet, Letters unchanged in mirror image are:

A, H, I, M, O, T, U, V, W, X, Y

Hence, Number of letters = 11.

Previous Paper (Solved)

Haryana Teacher Eligibility Test (HTET)

PGT (Level-3), Common Subjects, Exam 2018*

PART-I

Child Development and Pedagogy

Directions: *Answer the following questions by selecting the* ***most appropriate*** *option.*

1. If one activity occurs more often than another, it can be used to reinforce the activity that occurs less often. This principle is known as:
A. Premack's principle
B. Thorndike's principle
C. Skinner's principle
D. Pavlov's principle

2. 'Modelling' is an effective teaching method for:
A. Children with visual impairment
B. Children with learning disability
C. Acid attack victims
D. Children with intellectual disability

3. Which law of 'Trial and Error' given by Thorndike is similar to the concept of 'reinforcement'?
A. Law of Use B. Law of Disuse
C. Law of Effect D. Law of Readiness

4. According to Ecological systems theory of Bronfenbrenner, which of the following does *not* belong to macro system of the child?
A. School B. Values
C. Laws D. Customs

5. Which of the following is *not* true about the socio-cultural theory of Vygotsky?
A. Children learn very little from performing tasks they can already do independently.
B. Concept of Zone of Proximal Development (ZPD) is a part of it.
C. It ignores the importance of language in cognitive development.
D. It emphasizes role of socio-cultural environment in cognitive development.

6. The feeling of adolescents, "Everyone is looking at me", can be termed as:
A. Personal fable
B. Imaginary audience
C. Anorexia Nervosa
D. Bulimia Nervosa

7. Which of the following is the founder of Child Study Movement?
A. Alfred Binet B. Theodore Simon
C. G. Stanley Hall D. B.F. Skinner

8. A child angrily hits a playmate in the same way that he has been punished at home. It is an example of:
A. Operant conditioning
B. Classical conditioning
C. Observational learning
D. Insightful learning

9. Which of the following is *not* a form of immaturity of thinking during adolescence as proposed by Elkind?
A. Idealism
B. Argumentativeness
C. Assertiveness
D. Specialness

10. The phrase, 'six on one hand, and half a dozen on other' best describes which of the following type of conflict?
A. Approach – Avoidance conflict
B. Avoidance – Avoidance conflict
C. Approach – Approach conflict
D. Double Approach – Avoidance conflict

11. Which of the following statement is *not* true about the theory of cognitive development given by Jean Piaget?
A. It believes that development is a discontinuous process.
B. It assumes that children learn through assimilation and accommodation.
C. It believes that development is a continuous process.
D. It believes that cognitive development takes place in four different stages.

12. What is the relationship between negative reinforcement and punishment?

A. Both tend to strengthen a response
B. Both tend to weaken a response
C. Negative reinforcement strengthens a response whereas punishment weakens a response
D. Negative reinforcement weakens a response whereas punishment strengthens a response

13. The 'investment theory of creativity' is given by:
A. Binet and Simons
B. Carrol and Cattle
C. Sternberg and Lubart
D. Watson and Ryner

14. Which of the following is best indicator of high intelligence?
A. Scoring 103 on an IQ test
B. Reciting poem from memory
C. Earning high grades
D. Not making the same mistakes after receiving feedback

15. Which of the following is *not* an example of fixed interval schedule of reinforcement?
A. Getting salary every month
B. Dialing a busy number
C. Having a periodic dental checkups
D. Getting increment every year

16. Which of the following is *not* true about Day Dreaming among adolescents?
A. It is a form of active play.
B. The roles adolescents adopt in day dreaming are heroic.
C. It involves more physical activity than mental.
D. It involves more mental activity than physical.

17. A teenager feels that no one has ever been as deeply in love as he is. It indicates:
A. Imaginary Audience
B. Personal fable
C. Self identity
D. Identity crisis

18. 'Young teen-agers often believe that they are completely unlike any one else.' This phenomenon is known as:
A. Personal fable B. Imaginary Audience
C. Self realization D. Self disclosure

19. The concept of 'Life Space' is a part of:
A. Classical conditioning
B. Operant conditioning
C. Insightful learning
D. Lewin's field theory

20. Which of the following option is *not* a characteristic of Autism Spectrum Disorder?
A. Problem in vision and hearing
B. Problem in social interaction
C. Problem in verbal and non-verbal communication
D. Repetitive behaviour

21. Which of the following concept is derived from famous 'Bobo Doll' experiment?
A. Insightful learning
B. Observational learning
C. Moral development
D. Conditioned response

22. Which of the following is *not* controlled by pre-frontal cortex of brain?
A. Body movement B. Thinking
C. Problem solving D. Vision & hearing

23. Applied Behaviour Analysis is based on principles of:
A. Classical conditioning
B. Operant conditioning
C. Insightful learning
D. Observational learning

24. What is the *correct* sequence of four elements of observational learning?
A. Attention → Motivation → Retention → Reproduction
B. Attention → Retention → Reproduction → Motivation
C. Attention → Reproduction → Retention → Motivation
D. Attention → Retention → Motivation → Reproduction

25. Kim changed her mobile number, and got a new number. When someone asked her new number she could recall only three digits of her new mobile number. The cause behind it may be:
A. Decay
B. Proactive Interference
C. Suppression
D. Regression

26. Which of the following is *not* true about a reward?
A. It is a type of bribe.
B. It increases desirable behaviour.
C. It is a pleasant stimulus.
D. It is given to strengthen the response.

27. Which of the following is *not* a democratic teaching strategy?
A. Problem solving B. Project
C. Discovery D. Demonstration

28. The age range of Genital Stage of Freud's theory of Psycho-sexual development is similar to which of the following stage of Erikson's theory of Psycho-social development?
A. Trust vs mistrust
B. Autonomy vs shame & doubt
C. Initiative vs guilt
D. Identity vs role confusion

29. "At this stage of development, children think with their eyes, ears, hands and other sense organs."

The above statement best describes which of the following stage of cognitive development?

A. Sensori motor stage
B. Pre-operational stage
C. Concrete operational stage
D. Formal operational stage

30. As classified by Bloom, which one of the following is ***not*** a subdomain of cognitive domain?

A. Application B. Analysis
C. Synthesis D. Responding

PART-II

भाषा-I : हिन्दी

निर्देश : *निम्नलिखित प्रश्नों के उत्तर देने के लिए* ***सबसे उचित*** *विकल्प चुनिए।*

31. 'हमसफर अगर एक-दूसरे को समझ लें तो जीवन आसान हो जाएगा' – उक्त वाक्य किस काल से संबंधित है?

A. हेतुहेतुमद् भविष्य B. संभाव्य भविष्यत्
C. सामान्य भविष्यत् D. संदिग्ध वर्तमान

32. किस विकल्प में 'अलुक् तत्पुरुष' समास का प्रयोग हुआ है?

A. मनसिज B. दिग्विजय
C. सर्वव्याप्त D. कूपमंडूक

33. सन्धि की दृष्टि से ***असंगत*** विकल्प चुनिएः

A. तोय + धार = तोयाधार
B. विश्व + मित्र = विश्वामित्र
C. मूसल + धार = मूसलाधार
D. सत्य + नाश = सत्यानाश

34. निम्न में से किस विकल्प में स्त्रीलिंग वाचक शब्द है?

A. आँसू B. टेसू
C. रतालू D. ससुराल

35. 'यह बालिका फूल से भी कोमल है' – उक्त वाक्य विशेषण की दृष्टि से किस अवस्था का वाचक है?

A. मूलावस्था B. उत्तरावस्था
C. उत्तमावस्था D. इनमें से कोई नहीं

36. प्रत्यय का दृष्टि से ***असंगत*** विकल्प चुनिएः

A. निपुण + य = नैपुण्य
B. ईश्वर + य = ऐश्वर्य
C. भगिनी + य = भागिनेय
D. विशिष्ट + य = वैशिष्ट्य

37. 'विशेषण पदों' के विकारक तत्व कौन-कौन-से हैं?

A. लिंग और वचन
B. लिंग, वचन और कारक
C. लिंग और कारक
D. काल, वाच्य एवं पुरुष

38. एकवचन से बहुवचन बने शब्दों में ***असंगत*** को छाँटिए :

A. डाकुओं B. तरबुजों
C. वधुएँ D. भालुओं

39. 'शब्दकोश' में शब्दानुक्रम की दृष्टि से निम्न में से ***सही*** (आरोही) क्रम वाला विकल्प हैः

A. क्लिष्ट, क्रम, क्लांति, क्षण
B. क्षण, क्रम, क्लांति, क्लिष्ट
C. क्रम, क्लांति, क्लिष्ट, क्षण
D. क्लांति, क्रम, क्लिष्ट, क्षण

40. 'करणकारक' युक्त वाक्य चुनिएः

A. कानों सुनी बात सत्य होती है।
B. वे सिनेमा देखने गए हैं।
C. ललिता गुरुजी से कत्थक सीखती है।
D. इस साहसी छात्र ने एक बच्चे को नदी में डूबने से बचाया।

41. 'कमरे में कोई हँस रहा है' – वाक्य में प्रयुक्त सर्वनाम हैः

A. निश्चयवाचक B. अनिश्चयवाचक
C. प्रश्नवाचक D. पुरुषवाचक

42. वर्ण-विचार की दृष्टि से ***असंगत*** विकल्प चुनिएः

A. एक ही स्थान से उच्चरित दो सवर्ण स्वरों के योग से निर्मित स्वर उत्पत्ति के आधार पर 'दीर्घ स्वर' कहलाते हैं; जबकि भिन्न-भिन्न स्थानों से उच्चरित दो विजातीय स्वरों के योग से निर्मित स्वर 'संयुक्त स्वर' कहलाते हैं।
B. अनुस्वार व्यंजनों की प्रकृति है; जबकि अनुनासिक स्वरों की प्रकृति है।
C. जिन स्वरों के उच्चारण में हवा नाक से नहीं अपितु केवल मुख से निकलती है उन्हें 'सानुनासिक' स्वर कहा जाता है जबकि जिन स्वरों के उच्चारण में वायु मुख के साथ-साथ नासिका से भी निकलती है उन्हें 'निरनुनासिक स्वर' कहा जाता है।
D. हिन्दी वर्णमाला में श ष स ह वर्ण संघर्षी हैं जबकि च छ ज झ आदि वर्ण स्पर्श संघर्षी हैं।

43. समास की दृष्टि से कौन-सा विकल्प ***असंगत*** है?

A. पंत द्वारा प्रणीत = पंत प्रणीत
B. पवन से चलने वाली चक्की = पनचक्की
C. वह जो चक्षु से श्रवण करे = चक्षुश्रवा
D. समाचार के लिए पत्र = समाचारपत्र

44. किस शब्द में 'वर्णागम व्यंजन सन्धि' का प्रयोग ***नहीं*** हुआ है?
A. श्रीच्छाया B. प्रच्छन्न
C. मृच्छकटिक D. मातृच्छाया

45. वार्तनिक दृष्टि से ***अशुद्ध*** शब्द छाँटिए:
A. प्राणिमात्र B. सम्पर्कित
C. आभिजात्य D. कार्रवाई

PART-II

Language-II : English

Direction: *Answer the following questions by selecting the* ***most appropriate*** *option.*

46. Complete the sentence using the ***correct*** option:
George has travelled a lot. He .... speak four languages.
A. may B. can
C. need D. must not

47. They rested when evening came.
The underlined group of words in the above sentence is a/an:
A. Adjective clause
B. Noun clause
C. Adverb clause
D. Conjunction clause

48. Choose the ***correct*** plural of the word 'species':
A. Specis B. Species
C. Speceis D. Specieses

49. Which of the options given below is the ***correct*** indirect form of the given sentence?
He said, 'I have passed the examination'.
A. He said that he had passed the examination.
B. He told I have passed.
C. He said he must have passed the examination.
D. He informed us of his passing.

50. Choose the word in which the prefix dis – is ***incorrectly*** used:
A. Disbelief
B. Disobedience
C. Discomfort
D. Discussion

51. Choose the ***correct*** synonym of the word 'contaminate':
A. Defile B. Rehabilitate
C. Detach D. Valid

52. The old man was tired of walking.
The underlined word in the sentence is used as a:
A. Participle B. Gerund
C. Noun D. Adverb

53. Choose the ***correct*** preposition for the blank given below:
She had great affection .... her grandchildren.
A. within B. into
C. against D. for

54. Choose the word with the ***incorrect*** suffix 'ship':
A. Friendship B. Membership
C. Relationship D. Argueship

55. Choose the ***correct*** form of the verb:
Gymnastics .... my favourite sport.
A. is B. are
C. were D. do

56. Choose the ***correct*** past tense and past participle of the verb 'Begin':
A. Began, Begun
B. Begun, Begun
C. Begin, Began
D. Begun, Began

57. Choose the ***correct*** form of the verb 'play' from the options below:
They .... (play) since four O'clock.
A. have played B. will play
C. play D. have been playing

58. Choose the ***correct*** synonym of the word 'Pinnacle':
A. Peak
B. Pass
C. Foothills
D. Deep

59. Choose the ***correct*** option of the underlined phrasal verb:
We must cut down expenses or we will be getting into debt.
A. Reduce in size or amount
B. Appear
C. Expose
D. Rise to the surface

60. Choose the ***correct*** option for the blank given:
He found her blue ford escort in the car park. .... vehicle was locked and the lights were off.
A. A B. An
C. The D. Zero article

PART-III

General Studies : Quantitative Aptitude, Reasoning Ability and GK & Awareness

Direction: *Answer the following questions by selecting the* ***most appropriate*** *option.*

61. Which of the following words ***cannot*** be formed by using letters of word "DICTIONARY"?

A. RATION
B. DAIRY
C. NATION
D. ACTION

62. How many pairs of the letters does the word "BRIGHTER" contain in such that the two letters of the pair have as many letters between them in the word as there are in the English alphabet?

A. 4 B. 2
C. 1 D. 3

63. If $\frac{x}{y}=\frac{4}{5}$, then value of $\left(\frac{4}{7}-\frac{2y-x}{2y+x}\right)$ is:

A. $\frac{1}{7}$ B. $\frac{3}{7}$
C. $\frac{1}{3}$ D. 1

64. In a business, A and C invested amounts in the ratio 2 : 1, whereas the ratio between amounts invested by A and B was 3 : 2. If their total profit is ₹ 1,573. How much amount B will receive?

A. ₹ 363 B. ₹ 484
C. ₹ 605 D. ₹ 726

65. A man is 14 years older than his son. After two years, his age will be twice the age of his son. The present age of his son is:

A. 8 years B. 10 years
C. 12 years D. 14 years

66. Find the wrong number in the series:
10, 12, 28, 90, 360, 1850

A. 12 B. 28
C. 90 D. 360

67. There are 28 mango trees, 42 apple trees and 21 orange trees have to be planted in rows such that each row contains the same number of trees of one variety only. The minimum number of rows in which the above trees may be planted is:

A. 9 B. 10
C. 11 D. 13

68. A is twice as fast as B and B is thrice as fast as C. If some distance is covered by C in 54 minutes, then in how much time will B cover?

A. 9 minutes
B. 18 minutes
C. 12 minutes
D. 15 minutes

69. If the length and breadth of a rectangular plot be increased by 50% and 20% respectively, then how many times will its area be increased?

A. $\frac{1}{3}$ B. $\frac{2}{3}$
C. $\frac{1}{5}$ D. $\frac{4}{5}$

70. 10 litres of milk contains 8% water. What quantity of pure milk should be added to this mixture to reduce this to 4% water?

A. 6 litres B. 8 litres
C. 10 litres D. 15 litres

71. If sin A – cos A = 0 then the value of $\sin^4 A + \cos^4 A$ is:

A. 0 B. 1
C. $\frac{1}{2}$ D. $\frac{3}{4}$

72. A boat covers a certain distance downstream in $\frac{1}{2}$ hour, while it comes back in $1\frac{1}{2}$ hours. If the speed of the stream be 5 kmph. What is the speed of the boat in still water?

A. 10 kmph B. 12 kmph
C. 13 kmph D. 15 kmph

73. If in a code language 'pit dar na' means "you are good" , 'dar tok pa' means "good and bad", 'tim na tok' means "they are bad". In the same language which word stands for "they"?

A. tim B. tok
C. na D. pit

74. If 'South-East' is called 'East', North-West is called 'West', 'South-West' is called 'South' and so on, what will 'North' be called?

A. South
B. North-West
C. North-East
D. North

75. A three digit number 4p3 is added to 984 to get a four digit number 13q7. If 13q7 is divisible by 11, then the value of $(q - p)$ will be:

A. 8 B. 9
C. 7 D. 11

76. Select the correct combination of mathematical signs to replace '*' signs and to balance the given equation:

9 * 7 * 2 * 3 * 10

A. × ÷ + = B. − + × =
C. + − × = D. × + = −

77. If P is brother of Q, R is father of P, S is brother of T. T is daughter of Q, then paternal uncle of S is:

A. R B. Q
C. T D. P

78. A is the father of C and D is the son of B. E is the brother of A. If C is the sister of D, how is B related to E?

A. Daughter
B. Brother-in-law
C. Husband
D. Sister-in-law

79. In a certain code, 'CERTAIN' is coded as 'XVIGZRM', 'SEQUENCE' is coded as 'HVJFVMXV', then how would 'MUNDANE' be coded?

A. NFMWZMX B. NFMWMZX
C. NFMWZMV D. NFWMZMV

80. The least perfect square number which is exactly divisible by:

10, 12, 15 and 18

A. 876 B. 900
C. 981 D. 1024

81. Which of the following is a Painted Grey Ware (POW) site?

A. Banawali B. Balu
C. Bhagawanpura D. Bhirrana

82. Match the following:

Center	District
(*a*) Center of Excellence for Vegetable	(*i*) Kurukshetra
(*b*) Center of Excellence for Flowers	(*ii*) Sirsa
(*c*) Center of Excellence for Fruits	(*iii*) Jhajjar
(*d*) Integrated Bee-keeping Development Center	(*iv*) Karnal

Choose the ***correct*** code:

	(*a*)	(*b*)	(*c*)	(*d*)
A.	(*i*)	(*ii*)	(*iii*)	(*iv*)
B.	(*i*)	(*iii*)	(*ii*)	(*iv*)
C.	(*iv*)	(*ii*)	(*iii*)	(*i*)
D.	(*iv*)	(*iii*)	(*ii*)	(*i*)

83. The player who won the Gold medal in the Asian Games-2018:

A. Neha Goyal
B. Bajrang Punia
C. Vikas Krishan Yadav
D. Seema Poonia

84. Consider the following statements about the 'Mukhya Mantri Vivah Shagun Yojana':

(*a*) For the marriage of the daughter of a widow a grant of ₹ 51,000 is provided.
(*b*) The income of such widow lady must be less than one lac per annum.

Which of the above statements is/are ***correct***?

A. Only (*a*) is correct.
B. Only (*b*) is correct.
C. Neither (*a*) nor (*b*) is correct.
D. Both (*a*) and (*b*) are correct.

85. Which of the following crops does ***not*** cover under the 'Bhavantar Bharpayee Yojana'?

A. Sugarcane B. Potato
C. Tomato D. Onion

86. The male literacy rate of Haryana as per the census-2011 is:

A. 75.6% B. 65.9%
C. 84.1% D. 71.4%

87. With which of the following states, the "Kalesar National Park" shares its boundary?

(*i*) Himachal Pradesh
(*ii*) Uttrakhand
(*iii*) Rajasthan
(*iv*) Punjab

Choose the ***correct*** answer:

A. (*i*) & (*iv*) B. (*i*) & (*ii*)
C. (*iii*) & (*iv*) D. Only (*iv*)

88. Which of the following rivulets does ***not*** converge into Sahibi?

A. Dohan B. Kasavati
C. Indori D. Drishadvati

89. Which of the following statements about Pt. Neki Ram Sharma is ***not*** true?

A. Pt. Neki Ram Sharma played a vital role in the Home Rule Movement of Lokmanya Tilak.
B. He organized a public meeting of Gandhiji at Bhiwani during Non-cooperation Movement.
C. He published a Hindi Weekly 'Sandesh' from Bhiwani.
D. He was a Rajya Sabha Member from 1952 to 1956.

90. The region in which Colonel Gerrard led the counter attack against 1857 revolutionaries:

A. Panipat B. Rohtak
C. Mewat D. Narnaul

Answers

1	2	3	4	5	6	7	8	9	10
A	D	C	A	C	B	C	C	C	C
11	**12**	**13**	**14**	**15**	**16**	**17**	**18**	**19**	**20**
C	C	C	D	B	C	B	A	D	A
21	**22**	**23**	**24**	**25**	**26**	**27**	**28**	**29**	**30**
B	D	B	B	B	A	D	D	A	D
31	**32**	**33**	**34**	**35**	**36**	**37**	**38**	**39**	**40**
A	A	A	D	B	C	A	B	C	A
41	**42**	**43**	**44**	**45**	**46**	**47**	**48**	**49**	**50**
B	C	B	C	B	B	C	B	A	D
51	**52**	**53**	**54**	**55**	**56**	**57**	**58**	**59**	**60**
A	B	D	D	A	A	D	A	A	C
61	**62**	**63**	**64**	**65**	**66**	**67**	**68**	**69**	**70**
C	D	A	B	C	D	D	B	D	C
71	**72**	**73**	**74**	**75**	**76**	**77**	**78**	**79**	**80**
C	A	A	B	A	C	D	D	C	B
81	**82**	**83**	**84**	**85**	**86**	**87**	**88**	**89**	**90**
C	D	B	D	A	C	B	D	D	D

Explanatory Answers

62. 

63. $\left(\frac{4}{7}-\frac{2y-x}{2y+x}\right)$

$$= \left(\frac{4}{7}-\frac{y\left(2-\frac{x}{y}\right)}{y\left(2+\frac{x}{y}\right)}\right)$$

$$= \left(\frac{4}{7}-\frac{\left(2-\frac{x}{y}\right)}{\left(2+\frac{x}{y}\right)}\right) \quad \text{Given that } \frac{x}{y}=\frac{4}{5}$$

$$= \left(\frac{4}{7}-\frac{\left(2-\frac{4}{5}\right)}{\left(2+\frac{4}{5}\right)}\right)$$

$$= \left(\frac{4}{7}-\frac{6}{14}\right)=\frac{4}{7}-\frac{3}{7}=\frac{1}{7}.$$

64. We have,

A : C = 2 : 1 = 3 × (2 : 1) = 6 : 3

A : B = 3 : 2 = 2 × (3 : 2) = 6 : 4

A : B : C = 6 : 4 : 3

The amount received by B = $1573\times\frac{4}{6+4+3}$

$= 1573\times\frac{4}{13}$ = ₹ 484.

65. Let the present age of son = x years

Then, the present age of man = $(x + 14)$ years

After two years,

$$(x + 14) + 2 = 2(x + 2)$$
$$x + 16 = 2x + 4$$
$$x = 16 - 4$$
$$x = 12$$

Hence, the present age of his son is 12 years.

66. 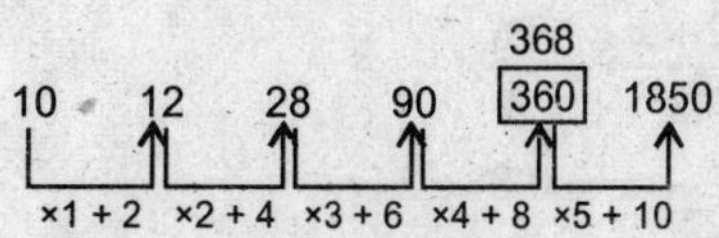

Hence, 360 is the wrong number in the series.

67. HCF (28, 42, 21)

Maximum trees in a row = 7

∴ Minimum no. of rows required

$$= \frac{28}{7}+\frac{42}{7}+\frac{21}{7}$$

= 4 + 6 + 3 = 13.

68. $\frac{\text{Speed of A}}{\text{Speed of B}} = \frac{2}{1} = \frac{6}{3}$

$\frac{\text{Speed of B}}{\text{Speed of C}} = \frac{3}{1}$

Speed of A : Speed of B : Speed of C = 6 : 3 : 1

If distance = constant the time $\propto \frac{1}{\text{Speed}}$

$t_A : t_B : t_C = \frac{1}{6} : \frac{1}{3} : 1 = 1 : 2 : 6$

$\therefore t_B = 54 \times \frac{2}{6} = 18$ minutes.

69. Let the initial length and breadth of rectangular plot are x unit and y unit respectively.

Initial area = $x \times y$ unit^2

$$\text{New length} = x \times 150\% = \frac{3}{2}x \text{ unit}$$

$$\text{New breadth} = y \times 120\% = \frac{6y}{5} \text{ unit}$$

$$\therefore \quad \text{New area} = \left(\frac{3}{2}x\right)\left(\frac{6}{5}y\right)$$

$$= \frac{9}{5}xy \text{ unit}^2$$

$$\text{Area increased} = \frac{9}{5}xy - xy = \frac{4}{5}xy$$

Hence, area increased by $\frac{4}{5}$ times.

70. Quantity of milk in 10 litres mixture

$= 10 \times 92\%$

$= 9.2$ litres

Quantity of water in 10 litres mixture

$= 10 - 9.2 = 0.8$ litres

Let x litres pure milk should be added

Then, milk : water = $(9.2 + x) : 0.8$

$$\frac{9.2 + x}{0.8} = \frac{(100 - 4)}{4}$$

$$\frac{9.2 + x}{0.8} = \frac{96}{4}$$

$$9.2 + x = 0.8 \times 24$$

$$9.2 + x = 19.2$$

$$x = 10 \text{ litres.}$$

71. $\because$ $\sin A - \cos A = 0$

$\therefore$ $\sin A = \cos A$

$$\sin A = \sin\left(\frac{\pi}{2} - A\right)$$

$$A = \frac{\pi}{2} - A$$

$$2A = \frac{\pi}{2}$$

$$A = \frac{\pi}{4}$$

$$\sin^4 A + \cos^4 A = \sin^4 \frac{\pi}{4} + \cos^4 \frac{\pi}{4}$$

$$= \left(\frac{1}{\sqrt{2}}\right)^4 + \left(\frac{1}{\sqrt{2}}\right)^4$$

$$= \frac{1}{4} + \frac{1}{4} = \frac{2}{4} = \frac{1}{2}.$$

72. Let the speed of boat in still water = x kmph

According to question,

Distance = Speed × time

$$(x + 5) \times \frac{1}{2} = (x - 5) \times \frac{3}{2}$$

$$x + 5 = 3x - 15$$

$$2x = 20 \Rightarrow x = 10 \text{ kmph}$$

73. 'pit dar na' → "you are good" ...(1)

'dar tok pa' → "good and bad" ...(2)

'tim na tok' → "they are bad" ...(3)

From equation (1) and equation (2)

dar → good

From equation (1) and equation (3)

na → are

From equation (2) and equation (3)

tok → bad

From equation (3)

tim → they.

77.

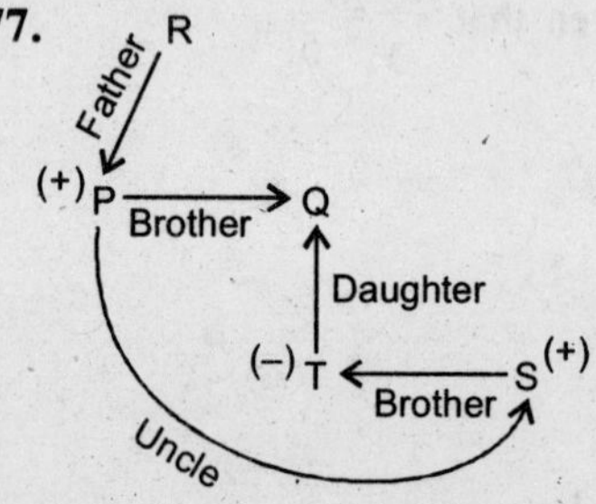

P is the uncle of S.

Previous Paper (Solved)

Haryana Teacher Eligibility Test (HT ET)

PGT (Level-3), Common Subject, Exam 2017*

PART-I

Child Development and Pedagogy

Directions: *Answer the following questions by selecting the **most appropriate** option.*

1. In the context of co-operative learning, STAD refers to:
A. Student Teacher Achievement Division
B. Students Team Achievement Division
C. Students Team Acknowledgement Division
D. Student Teacher Acquired Division

2. During which of the following stage, children develops 'Object Permanence'?
A. Sensory Motor Stage
B. Pre-operational Stage
C. Concrete Operational Stage
D. Formal Operational Stage

3. The feeling of an adolescent 'everyone noticed that I wore this shirt twice a week', is an example of:
A. His awareness   B. Imaginary audience
C. Self-regulation   D. None of the above

4. Which of the following is ***not*** true about negative reinforcement?
A. It increases desirable behaviour.
B. It is not similar to punishment.
C. It never increases desirable behaviour.
D. It can be used for children with Special Needs.

5. The 'good boy - good girl' orientation indicates:
A. Pre-conventional level morality
B. Conventional level morality
C. Post-conventional level morality
D. Both A and C are correct

6. Through conditioning a neutral stimulus acquires the power of a reinforcer, is known as:
A. Primary reinforcer   B. Secondary reinforcer
C. Neutral reinforcer   D. None of the above

7. According to Piaget, at which age the morality of co-operation develops?
A. 5-6 years to 8 years   B. 9-10 years to older
C. 12-13 years to older   D. Below 6 years

8. Two students 'A' & 'B' were tested a standardized I.Q. test. 'A' has an I.Q. of 60 and 'B' has an I.Q. of 30. Which of the following statement is ***not*** true about 'A' and/or 'B'?
A. 'A' has mild intellectual disability.
B. 'B' has a severe intellectual disability.
C. 'A' has a severe intellectual disability.
D. Both A and B are true

9. From Bronfenbrenner's perspective which of the following does ***not*** belong to the Macro system of the child?
A. Culture   B. School
C. Rules & Laws   D. Values

10. You greet your parents every morning and your kid learnt the same by watching it. It is an example of:
A. Observational learning
B. Operant conditioning
C. Classical conditioning
D. Learning by insight

11. The expectation based on previous experiences, with a lack of control that all one's efforts will lead to failure, is known as:
A. Depression   B. Learned helplessness
C. Negative Attitude   D. Mania

12. The concept of 'Life Space' was given by:
A. B.F. Skinner   B. J.B. Watson
C. Lewin   D. E.L. Thorndike

13. The application of an 'aversive stimulus' is:
A. Negative reinforcement
B. Punishment
C. Reward
D. Shaping

14. A student works hard to get first rank in his class. The type of motivation behind his hard work is:
A. Intrinsic motivation
B. Extrinsic motivation
C. Zero motivation
D. None of the above

*Exam held on 23-12-2017.

15. The phase at which a child can master a task if given appropriate help and support, is known as:
A. Zone of mastery
B. Zone of proximal development
C. Zone of learning
D. None of the above

16. The 'two factor theory of Intelligence' was given by:
A. Thurston B. Spearman
C. Binet D. Piaget

17. The statement 'first do what I want you to do, then you may do what you want to do', best describes:
A. Premack Principle B. Law of Readiness
C. Law of Exercise D. Law of Continuity

18. The term used to describe 'reading disability' is:
A. Dyslexia B. Dysgraphia
C. Dyscalculia D. Dysparaxia

19. The rules for when and how to use language to be an effective communicator in a particular culture, is known as:
A. Phonetics B. Phoenix
C. Pragmatics D. Semantics

20. Cognition about one's own cognitive processes can be termed as:
A. Recognition B. Meta cognition
C. Identity D. Perception

21. Reinforcing each small step of progress toward a desired goal until it is learnt completely, is known as:
A. Chaining B. Shaping
C. Cuing D. Modelling

22. The first stage of development of 'Gender Constancy' is:
A. Gender Stability
B. Gender Labelling
C. Gender Consistency
D. None of the above

23. Application of abstract knowledge learnt in one situation to a different situation can be termed as:
A. Negative Transfer B. High Road Transfer
C. Zero Transfer D. None of the above

24. You have introduced 'weekly quiz' in your class to assess student's progress. You are using which schedule of reinforcement?
A. Fixed Ratio B. Variable Ratio
C. Fixed Interval D. Variable Interval

25. PECS is a method of teaching, which may be used for:
A. Children with Autism Spectrum Disorders
B. Children with Communication Impairment
C. Both A and B
D. None of the above

26. Building 'schemes' through direct interaction with environment is known as:
A. Organisation B. Equilibration
C. Adaptation D. Ego-centricism

27. Which of the following is ***not*** a component of Reciprocal Teaching?
A. Questioning B. Clarifying
C. Predicting D. None of the above

28. The ability of 'Seriation' is the characteristic of the:
A. Sensory Motor Stage
B. Pre-operational Stage
C. Concrete Operational Stage
D. None of the above

29. The first person who used the term 'Learning Disabilities' was:
A. Skinner B. Samuel Kirk
C. Sigmund Freud D. Wilhelm Wundt

30. The view "children speak to themselves for self guidance", was given by:
A. Piaget B. Vygotsky
C. Freud D. Bronfenbrenner

PART-II

भाषा-I : हिन्दी

निर्देश : *निम्नलिखित प्रश्नों के उत्तर देने के लिए सबसे उचित विकल्प चुनिए।*

31. वर्णों की ध्वनिगत विशेषता के संदर्भ में निम्न में से कौन-सा युग्म सुमेलित ***नहीं*** है?
A. ताड़नजात – ड़ ढ़ B. ईषत्स्पृष्ट – श ष
C. विवृत्त – ज, झ D. ईषद् विवृत्त – य व

32. समास के संदर्भ में ***असंगत*** विकल्प को चुनिए :
A. समास में विग्रह वाक्य में प्रयुक्त विभक्ति चिह्न व अव्ययादि का लोप करने के उपरान्त शेष रहे दोनों पदों के मध्य संधि की जा सकती है।
B. हिंदी भाषा में समासों का प्रचलन सरल अभिव्यक्ति व भाषिक सौंदर्य की अभिवृद्धि के निमित्त किया जाता है।
C. पदों की प्रधानता व अप्रधानता के आधार पर समास के मुख्य रूप से छह भेद किए गए हैं।
D. तत्पुरुष का ही भेद कर्मधारय है तथा कर्मधारय का भेद द्विगु है।

33. कौन-सा शब्द कर्तृवाचक तृच् [ता] प्रत्यय के योग से निर्मित ***नहीं*** है?
A. रचयिता B. प्रदाता
C. व्याख्याता D. विद्वत्ता

34. संधि नियमानुसार प्रथम पद के अंतिम वर्ण 'म्' का योग 'क' से 'भ' तक किसी वर्ण में होगा तो 'म्' अंतिम पद के प्रथम वर्ण का पंचम वर्ण बनेगा। निम्न विकल्पों में से किस संधि शब्द का निर्माण उक्त नियम के तहत ***नहीं*** हुआ है?

A. हृदयङ्गम B. अकिञ्चन
C. दिङ्नाग D. दिवङ्गत

35. संरचना की दृष्टि से कौन-सा वाक्य सरल वाक्य ***नहीं*** है?

A. दूसरों के साथ मीठा बोलने वाले व्यक्ति सबके मन को भाते हैं।
B. पिताजी ने मुझसे कहा कि वे बहुत बीमार हैं।
C. स्वागतार्थ आए हुए लोगों से घिरे श्रीकृष्ण ने नगर में प्रवेश किया।
D. सभी आंदोलनकर्ता शांतिपूर्ण प्रदर्शन कर रहे थे।

36. कौन-सा शब्द वर्णागम संधि से निर्मित ***नहीं*** है?

A. आच्छादित B. परिष्क्रिया
C. प्रतिष्ठान D. संस्कृत

37. जो आँखों से परे है–के लिए कौन-सा शब्द ***सही*** है?

A. दर्शनीय B. इन्द्रियातीत
C. अकथनीय D. परोक्ष

38. शुद्ध वर्तनी वाला विकल्प चुनिए :

A. सौन्दर्यता B. पिशाचिनी
C. शुपर्णखा D. गार्हस्थ्य

39. उस सामासिक पद को छाँटिए जो कि दो भिन्न-भिन्न भाषाओं के मेल से निर्मित है :

A. आरामगाह B. राष्ट्रपिता
C. स्नानगृह D. जिलाधीश

40. निम्न विकल्पों में से कौन-सा विकल्प 'गिरि' का पर्याय ***नहीं*** है?

A. शैलजा B. महीधर
C. नग D. अद्रि

41. वर्णोच्चारणस्थल की दृष्टि से बेमेल को छाँटिए :

A. कंठनासिका – ङ B. कंठतालु – ए
C. दंतोष्ठ – फ़ D. दन्तनासिका – ण

42. 'पोखर' का तत्सम रूप है :

A. प्रखर B. पोषक्र
C. पुष्कर D. प्रवीण

43. किस विकल्प में दो उपसर्गों का योग ***नहीं*** है?

A. समाधि B. व्याधि
C. स्वागत D. अध्यापक

44. किस समस्तपद का विग्रह सम्यक् ***नहीं*** है?

A. अभूतपूर्व–जो पूर्व में नहीं हुआ हो।
B. अत्यावश्यक–आवश्यकता से परे।
C. अतीन्द्रिय–इन्द्रियों से अतीत (परे)।
D. निरामिष–आमिष से रहित।

45. किस शब्द में उपसर्ग व प्रत्यय दोनों का योग हुआ है?

A. पाशविक B. पारिवारिक
C. रासायनिक D. काल्पनिक

PART-II

Language-II : English

Directions: *Answer the following questions by selecting the* ***most appropriate*** *option.*

46. Choose the ***correct*** option for the blanks given:
I was going to Rishikesh when on .... way I met .... European.

A. a, the B. the, a
C. the, the D. a, a

47. Delayed by an hour, he reached Leh when it was already quite dark.
The word 'delayed' in the above sentence is used as a/an:

A. Infinitive B. Present Participle
C. Past Participle D. Gerund

48. Choose the option in which the prefix 'un' is ***correctly*** used:

A. uncapable B. unpunctual
C. unpatient D. unregular

49. Which of the options given below is the ***correct*** passive form of the given sentence?
They crowned him king.

A. He was crowned king by us.
B. He crowned king.
C. He was crowned king.
D. He had been crowned king.

50. Choose the ***correct*** option for the blank given below:
Ever since my brother joined the company as the CEO, he .... for almost twelve hours a day.

A. was working B. had been working
C. worked D. has been working

51. Choose the sentence that is grammatically ***correct***:

A. New houses have being built for the homeless.
B. New houses have been built for the homeless.
C. New house have being built for the homeless.
D. New houses has being build for the homeless.

52. You should not .... unfair means even if you fail.
Fill in the blank using the ***correct*** option.

A. adopt B. adept
C. adapt D. adapted

53. Choose the ***correct*** indirect form of speech of the given sentence:

Father said to me, "Let the child play in the garden."
A. Father told me to let the child play in the garden.
B. Father said to me let the child play in the garden.
C. Father asked me to allow the child to play.
D. Father asked me not to allow the child to play in the garden.

54. Choose the ***correct*** option for the blank given:

A post without remuneration is a/an .... post.
A. Voluntary
B. Sinecure
C. Honorary
D. Involuntary

55. Choose the ***correct*** option for the blank in the sentence given below:

There has been a .... decline in the case of infanticide in some of the districts of Haryana.
A. signified
B. signify
C. significantly
D. significant

56. The match was stopped <u>when it started raining</u>:

The underlined group of words in the above sentence is a/an:
A. Adverb clause of place
B. Adverb clause of manner
C. Adverb clause of time
D. Adverb clause of reason

57. The present government has come up with fabulously novel schemes.

In the sentence the word 'Novel' is used as:
A. Verb
B. Adjective
C. Noun
D. Adverb

58. Choose the ***correct*** option which gives the correct meaning of the underlined idiom/phrase:

He wants his son <u>to know the ropes</u> of the trade.
A. To know the techniques or ways of doing a job
B. To know how to tie ropes
C. To know how to untie ropes
D. To know how to make ropes

59. Choose the ***correct*** antonym of the word 'Kindle':
A. Extinguish
B. Light
C. Fade
D. Burn

60. .... students had gathered in the quadrangle on the reopening day of the college.

Fill in the blank using the ***correct*** option.
A. Every
B. Lot
C. Much
D. Many

PART-III

General Studies : Aptitude, Reasoning Ability and GK & Awarness

Directions: *Answer the following questions by selecting the **most appropriate** option.*

61. If fresh grapes contain 95% water, and dry grapes contain 5% water, how many kilograms fresh grapes are required to get 400 gm of dry grapes?
A. 7.6 kgms
B. 8 kgms
C. 8.2 kgms
D. 7.2 kgms

62. A two digit number is such that the product of its digits is 12. When 36 is added to the number, the digits interchange their places. Find the number:
A. 62
B. 60
C. 26
D. 20

63. Length of a rectangular hall is 4/3 times of its breadth. If area of a hall is 300 square meter, then what is the difference between length and breadth of hall?
A. 20 meters
B. 4 meters
C. 3 meters
D. 5 meters

64. Find the value of θ:

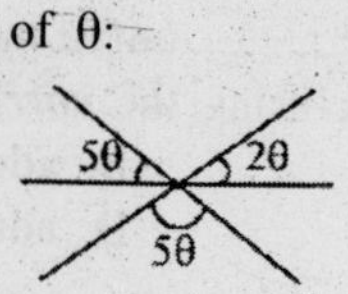

A. 15°
B. 60°
C. 90°
D. 45°

65. A river flows at 4 km/hr. The speed of a boat in downstream is thrice the speed of that boat in upstream. Find out the speed of the boat in still water?
A. 8 km/hr
B. 4 km/hr
C. 6 km/hr
D. 12 km/hr

66. A and B divided a profit of ₹ 1210 such that $\frac{2}{5}$ part of A was equal to $\frac{1}{3}$ part of B. How much amount did B get?
A. ₹ 550
B. ₹ 560
C. ₹ 650
D. ₹ 660

67. Find the number of triangles in the given figure:

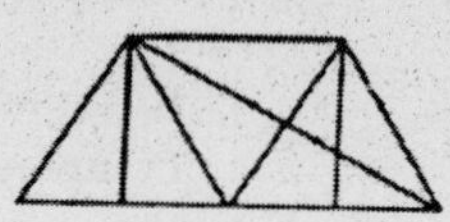

A. 18
B. 19
C. 20
D. 21

68. How many dots lie opposite to the face having three dots, when the given figure is folded to form a cube?

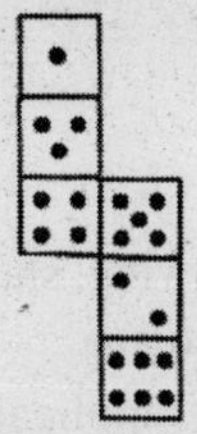

A. 2 B. 4
C. 5 D. 6

69. Statements:
1. A and B are friends.
2. B has friendship with all.
3. A has many enemies.
4. A & C does not like each other.

Conclusions:
I. A and C are friends of B.
II. B has friendship with A's friends.
III. C & B are friends.
IV. A, B & C are three friends.

Then which of the following is right conclusions?
A. I and II B. II and III
C. I, II, III & IV D. I, II and III

70. Starting from her house, Savita travelled 8 m towards west, then turned right and travelled 15 m. She then travelled 20 m towards east, followed by 20 m south to reach a hostel. How far is her house from the hostel and in which direction?
A. 13 m, north-west
B. 13 m, south-east
C. 28 m, north-west
D. 15 m, south-west

71. Akash goes to house of Seema who is the neighbour of Geeta. Geeta has a daughter Meena who is studying in school. Arman is the father of Aman and is married to Anjali. Arman's sister is Geeta, then how Geeta is related to Anjali?
A. Sister
B. Sister-in-law
C. Aunty
D. Mother-in-law

72. If □ means "<", Δ means ">", O means "=" and $2x \, \Delta \, 3y$, $2y$ O z, then which one is ***correct***?
A. x □ z B. $4x$ □ $3z$
C. $x \, \Delta \, z$ D. $4x \, \Delta \, 3z$

73. If code word of HEATER is KBDQHO and code word of AIRY is DFUB, then code word of COOLER is:
A. FLRIHO
B. ALRIHV
C. FRLIHO
D. FLLIHO

74. Find the wrong number in the series.
3, 3, 6, 18, 72, 380, 2160
A. 3 B. 18
C. 72 D. 380

75. Which of the following words can be formed by using letters of word "VENTURESOME"?
A. ROSTRUM
B. SERMOUNT
C. TRAVERSER
D. SEVENTEEN

76. How many pairs of the letters does the word DIFFICULT contain in such that the two letters of the pair have as many letters between them in the word as there are in the english alphabet?
A. 5 B. 4
C. 2 D. 3

77. If $\dfrac{1-9y}{19-3y} = \dfrac{5}{8}$, then y is equal to:
A. $\pm\dfrac{39}{19}$ B. $\dfrac{19}{29}$
C. $-\dfrac{29}{19}$ D. $\dfrac{29}{19}$

78. The least perfect square, which is divisible by each of 21, 36 and 66, is:
A. 231444 B. 214344
C. 213444 D. 214434

79. Five years ago, the age of A was twice the age of B. After five years, their age would be in the ratio 3 : 2. Their present ages are:
A. 15 years and 10 years
B. 45 years and 35 years
C. 19 years and 12 years
D. 25 years and 15 years

80. A person leaves a place P for place Q at 5 AM and reaches place at 9 AM. Another person leaves Q for P on the same track at 6 AM and reaches P at 10 AM. They will meet each other at ....
A. 8 AM B. 8 : 30 AM
C. 7 AM D. 7 : 30 AM

81. How many athlete/s of Haryana origin won the medal at '2016 Summer Paralympic'?
A. One B. Two
C. Three D. None

82. Who among the following has never been the Governor of Haryana?
A. B.N. Chakraborty
B. Harcharan Sing Barar
C. Shivraj Patil
D. Dhanik Lal Mandal

83. Match the following:

Sanctuaries	***Districts***
(*a*) Khaparwas	(*i*) Jhajjar
(*b*) Nahar	(*ii*) Rewari
(*c*) Bir Shikargarh	(*iii*) Panchkula
(*d*) Abubashahar	(*iv*) Sirsa

Code:

	(*a*)	(*b*)	(*c*)	(*d*)
A.	(*i*)	(*ii*)	(*iii*)	(*iv*)
B.	(*ii*)	(*i*)	(*iii*)	(*iv*)
C.	(*iv*)	(*ii*)	(*iii*)	(*i*)
D.	(*ii*)	(*iii*)	(*i*)	(*iv*)

84. Decadal population growth rate of Haryana as per the 2011 Census is:

A. 17.64% B. 28.43%
C. 21.34% D. 19.90%

85. As on November 1, 2017, how many women members are there in the 13th Legislative Assembly of Haryana?

A. Twelve B. Thirteen
C. Twenty Two D. Sixteen

86. Which one of the following is ***not*** correctly matched?

Leader of revolution of 1857		***Area of activity***
A. Sadruddin	–	Mewat
B. Nahar Singh	–	Ballabhagarh
C. Ghafur Ali	–	Pataudi
D. Ahamad Ali	–	Farrukh Nagar

87. 'City of Handloom' is:

A. Ambala
B. Faridabad
C. Hissar
D. Panipat

88. Consider the following statements regarding 'Deen Dayal Jan Awas Yojana':

(*i*) The scheme is applicable in low and medium potential towns.
(*ii*) Policy aims to encourage the development of low priced housing in towns.
(*iii*) Under the scheme 15 acres shall be the maximum planned area.
(*iv*) 150 square meter shall be the maximum plot size.

Which of the above statements are ***true***?

A. (*i*) & (*ii*)
B. (*ii*) & (*iii*)
C. (*i*), (*ii*) & (*iii*)
D. (*i*), (*ii*), (*iii*) & (*iv*)

89. The district, where Yamuna river does ***not*** flow:

A. Kurukshetra
B. Panipat
C. Sonipat
D. Palwal

90. 'Mango-Mela' is organized at:

A. Pinjore B. Surajkund
C. Sohna D. Gohana

Answers

1	2	3	4	5	6	7	8	9	10
B	A	B	C	B	B	B	C	B	A
11	**12**	**13**	**14**	**15**	**16**	**17**	**18**	**19**	**20**
B	C	B	B	B	B	A	A	C	B
21	**22**	**23**	**24**	**25**	**26**	**27**	**28**	**29**	**30**
B	B	B	C	C	C	D	C	B	B
31	**32**	**33**	**34**	**35**	**36**	**37**	**38**	**39**	**40**
C	C	D	C	B	C	D	B & D	D	A
41	**42**	**43**	**44**	**45**	**46**	**47**	**48**	**49**	**50**
D	C	D	B	B	B	C	B	C	D
51	**52**	**53**	**54**	**55**	**56**	**57**	**58**	**59**	**60**
B	A	A	C	D	C	B	A	A	D
61	**62**	**63**	**64**	**65**	**66**	**67**	**68**	**69**	**70**
A	C	D	A	A	D	B	A	D	A
71	**72**	**73**	**74**	**75**	**76**	**77**	**78**	**79**	**80**
B	D	A	D	B	D	C	C	D	D
81	**82**	**83**	**84**	**85**	**86**	**87**	**88**	**89**	**90**
A	C	A	D	B	C	D	D	A	A

Explanatory Answers

61. Fresh Grapes = Water + Pulp

$(95\% + 5\%) \times 19$

$= 1900\%$

[Multiply by 19 because pulp quantity is same]

Dry grapes = 5% + 95% = 100%

100% Value = 400 gm

$$1900\% \text{ Value} = \frac{400}{100} \times 1900$$

$= 7600$ gm $= 7.6$ kg.

62. Let the number $= 10x + y$

$$xy = 12$$

$$(10x + y) + 36 = (10y + x)$$

$$9x - 9y = -36$$

$$x - y = -4 \quad ...(i)$$

$$x + y = \sqrt{(x-y)^2 + 4xy}$$

$$= \sqrt{16+48} = \sqrt{64}$$

$$x + y = 8 \quad ...(ii)$$

After solving equation (*i*) and equation (*ii*), we get

$$x = 2, y = 6$$

$\therefore$ Number $= 10 \times 2 + 6 = 26$.

63. Let, the breadth of the hall $= x$

Then, length of the hall $= \frac{4}{3}x$

Area of rectangular hall $= l \times b$

$$x \times \frac{4}{3}x = 300$$

$$x^2 = \frac{900}{4}$$

breadth, $x = \frac{30}{2} = 15$ meters

length $= \frac{4}{3}x = \frac{4}{3} \times 15$

$= 20$ meters

Difference $= 20 - 15 = 5$ meters.

64. $x° = 5\theta$ (Vertically opposite Angle)

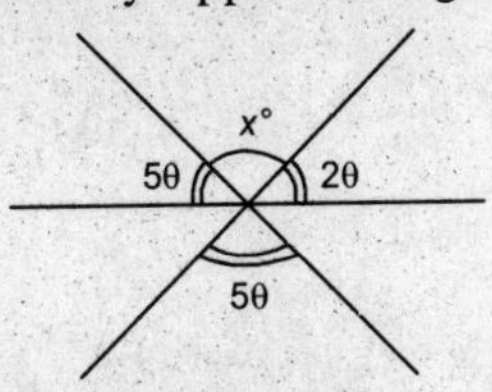

$\therefore \quad 5\theta + x° + 2\theta = 180°$

$$5\theta + 5\theta + 2\theta = 180°$$

$$12\theta = 180°$$

$$\theta = 15°.$$

65. Let, the speed of Boat in still water $= x$ km/h

$$x + 4 = 3(x - 4)$$

$$x + 4 = 3x - 12$$

$$16 = 2x$$

$$x = 8 \text{ km/h}.$$

66. $$\frac{2}{5} \times A = \frac{1}{3} \times B$$

$$\frac{A}{B} = \frac{5}{6}$$

$$B \text{ get} = 1210 \times \frac{6}{11} = 660.$$

67.

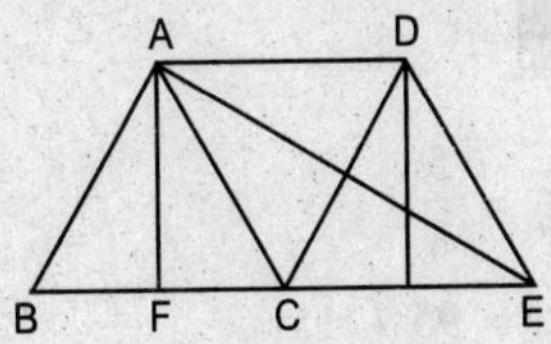

Base Figure,

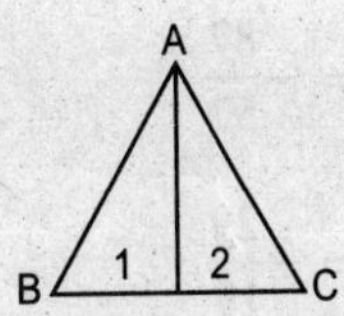

$= 1 + 2 + 3$

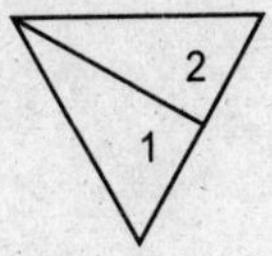

$= 3$

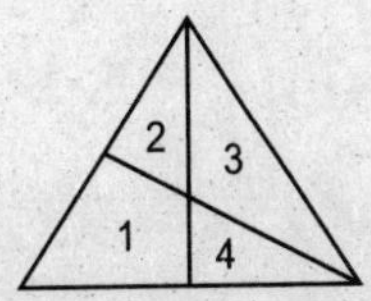

$= 1 + 2 + 3 + 4 = 10$

Total $\Delta = 3 + 3 + 10 + 1(\Delta ABC) + 1(AFE) + 1(ACE)$

$= 19.$

71.

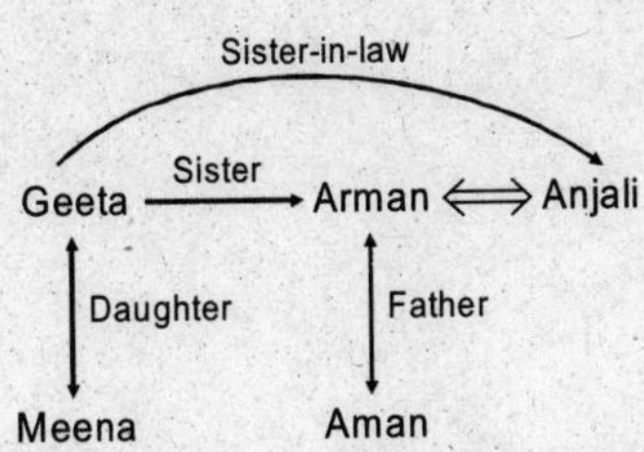

Geeta is Sister-in-law of Anjali.

72. $2x \Delta 3y \Rightarrow 2x > 3y$

$2y \bigcirc z \Rightarrow 2y = z$

$$y = \frac{z}{2}$$

$$2x > 3 \times \frac{z}{2}$$

$$4x > 3z$$

$$4x \Delta 3z.$$

73. As, H E A T E R → (+3, −3, +3, −3, +3, −3) → K B D Q H O

A I R Y → (+3, −3, +3, −3) → D F U B

Similarly, C O O L E R → (+3, −3, +3, −3, +3, −3) → **F L R I H O**

74. 3 (×1) 3 (×2) 6 (×3) 18 (×4) 72 (×5) **360** (×6) 2160

Hence, 380 is wrong number in the series.

76.

4	9	6	6	9	3	21	12	20
D	I	F	F	I	C	U	L	T

77.
$$\frac{1-9y}{19-3y} = \frac{5}{8}$$

$$8 - 72y = 95 - 15y$$

$$-57y = 87$$

$$y = -\frac{87}{57}$$

$$= -\frac{29}{19}.$$

78. LCM (21, 36, 66) = 2772

$(462)^2 = 213444$ is divisible by 2772

79. Let the present Age of A and B are x and y years respectively

$$(x - 5) = 2(y - 5)$$

$$x - 2y = -5 \quad ...(i)$$

$$\frac{x+5}{y+5} = \frac{3}{2}$$

$$2x + 10 = 3y + 15$$

$$2x - 3y = 5 \quad ...(ii)$$

Equation $(i) \times 2$ – equation (ii) we get

$$-y = -15$$

$$y = 15$$

Put in equation (i)

$$x - 30 = -5$$

$$x = 25$$

$\therefore$ x and y present age are 25 years and 15 years.

80. (5 am) ⟶ 4 hour (9 am)

P ———————— Q

(10 am) 4 hour ⟵ (6 am)

$\because$ Both take same time to reach their destination (distance same). It means speed of both person is same.

$$\therefore \quad \text{time} = 6 \text{ AM} + \frac{(9 \text{ AM} - 6 \text{ AM})}{2}$$

$$= 6 \text{ AM} + \frac{3}{2}$$

$$= 6 \text{ AM} + 1 \text{ h } 30 \text{ min}$$

$$= 7 : 30 \text{ AM}.$$

Previous Years Paper (Solved)

HTET-Post Graduate Teacher (Level-3), 2016*

PART- I

Child Development and Pedagogy

Directions: *Answer the following questions by selecting the **most appropriate** option.*

1. To cooperate the adolescent it is essential to
   A. Inspire
   B. Indicate his mistakes
   C. Criticise him
   D. Do negative behaviour

2. Which of the following is ***not*** a suitable technique used by teachers for socializing the child?
   A. Direct teaching
   B. Identification
   C. Democratic discipline
   D. Over-protection

3. Which of the following is a ***wrong*** statement about emotions of an adolescent?
   A. Emotional expressions are modified by learning.
   B. Emotions are permanent.
   C. Every emotion is accompanied by a feeling.
   D. Emotions are aroused by external stimuli.

4. Inclusive education means
   A. Meeting individual differences in general classroom.
   B. Meeting individual differences in different classroom.
   C. Meeting individual differences in special schools.
   D. Meeting individual differences in home based instruction.

5. In adolescence behaviour and attitude are affected mostly by
   A. Teacher B. Parents
   C. Peer Groups D. Films

6. Moral values can be effectively inculcated among the students when teacher
   A. Frequently talks about values.
   B. Himself practices them.
   C. Tells stories of good persons.
   D. Talks of Gods and Goddesses.

7. Critical thinking helps a person in developing abilities and skills for
   A. providing concrete experiences.
   B. proper interpretation, analysis, evaluation and inference.
   C. creating and constructing something.
   D. thinking about ways of reacting.

8. Best method of dealing with adolescent by parents and teachers is
   A. Autocratic B. Permissive
   C. Democratic D. Restrictive

9. Which of the following is ***not*** a characteristic of social development in adolescence?
   A. Active member of their peer group
   B. Being an attraction towards opposite sex
   C. High decrease in friendly relationship
   D. Extension of special interests

10. An adolescent uses her/his left hand for performing act like taking food or writing, this is developed due to
    A. Inherited behaviour
    B. Developmental behaviour
    C. Wrong behaviour
    D. All options are right

11. Discalculia is a problem related to the problem of
    A. Speaking accurately
    B. Writing without committing mistakes
    C. Listening message properly
    D. Doing mathematical calculations

12. Continuous and Comprehensive Evaluation (CCE) aims to evaluate
    A. The reasoning of child only.
    B. All aspects of development of child.
    C. The knowledge of child only.
    D. The understanding of child only.

13. Which of the following is ***not*** a trait (ability) of a creative child?
    A. Elaboration B. Originality
    C. Accuracy D. Novelty

* *Exam held on 18-06-2016.*

14. Learning outcomes means
A. Change in the behaviour of the student.
B. Change in teaching method of the teacher.
C. Recognization of the subject matter.
D. Completion of content.

15. Differentiation of emotions takes place at the time of
A. Birth of child
B. During infancy
C. During the period of adolescence
D. During adulthood

16. Which of the following provision is ***not*** suitable to meet individual differences among learners?
A. Their abilities should be assessed.
B. Adequate facilities and material should be provided.
C. Labelling them.
D. Making Individualisation necessary.

17. Working with adolescents, particularly maladjusted one, which is ***not*** appropriate?
A. Critical approach
B. Democratic approach
C. Collective approach
D. Ideal approach

18. Heredity plays most important role in the
A. Emotional development of the child
B. Social development of the child
C. Physical development of the child
D. Cultural development of the child

19. The knowledge of principles of learning is must for a good teacher, because
A. It helps in maintaining discipline.
B. It helps to make content interesting.
C. It helps to understand the content by simple methods.
D. It saves time

20. Which of the following characteristic is ***not correct*** about objective type testing?
A. Reliability B. Objectivity
C. Validity D. Subjectivity

21. Which of the following is the characteristics of constructivist classroom?
A. Students design experiments, draws conclusions and compare their findings.
B. Knowledge is objective, universal and complete.
C. Teacher transmits authoritative knowledge to students.
D. Students look for the 'right' answer.

22. Which of the following is the primary law of learning propounded by Thorndike?
A. Law of analogy B. Law of exercise
C. Law of assimilation D. Law of disposition

23. According to Piaget the child is able to apply logical thoughts to all classes of problems, this development occurs in which of the following periods?
A. The formal operational period
B. The concrete operational period
C. The pre-operational period
D. The sensory motor period

24. A child is average on creativity, high in academic achievement, poor in social development. This is an example of
A. Inter individual differences
B. Intra individual differences
C. Individual differences
D. Measurable individual differences

25. That internal state of mind that arouses, directs and maintains behaviour is called
A. Interest B. Opinion
C. Attitude D. Motivation

26. Some people adjust easily with new people because they have high
A. Intelligence Quotient (I.Q.)
B. Academic Quotient (A.Q.)
C. Emotional Quotient (E.Q.)
D. Spiritual Quotient (S.Q.)

27. Development generally proceeds from head to foot, this principle of development is called
A. Bilateral to unilateral
B. Proximodistal
C. General to specific
D. Cephalo Caudal

28. A student is working hard for Board Examination, his father has promised to give him a motor cycle if he gets good marks. This is
A. Intrinsic motivation
B. Extrinsic motivation
C. Mathematical motivation
D. Intrinsic and extrinsic motivation

29. Which of the following statements is ***not correct*** about learner centred approach?
A. It takes into account learner's capabilities, capacities and learning styles.
B. It stresses the importance of enquiry, observation and investigation.
C. It emphasises transmitting knowledge to the learner by the teacher.
D. It uses methods like experiential learning, problem solving, concept mapping and creative writing.

30. A child's attitude 'I do not care' is a type of behaviour which can be called
A. Aggression B. Defence
C. Denial D. Retrogression

PART- II

भाषा-I : हिन्दी

निर्देश : *सबसे उचित विकल्प चुनिए :*

31. अशुद्ध विकल्प को पहचानिए
A. विश्वामित्र = विश्व + मित्र
B. मूसलाधार = मूसल + धार
C. सभी = सब + ही
D. दीनानाथ = दीना + नाथ

32. 'वार्ष्णेय' शब्द में कौन-सा प्रत्यय लगा है?
A. य B. एय
C. इय D. अय

33. 'वह जिस पर हमला किया गया हो'—के लिए शब्द चुनें—
A. आत्मघात B. आघात
C. आक्रांत D. आक्रांता

34. 'जो नायिका अपने प्रेमी से मिलने स्वयं जाए'—के लिए एक शब्द है—
A. दुहिता B. अभिसारिका
C. प्रोषितपतिका D. स्वयंगमना

35. निम्न शब्दों में से कौन-सा शब्द 'रूढ़' है?
A. गाय B. विद्यालय
C. लम्बोदर D. पंकज

36. ''यदि तुम आते तो मैं भी तुम्हारे साथ चलता।''
इस वाक्य हेतु ***सही*** काल है—
A. आसन्न भूतकाल
B. हेतुहेतुमद् भूतकाल
C. संदिग्ध भूतकाल
D. अपूर्ण भूतकाल

37. 'जिसका जन्म अविवाहित कन्या के गर्भ से हुआ हो'— के लिए शुद्ध शब्द है
A. कन्यापुत्र B. कानीन
C. अवैध पुत्र D. कुमारीसुत

38. किस शब्द में समास की दृष्टि से विभक्ति का लोप नहीं, अपितु विभक्ति सहित प्रयोग किया गया है?
A. सरसिज B. कृतघ्न
C. स्वस्थ D. स्वर्णकार

39. किस शब्द में 'वी' प्रत्यय का प्रयोग शुद्ध रूप से ***नहीं*** हुआ है?
A. ऊर्जस्वी
B. साध्वी
C. तपस्वी
D. मायावी

40. 'मैं खाना खा चुका हूँ।' इस वाक्य में भूतकालिक भेद इंगित कीजिए।
A. पूर्ण भूत B. सामान्य भूत
C. आसन्न भूत D. संदिग्ध भूत

41. व्याकरण की दृष्टि से 'प्रेम' शब्द क्या है?
A. अव्यय B. भाववाचक संज्ञा
C. विशेषण D. शुद्धता

42. कौन-सा शब्द 'धनुष' का पर्यायवाची ***नहीं*** है?
A. कोदंड B. विशिखासन
C. चाप D. विशिख

43. 'गौरव' शब्द की ***सही*** व्युत्पत्ति है
A. गुरु + व B. गुरु + अ
C. गुरु + अव D. गौर + व

44. 'योगीश्वर' शब्द का सम्यक् संधि विच्छेद होगा
A. योगी + इश्वर B. योगि + ईश्वर
C. योगि + श्वर D. योगिन् + ईश्वर

45. हिन्दी की 'क' ध्वनि व्याकरण की दृष्टि में है
A. अल्पप्राण-सघोष B. महाप्राण-सघोष
C. अल्पप्राण-अघोष D. महाप्राण-अघोष

46. 'यज्ञशाला' शब्द में उपयुक्त समास का चयन करें
A. द्वितीया तत्पुरुष
B. तृतीया तत्पुरुष
C. षष्ठी तत्पुरुष
D. चतुर्थी तत्पुरुष

47. *'भूल गए राग रंग भूल गए छकड़ी, तीन चीज याद रही नून, तेल, लकड़ी'*—लोकोक्ति के लिए ***सही*** अर्थ का चयन कीजिए
A. महँगाई क आगे की विवशता
B. नून, तेल, लकड़ी के बिना संसार अधूरा है
C. अत्यावश्यक वस्तुओं से ही प्रेम
D. गृहस्थी के चक्कर में फँस जाना

48. उपसर्ग रहित शब्द है
A. सुरेश B. सुयोग
C. अत्यधिक D. विदेश

49. ***अशुद्ध*** विकल्प को चुनें
A. आर्ष-अनार्ष B. उद्धत-समुद्धत
C. उन्मीलन-निमीलन D. अर्पण-ग्रहण

50. 'किताब' किस भाषा का शब्द है?
A. अरबी B. फारसी
C. अंग्रेजी D. हिन्दी

51. 'बंदूक एक उपयोगी .... है।' रिक्त स्थान के लिए ***उचित*** शब्द का चयन करें।

A. अस्त्र
B. शस्त्र
C. रक्षक
D. औजार

52. किस शब्द में कर्मधारय समास का प्रयोग ***नहीं*** हुआ है?

A. कदाचार
B. जवाँमर्द
C. क्रोधाग्नि
D. कर्त्तव्याकर्त्तव्य

53. 'नेत्री' शब्द का पुल्लिंग क्या होगा?

A. नेताइन
B. नेतृ
C. नेता
D. अभिनेता

54. किस शब्द में विसर्ग संधि का प्रयोग ***नहीं*** हुआ है?

A. नभोमण्डल
B. शिरोभाग
C. क्षुधोत्तेजन
D. सर्वतोमुखी

55. ***अशुद्ध*** वर्तनी वाला शब्द छाँटिए

A. व्यवसायिक
B. कार्मिक
C. सांघातिक
D. षाण्मासिक

निर्देश (प्र.सं. 56-60) : *निम्नलिखित गद्यांश को पढ़कर दिये गये प्रश्नों के उत्तर दीजिए।*

भारत में परंपरा के प्रयोजन और औचित्य को लेकर दो अतिरेकवादी और परस्पर घोर विरोधी स्वर अकसर सुनाई पड़ते हैं। एक स्तर पर वो परंपरा प्रेमी हैं जो अतीत के प्रत्येक चिह्न को परंपरा मानने की जिद पकड़े हैं और दूसरे स्तर पर वो 'आधुनिक' हैं जो देश के प्रत्येक प्राचीन को संदेह की दृष्टि से देखते हैं और एक कथित आधुनिक राष्ट्र के निर्माण में उसे बाधा की तरह पाते हैं।

भारतीय मनीषा ने परंपरा को महत्व तो सदैव दिया है परन्तु इसे उचित ही प्रश्नांकित और तदनुसार परिमार्जित भी किया है। भारतीय समाज को एक परंपरावादी समाज के रूप में अभिहित किया जाता है जिससे कुछ लोग यह धोखा खा जाते हैं कि प्राचीनतम समय से यहाँ कुछ नहीं बदला है। परंपरा के साथ परिवर्तन ही भारतीय समाज की खूबी है।

वैदिक संहिताओं की कतिपय मान्यताओं का विरोध उपनिषदों में ही हो गया जो कि वैदिक वाङ्मय के ही भाग थे। महावीर स्वामी व गौतम बुद्ध ने उस वर्ण व्यवस्था का विरोध किया जिसमें वे स्वयं जन्मे थे। बौद्ध धर्म की नितान्त नीरस हीनयान परंपरा का विरोध महायान संप्रदाय के रूप में सामने आया और महायान संप्रदाय ने सृष्टिविषयक परिकल्पना का वह दार्शनिक वितान रचा जिसका गौतम बुद्ध सदैव विरोध करते रहे थे। जब पारसिकों एवं शकों से संपर्क हुआ तो उनका क्षत्रप-महाक्षत्रप का ढांचा भारत की राजनीतिक प्रणाली क. हिस्सा बन गया। गांधार कला का शिल्प शास्त्र हम भारतीयों को यूनानियों से लेने में कोई संकोच नहीं हुआ। इसी प्रकार ज्योतिष में यवन सिद्धान्त को आदर के साथ स्थान मिला। अचकन और बूट मध्य एशिया के ठंडे प्रदेशों से आये कुषाण लाये थे। भारतीय वस्त्र विन्यास में ये इस प्रकार समाहित हो गए कि इन्हें पृथक परंपरा के रूप में देखना संभव नहीं।

यह बदलाव ही भारतीय परंपरा की पूँजी है। जब कभी बदलाव को छोड़कर वह जड़ता की ओर उन्मुख हुई है, उसने दीर्घकालीन प्रगति को नुकसान पहुँचाया है। सामाजिक इतिहासकारों के अनुसार गुप्तोत्तर काल एक ऐसा युग था जब परंपराओं के पिष्टपेषण का बोलबाला था। परिवर्तन और परिमार्जन की कोई प्रेरणा नहीं थी। उस समय परंपरा के नाम पर कुछ ऐसी बद्धमूल धारणाएँ विकसित हुईं जिनका दुष्परिणाम हम आज भी भोग रहे हैं।

यद्यपि यह सही है कि अतीत की कुछ बद्धमूल परंपराओं का खामियाजा हमें उठाना पड़ा परंतु यह अभीष्ट नहीं है कि संपूर्ण अतीत और तद्जनित परंपरा सर्वथा त्याज्य हो जाए। स्वातंत्र्योत्तर भारत में आधुनिकता एवं बौद्धिकता के नाम पर समृद्ध अतीत को कटघरे में खड़ा करना एक बौद्धिक विलास बन गया है। हर वह चिह्न और धरोहर जो प्राचीन व परंपरा से जुड़ी हुई है, बौद्धिक समाज के एक वर्ग के लिये हेय बन गई है। परंपरा को प्रश्नांकित और तदनुसार परिमार्जित करना तो आवश्यक है परन्तु उसकी पूर्व शर्त यह है कि परंपरा का ठीक से अवगाहन किया जाए।

56. भारतीय समाज की विशेषता है :

A. घोर परंपरावाद
B. परंपरा विरोध
C. परंपरा के साथ परिवर्तन
D. सभी विकल्प गलत हैं

57. गौतम बुद्ध विरोधी थे :

(*i*) हीनयान सम्प्रदाय के
(*ii*) महायान सम्प्रदाय के
(*iii*) वर्ण व्यवस्था के
(*iv*) सृष्टि विषयक परिकल्पना के

उचित उत्तर विकल्प को चुनिए :

A. (*i*) एवं (*iv*)
B. (*iii*) एवं (*iv*)
C. केवल (*iii*)
D. केवल (*ii*)

58. भारत की राजनीतिक प्रणाली को अवदान दिया :

A. शकों ने
B. यूनानियों ने
C. कुषाणों ने
D. बौद्धों ने

59. पिष्टपेषण से भावार्थ है :

A. दोहराव
B. पिसाई
C. व्याख्या
D. महिमा मंडन

60. स्वातन्त्र्योत्तर भारत में बौद्धिक विलास है :

A. आधुनिकता
B. परंपरा का अवगाहन
C. अतीत को कटघरे में खड़ा करना
D. धरोहर और चिह्न

PART- III

Language-II : English

Directions: *Answer the following questions by selecting the* ***most appropriate*** *option.*

61. Choose the ***correct*** passive form of the verb in bracket in the given sentence:

I suddenly realized I (watch).

A. am being watched
B. have been watched
C. am watched
D. was being watched

62. I must finish this.

The underlined word in the above sentence indicates

A. Necessity B. Determination
C. Wish D. Habit

63. Choose the ***correct*** suffix to form the word. The meaning of the word is given:

Copi .... = Plentiful

A. ous B. some
C. ose D. ful

64. 'I don't enjoy going to the dentist.' The word 'going' in the above sentence is a/an :

A. Present participle
B. Infinitive
C. Perfect participle
D. Gerund

65. Choose the ***correct*** indirect speech of the given sentence:

Mother said, "Don't go to the park".

A. Mother asked us not to go to the park.
B. Mother told us not to go to the park.
C. Mother said us not to go to the park.
D. Mother said to us to not to go to the park.

66. Which of the following expression means 'extremely happy'?

A. be a basket case
B. fall off your perch
C. be off your trolley
D. on cloud nine

67. Choose the ***correct*** passive construction of the sentence:

Auctioneer will sell the painting at auction.

A. The painting would be sold at auction.
B. The painting will be sold by the auctioneers at auction.
C. The painting will be sold at auction.
D. The painting will be selling at auction.

68. Identify the figure of speech in the following sentence:

I must be cruel, only to be kind.

A. Epigram B. Paradox
C. Analogy D. Metaphor

69. Which of the following words is ***misspelt***?

A. incongruous B. chronological
C. synchronus D. sympathetic

Directions (Qs. 70 to 74): *Select the sentence that is grammatically* ***correct.***

70. A. My brother is the student in Mayo College.
B. My brother is student of Mayo College.
C. My brother is a student in the Mayo College.
D. My brother is a student in Mayo College.

71. A. Neither of them were present there.
B. Neither of them was present there.
C. Neither of them present there.
D. Neither of them are present there.

72. A. The roses smell sweet.
B. The roses smell sweetly.
C. The roses are smelling sweetly.
D. The roses are sweetly smelling.

73. A. You certainly did not ought to do it.
B. You certainly ought not to have done it.
C. You certainly did not ought to have done it.
D. You certainly ought not to have been done it.

74. A. Who was the book given to?
B. Who the book was given to?
C. The book was given to who?
D. Whom was the book given to?

75. Choose the ***correct*** phonetic transcription of the word 'Locate'.

A. /luket/ B. /lokeit/
C. /ləu'keit/ D. /ləuket/

76. Choose the ***correct*** direct speech of the given reported speech:

He said I'd better go because it was late.

A. He said, "You'd better go because it's late."
B. He said, "I'd better go because it was late."
C. He said, "You'd better be gone because it was late."
D. He said, "You'd better go because it was late."

77. Which of the following is ***spelt correctly***?

A. Pediatrician B. Padritician
C. Pedaitrician D. Pidiatrician

78. In which of the following sentences do we need to insert the definite article 'the'?
A. They are all busy growing things.
B. We do not generally speak of farmers 'growing animals'.
C. Why do people work?
D. They are different from rest.

79. Which of the following sentences is ***correct***?
A. My father's foot was put down when I said I wanted a car for my seventeenth birthday. He said I was too young.
B. My father down put the foot when I said I wanted a car for my seventeenth birthday. He said I am too young.
C. My father put his foot down when I said I wanted a car for my seventeenth birthday. He said I was too young.
D. All options are wrong

80. Since you were not there, I left a message with your sister.

The underlined group of words in the above sentence is a/an :
A. Noun Clause
B. Adverb Clause of place
C. Adverb Clause of time
D. Adverb Clause of reason

Directions (Qs. 81-85): *Read the following passage and answer the questions by choosing* ***most appropriate*** *option:*

Common sense is a rare and enviable quality. It may be truly said that 'Its price is above rubies'. How many learned men, how many wits, how many geniuses, how many dull and ignorant people, how many cunning knaves, how many well-meaning fools are without it! How few have it, how little do they or others know of it, except from the infalliable results—for one of its first requisites is the utter absence of all pretension.

The vulgar laugh at the pedant and enthusiast for the want of it, while they themselves mistake bigotry and narrow minded notions for it. It is not one of the sciences, but has been well pronounced to be 'fairly worth the seven'. It is a kind of mental instinct, that feels the air of truth and propriety as the fingers feel objects of touch. It does not consist with ignorance for we cannot pronounce on what we do not know; and on the other hand, the laying in of a stock of knowledge, or mastering any art or science seems to destroy that native simplicity and to warp and trammel the unbiased freedom of mind which is necessary to its receiving and giving their due weight to ordinary and casual impressions.

81. Common sense is a rare and enviable quality because:
A. Its price is above rubies
B. All learned men have it
C. All men are without it
D. Very few have it

82. What is ***not*** a requisite of common sense?
A. The utter absence of all pretension
B. Bigotry and narrow minded notions
C. Truth and propriety
D. An unbiased freedom of mind

83. Which of the following is ***not*** stated by the writer in the passage?
A. Affectation destroys common sense.
B. Common sense requires the utmost simplicity and sincerity.
C. Common sense feels the air of truth and propriety as the fingers feel objects of touch.
D. Common sense destroys the native simplicity and warps and trammels the freedom of mind.

84. Fill in the blank with the ***most appropriate*** word:

Common sense has been well pronounced to be 'fairly worth the seven' ....
A. Notions B. Sciences
C. Talents D. Wits

85. Which is ***not*** a synonym of the word 'pedant'?
A. dogmatist B. formalist
C. perfectionist D. down-to-earth

Directions (Qs. 86 and 90): *Fill in the blanks with the* ***most suitable*** *option.*

86. .... child should learn to read and write.
A. All B. Every
C. Whole D. Both

87. Can I ask your ...., do you think TV violence is harmful?
A. opinion B. favour
C. question D. advice

88. Where is my wallet? I left it .... the kitchen table.
A. at B. in
C. on D. by

89. Take some medicine and the pain will go ....
A. back B. off
C. out D. away

90. The walkers finally arrived at their destination. They .... all day, and they certainly needed a rest. They .... thirty miles.
A. had been walking; had walked
B. had walked; had been walking
C. walked; walked
D. have been walking; had walked

Note: *In addition to these 90 Questions, 60 Questions will be asked from Concerned Subjects.*

Answers

1	2	3	4	5	6	7	8	9	10
A	D	B	A	C	B	B	C	C	B
11	12	13	14	15	16	17	18	19	20
D	B	C	A	B	C	A	C	C	D
21	22	23	24	25	26	27	28	29	30
A	B	A	B	D	C	D	D	C	D
31	32	33	34	35	36	37	38	39	40
D	B	C	B	A	B	B	A	B	A
41	42	43	44	45	46	47	48	49	50
B	D	B	D	C	D	D	A	B	A
51	52	53	54	55	56	57	58	59	60
B	D	C	C	A	C	B	A	A	C
61	62	63	64	65	66	67	68	69	70
D	A	A	D	B	D	C	B	C	C
71	72	73	74	75	76	77	78	79	80
B	A	B	D	C	A	A	D	C	D
81	82	83	84	85	86	87	88	89	90
D	B	D	B	D	B	A	C	D	A

Previous Years Paper (Solved)

HTET-Post Graduate Teacher (Level-3), 2014

PART- I

Child Development and Pedagogy

Directions: *Answer the following questions by selecting the* ***most appropriate*** *option.*

1. Libido is
   A. Physical energy
   B. Sexual energy
   C. Mental energy
   D. Emotional energy

2. Which of the following is ***not*** a primary law of learning, according to Thorndike?
   A. Law of exercise
   B. Law of proximity
   C. Law of effect
   D. Law of readiness

3. Learning disabilities include
   A. Hearing or motor disabilities
   B. Mental retardation
   C. Emotional disturbances
   D. Disorder of understanding or using language (spoken or written)

4. Hermann Ebbinghaus is a well-known name in the field of
   A. Verbal Learning B. Personality
   C. Intelligance D. Perception

5. Which of the following theories is given by Leon Festinger?
   A. Functional theory
   B. Balance theory
   C. Social equity theory
   D. Cognitive dissonance theory

6. Images frozen in memories and tied to particular places, dates & times are known as
   A. Flash bulb memories
   B. Autobiographical memories
   C. Tip of Tongue (TOT) memories
   D. False memories

7. Values that are learnt from our family and society influence our behaviour as
   A. Internal motivating factors
   B. External motivating factors
   C. Mental motivating factors
   D. Physical motivating factors

8. Which of the following is ***not*** a scale of attitude measurement?
   A. Bogardus social distance scale
   B. Osgood's semantic differential scale
   C. Thurstone's Equal appearing scale
   D. Guttman's picture frustration scale

9. What is more important to be successful in life according to Daniel Goleman?
   A. Cultural intelligence
   B. Spiritual intelligence
   C. Emotional intelligence
   D. Cognitive intelligence

10. The aim of remedial teaching is to
    A. understand pupil's uniqueness in learning abilities and performance
    B. detaining the pupil for longer school hours so that he studies more
    C. provide extra coaching for competition
    D. reduce the burden of parents in getting their children's homework done

11. How many primary mental abilities are given by Thurstone?
    A. 7 B. 3
    C. 10 D. 14

12. Which of the following statements is ***not true*** about learning process according to Thorndike?
    A. Learning is a gradual process
    B. Learning is a trial and error process
    C. Learning comes through insight only
    D. Practice is an important principle of learning

13. In modern times, Psychology is considered the study of
    A. Spirit B. Soul
    C. God D. Human behaviour

14. If the chronological age of a child is 60 months and the mental age of the child is 72, what shall be his IQ?

A. 84 B. 100
C. 120 D. 92

15. Which of the following type of personality is known as the coronary heart disease prone personality?
A. Type A personality
B. Type B personality
C. Type C personality
D. Type Z personality

16. Carl Rogers does ***not*** emphasize on
A. Unconditional positive regard
B. Client centered approach
C. Growth of Self as an important aspect of personality
D. Unconscious mind

17. When the laws of primary and recency both operate in the learning process (serial position effect), what kind of learning curve do we get?
A. Curve of positive return
B. 'U' shaped Curve
C. Inverted 'U' shaped Curve
D. Sigmoid ('S' shaped) Curve

18. Kohler's experiment on Chimpanzee demonstrated
A. Learning through conditioning
B. Trial and error learning
C. Learning through insight
D. Latent learning

19. Dyslexia is a
A. Learning disability
B. Rigid personality
C. Malfunction of sense organs
D. Forgetfulness

20. Which of the following is ***not*** a component of an attitude?
A. Moral component
B. Affective component
C. Behavioural component
D. Cognitive component

21. Which of the following is an example of social motive?
A. Sex drive
B. Maternal drive
C. Exploratory motive
D. Achievement motive

22. The average IQ of a student ranges between
A. 110-120 B. 90-110
C. 120-130 D. 80-90

23. How many pairs of chromosomes an infant has?
A. 12 B. 15
C. 23 D. 48

24. According to Freud, Phallic Stage of personality emerges at the age of
A. 1-3 years B. 3-6 years
C. 7-11 years D. After 11 years

25. Which of the following is an important element of creativity?
A. Divergent Thinking
B. Convergent Thinking
C. Critical Thinking
D. Abstract Thinking

26. 'Perception is learnt behaviour.' This view is given by
A. Psychoanalysts B. Behaviourists
C. Functionalists D. Gestaltists

27. The aim of curriculum flexibility is to
A. improve pupil's school experience and his achievement
B. give more free time to the teachers
C. give free periods to the pupils
D. give the pupil an opportunity to attend or miss the class as he wishes

28. Which of the following is the lowest level of measurement?
A. Interval scale B. Ratio scale
C. Nominal scale D. Ordinal scale

29. Who was the founder of Psychoanalysis?
A. B.F. Skinner B. Sigmund Freud
C. G. Allport D. J.B. Watson

30. Which of the following is ***not*** a projective test?
A. Rorschach Ink Blot Test
B. Sentence Completion Test
C. Situational Test
D. TAT Test

PART- II

भाषा-I : हिन्दी

निर्देश : *सबसे उचित विकल्प चुनिए :*

31. निम्नलिखित में से ***अशुद्ध*** छाँटिए
A. गुंजन B. सङ्गत
C. सन्यासी D. संचय

32. प्रत्यय के योग से बना शब्द ***नहीं*** है
A. बुढ़ापा
B. पीछे
C. अगला
D. भूखा

33. 'चतुर्दश' शब्द में 'समास' का प्रकार है

A. अव्ययीभाव B. द्विगु

C. द्वन्द्व D. तत्पुरुष

34. 'सबके साथ एक-सा व्यवहार करना' के लिए उचित मुहावरा है

A. अन्धेर नगरी चौपट राजा

B. एक लाठी से सबको हाँकना

C. आटे के साथ घुन भी पिसता है

D. सावन हरे ना भादो सूखा

35. 'अपनी प्रशंसा करने वाला' वाक्यांश के लिए सार्थक शब्द होगा

A. आत्मवादी B. आत्मश्लाघी

C. आत्मद्रष्टा D. आत्मभू

36. 'वृष्टि न होने पर सूखा पड़ने की .... है।' प्रस्तुत वाक्य मे खाली स्थान पर कौन-सा शब्द आयेगा?

A. अपेक्षा B. आशा

C. आशंका D. सम्भावना

37. 'बच्चे छत पर खेल रहे हैं' इस वाक्य में रेखांकित शब्द में प्रयुक्त कारक को बताइए

A. करण B. सम्प्रदान

C. अपादान D. अधिकरण

38. निम्नलिखित में से *शुद्ध* शब्द छाँटिए

A. आयुषमान B. आयुश्मान्

C. आयुष्मान् D. आयुश्मान

39. ''मीठा'' शब्द से जातिवाचक संज्ञा बनेगी

A. 'आस' प्रत्यय के योग से

B. 'आई' प्रत्यय के योग से

C. 'पन' प्रत्यय के योग से

D. उपरोक्त सभी

40. 'वह तो विभीषण निकला।' रेखांकित पद में संज्ञा का प्रकार है

A. व्यक्तिवाचक B. जातिवाचक

C. भाववाचक D. समूहवाचक

41. जिन शब्दों का स्रोत पता नहीं हो, वे कहलाते हैं

A. तत्सम B. तद्भव

C. देशज D. विदेशी

42. 'अपेक्षा' का विलोम बनेगा

A. 'अव' उपसर्ग के योग से

B. 'उप' उपसर्ग के योग से

C. 'परा' उपसर्ग के योग से

D. 'वि' उपसर्ग के योग से

43. किस विकल्प में शब्दों का वही क्रम है जिस क्रम से वे शब्दकोश में मिलते हैं?

A. नलिनी, नवग्रह, नशा, नश्वर

B. खड़ाऊँ, खरोंच, ख़मीरा, खल

C. चंद्रहास, चकोरी, चक्रांक, चक्का

D. भारी, भाल, भारत, भाषा

निर्देश (प्र.सं. 44-53) : *निम्नलिखित गद्यांश को पढ़कर दिये गये प्रश्नों के* ***सबसे उचित*** *विकल्प को चुनियेः*

महाभारत में कहा गया है– ''*मुहूर्तं ज्वलितं श्रेयः, न तु धूमायितं चिरम्।*'' जीवन के लिये श्रेयस्कर है एक मुहूर्त में भभक कर जल उठना, बहुत समय तक धुआँना ठीक नहीं है। सच्चा जीवन वही है जो जीवन भर दीपक की तरह जलता रहे किन्तु आज सम्पूर्ण विश्व चौबीसों घण्टे धुआँ-सा नजर आ रहा है। इस धुआँती जिन्दगी ने खुद की आँखें भी आँसुओं से भरी हैं और दूसरों की भी। सच तो यह है कि अगर धुआँ न हो तो अन्धेरा भी बेहतर था। चले थे रोशनी की तलाश में, अंधेरे को भी विक्षिप्त कर दिया। जीवन को धुआँ-धुआँ-सा कर दिया। समस्त आज गीली लकड़ी की तरह बनकर रह गया है। जलाओ तो सिर्फ धुआँ ही उठता है। जितना गीलापन, उतना धुआँ। धुआँ कोई अग्नि का रूप नहीं है। मूल शिक्षा का सार तत्व यही है कि वह समाज को सूखी लकड़ी में परिणित कर दे। उससे अविवेक, हिंसा, बेईमानी की आर्द्रता सोख ले। ताकि लकड़ी अग्नि प्रज्वलन का आधार बन सके। आग हमेशा ऊपर ही उठती है। पानी हमेशा नीचे ही बहता है। चाहे मशाल को औंधी कर दें, अग्नि ऊपर ही उठेगी। चाहे दरिया को ऊपर ही उठा दें, पानी नीचे ही बहेगा। पानी लकड़ी की आर्द्रता है। अग्नि लकड़ी का आत्मतत्व है। तभी सूखी लकड़ियों की रगड़ से अग्नि का उद्घाटन होता है। शिक्षा का कार्य आत्मतत्व की अग्नि का उद्घाटन मात्र है ताकि व्यक्ति *'सम्यक् ऊर्ध्व गति'* कर सके। ऊर्ध्व जिसकी गति के लिए अनंत आकाश है। लेकिन हम ऊर्ध्व तो दूर क्षैतिज विकास भी नहीं कर पाए। उल्टे हमने अधोगामी विकास जरूर कर लिया। पानी की गति-सा। पाताल की ओर। विकास के लबादे में बैठा विनाश। शान्ति के कपड़ों में छुपी अशांति। निश्चित ही हमारी शिक्षा को शांति के लिए – *'मुहूर्तं ज्वलितं श्रेयः'* की ओर बढ़ना।

44. 'पानी की गति-सा' पदबंध विकास की किस प्रकृति को इंगित करता है?

A. धनात्मक B. ऋणात्मक

C. क्षैतिज D. ऊर्ध्व

45. 'इस धुआँती जिंदगी ने ...' वाक्य में रेखांकित पद है

A. संज्ञा B. सर्वनाम

C. विशेषण D. क्रियाविशेषण

46. 'लबादे' शब्द 'लबादा' से निर्मित है। स्रोत के आधार पर 'लबादा' शब्द है

A. तत्सम B. तद्भव

C. देशज D. विदेशी

47. 'समस्त समाज आज गीली लकड़ी की तरह बनकर रह गया है।' अवतरण के आधार पर रेखांकित पद से तात्पर्य है

A. अविवेक B. हिंसक

C. बेईमान D. पतनशील

48. लकड़ी का आत्मतत्व है

A. पानी B. सूखापन

C. आर्द्रता D. अग्नि

49. अवतरण के आधार पर 'धुएँ' का कारण है

A. अग्नि B. दीपक

C. गीलापन D. लकड़ी

50. आर्द्र से आर्द्रता का बनना उदाहरण है

A. संज्ञा से विशेषण बनना

B. विशेषण से संज्ञा बनना

C. संज्ञा से संज्ञा बनना

D. विशेषण से विशेषण बनना

51. 'सच्चे जीवन के लिए' प्रयुक्त रूपक है

A. सूखी लकड़ी B. जलता दीपक

C. अनंत आकाश D. मशाल

52. निम्न में से कौन-सा विलोम युग्म के रूप में अवतरण में प्रयुक्त ***नहीं*** हुआ है?

A. शांति – अशांति B. सूखी – गीली

C. गीलापन – आर्द्रता D. अंधेरा – रोशनी

53. 'चौबीसों घंटे धुआँ-सा नजर आ रहा है।' वाक्य में रेखांकित पद है

A. विशेषण B. संज्ञा

C. क्रियाविशेषण D. क्रिया

54. निम्नलिखित में से ऊष्म ध्वनि है

A. त् B. ड़्

C. फ् D. ष्

55. जरा-ज़रा शब्द युग्म का सही अर्थ है

A. थोड़ा – बुढ़ापा B. कुछ – थोड़ा

C. बुढ़ापा – थोड़ा D. थोड़ा – कुछ

56. 'आभूषण' का पर्यायवाची शब्द ***नहीं*** है

A. अलंकार B. विभूषण

C. भूषण D. हार

57. 'तद्रूप' में संधि का प्रकार है

A. स्वरगुण B. स्वर यण

C. व्यंजन D. विसर्ग

58. 'बे' उपसर्ग का प्रयोग कहाँ ***अनुचित*** है?

A. बेफिक्र B. बेफिज़ूल

C. बेचारा D. बेरोकटोक

59. निम्नलिखित में से ***अशुद्ध वर्तनी*** वाले शब्द का चयन कीजिए

A. उद्वहन B. उद्वात

C. उद्घोषित D. उद्भव

60. 'जिस पर किसी का उपकार हो' वाक्यांश के लिए निम्नलिखित में से उपयुक्त शब्द कौन-सा होगा?

A. उपकारी B. उपकृत

C. कृतज्ञ D. परोपकारी

PART- III

Language-II : English

Directions (Qs. 61-65): *Fill in the blanks with the correct alternative:*

61. I .... hardly hear you.

A. can B. can't

C. do D. don't

62. .... do you think you are, any way?

A. Why B. Which

C. Who D. Whether

63. This is strictly between you and ....

A. I B. me

C. we D. us

64. Almost the entire social and administrative structure reeks .... corruption.

A. in B. from

C. of D. about

65. The cost of State funding of election in India runs .... thousands of crores.

A. for B. into

C. about D. in

66. What is the sentence structure of the following sentence?

'Anil very carefully searched the room.'

A. SVOA B. SOVA

C. SVCO D. SAVO

67. Choose the correct ***indirect speech of*** the sentence: He said, "You would not believe me if I told you the real secret."

A. He said that I would not believe him if he told me the real secret.

B. He said that you would not believe me if I told you the real secret.

C. He said that he would not believe him if he told me the real secret.

D. He said that I would not believe it if he told me the real secret.

68. She stumbled over her words <u>so that the audience had difficulty in understanding her.</u>

The underlined group of words is an

A. Adverbial clause of reason

B. Adverbial clause of manner

C. Adverbial clause of condition

D. Adverbial clause of result

69. Give the opposite of 'Zenith'

A. Highest B. Nadir

C. Bottom D. Lower

70. Which of the following is ***not*** an example of a gerund?

A. Running is his idea of relaxation.

B. We were told that smoking is bad for our health.

C. I like sleeping children.

D. The old man was tired of walking.

71. We did it <u>ourselves.</u> The underlined word in the sentence is

A. A pronoun B. An adjective

C. An adverb D. A noun

72. Select the ***correct*** spelling of the following word

A. Haemorhage B. Haemorrhage

C. Heamorhage D. Heamorrhage

73. Choose the correct ***suffix*** to form the word. The meaning of the word is given.

Mani .... = many and various

A. festo B. fold

C. cure D. kin

74. Choose the correct ***passive construction*** of the sentence:

"Hard work and patience can solve even the most difficult problem in this world."

A. Even the most difficult problem in this world could be solved by hard work and patience.

B. Even the most difficult problem in this world can be solved by hard work and patience.

C. Even the most difficult problem in this world had been solved by hard work and patience.

D. Even the most difficult problem in this world would be solved by hard work and patience.

Directions (Qs. 75-79): *Read the following passage carefully and answer the questions given below in the context of the passage:*

The phenomenon of terrorism signifies violence by disgruntled groups of people determined to achieve certain political goals which they find are not attainable by lawful means. This menace has lately assumed a global character and many countries including the U.S.A. are affected by it. Terrorism is actually an infantile attitude, a sign of immaturity. just as certain other movements indicate political senility. It is wrong, however, to believe that terrorists are born. Like Naxalites, radicals and reformers, they are creatures of certain unfavourable conditions and circumstances. These circumstances in turn are often the result of tectless government policies, prolonged delays in redressing political, economic and other grievances. Bitterly disappointed individuals or groups resort to violence in order to focus attention on their problems. Terrorism sprouts and flourishes where there is intense anger and resentment against the administration, the Government's lapses and postures of neglect towards certain discordant elements feed the unrest, and when this reaches a high level it bursts into terrorism. Terrorists generally belong to the lower middle-class but sometimes even to well placed families.

75. Terrorism has lately assumed a

A. serious threat

B. global character

C. national character

D. insular character

76. Like naxalites, terrorists are victims of

A. political interference

B. unemployment and poverty

C. religious discrimination

D. unfavourable and disappointing circumstances

77. What, according to the writer, feeds, terrorism?

A. uncongenial living conditions

B. lower middle-class mindset

C. anger, resentment and neglect

D. ignorance

78. Terrorism is a/an .... trait.

A. inherent B. generic

C. tactless D. acquired

79. Terrorists resort to violence in order to

A. dislodge a ruling party

B. draw attention to their problems

C. get employment

D. terrorise innocent people

Directions (Qs. 80 and 81): *Pick out the word from the given choices that is nearest in meaning to the given word:*

80. Colossal

A. amazing B. huge

C. disclosure D. great losses

81. Obnoxious

A. filthy B. disgusting

C. traumatic D. nocturnal

Directions (Qs. 82 and 83): *Each of the following idioms has four choices. Select the one which gives the correct meaning:*

82. To rest on one's laurels

A. to depend on one's ability

B. to become a parasite
C. to retire from active life
D. to crave for popularity

83. A blue stocking
A. an unhealthy person
B. someone with literary tastes and learning
C. one who discourages others
D. an unreliable person

Directions (Qs. 84 to 90): *Select the sentence that is grammatically correct:*

84. A. The plea for a separate state is too serious a matter to be treated lightly.
B. The plea for a separate state is too serious matter to be treated lightly.
C. The plea for a separate state is too serious a matter to treat lightly.
D. The plea for a separate state is too serious matter to be treat lightly.

85. A. One of our cats have disappeared.
B. One of our cats has disappeared.
C. One of our cat has disappeared.
D. One of our cats has been disappeared.

86. A. Hardly had he left the house than the message came.
B. Hardly had he left the house then the message came.
C. Hardly had he left the house when the message came.
D. Hardly had he left the house and the message came.

87. A. Unless he does not behave well, you should not pardon him.
B. Unless he behaves well, you should not pardon him.
C. Unless he behaves well, you should pardon him.
D. Unless he does not behaves well, you should not pardon him.

88. A. He asked his son are you studying seriously for the examination.
B. He asked his son if he is studying seriously for the examination.
C. He asked his son whether he is studying seriously for the examination.
D. He asked his son whether he was studying seriously for the examination.

89. A. There was hardly anyone at the party, isn't it?
B. There was hardly anyone at the party, wasn't there?
C. There was hardly anyone at the party, was there?
D. There was hardly no one at the party, was there?

90. A. Are you going to invite Ram and myself to your house?
B. Are you going to invite Ram and I to your house?
C. Are you going to invite Ram and me to your house?
D. Are you going to invite both Ram and I to your house?

Answers

1	2	3	4	5	6	7	8	9	10
B	B	D	A	D	A	A	D	C	A
11	**12**	**13**	**14**	**15**	**16**	**17**	**18**	**19**	**20**
A	C	D	C	A	D	B	C	A	A
21	**22**	**23**	**24**	**25**	**26**	**27**	**28**	**29**	**30**
D	B	C	B	A	B	A	C	B	C
31	**32**	**33**	**34**	**35**	**36**	**37**	**38**	**39**	**40**
C	B	C	B	B	C	D	C	B	B
41	**42**	**43**	**44**	**45**	**46**	**47**	**48**	**49**	**50**
C	B	A	B	C	D	A	D	C	B
51	**52**	**53**	**54**	**55**	**56**	**57**	**58**	**59**	**60**
B	C	C	D	C	D	C	B	B	B
61	**62**	**63**	**64**	**65**	**66**	**67**	**68**	**69**	**70**
A	C	B	C	B	D	A	D	B	C
71	**72**	**73**	**74**	**75**	**76**	**77**	**78**	**79**	**80**
A	B	B	B	B	D	C	D	B	B
81	**82**	**83**	**84**	**85**	**86**	**87**	**88**	**89**	**90**
B	C	B	A	B	C	B	D	C	C

Note: *In addition to these 90 Questions, 60 Questions will be asked from Concerned Subjects.*

Previous Years Paper (Solved)

HTET-Post Graduate Teacher (Level-3), 2013

PART-I

CHILD DEVELOPMENT AND PEDAGOGY

Directions: *Answer the following questions by selecting the **most appropriate** option.*

1. In a group situation generally the performance of a student

A. remains same B. become better
C. deteriorate D. None of these

2. Which of the following is ***not*** the tool for formative assessment in scholastic domain?

A. Oral questions
B. Multiple choice questions
C. Projects
D. Assignments

3. What term is used for these characteristics?

(*i*) Consistent in different situations
(*ii*) Relatively stable over time
(*iii*) Variations in their strength leading to individual differences in personality

A. Factor B. Trait
C. Dimensions D. Levels

4. Thurston's primary mental abilities classsification does ***not*** include

A. Memory ability B. Musical ability
C. Word fluency D. Reasoning

5. What is the aim of reinforcement in Clark Hull's learning theory?

A. Reduction of need
B. Reduction of drive
C. Reduction of incentive
D. Reduction of motive

6. As a teacher what do you think about sex education?

A. Should be made compulsory in all schools because it helps children in making adjustments to their new bodily changes
B. Should be banned and not given in schools
C. It is the duty of parents to teaching these things to their children
D. There is possibility that it may disturb the environment of school

7. Among the following, which is ***not*** the other name of Hull's reinforcement theory?

A. Mathematical Theory
B. Need Reduction Theory
C. Biological Adaptation Theory
D. Contiguous Conditioning Theory

8. Which of the following is ***not*** correctly matched?

A. Humanism — Carl Rogers
B. Functionalism — William James
C. Structuralism — John B. Watson
D. Psychoanlysis — Sigmund Freud

9. Who among the following has applied reinforcement in shaping of the behaviour?

A. B.F. Skinner
B. Kurt Koffka
C. Max Wertheimer
D. Gagne

10. Which one is a ***correct*** sequence of stages of creative thinking?

A. Preparation, Illumination, Verification, Incubation
B. Incubation, Verification, Illumination, Preparation
C. Illumination, Preparation, Verification, Incubation
D. Preparation, Incubation, Illumination, Verification

11. Which is the ***correct*** statement about negative reinforcer?

A. Negative reinforcer and punishment both are same thing
B. Due to the presence of negative reinforcer, probability of repetition of response increases
C. Negative reinforcer decreases the probability of unwanted response
D. Negative reinforcer increases the probability of wanted response

12. In which type of learning, a new behaviour is learned but not demonstrated until reinforcement is provided for displaying it?

A. Latent Learning B. Insight Learning
C. Social Learning D. Verbal Learning

13. Respondent behaviour is related to
A. Elicited behaviour
B. Voluntary behaviour
C. Emitted behaviour
D. Operant behaviour

14. The role of cognitive processes in development relate to which of the following?
A. Knowing, experiencing and related mental activities
B. Activities related to physical development
C. Activities related to morality
D. Socio-emotional process

15. During a classroom interaction a student raises a question which you cannot answer there and then. How will you react?
A. Ignore the question and move ahead
B. Admit your inability and promise to answer next day
C. Ask the student not to raise question in the class
D. Scold the student for asking such question

16. A student with high intelligence is not doing well at studies. What is the best course of action for the teacher?
A. Wait till he performs better
B. Find out reasons for his under achievement
C. Give him grace marks in the examination
D. Ask his parents to withdraw him from the school

17. According to Piaget's theory of cognitive development, when does abstract thinking emerge?
A. Concrete operational stage
B. Pre-operational stage
C. Sensory motor stage
D. Formal operational stage

18. According to Kohlberg's Moral Development Theory, at which level, decisions of individual are inter-personal concordance oriented?
A. Post-conventional level
B. Conventional morality level
C. Pre-conventional level
D. Specific response level

19. Concept of curriculum flexibility was introduced to benefit
A. Disabled children
B. Madarsas and Maktabs
C. Scheduled Castes, Scheduled Tribes and Other Backward Classes
D. All of the above

20. The instructional process where the adult adjusts the amount and type of support offered so that it is best suited to the child's level of development is called
A. Assessment B. Adjustment
C. Scaffolding D. Instructing

21. Which one of the following is ***not*** a step of motivational cycle?
A. Drive B. Incentive
C. Need D. Inspiration

22. Among the following test, which one is an example of intelligence test?
A. Thematic Apperception Test
B. Rorschach Ink Blot Test
C. Raven's Progressive Matrices
D. Psycho-drama

23. Which statement is ***incorrect?***
A. Attitudes shape our identity
B. Family has a major influence in the formation of attitudes
C. Learning helps to acquire attitudes
D. Attitudes can not be changed by explaining and talking at all

24. Who gave the concept of mental age?
A. Terman B. Binet
C. Stern D. Spearman

25. When a child sees a world only in terms of their ownselves and are not able to appreciate others point of view, it is called
A. Decentering B. Egocentrism
C. Intuitive thought D. Animism

26. Which one is the highest stage of Gagne's hierarchical structure of learning?
A. Principle learning
B. Chain learning
C. Problem solving learning
D. Concept learning

27. Kohs block design test is an example of
A. Verbal test B. Creativity test
C. Performance test D. Personality test

28. According to Binet, the maximum age level, to which a child solve all the questions correctly, is known as
A. Terminal Year B. Basal Year
C. Credit D. Real Age

29. In which one of the following areas McClelland has major contribution?
A. Achievement Motivation
B. Need for Affiliation
C. Aggression Motivation
D. Power Motivation

30. A female student of your class complains of being teased by a male classmate, you will
A. ask her parents to teach the culprit a lesson
B. ignore her complaint
C. assure girl of the cognizance of her complaint, condemn such behaviour, warn him against such behaviour in future and teach gender sensitivity
D. find fault infemale student for which she has been teased

भाग-II

भाषा-I हिन्दी

निर्देश : *निम्नलिखित के उत्तर देने के लिए सबसे उचित विकल्प चुनिए:*

31. 'आदर' शब्द से विशेषण बनेगा
A. आदरकारी
B. आदरपूर्वक
C. आदरणीय
D. इनमें से कोई नहीं

32. कौन-सा शब्द 'अनु' उपसर्ग के मेल से *नहीं* बना है?
A. अनुगामी
B. अनूठा
C. अनुपात
D. अनुकरण

33. 'राजन' का स्त्रीलिंग है
A. रानी B. राज्ञी
C. राजनी D. राजिन

34. प्रत्यय के योग से बना शब्द *नहीं* है
A. बुढ़ापा B. पीछे
C. अगला D. भूखा

35. 'नौका झील में डूब गई' रेखांकित पद में कारक है
A. अधिकरण B. कर्म
C. अपादान D. करण

36. 'जानबूझ कर संकट में पड़ना' के लिए लोकोक्ति है
A. उड़ता तीर झेलना
B. अंगारों पर पैर रखना
C. आकाश के तारे तोड़ना
D. आ बैल मुझे मार

37. 'न अंधे को न्योतते न दो जने आते' लोकोक्ति का अर्थ है
A. अंधे को बुलावा देने पर तो दो आएँगे
B. न ऐसा कार्य करते न मुसीबत खड़ी होती
C. अनजाने में गलत कार्य करना
D. कोई नहीं

38. निम्न में से सही विलोम शब्दों के युग्म को चुनिए :
A. दुर्जन — साधुजन
B. मेहमान — अतिथि
C. रूक्ष — स्निग्ध
D. वैमनस्य — नवैमनस्य

39. 'बंदर' शब्द का पर्यायवाची *नहीं* है
A. हरि B. शक्र
C. मर्कट D. शाखामृग

40. 'सम् + धि' शब्द की सन्धि होगी
A. समधि B. समधी
C. सन्धि D. समाधि

41. निम्नलिखित मुहावरे का सही अर्थ चुनिए :
'आग लगने पर कुँआ खोदना'
A. संकट आने पर घबराना
B. हाथ-पाँव फूलना
C. आपत्ति आने के बाद बचाव हेतु प्रयत्न
D. पानी ढूँढना

42. 'यथाक्रम' समस्त पद किस समास का उदाहरण है?
A. कर्मधारय
B. बहुव्रीहि
C. तत्पुरुष
D. अव्ययी भाव

43. 'घृतान्न' पद में समास होगा
A. तत्पुरुष
B. बहुव्रीहि
C. द्वन्द्व
D. द्विगु

44. 'आभ्यन्तर' का विलोम शब्द है
A. बाह्य
B. अंतर
C. भीतर
D. अभ्यन्तर

45. 'स्वामी विवेकानन्द ने सभा में उपदेश दिया'—यह किस प्रकार का वाच्य है?
A. कर्मवाच्य
B. भाववाच्य
C. कर्तृवाच्य
D. इनमें से कोई नहीं

निर्देश : *निम्नलिखित गद्यांश को पढ़कर दिए गए प्रश्नों (प्रश्न सं.* **46** *से* **55** *तक) के सबसे उचित विकल्प को चुनिए :*

दूब पशुओं के खुर से कुचली जाती है, खुरपी से छीली जाती है, कुदाली से खोदी जाती है, हल की नोक से उलटी जाती है, अहिंस्र कहे जाने वाले पशुओं से निर्ममता के साथ चरी जाती है और मानवों के सबसे उत्तम वृत्ति रखने वाले खेतिहर से सतायी जाती है; पर वह प्रत्येक जीवन यात्री को वर्षा में फिसलने से बचने के लिए पाँवड़े बिछाती है। जरा-सा भी मौका मिल जाए, तो फैलकर मखमली फर्श बन जाती है, पनघट के मंगल गीतों का उच्छ्वास पाकर वह मरकत की राशि बन जाती है, शरद् का प्रसन्न आकाश जब रीझकर मोती बरसाता है, तब वह धरती की छितरायी आँचर बन जाती

है और जब ग्रीष्म का कुपित रवि आग बरसाता है, तब वह धरती के धीरज की छाँह बन जाती है। उस दूब को यदि नारी पूजा की थाली में सजाती है तो उन समस्त अत्याचारों का क्षण-भर के लिए उपशम हो जाता है जिन्हें दूब प्रतिक्षण सहती रहती है। भारतीय संस्कृति का मूल आधार है तितिक्षा, जिसकी सही अर्थ में मूर्त व्यंजना ही दूर्वा है। तितिक्षा ही के कारण उस संस्कृति की एक शाखा उच्छिन्न होते ही दूसरी शाखा निकल आयी है। जितने ही उस पर मार्मिक आघात हुए हैं, उतने ही शत-सहस्र उमंगों के साथ वह पनपी है। इसी के कारण उसे अप्रतिहत मांगलिक स्वरूप प्राप्त हुआ है। दूर्वा की नोक से जब हल्दी छिड़की जाती है तो ऐसा लगता है कि तितिक्षा के अग्रभाग से साक्षात् सौभाग्य छिड़का जा रहा हो। हल्दी-दूब का यह संयोग सत्व को चिद् और आनंद का मंगलमय परिधान देता है, नहीं तो अपने में सत्व निरापद और अशिव है। उसको अपना गौरव चिद् और आनंद के सुखद संयोग में ही प्राप्त होता है। शायद इसीलिए वह सत्व, राष्ट्र के प्रतीक में हल्दी और दूब के योग का मध्यमान बन गया है।

46. गद्यांश के अनुसार श्रेष्ठ व्यवसाय है
A. व्यापार
B. अध्यापन
C. कृषि
D. कोई नहीं

47. वर्षा में दूब की उपयोगिता है
A. मखमली घास के रूप में
B. फिसलने से बचाने के रूप में
C. आँचर के रूप में
D. शांति-रेखा के रूप में

48. 'शरद के मोती' कहा गया है
A. बर्फ को
B. ओस को
C. पाला को
D. उपर्युक्त सभी को

49. 'तितिक्षा' का अर्थ है
A. प्रतीक्षा
B. निरन्तरता
C. सहिष्णुता
D. प्राचीनता

50. मार्मिक आघातों के बावजूद भारतीय संस्कृति क्यों नहीं नष्ट हुई?
A. क्योंकि यह बहुत मोहक है
B. क्योंकि यह बहुत प्राचीन है
C. क्योंकि इसमें बहुत सहनशीलता है
D. क्योंकि इसमें उमंग है

51. अप्रतिहत मांगलिक वस्तु है
A. भारतीय संस्कृति
B. दूब
C. भारत की धरती
D. इनमें से कोई नहीं

52. सत्व कल्याणकारक होता है
A. हल्दी व दूब के संयोग से
B. चिद् व आनंद के संयोग से
C. शिव के संयोग से
D. उपर्युक्त सभी

53. गद्यांश में किस राष्ट्रीय चिह्न की ओर संकेत है?
A. चतुर्भुज सिंह
B. कमल
C. तिरंगा
D. उपर्युक्त सभी

54. भारतीय संस्कृति व दूब में क्या साम्य है?
A. सहिष्णुता
B. प्राचीनता
C. कोमलता
D. धैर्य

55. 'उपशम' का अर्थ है
A. शान्ति
B. निवारण
C. समाप्ति
D. समायोजन

56. 'सारंग' शब्द का सही अर्थ समूह चुनिए
A. बिजली, मोर, सर्प
B. राग, बादल, हिरन
C. कपूर, सिंह, शंख
D. उपर्युक्त सभी

57. किस शब्द में 'नि' उपसर्ग प्रयुक्त *नहीं* हुआ है?
A. निवेश
B. निस्तार
C. निहित
D. निलम्बित

58. 'मैं इस माह के अन्त तक घर जाने वाला हूँ।'
उपर्युक्त वाक्य में 'इस माह के अन्त तक' है
A. पद बन्ध
B. सामासिक पद
C. पद
D. उपवाक्य

59. शब्द युग्म 'राज़–राज' का सही अर्थ युग्म चुनिए :
A. रहस्य – राज्य
B. राज्य – रहस्य
C. मिस्त्री – राज्य
D. राज्य – गुप्त

60. 'ढ' वर्ण का उच्चारण स्थान है
A. कंठ-तालु
B. तालु
C. दंत
D. मूर्धा

भाग-III

भाषा-II अंग्रेजी

Direction (Q. Nos. 61 to 64) : *Choose the correct option to replace the group of words in* **italics:**

61. The company's profits have increased by 5% *in each of the last* three years.
A. Successive B. Preceding
C. Following D. Respective

62. Appearances can often be *liable to mislead.*
A. Evasive B. Deceptive
C. Defective D. Discursive

63. Having been officially banned, the political party was obliged to meet and operate *in secret.*
A. Stealthily B. Implicitly
C. Vicariously D. Clandestinely

64. The woman trapped in the blazing house was screaming *with uncontrollable emotion and fear.*
A. Tirelessly B. Tremulously
C. Hysterically D. Emotionally

Direction (Q. Nos. 65 & 66) : *Choose the part of the sentence that has an error. If there is no mistake, the answer is 'No error' :*

65. We are not sure (A)/ he is coming (B)/ to the party. (C) / No error. (D)

66. None of my friends (A)/ are applying (B)/ for this job. (C) / No error. (D)

Direction (Q. Nos. 67 & 68) : *Choose the correct option that describes the group of words in* **bold** *type :*

67. Jack has made Jill **an excellent husband.**
A. Direct object B. Object complement
C. Subject complement D. Indirect object

68. The jury declared our team **the winner.**
A. Direct object B. Indirect object
C. Object complement D. Subject complement

Direction (Q. Nos. 69 & 70) : *Choose the option that conveys almost the same meaning as the word in* **bold** *type:*

69. The Government did all it could to bring the **recalcitrant** opposition round to its views.
A. Rebellious B. Conciliatory
C. Accommodating D. Obstinate in opposition

70. I cannot stand his **supercilious** manners.
A. Proud and haughty B. Unfriendly
C. Barbaric D. Intriguing

Direction (Q. Nos. 71 & 72) : *Choose the most suitable 'one word' for the given expression :*

71. A violent and bad-tempered woman
A. Prostitute B. Concubine
C. Virago D. Amazon

72. Clumsy or ill-bred fellow
A. Boor B. Oaf
C. Lout D. Yokel

Direction (Q. Nos. 73 to 75) : *Pick out the best option which can complete the statement correctly and meaningfully:*

73. The more we looked at the piece of modern art ....
A. it looked better.
B. the more we like it.
C. we liked it less.
D. the less we liked it.

74. .... at all is doubtful.
A. If he will come
B. His coming
C. Whether he will come
D. Will he come

75. Experts fail to understand the .... behind the decision to move coal by road when there is enough rail capacity in this sector.
A. Ideology B. Judgement
C. Rationale D. Politics

Direction (Q. Nos. 76 to 85) : *Read the passage given below and answer the questions that follow by choosing the best* **option** *:*

Motivation for ruralism in underdeveloped countries are understandably different from those in developed countries. There, it is a sheer physical necessity for the very act of man's survival. In the Third World countries, which are predominantly rural, the only *lever* that can lift human life above its subhuman level, is rural development. Rural life, in such countries has been stagnating for centuries on end. Nothing worthwhile has been done to ameliorate the conditions of the rural population which is only slightly different from that of their quadruped counterparts. Ignorance, ill health and poverty have become synonyms of rural life in the underdeveloped and undeveloped countries. But the worst tragedy is that the unconcerned human populations have taken this state of affairs for granted, as something unalterable, something for which there is no remedy. Every ray of hope has gone out of their lives. In such countries, rural development is the inevitable condition of any material or non-material advancement. As such, enlightened sections of all such countries have been taking ever growing interest in the question of Rural Development.

This was also part of the legacy of their freedom struggle. In countries like India, it is well-known that attempts at rural development were an inseparable part of the Independence Movement. Leaders like Mahatma Gandhi realized quite well that Real India lived in her stagnating villages. Cities, which were mostly the products of Western colonialism, were just artificial showpieces. Even there, there were two worlds The posh areas, where the affluent few, moslty the products and custodians of imperial interest lived, were little islands engulfed by the vast ocean of dirt, represented by the vast majority of people.

Cities were by no means unknown to India, but in ancient India, they were integral parts, organically related to the rest of the country and society. But modern cities are exotic centres of commerical and industrial exploitation. Cities in ancient India were the flowers of cultural and artistic excellence of the nation, modern cities are just parasites, preying on and *debilitating* the country.

Hence, Gandhiji started the 'Go to Village Movement' which alone, according to him, could bring freedom to India and sustain it. Rural Development had the pride of place in his strategy for the nation's freedom. Thus it had its origin in the freedom struggle.

76. People are taking growing interest in Rural Development because
A. Nothing worthwhile can be done in the near future
B. They have now become optimistic about it
C. They have realized the indispensability of it
D. They have been suffering from severe health problems

77. Which of the following is the 'lever' according to the passage?
A. Upliftment of the rural people
B. Enlightenment of certain sections of the society
C. Non-material advancement
D. Stagnation of rural life

78. Which of the following is the worst tragedy according to the author?
A. Lack of realization of the importance of rural development
B. Exploitation of the rural people by the city-dwellers
C. The subhuman condition of the people
D. The pessimism of the rural people about their own conditions

'9. Which of the following statements is ***not true*** in the context of the passage?
A. Most of the rich people dwelling in modern cities are genuinely concerned about rural development
B. Rural development is a prerequisite of any other advancement and progress
C. The rural folk in the Third World countries feel that their subhuman condition cannot be improved
D. Only rural development can raise the standard of living of people in the Third World countries

80. Rural Development was considered as a part of India's freedom movement because
A. Gandhiji was against the Western colonialism
B. Real India was then under the British rule
C. Imperial interest lived only in villages
D. The country comprised of mainly villages

81. The standard of living of human beings in the Third World countries is
A. Subhuman despite best efforts for improvement
B. Not better than that of animals
C. Improving very rapidly
D. Immune to any improvement

82. In which of the following aspects were the ancient Indian cities different from the modern ones?
A. Wealth
B. Growing population
C. Trade and commerce
D. Oneness with the society

83. Which of the following best describes the two divergent worlds of the modern cities?
A. Commercial and industrial exploitation
B. Patrons of Western products and custodians of imperial interests
C. A few rich people and many poor people
D. Posh area and affluent people

84. Which of the following statements is ***true*** in the context of the passage?
A. The rural folk are very optimistic about improvement in their condition
B. In the present context, ignorance, poverty and ill-health are inseparable parts of rural life
C. Most of the Third World countries are undergoing fast urbanization
D. India's struggle for freedom has been considered as a part of rural development

85. Choose the word which is ***opposite*** in meaning to the given word as used in the passage

DEBILITATING

A. Inhabiting
B. Strengthening
C. Enfeebling
D. Occupying

Direction (Q. Nos. 86 & 87) : *Do as directed :*

86. Who is creating this mess? (Change the voice)
A. Who has created this mess?
B. By whom has this mess been created?
C. By whom this mess is being created?
D. By whom is this mess being created?

87. The spectators said, "Bravo! Well played, Ravi." (Change the narration)
A. The spectators called Ravi bravo because he had played well
B. The spectators said that Ravi played well and applauded him

C. The spectators encouraged Ravi saying that he played well

D. The spectators applauded Ravi saying that he had played well

Direction (Q. Nos. 88 & 89) : *One of the four sentences given in each question is grammatically* ***wrong.*** *That alternative is your answer:*

88. A. Politics is a dirty game.
B. Twenty miles is a long distance.
C. She did nothing but sang.
D. His father is an S.D.O.

89. A. I prefer to read than to write.
B. Each student must bring his pen and paper.
C. Several years have passed since I saw you
D. I have purchased a pair of socks.

90. The cloze technique would be least useful for testing a student's ability to
A. Comprehend a reading passage
B. Project expectations about the outcome of a situation
C. Use structural clues in determining meaning
D. Use socio-cultural clues in learning vocabulary

Answers

1	2	3	4	5	6	7	8	9	10
B	B	B	B	B	A	D	C	A	D
11	**12**	**13**	**14**	**15**	**16**	**17**	**18**	**19**	**20**
D	A	A	A	B	B	D	B	A	C
21	**22**	**23**	**24**	**25**	**26**	**27**	**28**	**29**	**30**
D	C	D	B	B	C	C	B	A	C
31	**32**	**33**	**34**	**35**	**36**	**37**	**38**	**39**	**40**
C	B	B	B	A	D	B	C	B	C
41	**42**	**43**	**44**	**45**	**46**	**47**	**48**	**49**	**50**
C	D	A	A	C	C	B	B	C	C
51	**52**	**53**	**54**	**55**	**56**	**57**	**58**	**59**	**60**
B	B	C	A	B	D	B	A	A	D
61	**62**	**63**	**64**	**65**	**66**	**67**	**68**	**69**	**70**
A	B	D	C	B	B	C	C	D	A
71	**72**	**73**	**74**	**75**	**76**	**77**	**78**	**79**	**80**
C	A	D	C	C	C	A	D	A	D
81	**82**	**83**	**84**	**85**	**86**	**87**	**88**	**89**	**90**
B	D	C	B	B	D	D	C	A	D

Child Development & Pedagogy

SECTION a

CHILD DEVELOPMENT

CONCEPT OF DEVELOPMENT AND ITS RELATIONSHIP WITH LEARNING

The discipline of Child Development is concerned with the changes in the behaviour of children over time and explains why and how they occur. It aims to describe and explain development in the areas of physical, social, emotional, language and cognitive functioning.

Development and Growth

The term 'development' is used for changes in a person's physical and behavioural traits that emerge in orderly ways and last for a reasonable period of time. The three main characteristics of these changes are progressive, orderly and long lasting. Development refers to both quantitative as well as qualitative changes. It includes changes not only in structure but also in function.

'Growth' refers to physical increase in the size of the body. Increase in weight, height and internal organs is growth. Growth refers to a quantitative change, that is, a change that can be measured.

Growth is only one aspect of the larger process of development. Development continues even when physical changes are not visible. Physical growth slows down considerably after adolescence but development does not.

Stages of Development

The human life span has been divided into the stages of infancy, childhood, adolescence and adulthood.

The period from birth to two years of age is referred to as the period of infancy. In this period the child is totally dependent on the caregiver for the fulfilment of his needs. After birth, this is the period of most rapid growth and development. The child's skills and abilities increase. By the end of infancy he is able to walk, run, communicate his needs verbally, feed himself, identify family members, recognise himself and venture confidently in familiar surroundings.

The period of childhood is from two to twelve years of age. Development at this stage is not as rapid as during infancy. During this period the child refines the skills he has acquired during infancy and learns new skill as well. During childhood he also learns the ways of behaviour that are considered appropriate by the society. The child meets many people outside the family and forms attachments with more people. As the child grows and his thinking capacities mature, he realises that he can do many things. This gives him a feeling of confidence. During this period he becomes more independent though adult guidance is constantly needed. The period of childhood is divided into two stages : the period of early childhood (2–6 years) and middle childhood (6–12 years). The period of early childhood is also referred to as the preschool age because at this age the child is learning skills that will help him to do tasks associated with schooling. The preschooler has mastered the words to ask questions about things and people. He learns about numbers, colours, shapes and the reasons for everyday events. All these concepts develop from actually seeing things and doing various activities. The child in the age group 6–12 years has matured a great deal and is expected to behave more responsibly than the preschooler.

The next stage is referred to as the period of adolescence (12–18 years). The beginning of this period is marked by puberty. Puberty refers to the stage around 11–14 years of the age, when there is a spurt in physical growth. This results in a rapid increase in height and weight and the emergence of secondary sexual characteristics. These rapid physical changes lead to a need for emotional readjustment.

At this age the peer group becomes very important and the adolescent follows the rules and the codes of her group. Feelings of loyalty and pride for the group are very strong. At times the values of the peer group may become more important than those of the family. During adolescence thinking develops further and becomes more complex. The individual can understand and deal with varied situations. He can think of abstract problems and work out their solutions. All this helps him to prepare for the roles and responsibilities, which he will be expected to carry out as an adult.

After the age of 18 years the person is referred to as an adult. Physical changes are completed in this stage and person becomes mature.

Areas of Development

The various developments that take place during the life span of an individual can be classified thus: physical and motor development, social development, emotional development, cognitive and language development.

Physical development refers to the physical changes in the size, structure and proportion of the parts of the body that take place from the moment of conception.

Motor development means the development of control over body movements. This results in increasing coordination between various parts of the body. As a result of physical and motor development the child acquires many abilities. These developments will bring about the change from an infant who at the time of birth is capable of only lying on his back to one who learns to roll over, hold his head, sit, walk, run and climb stairs. The improving coordination between the eye and the hand movements will help him to eat food without smearing it on his face. Gradually he will learn to clothe himself, draw, skip, paint, ride a bicycle and type. As he grows he will refine the skills already acquired as well as develop new ones.

Language development refers to those changes that make it possible for an infant, who in the early months uses crying for communication, to learn words and then sentences to converse fluently. How the child learns to speak grammatically correct sentences is amazing! At first the child indicates his need for water through crying. Then he learns to say ''water''. A little later he says, ''Mummy water'' and finally he speaks a complete sentence, ''Mummy, I want to drink water''. He will be about three years by this time.

Cognitive development concerns the emergence of thinking capabilities in the individual. We can see how the child's thinking develops and changes from one age to the next. The infant is not born with the reasoning and thinking, abilities of adults. In fact, the infant acts as if an object that is removed from his sight has ceased to exist. Gradually he learns that objects and people are permanent and they exist even if he cannot see them. Around five years of age he can understand concepts such as heavy and light, fast and slow, colours and sizes which he did not comprehend earlier. Exploration of the surroundings and the questions regarding the 'why' and 'how' of things result in an increasing store of information. His thought develops but he is still unable to see a situation from another person's point of view. For example, he is unable to understand why another child cannot climb the tree when he can do so. He thinks that everybody else should be able to do what he can and feel the way he does. He believes that all things have life and feelings like him including the sun, stone, pencil and table. A ten year old has learnt to reason and analyze but this ability is limited to real life concrete situations. He cannot usually think in abstract terms or predict future event. The capacity for abstruct thinking develops fully during the period of adolescence. He can now handle complex situations. Thus at each stage of a person's life, the ability to think is qualitatively different and more developed compared to the earlier stage.

Cognitive development is the process of mental development from infancy to adulthood. Cognition refers to the process of 'coming to know', which is accomplished through the gathering and processing of information. It includes perceiving, learning, remembering, problem solving, and thinking about the world. Intelligence is a term difficult to define. Nevertheless, according to a well known definition, it refers to the individual's ability to ''act purposefully, think rationally and deal effectively with the environment''.

Social development refers to the development of those abilities that enable the individual to behave in accordance with the expectations of the society. It is concerned with the child's relationships with people and his ways of interaction with them. The infant instinctively reaches out to the person who approaches him with love and affection. Gradually he learns to recognize his mother and other caregivers and forms attachment to them.

Emotional development refers to the emergence of emotions like anger, joy, delight, happiness, fear, anxiety and sorrow and the socially acceptable ways of expressing them. As the child grows up and becomes aware of acceptable ways of behaviour, a variety of emotions also emerge. As an infant he expresses only discomfort and delight. As he grows older, expressions of joy, happiness, fear, anger and disappointment appear. He learns to express these emotions in a healthy manner. For example, initially the child hits out when angry. Gradually he learns to control this and expresses anger in other ways.

Theories of Child Development and Learning

Maturationist Theory

The maturationist theory was advanced by the work of Arnold Gessell. Maturationists believe that development is a biological process that occurs automatically in predictable, sequential stages over time. This perspective leads many educators and families to assume that young children will acquire knowledge naturally and automatically as they grow physically and become older, provided that they are healthy.

School readiness, according to maturationists, is a state at which all healthy young children arrive when they can perform tasks such as reciting the alphabet and counting; these tasks are required for learning more complex tasks such as reading and arithmetic. Because development and school readiness occur naturally and automatically, maturationists believe the best practices are for parents to teach young children to recite the alphabet and count while being patient and waiting for children to become ready for kindergarten. If a child is developmentally unready for school, maturationists might suggest referrals to transitional kindergartens, retention, or holding children out of school for an additional year. These practices are sometimes used by schools, educators, and parents when a young child developmentally lags behind his or her peers. The young child's underperformance is interpreted as the child needing more time to acquire the knowledge and skills needed to perform at the level of his or her peers.

Environmentalist Theory

Theorists such as John Watson, B.F. Skinner, and Albert Bandura contributed greatly to the environmentalist perspective of development. Environmentalists believe the child's environment shapes learning and behaviour in fact, human behaviour, development, and learning are thought of as reactions to the environment. This perspective leads many families, schools, and educators to assume that young children develop and acquire new knowledge by reacting to their surroundings.

Kindergarten readiness, according to the environmentalists, is the age or stage when young children can respond appropriately to the environment of the school and the classroom (*e.g.*, rules and regulations, curriculum activities, positive behaviour in group settings, and directions and instructions from teachers and other adults in the school). The ability to respond appropriately to this environment is necessary for young children to participate in teacher-initiated learning activities. Success is dependent on the child following instructions from the teacher or the adult in the classroom. Many environmentalist-influenced educators and parents believe that young children learn best by rote activities, such as reciting the alphabet over and over, copying letters, and tracing numbers. This viewpoint is evident in kindergarten classrooms where young children are expected to sit at desks arranged in rows and listen attentively to their teachers. At home, parents may provide their young children with workbooks containing such activities as colouring or tracing letters and numbers—activities that require little interaction between parent and child. When young children are unable to respond appropriately to the classroom and school environment, they often are labelled as having some form of learning disabilities and are tracked in classrooms with curriculum designed to control their behaviours and responses.

Constructivist Theory

The constructivist perspective of readiness and development was advanced by theorists such as Jean Piaget, Maria Montessori, and Lev Vygotsky. Although their work varies greatly, each articulates a similar context of learning and development. They are consistent in their belief that learning and development occur when young children interact with the environment and people around them. Constructivists view young children as active participants in the learning process. In addition, constructivists believe young children initiate most of the activities required for learning and development. Because active interaction with the environment and people are necessary for learning and development, constructivists believe that children are ready for school when they can initiate many of the interactions they have with the environment and people around them.

Constructivist-influenced schools and educators pay a lot of attention to the physical environment and the curriculum of the early childhood classroom. Kindergarten classrooms often are divided into different **learning centers** and are equipped with developmentally appropriate materials for young children to play with and manipulate. Teachers and adults have direct conversations with children, children move actively from one center to another, and daily activities are made meaningful through the incorporation of children's experiences into the curriculum. At home, parents engage their young children in reading and storytelling activities and encourage children's participation in daily household activities in a way that introduces such concepts as counting and language use. In addition, parents may provide young children with picture books containing very large print, and toys that stimulate interaction (such as building blocks and large puzzles). When a young child encounters difficulties in the learning process, the constructivist approach is neither to lable the child nor to retain him or her; instead, constructivists give the child some individualized attention and customize the classroom curriculum to help the child address his or her difficulties.

Today, most researchers have come to understand child development and the learning process as articulated by the constructivists. However, this view has not been widely translated into practice. Many kindergarten teachers and parents still believe that young children are not ready for school unless they can recite the alphabet, count, and have the ability to follow instructions from adults.

PRINCIPLES AND THEORIES OF CHILD DEVELOPMENT

Studying and understanding child growth and development are important parts of teaching young children. No two children are alike. Children differ in physical, cognitive, social and emotional growth patterns. Even identical twins, who have the same genetic makeup, are not exactly alike. They may differ in the way they respond to play, affection, objects and people in their environment.

Knowledge of the areas of child development is basic to guiding young children. Linked to this is the understanding of healthy brain development. These stimuli begin at birth. Therefore, it is vital for children to have loving caregivers. Young children need dependable, trusting relationships. They thrive in environments that are predictable and nurturing. Understanding theories about how people develop helps form your knowledge base in caring for young children.

Child Development

Development refers to change or growth that occurs in children. It starts with infancy and continues to adulthood. By studying child development, you will form a profile of what children can do at various ages.

Different names are used to describe young children at different ages. From birth through the first year, children are called **infants. Toddlers** are children from age one up to the third birthday (Because of an awkward style of walking, the name toddler describes this age group). The term **preschooler** is often used to describe children ages three to six years of age.

Areas of Development

The study of child development is often divided into three main areas. These include physical, cognitive and social-emotional development. Dividing development into these areas makes it easier to study.

Physical development refers to physical body changes. It occurs in a relatively stable, predictable sequence. It is orderly, not random. Changes in size and weight are also part of physical development.

Physical skills, such as crawling, walking and writing, are the result of physical development. These skills fall into two main categories:

1. **Grossmotor development :** It involves improvement of skills using the large muscles in the legs and arms. Such activities as running, skipping and bike riding fall into this category.
2. **Fine-motor development :** It involves the small muscles of the hands and fingers. Grasping, holding, cutting and drawing are some activities that require fine-motor development.

Environmental factors also affect what children can do physically. These factors include proper nutrition and appropriate toys and activities.

Cognitive development, sometimes called **intellectual development,** refers to processes people use to gain knowledge. Language, thought, reasoning and imagination are all included. Identifying colours and knowing the difference between one and many are examples of cognitive tasks.

Language and thought are a result of cognitive development. These two skills are closely related. Both are needed for planning, remembering and problem solving. As children mature and gain experience with their world, these skills develop.

The third area of development is called social-emotional development. These two areas are grouped together because they are so interrelated. Learning to relate to others is social development. Emotional development, on the other hand, involves feelings and expression of feelings. Trust, fear, confidence, pride, friendship and humor are all part of social-emotional development. Other emotional traits include timidity, interest and pleasure.

Learning to express emotions in appropriate ways begins early. Caregivers promote this learning when they positively model these skills. A person's self-concept and self-esteem are also part of this area. As children have success with all skills confidence flourishes. This leads to a healthy self-concept and sense of worth.

The physical, cognitive and social-emotional areas of development are linked to one another. Development in one area can strongly influence another area. For instance, writing words requires fine-motor skills. It also requires cognitive development. Language, a part of cognitive development, is needed to communicate with others. It is also necessary for growing socially and emotionally.

Principles of Development

Although each child is unique, the basic patterns or principles of growth and development are universal, predictable and orderly. Through careful observation and interaction with children, researchers and those who work with children understand the characteristics of the principles that follow:

1. Development tends to proceed from the head downward. This is called the **cephalocaudal principle.** According to this principle, the child first gains control of the head, then the arms, then the legs. Infants gain control of head and face movements within the first two months after birth. In the next few months, they are able to lift themselves up using their arms. By 6 to 12 months of age, infant start to gain leg control and may be able to crawl, stand or walk.
2. Development also proceeds from the center of the body outward according to the **proximodistal principle**. Accordingly, the spinal cord develops before other parts of the body. The child's arms develop before the hands and the hands and feet develop before the fingers and toes. Fingers and toes are the last to develop.
3. Development also depends on maturation. **Maturation** refers to the sequence of biological changes in children. These orderly changes give children new abilities. Much of the maturation depends on changes in the brain and the nervous system. These changes assist children to improve their thinking abilities and motor skills. A rich learning environment helps children develop to their potential.

Children must mature to a certain point before they can gain some skills. For instance, the brain of a four-month-old has not matured enough to allow the child to use words. A four-month-old will babble and coo. However, by two years of age, with the help of others, the child will be able to say and understand many words. This is an example of how cognitive development occurs from simple tasks to more complex tasks. Likewise, physical skills develop from general to specific movements. For example, think about the way an infant waves its arms and legs. In a young infant, these movements are random. In several months, the infant will likely be able to grab a block with his or her whole hand. In a little more time, the same infant will grasp a block with the thumb and fore finger.

INFLUENCE OF HEREDITY AND ENVIRONMENT

Heredity and environment greatly influence the growth, development and behaviour of a child. Each child inherits certain capacities for growth. The way in which these capacities develop is influenced by the opportunities afforded by the environment, for example, the height to which the individual is capable of growing is determined by heredity. The environment cannot change the limits imposed by heredity. Whereas a poor environment *i.e.*, lack of exposure will slow down a child who is genetically clever, a rich environment which provides and exposes a child to a lot of educational facilities will not change a child who is genetically born not clever to become clever. A good environment will enable the individual to reach these limits. The environment influences the speed with which the child develops. The environment shapes the individual's development in the sense that it promotes the growth of certain capacities and neglects the growth of others. For instance, if the child experiences more emphasis on academic and no attachment to physical education, the child's capacity to develop certain skills will be neglected.

Effects of Heredity and Environment on Development of Personality

Before discussing the contribution of hereditary factors let us see what is meant by heredity when we talk of heredity we usually have biological heredity in mind. The term 'heredity' may also be used in another sense, for example, if a child is brought up in a particular social environment say of a tribe, the value of that tribe and the norms of that tribe are inculcated in him through other members of that social group and we call it **social heredity.** In the same way, a student in a classroom situation brings with him a specific cultural heredity also. Here our discussion will be focused on the influence of only biological heredity on individual differences. Each individual has a specific set of potentials which are developed through the environment. These potentialities and characteristics possessed by the individual are the result of his biological heredity. The influence of heredity is so strong that twins brought up in drastically different environment show very much similarity in terms of their mental abilities and other traits. This shows that even drastically different environments are not capable of overcoming hereditary influences.

Hereditary, or the genetic transmission of characteristics from parents to offspring, determine personality to a certain extent. Hereditary characteristics manifest at birth such as hair and eye colour, skin colour and body type. Hereditary also includes aptitude or the capacity to learn a skill or inclination for a particular body of knowledge. It establishes the limits of one's personality traits that can be developed. This aptitude creates the desire for a person to learn something. For instance, the son of a sports hero like a boxer superstar is expected to inherit the genes of his father. His capacity for growth in the boxing arena is immense because he is born with the ability.

Behavioural geneticists, Dr. David Reiss and colleagues from George Washington University, conducted a thorough and long-term study on the effects of genetics to a person's personality. The result of their study revealed that 'it seems that genetic influences are largely responsible for how 'adjusted' kids are : how well they do in school, how they get along with their peers, whether they engage in dangerous or delinquent behaviour'.

Effect of Environment on Personality Development

Apart from heredity, environment also effects the child development. The concept of environment needs little clarification when we say the environment of the child is not good, sometimes we mean that he is living in a locality which does not have desirable people or we mean that he is living in the rural area where he does not have access to many things which an urban environment may provide. As has rightly been said, the psychological environment consists of the sum total of the stimulation the individual receives from conception till death. This is an active concept of environment *i.e.*, the physical presence of objects does not in itself constitute environment unless the objects serve as stimuli for the individual.

The role of the prenatal environment on the development of the child is well known and has been demonstrated through various experiments. The diet a mother takes at the time of pregnancy, her mental status, glandular secretions and even the thinking process influence the development of the child. Environmentalists firmly believe that, under favourable circumstances, every individual is almost infinitely improvable.

Newman, Freeman and Holzinger conducted thorough research on nineteen pairs of identical twins reared in different environments. Initially they found that the pairs reared apart show mere differences in I.Q. But Woodworth (1941) in his analysis of the results pointed out a factor called error of measurement that is always involved in intelligence testing. When this factor was taken into account and results interpreted, Woodworth concluded that environmental differences do operate to produce I.Q. differences in persons with exactly the same hereditary potentialities. But the magnitude of these differences is not as large as those found among children whose heredity is not alike.

Environment and its Interaction with Hereditary Factors

Nature refers to what a child has inherited genetically, from the parents (*e.g.* eye colour, appearance, etc). The influence of environment on the development of the child (*e.g.* liking for a type of music) is referred to as nurture. The earlier view of child development focused either entirely on nature or nurture. Many favoured heredity, and believed that we are born with certain talents and personalities. These determine who we are and what we become.

In the other view, the focus was on the role of environment. We learn to do things for which we get rewards (or praises) and do not do things for which we are punished (including disapproval from elders). Both views contained some truth but neither is complete. To understand the development of a person, we have to study the complex interaction between nature and nurture (or heredity and environment).

Let us consider an example. A child is born with a talent for music. In the child's family, this talent for music is expressed by the child at an early age, through his activities of singing and listening to music. The parents notice the child's interest in music and expose the child to more music and give him a toy musical instrument (*e.g.* ek tara or flute). The child's interest in music grows further and his talent develops and this make the parents offer even more musical experiences (*e.g.* playing music on stage, attending music concerts etc.). This has a further positive effect on the child's talent and his desire to play music.

It is thus clear that both the child's inherited talent and environment shaped his/her development. The child had the talent for music, but this led to a change in the environment by making her parents provide more musical experiences at home. Now these experiences in the environment further developed the child's talent and motivation and made the parents introduce more musical experiences to the child. The process goes on and on like this in a form of transaction. This approach to understanding development is called a transactional model (TA).

The TA model is able to explain why brothers and sisters, though physically in the same environment, always grow up in 'different' ways. This simply means that the environment of family life is always changing in the process of adjusting to the personalities of its members. A first born child grows up with very different experiences than a middle born or youngest child. A child who displays temper tantrums (getting angry easily, without sufficient cause) has a very different experience with her parents as compared to her easy going brother.

Let us take another example to make the point more clear. Suppose you as a parent (if not today, then in the future) are facing difficulty with your argumentative 12-year-old. The TA model reminds you that you must first think about the factor which has brought your child to this point. Is it a personality trait that is troubling you? Is she stubborn (does not listen to others) all the time and is thus part of her nature? Does she resist any change in her usual routine? Does she lack the ability to talk to you about what's troubling her, and could that be upsetting her? The child represents one part of the puzzle or problem which has to be solved.

The next questions you have to ask are : What is my role in all this? Am I somehow rewarding the very behaviours? Am I trying to stop by paying too much attention to them? Am I having too much expectation from a 12-year old? Am I reminded of my younger sister with whom I had faced a similar problem, and could be causing irritation in me now? The environment which includes you forms the other-part of the picture.

Finally, you need to put the two together to obtain a full picture of what is going on and how to bring about a positive change. In which way my behaviour is affecting my child? And most importantly, what do I need to change to break this pattern of behaviour (argumentation in the child) located in its transactions with nurture? How can I better understand the forces behind my child's behaviour so as to improve my response to it?

This may sound very theoretical to some of you but it's exactly the questions which many parents are always asking themselves, even if they are not aware of it. By understanding the TA-model you will be in a better position to understand the interaction between nature and nurture which is responsible for your child's behaviour and development. This will help you in deciding which role you can play for effective development and improve the child's behaviour.

In summary according to the transactional model of development, the child changes the environment which in turn changes the child. The child's development is like a complex dance in which nature and nurture both lead, and are led.

SOCIALISATION PROCESS

As a child grows up, there is a deliberate and conscious effort made through active training to make the child learn the values and expectations of the society he or she lives in. The child has to learn to adjust and accommodate her behaviour according to the rules for appropriate behaviour in the society. Parents, teachers, elders as well as the peers (same age group children) all influence and control the behaviour of a child.

According to the Indian view, a child comes to this world with certain behavioural tendencies which carry over from previous birth. The role of the family is to bring up the child in such a way that her positive capacities are developed fully and negative tendencies are controlled. Apart from the family, there are also other influences on the child from the outside environment. The important agents of socialisation include media, day-care centers, peer group, school and religion.

Parents have the most direct effect on the socialisation of the child. They are role models for children. Their responses to child behaviour, giving approval or disapproval etc. mould the personality of child and plays a very important role in acquiring rules. In addition, parents arrange the environment of a children in different ways. They take the child outside in specific settings like museum, church, temple, mosque, hill station, sea beach. The grand parents and aunts and uncles of the child also contribute in the socialisation process. Children learn manners and skills by observing parents. During the life span of a person, at different ages, specific rituals are performed. These rituals represent the changes in the child from one stage to another. They contribute in forming the identity of the child.

The influence of the **peer group** of the child, particularly during middle childhood is very important. In the interactions with the children of the same age group, a child learns the importance of team work, sharing and trust. One of the significant effects of this is that the child learns to adjust and accommodate to the view point of the others.

The school which the child attends is another very important socializing agent. The child learns different types of social, intellectual and physical skills in school. The school provides the child with a miniature society where he or she has to learnt the right values and rules and follow them. Values such as honesty, democracy and fairness etc. are learnt in the school setting.

Now-a-days, children search and know the world through TV, magazines, books, comics, radio and films. This media influences the socialisation of the child in significant ways. A positive influence can be learning the importance of family values by watching good and informative programmes. Watching aggressive programmes and programmes based on violence can influence the child negatively.

In the present way of life, when both parents are doing jobs, very young children have to be left at day-care centers. These centers, therefore, play an important role in the socialisation of the child because the child will learn many things about appropriate behaviour in the society. For children from poor background the Aganwadis under the programme of Integrated Child Developments (ICDs) help children to learn about appropriate social behaviour and the importance of community life.

Theories of Development

Psychologists continue to study human development. They are learning more about what people are like and how they develop. Over the past century, many psychologists have provided theories that are considered practical guides. A theory is a principle or idea that is proposed, researched and generally accepted as an explanation. Developmental theories provide insights into how children grow and learn. Theories are helpful for understanding and guiding developmental processes.

Theories can be useful decision-making tools. Since a variety of theories exists, teachers need to understand these different approaches for working with children. Theories will help you understand strategies for promoting children's development. Four major theories about how children learn are important. These include theories of mid-twentieth century psychologists Erik Erikson, Jean Piaget and Lev Vygotsky. The final theorist, Howard Gardner, is a twenty first century developmental psychologist. These theories are based on observation and experiences with children.

Erikson's Psychosocial Theory

Erik Erikson proposed a theory of psychosocial development. He believed development occurs throughout the life span. His theory provided new insights into the formation of a healthy personality. It emphasizes the social and emotional aspects of growth. Children's personalities develop in response to their social environment. The same is true of their skills for social interaction.

Erikson's theory includes eight stages. At each stage, a social conflict or crisis occurs. These are not generally tragic situations; however, they require solutions that are satisfying both personally and socially. Erikson believed that each stage must be resolved before children can ascend to the next stage.

Maturity and social forces help in the resolution of the crisis or conflict. Therefore, teachers and parents play a powerful role in recognizing each stage. By providing social opportunity and support, teachers and parents can help children overcome each crisis. Following table contains the first four stages of Erikson's theory. These stages occur during the early childhood years. The paragraphs that follow give a brief overview of these early stages.

Erikson's Stages of Development During Early Childhood

Stage	Approximate Age	Psychosocial Crisis
I	Birth–18 months	Trust versus mistrust
II	18 months–3 years	Autonomy versus shame and doubt
III	3–5 years	Initiative versus guilt
IV	6–12 years	Industry versus inferiority

Note : *The first four stages of Erikson's theory concern children from birth to twelve years.*

Stage 1 : Trust Versus Mistrust

During the first eighteen months of life, children learn to trust or mistrust their environment. To develop trust, they need to have warm, consistent, predictable, and attentive care. They need caregivers who will accurately read and respond to their signals. When infants are distressed, they need to be comforted. They also need loving physical contact, nourishment, cleanliness, and warmth. Then they will develop a sense of confidence and trust that the world is safe and dependable. Mistrust will occur if an infant experiences an unpredictable world and is handled harshly.

Stage 2 : Autonomy Versus Shame and Doubt

This second stage occurs between eighteen months and three years of age. During this stage, toddlers use their new motor and mental skills. They want to be independent and do things for themselves. They are in the process of discovering their own bodies and practicing their developing locomotor (physical movement) and language skills.

The objective of this stage is to gain self-control without a loss of self-esteem. Fostering independence in children is important. At this age, toddlers start to become self-sufficient. They need to learn to choose and decide for themselves. To do this, toddlers need a loving, supportive environment. Positive opportunities for self-feeding, toileting, dressing and exploration will result in *autonomy,* or independence. On the other hand, overprotection or lack of adequate activities results in self-doubt, poor achievement, and shame.

Stage 3 : Initiative Versus Guilt

Between three and five years of age, the third stage occurs. According to Erikson, it emerges as a result of the many skills children have developed. Now children have the capacity and are ready to learn constructive ways of dealing with people and things. They are learning how to take initiative without being hurtful to others. They are also busy discovering how the world works. Children begin to realize that what they do can have an effect on the world, too. Challenged by the environment, children are constantly attempting and mastering new tasks. Aided by strong initiative, they are able to move ahead energetically and quickly forget failures. This gives them a sense of accomplishment.

Children at this stage need to develop a sense of purpose. This happens when adults direct children's urges toward acceptable social practices. If children are discouraged by criticism, feelings of incompetence are likely to emerge. This can also occur if parents demand too much control.

Stage 4 : Industry Versus Inferiority

The major crisis of this stage occurs between six and twelve years of age. At this time, children enjoy planning and carrying out projects. This helps them learn society's rules and expectations. During this stage, children gain approval by developing intellectual skills such as reading, writing, and math.

The way family, neighbours, teachers, and friends respond to children affects their future development. Realisfic goals and expectations enrich children's sense of self. Children can become frustrated by criticism or discouragement, or if parents demand too much control. Feelings of incompetence and insecurity will emerge.

PIAGET'S COGNITIVE DEVELOPMENT THEORY

Jean Piaget's thinking has challenged teachers to focus on the *ways* children come to know as opposed to *what* they know. His theory of cognitive development focuses on predictable cognitive (thinking) stages. Piaget believed that thinking was different during each stage of development. His theory explained mental operations. This includes how children perceive, think, understand and learn about their world.

Piaget believed that children naturally attempt to understand what they do not know. Knowledge is gathered gradually during active involvement in real-life experience. By physically handling objects, young children discover that relationships exist between them. Terms Piaget used to describe these processes were *schemata, adaptation, assimilation* and *accommodation.* These processes occur during each stage of development.

Schemata are mental representations or concepts. As children receive new information, they are constantly creating, modifying, organizing and reorganizing schemata.

Adaptation is a term Piaget used for children mentally organizing what they preceive in their environment. When new information or experiences occur, children must adapt to include this information in their thinking. If this new information does not fit with what children already know, a state of imbalance occurs. To return to balance, adaptation occurs through either assimilation or accommodation.

Assimilation is the process of taking in new information and adding it to what the child already knows.

Accommodation is adjusting what is already known to fit the new information. This process is how people organize their thoughts and develop intellectual structures.

Piaget's stages of cognitive development are the same for all children. Most children proceed through the stages in order. Each stage builds on a previous stage. However, the age at which a child progresses through these stages is variable due to differences in maturation.

Although Piaget did not apply his theory directly to education, he did strongly influence children's early education. Many teaching strategies have evolved from his work. Caregivers and teachers now know that learning is an active process. Providing children with stimulating, hands-on activities helps them build knowledge. Piaget's theory includes four stages: sensorimotor, preoperational concrete, and formal operations. The first three stages occur during early childhood and the early school-age years. The following paragraphs describe these stages.

Piaget's Stages of Development

The **sensorimotor stage** takes place between birth and two years of age. Infants use all their senses to explore and learn. In this way, sensory experiences and motor development promote cognitive development. Babies' physical actions, such as sucking, grasping and hitting, help them learn about their surroundings. Movements are random at first. Gradually they become intentional as behaviours are repeated. Children begin to learn that objects still exist even when they are out of sight. This is known as *object permanence.* Through exploration and exposure to new experiences, new concepts are learned.

The **preoperational stage** takes place between ages two and seven. Children during this stage are very *egocentric*. This means that they assume others see the world the same way they do. Children do not yet have the ability to see others' points of view. During this time, representation skills are learned. These skills include language, symbolic play, and drawing. Children learn to use symbols and internal images, but their thinking is illogical. It is very different from that of adults. Children begin to understand that changing the physical appearance of something does not change the amount of it. They are able to recognize the difference between size and volume. For example, a ball of clay can be stretched into a long rope. Even if the physical appearance changes, the amount of the object does not change. This skill is called *conservation.* At this stage, children can also classify groups of objects and put objects in a series in order.

During the ages of seven to eleven years, **concrete operations** begin. Children develop the capacity to think systematically, but only when they can refer to actual objects and use hands-on activities. Then they begin to internalize some tasks. This means they no longer need to depend on what is seen. They become capable of reversing operations. For example, they understand that 3 + 1 is the same as 1 + 3. When real situations are presented, they are beginning to understand others' points of view.

The fourth stage, *formal operations,* takes place from eleven years of age to adulthood (the age range you are in right now). According to Piaget, young people develop the capacity to think in purely abstract ways. They no longer need concrete examples. Problem solving and reasoning are key skills developed during this stage.

VYGOTSKY'S SOCIOCULTURAL THEORY

Both Jean Piaget and Lev Vygotsky believed that children build knowledge through experiences. Piaget believed this happened through exploration with hands-on activities. Vygotsky, on the other hand, believed that children learn through social and cultural experiences. Interactions with peers and adults help children in this process. While interacting with others, children learn the customs, values, beliefs, and language of their culture. For this reason, families and teachers should provide plently of social interaction for young children.

Vygotsky believed language is an important tool for thought and plays a key role in cognitive development. He introduced the term ***private speech,*** or self-talk. This refers to when children ''think out loud''. After learning language, children engage in this self-talk to help guide their activity and develop their thinking. Generally, self-talk continues until children reach school age.

One of Vygotsky's most important contributions was the *zone of* ***proximal development*** (ZPD). This concept presents learning as a scale. One end of the scale or ''zone'' includes the tasks that are within the child's current development level. The other end of the scale includes tasks too difficult for children to accomplish, even with help. In the middle are the tasks children cannot accomplish alone. These are achieved with help from another knowledgeable peer or adult. The term used for this assistance is ***scaffolding.*** Just as a painter needs a structure on which to stand and point a building, scaffolding provides the structure for learning to occur. For example, a teacher could scaffold a child's learning while constructing a puzzle. The teacher might demonstrate how a piece fits or provide clues regarding colour, shape or size. The ''zone'' is constantly changing. In contrast to Piaget, Vygotsky believed that learning was not limited by stage or maturation. Children move forward in their cognitive development with the right social interaction and guided learning.

KOHLBERG'S THEORY OF DEVELOPMENT

According to him moral development of the child proceeds in sequential but distinctive stages. These stages are given below:

(a) **Stage-I :** In the early years of a child's life (from zero-four years) the physical consequences of an action determines its goodness or badness. If fire burns the child, he does not touch it. The child is ego-centric and standards of morality are external here.

(b) **Stage-II :** The child gives importance to his own point of view, (his self) and is able to take account of other's roles insofar as he can use them in his own way. This is a period of make belief. Right action is what which satisfies the needs of the child. The role of others is also important in the sense that a child does only what can bring approval of others. Thus, only that behaviour is moral which can satisfy not only self needs of the child but it must please others also.

(c) **Stage-III :** At this stage the child adopts the view pints of others on the basis of their consequences. He does not question the views of others. The child considers only that thing as right which are considered as right by others. Thus, the child is totally conformist to the standard of the society.

(d) **Stage-IV:** At this stage, the child is able to make any moral decision on his own without caring for the thinking of others. Though he considers laws and regulations set by the society as the essence of morality, yet he develops his own principles of morality on various occasions. Thus, he is a non-conformist to the norms of the society to a great extent.

(e) **Stage-V :** Standards and norms are more internalized here. The adolescents examine various view points prepared by different societies and recognize them. They think that the laws prepared by their own society are correct. Other societies may have good moral principles that must be adopted after careful appraisal.

(f) **Stage-VI :** This is the last stage of moral development according to Kohlberg. Here the universality of the view points of the individual is seen. He formulates his own universal moral principles which he thinks that all societies should adhere to it. True understanding of right and wrong is developed at this stage.

Gardner's Multiple Intelligences Theory

Howard Gardner has helped teachers rethink how they work with young children. Traditional intelligence tests mainly focus on language and math/logic skills. In contrast, Gardner's theory of **multiple intelligences** emphasizes that there are different kinds of intelligences used by the human brain. Gardner believes intelligence is the result of complex interactions between children's heredity and experiences. This theory focuses on how cultures shape human potential.

Gardner claims that children learn and express themselves in many different ways. In the process, they are using several types of intelligence. Each intelligence functions separately, but all are closely linked. According to Gardner, a potential intelligence will not develop unless it is nurtured. Learning can best be achieved by using a child's strongest intelligence. Gardner claims, however, that all children need opportunities to develop all areas of intelligence.

The multiple intelligence theory allows teachers to see the positive attributes of all children. Teachers also view Gardner's theory as a meaningful guide for making curriculum decisions. It gives them a chance to assess children's learning strengths. From this data, teachers can plan a wide variety of learning experiences. Following chart lists Gardner's eight intelligences. The paragraphs that follow explain these intelligences in detail.

(i) Bodily-Kinesthetic Intelligence

Bodily-kinesthetic intelligence involves the ability to control body movements. This includes using parts of the body to solve problems, handle objects, and express emotions. People with this type of intelligence typically enjoy sports, dance or creative drama. They are able to express themselves with their entire bodies. Children will benefit from creative-movement experiences and role-playing.

Children with this type of intelligence process knowledge through sensation. They enjoy touch and creating with their hands. Therefore, daily opportunities should be provided for hands-on activities. Clay, sand, dough, feely boxes and other sensory activities help them develop fine-motor skills. Movement is also needed for gross-motor skills and coordination. It is important for caregivers and teachers to provide activities involving physical challenges. These may include playing kickball, jumping rope, and moving to music.

(ii) Musical-Rhythmic Intelligence

Musical-rhythmic intelligence involve the ability to recognize musical patterns. It also includes the ability to produce and appreciate music. Since music evokes emotion, this is one of the earliest intelligences to emerge. Composers and musicians are examples of people with this type of intelligence.

Children with this type of intelligence love listening to music. They are drawn to the art of sound and appreciate all forms of musical expression. They have a well-developed auditory sense and can discriminate tone, pitch and rhythmic patterns. As a result, they often cannot get songs out of their minds. You will hear them repeatedly singing or humming. This helps them understand concepts and remember information.

Activities to support musical intelligence can be included throughout the day. Offer opportunities for sound exploration through listening and singing. Use songs for directions and moving children from one activity to another. Play background music during self-selected play. Include songs during large and small group activities. Record the children creating their own music while singing or chanting. Explore rhythm by moving to recorded music. Use different instruments and instruments from other cultures to add variety.

(iii) Logical-Mathematical Intelligence

Logical-mathematical intelligence is more than just the ability to use math. It is the ability to use logic and reason to solve problems. Math experts have this form of intelligence. Scientists and composers may also have it. This intelligence involves the ability to explore categories, patterns and other relationships. It includes applying the principle of cause and effect. It also involves the skill to make predictions about patterns.

Children with this type of intelligence take pleasure in finding patterns and relationships. They enjoy discovering similarities and differences. Manipulatives for matching, measuring, and counting should be provided. Blocks can encourage the children's problem-solving and reasoning skills. Storybooks that show a sequence of events hold appeal for this type of intelligence. Water and sand activities with different-size containers help teach the concept of volume.

(iv) Verbal-Linguistic Intelligence

Verbal-linguistic intelligence involves the ability to use language for expression. People with this type of intelligence have well-developed language skills. They demonstrate sensitivity to the meaning, sound and rhythm of words. Lawyers, poets, public speakers and language translators have this type of intelligence.

Young children with this intelligence learn best by talking, listening, reading and writing. These children quickly learn the words to new stories, songs and finger plays. They enjoy talking to other people and are able to speak in an interesting and engaging manner. They are also able to learn a second language with ease.

This intelligence can be nurtured by environments rich with language opportunities. Children learn language in setting where it is used. Teachers need to follow the children's interests. They can then use these interests to engage children in meaningful conversations. Children's storybooks, songs, poetry, chants, and rhymes can serve as means for learning new vocabulary words. Listening to and telling stories can also promote language development.

(v) Interpersonal Intelligence

People with *interpersonal intelligence* display excellent communication and social skills. These people have a gift for understanding the feelings, behaviours, moods and motives of others. They make friends easily. They use language to develop trust and bonds with others. They are also skilled in supporting others and empathizing with them. These skills are important for teachers, politicians, salespeople and people working in the service industry.

These skills are nurtured in young children when caring behaviours are modeled for them. Teachers should keep this in mind. They can share experiences and provide the children with chances for verbal interaction. Books focusing on emotions can be acted out.

(vi) Intrapersonal Intelligence

Intrapersonal intelligence is the ability to understand the inner self. This is also known as *self-awareness.* It involves knowing your skills, limits, and feelings. It includes understanding your desires and motives. The ability to organize groups of people is part of this strength. Communicating needs clearly is another aspect. Psychologists, social workers, religious leaders, and counsellors are examples of people with this type of intelligence.

How can you foster this type of intelligence? In the classroom, share emotions that all children experience. These include joy, sadness, regret and disappointment. Classroom examples should be shared as well as storybooks that contain emotional concepts.

(vii) Visual-Spatial Intelligence

Visual-spatial intelligence allows people to use their vision to develop mental images. People who have this type of intelligence show a preference for pictures and images. Photographers and artists are some examples. Architects, engineers, and surgeons also need this ability. They use it to see the relationship of objects in space.

Teachers can foster this intelligence by providing children with unstructured materials. Building blocks and puzzles strengthen this type of intelligence, 4-18. Make and use visual aids wherever possible. For example, classroom schedules, recipes, and stories can all be displayed on charts. Shelving units can be labelled with pictures cut from equipment catalogs.

(viii) Naturalistic Intelligence

Naturalistic intelligence is developed from the need to survive. This is the ability to classify objects in nature such as animals and plants. It depends on a type of pattern recognition. This strength also includes the ability to distinguish among types and brands of objects. Sailors, gardeners, chefs, and farmers are people who have this intelligence.

To build on this intelligence, provide cooking activities and nature walks. These help develop use of the senses to gather information. Planting and growing a garden helps the children observe cycles. Rocks, seashells, flowers, leaves, seeds, and coins can also be collected. In the classroom, they can be sorted and classified. Post picture collections and share books about natural events.

CONCEPTS OF CHILD-CENTERED AND PROGRESSIVE EDUCATION

Child-Centered Education

Child-centered education is the idea that the needs and desires of the child should take precedence in structuring the learning day. The whole idea is that learning should be fun and engaging for the child, and is most likely to be that way if the child is incharge of the learning experience, rather than the adult parent or teacher.

Child-centered education is most characterised by learning 'centers' in a classroom that promote hands-on, active participation by the child. There may be magnifying glasses and bug slides in the science center, books and puppets that could be used to re-tell the stories in the language arts center, and wood blocks and shapes in the math center. The children are free to manipulate the objects in these centers. It is the process, the activity, the experience, that is valuable, not the facts, ideas, concepts or skills.

It is a relatively new approach to education. For centuries past, adults defined what education should be and children were the ones who did the adjusting. Education was considered work, not play.

Then came the softening influences of child psychologist Jean-Jacques Rousseau, as well as Dr. Marria Montessori, John Dewey, Jean Piaget and Lev Vygotsky, who all contended that a child's self-esteem and self-concept should be built up in order to create a better learner. Soon, the colleges of education were promoting child-centered education instead of instructionally centered education.

Role of Learner in Child-Centered Education

Learners are active as opposed to passive recipients of knowledge. Learners may assume a decision-making role in the classroom. Learners often decide what is to be learned, through which activities and at what pace. Learners can also produce materials and provide activities for the classroom.

Role of Teacher in Child-Centered Education

To put this approach into practice, teachers need to help students set achievable goals; they encourage students to assess themselves and their peers; help them to work co-operatively in groups and ensure that they know how to make use of all the available resources for learning.

Progressive Education

During most of the twentieth century, the term 'progressive education' has been used to describe ideas and practices that aim to make schools more effective agencies of a democratic society. Although there are numerous differences of style and emphasis among progressive educators, they share the conviction that democracy means active participation by all citizens in social, political and economic decisions that will affect their lives. The education of engaged citizens, according to this perspective, involves two essential elements: (1) respect for diversity, meaning that each individual should be recognised for his or her own abilities, interests, ideas, needs, and cultural identity, and (2) the development of critical, socially engaged intelligence, which enables individuals to understand and participate effectively in the affairs of their community in a collaborative effort to achieve a common good. These elements of progressive education have been termed 'child-centered' and 'social reconstruction' approaches, and while in extreme forms they have sometimes been separated, in the thought of John Dewey and other major theorists they are seen as being necessarily related to each other.

The term 'progressive' arose from a period (roughly 1890–1920) during which many Americans took a more careful look at the political and social effects of vast concentrations of corporate power and private wealth. Dewey, in particular, saw that with the decline of local community life and small scale enterprise, young people were losing valuable opportunities to learn the arts of democratic participation, and he concluded that education would need to make up for this loss. In his Laboratory School at the University of Chicago, where he worked between 1896 and 1904, Dewey tested ideas he shared with leading school reformers such as Francis W. Parker and Ella Flagg Young. Between 1899 and 1916 he circulated his ideas in works such as The School and Society, The Child and the Curriculum, Schools of Tomorrow, and Democracy and Education, and through numerous lectures and articles. During these years other experimental schools were established around the country, and in 1919 the Progressive Education Association was founded, aiming at "reforming the entire school system of America".

Therefore, progressive education is a reaction against the traditional style of teaching which teaches facts largely at the expense of understanding what is being taught. According to **John French,** "The progressive school teaches the child to think for himself instead of passively accepting stereotyped ideas. It keeps always in mind that each child is different from every other, and that what makes an educated person useful in his particular walk of life, what makes him interesting, what makes him an individual, is not his resemblance to other people, but his differences".

Philosophies and Practices of Progressive Education

1. Curriculum is strongly influenced by what the children are interested in, and is child-centered rather than adult driven.
2. Learning is 'hands-on', experiential and the emphasis is on process rather than product children are 'learning to learn'.
3. Children learn through integrated, theme-based units or inquiry projects and the 'theme' often emerges from the children.
4. Assessment is authentic and holistic. Children are well known by their teachers and peers.

There are no tests or letter grades. Instead, narrative reports are written about children that cover all aspects of their development: social, emotional, personal, physical and intellectual level.

5. Classes are usually of mixed ages and no ability grouping is used. Children are able to work at their own pace and cross-age friendships are encouraged.
6. Progressive education practices a developmental approach which holds that each child is a unique being unfolding and developing at their own pace according to a specific pattern. At each stage of development there are things that can be learned and things that should not be learned. Respecting a child's development is central to progressive education.

Types of Progressive Education

1. **Humanistic :** The humanistic form of progressive education focuses on the humanities, arts and social sciences. Its emphasis is on the individual child and not the curriculum. This type of progressivism aims to build a well-rounded individual with highly developed critical thinking and reasoning skills. The children learn think for themselves instead of accepting everything teachers tell them. Social development and interaction among the students are seen as valuable learning techniques.
2. **Constructivism :** Constructivism is a type of child-centered progressivism. It focuses on the child's creativity and learning abilities. Teachers should build the curriculum around the requirements and interests of the child. It maintains that education should consider children's developmental stages. Swiss psychologist **Jean Piaget** influenced the theories of constructivist education. Experiential learning, or learning by doing, allows students to construct their own knowledge.
3. **Montessori :** Italian doctor Marria Montessori started the Montessori progressive educational system. She developed her teaching theories by clinical observation and analysis of how children learn. Her method of education focused on how children naturally learn, all by themselves, without the help of adults. Maria Montessori concluded that children teach themselves, and it's the job of teachers to facilitate this process, not dominate it. Montessori teachers provide a sensory-rich environment and hands-on activities.

CRITICAL PERSPECTIVE OF THE CONSTRUCT OF INTELLIGENCE

Introduction

The most important variable that affects schooling or performance on a job is intelligence. Psychologists have interpreted the term intelligence in different ways and there is no consensus among them on the term even so far. In psychology this term is treated as a construct whose structure is different in different individuals.

The vagueness of the term arises due to the fact that intelligence is not a concrete material. It is rather abstraction from the behaviour of the individual which is indirectly inferred and elaborated as an adjective.

The dictionary meaning of term "intelligence" is the capacity to acquire and apply knowledge. **Boring** defines intelligence as intelligence is what an intelligence test measures.

Definitions of Intelligence

Several psychologists have classified and defined intelligence in several ways. Some of them are given below:

1. Vernon's Classification of Intelligence

(a) *Biological Approach:* Man is an organism among millions living on earth. Environment works as a foe for him. Intelligence is the capacity to adapt to the environment or new situations of life at every moment.

This definition of intelligence can be criticized on the ground that there have been many intelligent and renowned persons who were ill adapted to their social and physical environment. Besides, if we want to study individual differences in a society, this definition serves no practical purpose.

(b) *Psychological Approach :* According to psychologists intelligence is the relative effects of heredity and environment both. An English psychologist, **C. Burt** defined intelligence as the innate general cognitive ability.

In support of psychological definitions of intelligence **Hebb** and **R.B. Catell** distinguished two kinds of intelligence. The first is intelligence "A" which is Fluid intelligence and which is related to genetic potentialities or innate qualities of the individual's nervous system. Second is intelligence "B" which is crystalised "intelligence" and which is related to experiences, learning and environmental factors. These two types of intelligence in normal circumstances so much overlap on each other that they are practically indistinguishable.

(c) *Operational Approach :* These definitions help us to understand the concept of intelligence in clear and definite terms. In this approach scientific terms are first of all defined operationally and then observations are conducted with reference to these terms. For example, in order to determine a child's IQ, we first administer a test of a specific kind. Then we observe his performance on the test and finally draw certain conclusions in the context of the pre-determined objectives.

2. Freeman's Classification

(a) *Ability of adjustment :* An individual is intelligent to the extent to which he is able to adjust to new situations and problems of life. The more a person is intelligent, the more he is able to adapt to his environment in antagonistic conditions. The person who is low in intelligence has less capacity to adjust to the new situations of life.

(b) *Ability of learning :* Learning ability is also an index of intelligence. The more a person is intelligent, the more he will be able to learn new things.

(c) *Ability to carry on abstract thinking :* This category of definitions of intelligence is related to the effective use of concepts and symbols in dealing with situations and solving the problems through the use of verbal and numerical symbols. According to **Terman**, an individual is intelligent to the extent he is able to carry on abstract thinking.

3. E.L. Thorndike's Classification

(a) *Concrete intelligence :* The intellectual ability in relation to concrete materials is called concrete intelligence. It is the ability of a person to comprehend the actual situations and react to them adequately. This kind of intelligence is measured by using performance tests or picture tests in which the subject manipulates the concrete materials.

(b) *Abstract intelligence :* It is the ability to respond to words, letters, numbers or symbols. This type of intelligence is required in all academic activities in schools or outside the schools. The highest level of abstract intelligence is manifested in the thoughts of philosophers or in the inventions of scientists and mathematicians.

(c) *Social intelligence :* It is the ability of an individual to react to social situations of life. It is the ability to understand others and to react to them in such a manner that they may not feel unjust attitude regarding them.

4. Intelligence as a Global Capacity

A comprehensive definitions of intelligence : **Stoddard** (1943) and **Wechsler** (1944) have defined intelligence in the following words :

"Intelligence is the aggregate or the global capacity of the individual to act purposefully, to think rationally and to deal with the environment effectively".

Stoddard further elaborated that intelligence is the capacity of a person to undertake such activities which are: (*i*) difficult (*ii*) complex (*iii*) abstract (*iv*) economical (*v*) goal directed (*vi*) valuable from social view points (*vii*) original. These activities demand concentration of energy and a resistance to emotional forces.

Characteristics of Intelligence

From the above definitions of intelligence, we can draw the following characteristics of intelligence:

(*i*) Intelligence is the composite of several intellectual skills, such as thinking, doing, reasoning, dealing, learning etc.

(*ii*) Intelligence is displayed by the behaviour of the individual as a whole and intelligent behaviour is always goal directed.

(*iii*) Intelligence is the ability to adjust to abnormal and challenging situations of life.

(*iv*) Intelligence is not related to ordinary tasks of life. It is always related to extra ordinary manipulation.

(*v*) Wechsler has included the concepts of drive and incentive which are implied in his statement. "To act purposefully" and "to deal effectively". But many psychologists are of the view that drive and incentive are non-intellectual traits of personality and if they are included in a test of mental ability, more confusions will be created thereof.

(*vi*) There are seven fundamental elements of intelligence according to **Stoddard.** Intelligent person can undertake difficult and abstract tasks with ease. He can manipulate and deal the abstract ideas and concepts efficiently. Similarly, economy refers to the rate at which a mental task is done or a problem is solved. If "A" solves a problem sooner than 'B' then 'A' will be considered more intelligent than 'B'. The term social value indicates whether a mental task performed by a person is in accordance with the socially desirable and acceptable norms or not. The last term original refers to a person's, ability to discover something new and different, *i.e.*, this term is directly related to creative potential of a person. Discovery of some new facts and principles and inventions of new concrete materials by the scientists are few examples of originality.

Stoddard's definition of intelligence has been criticized on two grounds :

(*a*) It includes social values in intelligence, *i.e.*, intelligent task must be socially desirable. Psychologists criticize this point by saying that social value is a subjective phenomenon, *i.e.*, what is desirable for me, may not be necessarily desirable for others. So, there is no scope of subjectivity in an objective intelligence test.

(*b*) He has included two conditions of intelligent behaviour in his definition. First is concentration of energy and second is resistance to emotional forces. Psychologists say that these elements are non-intellectual traits and hence they should not be included in mental abilities at any cost.

Theories of Intelligence

1. Faculty theory of intelligence:

This is the oldest theory of intelligence given during the period of pre-experimental psychology. According to this theory mind is made up of different faculties like reasoning, logic, memory, imagination and discrimination. These faculties are independent of each other and can be developed by rigorous mental exercises of the difficult subject-matter.

This theory does not take the hereditary factors of intelligence into account and thus this theory was discarded by the later psychologists who believed that we can never improve the intellectual capacity of a person if he is mentally slow by birth.

2. Unifactor theory:

According to Alfred Binet (1916) intelligence is a general intellectual ability which is made up of several discrete abilities. These abilities include

(*i*) to reason well with abstract material

(*ii*) to comprehend well

(*iii*) to have a clear direction of thoughts

(*iv*) to relate thinking with the attainment of a desirable end and

(*v*) to be self-critical.

All these abilities combined together is called general mental ability. Thus, intelligence is a single but complex mental process which can be measured by different kinds of materials designed for the purpose.

3. Two factors theory:

This theory was developed by an English psychologist, **Charles Spearman** in 1904. According to him, intellectual abilities consist of two factors, general ability known as 'G' factors and specific abilities known as 'S' factors.

Characteristics of G factors

(*i*) It is universal inborn ability.

(*ii*) It is general mental energy.

(*iii*) It is constant, *i.e.*, it remains the same in all the individuals and does not change with time.

(*iv*) The amount of G differs from person to person depending on his genes.

(*v*) It is used in every life activity.

(*vi*) Greater the amount of G in an individual, larger is the chance of his success in life.

Characteristics of 'S' factors

(*i*) It is learnt and hence acquired in the environment.

(*ii*) It varies from activity to activity in the same individual.

(*iii*) The amount of S also differs from person to person due to his accessibility to learning situations.

(*iv*) 'S' factors are related to the specific activity. A low correlation between two or more functions or activities indicates the presence of 'S' factor involved in the activity. A person can be expert only in one or few activities because of the specific factors involved in the activity.

According to Spearman, out of these two factors 'G' factor is more important and thus it is an important measure of intelligence. So, any intelligence test should measure only 'G' factor because it provides most important basis of predicting a person's behaviour in different situations. Raven's Progressive Matrices and Catell's Culture Fair Test both measure 'G' factor.

Spearman has explained his theory with the help of a tetrad equation which is given below :

rap × rbq – raq × rbp = 0

Here,

a = opposites

b = discrimination

p = completion

q = cancellation

Thus, rap means correlation between opposites and completions, rbq means correlation between cancellation and discrimination, raq means correlation between opposite and cancellation and rbp means correlation between discrimination and completion. This theory can also be explained with the help of a diagram given below :

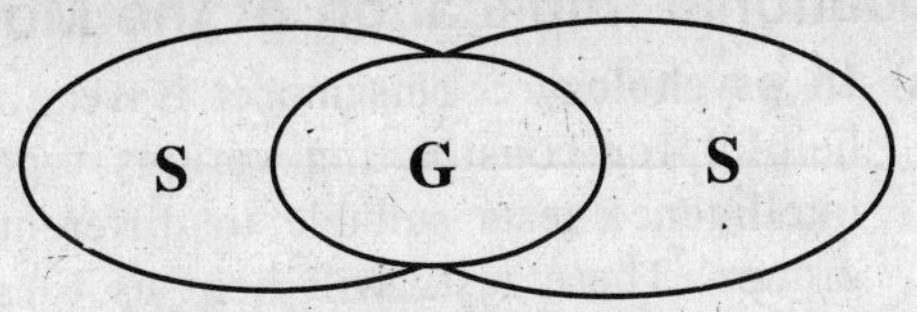

4. Multi-factors theory :

This theory was developed by an American psychologist, **E.L. Thorndike.** He opposed the theory of general intelligence by saying that there are specific stimuli and specific mental responses. Intelligence is nothing more than a potential specific connections between these stimuli and responses. Differences of intelligence among people are due to the different number of such connections in the neurological system. This theory is also called **atomistic theory** of intelligence. There are **four attributes of intelligence** according to him:

(a) *Level :* It refers to the difficulty of a task that can be removed by using intelligence. If different tasks are arranged in increasing difficulty order, then the height that a person can attain determines his level of intelligence. — It is a kind of power test.

(b) *Range :* It refers to the number of tasks of the same difficulty value that a person can do in a certain period of time. Theoretically, an individual possessing a certain level of intelligence should be able to solve the whole range of tasks at a given level. It is a kind of speed test.

Range and level can not be completely isolated from each other. We can not measure range without altitude (level) and vice versa.

(c) *Area :* It refers to the total numbers of situations at each level to which the individual is able to respond. Area is the summation of all ranges at each level of intelligence. Area = Level × Range.

(d) *Speed :* It refers to the rapidity with which an individual can respond to a test items. Speed and level are positively correlated. It is different from range in the sense that no specific time is given here to complete a task.

Every intelligence test should consist of these four attributes.

5. Group factor structure of intelligence (PMA Test) :

This theory was developed by **L.L. Thurstone.** According to him, intelligence is not an expression of general factor but a combination of group of traits. They are intermediate factors, *i.e.*, they are not so universal as 'G' factor and they are not so specific as 'S' factor. This primary group of factors give the common mental abilities, a functional cohesiveness and then constitute a group. Another group of common mental abilities is said to have another primary factor and so on. In this way, there are a number of groups of mental abilities each of which has its own primary factors. On the basis of factor analysis of these groups, Thurstone identified the following seven group factors which are termed as primary mental abilities (PMA).

1. Number factor (N) : It is the ability to do numerical calculations rapidly and accurately.
2. Verbal factor (V) : They are related to the operations involving verbal comprehension.
3. Space factor (S) : It is related to the tasks in which subject manipulates an object imaginary in space.
4. Word fluency factor (W) : It is involved to the situation when the subject is asked to think of isolated words at a fast rate.
5. Reasoning factors (R) : It is used in those tasks that require the subject to discover a rule or principles involved in series or groups of letters.
6. Rote memory (M) : It is the ability to memorize a fact quickly.
7. Perceptual speed (P) : It is the ability to note perceptual (visual) details rapidly.

The point to be noted here is that these seven abilities are significantly correlated with each other.

6. Structure of intelligence (SI) model :

This model was given by **J.P. Guilford** in 1966 in the University of California on the basis of factor analysis of many tests. According to him human mind is composed of at least three dimensions—operations, contents and products, and each dimension of intellect is sufficiently distinct which can be detected by factor analysis. These three dimensions of mind are given below:

(A) Operations : Operations can be divided into five major groups of intellectual abilities.

- **Cognition :** It includes discovery, recognition of informations and new understanding of the facts.
- **Memory :** It is the ability to recognize or recall previously learnt material.
- **Divergent thinking :** This operation is closely associated with creative potential.

It refers to the ability to search out and think in a novel out of track way.

- **Convergent thinking :** It refers to the generation of information from given information and drawing conclusion from the given facts.
- **Evaluation :** It is the ability to make judgement on the basis of merits and demerits of a phenomenon. Here, value judgement on knowledge and thoughts is placed after critically examining them.

(B) Contents : Five kinds of contents are involved here. Operations are performed on these contents.

- **Figural content :** It is the concrete material perceived through the senses. Visual materials have three properties, size, form and colour.
- **Auditory content :** It includes nature and characteristics of sound perceived.
- **Symbolic content :** It includes letters, digits and other conventional signs usually organised in general pattern.
- **Semantic content :** It refers to those verbal meanings, ideas and concepts for which no examples are necessary.
- **Behavioural content :** It includes knowledge regarding other persons.

(C) Products : When five operations are applied to five types of contents, six kinds of products are made.

- **Units :** It refers to the production of a single word, definition or isolated bits of informations.
- **Classes :** It refers to the production of a concept.
- **Relations :** It refers to the production of any form of relationship, such as, analogy, opposite or similar ones.
- **System :** It refers to the production of internally consistent set of classification of various forms.
- **Transformation :** It refers to the production of changes in meaning, organisation or some other arrangement.
- **Implication :** It refers to the production of such information which is beyond the data given.

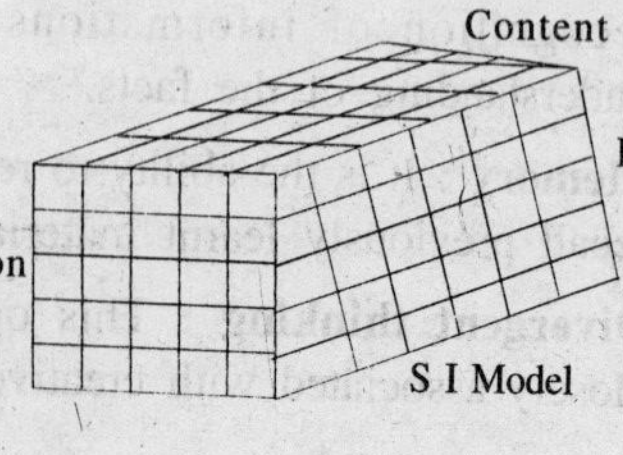

S I Model

On the basis of the model given above it can be stated that there are $5 \times 5 \times 6 = 150$ factors involved in intelligent acts.

Educational Implication of the Model

(a) In psychology : This model is very much helpful for constructing various types of intelligence tests suitable to different age groups. These tests will help us to study individual differences in the society. This model is taxonomic in nature and has discovered many abilities which were not known before. If test maker has included items representing contents and operations, he can see whether products are same or different. Conversely, if products are shown by the subject through the test, the test maker can find out the content and operation and match them with the items given in the test.

(b) In vocational testing : This model shows that there are 150 intellectual abilities. This model predicts five kinds of mental abilities classified as content. This means that different kinds of test items are needed in vocational testing. Six types of products are also tested on the basis of items representing the products. For example, if a person is able to deal with items of figural contents, he can deal with machines, operators, engineers etc. and any or all of the six types of products can be made by him, such as, he can define a machine or any operator. He can give clear concept about how a machine is operated and so on.

(c) In the field of education : Conventionally, learner was considered to be a kind of stimulus response device. Once the stimulus is given to him, he will respond but the new conception of the learner in the light of SI model is that of electronic computer which not only stores information but uses that information to generate new information either by divergent or convergent thinking.

Thus, this model gives the idea that learning is not merely the association of informations but it is the discovery of information as well. Model suggests that in order to understand human learning and higher mental processes of thinking, some drastic modifications are to be made in our theory of curriculum construction and pedagogy of instruction. Similarly, education is no longer considered to be the training of mind. Now, main emphasis on education is given to the learning of specific skills and modification of behaviour and all these materials are not taught merely for the purpose of training the mind of humans.

7. Two Level Process Theory of Intelligence :

This theory was developed by **Jensen** in 1968. According to him intelligence is a combination of two levels of processes. One is associative intelligence and the other is abstract intelligence. Associative intelligence includes those kinds of tests that depend upon memory and simple verbal association. Abstract intelligence includes those factors as concept learning, thinking, problem solving skills, multiple discrimination, principle learning etc.

8. Burt and Vernon's hierarchy theory :

Burt (1940) separated four factors of intelligence by using statistical techniques :

- General factors (common to all traits)
- Group factors (common to some of the traits)
- Specific factors (limited to few traits)
- Error factors (limited to a particular trait when it is measured)

When human mind is put at the top, there will be 5 level hierarchical model of intelligence where general factors will come next to intelligence and error factors will come in the last.

Vernon, on the other hand, suggested that intelligence tests measure an overall factor G as well as two other mental abilities. First are related to verbal, numerical and educational. Second are related to practical, mechanical, spatial and physical. These two major factors can be divided into minor group factors. These minor factors can further be divided into various specific factors and so on.

MEASUREMENT OF INTELLIGENCE

Historical development of mental testing can be divided into three periods for the purpose of convenience.

(A) Pre-Binet Period :

In the 19th century, there was a good deal of interest in the field of psychophysics in which attempts were made to develop general rule of sensory judgement. The functioning of sensory reactions of the typical individuals is actually studied in psycho-physics. Method of limits procedure was used here to measure the extent to which people were able to differentiate between stimuli. But the limitation of these experiments was that accurate generalization of the result was not possible.

Francis Galton was the first psychologist who took interest in studying whether individual characteristics are acquired or inherited. For this purpose, he studied the lives of prominent English men and in his book "Hereditary Genius" he demonstrated that personal characteristics, (mental and physical) of men are inherited. He developed a series of tests to measure these characteristics. It was the starting point of mental measurement.

The first laboratory of experimental psychology was established by **Wundt** in 1879 in Leiping. He employed two methods to test vision, hearing, reaction time and psychosomatic problems—*(i)* psycho-physical method *(ii)* Introspection method. He also developed mental tests which could measure the keenness of vision and hearing, muscular strength, reaction time and other sensory motor functions of body.

Many of **Galton's** ideas were brought to USA by an American psychologist **J.M. Catell.** Like **Galton** he also believed that intellectual functions can best be measured by the reaction time and sensory discrimination tests.

In the last quarter of the 19th century, many psychological laboratories came into existence and studies of individual differences in mental abilities started.

The word "**Mental Test**" was first used by Catell in 1890 but his tests were actually tests of sensory discrimination, speed of motor responses and the like.

Thus, upto this period mental ability was identified as sensory acuity of an individual. The correlation between mental abilities and academic achievements was not known at the time.

Drawbacks of this period:

- Psychologists were unable to identify and define the nature of intelligence. Keenness of sensory motor reactions were related to intelligence.
- They were unable to measure the complex functions of the body.
- Intelligence tests developed during this period were measuring other than intelligence.

(B) Binet Period :

An important incident led the people to think about mental measurement during this period. In the beginning of the 20th century in France, a large number of students failed in the examination. For this teachers and students blamed each other. Seeing this, superintendent of public instruction appointed a committee to device some techniques to screen out slow learners in the schools. Binet and Simon were among members of the committee. They developed a variety of paper pencil tests in their psychological laboratory established in 1889, to administer them on children of different ages. Through these tests Binet tried to measure more complex mental functions such as power of judgement and reasoning, memory, arithmetic ability, etc.

An important contribution of Binet and Simon is that they categorised their tests in terms of age levels by administering their test items to children of different ages. In this way, an age scale of intelligence was also developed. For example, if an item was correctly answered by majority of seven years old children but only few six years old children could respond it correctly, then this item was reserved for seven years old children. In this way, Binet and Simon developed separate tests for different ages.

Similarly, if an item suited to eight years old child was correctly answered by a child of 6 years and if the same trend was shown by the six years old child in most of the cases of a test, then the mental age of the child was considered to be eight years not six years, though his chronological age is six years only. Thus, the concept of mental age was also introduced by Binet and Simon for the first time in the history of mental testing and with the help of this concept we could assess the intellectual ability of a person. Some of the tests developed during this period are given below:

Binet-Simon Scale

The first scale of Binet-Simon was published in 1905. This scale consisted of 30 items arranged in increasing order of difficulty. This scale was a crude measure of intelligence of school going children.

In order to remove some of its defects they revised their scale in 1908. It was the first age based scale and it created a lot of interest among the psychologists across the world. The items in the tests were grouped according to the appropriate age levels from 3 to 13 years.

Some items for three years age

- Point to your nose, eyes and mouth.
- Repeat two digits 3, 5.
- Repeat sentences of six syllables.
- Enumerate objects in a picture.
- Give family names.

Some items of eight years age

- Read a passage and remember two lines.
- Add up the value of five coins.
- Name four colours.
- Count reverse from 20 to zero.
- Give differences between two objects.

1908 revision of Binet-Simon Scale was adopted by many psychologists of America, Switzerland and Germany and many suggestions were given by them for the improvement of the scale. Binet-Simon accepted their suggestions and revised their scale again in 1911.

Some sample items of 1911 scale are given below:

(A) Age = 8 years

- Gives difference between two objects.
- Counts reverse from 20 to zero.
- Points out omissions from unfinished pictures.
- Tells the dates correctly.
- Repeats the digits.

(B) Age = 10 years

- Arranges five blocks in order of increasing weights.
- Reproduces two geometric designs by using memory.
- Criticizes absurd statements.
- Comprehends and answers difficult questions.
- Uses three given words in two sentences.

Main Features of Binet-Simon Scale

(i) They are really scales, *i.e.*, items of the tests are arranged in the increasing difficulty order. Easiest items are put in the beginning and the most difficult item is put in the last. Thus, these scales measure the level or aptitude of an examinee and not their speed.

(ii) These tests measure the general abilities of intelligence instead of specific abilities.

(iii) They can also measure the mental growth of the subject because they are arranged according to different ages from 3 to 14 years.

(iv) They are administered on subjects individually.

(v) Their system of scoring is tied to age norms. A child's performance on the scale will be compared to that of children of his own age.

L.M. Terman's revision of Binet–Simon Scale: L.M. Terman of **Stanford** University revised this scale in 1916 to adapt to American situations. He introduced one new concept which was intelligence Quotient (IQ) in his revision. His scale consisted of 90 items ranging from 3 to 14 years of age. Some items of this scale are given below:

Age = 7 years

- Knows number of fingers on both hands.
- Describes pictures.
- Repeats five digits.
- Gives differences between paired objects.
- Ties a bowknot.

1937 Revision of Binet-Simon Scale : Terman along with his associate Merill revised 1916 scale again in 1937. This revision had two equivalent forms L and M. The number of items in the test was raised to 129 in each L M. forms. A new change was also introduced in the test which was the calculation of chronological age. Upto 13 years CA was taken to be as original but after 13 years CA was computed in the following manner.

At 14 years = 13 yrs+2/3 of 14th year = 13 2/3

At 15 years = 13+2/3 of 2 years = 14 1/3 years.

At 16 years = 13+2/3 of 3 years = 15 years.

Besides, 16 years was taken to be the last age for calculation of IQ. After that, CA was taken to be constant.

LM form revision of 1960 : Binet-Simon scale was last revised in 1960 in which items of both L and M forms were included in the scale. This revision has a range of 2 years of mental age scores to 22 years and 11 months of mental age score. This form of the test measures abilities from 7 categories namely, language, memory, reasoning, social intelligence, conceptual phenomenon, numerical, reasoning and visual motor. Test items are in the form of words, objects and pictures and the responses given by the examinees are in the form of drawing, calculating, writing and speaking. Administration of the test requires one full hour. In this revision intelligence is expressed in terms of standard scores of the deviation IQ.

Wechsler Scale : This scale may be considered an improvement over Binet-Simon scale as it can measure the intelligence of adults very effectively. David Wechsler developed this scale in 1939. This scale was developed in two equivalent forms, each form consisted of ten subtests of which five tests were verbal and five were non-verbal or performance type. This scale was revised in 1955 and was renamed as Wechsler Adult Intelligence Scale (WAIS). It comprised of 11 sub tests of which six were verbal and five were non-verbal. This scale is used on persons above 16 years of age upto 64 and administration time of the scale is one hour. The detail of these 11 subtests are given below:

(a) Verbal subtests :

1. *Information* : 29 questions are given here to test the recall of knowledge concerning wide varieties of information.
2. *Comprehension* : 14 questions are given here to test understanding of knowledge concerning a particular subject or event.
3. *Arithmetic* : 14 questions are given here to test numerical ability. These questions are solved orally without using paper and pencil at all.
4. *Similarity* : 13 questions are given here to measure abstract verbal reasoning. Examinees are required here to compare two objects and find out the relationship between them.
5. *Digit span* : Memory for digits are measured here. In the first half, the examinee is asked to repeat in the same order, three to nine digits presented in the forward directions and in the second half, the digits are repeated in a backward direction.
6. *Vocabulary* : 40 words of increasing difficulty value are presented before the examinees here and they are asked to tell the meaning of these words.

(b) Non-verbal or performance subtests:

1. *Digit symbol* : Nine digits each with different digit symbols are given to the examinees here and they are asked to give the right code for each digits or symbols.
2. *Picture completion* : This subtest measures the ability of the examinees to analyse the parts from the whole. Examinees are given 21 cards containing incomplete pictures and they are asked to fill the missing part of each picture.
3. *Block design* : Its purpose is to measure the ability to analyse the complex whole. There are only 7 designs in these blocks which have red, white and red-white sides. Examinees are asked to produce a given design with the help of these blocks.
4. *Picture arrangement* : Its purpose is to measure the ability to identify the whole from the parts. Here six set of pictures are given to the examinees and they are asked to arrange them in an order which tells a meaningful story.
5. *Object assembly* : Its purpose is to measure the ability to synthesise the whole with the help of parts. Here examinees are given some puzzle pictures each representing some parts of the human body and they are asked to assemble them in the form of a complete man.

Speed and accuracy factors are also scored in Arithmetic, digit symbol, block design, picture arrangement and object assembly. Raw scores of each subject are converted into normalized standard scores with a mean of 10 and SD of 3. This makes the scores of each sub tests comparable. Separate IQ for verbal and non-verbal subtest forms is calculated by adding up the respective subtests of the two forms and if we add up scores on all the 11 subtests, we obtain total scale score. These standard scores are expressed in the form of deviation IQ with a mean of 100 and SD of 15.

Wechsler developed another scale known as Wechsler intelligence Scale for Children in 1949 to test the intelligence of children from 5 to 15 years of age. It also takes one hour to administer, though there are 12 subtests in this scale. Maze test is the only test which is extra in WISC. Maze subtest has eight mazes to be traced by the examinee with a pencil. These mazes are given in increasing order of difficulty.

The scoring system of both the tests WAIS and WISC are the same. Here also the total scores are converted into deviation IQ with a mean of 100 and SD of 15.

Advantages of Wechsler Scales

(i) Though Binet's scale and Wechsler's scale both are individual scales, yet the later can be administered on small groups of children and adults.

(ii) Wechsler's scale is easier to administer than Binet's Scale and its scoring is also less complex than the former.

(iii) Wechsler has prepared separate scales for children and adults Binet's scale does not possess this advantage.

Other differences of Wechsler Scales and Stanford Binet Scale

(i) In Wechsler scale, items are not grouped in terms of mental age as is the case of Stanford-Binet scale. Points are given here for all correct responses. Thus, WAIS or WISC is a point scale.

(ii) In Stanford-Binet scale items are interpreted in terms of different age levels of the examinees but in WAIS or WISC similar types of items are grouped together to form subtests.

(iii) WAIS has separate age norms for adults but in SB Scale all the individuals above 18 are treated in a similar manner as far as computation of IQ is concerned. Thus, people of all age levels are treated as 18 years of age after 18.

(iv) In SB tests items are varied, unrelated and upgraded but in WAIS and WISC tests, items are graded according to various range of ages.

(v) SB scale is internally standardized and rigid but WAIS is externally standardized and flexible.

(vi) SB scale refers to qualitative evaluation while WAIS refers to quantitative evaluation.

(vii) Slight chance of statistical treatment is possible in SB scale but WAIS is fully subject to all statistical analysis.

(c) Post Binet period :

This period is particularly known for testing intelligence in groups and thus group test of intelligence became popular during this periods.

A group test is one that can be given to a number of subjects at a time by a single examiner. This type of test came into being during first World War for the purpose of classifying soldiers for various jobs in accordance with their mental abilities. Army Alpha and Army Beta, two tests were developed during this period. Army Alpha is a verbal group test of intelligence meant for literate people. Army beta is a non-verbal group test of intelligence meant for illiterate persons.

We will discuss here some more group test of intelligence :

1. **Catell's Culture Fair Test :** This test was developed by RB Catell and was published by IPAT (Institute for Personality and Ability Testing) in 1961. The test has three scales and can be administered on children and adults both.

   Scale I meant for 4-8 years

   Scale II meant for 8-15 years

   Scale III meant for 15 years and above

   This test measures the general intelligence factor and takes 30-60 minutes to administer. The test has been prepared in such a manner that previously learnt skill or knowledge does not help the examinee to score more on this test. That is why, it is said to be independent of school achievement, social advantages and environmental influences.

2. **Large Thorndike's Intelligence Test :** This test is meant for primary and secondary school children graded into five different levels. The purpose of the test is to measure verbal comprehension, numerical skill and reasoning abilities. Test has verbal as well as non-verbal items. Only non-verbals items are, however, included at the lower levels. The administration of the test takes 30 minutes in all.

3. **Raven Progressive Matrices Test :** This test was developed in England. It consists of geometric figures and designs. The subjects find out the relationship between figures and select appropriate parts for completion of each pattern of relations.

Classification of Intelligence Test

(A) Classification from the point of view of administration

1. **Individual intelligence test :** An individual intelligence test is one which is administered to only one person at a time. Binet-Simon is an example.

2. **Group intelligence test :** A group intelligence test is one which can be administered to more than one persons at a time. Army Alpha and Army Beta are two examples of such tests.

Some general characteristics of group intelligence tests are as follows :

(i) They have been developed on the assumption that intelligence is a general capacity and can be measured by sampling a variety of mental activities.

(ii) In group tests the similar types of items are pooled together in different subtests.

(iii) Every group test is standardized for a special range of ages or school grades.

(iv) Construction of individual test is also very difficult and costly as compared to group tests. Their scoring and standardization is also time consuming process.

(v) It is very difficult to establish rapport between the examiner and the examinees and hence examinees can not be motivated properly in group tests of intelligence. These two limitations are not seen in individual tests.

(vi) Group tests are superior to individual tests in the sense that norms established here are more dependable than that of individual tests. It is because these norms are calculated on the basis of a very large sample.

(vii) Individual test provides qualitative performance of the individual while group tests are mostly point scale and express the performance in quantities.

(B) Classification from the point of view of nature of items of the test

1. **Verbal test :** Verbal test of intelligence is one in which instructions and items are produced before the examinees through the written language. So, examinees must be literate to take these tests. Mohsin's General intelligence Test, Joshi's General Mental Ability test and Jalota's Group General Mental Ability Test are some examples of verbal tests of intelligence of Indian origin.

2. **Non-verbal test :** A non-verbal test is one which requires the use of language only to impart instructions. The examinees are asked to manipulate the test materials in their own way. Since language is not needed to respond to items here, it can be administered to illiterate persons as well. They are also culturally free and hence they can be applied to any situation representing any culture. Test items are usually of figured relation type. Army Beta is a good example of non-language test.

3. **Performance test :** A performance test is one in which a subject has to perform some thing or to manipulate some concrete materials without much use of the language ability. Non-verbal and performance tests are useful for the following groups of people:

(a) *Deaf and Dumb :* Those children who cannot hear or speak can be tested with the help of performance test.

(b) *Illiterates :* Verbal test of intelligence is useless for those who cannot read or write. Performance test is useful for them.

(c) *Shy children :* Many withdrawn children are hesitant to express before others. Performance and non-verbal test of intelligence will suit them very much.

(d) *Educationally deficient children :* Verbal test of intelligence generally measure learning along with intelligence. If children are educationally poor, they will perform poorly on intelligence test too and thus they will be wrongly declared as children of below average intelligence. Such a problem can be overcome by using performance test or non-verbal intelligence test.

(e) *Useful for children of other culture :* A particular culture dominates in every verbal intelligence test and thus the test can not be adopted by other cultures. Due to free from culture, performance test is suitable for these foreign students.

Some performance tests of intelligence are given below :

(a) **Pintner Paterson Scale :** This is the first systematic performance test. This scale was standardized in 1917. It consists of 15 subtests.

(b) **Goodenough Drawing Test :** This scale was developed by Florence Goodenough in 1926. Here child is asked to draw the picture of a man as best as possible without any time limit. This is especially useful for those children who are suspected to be mentally retarted.

Weaknesses of performance test :

- Here the subject can score high due to practice effect and chance success is more frequent than verbal tests. Because of this reason, reliability coefficient is very low.
- They fail to distinguish between gifted and average children due to limited scope of these tests.
- These scales fail to test fine mental abilities such as, ability to make abstraction or concept formation or evaluation abilities of mind.

Interpretation of Intelligence Test Scores : Intelligence test scores can be interpreted in the following three ways:

1. **Mental age :** This concept was first introduced by **Afred Binet** of France in 1908. It refers to a score that is determined by comparing a child's score with the scores obtained by younger or older children in the norming group. Here a child's score is compared with the average score of his own age. For example, if a 9-year-old child scores 60 on an

intelligence test and suppose mental age norms for that scale are as follows:

Mental age of 8 years = 60

Mental age of 9 years = 70

Mental age of 10 years = 80

Then, in that case, mental age of the child will be considered as 8 years instead of 9 though his chronological age is 9 years.

Similarly, if another child of 8 years obtains a score of 80, then his mental age will be 10 years, though his chronological age is 8 years only.

Thus, we can say that the mean performance of each age level becomes the mental age for that age level.

2. **Intelligent Quotient (IQ) :** IQ is also based on the concept of mental age. It is the ratio of mental age to the chronological age multiplied by 100.

$$IQ = \frac{MA}{CA} \times 100.$$

Suppose, the mental age of a 10-year-old child is 12 years on the basis of his scores on an intelligence test, his IQ will be

$$\frac{12}{10} \times 100 = 120.$$

Similarly, if mental age of a person is nine years two months and his age is 12 years 6 months, then his IQ will be

$$\frac{110}{150} \times 100 = 73.3.$$

General classification of persons in terms of IQ

IQ	Classification
140 and above	Genius
130-140	Very superior
120-130	Superior
110-120	Bright
90-110	Average
80-90	Dull
70-80	Borderline
Below 70	Mentally retarded.

Shortcomings of IQ: Some of the main short comings of IQ are as follows:

(*i*) It is a well-known fact that after 18 years, the mental age of a person tends to stabilize. Thus, if IQ is calculated after this age, the result will be misleading, *i.e.*, a person will be less intelligent if he grows in age.

(*ii*) Variability of IQ scores from one test to another is not the same. As a result IQ scores for different tests would not be directly comparable.

(*iii*) It has also been found that variability in IQ scores for the different age levels on the same test is not the same. In that case IQ scores would be a misleading index because it would indicate that a person's IQ may increase or decrease as he grows in age. An example will illustrate this point.

Age	IQ	SD
9 years old child	120	12
7 years old child	120	9

Here IQ of 120 of both the children is not the same due to difference in SD.

3. **Deviation IQ :** Now-a-days IQ ratio is converted into a normalized standard score with a fixed mean of 100 and SD of 15. This is known as DIQ. This fixed mean and SD remain constant through all the age levels. It means that if a child's score is 1 SD above the mean his DIQ will be 100 + 15 = 115. Similarly, if his score is 1 SD below the mean his DIQ will be 100 – 15 = 85 and so on. Thus, with the help of these **DIQ** scores inter age comparison is also possible.

Uses of Intelligence Test

Intelligence tests can be applied in the following situations.

1. **Measurement of general learning abilities:** Intelligence and achievement in schools are highly correlated. If a person is high on an intelligence test, he is expected to score high on school achievements also. Conversely if a person scores high on an intelligence test and still his school achievement is very poor, we can find out other reasons for his educational backwardness.
2. **Assessment of individual differences and categorization :** With the help of intelligence tests we can categories a particular class into several convenient groups and plan our instructional strategies accordingly. Thus, intelligence testing is very useful for educational guidance.
3. **Exact definition of mental retardation is possible :** It is said that those who are below 70 in IQ are retarded but to what extent they are mentally retarded can further be studied with the help of higher screening. We may define the three groups of mentally retarted in the following ways.

Category	IQ level
Morons	45-69
Imbeciles	25-45
Idiots	Below 25

4. **Identification of gifted children :** Gifted children are the treasure of the society. They must be identified in the earlier stages of their lives so that they can be fully guided and helped for their better advancement which is directly related to the advancement of the society as well. Intelligence testing will help the concerned organisations to chalk out plans in the desired manner.
5. **Vocational guidance :** Some children are very forward in verbal abilities and some are superior in non-verbal abilities. This identification is possible only with the help of intelligence tests. Since academic subjects need verbal intelligence and technical subjects need non-verbal or performing abilities, hence children may be guided accordingly.
6. **Screening :** In today's age of competition and rush, screening has become a necessity. Every school has limited seats of admission and it has to select only those students who can raise the academic level of the school high and get name for it. Same is the case with appointments in jobs. For all these purposes, intelligence testing is a must.
7. **Study of mental growth :** Mental abilities develop in a sequential order onward. We can use intelligence tests for studying the trends of mental development of individuals. Intelligence tests have made it clear that mental development of children is a steady consistent process from year-to-year till the age of 25. Intelligence tests show that mind does not develop rapidly in the period of adolescence like the physical and emotional development, but in childhood, it develops rapidly.

Limitations of Intelligence Tests

1. Generally intelligence test shows what a person can do at a certain point of time. These abilities are tested on the basis of certain items included in the test. In order to make the results dependable, a proper size of the sample must be selected for standardization of the test.
2. Some people may be fatigued earlier than others when take a test. This extent of fatigue may reduce their scores and hence intelligence testing will not be accurate. So scores should be taken with caution.
3. No intelligence test is fully free from cultural influences. So, home or school background may affect the intelligence test scores of subjects.
4. Administration of the test also affects the scores of subjects. If proper rapport is there between the examiner and the examinee. IQ scores may be high. On the other hand, if children are frightened with the testing situation as is case of slow learners they will perform poorly on the test.
5. Taking intelligence scores in absolute form is misleading. Intelligence tests do not reveal all the mental abilities in most of the cases. So, intelligence test must be supplemented with clinical setting and case history method to collect detailed information about a subject as is done in clinics by physician who does not entirely believe in physical investigations. He rather takes the help of clinical diagnosis before giving remedial treatment to the patients.

THOUGHT AND LANGUAGE

In this section we examines the relationship between language and thought: that language determines thought, that thought determines language, and that thought and language have different origins. Let us examine these three viewpoints in some detail.

Language as Determinant of Thought

In Hindi and other Indian languages we use a number of different words for various kinship relationships. We have different terms for mother's brother, father's elder brother, father's younger brother, mother's sister's husband, father's sister's husband and so on. An English person uses just one word *uncle* to describe all these kinship relationships. In the English language there are dozens of words for colours whereas some tribal languages have only two to four colour terms. Do such differences matter for how we think? Does an Indian child find it easier to think about and differentiate between various kinship relationships compared to her English-speaking counterpart? Does our thinking process depend on how we describe it in our language?

Benjamin Lee Whorf was of the view that language determines the contents of thought. This view is known as **linguistic relativity hypothesis**. In its strong version, this hypothesis holds what and how individuals can possibly think is determined by the language and linguistic categories they use **(linguistic determinism).** Experimental evidence, however, maintains that it is possible to have the same level or quality of thoughts in all languages depending upon the availability of linguistic categories and structures. Some thoughts may be easier in one language compared to another.

Thought as Determinant of Language

The noted Swiss psychologist, Jean Piaget believed that thought not only determines language, but also precedes it. Piaget argued that children form an internal representation of the world through thinking. For example, when children see something and later copy it (a process called imitation), thinking does take place, which does not involve language. A child's observation of other's behaviour and imitation of the same behaviour, no doubt involves thinking but not language. Language is just one of the vehicles of thinking. As actions become internalised, language may affect children's range of symbolic thinking but is not necessary for the origins of thought. Piaget believed that though language can be taught to children, understanding of the words require knowledge of the underlying concepts (*i.e.* thinking). Thus, thought is basic, and necessary if language is to be understood.

Different Origins of Language and Thought

The Russian psychologist, Lev Vyogotsky, argued that thoughts and language develop in a child separately until about two years of age, when they merge. Before two years thought is preverbal and is experienced more in action (Piaget's sensory motor stage). The child's utterances are more automotic reflexes—crying when uncomfortable—than thought-based. Around two years of age, the child expresses thought verbally and her/his speech reflects rationality. Now children are able to manipulate thoughts using soundless speech. He believed that during this period the development of language and thinking become interdependent; the development of conceptual thinking depends upon the quality of inner speech and vice versa. Thought is used without language when the vehicle of thinking is non-verbal such as visual or movement-related. Language is used without thought when expressing feelings or exchanging pleasantries, for example ''Good morning! How are you?'' ''Very well, I am fine''. When the two functions overlap, they can be used together to produce verbal thought and rational speech.

Development of Language

Language is a complex system and unique to human beings. Psychologists have tried to teach sign language, use of symbols to chimpanzees, dolphins, parrots, etc. But it is observed that, human language is more complex, creative, and spontaneous than the system of communication other animals can learn. There is also a great deal of **regularity** with which children all over the world seem to be learning the language or languages to which they are exposed. When we compare individual children, we find that they differ a great deal in the rate of their language development as well as in how they go about it. But when we take a general view of children's acquisition of language all over the world we find some *predictable pattern* in which children proceed from almost no use of language to the point of becoming competent language users. Language develops through some of the stages discussed below.

Newborn babies and young infants make a variety of sounds, which gradually get modified to resemble words. The first sound produced by babies is crying. Initial crying is undifferentiated and similar across various situations. Gradually, the pattern of crying varies in its pitch and intensity to signify different states such as hunger, pain, and sleepiness, etc. These differentiated crying sounds gradually become more meaningful *cooing sounds* (like 'aaa', 'uuu', etc). usually to express happiness.

At around six months of age children enter the *babbling* stage. Babbling involves prolonged repetition of a variety of consonants and vowel sounds (for example, da—, aa—, ba—). By about nine months of age these sounds get elaborated to strings of some sound combinations, such as 'dadadadadada' into repetitive patterns called *echolalia.* While the early babblings are random or accidental in nature, the later babblings seem to be imitative of adult voices. Children show some understanding of a few words by the time they are six months old. Around the first birthday (the exact age varies from child-to-child) most children enter the *one-word-stage.* Their first word usually contains one syllable—*ma or da*, for instance. Gradually they move to one or more words which are combined to form whole sentences or phrases. So they are called *holophrases*. When they are 18 to 20 months of age, children enter a *two-word stage* and begin to use two words together. The two-word stage exemplifies *telegraphic speech.* Like telegrams (got admission, send money) it contains mostly nouns and verbs. Close to their third birthday, *i.e.* beyond two-and-a-half years, children's language development gets focused on rules of the language they hear.

How is language acquired? You must be wondering: ''How do we learn to speak?'' As with many other topics in psychology, the questions of whether a behaviour develops as a result of inherited characteristics (nature) or from the effects of learning (nurture) has been raised with regard to language. Most psychologists accept that both nature and nurture are important in language acquisition.

Behaviourist B.F. Skinner believed we learn language the same way as animals learn to pick keys or press bars. Language development, for the behaviourists follow the learning principles, such as association (the sight of bottle with the word 'bottle'), imitation (adults use of word ''bottle''), and reinforcement (smiles and hugs when the child says something right). There is also evidence that children produce sounds that are appropriate to a language of the parent or care-giver and are reinforced for having done so. The principle of shaping leads to successive approximation of the desired responses so that the child eventually speaks as well as the adult. Regional differences in pronunciation and phrasing illustrate how different patterns are reinforced in different areas.

Linguist Noam Chomsky put forth the innate proposition of development of language. For him the *rate at which children acquire words and grammar* without being taught can not be explained only by learning principles. Children also *create all sorts of sentences* they have never heard and, therefore, could not be imitating. Children throughout the world seem to have a *critical period*—a period when learning must occur if it is to occur successfully—for learning language. Children across the world also go through the same stages of language development. Chomsky believes language development is just like physical maturation given adequate care, it ''just happens to the child''. Children are born with ''universal grammar''. They readily learn the grammar of whatever language they hear.

Skinner's emphasis on learning explains why infants acquire the language they hear and how they add new words to their vocabularies. Chomsky's emphasis on our built-in readiness to learn grammar helps explain why children acquire language so readily without direct teaching.

GENDER AS A SOCIAL CONSTRUCT; GENDER ROLES, GENDER-BIAS AND EDUCATIONAL PRACTICE

Gender refers to the social distinctions between boys and girls and men and women that are socially constructed rather than biologically determined. These distinctions are reflected in the roles that boys and girls play in society and the status that they occupy within it. Gender roles tend to be dynamic. They vary from one culture and time period to another and are characterized by unequal power relationships.

Ending gender bias and discrimination is crucial to the empowerment of women and girls and to the achievement of gender equality in education. Applying a gender perspective helps to make differences in power relations visible. It also helps us to see more clearly the needs and rights of girls and boys in particular geographical, cultural and economic contexts.

The ultimate goal is to eliminate gender biases and discriminatory practices and policies, both overt and covert. This is at the heart of gender analysis. Gender analysis should therefore be a prerequisite for identifying and understanding problems as they relate to education, and especially to the continued exclusion of girls from quality schooling. Gender analysis guides the process of finding viable and sustainable solutions to the problems of access, quality and learning achievement.

Gender analysis of what learners bring to education (including early childhood socialization, feeding and health access, cultural heritage and language), the content of education, teaching and learning processes, learning environments and learning outcomes help to highlight bad (and good) educational practices and policies. This analysis, in turn, should form the basis for educational interventions that are sensitive to both gender and human rights.

Gender Bias in Teaching

A common response from teachers when asked about gender inequity in classrooms is that they treat all their students the same. There are two problems with this statement. First, students are diverse and have different learning issues, thus treating all students in the same way means that some students will have a better learning experience than their peers. Second, teachers may be ignoring their unconscious gender biases towards their students, their schools and themselves. If ignored, these gender biases, which may have developed from cultural norms, may lead to bias in the classroom.

Gender bias occurs when people make assumptions regarding behaviours, abilities or preferences of others based upon their gender. Because there are strong gender role stereotypes for masculinity and femininity, students who do not match them can encounter problems with teachers and with their peers. For example, the expectation is that boys naturally exhibit boisterous, unruly behaviour, are academically able, rational, and socially uncommunicative, whereas girls are quiet, polite, and studious. Girls are also expected to possess better social skills than boys and to excel at reading and the language arts. So girls who present discipline problems for teachers, or quiet, studious boys, may encounter a lack of understanding from peers and teachers. Within the classroom, these biases unfold in students' practices and teachers' acceptance of certain behaviours from one student or another based upon the students' gender. Also, bias due to a person's gender is not mutually exclusive of other social categories such as race, ethnicity, class, religion, and language. For example, some teachers may perceive African American or other Black girls as loud and uncontrollable because the girls do not exhibit the feminine behaviours associated with White women, such as quiet, self-effacing and malleable.

Gender bias can occur within subject areas and school activities. For example, in subjects such as mathematics and the sciences, there are different participation patterns for girls and boys. Gender bias promulgates a myth that boys are naturally better at mathematics and science than girls. The implications are that if girls succeed in these subjects it is due to their hard work, not their intelligence, whereas boys' success is credited to their natural talent. There are some signs that gender bias in schools may be decreasing in some areas. The percentage of girls participating in science has increased and achieved parity with boys in biology, chemistry and algebra. However, subjects that are prerequisites for college majors such as engineering or physics remain dominated by men. Only 25% of high school students enrolled in physics are female. Moreover, there has been little increase in the percentage of women in engineering programs.

Males are also more likely than females to be in remedial programs and students' race also impacts these patterns. For example, African American males are more likely than White or female peers to enroll in remedial reading and mathematics courses. And non-White students have a higher representation in vocational and noncollege preparatory courses than their White peers. Teachers are critical components in challenging gender bias in schooling, but they also can be major contributors to it as well, through their pedagogical practices, curriculum choices, and assessment strategies.

Gender Bias in Teachers

Teachers' unconscious gender biases can produce stereo-typic expectations for students' success and participation in the classroom. Teachers view male students' domination of the classroom and their time as typical masculine behaviour. However, these biases have consequences for the students and the classroom climate. More than two decades ago, researchers identified and named groups of students who dominated the teacher's time and the classroom resources as ''target students'' (Tobin & Gallagher, 1987). Target students were typically white and male. They answered most of the teacher's questions and also asked most of the questions. This behaviour pattern was particularly insidious in mathematics and science classrooms because teachers did not expect girls to have competent knowledge in these subject areas. Classroom observations documented that target students typically called out answers to the teacher's questions, thus denying other students the opportunity to engage in dialogue with the teacher or get to grips with the subject matter. Furthermore, because boys are perceived as having natural talent in science, teachers asked boys harder and more complicated questions than girls. If girls attempted to answer more difficult questions than boys and faltered, teachers often repeated the question and asked that another student, typically a boy, provide the answer. However, if a boy failed to answer correctly, teachers reframed the question or broke it into a series of simpler questions that could help the student find the answer. Teachers' unconscious stereotyped gender bias that boys are smarter than girls, especially in mathematics and the sciences, meant they were willing to work with boys to reach the answer because they perceived boys were capable of achieving that goal but girls were not. Conversely, teachers of subjects perceived as feminine will spend more time engaged with girls.

Teachers' gendered perceptions of students' ability is also reflected in the type of praise and expectations they have of their students. Teachers often give girls less meaningful and less critical praise than boys. Boys' work is described as unique or brilliant, while girls' work is often undervalued, critically ignored and praised for its appearance. This aspect of teachers' behaviour is particularly detrimental to girls because it means they do not receive feedback on their work that could help them develop deeper understandings of concepts (Liu, 2006).

Teachers also use target students to maintain the tempo and pace of classroom instruction. For example, in a lecture or whole class discussion when a teacher is posing questions to the class, he or she may encourage target students to call out answers in order to keep the lesson moving, rather than wait for the other students to process the question and provide an answer. This short ''wait time'' may be detrimental to learning. More than three decades ago, researchers found that if teachers waited three to five seconds before accepting a student's answer, more students became engaged in the classroom and also improved their understanding of the content. Moreover, the longer wait time meant that teachers began to ask more cognitively challenging questions. However, the existence of target students in classes who often call out answers without direction from teachers meant that fewer students, especially girls, engaged in the lessons. In the absence of proactive teacher intervention, these patterns in which males dominate classroom interactions also occur in mixed-gender, small groups.

Target students dominate classroom interactions and exchanges at all education levels. In the early

2000s, researchers identified these same patterns of engagement in a professional development program for science teachers. When alerted to the invasive behaviours of the male teachers in the cohort, faculty began using overt breaching strategies to stop the target students calling out answers, dominating the human and materials resources of the classroom, and showing disrespect to their peers (Martin Milne & Scantlebury, 2006).

Teachers' gender bias towards students can also extend to their response to students who challenge their authority. Such risk-taking behaviour in boys is expected and at times praised, but assertiveness in girls is viewed negatively and labelled unfeminine. Similarly, boys who do not exhibit stereotypic masculine behaviours may be ridiculed (Renold, 2006).

Teachers use gender expectations as a means of maintaining classroom control. For example, teachers will seat undisciplined boys next to girls as a classroom management strategy. Further, teachers use the gendered expectation that girls' nurturing characteristics will lead them to place others' needs before their own. In other words, teachers often ask girls to assume mothering roles towards students who have fallen behind with learning because of inattentiveness, absenteeism through truancy, or in-school disciplinary procedures, and often those students are male.

Effects of Gender Bias

Gender bias can impact students' attitudes towards learning and their engagement with the subject. If affected by gender bias, girls will tend to believe that any success they have is due to hard work rather than any innate talent or intelligence. Boys may be encouraged to believe that success in science and mathematics should come easily to them because of their gender. Some males report dropping out of college science and mathematics programs because they no longer perceive these subjects as easy. Overall, teachers have lower expectations for girls' academic success compared to boys, and their attitudes are shown through the type and quality of the student-teacher interaction. The type and quality of critique teachers give their students can also have an impact. Teachers' comments on girls' work focuses on its appearance but with boys' work teachers focus on the content. Girls often do not receive substantive comments or criticism from teachers from which they could improve their ability to learn. During the many hours spent in classrooms, girls receive less time and attention from teachers than their male peers. Teachers usually ask girls easier questions than they ask boys. Typically, girls receive fewer opportunities to engage in classroom discourse, use equipment and assert their knowledge in classrooms.

Reducing Gender Bias

Gender bias in education is a series of microinequities whose impact is cumulative and often ignored. Girls are rewarded and praised for compliant behaviour. Teachers do not challenge girls with questions and rarely offer criticisms of their works. Teachers can reduce and challenge gender bias through an examination of their pedagogical practices and by posing simple questions about their practices. For example, which students do they frequently interact with? Are target students evident in their classroom? If so, how does the teacher deal with those students? What questioning techniques does the teacher use to engage students? Does the teacher ask complicated questions to girls as well as boys? Does the teacher use a variety of pedagogical and assessment practices? Which students are engaged with the curriculum?

Another way of reducing gender bias would be for teachers to videotape their classes and review their interactions with the students. Or they could invite a colleague to watch their teaching and record which students are being asked questions and what type of questions. However, teachers must also prepare for the consequences of changing their practices. Girls are conditioned to receiving less of the teacher's attention, and they do not usually cause discipline problems if they are not receiving their fair share, but boys can react negatively to losing the teacher's attention, causing disruption to lessons and becoming discipline problems. Moreover, research has also shown that boys avoid written work and often have poor communication skills when asked to work in singlesex groups.

However, the gains in reducing gender bias in education may disappear with the requirements of high-stakes testing required by No Child Left Behind (NCLB). NCLB requires that states report academic achievement data in most social categories, except gender (Kahle, 2004). This may result in less attention being placed on gender bias and less data that might reveal it. Continued monitoring of gender bias is necessary to minimize its impact on students' opportunities for learning and achievement.

INDIVIDUAL DIFFERENCES AMONG LEARNERS

It is not unusual to find a wide range of differences among students in a class or a group. These differences are invariably identified in terms of student's characteristics such as physical (appearance, height, size, sex, colour, etc.), demographic (age, caste, socio-economic status, etc.) and cognitive behaviour (thinking, remembering, problem solving, creating idea, etc.). The differences that exist among students due to physical, demographic, affective behaviour and cognitive behaviour characteristics are referred to as individual differences.

Differences due to physical and demographic characteristics are conspicuous and easy to identify. However, the differences that exist in the way they solve problem in Mathematics or in their ability to interpret and explain ideas are not easily visible but are identified through their performance. Let us examine, for instance, the answers given by Bitto and Neha, two students of the same class to the following proverb.

Interpret the saying, "Pen is mighter than the sword".

Bitto's Interpretation

It means that writing had always been able to influence mankind more than any amount of sheer physical strength; writing undoubtedly makes a more lasting impact in the minds of the people than any form of physical demonstration. In the case of the latter the impact might be forceful though less lasting. Great thinkers, writers and philosophers have from time immemovial been able to hold sway over the minds of the people by means of their profound knowledge through their writings. For example, Socrates won the wrath of a powerful state, because of his great ability to hold spellbound the young through his discourses. Similarly, the writing of Voltaire and Rousseau inspired the French to rise up in revolt.

Neha's Interpretation

It is a common proverb which simply means that through writing it is possible to win more victories than by using physical force and weapons. When any good book is read it is possible to retain in our memory the message it contains. On the other hand, success achieved through physical might is not for mankind.

The above illustration reflects the differences between Bitto and Neha in their interpretation of the proverb. While Bitto delves deep in her interpretation, Neha states only the meaning.

According to Skinner, individual differences in learner behaviours are the result of the organism's genetic endowment and reinforcement. Thus, Skinner believed that defective genetic endowment and/or defective reinforcement contingencies in an individual's experience result in a failure to acquire a variety of learned behaviours.

The process of an individual's mental activities such as remembering, analysing, interpreting, reasoning, problem solving and thinking are cognitive domain behaviours and are essential for learning and achievement. How we think, what and how we remember, how we solve problem and how we create ideas are cognitive domain behaviours and individuals differ by these behaviours. Such differences are often identified by psychologists in terms of intelligence, aptitude, creating and academic achievement.

Individual differences are crucial for teachers who are responsible for guiding all forms of learning. In fact, many educators would suggest that the primary role of teachers is to provide education to meet the individual differences and to develop student cognitive process.

Do Individuals Differ in Intelligence?

Well, they do differ. But how? Differences are due to the differences in the level of general intellectual ability and the underlying cognitive process among individuals.

How do we identify differences in intelligence?

Using suitable intelligence tests we can measure and identify the difference. An intelligence test may contain sub-tests (sub-sections) and each sub-test represents a different set of ability. The scores obtained in all sub-tests are added up to obtain a single score to represent the general ability of the student. Thus, the single score obtained for each individual in a test is expressed in terms of **intelligence quotient** (IQ). IQ is a measure of intelligence and is defined as the ratio of mental age (average age of children who give correct responses/ answers in an intelligence test) to the chronological age (actual age) multiplied by 100 (to avoid fraction). Thus mental age is:

$$IQ = \frac{\text{Mental age}}{\text{Chronological age}} \times 100$$

IQ scores help us estimate individual differences by categorising individuals on the basis of their IQs. These differences have important consequences for learning and performance. Let us examine the different categories of students based on their intelligence level.

Gifted : Those students who possess IQs of 130 or above are called gifted students. They are superior in intelligence and have high ability to reason. As compared to other children, they can perform academic activities grasping concepts, memorising, perceiving, seeing relationships, generalising, dealing with abstract ideas, critical thinking and solving problems more effectively and quickly. They have a broad attention span that permits concentration and the ability for a high level of academic performance. They take initiative in intellectual work and follow complex directions. Such individuals are small in number as compared to normal or average children. Normal groups have those children whose IQs range from 90 to 110 and they are able to profit from regular school programmes with varying degrees of effort.

Disabled : There are children with **disability** due to low level to intellectual functioning or specific learning deficits. Children with low level or below-average intellectual functioning are called mentally retarded. The children with inadequate level of intelligence are impaired in their ability to learn and to adapt to the demands of society. Mentally retarded children are of different categories. They can be:

- **Border line** (IQ ranges 90-70) and **educable mentally retarded** (IQ ranges 70-50) children can perform academic activities but are slow in their learning. Special instructional strategies can help them to profit from learning activities. They can take care of themselves and live independently as adults.
- **Trainable mentally retarded** (IQ ranges 50-35) are capable of learning only certain rudimentary literacy materials and simple occupational skills. They possess some ability to take care of their personal needs and can be trained in daily living skills. Such children require special classes or schools to study in.
- **Severely retarded** (IQ below 35) have quite limited adaptive behaviour and are never found in school. They are dependent on their families for their personal needs.

Children with specific learning defects are called learning disabled group. They are normal to above-average on intelligence but have difficulties in one or more psychological processes involved in understanding or in using language or numbers (written or spoken). The difficulties manifest in their ability to listen, think, speak, read, write, spell or do mathematical calculations. These difficulties are identified as **aphasia** (difficulty in grasping spoken language), **dylesia** (difficulty in reading), **hyperiexia** (little or no comprehension), **dyscalculia** (difficulty in doing arithmetic) and **dysgraphia** (difficulty in writing). Some are hyperactive in the sense that they are excessively active inattentive and behave impulsively. They follow instructions poorly and do not often complete the assigned tasks.

Instructional Strategies for Handling Individual Differences

- Organise instruction for the development of cognitive process.
- Use existing cognitive level as base.
- Strengthen memory.
- Formulate level specific instructional strategy.
- Use individual meeting.
- Provide instructions to overcome learning disability.

Do Individuals Differ in Aptitude?

Yes, they do differ. An individual may have a mechanical aptitude, another may have an aptitude for mathematics or yet another may have an aptitude for language, music or athletics. Such differences are due to the differences in the combination of abilities related to the cognitive processes, and the sensory and psychomotor components. For instance, when we talk of mechanical aptitude, we may deal with ability for spatial relations, ability to acquire information on mechanical matters and ability to comprehend mechanical relations, besides sensory and psychomotor abilities. Similarly, when we discuss aptitude in music, we may identify ability for musical memory, pitch discrimination, loudness discrimination, time discrimination and judgement of rhythm. Likewise, abilities required for science or mathematics are different and each requires a separate set of abilities.

The differences in aptitude can be identified using aptitude tests. Aptitude tests for areas such as mechanical skills, mathematics, science, language, music and graphic art can be used to identify the aptitude of students in each area of performance. You might have heard of the use of aptitude tests in medicine, engineering, business management, law or teacher training for selection of students for studies in the respective fields. The aptitude test, in fact, provides a measure of the candidates promise or teachability in a field of study, say, medicine. In other words, the test would tell whether the candidate possesses the required aptitude or readiness to profit from studies in the concerned field of study.

Instructional Strategy for Handling Individual Differences

The suggested approach for handling individual differences is **adaptive instructional system**. In this approach at least two alternative instructional treatments are needed to ensure academic success. Which is the most appropriate instructional treatment for the student depends upon his or her existing level of aptitude (learning readiness). Students with high aptitude may choose unstructured instructional strategy. With minimum guidance from teacher, they may be encouraged to learn through the discovery oriented approach. You may use the inductive process but instructional treatment is essentially learner-centered.

In contrast, highly structured instructional treatment for low aptitude learners is designed in small units through sequential steps and feedback. Frequent summary and review with simplified illustration, analogy and precise explanation of concepts and principles to be learned will facilitate progressive learning. Periodic achievement and aptitude assessments and comparison of these scores with the aptitude scores obtained at the start of instruction would tell the degree to which each learner in the specific treatment group has achieved.

However, for those who are unable to profit from either of the alternative treatments presented above, **compensatory aptitude training** is suggested. This consists of directed reading skill, study habits, self-learning skills, note taking and related activities. The main aim of compensatory aptitude training is to develop readiness for entry into structured treatment. Periodic monitoring should be formulated to identify the students who reach the required level for entry into alternative treatment.

Do Learners Differ in their Academic Achievements?

They do differ, but how? We have seen that those who possess appropriate pre-requisite knowledge learn more effectively than those who lack such knowledge. Differences in pre-requisite knowledge possessed by students create differences in the attainment of knowledge. Further, knowledge is attained progressively. Progressive differences in knowledge attainment leads to cumulative differences in knowledge attainment and this form of differences is often called **Mathew Effect.** It means that academically rich get richer and those who are poor continue to be poor. Thus, differences in pre-requisites and cumulative knowledge lead to differences in the knowledge possessed by the students likewise, they also differ in their capabilities to manipulate the knowledge in a given situation and the differences are identified in terms of the abilities to apply, analyse, synthesise and evaluate knowledge. In fact, ability is an essential condition for learning and the abilities related to intelligence, aptitude and creativity are important for academic achievement. We have seen the instructional strategies for meeting the differences in intelligence, aptitude and creativity through classroom situations. It means that differences in intelligence, aptitude and creativity do create differences in academic achievement.

The differences in academic achievement can be identified using an achievement test in the concerned subject. However, if the achievement test contains only knowledge level items (questions), it tells only knowledge level differences. On the other hand, if it contains items (questions) on knowledge and capabilities—comprehension, application, analysis, synthesis and evaluation—the various levels of differences can be identified. Besides, the total marks, each level-wise total is needed to identify the strengths and weaknesses of every student as well as the differences among students. As a teacher, if you know the strengths and weaknesses of your students in a subject, you may be able to adopt appropriate instructional strategies to suit their strenghts and weaknesses in that subject.

Apart from these achievement differences are quite often identified in terms of categories of achievers by classifying students as high, average and low achievers. Though there is no strict cut-off points, these categories can be created using marks. High achievers are those who possess higher level of knowledge and capabilities (say, with marks 66% and above) than the rest and those who possess average level of knowledge and capabilities (say, with marks 36% to 65%) are called average achievers. On the other extreme, you may find learners with low level knowledge and capabilities (with 35% and below marks). They are called low achievers. If you are interested in identifying the high, average and low achievers in a subject, say Science or language, the categories are created using the marks obtained in the concerned subject. However, categories can also be created based on the overall achievement in a class.

As a teacher, you may be curious to know the strategies for meeting the achievement differences in your classroom or the challenges posed by the strengths and weaknesses of the students in teaching-learning situations. Let us discuss important instructional strategies.

What are Instructional Strategies?

Let us discuss the major strategies to cope up with the differences in academic achievement.

- Provide appropriate pre-requisites to organise and learn new information.
- Use visual aids.
- Use analogy, example and illustration.
- Ensure learner's active involvement in learning.
- Periodic assessment.

EVALUATION AND ASSESSMENT

Evaluation

Evaluation, particularly educational evaluation is a series of activities designed to measure the effectiveness of the teaching-learning systems as a whole. According to Mary Thorpe (1980), "Evaluation is the collection, analysis and interpretation of information about any aspect of a programme of education." Teaching-learning process is a continuous activity. It needs to be evaluated from beginning to end. Evaluation during the learning process (continuous assessment), often termed as "formative evaluation", is important for learners and teachers alike.

The bases of evaluation are learning objectives, performance standards and achievement tests on the one hand, and learners' and experts' opinions on the other. Evaluation helps to build an educational programme, assess its achievement and improve upon its effectiveness. It also provides valuable feedback on the design, development and implementation of the programme. It is, of course, an important component of the teaching-learning process. It helps in making the value judgement, determining educational status, or measuring achievement of learners.

The scope of evaluation in schools extents to almost all the areas of learner's personality development. It includes both scholastic and non-scholastic areas. It reveals the strengths and weaknesses of the learners, so that the learners have better opportunity to understand and improve themselves.

Evaluation is helpful to teachers also. It provides feedback to them to reshape their teaching strategies according to the needs of the learners. Evaluation in education in general and in distance education in particular becomes imperative to know as to what extent the goals of education have been achieved.

Thus, evaluation is not merely assigning grades to learners. It is a continuous process of acquiring and processing information in order to improve one's learning and to assess decisions made in designing an instructional system. If we analyse the above statement we easily notice that it has three important implications for the entire teaching-learning system. They are as follows:

1. Evaluation is a continuous process and not a one time performance measurement, effected at the end of a course/programme. It starts at the stage of curriculum development and continues until the instruction ends.
2. Evaluation process is goal-directed. It is aimed at finding ways and means to improve learning and thereby to achieve learning objectives more effectively and more efficiently.
3. Evaluation requires the use of accurate and appropriate measuring instructions to collect information for taking decisions about the quality and operation of education.

It is clear that in designing an effective learning system, one of the earliest steps we need to take is to prepare a comprehensive evaluation plan, which should be developed soon after the learning objectives have been formulated. This practice will help us to:

- determine whether the objectives are attainable or need revisions before we start designing the instructional system;
- collect data/information in a form that suits our purposes adequately and at a time when it is available, otherwise the opportunity to collect specific information may be lost; and
- have sufficient time to test the effectiveness of a design.

Continuous and Comprehensive Evaluation (CCE)

Continuous and Comprehensive Evaluation (CCE) refers to a system of school based evaluation of a student that covers all aspects of a student development. It is a developmental process of student which emphasizes on two fold objectives. These objectives are continuity in evaluation and assessment of broad based learning and behaviourial outcomes on the other.

The term **'continuous'** is meant to emphasise that evaluation of identified aspects of students **'growth and development'** is a continuous process rather than an event, built into the total teaching-learning process and spread over the entire span of academic session. It means regularity of assessment, frequency of unit testing, diagnosis of learning gaps, use of corrective measures, retesting and feedback of evidence to teachers and students for their self evaluation.

The second term **'comprehensive'** means that the scheme attempts to cover both the scholastic and the co-scholastic aspects of the students' growth and development. Since abilities, attitudes and aptitudes can manifest themselves in forms other than the written word, the term refers to application of variety of tools and techniques (both testing and non-testing) and aims at assessing a learner's development in areas of learning, like:

- Knowledge
- Understanding
- Applying
- Analyzing
- Evaluating
- Creating

Objectives of CCE

- To help develop cognitive, psychomotor and affective skills.
- To lay emphasis on thought process and de-emphasise memorization.
- To make evaluation an integral part of teaching-learning process.
- To use evaluation for improvement of students achievement and teaching-learning strategies

on the basis of regular diagnosis followed by remedial instructions.

- To use evaluation as a quality control device to maintain desired standard of performance.
- To determine social utility, desirability or effectiveness of a programme and take appropriate decisions about the learner, the process of learning and the learning environment.
- To make the process of teaching and learning a learner-centered activity.

Features of CCE

- The **'continuous'** aspect of CCE takes care of **'continual'** and **'periodicity'** aspect of evaluation.
- Continual means assessment of students in the beginning of instructions (placement evaluation) and assessment during the instructional process (**formative evaluation**) done informally using multiple techniques of evaluation.
- Periodicity means assessment of performance done frequently at the end of unit/term (**summative evaluation**).
- The **'comprehensive'** component of CCE takes care of assessment of all round development of the child's personality. It includes assessment in **Scholastic as well as Co-Scholastic** aspects of the pupil's growth.
- Scholastic aspects include curricular areas or subject specific areas, whereas Co-Scholastic aspects include Life Skills, Co-Curricular Activities, Attitudes and Values.
- Assessment in Scholastic areas is done informally and formally using multiple techniques of evaluation continually and periodically. The diagnostic evaluation takes place at the end of unit/term test. The causes of poor performance in some units are diagnosed using diagnostic tests. These are followed with appropriate interventions followed by retesting.
- Assessment in Co-Scholastic areas is done using multiple techniques on the basis of identified criteria, while assessment in Life Skills is done on the basis of Indicators of Assessment and Checklists.

Functions of CCE

- It helps the teacher to organize effective teaching strategies.
- Continuous evaluation helps in regular assessment to the extent and degree of Learner's progress (ability and achievement with reference to specific Scholastic and Co-Scholastic areas).
- Continuous evaluation serves to diagnose weaknesses and permits the teacher to ascertain an individual learner's strengths and weaknesses and her needs. It provides immediate feedback to the teacher, who can then decide whether a particular unit or concept needs a discussion again in the whole class or whether a few individuals are in need of remedial instruction.
- By continuous evaluation, children can know their strengths and weaknesses. It provides the child a realistic self assessment of how he/she studies. It can motivate children to develop good study habits, to correct errors, and to direct their activities towards the achievement of desired goals. It helps a learner to determine the areas of instruction in where more emphasis is required.
- Continuous and comprehensive evaluation identifies areas of aptitude and interest. It helps in identifying changes in attitudes and value systems.
- It helps in making decisions for the future, regarding choice of subjects, courses and careers.
- It provides information/reports on the progress of students in Scholastic and Co-Scholastic areas and thus helps in predicting the future success of the learner.

Continuous evaluation helps in bringing awareness of the achievement to the child, teachers and parents from time-to-time. They can look into the probable cause of the fall in performance if any, and may take remedial measures of instruction in which more emphasis is required. Many times, because of some personal reasons, family problems or adjustment problems, the children start neglecting their studies, resulting in sudden drop in their performance. If the teacher, child and parents do not notice the sudden drop in the performance of the child in academics, it could result in a permanent deficiency in the childs' learning.

The major emphasis of CCE is on the continuous growth of students ensuring their intellectual, emotional, physical, cultural and social development and therefore, it will not be merely limited to assessment of learner's scholastic attainments. CCE uses assessment as a means of motivating learners to provide feedback and follow up work to improve upon the learning in the classroom and to present a comprehensive picture of a learner's profile. It is this that has led to the emergence of the concept of **School Based Continuous and Comprehensive Evaluation.**

Scholastic and Co-Scholastic Assessment

In order to have Continuous and Comprehensive Evaluation, both Scholastic and Co-Scholastic aspects need to be given due recognition. Such a holistic assessment requires maintaining an ongoing and comprehensive profile for each learner that is honest, encouraging and discreet. While teachers frequently reflect, plan and implement remedial strategies, the child's ability to retain and articulate what has been learned over a period of time also requires periodic assessment. These assessments can take many forms but all of them should be as comprehensive and discreet as possible. **Weekly**, **fortnightly**, or **quarterly** reviews (depending on the learning area), that do not openly compare one learner with another are generally recommended. The objective is to promote and enhance not just learning and retention among children, but their soft skills as well.

Scholastic Assessment

The objectives of the Scholastic domain are:-

- Desirable behaviour related to the learner's knowledge, understanding, application, evaluation, analysis and the ability to apply it in an unfamiliar situation.
- To improve the teaching learning process.
- Assessment should be both **Formative** and **Summative**.

Summative and Formative Assessment

Assessment is often divided into formative and summative categories for the purpose of considering different objectives for assessment practices.

Summative Assessment

Summative assessment is intended to measure learning outcomes and report those outcomes to students, parents and administrators. In an educational setting, it generally occurs at the conclusion of a class, course, semester or academic year. In the context of a course summative assessments are typically used to assign students a course grade. It is also referred to in a learning context as **"assessment of learning"**. **Performance-based assessment** is similar to summative assessment, as it focuses on achievement. A well-defined task is identified and students are asked to create, produce, or do something, often in settings that involve real-world application of knowledge and skills. Proficiency is demonstrated by providing an extended response. Performance formats are further differentiated into products and performances. The performance may result in a product, such as a painting, portfolio, paper, or exhibition, or it may consist of a performance, such as a speech, athletic skill, musical recital, or reading.

Definitions of Summative Assessment

- "Good summative assessments—tests and other graded evaluations—must be demonstrably reliable, valid, and free of bias" (Angelo and Cross, 1993).
- '...assessment (that) has increasingly been used to sum up learning' (Black and William, 1999).
- '...looks at past achievements ... adds procedures or tests to existing work ... involves only marking and feedback grades to student ... is separated from teaching ... is carried out at intervals when achievement has to be summarized and reported.' (Harlen, 1998).

Features of Summative Assessment

- Assessment of learning.
- Generally taken by students at the end of a unit or semester to demonstrate the **"sum"** of what they have or have not learned.
- Summative assessment methods are the most traditional way of evaluating student work.

Formative Assessment

Formative assessment is generally carried out throughout a course or project. In an educational setting, formative assessment is used by teachers to consider approaches to teaching and next steps for individual learners and the class, and would not necessarily be used for grading purposes. Formative assessment, also referred to as **"educative assessment"** or **"assessment for learning"**, is used to aid learning. Assessment for learning is defined as "all those activities undertaken by teachers and/or students, which provide information to be used as feedback to modify the teaching and learning activities in which they are engaged" (Black and William 2004).

Definitions of Formative Assessment

- '... often means no more than that the assessment is carried out frequently and is planned at the same time as teaching'. (Black and William, 1999)
- '... provides feedback which leads to students recognizing the (learning) gap and closing it ... it is forward looking ...' (Harlen, 1998).
- '... includes both feedback and self-monitoring'. (Sadler, 1989)
- '... is used essentially to get a feedback into the teaching and learning process.' (Tunstall and Gipps, 1996)

Features of Formative Assessment

- Is diagnostic and remedial.
- Makes provision for effective feedback.

- Provides a platform for the active involvement of students in their own learning.
- Enables teachers to adjust teaching to take account of the results of assessment.
- Recognizes the profound influence assessment has on the motivation and self-esteem of students, both of which are crucial influences on learning.
- Recognizes the need for students to be able to assess themselves and understand how to improve.
- Builds on students' prior knowledge and experience in designing what is taught.
- Incorporates varied learning styles to decide how and what to teach.
- Encourages students to understand the criteria that will be used to judge their work.
- Offers an opportunity to students to improve their work after they get the feedback.
- Helps student to support their peer group and vice-versa.

A common form of formative assessment is **"diagnostic assessment"**. Diagnostic assessment measures a student's current knowledge and skills for the purpose of identifying a suitable program of learning. **"Self-assessment"** is a form of diagnostic assessment which involves students assessing themselves. **"Forward-looking assessment"** asks those being assessed to consider themselves in hypothetical future situations.

Co-Scholastic Assessment

The desirable behaviour related to learner's life skills, attitudes, interests, values, co-curricular activities and physical health are described as skills to be acquired in co-scholastic domain.

The process of assessing the students' progress in achieving objectives related to scholastic and co-scholastic domain is called comprehensive evaluation. It has been observed that usually under the scholastic domain such as knowledge and understanding of the facts, concepts, principles etc. of a subject are assessed. The Co-Scholastic elements are either altogether excluded from the evaluation process or they are not given adequate attention. For making the evaluation comprehensive, both Scholastic and Co-Scholastic aspects should be given importance. Simple and manageable means of assessment of Co-Scholastic aspects of growth must be included in the comprehensive evaluation scheme.

Comprehensive evaluation would necessitate the use of a variety of tools and techniques. This will be so because both different and specific areas of learner's growth can be evaluated through certain special techniques.

School Based CCE

School based Evaluation is held at school level unlike external examination conducted by the Boards of School Education. This is done by the teachers according to the schedule developed by the school and guidelines given by the Board. Though this evaluation has been done at school level all along, certain shortcomings have crept into this system. These shortcomings can be attributed to various factors. The basic factor is the misconception of teachers regarding the place of evaluation and its importance in the educational process. The other factor has been the imitation of the practice of external examination which is generally held at the end of the session.

In the School Based System of evaluation, the focus on the purpose of assessment has changed. Now, it includes readiness testing, screening of development, evaluation of performance in cognitive, affective and psychomotor domains more frequently, systematically and effectively.

In other words, School Based Evaluation is child-centred, school-centred and multidimensional evaluation. Hence, in its true spirit, it triggers an all round development of the learner. It encourages all kinds of learning in life both inside the school as well as outside it. It is child-centered as it attempts to consider the learner as a unique entity for its individual pattern of development. It builds on individual child's abilities, progress and development in achieving already set goals and objectives of education as an individual and not just his/her position in relation to other learners.

Further, this evaluation helps a learner to use his/her potential in a better manner and also provides insight to the teachers to discover the methods which may be helpful to the individual learner in resolving his/her problems and difficulties.

Besides being ***child-centred,*** this evaluation is ***school-centred*** as well. It means that no outside agency interferes in this evaluation process. It is entirely school based and done by the teacher. The teacher is trusted and given full responsibility of evaluating students with the brief that the teacher knows best about his/her students.

School Based Evaluation is ***multidimensional.*** Its multidimensional nature is reflected in recognizing and taking care of learners' social, emotional, physical, intellectual and other areas of development which are interrelated and cannot be considered in isolation. It also calls for the use of multiple techniques and tools of evaluation.

Aim of School Based CCE

- Elimination of chance element and subjectivity (as far as possible), de-emphasis on memorization, encouraging comprehensive evaluation incorporating both Scholastic and Co-Scholastic aspects of learners development.
- Continuous evaluation spread over the total span of the instructional time as an integral built-in aspect of the total teaching-learning process.
- Functional and meaningful declaration of results for effective use by teachers, students, parents and the society.
- Wider uses of test results for purposes not merely of the assessment of levels of pupils' achievements and proficiencies, but mainly for their improvement, thorough diagnosis and remedial/enrichment programmes.
- Improvement in the mechanics of conducting examinations for realizing a number of other allied purposes.
- Introduction of concomitant changes in instructional materials and methodology.
- Introduction of the semester system.
- The use of grades in place of marks in determining and declaring the level of pupil performance and proficiency.

Its Characteristics

School Based Evaluation has the following characteristics:

- Is broader, more comprehensive and continuous than traditional system.
- Aims primarily to help learners for systematic learning and development.
- Takes care of the needs of the learner as responsible citizens of the future.
- Is more transparent, futuristic and provides more scope for association among learners, teachers and parents.

School based evaluation provides opportunities to teachers to **know the following about their learners:**

- What they learn?
- How they learn?
- What type of difficulties/limitations they face in working in tandem?
- What do the children think?
- What do the children feel?
- What are their interests and dispositions?

The focus has shifted to developing a deep learning environment. There is a paradigm shift in the pedagogy and competencies from 'controlling' to 'enriching' to 'empowering' schools.

Traditional Schooling	**Enriching Schooling**	**Empowering Schooling**
• Teacher centred • Subjects and classes-teacher directed • Sorting and ranking individuals **Competency:** • Memory • Competitive	• Student centred • Self directed • Continuous assessment **Competency:** • Critical thinking • Collaborative • Creative	• Experience centred • Virtual authenticity • Multi literacies **Competency:** • Risk taking • Ethical • Interactive

Implementing School Based Assessment would mean:

- Elimination of chance element and subjectivity (as far as possible), de-emphasis of memorization, encouraging Comprehensive evaluation incorporating both scholastic and co-scholastic aspects of learners development.
- Continuous evaluation spread over the total span of the instructional time as an integral built-in aspect of the total teaching-learning process.
- Functional and meaningful declaration of results for effective use by teachers, students, parents and the society.
- Wider uses of test results for purposes not merely of the assessment of levels of pupils' achievements and proficiencies, but mainly for its improvement, through diagnosis and remedial/enrichment programmes.
- Improvements in the mechanics of conducting examinations for realizing a number of other allied purposes.
- Introduction of concomitant changes in instructional materials and methodology.

- Introduction of the semester system from the secondary stage onwards.
- The use of grades in place of marks in determining and declaring the level of pupil performance and proficiency.

The above goals are relevant for both external examination and evaluation in schools.

Shortcoming of Traditional External Examination

- It is a one shot examination at the end of a year at the terminal stage of schooling.
- It mainly evaluates only the scholastic aspects of learning of the students.
- It does not evaluate all the abilities of the children. On the basis of marks obtained in written examination the students are declared pass or fail and further classified into predetermined divisions.
- Pass and fail system causes frustration and is inhumane because the failed candidates come to feel that they are good for nothing.
- Co-scholastic areas are almost totally ignored and have no place in the currently prevalent scheme of education and evaluation.
- The practice of testing of untaught content also reflects poor learning achievement.
- Only limited techniques of evaluation without potential for judging a student are being used.
- The aim of evaluation is to improve learner's quality which is not served by external examination.
- The current practice of awarding marks suffers from many discrepancies due to variety of errors.
- The varied ranges of obtained scores of students in different subjects create the problem in declaring reliable results.
- Analysis and interpretation of test results is not done in a scientific way.

School Based Continuous and Comprehensive Evaluation System should be Established to:

- reduce stress on children.
- make evaluation comprehensive and regular.
- provide space for the teacher for creative teaching.
- provide a tool of diagnosis and remediation.
- produce learners with greater skills.

Four Assessment Paradigms

Assessment *of* Learning

The 'assessment **of** learning' is defined as a process whereby someone attempts to describe and quantify the knowledge, attitudes or skills possessed by another. Teacher direction is paramount and the student has little involvement in the design or implementation of the assessment process in these circumstances.

- Teacher designs learning
- Teacher collects evidence
- Teacher judges what has been learnt (and what has not been learnt)

Assessment *for* Learning

The 'assessment **for** learning' involves increased level of student autonomy, but not without teacher guidance and collaboration. The assessment **for** learning is sometimes seen as being akin to 'formative assessment'. There is more emphasis towards giving useful advice to the student and less emphasis on the giving of marks and the grading function.

- Teacher designs learning
- Teacher designs assessment with feedback to student
- Teacher judges what has been learnt (student develops insight into what has not)

Assessment *as* Learning

The 'assessment **as** learning' is perhaps more connected with diagnostic assessment and can be constructed with more of an emphasis on peer learning. Assessment **as** learning generates opportunities for self assessment and peer assessment. Students take on increased responsibility to generate quality information about their learning and that of others.

- Teacher and student co-construct learning
- Teacher and student co-construct assessment
- Teacher and student co-construct learning progress map

Assessment **for** learning and assessment **as** learning activities should be deeply embedded in teaching and learning and be the source of interactive feedback, allowing students to adjust, re-think and re-learn.

Assessment *in* Learning

The 'assessment **in** learning' places the question at the centre of teaching and learning. It deflects the teaching from its focus on a 'correct answer' to a focus on 'a fertile question'. Through enquiry students engage in processes that generates feedback about their learning, which come from multiple sources and activities. It contributes to the construction of other learning activities, line of enquiry and the generation of other questions.

- Student as the centre of learning

- Student monitors, assesses and reflects on learning
- Student initiates demonstration of learning (to self and others)
- Teacher as coach and mentor.

Teachers and students need to understand the purpose of each assessment strategy. The overall assessment 'package' being used by learners and teachers should accurately capture, generate and use meaningful learning information to generate deep learning and understanding.

ASSESSING LEARNERS

Any meaningful report on the quality and extent of a child's learning needs to be comprehensive. We need a curriculum whose creativity, innovativeness, and development of the whole being, the hallmark of a good education makes uniform tests that assess memorised facts and textbook-based learning obsolete. We need to redefine and seek new parameters for and ways of evaluation and feedback. In addition to the learner's achievements in specific subject areas that lend themselves to testing easily, assessment would need to encompass attitudes to learning, interest, and the ability to learn independently.

ASSESSMENT IN THE COURSE OF TEACHING

Preparing report cards is a way for the teacher to think about each individual child and review what she/he has learnt during the term, and what she/he needs to work on and improve. To be able to write such report cards, teachers would need to think about each individual child, and hence pay attention to them during their everyday teaching and interaction. One does not need special tests for this; learning activities themselves provide the basis for such ongoing observational and qualitative assessments of children. Maintaining a daily diary based on observation helps in continuous and comprehensive evaluation. An extract from the diary of a teacher for a week notes the following: "Kiran enjoyed his work. He took an instant liking to the books that were informative and brief. He says that he likes simple and clear language. In noting down facts, he goes for short answers. He says that it helps him understand things easily. He favours a practical approach." Similarly, keeping samples and notes of the child's work at different stages provides both the teacher and the learner herself or himself with a systematic record of his/her learning progress.

The belief that assessment must lead to finding learning difficulties to then be remediated is often very impractical and not founded on a sound understanding of pedagogic practice. Problems regarding conceptual development cannot and do not wait for formal tests in order to be detected. A teacher can, in the course of teaching itself, come to know of such problems by asking questions that make children think or by giving them small assignments. She can then attend to them in the process of teaching—by ensuring that her planning is flexible and responsive to the learners and their learning.

CURRICULAR AREAS THAT CANNOT BE 'TESTED FOR MARKS'

Each area of the curriculum may not lend itself to being 'tested'; it may even be antithetical to the nature of learning in the curricular area. This includes areas such as work, health, yoga, physical education, music and art. While the skill-based component of physical education and yoga could be tested, the health aspect needs continuous and qualitative assessments. Currently, this has the effect of making these subjects and activities 'less important' in the curriculum; these areas are inadequately provided for in terms of material resources and curricular planning, and marked by a lack of seriousness. Further, the time allocated for them is also frequently sacrificed to accommodate special classes. This is a serious compromise with parts of the curriculum that have deep educational significance and potential.

Even if 'marks' cannot be given, children can be assessed for their development in these areas. Participation, interest, and level of involvement, and the extent to which abilities and skills have been honed, are some markers that can help teachers to gauge the benefits of what children learn and gain through such activities. Asking children to self-report on their learning can also provide teachers with insight into children's educational progress and give them feedback on improving curriculum or pedagogy.

DESIGN AND CONDUCT OF ASSESSMENT

Assessments and examinations must be credible, and based on valid ways of gauging learning.

As long as examinations and tests assess children's ability to remember and recall textbook knowledge, all attempts to redirect the curriculum towards learning will be thwarted. First, tests in knowledge-based subject areas must be able to gauge what children have learnt, and their ability to use this knowledge for problem solving and application in the real world. In addition, they must also be able to test the processes of thinking to gauge if the learner has also learnt where to find information, how to use new information, and to analyse and evaluate the same.

The types of questions that are set for assessment need to go beyond what is given in the book. Often children's learning is restricted as teachers do not accept their answers if they are different from what is presented in the guidebooks.

Questions that are open-ended and challenging could also be used. Designing good test items and questions is an art, and teachers should spend time thinking about and devising such questions. The interest and ability of teachers to design good questions can be promoted through district—or state-level competitions. All question papers must be designed graded for difficulty in order to permit all children to experience a level of success, and to gain confidence in their ability to answer and solve problems.

Trying to devise a good and effective open-book examination can be a challenge that we must try to take up in our curricular efforts at all levels of school. This would require teachers and examination setters to emphasise the interpretation and application of learning over the arguments and facts that can be located in the book. There have been successful demonstrations that such examinations can be carried out on a large scale, and that teachers can themselves be trusted with moderating the results of such examinations. In this way, the assessment of projects and lab work can also be made credible and sound.

It is important that after receiving their corrected papers, children rewrite the answers and that these are again reviewed by teachers to ensure that children have learnt and gained something out of the ordeal.

Competition is motivating, but it is an extrinsic rather than intrinsic form of motivation. It is, of course, much easier to establish and to manipulate, and therefore frequently resorted to by teachers and school systems as a way creating and nurturing the drive for excellence. Schools begin 'ranking' children as early as their pre-primary years as a way of inculcating in them a competitive spirit. Such a competitive drive has several negative side effects on learning, often superficial learning is sufficient to create and maintain impressions, and over time students lose their ability to take initiative or do things for the fulfilment of one's own interest; hence, areas that cannot be 'marked' are neglected. This has unhealthy consequences for classroom culture, making children individualistic and unsuited to team work. There is an absurd and unnecessary importance given to term examinations, often accompanied by extreme arrangements of invigilation and secrecy. While the physical and psychological effects of this may not be readily visible until middle school, they frequently lead to high levels of stress in children, and cause early burnout. Schools and teachers need to ask themselves whether there is really much to be gained out of such practices and to what extent learning requires such systems of marking and ranking.

SELF-ASSESSMENT AND FEEDBACK

The role of assessment is to gauge the progress that both learner and teacher have made towards achieving the aims that have been set and appraising how this could be done better. Opportunity for feedback, leading to revision and improvement of performance, should constantly be available, without exams and evaluations being used as a threat to study.

Grading and correction carried out in the presence of students and providing feedback on the answers they get right and wrong, and why. Asking children about why they answered what they did assists teachers in going beyond the written answer to engage with children's thinking. Such processes also take away the frightening judgemental quality of marks obtained in a test, and enable children to understand and focus on their mistakes and learn through these mistakes. Sometimes head teachers object, claiming that correction in the presence of the child reduces 'objectivity'. This is a misplaced concern for 'objectivity', stemming from a competitive system that believes in judging children. Such a concern for 'objectivity' is misplaced in evaluation, which is consistent with educational goals.

Not only learning outcomes but also learning experiences themselves must be evaluated. Learners happily comment on the totality of their experience. Exercises, both individual and collective, can be designed to enable them to reflect on and assess their learning experiences. Such experiences also provide them with self-regulatory capabilities essential for 'learning to learn'. Such information is also valuable feedback to the teacher, and can be used to modify the learning system as a whole.

Every classroom interaction with children requires their evaluation of their own work, and a discussion with them about what should be tested and the ways of finding out whether the competencies are being developed or not. Even very young children are able to give correct assessments of what they can or cannot do well. The role of teaching is to provide an opportunity to each child to learn to the best of his or her ability and provide learning experiences that develop cognitive qualities, physical well-being and athletic qualities, as also affective and aesthetic qualities.

Report cards need to present to children and parents a comprehensive and holistic view of the child's development in many fields. Teachers must be able to say things about each child/student, that conveys to them a sense of individualised attention, reaffirms a positive self-image, and communicates personal goals for them to work towards. Whether it is marks or grades that are reported, a qualitative statement by the teacher is necessary to support the assessment. Only through such a relationship with each child can any teacher succeed in influencing him/her, and contributing to his/her learning. Along with the teacher assessing each child, each student could also assess himself or herself and include this self-assessment in the report card.

Currently, many report cards carry information on subject areas and have nothing to say about other aspects of the child's development, including health, physical fitness and abilities in games, social skills, and abilities in art and craft. Qualitative statements about these aspects of children's education and development would provide a more holistic assessment of educational concerns.

AREAS THAT REQUIRE FRESH THINKING

There are many areas of the curriculum that can be assessed but for which we still do not have reliable and efficient instruments. This includes assessing learning that is carried out in groups, and learning in areas such as theatre, work and craft where skills and competencies develop over longer time scales and require careful observation.

Continuous and comprehensive evaluation has frequently been cited as the only meaningful kind of evaluation. This also requires much more careful thinking through about when it is to be employed in a system effectively. Such evaluation places a lot of demand on teachers' time and ability to maintain meticulous records if it is to be meaningfully executed and if it is to have any reliability as an assessment. If this simply increases stress on children by reducing all their activities into items for assessment, or making them experience the teacher's 'power', then it defeats the purpose of education. Unless a system is adequately geared for such assessment, it is better for teachers to engage in more limited forms of evaluation, but incorporating into them more features that will make the assessment a meaningful record of learning.

Finally, there is a need to evolve and maintain credibility in assessment so that they perform their function of providing feedback in a meaningful way.

ASSESSMENT AT DIFFERENT STAGES

ECCE and Classes I and II of the Elementary Stage: At this stage, assessment must be purely qualitative judgements of children's activities in various domains and an assessment of the status of their health and physical development, based on observations through everyday interactions. On no account should they be made to take any form of test, oral or written.

Class III to Class VIII of the Elementary Stage: A variety of methods may be used, including oral and written tests and observations. Children should be aware that they are being assessed, but this must be seen by them as a part of the teaching process and not as a fearful constant threat. Grades or marks along with qualitative judgements of achievement and areas requiring attention are essential at this stage. Children's own self-evaluation can also be a part of the report card from Class V onwards. Rather than examinations, there could be short tests from time-to-time, which are criterion based. Term-wise examinations could be commenced from Class VII onwards when children are more psychologically ready to study large chunks of material and, to spend a few hours in an examination room, working at answering questions. Again, the progress card must indicate general observations on health and nutrition, specific observations on the overall progress of the learner, and information and advice for the parents.

Class IX to Class XII of the Secondary and Higher Secondary Stages: Assessment may be based more on tests, examinations and project reports for the knowledge-based areas of the curriculum, along with self-assessment. Other areas would be assessed through observation and also through self-evaluation.

Reports could include much more analysis about the students, various skill/knowledge areas and percentiles, etc. This would assist them by pointing out the areas of study that they need to focus on, and also help them by providing a basis for further choices that they make regarding what to study thereafter.

SECTION b CONCEPT OF INCLUSIVE EDUCATION & UNDERSTANDING CHILDREN WITH SPECIAL NEEDS

INCLUSIVE EDUCATION: DEFINITION AND CONCEPT

Inclusive Education denotes that all children irrespective of their strengths and weaknesses will be part of the mainstream education. Thus, inclusive education means, "the act of ensuring that all children despite their differences, receive the opportunity of being part of the same classroom as other children of their age, and in the process get the opportunity to being exposed to the curriculum to their optimal potential."

Every child is special for his/her parent and, every child has a special need for love, acceptance and a feeling of belongingness. Here, we call **children with special needs** to those who are "different" from their cohorts. They are born equal with some limitations and with the help of inclusion be able to actively participate as equal citizens in all aspects of society and community life. Thus, children with special needs refer to "all those children who require adaptations to the normal process of education due to problems of vision, hearing, movement, learning and intellect." In other words, these children have some kind of **disability**.

Disability: Definitions

Disability refers to any limitations experienced by the disabled in comparisons to able persons of similar age, sex and culture. The UN Declaration on the Rights of Disabled Persons has defined disabled person as "any person unable to ensure by himself or herself, wholly or partly, the necessities of a normal individual and/or social life, as a result of a deficiency, either congenital or not, in his or her physical or mental capabilities".

DISTINCTIONS AMONG IMPAIRMENT, DISABILITY AND HANDICAP

The World Health Organisation (WHO) has made distinctions between the definitions of impairment, disability and handicap as follows:

- Impairment is any loss or abnormality of psychological, physiological or anatomical structure or function generally taken to be at organ level. Impairment is a damage to tissue due to disease or trauma.
- A disability is any restriction or lack of ability (resulting from an impairment) to perform an activity in the manner or within the range considered normal for a human being.
- A handicap is a disadvantage for an individual, resulting from impairment or disability that limits or prevents fulfilment of a role that is normal (depending on age, sex and social cultural factors) for that individual. Handicap is a condition or burden, which is imposed on the person confronted with the disability.

Types of Disability According to PWD Act, 1995

The PWD Act, 1995 has given the following seven types of disability as:

1. Blindness
2. Low Vision
3. Leprosy-cured
4. Hearing impairment
5. Locomotor disabilities
6. Mental retardation
7. Mental illness

EDUCATIONAL PROVISIONS FOR CHILDREN WITH SPECIAL NEEDS

The last two decades of the 19th century has witnessed the knowledge and processes of educating the disabled children through Christian Missionaries. The first school for the deaf was established in Mumbai in 1883 and the first school for the blind in Amritsar in 1887. At that time, it was believed that children with disabilities could not be educated alongwith normal children. Therefore, education to disabled children was offered through special school. This trend continued early sixties of the last century with the help of some international agencies who developed programme of integrated education. Here, children disabilities were placed in regular school so that they could study alongwith their non-disabled 'peers". The integrated education adopts various models for service deliver. Presently the emphasis is on the need to provide education for all in appropriate environment with inclusive philosophy through inclusive education.

Integrated Education for the Disabled Children (IEDC)

With the development of science and technology and improvement in Medical Services and Aggressive neo-natal intervention has ensured that a large number of babies who would earlier have not survived but often with different abilities. The number of differently abled children is on the increasing trend but it is not possible to create the required number of special schools throughout the country to meet this challenge due to the high cost and also due to the fact that the population is so scattered. The best alternative under these situations is to make use of the infrastructural facilities already present in terms of regular schools and integrate children into the mainstream of education.

Consequent on the success of international institutions in introducing differently abled children in regular schools, the planning commission, Govt. of India, in 1971 includes in its plan a programme for integrated education. In 1974, the Union Government introduced a scheme called "Integrated Schools" to do just this. This scheme was later revised and a plan of action formulated. The important aims of IEDC includes:

- Provide educational opportunity to differently abled children in regular schools.
- Facilitate retention of differently abled in the school system.
- Integrate children from special school to common schools.

The scope of the scheme of IEDC includes pre-school training, counselling for the parents, and special training in skills for all kinds of differently abled children. It provides facilities in the form of books, stationary, uniforms and allowances for transport, reader and escort etc.

Project Integrated Education for the Disabled (PIED)

This scheme was launched by MHRD Govt. of India in collaboration with UNICEF in 1987 to strengthen the integration of differently abled into regular schools. Under this scheme, a cluster instead of individual school is given importance. This scheme is an improvement over the special schools in one or many ways and provides a way towards universalisation of elementary education and Education for All including for differently abled children.

ASSUMPTION ABOUT INTEGRATED EDUCATION

Integrated education assumes a process of bringing disabled children into mainstream schools, where the system remains the same. As per the system, the child is the problem. So, it is essential to change the child where the resources are focused on the individual child. The failure is due to the child's problem; he is not able, not ready, not good enough to cope up with the system.

In integrated education; it is the children with disabilities who are seen as the problem, who must be "fixed", "changed" & "adapted" to suit the existing regular, mainstream school. It is the disabled child who is seen as a square peg in a round table. The system remains the same. The onus for successful integration therefore, is on the disabled child.

ASSUMPTION ABOUT INCLUSIVE EDUCATION

Assumptions of inclusive education is opposite to integrated education. Inclusive education assumes that changes the system to fit the child. It is essential to addresses all types of individual needs, not just disability. Teachers and schools are held responsible for children's learning. It focuses on flexibility of curriculum, teacher training and change in environmental. Failure is the problem with the system not with the child. It is quite essential to assumes that all children can learn and that all children need their learning to be supported in diverse ways.

In this model of inclusive education, it is not the child, but the education system, which is seen as a problem. Therefore, it is the system (with all its components) with should be changed, modified & made flexible enough to accommodate the diverse needs of all learners, including children with disabilities. The onus for success is therefore on the flexibility of the system. It focuses on the environment, as the "disabling" cause because it fails to provide appropriate access to equal opportunities for all persons to participate fully in social life.

Though integrated education of differently abled children has gained momentum all over the country since 1974, there are some other possibilities too for these children to get education. For example, the NIOS (National Institute of Open Schooling) offers education which have the advantage of being specially adopted to the needs of every child as well as aimed at giving the child every opportunity to progress at his/her pace. Another example is alternative schooling and community-based rehabilitation programmes.

EDUCATION FOR A COHESIVE SOCIETY

Despite more than half a century of independence, India is struggling for freedom from various kinds of biases and imbalances such as rural/urban, rich/poor, and differences on the basis of caste, religion, ideology, gender etc. Education can play a very significant role in minimising and finally eliminating these differences by providing equality of access to quality education and opportunity.

Equality of opportunity means ensuring that every individual receives suitable education at a pace and through methods suited to his/her being. Children of the disadvantaged, and socially discriminated groups and also those suffering from specific challenges must be paid special attention.

Provision for equal opportunity to all not only in access, but also in the conditions for success is a precondition for the promotion of equality. The curriculum must create an awareness of the inherent equality of all with a view to removing prejudices and complexes transmitted through the social environment and the factor of birth.

EDUCATION OF GIRLS

Equality among sexes is a fundamental right under the constitution of India. The state, however, also has the right to exercise positive protective discrimination in favour of the disadvantaged population groups including women. Emphasis in education has moved from 'Equality of Educational Opportunity' (NPE, 1968) to 'Education for Women's Equality and Empowerment' (1986). As a result, the curricular and training strategies for the education of girls now demand more attention. Besides, making education accessible to more and more girls, especially rural girls, removing all gender discrimination and gender bias in school curriculum, textbooks and the process of transaction is absolutely necessary. There is a need to develop and implement gender inclusive and gender sensitive curricular strategies to nurture a generation of girls and boys who are equally competent and are sensitive to one another, and grow up in a caring and sharing mode as equals, and not as adversaries.

EDUCATION OF LEARNERS FROM DISADVANTAGED GROUPS

For achieving a cohesive society it would be essential to respond to specific educational needs of learners from different sections of the society with special emphasis on the Scheduled Castes, the Scheduled Tribes and the other socially and economically disadvantaged groups. In order to do so, there is a need for integrating the socio-cultural perspectives partly by showing concern for their linguistic specificities and pedagogic requirements. Implications of the multilingual and multicultural environment shall have to be taken care of through specifically devised methodology. Contextualisation of curriculum shall have to be effected through curricular materials. The fundamental rights of the disadvantaged groups have to be consciously incorporated in the curriculum. Even the problem of educating the migrating population shall have to be handled through specific condensed educational programmes based on the main ingredients of the national curriculum.

EDUCATION OF THE GIFTED AND TALENTED

An educational system has the dual role of promoting equality as well as excellence. Education is increasingly called upon to liberate all the creative potentialities of human consciousness. Man essentially fulfils himself in and through creation. It is in the context of this, that education of gifted and talented children assumes great importance. A curricular programme while on the one hand should identify such children, on the other it should also nurture their diverse creative abilities by paying them special attention. It is also important that the identification and nurturance begins right from the earliest stage of education. Moreover, the task of identifying the gifted and talented must be accomplished on the basis of a broad conceptualisation of the process from multiple perspectives rather than as a search for a unitary human attribute. Not only their IQ (Intelligence Quotient) but also their EQ (Emotional Quotient) and SQ (Spiritual Quotient) ought to be assessed.

NATIONAL LEVEL POLICY AND LEGISLATION

Kothari Commission (1964-66)

The Kothari Commission first suggested that the education of handicapped children has to be organised not merely on humanitarian grounds, but also an aspects of utility. The commission emphasised that the education of children with disability should be "an inseparable part of the general education system. The commission also specifically emphasised that the education of children with disability should be "an inseparable part of the general education system. The commission also specifically emphasised. the importance of integrated education in meeting this target as it is cost effective and useful in developing mutual understanding between children with and without disabilities.

National Policy on Education (1986)

The National Policy on Education was adopted by Indian Parliament in 1986. The policy emphasized the removal of disparities, and ensuring equalisation of educational opportunity under its para education of the disabled.

National Policies for Persons with Disabilities (2006)

This recognises that persons with disabilities are valuable human resources for the country and seek to create an environment that provides them equal opportunities, protection of their rights and full participation in society.

Persons with Disabilities (Equal Opportunities, Protection of Rights & Full Participation) Act, 1995

Landmark legislation in the history of special education in India is the persons with Disabilities Act, 1995. This comprehensive Act covers seven disabilities, namely blindness, low vision, hearing impaired, loco-motor impaired, mental retardation, leprosy cured and mental illness.

The Rehabilitation Council of India (RCI) Act, 1992

This Act was passed in 1992 for the purpose of constituting the Rehabilitation Professionals and for maintenance of a Central Rehabilitation Register. It was amended by Rehabilitation Council of India (Amendment) Act, 2000 to provide for monitoring the training of rehabilitation professionals and personal, promoting research in rehabilitation and special education as additional objectives of the council.

SECTION C LEARNING AND PEDAGOGY

HOW CHILDREN THINK AND LEARN

Children learn from anything and everything they see and act upon. They have learnt a lot before they join school, and they continue to learn outside the school hours. If we believe that children learn only in school, it is because of what we wrongly regard as learning. When a child spends hours on trying to solve a Jigsaw puzzle (say), he/she is often reprimanded by adults for wasting study time. Little do the grown-ups realise that it is through such interesting games that this child may be increasing his/her understanding of shapes and size. And, this learning is taking place outside the school hours, without formal instruction. A curriculum built upon assumptions about children's learning, that ignore this aspect, is also responsible for children losing interest in mathematics or in any formal learning.

From the time a child is born, his/her interaction with the world around his/her starts. He/she perceives things around his/her, and gradually makes sense of them. He/she slowly begins to recognise people and objects, relate more and more to the environment, and observe things through the senses of touch, sight, taste, smell and sound. There are **four different stages** of learning or development that each child goes through.

Sensorimotor

This is from the ages of birth to about two years old. During this time the child's primary mode of learning occurs through the five senses. He/she learns to experience environment. The child touches things, holds, looks, listens, tastes, feels, bangs, and shakes everything in sight. When the child adds motor skills such as creeping, crawling and walking, his/her environment expands by leaps and bounds. The child is now exploring their environment with both senses and the ability to get around.

Preoperational

This is the stages between ages two and seven. During this stage the child is busy gathering information or learning, and then trying to figure out ways that they can used what they have learned to begin solving problems.

During this stage of his/her life child will be thinking in specifics and will find it very difficult to get generalise anything. This is the time when a child learns by asking questions. The child generally will not want a real answer to his question at this point. When he asks why do we have grass .... He simply wants to know that it is for him to play in. No technical answers for know. The child in this age group judges everything on the 'me' basis—How does it affect me? Do I like it?

Concrete Operations Period

This is the period of time when child is between the ages of seven to ten. This is a wonderful age as this is when children begin to manipulate data mentally. They take the information at hand and begin to define, compare and contrast it. They, however, still think concretely.

The concrete operational child is capable of logical thought. This child still learns through their senses, but no longer relies on only them to teach him. He now thinks as well. A good teacher for this age group would start each lesson at a concrete level and then more toward a generalised level. The child, during this period, is very literal in their thinking.

Formal Operations Period

The period begins at about age eleven. At this time the child will break through the barrier of literalism and more on to thinking in more abstract terms. He no longer restricts thinking to time and space. This child now starts to reflect, hypothesize and theorize.

In the formal operation period, children need to develop cognitive abilities. The following is a list of six simple categories of cognitive abilities. The following is a list of six simple categories of cognitive abilities:

1. **Knowledge of facts and principals:** This is the direct recall of facts and principals. **Examples:** memorisation of dates, name, definition, vocabulary words.
2. **Comprehension:** Understanding of facts and ideas.
3. **Application:** Needs to know, rules, principles, and procedures and how to use them.
4. **Analysis:** Breaking down concepts into parts.
5. **Synthesis:** Putting together information or ideas.
6. **Evaluation:** Judging the value of information.

BASIC PROCESSES OF TEACHING AND LEARNING

Teaching-learning process is the heart of education. On it depends the fulfilment of the airns & objectives of education. It is the most powerful instrument of education to bring about desired changes in the students. Teaching learning are related terms. In teaching-learning process, the teacher, the learner, the curriculum & other variables are organised in a systematic way to attain some pre-determined goal.

Essential Aspects of the Teaching-learning Process

According to Diana Laurillard, there are four aspects of the teaching-learning process:

1. **Discussion**—between the teacher and learner.
2. **Interaction**—between the learner and some aspect of the world defined by the teacher.
3. **Adaptation**—of the world by the teacher and action by the learner.
4. **Reflection**—on the learner's performance by both teacher and learner.

According to **Burton** in the figure above

1. Teaching can become effective only by relating it to process of learning.
2. Teaching objective cannot be realised without being related to learning situation.
3. We may create and use teaching aids to create some appropriate learning situation.
4. The strategies and devices of teaching may be selected in such a manner that the optimal objectives of learning area achieved.
5. To understand principles, goals, objectives of education in right perspective.
6. Appropriate learning situation condition may be created for congenial and effective teaching.

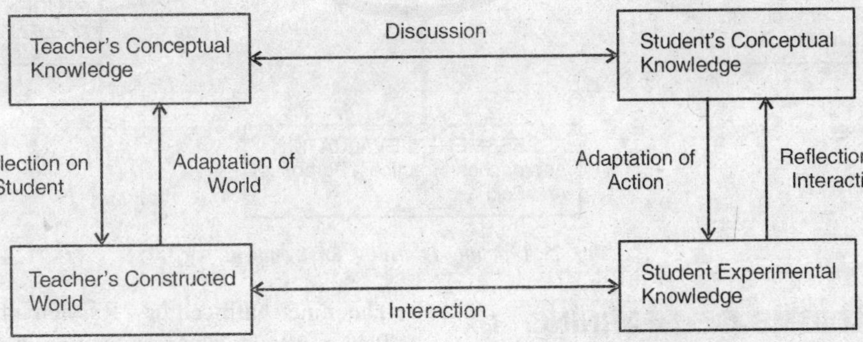

Fig. 1: *Essential aspects of the ideal teaching-learning process*

Approaches to Learning Theories

Aspect	Behaviourist	Cognitivist	Humanist
Learning theorists	Thorndike, Pavlov, Watson, Guthrie, Hull, Tolman, Skinner	Koffka, Kohler, Lewin, Piaget, Ausubel, Bruner, Gagne	Maslow, Rogers
View of the learning process	Change in behaviour	Internal mental process (including insight, information processing, memory, perception)	A personal act to fulfil potential
Locus of learning	Stimuli in external environment	Internal cognitive structuring	Affective and cognitive needs

Aspect	Behaviourist	Cognitivist	Humanist
Purpose in education	Produce behavioural change in desired direction	Develop capacity and skills to learn better	Become self-actualized autonomous
Educator's role	Arranges environment to elicit desired response	Structures content of learning activity	Facilitates development of the whole person
Manifestations in adult learning	Behavioural objectives	Cognitive development	Andragogy
	Competency-based education	Intelligence, learning and memory as function of age	Self-directed learning
	Skill development and training	Learning how to learn	

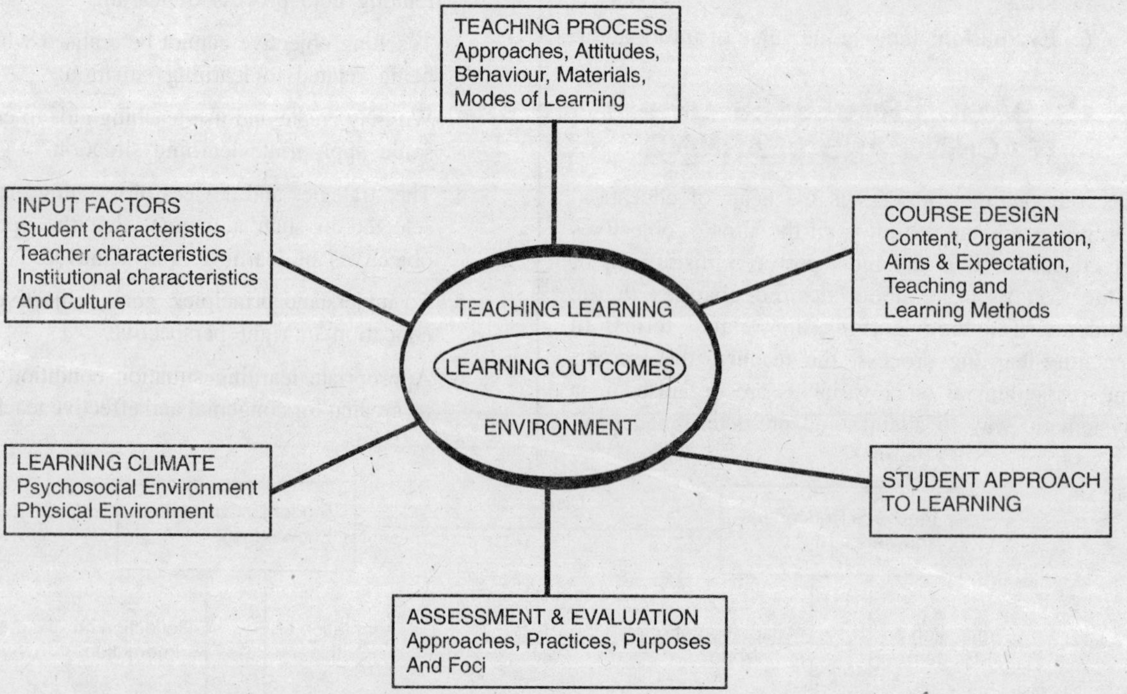

Fig. 2: *Teaching-Learning Environment*

PARADIGMS OF LEARNING

Learning takes place in many ways. There are some methods that are used in acquisition of simple responses while other methods are used in the acquisition of complex responses. The simplest kind of learning is called conditioning. Two types of conditioning have been identified. The first one is called classical conditioning and the second instrumental/operant conditioning. In addition, we have observational learning, cognitive learning, verbal learning, concept learning and skill learning.

Classical Conditioning

This type of learning was first investigated by Ivan P. Pavlov. Like many great scientific advances, classical conditioning was discovered accidentally. The nineteenth-century Russian physiologist Ivan Pavlov was looking at salivation in dogs in response to being fed, when he noticed that his dogs would begin to salivate whenever he entered the room, even when he was not bringing them food. However, when Pavlov discovered that any object or event which the dogs learnt to associate with food (such as the food bowl) would trigger the same response, he realised that he had made an important scientific discovery, and he devoted the rest of his career to studying this type of learning.

Classical conditioning is 'classical' in that it is the first systematic study of basic laws of learning. Classical conditioning involves learning to associate an unconditioned stimulus that already brings about a particular response (*i.e.* a reflex) with a new (conditioned) stimulus, so that the new stimulus brings about the same response. The unconditioned stimulus (or UCS) is the object or event that originally produces the reflexive/natural response.

Once the neutral stimulus has become associated with the unconditioned stimulus, it becomes a conditioned stimulus (CS). The conditioned response (CR) is the response to the conditioned stimulus. Thus, learning situation in classical conditioning is one of S-S learning in which one stimulus becomes a signal of another stimulus.

Determinants of Classical Conditioning

How quickly and strongly acquisition of a response occurs in classical conditioning depends on several factors. Some of the major factors influencing learning a CR are described below:

1. Time Relations between Stimuli: The classical conditioning procedures, discussed below, are basically of four types based on the time relations between the onset of conditioned stimulus (CS) and unconditioned stimulus (US). The first three are called forward conditioning procedures, and the fourth one is called backward conditioning procedure. The basic experimental arrangements of these procedures are as follows:

(*a*) When the CS and US are presented together, it is called simultaneous conditioning.

(*b*) In delayed conditioning, the onset of CS precedes the onset of US. The CS ends before the end of the US.

(*c*) In trace conditioning, the onset and end of the CS precedes the onset of US with some time gap between the two.

(*d*) In backward conditioning, the US precedes the onset of CS.

It is now well established that delayed conditioning procedure is the most effective way of acquiring a CR. Simultaneous and trace conditioning procedures do lead to acquisition of a CR, but they require greater number of acquisition trials in comparison to the delayed conditioning procedure. It may be noted that the acquisition of response under backward conditioning procedure is very rare.

2. Type of Unconditioned Stimuli: The unconditioned stimuli used in studies of classical conditioning are basically of two types, *i.e.* appetitive and aversive. Appetitive unconditioned stimuli automatically elicits approach responses, such as eating, drinking, caressing, etc. These responses give satisfaction and pleasure. On the other hand, aversive US, such as noise, bitter taste, electric shock, painful injections, etc. are painful, harmful, and elicit avoidance and escape responses. It has been found that appetitive classical conditioning is slower and requires greater number of acquisition trials, but aversive classical conditioning is established in one, two or three trials depending on the intensity of the aversive US.

3. Intensity of Conditioned Stimuli: This influences the course of both appetitive and aversive classical conditioning. More intense conditioned stimuli are more effective in accelerating the acquisition of conditioned responses. It means that the more intense the conditioned stimulus, the fewer are the number of acquisition trials needed for conditioning.

Operant/Instrumental Conditioning

B.F. Skinner is regarded as the father of operant conditioning, but his work was based on **Thorndike's law of effect.** In the late nineteenth century, psychologist Edward Thorndike proposed the law of effect. The law of effect states that any behaviour that has good consequences will tend to be repeated, and any behaviour that has bad consequences will tend to be avoided. In the 1930s, B.F. Skinner, extended this idea and began to study operant conditioning. Operant conditioning is a type of learning in which responses come to be controlled by their consequences.

Operants are those behaviours or responses, which are emitted by animals and human beings voluntarily and are under their control. The term operant is used because the organism operates on the environment. Conditioning of operant behaviour is called operant conditioning. Skinner conducted his studies on rats and pigeons in specially made boxes, called the Skinner Box.

Determinants of Operant Conditioning

The operant or instrumental conditioning is a form of learning in which behaviour is learned, maintained or changed through its consequences. Such consequences are called **reinforcers**. A reinforcer is defined as any stimulus or event, which increases the probability of the occurrence of a (desired) response. A reinforcer has numerous features, which affect the course and strength of a response. They include its type—positive or negative, number or frequency, quality—superior or inferior, and schedule—continuous or intermittent (partial).

Reinforcement may be positive or negative. Positive reinforcement involves stimuli that have pleasant consequences. They strengthen and maintain the responses that have caused them to occur. Positive reinforcers satisfy needs, which include food, water, medals, praise, money, status, information, etc. Negative reinforcers involve unpleasant and painful stimuli. Responses that lead organisms to get rid of painful stimuli or avoid and escape from them provide negative reinforcement. Thus, negative reinforcement leads to learning of avoidance and escape responses. For instance, one learns to put on woollen clothes, burn firewood or use electric heaters to avoid the unpleasant cold weather. One learns to move away from dangerous stimuli because they provide negative reinforcement. It may be noted that negative reinforcement is not punishment. Use of punishment reduces or suppresses the response while a negative reinforcer increases the probability of avoidance or escape response. For instance, drivers and co-drivers wear their seat belts to avoid getting injured in case of an accident or to avoid being fined by the traffic police.

Classical and Operant Conditioning : Differences

1. In classical conditioning, the responses are under the control of some stimulus because they are reflexes, automatically elicited by the appropriate stimuli. Such stimuli are selected as US and responses elicited by them as UR. Thus Pavlovian conditioning, in which US elicits responses, is often called respondent conditioning.

   In instrumental conditioning, responses are under the control of the organism and are voluntary responses or 'operants'. Thus, in the two forms of conditioning different types of responses are conditioned.

2. In classical conditioning, the CS and US are well-defined, but in operant conditioning CS is not defined. It can be inferred but is not directly known.

3. In classical conditioning, the experimenter controls the occurrence of US, while in operant conditioning the occurrence of the reinforcer is under the control of the organism that is learning. Thus, for US in classical conditioning the organism remains passive, while in operant conditioning the subject has to be active in order to be reinforced.

4. In the two forms of conditioning, the technical terms used to characterise the experimental proceedings are different. Moreover what is called reinforcer in operant conditioning is called US in classical conditioning. An US has two functions. In the beginning, it elicits the response and also reinforces the response to be associated and elicited later on by the CS.

OBSERVATIONAL LEARNING

The other form of learning takes place by observing others. Earlier this form of learning was called **imitation**. Bandura and his colleagues in a series of experimental studies investigated observational learning in detail. In this kind of learning, human beings learn social behaviours, therefore, it is sometimes called **social learning**. In many situations individuals do not know how to behave. They observe others and emulate their behaviour. This form of learning is called **modelling**.

Examples of observational learning abound in our social life. Fashion designers employ tall, pretty, and gracious young girls and tall, smart, and well-built young boys for popularising clothes of different designs and fabrics. People observe them on televised fashion shows and advertisements in magazines and newspapers. They imitate these models. Observing superiors and likeable persons and then emulating their behaviour in a novel social situation is a common experience.

The children observe adults' behaviours, at home and during social ceremonies and functions. They enact adults in their plays and games. For instance, young children play games of marriage ceremonies, birthday parties, thief and policeman, house keeping, etc. Actually they enact in their games what they observe in society, on television, and read in books.

Children learn most of the social behaviours by observing and emulating adults. The way to put on clothes, dress one's hair, and conduct oneself in society are learned through observing others. It has also been shown that children learn and develop various personality characteristics through observational learning. Aggressiveness, prosocial behaviour, courtesy, politeness, diligence, and indolence are acquired by this method of learning.

COGNITIVE LEARNING

Some psychologists view learning in terms of cognitive processes that underlie it. They have developed approaches that focus on such processes that occur during learning rather than concentrating solely on S-R and S-S connections. Thus, in cognitive learning, there is a change in what the learner knows rather than what he/she does. This form of learning shows up in insight learning and latent learning.

Insight Learning

Kohler demonstrated a model of learning which could not be readily explained by conditioning. He performed a series of experiments with chimpanzees that involved solving complex problems. Kohler placed chimpanzees in an enclosed play area where food was kept out of their reach. Tools such as poles and boxes were placed in the enclosure. The chimpanzees rapidly learned how to use a box to stand on or a pole to move the food in their direction. In this experiment, learning did not occur as a result of trial and error and reinforcement, but came about in sudden flashes of insight. The chimpanzees would roam about the enclosure for some time and then suddenly would stand on a box, grab a pole and strike a banana, which was out of normal reach above the enclosure. The chimpanzee exhibited what Kohler called insight learning—the process by which the solution to a problem suddenly becomes clear.

In a normal experiment on insight learning, a problem is presented, followed by a period of time when no apparent progress is made and finally a solution suddenly emerges. In insight learning, sudden solution is the rule. Once the solution has appeared, it can be repeated immediately the next time the problem is confronted. Thus, it is clear that what is learned is not a specific set of conditioned associations between stimuli and responses but a cognitive relationship between a means and an end. As a result, insight learning can be generalised to other similar problem situations.

Latent Learning

Another type of cognitive learning is known as latent learning. In latent learning, a new behaviour is learned but not demonstrated until reinforcement is provided for displaying it. Tolman made an early contribution to the concept of latent learning. To have an idea of latent learning, we may briefly understand his experiment. Tolman put two groups of rats in a maze and gave them an opportunity to explore. In one group, rats found food at the end of the maze and soon learned to make their way rapidly through the maze. On the other hand, rats in the second group were not rewarded and showed no apparent signs of learning. But later, when these rats were reinforced, they ran through the maze as efficiently as the rewarded group.

Tolman contended that the unrewarded rats had learned the layout of the maze early in their explorations. They just never displayed their latent learning until the reinforcement was provided. Instead, the rats developed a cognitive map of the maze, *i.e.* a mental representation of the spatial locations and directions, which they needed to reach their goal.

LEARNING AS A SOCIAL ACTIVITY

Learning is a social activity. Our learning is intimately associated with our connection with other human beings, our teachers, our peers, our family as well as casual acquaintances, including the people before us or next to us. We are more likely to be successful in our efforts to educate, if we recognise this principle rather than try to avoid it. Much of traditional education, as Dewey pointed out, is directed towards isolating the learner from all social interaction, and towards seeing education as a one-on-one relationship between the learner and the objective material to be learned. In contrast, progressive education (to continue to use Dewey's formulation) recognizes the social aspect of learning and uses conversations interaction with others, and the application of knowledge as an integral aspect of learning.

SOCIAL CONTEXT OF LEARNING

Social Learning theory

Social learning theory focuses on the learning that occurs within a social context. It considers that people learn from one another, including such concepts as observational learning, imitation, and modelling. Among others **Albert Bandura** is considered the leading proponent of this theory.

General Principles of Social Learning Theory Follows:

1. People can learn by observing the behaviour is of others and the outcomes of those behaviours.
2. Learning can occur without a change in behaviour. Behaviourists say that learning has to be represented by a permanent change in behaviour, in contrast social learning theorists say that because people can learn through observation alone, their learning may not necessarily be shown in their performance. Learning may or may not result in a behaviour change.
3. Cognition plays a role in learning. Over the last 40 years social learning theory has become increasingly cognitive in its interpretation of human learning. Awareness and expectations of future reinforcements or punishments can have a major effect on the behaviours that people exhibit.
4. Social learning theory can be considered a bridge or a transition between behaviourist learning theories and cognitive learning theories.

How the Environment Reinforces and Punishes Modelling:

People are often reinforced for modelling the behaviour of others. Bandura suggested that the environment also reinforces modelling. This is in several possible ways:

1. The observer is reinforced by the model. For example, a student who changes dress to fit in with a certain group of students has a strong likelihood of being accepted and thus reinforced by that group.
2. The observer is reinforced by a third person. The observer might be modelling the actions of someone else, for example, an outstanding class leader or student. The teacher notices this and compliments and praises the observer for modelling such behaviour thus reinforcing that behaviour.
3. The imitated behaviour itself leads to reinforcing consequences. Many behaviours that we learn from others produce satisfying or reinforcing results. For example, a student in my multimedia class could observe how the extra work a classmate does is fun. This student in turn would do the same extra work and also receive enjoyment.
4. Consequences of the model's behaviour affect the observers behaviour vicariously. This is known as vicarious reinforcement. This is where in the model is reinforced for a response and then the observer shows an increase in that same response. Bandura illustrated this by having students watch a film of a model hitting a inflated clown doll. One group of children saw the model being praised for such action. Without being reinforced, the group of children began to also hit the doll.

Contemporary Social Learning Perspective of Reinforcement and Punishment

1. Contemporary theory proposes that both reinforcement and punishment have indirect effects on learning. They are not the sole or main cause.
2. Reinforcement and punishment influence the extent to which an individual exhibits a behaviour that has been learned.
3. The expectation of reinforcement influences cognitive processes that promote learning. Therefore, attention pays a critical role in learning. And attention is influenced by the expectation of reinforcement. An example would be, where the teacher tells a group of students that what they will study next is not on the test. Students will not pay attention, because they do not expect to know the information for a test.

Cognitive Factors in Social Learning

Social learning theory has cognitive factors as well as behaviourist factors (actually operant factors).

1. **Learning without performance:** Bandura makes a distinction between learning through observation and the actual imitation of what has been learned.
2. **Cognitive processing during learning:** Social learning theorists contend that attention is a critical factor in learning.
3. **Expectations:** As a result of being reinforced, people form expectations about the consequences that future behaviours are likely to bring. They expect certain behaviours to bring reinforcements and others to bring punishment. The learner needs to be aware however, of the response reinforcements and response punishment. Reinforcement increases a response only when the learner is aware of that connection.
4. **Reciprocal causation:** Bandura proposed that behaviour can influence both the environment and the person. In fact each of these three variables, the person, the behaviour, and the environment can have an influence on each other.
5. **Modelling:** There are different types of models. There is the live model, and actual person demonstrating the behaviour. There can also be a symbolic model, which can be a person or action portrayed in some other medium, such as television, videotape, computer programs.

Behaviours that can be learned through modelling:

Many behaviours can be learned, at least partly, through modelling. Examples that can be cited are, students can watch parents read, students can watch the demonstrations of mathematics problems, or seen someone acting bravely and a fearful situation. Aggression can be learned through models. Much research indicate that children become more aggressive when they observed aggressive or violent models. Moral thinking and moral behaviour are influenced by observation and modelling. This includes moral judgments regarding right and wrong which can in part, develop through modelling.

Conditions Necessary for Effective Modelling to Occur:

Bandura mentions four conditions that are necessary before an individual can successfully model the behaviour of someone else:

1. **Attention:** the person must first pay attention to the model.
2. **Retention:** the observer must be able to remember the behaviour that has been

observed. One way of increasing this is using the technique of rehearsal.

3. **Motor reproduction:** the third condition is the ability to replicate the behaviour that the model has just demonstrated. This means that the observer has to be able to replicate the action, which could be a problem with a learner who is not ready developmentally to replicate the action. For example, little children have difficulty doing complex physical motion.
4. **Motivation:** the final necessary ingredient for modelling to occur is motivation, learners must want to demonstrate what they have learned. Remember that since these four conditions vary among individuals, different people will reproduce the same behaviour differently.

Effects of Modelling on Behaviour:

Modelling teaches new behaviours.

Modelling influences the frequency of previously learned behaviours.

Modelling may encourage previously forbidden behaviours.

Modelling increases the frequency of similar behaviours. For example, a student might see a friend excel in basketball and he tries to excel in football because he is not tall enough for basketball.

Educational implications of social learning theory:

Social learning theory has numerous implications for classroom use.

1. Students often learn a great deal simply by observing other people.
2. Describing the consequences of behaviour is can effectively increase the appropriate behaviours and decrease inappropriate ones. This can involve discussing with learners about the rewards and consequences of various behaviours.
3. Modelling provides an alternative to shaping for teaching new behaviours. Instead of using shaping, which is operant conditioning, modelling can provide a faster, more efficient means for teaching new behaviour. To promote effective modelling a teacher must make sure that the four essential conditions exist; attention, retention, motor reproduction, and motivation.
4. Teachers and parents must model appropriate behaviours and take care that they do not model inappropriate behaviours.
5. Teachers should expose students to a variety of other models. This technique is especially important to break down traditional stereotypes.
6. Students must believe that they are capable of accomplishing school tasks. Thus, it is very important to develop a sense of self-efficacy for students. Teachers can promote such self-efficacy by having students receive confidence-building messages, watch others be successful, and experience success on their own.
7. Teachers should help students set realistic expectations for their academic accomplishments. In general in my class that means making sure that expectations are not set too low. I want to realistically challenge my students. However, sometimes the task is beyond a student's ability, example would be the cancer group.
8. Self-regulation techniques provide an effective method for improving student behaviour.

CHILD AS A PROBLEM SOLVER AND A SCIENTIFIC INVESTIGATOR

Problem solving is the foundation of a young child's learning. It must be valued, promoted, provided for and sustained in the early childhood classroom. Opportunities for problem solving occur in the everyday context of a child's life. By observing the child closely, teachers can use the child's social, cognitive, movement and emotional experiences to facilitate problem solving and promote strategies useful in the lifelong process of learning.

Problem solving is thinking that is goal-directed. Almost all our day-to-day activities are directed towards a goal. Here, it is important to know that problems are not always in the form of obstacles or hurdles that one faces. It could be any simple activity that you perform to reach a defined goal, for example, preparing a quick snack for your friend who has just arrived at your place. In problem solving there is an initial state (*i.e.* the problem) and there is an end state (the goal). These two anchors are connected by means of several steps or mental operations. Following table would clarify our understanding of various steps through which one solves a problem.

Table: Mental Operations Involved in Solving a Problem

Let us look at the problem of organising a play in school on the occasion of Teachers' Day. Problem solving would involve the following sequence.

Mental operation	Nature of problem
1. Identify the problem	A week is left for teachers' day and you are given the task of organising a play.
2. Represent the problem	Organising a play would involve identification of an appropriate theme, screening of actors, actresses, arranging money, etc.
3. Plan the solution: Set sub-goals	Search and survey various available themes for a play, and consult teachers and friends who have the expertise. The play to be decided, based on such considerations as cost, duration, suitability for the occasion, etc.
4. Evaluate all solutions (plays)	Collect all the information/stage rehearsal.
5. Select one solution and execute it	Compare and verify the various options to get the best solution (the play).
6. Evaluate the outcome	If the play (solution) is appreciated, think about the steps you have followed for future reference for yourself as well as for your friends.
7. Rethink and redefine problems and solutions	After this special occasion you can still think about ways to plan a better play in future.

Learning Through Problem Solving

By exploring social relationships, manipulating objects, and interacting with people, children are able to formulate ideas, try these ideas out, and accept or reject what they learn. Constructing knowledge by making mistakes is part of the natural process of problem solving. Through exploring, then experimenting, trying out a hypothesis, and finally, solving problems, children make learning personal and meaningful. Piaget states that children understand only what they discover or invent themselves. It is this discovery within the problem solving process that is the vehicle for children's learning. Children are encouraged to construct their own knowledge when the teacher plans for problem solving; bases the framework for learning in problem solving; and provides time, space, and materials.

Teacher's Role

Changing through problem solving is modelled by adults and facilitated by the teacher in the classroom environment. When teachers articulate the problems they face and discuss solutions with children, children become more aware of the significance of the problem-solving process. Being a problem solver is modelled by the teacher and emulated by the children. The teacher's role is two-fold: first, to value the process and be willing to trust the learner, and second, to establish and maintain a classroom environment that encourages problem solving. It is the attitude of the teacher that must change first in the problem-solving classroom. Values and goals must be clearly defined to include a child-centered curriculum, the development of communication skills, promotion of cooperative learning, and inclusion of diverse ideas.

The teacher must be willing to become a learner, too. By being curious, observing, listening, and questioning, the teacher shares and models the qualities that are valued and promoted by the problem-solving process.

Planning for Problem Solving

A curriculum that accommodates a variety of developmental levels as well as individual differences in young children sets the stage for problem solving. Choices, decision-making, and a curriculum framework that integrates learning, such as Katz and Chard's project method, are especially appropriate for young learners. The project approach facilitates cooperative learning and promotes diverse ideas. Donna Ogle's K-W-L (what you KNOW, what you WANT to know, and what you have LEARNED) is another method of organizing work that promotes problem solving. Themes, units, webbing, and the KWL method are all ways of organizing curriculum that can support problem solving. Beginning with the needs and interests of the children, problem solving develops from meaningful experiences important to the children. The teacher-designed curriculum provides the classroom basis for these experiences.

For example, a second grade investigation of waste materials from a classroom led one group of young children to explore the topic in an integrated way. Reading, writing, counting, measuring, interviews of community people, and science experiments were planned, initiated and reported. Solutions to many problems posed during the investigation were tried out and some were found to be successful. Through group work, individuals were able to participate and communicate as cognitive and social needs were met. Each child, at individual levels and in individual ways, was successful within the group experience. Problem solving empowers children.

Providing for Problem Solving

Problem solving is a skill that can be learned and must be practiced. It is facilitated by a classroom schedule that provides for integrated learning in large blocks of time, space for ongoing group projects, and many open-ended materials. The teacher provides the time, space, and materials necessary for in-depth learning.

1. Time: Teachers can provide for problem solving by enlarging blocks of learning time during the school day. Because making choices, discussing decisions, and evaluating mistakes takes time, large time blocks best suit the problem-solving process. It is important that children know they have time to identify and solve problems.

2. Space: Projects and group meetings may require an assessment of classroom space. Moving desks and tables together facilitates communication and cooperation in the classroom. Once the teacher has observed the patterns of traffic in the classroom, equipment can be moved or eliminated to promote problem solving.

3. Materials: The open-ended materials that are needed for the construction and concrete solving of problems should be safe, durable, and varied. Well-marked storage units should be easily accessible to children, and materials should be available for ongoing exploration and manipulation. Access to a variety of materials encourages children to use materials in new and diverse ways. This freedom promotes problem solving.

The Problem-Solving Model

Individuals or groups can solve problems. Group problem solving is important to young children because many diverse ideas are generated. Both individual and group processes should be included in the early childhood classroom. Becoming skillful at problem solving is based on the understanding and use of sequenced steps. These steps are:

1. Identifying the problem,
2. Brainstorming a variety of solutions,
3. Choosing one solution and trying it out, and
4. Evaluating what has happened.

Choosing Good Problems

Goffin provides teachers with guiding questions that will help them identify appropriate problems for young children. Some of these are:

1. Is the problem meaningful and interesting?
2. Can the problem be solved at a variety of levels?
3. Must a new decision be made?
4. Can the actions be evaluated?

Problem solving is a way to make sense of the environment and, in fact, control it. The process allows children in an increasingly diverse world to be active participants and to implement changes. By including problem solving in the early childhood classroom, we equip children with a life-long skill that is useful in all areas of learning.

Obstacles to Solving Problems

Two major obstacles to solving a problem are mental set and lack of motivation.

Mental Set

Mental set is a tendency of a person to solve problems by following already tried mental operations or steps. Prior success with a particular strategy would sometimes help in solving a new problem. However, this tendency also creates a mental rigidity that obstructs the problem solver to think of any new rules or strategies. Thus, while in some situations mental set can enhance the quality and speed of problem solving, in other situations it hinders problem solving. You might have experienced this while solving mathematical problems. After completing a couple of questions, you form an idea of the steps that are required to solve these questions and subsequently you go on following the same steps, until a point where you fail. At this point you may experience difficulty in avoiding the already used steps. Those steps would interfere in your thought for new strategies. However, in day-to-day activities we often rely on past experiences with similar or related problems.

Like mental set, **functional fixedness** in problem solving occurs when people fail to solve a problem because they are fixed on a thing's usual function. If you have ever used a hardbound book to hammer a nail, then you have overcome functional fixedness.

Lack of Motivation

People might be great at solving problems, but all their skills and talents are of no use if they are not motivated. Sometimes people give up easily when they encounter a problem or failure in implementing the first step. Therefore, there is a need to persist in their effort to find a solution.

ALTERNATIVE CONCEPTIONS OF LEARNING

When teachers provide instruction on concepts in various subjects, they are teaching students who already have some pre-instructional knowledge about the topic. Student knowledge, however, can be erroneous, illogical or misinformed. These erroneous understandings are termed alternative conceptions or misconceptions (or intuitive theories). Alternative conceptions (misconceptions) are not unusual. In fact, they are a normal part of the learning process. We quite naturally form ideas from our everyday experience, but obviously not all the ideas we develop are correct with respect to the most current evidence and scholarship in a given discipline. Moreover, some concepts in different content areas are simply very difficult to grasp. They may be very abstract, counterintuitive or quite complex. Hence, our understanding of them is flawed. In addition, things we have already learned are sometimes unhelpful in learning new concepts/theories. This occurs when the new concept or theory is inconsistent with previously learned material. Accordingly, as noted, it is very typical for students (and adults) to have misconceptions in different domains (content knowledge areas). Indeed, researchers have found that there is a common set of alternative conceptions (misconceptions) that most students typically exhibit. There is one class of alternative theories (or misconceptions) that is very deeply entrenched. These are "ontological misconceptions," which relate to ontological beliefs (*i.e.*, beliefs about the fundamental categories and properties of the world).

Alternative conceptions (misconceptions) can impede learning for several reasons. First, students generally are unaware that the knowledge they have is wrong. Moreover, misconceptions can be very entrenched in student thinking. In addition, new experiences are interpreted through these erroneous understandings, thereby interfering with being able to correctly grasp new information. Also, alternative conceptions (misconceptions) tend to be very resistant to instruction because learning entails replacing or radically reorganizing student knowledge. Hence, conceptual change has to occur for learning to happen. This puts teachers in the very challenging position of needing to bring about significant conceptual change in student knowledge. Generally, ordinary forms of instruction, such as lectures, labs, discovery learning, or simply reading texts, are not very successful at overcoming student misconceptions. For all these reasons, misconceptions can be hard nuts for teachers to crack. However, several instructional strategies have been found to be effective in achieving conceptual change and helping students leave their alternative conceptions behind and learn correct concepts or theories.

Instructional strategies that can lead to change in students' alternative conceptions (misconceptions) and to learning of new concepts and theories

1. Present new concepts or theories that you are teaching in such a way that students see as plausible, high-quality, intelligible and generative.
2. Use students' correct conceptions and build on those by creating a bridge of examples to the new concept or theory that students are having trouble learning due to misconceptions they hold.
3. Use model-ased reasoning, which helps students construct new representations that vary from their intuitive theories.
4. Use diverse instruction, wherein you present a few examples that challenge multiple assumptions, rather than a larger number of examples that challenge just one assumption.
5. Help students become aware of (raise student metacognition about) their own alternative conceptions (misconceptions).
6. Present students with experiences that cause cognitive conflict in students' minds. Experiences (as in strategy 3 above) that can cause cognitive conflict are ones that get students to consider their erroneous (misconception) knowledge side-by-side with, or at the same time as, the correct concept or theory.
7. Engage in Interactive Conceptual Instruction (ICI).
8. Develop students' epistemological thinking, which incorporates beliefs and theories about the nature of knowledge and the nature of learning, in ways that will facilitate conceptual change. The more naive students' beliefs are about knowledge and learning, the less likely they are to revise their misconceptions.
9. Help students "self-repair" their misconceptions.
10. Once students have overcome their alternative conceptions (misconceptions).

Presenting new concepts or theories

In presenting new concepts or theories, teachers should be sure to show these theories or concepts as:

1. Plausible: The new information should be shown to be consistent with other knowledge and able to explain the available data. Learners must see how the new conception (theory) is consistent with other knowledge and a good explanation of the data.

2. High quality: Of course, the theory/concept to be taught is of high quality from a scientific point of view, since it is a correct theory. However, the presented theory should take a better account of the data than what students currently have available to them. For example, the instructor should deal with the problem from the perspective of the students (*e.g.*, students for whom a "flat earth" theory provides a better account of the data available than does a "spherical earth" theory). Hence, the quality of the new theory must be considered along with the kind of data that students know about.

3. Intelligible: Teachers should do what they can to increase the intelligibility of the new theory. Learners must be able to grasp how the new conception works. To increase intelligibility, teachers can use methods such as use of:

(*a*) analogies,

(*b*) models, and

(*c*) direct exposition.

4. Generative/fruitful: Teachers should show that the new concept/theory can be extended to open up new areas of inquiry. Learners must be able to extend the new conception to new areas of inquiry. Teachers might accomplish this by illustrating the application of the new concept/theory to a range of problems. These problems can include familiar ones and new ones.

UNDERSTANDING CHILDREN'S 'ERRORS' AS SIGNIFICANT STEPS IN THE LEARNING PROCESS

The legacy of Jean Piaget to the world of early childhood education is that he fundamentally altered the view of how a child learns. And a teacher, he believed, was more than a transmitter of knowledge she was also an essential observer and guide to helping children build their own knowledge.

As a university graduate, Swiss-born Piaget got a routine job in Paris standardizing Binet-Simon IQ tests, where the emphasis was on children getting the right answers. Piaget observed that many children of the same ages gave the same kinds of incorrect answers. What could be learned from this?

Piaget interviewed many hundreds of children and concluded that children who are allowed to make mistakes often go on to discover their errors and correct them, or find new solutions. In this process, children build their own way of learning. From children's errors, teachers can obtain insights into the child's view of the world and can tell where guidance is needed. They can provide appropriate materials, ask encouraging questions, and allow the child to construct his own knowledge.

Piaget's continued interactions with young children became part of his life-long research. After reading about a child who thought that the sun and moon followed him wherever he went, Piaget wanted to find out if all young children had a similar belief. He found that many did indeed believe this. Piaget went on to explore children's countless "why" questions, such as, "Why is the sun round?" or "Why is grass green?" He concluded that children do not think like adults. Their thought processes have their own distinct order and special logic. Children are not "empty vessels to be filled with knowledge" (as traditional pedagogical theory had it). They are "active builders of knowledge-little scientists who construct their own theories of the world."

COGNITION & EMOTIONS

What is Cognition?

Cognition is the ability to preceive, memorise, reason and understand. These abilities change with age. As the child grows, her thinking becomes more mature and efficient. Therefore, cognition can simply be defined as the process of acquiring, processing, organising and using knowledge. The development of cognition means development of all these abilities. A child's thinking changes as result of both age (maturation) and increased experiences.

Major Cognitive Characteristics of Children

Infancy

It is interesting to see the number of changes that take place in the first two years. Children at this stage are very active learners. Even when it seems the child is only lying and looking at nothing (e.g. 2 month old) she is actually looking at and trying to understand the things around her.

The first two years children begin by exploring their own bodies and move to the outside objects. Children at 2/3 months discover their thumb or hand or occasionally their own foot. These fascinate them they try to play with them. For a two month old a toy is not as satisfying as her/his own thumb in her/his mouth. Gradually, by about six months, children begin to play with objects outside the body. This could be the toy, the sheet, the bottle, etc. Later, by two years they can even indulge in pretend play [example doctor-doctor, house-house, etc.].

What children also achieve by two years is the understanding of object permanance. **Object**

permanance is the understanding that things exist even if you can not see them. Let us take an example. If you show a five month old a toy she gets excited. If you hide the toy the child soon forgets that any toy even existed. This is because she thinks out of sight is out of mind. Do the same thing with a 1½ year old and you will find the child is either looking for it or asks you to find it. This is because she knows the toy exists even if she can not see it. This understanding, that things exist even if you can not see them, is called object permanance.

The other major development that happens by two years is that children begin to learn the symbols. What are symbols? A two year old can convey her thoughts and desires through language. All these are essential processes of cognition.

Early Childhood

This is a period when the childs mastery in use of symbols increases. We can observe this in the everyday behaviour and activities of the child, *i.e.* in what she plays, her language etc. Gradually her representations of objects become more flexible and less self centred. A one year old while playing does not need a toy phone to pretend speaking on the phone. She can use any object. This is indicative of flexibility in thinking. Gradually, children also start directing play between dolls, *e.g.,* one doll is the mother and the other doll the child. This is indicative of the child moving away from self to becoming less self centred.

Children at this stage also believe that all objects have feelings like human beings. That is why you will often see the child feeding her teddy bear.

Children at this stage can also focus on only one aspect of a situation and can not go back. Let us now take an example. You offer cola to a 4 yr old in a tall glass. You then change your mind and pour the coke from the tall glass to a short glass and give it to the child. You will find the child will say I want the big glass. This is because she can only focus on one aspect (height) at a time. Also, she is not able to go back mentally and realise that in the process of pouring from big to small glass, no cola was taken away.

Similarly, take two plates and put in one 6 pieces of chocolate spreadout and in the other make a tower of 6 pieces of chocolate. You will find the child thinking the spread out chocolate is more. This is because the child can only focus on one aspect at a time. This limitation seriously restricts the problem solving and logical thinking abilities of the child.

It also indicates the child's inability to understand that another point of view different from her own can exist, *e.g.,* you often find children responding to your question by nodding their heads, even if they are not in the same room as you. This is because they do not see another's point of view.

Middle Childhood

During this period, children begin to understand that another view point can exist. They are also able to focus on more than one aspect of a situation and go back and forth on their thinking. This makes their thinking more logical and efficient. However, children are only comfortable with concrete ideas/objects. It means, something that is real for them, *i.e.,* either something they have seen, *e.g.,* a house or sometning is in front of them, a plant or something linked to what they know, *e.g.,* blue like the sky. They are not able to think about abstract ideas, *e.g.,* what would happen if everyone could fly?

Emotion

Emotions, put simply, are feelings. In infants we can see these very clearly in the form of joy, anger and fear. These are similar to the emotions that adults have.

1. **The variety of emotions increases with age:** The basic emotions of joy, fear, anger are visible in infants. Gradually, as a sense of self develops; children begin to relate with people around them and value their opinions. Then we can see the emotion like pride, shame, sympathy, guilt also developing in them.
2. **The expression of emotion also changes with age:** Emotions are both innate and learnt. The instinctive response to a stimulus is innate but how to express that feeling is learnt, *e.g.* taking away of a toy makes the child angry (innate) but instead crying she is encouraged to ask for it back (learnt). Frustration tolerance increases with age. As children grow older, their responses change in both as well as instinctive method of expression, *e.g.,* when 2 year old falls downs she cries loudly and later forgets quickly. A 6 year old on the other hand, may not cry but forgets far less easily.
3. **The triggers or cause of emotions change with age:** The stimuli that elicit emotion also change with age, *e.g.,* an infant may cry on hearing the loud explosion of a cracker but a middle childhood child may laugh. Sucking a thumb may give great joy to an infant but provides no pleasure to a child is middle childhood.
4. **The coping techniques change with age:** Methods of coping with frustration and stress change with age. While a younger child may cry, or cling to the adult, an older child is likely to suppress the emotion.

Factors Affecting Emotional Development

If we look round in our environment, we will find that people differ in the emotions they experience and express. Some are happy, some are angry, some moody, some helpful. What then affects our emotional development?

1. **Parenting style:** Democratic parenting where induction is used as a method of disciplining allows for more mature emotional development and also for development of personal behaviour.
2. **Role model:** There are two factors which influence what a child ultimately learns:
   (i) How adults and others in the child's environment handle their emotions.
   (ii) How successful is the emotional expression in achieving their needs.
3. **Violence in the child's environment:** The kind of behaviour the child see in the community (*e.g.* during riots) or on TV will affect her expressions of emotions.
4. **Cultural norms:** Emotional expressions are learnt from the environment. It is the environment that tells us how to react in a situation (*e.g.* some people feel the emotion of fear when a black cat crosses their path). It is also the environment that tells us the acceptable way of expressing ones emotions (*e.g.* in many families it is unacceptable for boys to express their distress by crying). Therefore, our cultural beliefs and values also influence our emotional development.

MOTIVATION AND LEARNING

Motivation

Motivation is the heart of the learning process. It generates the will in an individual to do something. Adequate motivation not only engages the student in an activity which results in learning, but also sustains and directs learning. Two types of motivation are commonly recognised. These are: intrinsic and extrinsic motivation.

Intrinsic motivation arises when the resolution of tension is to be found in mastering the learning task itself; the material learned provides its own reward. For example, the student who studies the construction of model aeroplanes diligently so that he can make a model, is experiencing a kind of intrinsic motivation.

Extrinsic motivation occurs when a student pursues a learning task, but for reasons which are external. If a student engages in construction of model aeroplanes because he thinks it will please his father, who is an ex-pilot, rather than because of intrinsic motivation. We should remember that in most learning situations motivation can not be dichotomised so neatly. It is the function of the total learning situation and hinges on some blend of personal concern for the work itself and the concern for some extrinsic factors as well. As a working principle, motivation is probably a function of an interactive situation where reward to a particular action acts as an incentive. Some of the common forms of extrinsic motivation are:

- **Purposive striving, goals and ideals:** The goal and purposes of learning clearly perceived by the individual, provide strong motivation for better action and learning.
- **Knowledge of results:** Knowledge of results in terms of success and failure provides incentive for greater efforts on the part of the student. If a student practices a task without knowing the accuracy or inaccuracy of his performance, he may practise wrong task. In such a case, all learning will be futile. Therefore, if results of performance are known to the student, he learns better as compared to when he does not know about the results. Mere repetition of a task without knowledge of its results fails to bring about learning. Knowledge of results serves two purposes: (i) it enables the subject to evaluate his efficiency and to change his responses in the direction of greater accuracy, and (ii) it adds to the satisfaction in reaching a goal, one tends of repeat rewarded responses.
- **Punishment and rewards:** Punishment can be understood as an act of inflicting pain deliberately with the purpose of affecting the future conduct of an individual being punished. Punishment is based on fear of physical pain, embarrassment and loss of status. Thus, punishment of fear of being punished is one of the common and obvious methods of keeping under control and guiding the students. Punishment or fear is a very strong stimuli, a negative incentive to learning especially when errors occur. Thorndike showed that generally punishment speeds up learning and reduces the number of errors as it produces emotional excitement which tends to fix at punished response. But it does not mean that punishment under all the circumstances and with all the students is equally effective. For example, it may prove disastrous and destructive when task is very difficult.

  Contrary to punishment, rewards are certainly better and positive incentives to learning. They are responsible for initiative, energy, competition, self-expression and creative ability. According to law of effect, reward is satisfying and pleasant, thus reward strengthens learning. Rewards may in the form of gifts, prizes, money, badges, cups, certificates of merit, or other objects of some value. Motivation through such objects feeds the natural drive in all the human beings. But, when these rewards are too much strived for, they degenerate the whole learning.

- **Praise and blame:** These are also strong incentives for effective learning. Praise stimulates average and inferior children, but has less effect on those of superior intelligence. Reproof is felt most by superior children, but girls seem more susceptible to praise than do boys. Regardless of age sex, or initial ability, praise is the most effective of the incentives. Reproof seems to be less effective for all students. Chase (1932) reported praise to be less effective than blame with young children, but Hurlock (1920) generalised, still accepted by contemporary investigators, that praise is more effective stimulus in motivating both immediate and long-continued tasks.
- **Rivalry:** The rivalry between students which leads to resentment, jealousy, etc., or rivalry between groups of students which creates hatred, is the least desirable type of incentive to be encouraged in the schools. Self-rivalry or rivalry in the form of healthy competition is the most valuable type. This tendency should be developed in the student. Though experimental researchers have shown rivalry to be a powerful motivation influence, the emotional and social consequences of rivalry must be considered by the teacher.

Functions of Motivation

The major functions of motivation in learning are as follows:

- To energies the students in learning
- To direct behaviour
- To select behaviour
- To help capture the attention
- To help in acquiring knowledge
- To help in character formation
- To develop social qualities

Attention in Relation to Motivation

Attention is the basic pre-requisite of all learning in the classroom. Learning is possible only if students concentrate their attention on the object or stimuli to be learnt. Attention increases the amount and rate of learning, and also the efficiency of work.

Attention is closely related to motivation. Attention is motivated behaviour, in which the student makes a variety of efforts for achieving the goal. Thus motivation helps in capturing attention. You can help your students by motivating them to concentrate their attention on the tasks to be learnt by them.

Between the two types of motivation, intrinsic motivation should be preferred to extrinsic motivation It produces better learning because it is related to interest. The learner pursues the activity in which he has interest without waiting for any external pressure. When the learner does not show any intrinsic motivation or interest in learning we have to resort to extrinsic motivation by the use of 'incentives'—whether financial or non-financial (monetary or non-monetary)--such as rewards, awards, prizes, competitions, praise, etc.

In-built Motivation

Another type of motivation is called in-built motivation. Whatever may be the type of motivation, it should be an in-built component of the whole programme of education/training. Right type of trainers, attractive and need-based reading materials, supportive training methodologies, constant awareness of the new dimensions of the programme will facilitate motivation in an in-built manner.

Theories of Motivation

The main theories of motivation are: (a) Psycho-analytic Theory, (b) Maslow's Theory of Self-actualisation, (c) Physiological Theory and (d) Achievement-Motivation Theory.

Psycho-Analytic Theory

According to this theory, motivation gives the vital life forces which are the prime mover of life and its activities. 'It is will power that motivates a person', *i.e.*, 'no will power—no activity'. All these versions agree on one point *i.e.*, 'building ego of man'.

Maslow's Theory of Self-Actualisation

This theory is based on human needs and their satisfaction. Maslow (1998) has arranged man's basic needs in a hierarchy, *i.e.*, some needs are strong or more important than others. According to him the five basic needs, progressing from physiological needs through safety needs, love, esteem needs and the need for self-actualisation. These basic needs are described here under:

- **Physiological needs:** Maslow states that physiological needs are undoubtedly the most powerful of all needs. Examples are the needs for food, sleep or rest. Until the biological needs are met, an individual may lack awareness of other needs. When a person is gratified he/she is released and higher needs can emerge. Some potential adult learners from low-economic background actually have unmet physiological needs, such as hunger, which prevent them from learning. An old person may not be able to see or hear well and he might not be open to satisfying other needs.

- **Safety Needs:** When physiological needs are satisfied, safety needs emerge, such as need for security, for physical safety, for stability in one's life. Safety needs are seen when a person prefers the familiar over the unfamiliar. An adult would rather go to a meeting in a building with which he is familiar than in a building new to him.
- **Love or Belongingness:** If both the physiological and safety needs are gratified, the needs for love, affection and belongingness emerge. Love needs involve both giving and receiving love. They involve the feeling of being wanted. The person who does not feel he belongs, no matter what the reason, probably will not continue with the group and discontinue his participation in adult education programme. The teacher should be affectionate towards adult learners and develop a group spirit among learners.
- **Esteem:** All people in our society have a need, a desire, for self-respect or self-esteem and for the esteem of others. There are two types: The desire for achievement and the desire for prestige or recognition from others. Satisfaction of the need for self-esteem leads to feelings of self-confidence and of being useful to the society. Thwarting of these needs produce feelings of inferiority or weakness. Fear or failure or lack of self-esteem might prevent an adult from participating in educational activities.
- **Self-Actualisation:** Even after the earlier needs are satisfied a person might still feel restless unless he becomes everything he is capable of becoming. This is called self-fulfilment or self-actualisation. The specific form of this needs varies from person-to-person. One person might desire to be an ideal mother or an ideal leader.
- **Implications for Adult Learning:** Before starting the adult education class, the basic needs of the learners should be studied. It may be possible that due to poverty and less per capita income, the basic biological needs of the learners may not be fulfilled. Then the main aim of adult education should be to provide regular income to the learners. This can be done by starting various income generating projects. The educators should also help by marketing of such products produced by the learners. The officials connected with adult education should take steps to start such programmes. This will make the classes more interesting to the learners. The teacher needs to strengthen the group spirit among learners and should identify himself/herself with the group. The learning experiences in the centres should promote the talents, attitudes capacities and potentialities of adults.

Physiological Theory of Motivation

This theory has been developed by Clifford Morgan and William James. According to this theory of the body determines attitudes and interests and explains activities and behaviour of people.

Implications for Adult Education: Participa-tion in physical activities decrease with age so also interests change as a person becomes older. Many physical limitations affect the amount of time an adult has for educational activities. After working all day at a job, some adults are too tired to participate in educational activity, such people can be motivated giving them work which gives them relaxation. Hearing and vision also decrease with age. The ages of the group members will determine the size of letters that a teacher writes on a black board, the colour of the chalk used, the size of the articles he holds for the adults to see, and how loudly and distinctly he speaks. The size, type and quality of handout material are also important.

Achievement-Motivation Theory

This theory has been developed by McClelland (1985). According to this theory all human behaviour is intended to reduce tension and reach a state of physiological and psychological equilibrium. It is a desire to do better, to achieve unique accomplishment, to compete with a standard of excellence and to involve oneself with long term achievement goals. It can be identified on the basic of individual expectation of success. It applies only when the individual knows that his/her performance will be evaluated by himself or by others in terms of excellence, and that the consequences of his action will either succeed or fail.

FACTORS CONTRIBUTING TO LEARNING

Introduction

Learning, can be considered as the process by which skills, attitudes, knowledge and concepts are acquired, understood, applied and extended. All human beings, whether grown ups or children engage in the process of learning, either consciously, sub-consciously or subliminally. It is through learning that their competence and ability to function in their environment get enhanced. It is important to understand that while we learn some ideas and concepts through instruction or teaching, we also learn through our feelings and experiences. Feelings and experiences are a tangible part of our lives and these greatly influence what we learn, how we learn and why we learn.

Learning has been considered partly a cognitive process and partly a social and affective one. It qualifies as a cognitive process because it involves the functions of attention, perception, reasoning, analysis, drawing of conclusions, making interpretations and giving meaning to the observed phenomena. All of these are mental processes which relate to the intellectual functions of the individual. Learning is a social and affective process, as the societal and cultural context in which we function and the feelings and experiences which we have, greatly influence our ideas, concepts, images and understanding of the world. These constitute inner subjective interpretations and represent our own unique, personalized constructions of the specific universe of functioning. Our knowledge, ideas, concepts, attitudes, beliefs and the skills which we acquire are a consequence of these combined processes.

CLASSIFICATION OF FACTORS: PERSONAL & ENVIRONMENT

To understand how we categorise the factors affecting learning, let us begin by considering the following examples:

- Ravi is sixteen year old and wants to please his mother by getting good results in his board examinations. He is so eager to please her, that he spends long hours of concentrated time and energy on his studies. He consciously tries to control other sources of distraction in his life and reduces the time spent on watching television, playing games and chatting with his friends.
- Rita Williams wants to be a famous tennis player. To achieve her goal, she practices tennis whenever she can, even though she gets no encouragement from her family. She makes it a point to watch tennis matches and maintain a good rapport with her sports teacher.
- Yuvraj is a good student, but lately he has been scoring very low marks at school. He is not able to concentrate or pay attention and his class work and home assignments reflect a very poor quality. Sources revealed that his parents fight a lot with each other and are about to get divorced.
- Arti and Kavita are two sisters. Arti is very good at art and craft and can sketch just about anything she sees. Kavita has a ear for music. She knows most songs and can sing them even if she has heard them only once. Both of them spend hours together pursuing their respective interest areas.
- Sayeeda is tall, attractive and has a very good figure. She wants to be a model or an air-hostess and nurtures this secretly as her dream. She is too scared to share her wishes with her family, since she belongs to an orthodox family, where girls at best can pursue teaching as a career. When she tries telling her mother what she wants, she is firmly told that she can only do her B.Ed and can go to the coaching classes for these.

The above cited examples illustrate that learning is a universal phenomenon mediated by a number of factors, both personal and environmental in nature. The dictum "everybody learns" is as true as its corollary, *i.e.*, everybody learns in accordance with his/her unique, individualized blend of personal and environmental factors. For example, in case of Ravi, the desire to please his mother, striving to do well in his board exams and managing his life situations appropriately constitute the key factors which influence him. For Rita Williams, it is her intrinsic desire to be a good tennis player which is paramount. She is not deterred by the lack of family support and continues to make efforts to promote her love for tennis on her own and fulfil her desire to be successful.

In case of Yuvraj, in spite of his innate capacity to study and perform well, his lack of achievement can be attributed to the emotional insecurity stemming from his parents' divorce. As far as Arti and Kavita are concerned, their special interests and talent in art and music respectively, seem to guide their activities.

For Sayeeda, the home environment and family culture and values determine her professional choice. Her own inner interests, desires and wishes are not to be taken into cognizance.

In all the examples cited, we can find evidence of both personal and environmental factors influencing the process of learning. Learning can thus be defined as a function of the interaction of personal and environmental factors.

$$L = f(EF \times PF)$$

L = learning; f = function; EF = environmental factors; PF = personal factors.

Personal factors are the intra individual factors like motivation, interests, abilities etc which predispose an individual towards learning as in the case of Rita Williams, Arti and Kavita. Environmental factors on the other hand, are those contextual factors which highlight the role of the environment in learning, such as the socio-emotional, societal and cultural factors as seen in the case of Yuvraj and Sayeeda. Although the two factors represent different categories, they operate in a common system. The environmental factors provide the context within which the personal factors, operate. The learner and the learning process can only be completely understood with reference to the interaction of both environmental and personal factors. This may be diagrammatically represented as follows:

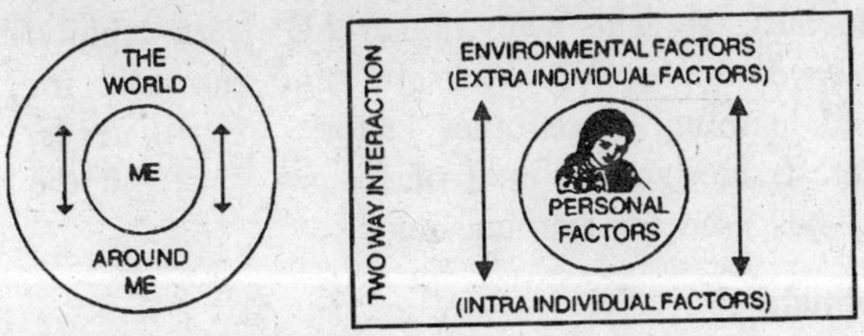

Fig: *Factors affecting learning*

Personal Factors Influencing Learning

The process of learning is influenced by a variety of personal factors. A thorough knowledge of these factors will prove very helpful for teachers and parents in understanding and guiding their children's learning. Some of the personal factors that influence the learning process may be classified as under : sensation and perception, fatigue and boredom, maturation, emotional condition, needs, interests, motivation, attention, intelligence, aptitude, attitude, etc. Let us discuss the important personal factors in the following sub-sections.

Sensation and Perception

Apart from the general health of the students, sensation and perception are the psychological factors which help in learning. Sensation is at the core of perception. There are five sense organs *i.e.*, skin, ears, tongue, eyes and nose. These sense organs are the gateways of knowledge and help in perception of various stimuli in the environment. Any defect in any of the sense organs will affect learning and hence acquisition of knowledge. For example, defects of vision such as myopia, hypermetropia, astigmatism, etc., cause headaches, nausia and general disinclination to study. A blind person depends upon the sense of touch or skin for learning and thus acquires knowledge and skills, as he can not visualise the objects. The stimuli are preceived and assimilated, and hence learnt through various sense organs. In this way we can say that sensation and perception is the bases of knowledge and learning.

Fatigue and Boredom

It is virtually boredom or lassitude rather than fatigue which bothers the students. The difference between the two is that fatigue is mental or physical tiredness which decreases in efficiency and competency to work. Boredom, on the other hand, is a lack of desire on an aversion to work. Such an aversion makes one feel fatigued without being actually fatigued. Studying seldom causes fatigue. It is mainly boredom which, besides causing the impression of fatigue, decreases student efficiency in learning.

Age and Maturation

Learning is directly dependent upon age and maturation. No learning can take place unless individual is matured enough to learn. Some children can learn better at earlier age while others take more time to learn the same content.

Mental age increases with the chronological age and ceases at about the age of sixteen years. Increase in age means intellectual maturation which helps in solving difficult problems. The principle of maturation warns us against enforcing learning on a child when he is not mature enough to learn the specific skills. Teachers should explain this principle to parents who are over ambitious or over enthusiastic in sending their children to school at the very early age.

Emotional Conditions

Desirable emotional conditions enhance the quality and speed of learning. Happiness, joy and satisfaction are always favourable for any type of learning. Adverse emotional conditons, on the other hand, hinder learning. Many studies have established the fact that emotional strain, stress, tensions, disturbances, etc., are extremely inimical to scholastic pursuits.

Needs

A need is the lack of something which, if provided, would facilitate child's usual behaviour. The lack of something is experienced by the child. The child then tries to perform that activity which culminates in the satisfaction of the need. Thus, the needs are associated with goals. Among human beings, the needs are realtively permanent tendencies which seek satisfaction in achieving certain specific goals. When these goals are achieved, the particular need is satisfied or met for the time being, but it recurs sooner or later and energises further activity. The needs in human beings can be physiological such as need for oxygen, food, water, etc. They may be social such as the need for affection, recognition, self-regard, etc. Social needs are however, quite different from physiological needs. Social needs might originate after physiological needs are satisfied. These needs have a complex structure and dominate the individual's behaviour.

There is not equal urgency in the satisfaction of all needs. Some have to be satisfied before others can manifest themselves.

In schools, children are not expected to do any intellectual thinking unless their physiological needs are satisfied. Poor, starved children may concentrate less on attainment of knowledge than on food. Similarly, very cold or hot classrooms or over-crowded seats will not be conducive to good learning. Likewise the need for safety, love and esteem, all act as powerful motives in the learning situations. If the child is afraid of the teacher or feels unsafe while in the school on account of too much beating or some other form of punishment, no learning can take place. Similarly, his needs for warmth and affection are very stimulating and hence results in effective learning.

Interests

Various types of interests of the students can be exploited to facilitate their learning. The interests during early infancy are mostly limited and short lived. As the child grows older his interests diversify and stabilize. You, a school teacher, should have thorough knowledge of children's interests. You can eliminate much drudgery, monotony and boredom from the school work if you make your instruction lively and stimulating and arouse student interest in it.

Once the students' interest is aroused in an activity you should expend more effort on it. No learning can be achieved without proper expenditure of effort on it. Students can even overcome distraction, fatigue and boredom if they feel interested in your instruction and class activities. It has often been found that, in most cases, fatigue in reality is loss of interest in the learning activity. Interest, should be exploited to yield results of greater quantity and quality learning in school.

Life is so exciting that many interesting things and activities often clamor to attract our attention. Children frequently face the dilemma of mutually conflicting interests. Immediate interests often seem to be clashing with the remoter ones. A student might be in a quandary at least for the time being when his interest in sports impels him towards the play-field and his interest in studies force him to concentrate on books.

In such cases of conflicting interests a lot of hesitancy, wastage, frustration and unhappiness is bound to follow. What is needed is education at home and school which helps/trains children to achieve a healthy balance in their interests. They should be trained to budget their time in such a manner as to pay a reasonable attention to various interests, scholastic, athletic, social etc., within the time at their disposal.

Motivation

Motivation is the heart of the learning process. It generates the will in an individual to do something. Adequate motivation not only engages the student in an activity which results in learning, but also sustains and directs learning. Two types of motivation are commonly recognised. These are: intrinsic and extrinsic motivation.

Intelligence

Intelligence as expressed by an I.Q. score on an intelligence test is positively related to learning. Generally, students with higher I.Q. learn rapidly. However, higher I.Q. in itself is no guarantee for rapid learning, since other factors such as needs, interest, motivation, etc., of the students and the methods used for learning are also important.

Aptitude

A student who possesses appropriate aptitude for a particular subject of study or skill, will learn better and retain it for a longer time. On the other hand, he will require relatively longer time to study a subject for which he lacks natural aptitude. He is liable to forget it soon besides feeling bored and unhappy all the time while learning it. Hence, it is extremely desirable to analyse the aptitude of students before prescribing courses of study for them.

Attitude

The learning process is also influenced considerably by the attitude of the student. If he is alert, attentive and interested in the material to be learnt, he is bound to have a favourable attitude towards it. Such an attitude will enable him to tackle the learning situation economically, pleasantly and effectively. Conversely, if he is inattentive and is uninterested in the material his attitude is bound to be unfavourable. This will hinder the smooth learning of the material in hand besides involving undue strain and tension in the learner.

Environmental Factors

Environmental influences begin since the time of the conception of the child in the womb of the mother. Mother's mental, physical and emotional conditions influence the development of foetus in the womb. The external environment starts from the time of birth of the child. It (external environment) refers to the surroundings which prevail in home, school and locality. At these places, the child interacts with members of the family, teachers, classmates or peers and neighbours and establishes relationship with them. The relationship with the members of the society, and the surroundings may affect the development of the child and also the way he learns. Some of the environmental factors are discussed as follows:

Surrounding : Natural, Social and Cultural

As the title of the sub-section indicates, we shall discuss here natural, social and cultural environment the child interacts with and get influenced.

Natural surrounding covers the climatic and atmospheric condition. These conditions affect learning directly. It has been found that high temperature and humidity reduces mental efficiency. For a limited time, humidity and high temperature can be tolerated but prolonged humidity and high temperature become unbearable and decrease mental efficiency. The intellectual productivity and creativeness of people living in hot regions are much low. Likewise, the morning time is always better for mastering difficult tasks. Mental efficiency decreases due to increased humidity and temperature. Studies on the academic progress of evening school students shows losses of efficiency varying from one to six per cent.

Social surrounding includes especially the environment of home, school and locality. Physical conditions at home such as large family, small family, (specific place of the study), insufficient ventilation, improper lighting, uncomfortable temperature, noisy home environment due to use of radio, TV, etc., noisy neighbourhood, constant visits by friends or relatives, etc., influence the intellectual learning of the student. The socio-emotional factors such as child rearing practices, reward and punishment, scope for freedom and independence in activities and decision making, play and study facilities, ambitions and aspirations of the parents, disorganisation and discord among birth positions such as eldest, youngest or single child have their definite influence on learning. For example, a student who comes from a very poor family and never had any intellectual stimulation at home remains dull and unresponsive in the class. In some societies there is a strong sex bias. Girls are directly or indirectly told that education is not meant for them. In the middle class families, on the other hand, parents are rather over-ambitious. They wish their children to make quick academic progress, grow-up and find a respectable vocation preferably a white collar job. Such children, therefore get sufficient incentive from their families. This, of course, is most favourable to scholastic learning, although an overdose of family emphasis on acquiring academic excellence might affect the child's mental and physical health adversely. Similarly, school activities, study facilities and teaching methods and behaviour of teachers, principals and non-teaching staff have an impact upon learning. If the school atmosphere is unconducive, it adversely affects the learning process. Locality also has an influence on a child. If the locality is bad, the learning will be ineffective to some extent.

Cultural demands and social expectations also influence learning. The spirit of culture is reflected in its social and educational institutions. Children's learning, therefore, is greatly determined by the demands and expectations of their culture. Thus, for instance, in an industrialized culture the emphasis mostly centres mechanical sciences and preparing children for highly mechanised vocations. In an agriculture based community, on the other hand, the educational process focusses on preparing its members for those skills which are suited to the needs of an agrarian community.

The philosophical elements of culture also influence the spirit of children's learning. Children in a democratic culture tend to acquire democrative and values and attitudes. A feudal, aristocratic or dictatorial culture, on the other hand, promotes autocratic modes of thought and behaviour.

Relationship with Teacher, Parents and Peers

The teacher is an important constituent in the instructional process. She/he plays an important role in shaping the behaviour of students. The way he teaches and manages the students has an affect on their learning. An authoritarian teacher will create an aggression and hostility among students while a democratic teacher will create a participatory climate for learning. The democratic environment leads students to constructive, thoughtful and cooperative behaviour. Generally, students learn better in a democratic set up because they like democratic procedures. The teacher is no more an instructor or the director of learning in a democratic set up. She/he helps his/her students in their learning. The teachers no more dominate the scene, they can get better results by decentralizing authority, increasing independence of students. They can attend to the comments and questions of the students. They can encourage students to participate in learning activities in and outside the class. There should be more emphasis on activity-centred classroom where student's active participation in the teaching-learning process is encouraged and the teacher acts as a guide to promote learning.

Relationship with parents plays a vital role in the learning process of the student. If the child-parents relationship is based on mutual respect and faith, it can provide the child a congenial atmosphere which in turn can facilitate his/her learning. A distorted and unhealthy environment, on the other hand, adversely affects the learning of the student. The upward mobility brings resistance on the part of the student to learn. Students in such families find themselves unable to cope up. A subtle but powerful influence on the growing child arises from his/her position among the children in the family. The parents of the first born expect the child to act like miniature adults and hence the first-born are found to encounter a variety of expectations and stresses. Whereas parents tend to be more relaxed in their do's and dont's with the last-born. Factors like traumatic events at home, separation or death can also precipitate learning problems in the normal child.

A healthy peer group relationship also plays an important role in learning. Student-student relationship in the classroom, school, society, etc., create a particular type of emotional climate. The climate solely depends upon their relationships. A sound relationships provides a tension free environment to the student to learn more and to compete in the class. If the relationship among peers is not good, it adversely affects their learning. Therefore, to improve the classroom learning climate, free discussion should be there. You should help your students understand each other in formal or informal meetings. They should be encouraged to meet each other and their teachers freely. If any mis-understanding is created or developed, it should be immediately clarified so as to maintain the healthy climate and cordial relationship among peers.

Media Influence on Learning

Media has been considered an important component of transmitting information. Media can be divided into two broad categories—print and non-print media. Print media refers to texts or printed materials. It is economical and has traditionally been used for pedagogical purposes.

But, it may not be the only or the perfect medium to impart education. Non-print media, also known as modern electronic media, have certain unique qualities which, in certain cases, facilitate learning much more faster than the print medium. These helps meet diverse learning objectives more efficiently than the printed matter.

Certain non-print media formats and delivery systems contribute well to student's learning actitivies, For example, audio tapes or computers can be used effectively to drill and practice in language and learning arithmatic. Electronic media can help promote the discovery approach to learning. For example, a film can be exploited for discovery teaching in the physical sciences. Students keep watching the various sections of the film until they perceive the relationships between the visuals. Then they are curious to find out the principles that explain those relationships. Likewise, in the social sciences various media can be used to present students with visual and auditory experiences that provide related inquiry. Films and stimulation are often used to present real-life or laboratory learning situations to students.

The role of the electronic media has proved effective for teaching students. These excite the student psychologically and prepare/motivate them to participate in teaching-learning activites. Non-print media perform following fuctions:

- direct attention,
- arouse motivation,
- increase student's concentration, and
- help them actively involve in the learning process.

PRACTICE PAPER

1. Mass media, cinema and library are passive agencies of education because
   (a) learner can not react to the feedback system of these agencies directly
   (b) they provide informal education
   (c) they can not come closer to the educant
   (d) all of these
2. Education of a child really begins
   (a) Once he takes birth
   (b) Once he attains the age of three
   (c) Once he is admitted to post nursery schools
   (d) Once he learns to speak
3. Family is the original social institution from which all other institutions emerged, who said this
   (a) Brown (b) Ballard
   (c) Machiver (d) None of them
4. Which of the following is not the primary function of schools
   (a) reorganization and reconstruction of Human experiences
   (b) all-round development of the child
   (c) to make the children self reliant
   (d) advancement of culture
5. In a democratic country, school should reflect
   (a) National aspirations
   (b) Community related local aspirations
   (c) Both of these
   (d) None of these
6. The best teacher in a village school is he who
   (a) carries community experiences to the class room
   (b) prepares instructional programmes in the interest of the community
   (c) carries classroom experiences to the community
   (d) all of these
7. Universalisation of education is the concept adopted by
   (a) modern state (b) democratic state
   (c) totalitarian state (d) religious state
8. Secular education in India means
   (a) an education opposed to religion
   (b) an education indifferent to religion
   (c) an education emphasizing equality of religions
   (d) none of these
9. School works as a social sub system for
   (a) transmission of culture
   (b) preservation of culture
   (c) advancement of culture
   (d) all of these
10. "Society is nothing but a process of interaction among people." Who said this?
    (a) Lapier (b) Cuber
    (c) Reuter (d) Payne
11. The best model of schooling is
    (a) Close interaction between education of society
    (b) Self reliant society by education
    (c) Reflection of openness by schools
    (d) All of these
12. Special provisions have been made for socially and educationally backward classes of the nation under article
    (a) 29 (b) 31
    (c) 15 (d) 19
13. Religious education is prohibited in government schools and colleges under Article
    (a) 29 (b) 28 (1)
    (c) 39 (2) (d) 15 (a)
14. Religious and linguistic minorities shall have the right to establish and administer their own educational institutions under Article
    (a) 30(1) (b) 31(2)
    (c) 40 (d) 41
15. Article 351 is about
    (a) education of tribals
    (b) promotion of Hindi
    (c) promotion of secularism
    (d) English as official language
16. Status of central university is given to any educational institution under union list of
    (a) Entry 65 (b) Entry 63
    (c) Entry 66 (d) None of these
17. Entry 25 of concurrent list states about
    (a) vocational and technical training of labour
    (b) the education of working class
    (c) the education of disabled
    (d) none of the above

18. Education in the mother tongue at primary stage to children belonging to linguistic minorities has been mentioned in Article
(*a*) 250 (*b*) 350
(*c*) 349 (*d*) 351

19. Educational and economic interests of SCs and STs have been safeguarded under Article
(*a*) 46 (*b*) 45(a)
(*c*) 351 (*d*) 52

20. Education of union territories is administered by the central government under Article
(*a*) 350 (*b*) 229
(*c*) 239 (*d*) 50

21. Education was transferred from state list of subjects to concurrent list in
(*a*) 1976 (*b*) 1972
(*c*) 1980 (*d*) 1950

22. Which of the following statements about growth and development is not correct?
(*a*) Growth generally refers to quantitative changes while development refers to qualitative changes
(*b*) Growth is a function of the environment
(*c*) Growth is not possible without development and vice versa
(*d*) Growth is determined by intrinsic and genetic factors of the organism

23. The limit of growth is fixed by
(*a*) internal factors of the organism
(*b*) nutrition and exercise
(*c*) both of these
(*d*) none of these

24. Development is
(*a*) Maturation
(*b*) Learning
(*c*) Synthesis of abilities
(*d*) All of these

25. Development takes place when
(*a*) environmental forces work on the organism
(*b*) environmental forces interact with the hereditary forces in an organism
(*c*) both of these
(*d*) none of these

26. Which of the following statements about development is correct?
(*a*) Process of development can be improved by exercise and nutrition
(*b*) Development may be positive and negative both
(*c*) Development proceeds from general to specific
(*d*) All of these

27. The son of a goldsmith becomes an expert goldsmith. It is an example of a
(*a*) biological heredity
(*b*) social heredity
(*c*) transfer of instinct
(*d*) none of these

28. All humans contain .... chromosomes.
(*a*) 26 (*b*) 36
(*c*) 46 (*d*) 42

29. DNA test helps us to know
(*a*) the genetic traits of a person
(*b*) nature of personality and its composition
(*c*) both of these
(*d*) none of these

30. The law of inheritance was discovered by Gregor Mendel in
(*a*) 1866 (*b*) 1911
(*c*) 1888 (*d*) 1920

31. Which of the following statements regarding personality traits is correct?
(*a*) Traits of personality can not be developed in isolation without taking the help of environment
(*b*) Subjective traits of the individual are determined by genetic factors
(*c*) Bad environment can surpass good inheritance but good environment is not a substitute for poor heredity
(*d*) All of these

32. Which of the following characteristics denote infancy period?
(*a*) Physical growth is curvilinear
(*b*) Physical growth is rapid
(*c*) Head grows at relatively slower rate as compared to other parts of the body
(*d*) All of these

33. Which of the following is not the characteristic of infancy period?
(*a*) From bilateral to unilateral trend in motor organs
(*b*) From general to specific trend in motor organs
(*c*) Emotional/social development is not associated with motor development
(*d*) Steady mental development

34. Which of the following illustrates conceptual development?
(*a*) Perception is the beginning of concept formation
(*b*) Concept changes with changes in experiences
(*c*) Concept changes with age
(*d*) All of these

35. There is one thing common in language and physical development what is that?
(*a*) Spurts of development at different ages
(*b*) Dependence on experience
(*c*) Dependence on training
(*d*) None of these

36. Which of the following characteristics is not associated with emotional development?
(*a*) Emotion is accompanied by physiological changes
(*b*) Emotions start immediately after birth
(*c*) Intense form of emotions are seen during early childhood period
(*d*) Emotions are unrelated to physical development

37. The child acquires about three fourth of the brain weight by the age of
(*a*) 2½ years (*b*) 2 years
(*c*) 6 years (*d*) 8 years

38. Social development of an infant depends on
(*a*) his chance of interaction with others
(*b*) love and affection shown to the child
(*c*) the extent to which he is able to attract the attention of others
(*d*) all of the above

39. In which of the following stages the child looks self centred?
(*a*) Infancy (*b*) Early childhood
(*c*) Adolescence (*d*) Adulthood

40. In the period of infancy, emotions are
(*a*) intense, frequent and unstable
(*b*) like an open book(overt)
(*c*) need based
(*d*) all of these

41. Which of the following organs of the body shows rapid growth in infancy?
(*a*) growth of hands (*b*) growth of head
(*c*) growth of legs (*d*) growth of fingers

42. In normal learning environment, forgetting is caused
(*a*) due to back of practice for a long time
(*b*) due to the interference of other learnt material
(*c*) due to lack of consolidation of memory traces
(*d*) all of these

43. Clear conception of size, weight, colour, time etc., is seen at the age of
(*a*) six (*b*) four
(*c*) four and half (*d*) five

44. Which of the following is not the characteristics of intellectual development of early childhood?
(*a*) increased span of attention
(*b*) exploration of the environment
(*c*) ability to verbalize all known concepts
(*d*) ability to distinguish past, present and future

45. Social development by the end of early childhood is marked by
(*a*) the feeling of autonomy
(*b*) the end of solitary plays
(*c*) the temperament of co-operation and friendliness
(*d*) all of these

46. Fictional world of the child starts at the age of
(*a*) 5-6 (*b*) 6-8
(*c*) 3-4 (*d*) 4-5

47. Girls are more dominating than boys in social situations in which of the following periods?
(*a*) pre-adolescent period
(*b*) early childhood period
(*c*) both of these
(*d*) none of these

48. In the period of early childhood, child is
(*a*) helpless to hide his emotions
(*b*) seen shifting his emotions very rapidly and frequently
(*c*) guided by his innate tendencies and instincts
(*d*) all of these

49. A nursery teacher should organize
(*a*) group games in the school
(*b*) those games which involve motor organs of the body
(*c*) those games which help the child to manipulate the environment
(*d*) all of these

50. Later childhood is called latency period because
(*a*) creative potentials are dormant
(*b*) sex remains dormant
(*c*) it is a period of inactivity
(*d*) all of these

51. Physical development of later childhood is marked by
(*a*) Auscification of bones
(*b*) Permanent teeth
(*c*) Excessive motor activity
(*d*) All of these

52. Girls surpass boys physically in
(*a*) infancy
(*b*) later childhood
(*c*) early childhood
(*d*) adolescence

53. The period of later childhood is marked by
(*a*) intellectual maturity
(*b*) high muscular energy
(*c*) hero worship
(*d*) all of these

54. Which of the following is not the characteristics of intellectual development of later childhood?
(*a*) High interest in science fiction
(*b*) Increased logical power
(*c*) Careful for future
(*d*) End of imaginary fears

55. Children are very much hateful or indifferent to opposite sex at the age of
(*a*) 11-12 (*b*) 13-14
(*c*) 10-11 (*d*) 15-16

56. Period of later childhood is marked by
(*a*) slow and steady physical growth
(*b*) stability in emotions
(*c*) anger against injustice
(*d*) all of these

57. At the end of later childhood period, the child
(*a*) feels himself superior to girls
(b) becomes independent of his family
(c) wants to become hero
(d) all of these

58. The best place of social development for a 12 years old child is
(*a*) neighbourhood
(*b*) family
(*c*) playground
(*d*) schooi

59. Group activities and group loyalties are at its peak at the age of
(*a*) 10-12 (*b*) 13-15
(*c*) 8-10 (*d*) 18-20

60. A teacher should not let a 12 years old child any time free because
(*a*) child is always interested to get involve in physical or mental activities
(*b*) spurts of creativity are seen at this age
(*c*) child is frustrated
(*d*) all of these

61. Elektra complex refers to
(*a*) daughter comes closer to the father
(*b*) son comes closer to the mother
(*c*) inferiority complex in the presence of girls
(*d*) none of these

62. According to Freud, super ego is properly developed during
(*a*) latency period (*b*) anal period
(*c*) phallic period (*d*) none of these

63. Development is a process of observable social interaction. This is the opinion of
(*a*) Erikson (*b*) Skinner
(*c*) Robert Sears (*d*) None of these

64. The secondary behaviour of the child according to Robert Sears starts with
(*a*) reinforcement (*b*) imitation
(*c*) modelling (*d*) none of these

65. The period of sensory motor adoptation of Piaget is
(*a*) 0-2 years (*b*) 1-3 years
(*c*) 3-5 years (*d*) 4-6 years

66. The child adopts the view points of others on the basis of consequences of these views in the
(*a*) third stage of Kohlberg's theory
(*b*) second stage of Kohlberg's theory
(*c*) fourth stage of Kohlberg's theory
(*d*) fifth stage of Kohlberg's theory

67. Which of the following is not the view point of cognitive theories of development?
(*a*) moral principles are acquired automatically with age
(*b*) super ego is formed during the period of adolescence
(*c*) Moral values are determined by culture
(*d*) Mural principles are universal

68. Organization of sensory experiences about a particular object is called
(*a*) percepts (*b*) reasoning
(*c*) concept (*d*) none of these

69. The concept building in a person depends on
(*a*) the age and maturity of the person
(*b*) past experiences of the learner
(*c*) intelligence of the learner
(*d*) all of these

70. Agreement on a concept is possible because
(*a*) concepts are subjective
(*b*) concepts are objective
(*c*) concepts are hierarchical
(*d*) b and c both

71. Which of the following statements about concepts is correct?
(*a*) Some concepts are more powerful than others
(*b*) All concepts are universal
(*c*) Concepts are differentiated on the basis of their attributes
(*d*) None of these

72. Which is the highest level of concept formation?
(*a*) formal level (*b*) sensory level
(*c*) concrete level (*d*) none of these

73. How many steps of problem solving has been given by Gates?
(*a*) Six (*b*) Seven
(*c*) Five (*d*) Ten

74. Freeman considers intelligence as an ability
(*a*) to adjust in an adverse situation
(*b*) to learn better and faster
(*c*) to manipulate abstract materials
(*d*) all of these

75. Single factor theory of intelligence was given by
(*a*) Alfred Binet (*b*) Thorndike
(*c*) Freeman (*d*) None of them

76. Which of the following is not the characteristics of 'S' factor according to Spearman ?
(*a*) It is the acquired capacity of the individual
(*b*) Specialization in only one trade is possible
(*c*) It varies from activity to activity in the same individual
(*d*) Individuals differ only in 'S' factor of intelligence

77. In multifactor theory, range is related to
(*a*) Number of tasks that a person can do in a limited period of time

(*b*) Difficulty level of items
(*c*) General intelligence of learners
(*d*) None of these

78. SI model of intelligence was given by J P Guilford in
(*a*) 1911 (*b*) 1904
(*c*) 1967 (*d*) 1975

79. Hierarchy theory of intelligence was given by
(*a*) Jenson
(*b*) Thorndike
(*c*) Burt and Vernon
(*d*) None of them

80. In the pre-Binet period, intelligence was considered as
(*a*) Sensory acuity of the individual
(*b*) Verbal ability of the individual
(*c*) Associative ability of the individual
(*d*) All of these

81. An age scale of intelligence was first developed by
(*a*) Spearman (*b*) Terman
(*c*) Binet-Simon (*d*) None of them

82. Binet-Simon scale of intelligence measures
(*a*) General mental abilities not specific ones.
(*b*) Mental growth of the individual over a period of time
(*c*) The aptitude or level of an examinee not their speed
(*d*) All of these

83. WAIS came into being in
(*a*) 1939 (*b*) 1955
(*c*) 1960 (*d*) 1964

84. Wechsler developed an intelligence test for children in
(*a*) 1939 (*b*) 1949
(*c*) 1955 (*d*) 1956

85. Catell's culture fair test of intelligence was developed in
(*a*) 1960 (*b*) 1961
(*c*) 1965 (*d*) 1955

86. Non-verbal test of intelligence is suitable for
(*a*) deaf and dumb
(*b*) illiterates
(*c*) backward children
(*d*) all of these

87. Intelligence testing is useful for knowing
(*a*) individual difference
(*b*) mental retardation
(*c*) educational backwardness
(*d*) all of these

88. Scores on intelligence tests can not be fully relied on because
(*a*) fatigue level can influence the performance
(*b*) cultural factors can influence the score
(*c*) they generally do not reveal all the mental abilities of a person
(*d*) all of these

89. Who among the following psychologists is of the view that a learner can be motivated by satisfying his needs?
(*a*) Henry Murray (*b*) Abraham Maslow
(*c*) Both of these (*d*) None of these

90. Permanent change in behaviour brought about by experience or training is called.
(*a*) Learning (*b*) Motivation
(*c*) Assimilation (*d*) None of these

91. The book "**A Theory of Motivation**" has been written by
(*a*) Maslow (*b*) K B Madson
(*c*) Murray (*d*) None of them

92. Motivated behaviour of a person is
(*a*) Well directed and well guided towards the goal
(*b*) Agitated until the goal is achieved
(*c*) Both of these
(*d*) None of these

93. Factors affecting motivations are
(*a*) Physiological factors only
(*b*) Psychological factors only
(*c*) Psycho-social factors
(*d*) All of these

94. Process of motivation is affected by all except
(*a*) Habits
(*b*) Mental sets and values
(*c*) Physical factors
(*d*) None of these

95. Which of the following does not come under the category of social motives?
(*a*) Prestige and Status
(*b*) Social approval
(*c*) Personal goal
(*d*) Money hoarding

96. Our action and behaviour is motivated by the desire for getting pleasure and avoiding pain. This is the opinion of
(*a*) Thomas Hobbes (*b*) Descartes
(*c*) Kant (*d*) John Locke

97. Fundamental instincts of humans are inherited rather than acquired. These instincts are the spring of human behaviour. The above opinion was held by
(*a*) Charles Darwin (*b*) Mc Dougall
(*c*) Both of these (*d*) None of these

98. Instinct theory of behaviour was rejected by psychologists on which of the following grounds?
(*a*) Adult behaviour is guided by experience and learning also. It is not always guided by instinct
(*b*) Human behaviour is affected by the cultural factors also

(*c*) Human being is a rational animal. He is not supposed to be directed by instincts only
(*d*) All of these

99. Central motive state was explained by
(*a*) Morgan
(*b*) Mc Dougall
(*c*) Murray
(*d*) None of them

100. Abraham Maslow was basically a
(*a*) Pragmatist (*b*) Humanist
(*c*) Realist (*d*) All of them

101. A self actualized person is one who
(*a*) Does not accept restrictions imposed by the society
(*b*) Always seeks perfection
(*c*) Is very good in inter personal relationship with others
(*d*) All of these

102. The theory of achievement motivation was developed by Mc Clelland of Harward University in
(*a*) 1949 (*b*) 1951
(*c*) 1965 (*d*) 1944

103. Achievement motive in a child can be developed by
(*a*) Proper guidance and high expectation from the child
(*b*) Telling the stories of great men to the child
(*c*) Setting a realistic goal for the child
(*d*) All of these

104. Which of the following is not a characteristic of learning?
(*a*) Learning is a relatively permanent change in behaviour
(*b*) Learning is a growth of the organism
(*c*) Learning is directly observed
(*d*) Learning is a goal directed process

105. In the beginning of life, the baby is guided by
(*a*) maturation
(*b*) instincts
(*c*) learning
(*d*) none of these

106. Accumulation of knowledge or facts becomes learning when
(*a*) It is applied in real life situation
(*b*) It is done by the learner himself
(*c*) It is provided by the teacher
(*d*) None of these

107. Dancing, driving, writing etc are the examples of
(*a*) Mechanical learning
(*b*) Perceptual motor learning
(*c*) Psychomotor learning
(*d*) both (*b*) and (*c*)

108. In Gagne's hierarchy, learning has been divided into
(*a*) eight parts (*b*) nine parts
(*c*) seven parts (*d*) none of the above

109. Match the following:

(A)	(B)
(*i*) Classical conditioning	1. Kohler
(*ii*) Drive reduction	2. Hull
(*iii*) Sign gestalt	3. Pavlov
(*iv*) Learning by insight	4. Tolman

	(*i*)	(*ii*)	(*iii*)	(*iv*)
(*a*)	1	2	3	4
(*b*)	3	2	4	1
(*c*)	2	1	3	4
(*d*)	4	3	2	1

110. Reflexes are of two types according to Pavlov. They are physiological and
(*a*) Psychic (*b*) Neural
(*c*) Mental (*d*) None of these

111. In classical conditioning, extinction will take place when
(*a*) Organism is poor in generalization
(*b*) CS is given without UCS for a long time
(*c*) CS > UCS
(*d*) None of these

112. Backward conditioning will take place when
(*a*) UCS is presented prior to CS
(*b*) CS is presented prior to UCS
(*c*) Reward is not given to the organism
(*d*) None of these

113. When connection is not established between a CS and CR, due to any factor, that is called
(*a*) Spontaneous recovery
(*b*) Extinction
(*c*) Inhibition
(*d*) None of these

114. When a child responds to all women who wear black suit because of the black suit of her mother, it is the example of
(*a*) internal inhibition
(*b*) generalization
(*c*) assimilation
(*d*) all of these

115. Which of the following is not a behaviourist?
(*a*) Watson
(*b*) Skinner
(*c*) Pavlov
(*d*) Lewin

116. Learning according to Watson is
(*a*) the shifting of old responses to the new stimuli
(*b*) the result of connection between S-R formed in the brain
(*c*) both of these
(*d*) none of these

117. Which of the following points differentiates the theories of Watson and Guthrie?
(*a*) law of contiguity
(*b*) law of recency
(*c*) generalization
(*d*) law of frequency

118. In operant conditioning reward works as motives but in Guthrie's theory motives are
(*a*) Stimuli given to the learner
(*b*) Actions done by the learner
(*c*) Both of these
(*d*) None of these

119. We forget something not by disuse but by other learning. This is the theory of
(*a*) contiguity
(*b*) trial and error
(*c*) learning by insight
(*d*) perception

120. Which of the following is not an essential requirement for trial and error learning?
(*a*) Drive
(*b*) Barrier
(*c*) Chance success
(*d*) Selective movement of the organism

121. According to the law of trial and error, learning occurs when
(*a*) it is satisfying for the learner
(*b*) bond between S-R is strengthened by the repeated use
(*c*) drive is there in the learner to act
(*d*) all of these

122. Which of the following facilitates learning according to Thorndike?
(*a*) Transfer of training
(*b*) Mental set of the learner
(*c*) Law of contiguity
(*d*) All of these

123. In Hull's theory, for learning to occur, the S-R connection must be associated with the
(*a*) cognitive field of the learner
(*b*) diminution of the need
(*c*) both of these
(*d*) none of these

124. Reinforcement in Skinner's theory is similar to drive reduction in which theory
(*a*) Hull's theory
(*b*) Guthrie's theory
(*c*) Lewin's theory
(*d*) None of these

125. Which of the following theories is most quantitatively measurable?
(*a*) Pavlov's
(*b*) Skinner's
(*c*) Hull's
(*d*) None of these

126. In drive reduction theory, the effective stimulus in learning is the trace. It is formed
(*a*) in the brain
(*b*) by the bond of S-R
(*c*) in the nervous system
(*d*) none of these

127. In drive reduction theory, habit formation is a function of
(*a*) stimulus potential
(*b*) stimulus generalization
(*c*) reaction potential
(*d*) all of these

128. Hull may be considered superior to other S-R Theorists in the sense that he was able to measure
(*a*) latency of response
(*b*) reinforcement potential
(*c*) both of these
(*d*) none of these

129. Which of the following points differentiates Skinner from other S-R theorists?
(*a*) His operant conditioning (type R learning)
(*b*) His schedule of reinforcement
(*c*) His way of shaping behaviour
(*d*) All of these

130. Skinner's theory is more objective in nature than the others because
(*a*) operant behaviour is external
(*b*) reflexes never have zero strength
(*c*) reinforcement is followed by responses
(*d*) all of these

131. Aversive stimuli in operant conditioning means
(*a*) individual will not do a particular act because of fear of such stimuli
(*b*) individual will not do a particular act because of the disapproval from others
(*c*) both of these
(*d*) none of these

132. In Skinner's theory, reinforcement is given to the learner when
(*a*) his response is 100% correct
(*b*) his response is closer to the correct behaviour
(*c*) both of these
(*d*) none of these

133. Which of the following statements regarding S-R theories is not correct?
(*a*) Man behaves like a machine
(*b*) Behaviour is overt and can be objectively measured
(*c*) Learning proceeds from simple to complex
(*d*) Things are perceived in the context of figure ground *i.e.*, in relation to other things

134. Which of the following statements regarding field theories are correct?
(*a*) Learning is not additive

(*b*) Molar approach of behaviour is followed here
(*c*) Interaction between organism and the environment is essential for learning
(*d*) All of these

135. Operant conditioning is different from respondent conditioning in which of the following points
(*a*) In OC reinforcement is given after the response is made
(*b*) In operant conditioning, behaviour is controlled by central nervous system
(*c*) A chain of responses is needed for shaping the behaviour (learning)
(*d*) All of these

136. Thorndike and Skinner do not differ at all in
(*a*) the law of effect
(*b*) law of readiness
(*c*) law of contiguity
(*d*) all of these

137. According to gestalt psychologists, behaviour can not be quantified because
(*a*) it is always changeable
(*b*) it is governed by the configuration produced in the mind
(*c*) it is rarely overt
(*d*) all of these

138. Law of pragnanz is the other name of the law of
(*a*) continuity
(*b*) closure
(*c*) contiguity
(*d*) none of these

139. How does the law of similarity work according to field theorists?
(*a*) Similar ideas and experiences get associated to form a whole
(*b*) Similar objects or experiences are easily learnt
(*c*) Both of these
(*d*) None of these

140. Learning by insight looks similar to some extent to which of the following theories?
(*a*) Need reduction theory
(*b*) R type of learning
(*c*) Trial and error theory
(*d*) None of the above

141. The other name of conditioned reflexes is
(*a*) psychic reflexes
(*b*) motor reflexes
(*c*) physiological reflexes
(*d*) none of the above

142. According to Renzuli, a gifted child is one
(*a*) Who possesses above average ability in almost every field
(*b*) Who is committed to task and highly motivated
(*c*) Who is definitely creative
(*d*) All of these

143. Gifted and talented children must be identified as early as possible because
(*a*) If their potentials are not developed by proper guidance of the teacher, it is a loss of the society
(*b*) They are likely to create problems for others, if they are not given work according to their ability
(*c*) Ordinary level of curriculum will not suit to these children
(*d*) All of these

144. Achievement test can be a good indicator of intellectual power if
(*a*) It is conducted immediately after the teaching is over
(*b*) A student shows good performance consistently on different achievement test
(*c*) Both of these
(*d*) None of these

145. Which of the following skills does not require high intellectual ability?
(*a*) Technical skills
(*b*) Mechanical skills
(*c*) Teaching skills
(*d*) Management skills

146. Cognitive abilities related to giftedness are all except
(*a*) High comprehensive and analytical abilities
(*b*) High level of verbal intelligence
(*c*) High retention power
(*d*) None of these

147. A superior child is advanced to a normal child by at least
(*a*) 2½ years
(*b*) Four years
(*c*) 1 years
(*d*) 1½ years

148. A gifted child is
(*a*) realistic in his approach
(*b*) highly interested in solving social problems
(*c*) more frequently chosen by his age mates and peers
(*d*) all of these

149. Which of the following enrichment programmes is suitable for gifted children in the school?
(*a*) Mathematics or Science Olympiad
(*b*) Challenging home assignments
(*c*) Map work during studies
(*d*) All of these

150. Which of the following does not come under the category of acceleration for gifted children?
(*a*) Skipping of classes

(b) Early admission
(c) Extra laboratory work
(d) Organizing summer camps

151. Under achievers are those who
(a) Score low on intelligence tests
(b) Achieve low in the class consistently despite their superior intelligence
(c) Are unable to correspond their achievement to the level of their innate abilities
(d) Both (b) and (c)

152. Which of the following conditions must be satisfied in order to designate a person mentally retarded?
(a) Sub-normal intellectual functioning
(b) Very poor adaptive ability
(c) Dependability on others
(d) All of these

153. The best measure of identifying mildly mentally retarded is
(a) Administration of standardized intelligence test
(b) Administration of behaviour test
(c) Administration of adjustment test
(d) A combination of all

154. Physical trauma during pregnancy may cause
(a) Mental retardation
(b) Blindness
(c) Deafness
(d) All of these

155. All of the following may cause mental retardation except
(a) Blood incompatibility
(b) Action of toxic agent
(c) Radio-activity
(d) None of these

156. Which of the following is an important postnatal cause of mental retardation?
(a) Brain injury
(b) Infection
(c) Severe malnutrition
(d) All of these

157. Dullers do not differ from normal children in
(a) Physical characteristics
(b) Level of social expectancy
(c) Both of these
(d) None of these

158. Which of the following things is not required for educating mildly mentally retarded children?
(a) Regular counseling
(b) Remedial teaching
(c) Modification in the curriculum
(d) Regular evaluation

159. Teaching of which of the following skills is not suitable to borderline cases?
(a) Electric fitting
(b) Repairing of electric or electronic equipments
(c) Oratory skills
(d) Activity based skills

160. IQ range of morons are in the range of
(a) 60-90 (b) 50-75
(c) 60-80 (d) 30-50

161. Morons are slow in
(a) Physical growth
(b) Thinking and planning
(c) Taking initiative
(d) All of these

162. Unsatisfactory relation of a mentally retarded child with the environment is technically called
(a) Autism
(b) Maladjustment
(c) Pseudo-dullness
(d) None of these

163. All of the following are characteristics of morons except
(a) They are restricted to unskilled or semi skilled occupations
(b) They are likely to be delinquent more easily
(c) They have stronger sex drives than the normals
(d) They are educable upto normal level but at a slower rate

164. Which of the following modifications in the curriculum is needed for morons?
(a) Activity based curriculum
(b) Skill dominated curriculum
(c) Emphasis on social training
(d) All of these

165. Which of the following things can not be taught to Imbeciles?
(a) Self help skills
(b) Unskilled job to be performed under supervision
(c) Writing skills
(d) Social skills

166. In which of the following cases divergent thinking is required?
(a) Attempting a multiple choice items
(b) Writing an essay
(c) Doing a research activity
(d) Both (a) and (c)

167. Which of the following tests is similar to Guilford's test of cognitive abilities?
(a) Word association test
(b) Things test
(c) Hidden shapes test
(d) None of these

168. In Hidden shapes test of creativity, which of the following things is used?
(a) Pictures

(*b*) Words
(*c*) Things
(*d*) None of them

169. A creative child in the class can not be satisfied unless
(*a*) He is given freedom to manipulate ideas or things
(*b*) He is allowed to ask questions in his own way
(*c*) Both of these
(*d*) None of these

170. A creative child is one who
(*a*) Is ideationally productive and unconventional
(*b*) Does not stick to social and religious norms in a hard manner
(*c*) Is all the time restless to do something uncommon and unique
(*d*) All of these

171. For the development of creative potential of a child, the teacher should
(*a*) Allow him to be critical to ideas and people
(*b*) Give them chance of problem solving
(*c*) Both of these
(*d*) None of these

172. New ideas (Eureka) suddenly comes in the minds of the creative children in the stage of
(*a*) Preparation
(*b*) Illumination
(*c*) Revision
(*d*) Incubation

173. The technique to foster creativity in children is
(*a*) Brain storming
(*b*) Problem solving
(*c*) Both of these
(*d*) None of these

174. A teacher can foster creativity in children by
(*a*) Developing confidence in them
(*b*) Giving them opportunity to express
(*c*) Both of these
(*d*) None of these

175. Learning disabled children are
(*a*) Deficient in using potentials
(*b*) Low in intelligence
(*c*) Slow in activity
(*d*) None of these

176. Learning disabled children perform very poorly in
(*a*) academic areas
(*b*) technical areas
(*c*) both of these
(*d*) none of these

177. Problem of learning disability is more complex than that of other disabilities because
(*a*) Its causes can not be easily ascertained by applying usual tests
(*b*) It is associated to behaviour problems
(*c*) Both of these
(*d*) None of these

178. Educationally, learning disabled look similar to
(*a*) dullers
(*b*) backward children
(*c*) both of these
(*d*) none of these

179. In which of the following physical characteristics learning disabled children differ from the normal ones?
(*a*) They are all the time clumsy and awkward
(*b*) Poor coordination of motor abilities
(*c*) Height, weight and health
(*d*) All of these

180. Which of the following methods is most suitable for learning disabled children?
(*a*) Behaviour guidance method
(*b*) Remedial teaching
(*c*) Brain storming
(*d*) None of them

181. In order to improve work habits of learning disabled what should be done?
(*a*) Unattending behaviour should be penalized
(*b*) Close monitoring of the behaviour is needed
(*c*) Cues and prompt should be given
(*d*) All of these

182. Those who are normal in intelligence but slow in academic achievement due to psycho-social reasons are called
(*a*) Backward children
(*b*) Gifted under achievers
(*c*) Both of these
(*d*) None of these

183. Consistent low achievement leads to low intelligence because
(*a*) 50% intellectual ability is expressed in verbal form
(*b*) Learning develops thinking and reasoning power
(*c*) Both of these
(*d*) None of these

184. Which of the following situations may lead to educational backwardness?
(*a*) Sensory impairment
(*b*) Motor disability
(*c*) Long diseases and health problems.
(*d*) All of these

185. Emotional disturbances may lead to educational backwardness because
(*a*) Proper emotional development is necessary for social interactions
(*b*) Emotions will develop intellectual power, *i.e.*, emotional intelligence

(c) Both of these
(d) None of these

186. Which of the following factors will not lead to educational backwardness?
(a) Poor socio economic status of the family
(b) Poor educational environment of the school
(c) Occupation of the family
(d) Poor emotional climate of the family

187. Which of the following is an important cause of educational backwardness at primary level of education in India?
(a) Poor school organisation
(b) Lack of accountability
(c) Attitude of the masses towards education
(d) All of these

188. Which of the following measures should be adopted by the teacher to check educational backwardness?
(a) Continuous evaluation and regular feedback
(b) Remedial teaching
(c) Adjustment and behaviour training
(d) All of these

189. Teaching by small steps and frequent short assignment techniques are useful for
(a) Slow learners
(b) Learning disabled
(c) Educationally backward children
(d) Children of all types of disabilities

190. Special schools are required for backward children when
(a) Backwardness is due to any serious physical handicap
(b) The size of population of backward children in the society is very large as is the case of Gujarat where the achievement of students in mathematics is always seen very low
(c) Both of these
(d) None of these

191. Which of the following should be considered the most important quality of a teacher at primary level?
(a) Patience and perseverance
(b) Competence in methods of teaching and knowledge of subjects
(c) Competence to teach in highly standardised language
(d) Eagerness to teach

192. A teacher, because of his/her democratic nature, allows students to sit all over the class. Some sit together and discuss or do group reading. Some sit quietly and read themselves. A parent does not like it. Which of the following may be the best way to handle the situation?
(a) Parents should request the principal to change the section of their ward
(b) Parents should show trust in the teacher and discuss the problem with the teacher
(c) Parents should take away the child from that school
(d) Parents should complain against the teacher to the principal

193. The stage in which a child begins to think logically about objects and events is known as
(a) Formal operational stage
(b) Pre-operational stage
(c) Concrete operational stage
(d) Sensori-motor stage

194. 'Mind mapping' refers to
(a) a plan of action for an adventure
(b) drawing the picture of a mind
(c) researching the functioning of the mind
(d) a technique to enhance comprehension

195. The best way, specially at primary level, to address the learning difficulties of students is to use
(a) expensive and glossy support material
(b) easy and interesting textbooks
(c) story-telling method
(d) a variety of teaching methods suited to the disability

196. Which of the following will foster creativity among learners?
(a) Providing opportunities to question and to nurture the innate talents of every learner
(b) Emphasizing achievement goals from the beginning of school life
(c) Coaching students for good marks in examination
(d) Teaching the students the practical value of good education

197. According to Piaget, at which of the following stages does a child begin to think logically about abstract propositions?
(a) Formal operational stage (11 years and up)
(b) Sensori-motor stage (Birth–02 years)
(c) Pre-operational stage (02–07 years)
(d) Concrete operational stage (07–11 years)

198. Learning can be enriched if
(a) more and more teaching aids are used in the class
(b) teachers use different types of lectures and explanation
(c) due attention is paid to periodic tests in the class
(d) situations from the real world are brought into the class in which students interact with each other and the teahcer facilitates

199. Which of the following statements ***cannot*** be considered as a feature of the process of learning?
(a) Learning is a comprehensive process
(b) Learning is goal-oriented
(c) Unlearning is also a learning process
(d) Educational institutions are the only place where learning takes place

200. A student of V-grade with 'visual deficiency' should be
(*a*) helped with his/her routine-work by parents and friends
(*b*) treated normally in the classroom and provided support through Audio CDs
(*c*) given special treatment in the classroom
(*d*) excused to do a lower level of work

201. Which of the following is ***not*** related to the socio-psychological needs of the child?
(*a*) Need for emotional security
(*b*) Regular elimination of waste products from the body
(*c*) Need for company
(*d*) Need for appreciation or social approval

202. Which is the place where the child's 'cognitive' development is defined in the best way?
(*a*) School and classroom environment
(*b*) Auditorium
(*c*) Home
(*d*) Playground

203. .... is considered a sign of motivated teaching.
(*a*) Remedial work given by the teacher
(*b*) Questioning by students
(*c*) Pin drop silence in the class
(*d*) Maximum attendance in the class

204. Which of the following is ***not*** a sign of an intelligent young child?
(*a*) One who has the ability to communicate fluently and appropriately
(*b*) One who carries on thinking in an abstract manner
(*c*) One who can adjust oneself in a new environment
(*d*) One who has the ability to cram long essays very quickly

205. "Children actively construct their understanding of the world" is a statement attributed to
(*a*) Pavlov (*b*) Kohlberg
(*c*) Skinner (*d*) Piaget

206. Kritika who does ***not*** talk much at home, talks a lot at school. It shows that
(*a*) teachers demand that children should talk a lot at school
(*b*) she does not like her home at all
(*c*) her thoughts get acknowledged at school
(*d*) the school provides opportunities to children to talk a lot

207. A teacher should make an attempt to understand the potentialities of her/his students. Which of the following fields is related to this objective?
(*a*) Social Philosophy
(*b*) Media – Psychology
(*c*) Educational Psychology
(*d*) Educational Sociology

208. Motivation, in the process of learning,
(*a*) differentiates new learning from old learning
(*b*) makes learners think unidirectionally
(*c*) creates interest for learning among young learners
(*d*) sharpens the memory of learners

209. The term 'curriculum' in the field of education refers to
(*a*) overall programme of the school which students experience on a day-to-day basis
(*b*) evaluation process
(*c*) text-material to be used in the class
(*d*) methods of teaching and the content to be taught

210. At lower classes, play-way method of teaching is based on
(*a*) principles of methods of teaching
(*b*) psychological principles of development and growth
(*c*) sociological principles of teaching
(*d*) theory of physical education programmes

211. "A young child responds to a new situation on the basis of the response made by him/her in a similar situation as in the past." This is related to
(*a*) 'Law of Effect' of learning
(*b*) 'Law of Attitude' of learning process
(*c*) 'Law of Readiness' of learning
(*d*) 'Law of Analogy' of learning

212. .... is ***not*** considered a sign of 'being gifted'.
(*a*) Fighting with others
(*b*) Novelty in expression
(*c*) Curiosity
(*d*) Creative ideas

213. Education of children with special needs should be provided
(*a*) by methods developed for special children in special schools
(*b*) in special schools
(*c*) by special teachers in special schools
(*d*) along with other normal children

214. To make assessment a 'useful and interesting' process, one should be careful about
(*a*) labelling students as intelligent or average learners
(*b*) using a variety of ways to collect information about the student's learning across the scholastic and co-scholastic boundaries
(*c*) using technical language to give feedback
(*d*) making comparisons between different students

215. 'Dyslexia' is associated with
(*a*) Mathematical disorder

(*b*) Reading disorder
(*c*) Behavioural disorder
(*d*) Mental disorder

216. Parents should play a .... role in the learning process of young children.
(*a*) proactive
(*b*) sympathetic
(*c*) neutral
(*d*) negative

217. "Development is a never ending process." This idea is associated with
(*a*) Principle of continuity
(*b*) Principle of integration
(*c*) Principle of interaction
(*d*) Principle of interrelation

218. The 'insight theory of learning' is promoted by
(*a*) Pavlov
(*b*) Jean Piaget
(*c*) Vygotsky
(*d*) 'Gestalt' theorists

219. In which of the following stages do children become active members of their peer group?
(*a*) Adulthood
(*b*) Early childhood
(*c*) Childhood
(*d*) Adolescence

220. Four distinct stages of children's intellectual development are identified by
(*a*) Erikson (*b*) Skinner
(*c*) Piaget (*d*) Kohlberg

ANSWERS

1	**2**	**3**	**4**	**5**	**6**	**7**	**8**	**9**	**10**
(*a*)	(*a*)	(*b*)	(*d*)	(*c*)	(*d*)	(*a*)	(*c*)	(*d*)	(*c*)
11	**12**	**13**	**14**	**15**	**16**	**17**	**18**	**19**	**20**
(*a*)	(*c*)	(*b*)	(*a*)	(*b*)	(*b*)	(*a*)	(*b*)	(*a*)	(*c*)
21	**22**	**23**	**24**	**25**	**26**	**27**	**28**	**29**	**30**
(*a*)	(*b*)	(*a*)	(*d*)	(*c*)	(*d*)	(*b*)	(*c*)	(*c*)	(*a*)
31	**32**	**33**	**34**	**35**	**36**	**37**	**38**	**39**	**40**
(*d*)	(*d*)	(*c*)	(*d*)	(*a*)	(*d*)	(*b*)	(*d*)	(*a*)	(*d*)
41	**42**	**43**	**44**	**45**	**46**	**47**	**48**	**49**	**50**
(*c*)	(*d*)	(*a*)	(*c*)	(*d*)	(*a*)	(*c*)	(*d*)	(*d*)	(*b*)
51	**52**	**53**	**54**	**55**	**56**	**57**	**58**	**59**	**60**
(*d*)	(*b*)	(*d*)	(*c*)	(*a*)	(*d*)	(*d*)	(*c*)	(*a*)	(*a*)
61	**62**	**63**	**64**	**65**	**66**	**67**	**68**	**69**	**70**
(*a*)	(*a*)	(*c*)	(*b*)	(*a*)	(*a*)	(*c*)	(*a*)	(*d*)	(*d*)
71	**72**	**73**	**74**	**75**	**76**	**77**	**78**	**79**	**80**
(*b*)	(*a*)	(*c*)	(*d*)	(*a*)	(*d*)	(*a*)	(*c*)	(*c*)	(*a*)
81	**82**	**83**	**84**	**85**	**86**	**87**	**88**	**89**	**90**
(*c*)	(*d*)	(*b*)	(*b*)	(*b*)	(*d*)	(*d*)	(*d*)	(*c*)	(*a*)
91	**92**	**93**	**94**	**95**	**96**	**97**	**98**	**99**	**100**
(*a*)	(*c*)	(*d*)	(*d*)	(*c*)	(*a*)	(*c*)	(*d*)	(*a*)	(*b*)
101	**102**	**103**	**104**	**105**	**106**	**107**	**108**	**109**	**110**
(*d*)	(*b*)	(*d*)	(*c*)	(*b*)	(*a*)	(*d*)	(*a*)	(*b*)	(*a*)
111	**112**	**113**	**114**	**115**	**116**	**117**	**118**	**119**	**120**
(*b*)	(*a*)	(*c*)	(*b*)	(*d*)	(*c*)	(*d*)	(*a*)	(*a*)	(*d*)
121	**122**	**123**	**124**	**125**	**126**	**127**	**128**	**129**	**130**
(*d*)	(*d*)	(*b*)	(*a*)	(*c*)	(*c*)	(*a*)	(*a*)	(*d*)	(*a*)
131	**132**	**133**	**134**	**135**	**136**	**137**	**138**	**139**	**140**
(*a*)	(*c*)	(*d*)	(*d*)	(*d*)	(*a*)	(*b*)	(*b*)	(*a*)	(*c*)
141	**142**	**143**	**144**	**145**	**146**	**147**	**148**	**149**	**150**
(*a*)	(*d*)	(*d*)	(*c*)	(*a*)	(*d*)	(*a*)	(*d*)	(*d*)	(*c*)
151	**152**	**153**	**154**	**155**	**156**	**157**	**158**	**159**	**160**
(*d*)	(*d*)	(*d*)	(*d*)	(*d*)	(*d*)	(*c*)	(*c*)	(*c*)	(*b*)

161	162	163	164	165	166	167	168	169	170
(d)	(a)	(d)	(d)	(d)	(d)	(b)	(a)	(c)	(a)
171	**172**	**173**	**174**	**175**	**176**	**177**	**178**	**179**	**180**
(c)	(b)	(c)	(c)	(d)	(a)	(a)	(b)	(b)	(a)
181	**182**	**183**	**184**	**185**	**186**	**187**	**188**	**189**	**190**
(d)	(a)	(c)	(d)	(c)	(c)	(d)	(d)	(d)	(c)
191	**192**	**193**	**194**	**195**	**196**	**197**	**198**	**199**	**200**
(a)	(b)	(c)	(c)	(d)	(a)	(d)	(d)	(d)	(b)
201	**202**	**203**	**204**	**205**	**206**	**207**	**208**	**209**	**210**
(b)	(a)	(b)	(d)	(d)	(c)	(c)	(c)	(a)	(b)
211	**212**	**213**	**214**	**215**	**216**	**217**	**218**	**219**	**220**
(a)	(a)	(d)	(b)	(b)	(a)	(a)	(d)	(d)	(c)

GLOSSARY

Accommodation : Piaget used this term for modification or reorganisation of existing cognitive structure (schemata) to deal with environmental demands. Accommodation is the adjustment the individual makes when incorporating external reality. Piaget uses this concept in conjunction with assimilation, which is the individual's response to the immediate and compelling environmental demands that have been and are being assimilated.

Advance organisers : Introductory information intended to facilitate a student's learning by providing a framework and organisation for the material to be learned.

Affective domain : One of the categories of educational objectives for students attitudes, values and emotional growth. The affective domain includes five basic categories: receiving, responding, valuing, organisation and characterisation by a value.

Assimilation : Assimilation is the process of taking within or internalising, one's environmental experience. The term is used by Piaget for the process of making sense of experiences and perceptions by fitting them into previously established cognitive structure (schemata). Assimilation is used by Piaget in conjunction with the concept of accommodation. Piaget believes that assimilation is a spontaneous process on the part of the child.

Attitudes : A learned predisposition to respond either positively or negatively to persons, situations, or things. Attitudes carry a strong emotional component and therefore can never be neutral.

Attribution theory : The term attribution refers to the explanation a person gives for his or her own or another person's actions or beliefs. An attribution based on internal factors is called a dispositional attribution, and one based on external factors is called a situational attribution.

Behaviourism : A school of thought in Psychology usually considered to have originated in the work and writings of John B. Watson in 1913. Watson argued against the use of introspection in gathering psychological data. He considered observable behaviour the only valid data in Psychology. According to Watson, any concepts, like mind or consciousness, that have mentalistic overtones must be purged from the field of psychology. The most famous current representative of this tradition is Harvard University's B.F. Skinner.

Classical conditioning : A procedure in which the conditioned stimulus after being paired with the unconditioned stimulus often enough, can then be substituted for it. It is often called ''stimulus substitution.''

Cognition : The process of faculties by which knowledge is acquired and manipulated (*e.g.*, thinking or remembering).

Cognitive domain : A part of Bloom's Taxonomy of educational objectives. Bloom divided the objectives in the cognitive domain into six categories: knowledge, comprehension, application, analysis, synthesis and evaluation.

Cognitive style : The consistent way in which an individual responds to a wide range of perceptual tasks.

Computer-assisted instruction (CAI) : The use of a computer as tutor to present information, give students opportunities to practice what they learn, evaluate student achievement, and provide additional instruction.

Concept learning : The acquisition of pattern-recognition knowledge involving the learning of a rule or rules for classifying a number of objects into mutually exclusive categories based on one or more salient characteristics of the objects.

Conditioned response : A response elicited by a conditioned stimulus. The response is similar but not identical to its associated unconditioned response.

Cognitive learning : The view that learning is based on a restructuring of perceptions and thoughts occurring within the organism is called cognitive learning. This restructuring allows the learner to perceive new relationships, solve new problems and gain understanding of a subject area. Cognitive learning theorists stress the reorganisation of one's perceptions in order to achieve understanding, as opposed to the behaviourist theorists, who stress the importance of associations formed between stimuli and responses.

Conditioned response : The term is used both in classical conditioning, and in operant conditioning. In classical conditioning, the conditioned response is the response being elicited by the conditioned stimulus. The stronger the conditioning, the greater the magnitude of the conditioned response and the shorter its latency. In Pavlov's experiment the conditioned response was the dog's salivation to the tone.

In operant conditioning, since the response must precede the reinforcer, the conditioned response is defined not in terms of magnitude or latency, but in terms of either the rate of response or its resistance to extinction. For example, a strongly conditioned operant will occur for more rapidly than one that has been only weakly conditioned. Also, a strongly conditioned operant will be far more difficult to extinguish.

Conditioned stimulus : In classical conditioning, the previously neutral stimulus takes on the power to elicit the response through association with an unconditioned stimulus. For this to occur, the conditioned stimulus must precede the unconditioned stimulus on enough occasions to cause the conditioned stimulus to serve as a signal that the unconditioned stimulus will follow. In Pavlov's experiment on conditioning the dog, the tone was used as the conditioned stimulus. The tone was consistently followed by the meat powder, until the dog began salivating to the tone alone.

Conditioning : Process of learning whereby stimuli and responses become associated through training. There are two general types of conditioning, classical and operant. In classical conditioning a conditioned stimulus is presented, followed by an unconditioned stimulus. Conditioning is exhibited when the organism learns to respond to the conditioned stimulus alone. In operant conditioning the operant is allowed to occur and then is followed by a reinforcing stimulus. Operant conditioning is exhibited when the rate of responding increases over the original, preconditioned rate.

Convergent thinking : A term used by Guilford to describe the type of thinking in which an individual produces a single response to a specific question or problem.

Creativity : The capacity of individuals to produce novel or original answers or products.

Culture : The ways in which a group of people think, feel, and react in order to solve problems of living in their environment.

Cumulative records : A file on a student that includes such information as family data, health, academic grades, standardized test scores, attendance and teacher comments.

Discovery learning : Term is used to describe a form of learning that results not from rote memorisation or conditioning but from the active exploration of alternatives on the part of the learner. This learning is largely a result of learner's own efforts. Learning attained through discovery is more meaningful and long-lasting than that from memorisation.

Divergent thinking : A term used by Guilford to describe the type of thinking wherein an individual produces multiple responses or solutions (often non-traditional) to a single question or problem. Divergent thinking is associated with creativity.

Egocentrism : Piaget's term for describing children in the preperational stage, who have difficulty in assuming the point of view of others.

Enactive : Bruner's first stage of cognitive development, in which children understand the environment through physical action on that environment.

Encoding : The short-term memory process of transforming incoming information into episodic or semantic form and associating it with old knowledge for storage in long-term memory.

Entry behaviour : The knowledge, skills, or attitudes that a learner brings into a new learning situation.

Formal-operations stage : This is a stage of cognitive development according to Jean Piaget, occurring during early adolescence. The period of formal operations (eleven to sixteen years) is the last of Piaget's stages and is characterised by the youth's ability to develop full, formal patterns of thinking based on abstract symbolism. The youth is able to reason things out logically at the abstract level, develop symbolic meanings, and generalize to other situations. This is the highest level of thinking and according to Piaget, must await the maturation of certain structures in the brain for its full development.

Equilibration : A motivation principle in Piaget's theory that identifies human beings as active and exploratory in attempting to impose order and meaningfulness on experiences. This order or balance occurs through the processes of assimilation and accommodation.

Evaluation : This is a process of obtaining information to form judgments so that educational decisions can be made.

External locus of control : A feeling that one has little control over one's and the failure to perceive a cause-and-effect relationship between actions and consequences.

Extrinsic motivation : Motivation influenced by external events such as grades, marks or money.

Gestalt psychology : A school of thought maintaining that the organised whole, configuration, or totality of psychological experience should be the proper object of study. Founded in Germany by Max Wertheimer in the early 1900s, gestalt psychology's first interest was in the field of perception. Later, under Wolfgang Kohler's direction, studies were done in the area of learning, and under Kurt Lewin's direction, in the area of motivation. Gestalt psychologists tend to emphasize cognitive processes in the study of learning. They stress that true understanding occurs only through the reorganisation of ideas and perceptions, not through memorisation or conditioning.

Information processing : Theory of learning and remembering that is based on the computer as a model. Information is seen as following into and within the organism. The sense organs respond to incoming information, and it is passed along and encoded in the memory and nervous system. The encoded information may then be stored and processed and finally retrieved and acted on. As with the computer, there is information input, storage and/or processing, and output.

Insight : A suddenly realised solution to a problem, sometimes called the ''a-ha! phenomenon''. Introduced by Wolfgang Kohler, the concept of insight is used to explain the apparently spontaneous appearance of a solution to a problem. Insight results from the reorganisation of ideas and perceptions rather than from simple trial-and-error behaviour. The concept of insight is used typically by gestalt psychologists.

Inquiry learning : A process that is similar to discovery learning. Students learn strategies to manipulate and process information, test hypothesis and apply their conclusions to new content or situations.

Intelligence : The capacity, or a set of capacities that allows an individual to learn, solve problems, and/or interact successfully with his or her environment. As hypothetical construct, intelligence has come to mean higher-level thought processes, or intellectual abilities. Statistical studies of intelligence utilise the concept of measured intelligence, which is the score received on a standardised intelligence test.

Intelligence Quotient (IQ) : Originally, a measure of intelligence calculated by dividing a student's mental age (MA) by the chronological age (CA) and multiplying by 100, that is, IQ = MA/CA × 100. This is called the ratio method of obtaining an IQ.

More recently, IQ has been computed by the deviation method. One's deviation IQ is defined by one's relative standing among peers. The deviation IQ is computed on the basis of how far one's score deviates from the mean score obtained for the entire group of individuals of the same chronological age. This technique is based on the standard, or z-score concept and assumes a normal distribution for each age group.

Law of effect : This is one of E.L. Thorndike's main laws of learning. It states that when an association between a stimulus and response is followed by a satisfying state of affairs, the association (or connection) is strengthened. When the association is followed by an annoying state of affairs, it is weakened. In brief, reward strengthens and punishment weakens any connection between stimuli and responses. In a later version of the law, Thorndike soft-pedaled the importance of punishment of a weakening agent. Thorndike's law of effect is considered by many psychologists to be the cornerstone on which B.F. Skinner built his system of operant conditioning.

Law of exercise : One of E.L. Thorndike's three main laws of learning. It states that the more frequently a stimulus response connection occurs, the stronger the resulting association and hence, the stronger the learning. The repetition of a learned response strengthens the bond between stimulus situation and the response. The law was later amended to incorporate the importance of the consequences of the action; thus, practice without knowledge of results is not nearly as effective as when the consequences become known to the learner.

Law of readiness : One of E.L. Thorndike's three main laws of learning. It states that learning occurs when the student is mentally ready to learn. The reference here is to momentary readiness rather than maturational readiness.

Learning : Learning is a very general term refering to a process that leads to a relatively permanent change in behaviour resulting from experience. Thus, such activities as acquiring physical skills, memorizing poems, acquiring attitudes, etc., are all examples of learning. Learning may be conscious or unconscious, adaptive or maladaptive, overt or covert. Although the learning process is typically measured on the basis of a change in performance, most psychologists agree that an accompanying change occurs within the nervous system. Though there are a great many theories and explanations concerning learning, there is general agreement regarding its definition.

Locus of control : The concept identifies the type of personal control used by an individual. When the locus of control is internal, individual views himself as personally in charge of his own destinies. When the locus of control is external, the person feels he is at the mercy of external circumstances.

Long-term memory (LTM) : In the information-processing system, LTM is the second of the two main storage systems. Information that is in short-term memory may, under certain conditions, be passed along for processing and consolidation into a more permanent storage site, long-term memory. Long-term memory has the potential for holding encoded information for long periods.

Mental age : Term first used by Alfred Binet as the unit for measuring intelligence. Binet defined mental age in terms of the age at which a given number of test items are passed by an average child. If, for example, the average six-year-old could correctly answer a certain number of items, then any other child correctly answering the same number of items would be assigned at least a mental age of six.

Motivation : A general psychological term used to explain behaviour initiated by needs and directed towards a goal. Motives may be biogenic (that is stemming from tissue needs within the organism) or acquired (that is, learned through interaction with the environment, especially the social environment).

Among learning theorists, Jerome Bruner makes much of the principle of motivation, assuming that almost all children have a built-in "will to learn".

Nature-nurture controversy : Debate over which component, nature (heredity) or nurture (environment), is more influential in determining behaviour. In Psychology the behaviourists consistently argued on behalf of nurture, and the intelligence testers favoured nature. Educational Psychology has long been the battleground on which this issue has been fought, since the psychologists primarily concerned with this issue were the learning theorists (largely behaviourists).

Need hierarchy : Theory proposed by Abraham Maslow that suggests that human beings place their needs on the following universal, order-of-importance scale: (*i*) physiological needs, (*ii*) safety needs, (*iii*) love needs, (*iv*) esteem needs, and (*v*) self-actualising needs.

Needs : The part of the motivational cycle seen as deficits that lie within the individual. These may be physiological (*e.g.*, the needs for food) or psychological (*e.g.*, the need for approval).

Non-verbal behaviour : Body language. Based largely on the theroy of Charles Galloway and some research by Robert Rosenthal, the teacher's non-verbal behaviour represents an important avenue for the transmission of teacher expectations. Galloway has shown how non-verbal behaviour can promote or reduce student learning. Rosenthal has shown how his test (Profile of Non-verbal Sensitivity) can identify the channels for communicating how teachers really feel about their students.

Operants : Responses, according to B.F. Skinner, for which the original stimuli are either unidentified or non-existent are called operants. The consequences of operant behaviour can be observed even though the stimulus is not known. For example, if a rat presses the lever in a Skinner box and this results in reinforcement, an increase in operant rate will be observed despite the fact that no stimulus could be identified as initiating the original stimulus could be identified as initiating the original lever pressing. In operant conditioning, reinforcement is contingent on the operant's first being emitted. The organism must in some way "operate" on the environment in order that the reinforcement will follow. Operant responding at one time was called instrumental responding by some psychologists.

Operant conditioning : A type of learning that involves an increase in the probability that a response will occur as a function of reinforcement. This is a forn of conditioning, described by B.F. Skinner, in which the free operant is allowed to occur and is followed by a reinforcing stimulus that is, in turn, followed by an increased likelihood of the operant's occurring again. For optimum conditioning the reinforcing stimulus should follow the operant immediately. The rate of responding for a conditioned operant may jump dramatically over the preconditioned rate (operant level).

Operant level : The original, or preconditioned, rate of operant responding before any reinforcing stimuli have been introduced. If a rat happens to press the lever in a Skinner box four times an hour (without being reinforced), the operant level for that response is established at four per hour. Thus, the operant level is the rate at which the free operant is typically emitted prior to conditioning.

Positive reinforcement : A procedure that maintains or increases the rate of a response by presenting a stimulus (a positive reinforcer) following the response.

Preoperational stage : The second stage in Piaget's theory of cognitive development, in which the lack of logical operations forces children to make decisions bases on their perceptions.

Primary reinforcement : The process of using a stimulus that is reinforcing in the absence of any learning. Such stimuli as food and water are primary reinforcers.

Programmed instruction (PI) : PI is an arrangement of instructional material in a step-by-step sequence designed to lead the student to a specified goal. The material being presented is broken down into small steps called frames. There are two general approaches to programming: (*i*) linear programmes, in which all students go through the entire programme and the frames gradually increase in difficulty, and (*ii*) branched programmes, in which the student skips forward or backward in the programme (the order of the frame presentation varies) as a result of the success or failure experienced in responding.

PI can be in book form, or it can be presented through the use of a teaching machine and/or computer. The concept of programmed instruction is credited to B.F. Skinner.

Psychoanalytic theory : This reveals the theory/method of studying and treating mental illness presented by Sigmund Freud. The theory attempts to give a rational explanation for irrational thoughts and responses. Psychoanalytic theory states (*i*) that all behaviour is determined by specific motives; (*ii*) that most human motives lie at the unconscious level, and therefore people are unaware of the reasons for most of their own behaviour; (*iii*) that neurotic symptoms result from an individual's inner conflicts; and (*iv*) that inner conflicts are a product of childhood trauma and anxiety. The technique is based on the therapist's revealing to the patient the source of his or her anxiety and helping the patient achieve insight and emotional release.

Puberty : The biological changes that lead to reproductive maturity. Its onset is identified by such factors as the growth of body hair, voice changes in males, and menstruation and breast development in females.

Punishment : A method for controlling behaviour through the use of aversive stimulation. In other words, punishment is a procedure in which an aversive stimulus is presented immediately following a response, resulting in a reduction in the rate of response. Punishment, though not itself causing the extinction of a conditioned response, does severely reduce the rate of responding while the punishment is in force. Punishment should not be confused with negative reinforcement.

Reinforcement : Any stimulus that increases the likelihood of a response's recurring. Reinforcement, as a Skinnerian concept, should not be confused with reward, feelings of pleasure, or any other concept with subjective of mentalistic overtones. Reinforcement may be used in either classical (respondent) or operant conditioning. In respondent condition the unconditioned stimulus serves as the reinforcement. In operant conditioning the presentation of any stimulus following the emitted response can be considered a reinforcement if it results in a higher response rate.

Schemata : Cognitive structures created through the abstraction of previous experience. Schemata function in the comprehension and recall of data and can aid learning or be responsible for many types distortion in recall.

Secondary reinforcement : A process that uses a stimulus that is not originally reinforcing but that acquires reinforcing properties when paired with a primary reinforcer. Money is a secondary reinforcer.

Self-actualization : Maslow's term for the psychological need to develop one's capabilities and potential in order to enhance personal growth. It refer to a person's constant striving to realise the potential within and to develop inherent talents and capabilities.

Self-concept : The total organisation of the perceptions individuals have of themselves.

Self-esteem : The value, or judgement, individuals place on their behaviour. Self-esteem and self-concept are often used interchangeably in educational literature.

Self-reinforcement : A procedure in which individuals reinforce their own behaviour.

Sensitive period : This is a time period when an organism is susceptible to a change in behaviour due to certain kinds of environmental stimulation. The sensitive periods typically occur early in the organism's life and tend to produce behaviour changes that are relatively long-lasting. The process of mother-infant bounding is said to occur only during the baby's first three days of life.

Short-term memory (STM) : In the information processing system, STM is the first of two main storage systems. Sometimes it is called working or active memory. Estimates of how long information may be retained in short-term memory vary from about twenty seconds to over a minute.

Social facilitation : The concept from the field of social psychology is used to explain the fact that in some circumstances individuals perform more quickly when in a group situation than when alone. Social facilitation is most pronounced in the case of fairly simple mechanical tasks. The more difficult and the more intellectual the task, the less the effect of social facilitation.

Social learning theory : Theory, proposed by Albert Bandura, suggests that a large part of what a person learns occurs through imitation or modelling. Bandura's major concern is with learning that takes place in the context of a social situation in which individuals come to modify behaviour as a result of how others in the group respond. Social learning does not require primary reinforcement.

Stimulus-response : A theory that stresses the importance of the build up of stimulus response associations in defining learning. Most behaviourists adhere to stimulus response learning theories, the major exception being E.C. Tolman. The leading stimulus response theorists are E.L. Thorndike, Ivan Pavlov, J.B. Watson, Edwin Guthrie, C.L. Hull, and B.F. Skinner. Stimulus response theorists stress the importance of nurture in the nature-nurture debate. Most theories of learning during the first half of the twentieth century were stimulus response theories. The cognitive-gestalt position, however, was not based on a stimulus-response theory.

Stimulus variety : Variation, at all sensroy modes, of stimulus inputs. Stimulus variety was seen by many early-experience theorists as the crucial ingredient in intellectual development. The more the child hears, sees, and touches, the more he or she will want to hear, see, and touch and the more intellectual growth will occur.

Teaching machine : A device used to present an instructional programme one step (or frame) at a time. The student either writes in answers or presses a button corresponding to the correct alternative. The advantages of the teaching machine are that (*i*) the student can proceed at his or her own pace; (*ii*) the student receives immediate feedback; (*iii*) for many students the machines are intrinsically motivating.

Unconditioned response : An unconditioned response is any response that can be elicited automatically by the presentation of a certain stimulus, without any training or learning. The term is used in classical conditioning and in Ivan Pavlov's original experiment the unconditioned response was salivation to the stimulus of meat powder being placed in the dog's mouth.

Unconditioned stimulus : Any stimulus that will elicit a given response automatically, without any training or learning. The term is used in classical conditioning and in the case of Ivan Pavlov's own experiment, the unconditioned stimulus was meat powder placed in the dog's mouth.

हिंदी

व्याकरण

व्याकरण वह शास्त्र है जिसके द्वारा किसी भी भाषा के शब्दों और वाक्यों के शुद्ध स्वरूपों एवं शुद्ध प्रयोगों का ज्ञान कराया जाता है।

व्याकरण के चार अंग हैं : (i) वर्ण विचार (ii) शब्द विचार (iii) पद विचार और (iv) वाक्य विचार

भाषा : भाषा अभिव्यक्ति का एक ऐसा साधन है जिसके द्वारा मनुष्य अपने विचारों को दूसरों पर प्रकट कर सकता है और दूसरों के विचार जान सकता है। भाषा के दो रूप हैं–(i) मौखिक और (ii) लिखित।

बोली : भाषा का क्षेत्रीय रूप बोली कहलाता है।

लिपि : किसी भी भाषा के लिखने की विधि को लिपि कहते हैं।

वर्ण : हिन्दी भाषा में प्रयुक्त सबसे छोटी ध्वनि वर्ण कहलाती है। जैसे–अ, आ, ई, क्, ख्, आदि

वर्णमाला : वर्णों के समुदाय को वर्णमाला कहते हैं। हिन्दी वर्णमाला में 44 वर्ण हैं। जिनमें 11 स्वर तथा 33 व्यंजन हैं।

स्वरवर्ण : उन वर्णों को कहते हैं, जिनका उच्चारण बिना किसी दूसरे वर्ण की सहायता से होता है। हिन्दी में 11 स्वर हैं–अ, आ, इ, ई, उ, ऊ, ए, ऐ, ओ, औ, ऋ।

व्यंजन वर्ण : उन वर्णों को कहते हैं, जिनका उच्चारण स्वर वर्णों की सहायता के बिना नहीं हो सकता है। इनकी संख्या 33 है–

क ख ग घ ड़ च छ ज झ ञ ट ठ

ड ढ़ ण त थ द ध न प फ ब भ

म य र ल व श ष स ह।

वर्ण : एक या अधिक वर्णों से बनी हुई स्वतन्त्र सार्थक ध्वनि शब्द कहलाती है।

शब्दों को तत्सम, तद्भव, देशज और विदेशी भागों में बाँटा जाता है।

तत्सम : जो शब्द संस्कृत भाषा से हिन्दी में बिना किसी परिवर्तन के लिए जाते हैं वे तत्सम कहलाते हैं, जैसे– अग्नि, क्षेत्र, मित्र, नासिका आदि।

तद्भव : उन शब्दों को कहते हैं, जो संस्कृत से ही लिए गए हैं, परन्तु हिन्दी में आने पर जिनका रूप बदल गया है। जैसे–आग, खेत, रात आदि।

देशज : उन शब्दों को कहते हैं, जो बोलचाल तथा देश की अन्य भाषाओं से लिए गए हैं। जैसे–कटोरा, झंझत, डिबिया, लोटा आदि।

विदेशज या विदेशी : उन शब्दों को कहते हैं, जो किसी विदेशी भाषा से आए हैं। जैसे–स्कूल, कार, कमरा, खुदा, जोश, सरकार आदि।

शब्द सम्पदा

तत्सम शब्दों के तद्भव रूप

तत्सम	तद्भव	तत्सम	तद्भव
अग्नि	आग	अद्य	आज
अष्ट	आठ	अक्षि	आँख
अर्ध	आधा	अस्थि	हड्डी
अश्रु	आँसू	आम्र	आम
ग्राम	गाँव	गर्दभ	गधा
गृध्र	गीध	गौर	गोरा
गृह	घर	घट	घड़ा
धातु	धात	धृत	घी
लक्ष	लाख	सप्त	सात
त्वम्	तुम	दुग्ध	दूध
रत्न	रतन	वर्ष	बरस
भक्त	भगत	मर्कट	बन्दर
रात्रि	रात	उलूक	उल्लू
अन्धकार	अन्धेरा	क्षीर	खीर
निद्रा	नींद	पृष्ठ	पीठ
ज्येष्ठ	जेठ	स्वर्ण	सोना
श्वास	साँस	काक	काग
कार्य	काज	कर्ण	कान

तत्सम	तद्भव	तत्सम	तद्भव
पाद	पाँव	हस्त	हाथ
नासिका	नाक	कंटक	काँटा
दश	दस	दधि	दही
दीप	दीया	निद्रा	नींद
नव	नौ	पत्र	पत्ता
प्रस्तर	पत्थर	जिह्वा	जीभ
हस्ती	हाथी	दन्त	दाँत
क्षेत्र	खेत	नृत्य	नाच
सूचिका	सूई	स्वर्णकार	सुनार
लोक	लोग	पर्यड़्क	पलंग
स्वप्न	सपना	कातर	कायर
पुत्र	पूत	मानव	मनुष्य
शत	सौ	पुष्प	फूल
पक्व	पक्का	कृषक	किसान
कर्म	कार्य	आम्र	आम
कर्ण	कान	अष्ट	आठ
घंटिका	घंटी	चन्द्र	चन्द
यव	जौ	धूम्र	धुआँ

विराम चिह्न

विराम का अर्थ रुकना। अपने विचारों को ठीक ढंग से प्रकट करने के पढ़ते अथवा लिखते समय हमें कुछ रुकना पड़ता है। इस प्रकार के रुकने को विराम कहते हैं।

प्रत्येक-विराम के लिए अलग-अलग चिह्न हैं–

पूर्ण विराम	[।]
अल्प विराम	[,]
अर्ध विराम	[;]
प्रश्न बोधक	[?]
विस्मयादि बोधक	[!]
योजक	[–]
उद्धरण	[" "]

कारक

कारक शब्द उस रूप को कहते हैं, जिससे संज्ञा या सर्वनाम वाक्य के साथ सम्बन्ध जाना जाता है। जैसे–शीला कलम **से** लिखती है।

यह सीमा **की** पुस्तक है।

कारक के भेद विभक्ति चिह्नों सहित

कारक	**विभक्ति**
कर्त्ता	ने
कर्म	को
करण	से
सम्प्रदान	के लिए
अपादान	से
सम्बन्ध	का, के, की
अधिकरण	में, पर
सम्बोधन	हे, अरे!

पर्यायवाची शब्द

जिन शब्दों से एक समान अर्थ का बोध होता है, उन्हें पर्यायवाची या समानार्थी शब्द कहते हैं।

कुछ पर्यायवाची शब्दों के उदाहरण निम्नलिखित हैं–

आग – अग्नि, अनल, पावक, हुताशन, ज्वाला।
आकाश – नभ, आसमान, गगन, लोभ।
असुर – राक्षस, दानव, निशाचर, दैत्य।
अमृत – अभिय, पीयूष, सुधा, सोम।
अन्धकार – अन्धेरा, तिमिर, तम, तमिस्त्र।
आँख – नेत्र, नयन, लोचन, चक्षु, दृग।
कमल – जलज, पंकज, नीरज, राजीव।
इन्द्र – सुरपति, देवेन्द्र, सुरेन्द्र, देवेश।
ईश्वर – प्रभु, भगवान, जगदीश, दीनबन्धु।
पक्षी – खग, विहग, चिड़िया, नभचर।
बादल – घन, जलधर, वारिद, नीरद।
गंगा – सुरसरि, जाह्नवी, त्रिपथगा, देवनदी, विष्णुपदी।
चन्द्रमा – शशि, मयंक, निशाकर, सुधाकर, सुधांशु, सोम हिमांशु, राकेश।
जल – पानी, नीर, लोभ, अम्बु, सलिल, क्षीर, वारि।
फूल – पुष्प, कुसुम, सुमन, प्रसून, सारंग।
पृथ्वी – भू, भूमि, धरा, वसुन्धरा, वसुधा, धरती क्षमा, लोक।
कपड़ा – पट, वस्त्र, चीर, अम्बर, दुकूल।
घर – गृह, गेह, निकेतन, आलय, निलय, भवन, शाला, धाम, सदन।
जंगल – वन, कानन, अरण्य, विपिन।
तालाब – सरोवर, ताल, जलाशय, तड़ाग।
दिन – दिवस, वासर, वार।
पहाड़ – गिरि, पर्वत, गूधर, नग, महीधर, मेरू।
पत्थर – पहाड़, प्रस्तर, पाहन।
पवन – वायु, समीर, हवा, मारुत, अनिल।
पुत्र – सुत, तनय, पूत, आत्मज।
बिजली – तड़ित, चपला, दामिनी।
वृक्ष – तरू, रूख, विटप, पेड़।
मनुष्य – नर, मानव, मनुज, आदमी।
हाथी – करि, हस्ती, गज।
मित्र – सखा, मीत, सहचर, दोस्त।
राजा – नरेश, नृप, महीप, भूप।
समुद्र – सागर, सिन्धु, जलधि, नीरधि।
सरस्वती – शारदा, वागेश्वरी, भारती, महाश्वेता।
साँप – पन्नग, सर्प, विषधर, अहि, व्याल।
सूर्य – दिनकर, दिवाकर, रवि, भानु, भास्कर।
स्त्री – नारी, महिला, दारा, वामा।
शरीर – देह, तन, काया, गात, बदन।
गणेश – गजानन, गणपति, विनायक, एकदन्त, गजवदन लम्बोदर, विघ्न नाशक।
घोड़ा – तुरंग, बाजि, हय, अश्व, घोटक।
युद्ध – समर, रण, संग्राम।
सिंह – केसरी, मृगराज, केहरी।
शत्रु – अरि, रिपु, बैरी।
विष्णु – हरि, कमलेश, रमापति, चक्रपाणि, केशव, माधव, पीताम्बर।
कोष – खजाना, भण्डार, निधि।
धन – दौलत, द्रव्य, मुद्रा।

तलवार – कृपाण, असि, खड्ग।
अंग – भाग, हिस्सा, अवयव।
चोर – तस्कर, दस्यु, रजनीचर।
पत्नी – भार्या, दारा, गृहिणी।
पुत्र – तनय, सुत, लड़का, बेटा।
पुत्री – तनया, सुता, लड़की, बेटी।
माता – जननी, अम्बा, अम्बिका, अम्मा, माँ, धात्री।
मोर – शिखी, नीलकण्ठ, मयूर।
मृत्यु – मौत, काल, देहान्त।
रक्त – रुधिर, शोणित, खून, लहू।
विष – जहर, हलाहल, गरल।
सोना – कंचन, स्वर्ण, कनक।
हृदय – उर, छाती, वक्ष, वक्षस्थल, हिय, हिया।
सभा – अधिवेशन, परिषद्, बैठक, महासभा, समागम, समिति, सम्मेलन।
यमुना – कालिन्दी, कृष्णा, जमुना, रविसुता तरणि-तनुजा।

विलोम-शब्द

शब्दों के अपने निश्चित अर्थ होते हैं। उन अर्थों के विपरीत अर्थ देने वाले शब्द को विलोम-शब्द कहते हैं।

शब्द	विलोम	शब्द	विलोम
अमृत	विष	उदार	संकीर्ण
अनुकूल	प्रतिकूल	अनुराग	विराग
आदि	अन्त	उत्थान	पतन
इच्छा	अनिच्छा	उचित	अनुचित
अल्पायु	दीर्घायु	अनुज	अग्रज
उन्नति	अवनति	आकाश	पाताल
अधिक	न्यून	आयात	निर्यात
एक	अनेक	अन्धकार	प्रकाश
अर्थ	अनर्थ	उदय	अस्त
परकीया	स्वकीया	जड़	चेतन
जय	पराजय	अनिवार्य	वैकल्पिक
नकद	उधार	अपेक्षा	उपेक्षा
उपस्थित	अनुपस्थित	आदर	अनादर
अन्धेरा	उजाला	अपना	पराया
उत्तम	अधम	आय	व्यय
सुपुत्र	कुपुत्र	स्वाधीन	पराधीन
आहार	निराहार	कठोर	कोमल
दाता	याचक	दोषी	निर्दोषि
खेद	प्रसन्नता	धनी	निर्धन
निकट	दूर	चर	अचर
देव	दानव	खरा	खोटा
गरीब	अमीर	प्रेम	घृणा
जीवन	मृत्यु	बुरा	भला
सजीव	निर्जीव	मित्र	शत्रु
सुगन्ध	दुर्गन्ध	मौखिक	लिखित
संक्षेप	विस्तार	कटु	मधुर
आरम्भ	अन्त	कड़वा	मीठा
कृतज्ञ	कृतघ्न	दिन	रात
साक्षर	निरक्षर	पवित्र	अपवित्र
पाप	पुण्य	जल	थल
धीर	अधीर	निर्मल	मलिन

शब्द	विलोम	शब्द	विलोम
गुण	अवगुण	नश्वर	अनश्वर
निन्दा	स्तुति	भारी	हल्का
मनुष्यता	पशुता	सरस	नीरस
मान	अपमान	क्रय	विक्रय
धर्म	अधर्म	गहरा	उथला
गुरु	शिष्य	पक्ष	विपक्ष
जन्म	मृत्यु	बन्धन	मुक्ति
यश	अपयश	ज्ञान	अज्ञान
आदर	अनादर	पूर्ण	अपूर्ण
सफल	असफल	शान्त	अशान्त
कीर्ति	अपकीर्ति	वादी	प्रतिवादी
आस्तिक	नास्तिक	स्वदेश	परदेश
सज्जन	दुर्जन	राग	द्वेष
ऊसर	उर्वर	उदार	कृपण
अगला	पिछला	अगम	सुगम
अग्नि	जल	अति	अल्प
अर्थ	अनर्थ	अतल	वितल
अत्यधिक	स्वल्प	अद्यः	उपरि
अधिकतम	न्यूनतम	अतिवृष्टि	अनावृष्टि
अनाथ	सनाथ	ईश्वर	जीव
अनुलोम	विलोम	अर्पण	ग्रहण
अवनि	अम्बर	अस्त	उदय
आकर्षण	विकर्षण	आगे	पीछे
आजाद	गुलाम	आदान	प्रदान
आधुनिक	प्राचीन	आना	जाना
आय	व्यय	आयात	निर्यात
आवश्यक	अनावश्यक	आशा	निराशा
आस्था	अनास्था	इहलोक	परलोक
उच्च	निम्न	उत्थान	पतन
उपकार	अपकार	उपयोग	दुरुपयोग
एकता	अनेकता	कल	आज
कृत्रिम	प्राकृत	कृष्ण	शुक्ल
कपूत	सपूत	कोमल	कठोर
गगन	धरा	ज्ञान	अज्ञान

लिंग

लिंग का अर्थ है 'चिह्न'। लिंग शब्द उस चिह्न को कहते हैं जिससे वस्तु के पुरुष या स्त्री होने की कल्पना हो। लिंग दो प्रकार के होते हैं— (1) पुल्लिंग (2) स्त्रीलिंग

पुल्लिंग–पुल्लिंग संज्ञा के उस रूप को कहते हैं जिससे उसके पुरुष होने का ज्ञान होता है। जैसे–राम, श्याम, घोड़ा, हाथी, कुत्ता आदि।

स्त्रीलिंग–स्त्रीलिंग संज्ञा के उस रूप को कहते हैं जिससे उसके स्त्री होने का ज्ञान हो। जैसे–भैंस, गाय, बकरी, सीता, रमा इत्यादि।

पुल्लिंग	स्त्रीलिंग	पुल्लिंग	स्त्रीलिंग
इन्द्र	इन्द्राणी	मेहतर	मेहतरानी
नौकर	नौकरानी	जेठ	जेठानी
देवर	देवरानी	सेठ	सेठानी
पण्डित	पण्डिताइन	ओझा	ओझाइन
बनिया	बनियाइन	दुबे	दुबाइन
हलवाई	हलवाइन	चौबे	चौबाइन
गुरु	गुरुआइन	लड़का	लड़की
दास	दासी	कबूतर	कबूतरी
हिरण	हिरणी	क्षत्रिय	क्षत्राणी
मुगल	मुगलानी	हिन्दू	हिन्दुआनी
चौधरी	चौधरानी	भव	भवानी
लाला	ललाइन	पण्डा	पण्डाइन
ठाकुर	ठकुराइन	बाबू	बबुआइन
घोड़ा	घोड़ी	गूँगा	गूँगी
बच्चा	बच्ची	चाचा	चाची
बकरा	बकरी	मामा	मामी
मुर्गा	मुर्गी	साला	साली
चींटा	चींटी	रस्सा	रस्सी
देव	देवी	ब्राह्मण	ब्राह्मणी
बेटा	बेटी	बूढ़ा	बुढ़िया
चूहा	चुहिया	डिब्बा	डिबिया
गुड्डा	गुड़िया	कुम्हार	कुम्हारिन
सुनार	सुनारिन	नाती	नातिन
जुलाहा	जुलाहिन	दर्जी	दर्जिन
पापी	पापिन	हाथी	हथिनी

पुल्लिंग	स्त्रीलिंग	पुल्लिंग	स्त्रीलिंग
पिता	माता	बैल	गाय
कवि	कवयित्री	विधुर	विधवा
बाप	माँ	बादशाह	बेगम
नर	मादा	मर्द	औरत
युवक	युवती	वर	वधू
सम्राट्	सम्राज्ञी	साढ़ू	साली
फूफा	बुआ	पुत्र	पुत्री
पहाड़	पहाड़ी	गोप	गोपी
गधा	गधी	तरुण	तरुणी
नर्तक	नर्तकी	बेटा	बिटिया
बछड़ा	बछिया	चिड़ा	चिड़िया
बन्दर	बन्दरिया	कुत्ता	कुतिया
नाई	नाइन	धोबी	धोबिन
ग्वाला	ग्वालिन	भंगी	भंगिन
स्वामी	स्वामिनी	विद्वान्	विदुषी
साधु	साध्वी	पुरुष	स्त्री
पति	पत्नी	वीर	वीरांगना
साहब	मेम	सास	ससुर
मियाँ	बीबी	राजा	रानी
बिलाड़	बिल्ली	अनुज	अनुजा
छात्र	छात्रा	महोदय	महोदया
प्रिय	प्रिया	मामा	मामी
लोटा	लुटिया	मोर	मोरनी
शेर	शेरनी	जाट	जाटिन
डाक्टर	डाक्टरनी	मालिक	मालकिन
माली	मालिन	बाघ	बाघिन
हाथी	हथिनी	स्वामी	स्वामिनी
बालक	बालिका	धनवान	धनवती
धावक	धाविका	नेता	नेत्री
गुणवान	गुणवती	नर	मादा
अभिनेता	अभिनेत्री	प्राचार्य	प्राचार्या
प्रबन्धकर्ता	प्रबन्धकर्ती	दाता	दात्री
ननदोई	ननद	अध्यापक	अध्यापिका

वचन

शब्द के जिस रूप से उसके एक अथवा अनेक होने का बोध हो, उसे वचन कहते हैं।

हिन्दी में दो वचन होते हैं–

(1) एकवचन और (2) बहुवचन

एकवचन–शब्द के जिस रूप से एक ही वस्तु का बोध हो, उसे एकवचन कहते हैं। जैसे–लड़का, गाय, बकरी, घोड़ा, राम, सीता आदि।

बहुवचन–शब्द के जिस रूप से अनेकता का बोध हो उसे बहुवचन कहते हैं। जैसे–लड़के, कपड़े, गायें आदि।

एकवचन	बहुवचन	एकवचन	बहुवचन
लड़का	लड़के	कौवा	कौवे
बेटा	बेटे	कमरा	कमरे
कपड़ा	कपड़े	बहन	बहनें
चीज	चीजें	गधा	गधे
रुपया	रुपये	घोड़ा	घोड़े
नहर	नहरें	रात	रातें
बात	बातें	सड़क	सड़कें
दाना	दाने	लोटा	लोटे
पैसा	पैसे	पुस्तक	पुस्तकें
कन्या	कन्याएँ	वधू	वधुएँ
नारी	नारियाँ	लड़की	लड़कियाँ
मुर्गा	मुर्गे	घण्टा	घण्टे
गद्दा	गद्दे	हीरा	हीरे
बच्चा	बच्चे	प्याला	प्याले
छाता	छाते	गाय	गायें
कथा	कथाएँ	कविता	कविताएँ
बहू	बहुएँ	टोपी	टोपियाँ
नाली	नालियाँ	बेटा	बेटे
ताला	ताले	जूता	जूते

एकवचन	बहुवचन	एकवचन	बहुवचन
डिबिया	डिबियाँ	नाक	नाकें
पूँछ	पूँछें	मूँछ	मूँछें
चिड़िया	चिड़ियाँ	सरिता	सरिताएँ
बालिका	बालिकाएँ	चाभी	चाभियाँ
कहानी	कहानियाँ	दरवाजा	दरवाजे
कलम	कलमें	कुटिया	कुटियाँ
रानी	रानियाँ	नाई	नाइयों
माता	माताएँ	बाल	बालों
हाथ	हाथों	मुख	मुख
कोट	कोट	दाँत	दाँतों
नाखून	नाखूनों	पैर	पैरों
बैल	बैलों	माली	मालियों
राजा	राजाओं	पिता	पिता
चन्द्रमा	चन्द्रमा	कवि	कवियों
मुनि	मुनियों	कौआ	कौए
छात्रा	छात्राएँ	सेना	सेनाएँ
दिशा	दिशाएँ	गुड़िया	गुड़ियाँ
मेज	मेजें	भैंस	भैंसें
अंगूर	अंगूरों	समुद्र	समुद्र

अनेक शब्दों के लिए एक शब्द

जिसकी कोई उपमा न हो : **अनुपम**
तेज बुद्धि वाला : **कुशाग्रबुद्धि**
कल्पना से परे हो : **कल्पनातीत**
जो उपकार नहीं मानता है : **कृतघ्न**
जो उपकार मानता है : **कृतज्ञ**
किसी की हँसी उड़ाना : **उपहास**
ऊपर कहा हुआ : **उपर्युक्त**
ऊपर लिखा हुआ : **उपरलिखित**
जिस पर उपकार किया गया हो : **उपकृत**
इतिहास का ज्ञाता : **इतिहासज्ञ**
आलोचना करने वाला : **आलोचक**
ईश्वर में आस्था रखने वाला : **आस्तिक**
बिना वेतन का : **अवैतनिक**
जो कहा न जा सके : **अकथनीय**
जो गिना न जा सके : **अगणित**
जिसका कोई शत्रु ही न जन्मा हो : **अजातशत्रु**
जिसके समान कोई दूसरा न हो : **अद्वितीय**
जो परिचित न हो : **अपरिचित**
आकाश में उड़ने वाला : **नभचर**
जो टुकड़े-टुकड़े हो गया हो : **खण्डित**

मछली की तरह आँखों वाली : **मीनाक्षी**
मयूर की तरह आँखों वाली : **मयूराक्षी**
बच्चों के लिए काम की वस्तु : **बालोपयोगी**
जिसकी बहुत अधिक चर्चा हो : **बहुचर्चित**
जिस स्त्री को कभी सन्तान न हुई हो : **बन्ध्या (बाँझ)**
फेन से भरा हुआ : **फेनिल**
प्रिय बोलने वाली स्त्री : **प्रियम्वदा**
जिसकी उपमा न हो : **निरुपम**
जो थोड़ी देर पहले पैदा हुआ हो : **नवजात**
जिसका कोई आधार न हो : **निराधार**
नगर में वास करने वाला : **नागरिक**
रात में घूमने वाला : **निशाचर**
ईश्वर में विश्वास न रखने वाला : **नास्तिक**
माँस न खाने वाला : **निरामिष**
बिल्कुल बर्बाद हो गया : **ध्वस्त**
जिसकी धर्म में निष्ठा हो : **धर्मनिष्ठ**
देखने योग्य : **दर्शनीय**
बहुत तेज चलने वाला : **द्रुतगामी**
जो किसी पक्ष में न रहे : **तटस्थ**
तत्त्व को जानने वाला : **तत्त्वज्ञ**

तप करने वाला	: **तपस्वी**
जिसे देखकर डर लगे	: **डरावना**
जो जन्म से अन्ध हो	: **जन्मान्ध**
जीने की प्रबल इच्छा	: **जिजीविषा**
जिसने इन्द्रियों को जीत लिया हो	: **जितेन्द्रिय**
चिन्ता में डूबा हुआ	: **चिन्तित**
जो बहुत समय तक ठहरे	: **चिरस्थायी**
जिसकी चार भुजाएँ हों	: **चतुर्भुज**
जिसके हाथ में चक्र हों	: **चक्रपाणि**
जिससे घृणा की जाए	: **घृणित**
जिसे गुप्त रखा जाए	: **गोपनीय**
गणित ज्ञाता	: **गणितज्ञ**
आकाश को चूमने वाला	: **गगनचुम्बी**
जिसका आदि न हो	: **अनादि**
जो कुछ न जानता हो	: **अज्ञ**
जो अनुकरण करने योग्य हो	: **अनुकरणीय**
जिसका अन्त न हो	: **अनन्त**
जो कभी न मरे	: **अमर**
जो कम बोलता हो	: **अल्पभाषी**
जिसका इलाज न हो	: **लाइलाज**
जिसका कोई नाथ न हो	: **अनाथ**
कम जानने वाला	: **अल्पज्ञ**
जहाँ जाना सम्भव न हो	: **अगम**
बड़ा भाई	: **अग्रज**
कम खाने वाला	: **अल्पाहारी**
जो बात पहले कभी न हुई हो	: **अभूतपूर्व**
दूसरों के पीछे चलने वाला	: **अनुचर**
जो पहले न पढ़ा हो	: **अपठित**
जिसके आर-पार दिखाई देता हो	: **पारदर्शी**
आज्ञा पालन करने वाला	: **आज्ञाकारी**
काम से जी चुराने वाला	: **कामचोर**
प्रतिदिन होने वाला	: **दैनिक**
जिसका कोई अर्थ न हो	: **निरर्थक**
हाथ से लिखा हुआ	: **हस्तलिखित**
आँखों के सामने होने वाला	: **प्रत्यक्ष**
जिसका आचरण अच्छा हो	: **सदाचारी**
वह पुरुष जिसकी पत्नी मर गई हो	: **विधुर**
वह स्त्री जिसका पति मर गया हो	: **विधवा**
जिसका रूप अच्छा न हो	: **कुरूप**
सदा सत्य बोलने वाला	: **सत्यवादी**
बड़ी इमारत के टूटे-फूटे भाग	: **खण्डहर**
प्रशंसा के योग्य	: **प्रशंसनीय**
जहाँ अनाथ रहते हों	: **अनाथालय**
प्रत्येक मास होने वाला	: **मासिक**
जहाँ पानी के जहाज आकर रुकते हैं	: **बन्दरगाह**
प्रत्येक सप्ताह होने वाला	: **साप्ताहिक**
प्रत्येक वर्ष होने वाला	: **वार्षिक**
जो कठिनाई से मिले	: **दुर्लभ**
जिसका आकार हो	: **साकार**
जिसका आकार न हो	: **निराकार**
जो कभी बूढ़ा न हो	: **अजर**
बहुत बोलने वाला	: **वाचाल**
पृथ्वी पर रहने वाला	: **थलचर**
जल में रहने वाला	: **जलचर**
नभ में विचरण करने वाला	: **नभचर**
जल-थल दोनों में रहने वाला	: **उभयचर**
जिसमें रस न हो	: **नीरस**
पढ़ने वाला	: **पाठक**
जो भाषण देता हो	: **वक्ता**
जो साथ में पढ़ता हो	: **सहपाठी**
जिसके नीचे रेखा खींची हो	: **रेखांकित**
जानने की इच्छा रखने वाला	: **जिज्ञासु**
जिसकी कोई सन्तान न हो	: **निःसन्तान**
जिसका कोई मूल्य न हो	: **अमूल्य**
जो वन में घूमता हो	: **वनचर**
जो इस लोक के बाहर की बात हो	: **अलौकिक**
जो इस लोक की बात हो	: **लौकिक**
जिसका सम्बन्ध पश्चिम से हो	: **पाश्चात्य**
जो स्थिर रहे	: **स्थावर**
दुःखान्त नाटक	: **त्रासदी**
ज्ञान देने वाली	: **ज्ञानदा**
भूत, वर्तमान भविष्य को देखने वाला	: **त्रिकालदर्शी**
जो क्षमा के योग्य हो	: **क्षम्य**
हिंसा करने वाला	: **हिंसक**
हित चाहने वाला	: **हितैषी**
सब कुछ जानने वाला	: **सर्वज्ञ**
जो स्वयं पैदा हुआ हो	: **स्वयंभू**
जो शरण में आया हो	: **शरणागत**
जिसका वर्णन न किया जा सके	: **वर्णनातीत**
व्याकरण जानने वाला	: **वैयाकरण**
रचना करने वाला	: **रचयिता**
खून से रंगा हुआ	: **रक्तरंजित**
अत्यन्त सुन्दर स्त्री	: **रूपसी**
कीर्तिमान पुरुष	: **यशस्वी**

महत्त्वपूर्ण शब्दों की भाववाचक संज्ञा

शब्द	भाववाचक संज्ञा	शब्द	भाववाचक संज्ञा	शब्द	भाववाचक संज्ञा	शब्द	भाववाचक संज्ञा
दास	दासता	क्षत्रिय	क्षत्रियत्व	अहं	अहंकार	अपना	अपनापन
पशु	पशुता	बालक	बालकपन	व्यक्ति	व्यक्तित्व	मीठा	मिठास
बन्धु	बन्धुत्व	मित्र	मित्रता	गरीब	गरीबी	सफल	सफलता
बूढ़ा	बुढ़ापा	सती	सतीत्व	बुरा	बुराई	स्वस्थ	स्वास्थ्य
सेवक	सेवा	शिशु	शैशव	सरल	सरलता	कंजुस	कंजुसी
अपना	अपनत्व	पराया	परायापन	कमजोर	कमजोरी	हरा	हरियाली
पण्डित	पाण्डित्य	पुरुष	पुरुषत्व	गर्म	गर्मी	मोटा	मोटाई
ब्राह्मण	ब्राह्मणत्व	बच्चा	बचपन	चालाक	चालाकी	गम्भीर	गम्भीरता
प्रभु	प्रभुता	नारी	नारीत्व	पढ़ना	पढ़ाई	लिखना	लिखाई
देव	देवत्व	लड़का	लड़कपन	थकना	थकावट	लिखना	लिखावट
मनुष्य	मनुष्यता	दानव	दानवता	लूटना	लूट	लड़ना	लड़ाई
निज	निजता	स्व	स्वत्व	हँसना	हँसी	आप	अपनत्व

महत्त्वपूर्ण शब्दों के विशेषण

शब्द	विशेषण	शब्द	विशेषण	शब्द	विशेषण	शब्द	विशेषण
अंक	अंकित	अर्थ	आर्थिक	वन	वन्य	विष्णु	वैष्णव
इतिहास	ऐतिहासिक	उदासी	उदास	शहर	शहरी	तप	तपस्वी
कलंक	कलंकित	कुसुम	कुसुमित	जापान	जापानी	तेज	तेजस्वी
जटा	जटिल	भार	भारी	तत्त्व	तात्त्विक	दया	दयालु
बनारस	बनारसी	बाजार	बाजारू	देव	दैविक	निंदा	निंदक
प्यास	प्यासा	पुराण	पौराणिक	नव	नवीन	पोषण	पोषक
पंक	पंकित	पक्ष	पाक्षिक	पेट	पेटू	पाप	पापी
धन	धनी	दो	दूसरा	पूजा	पूज्य	भूख	भूखा
तीन	तीसरा	झगड़ा	झगड़ालू	फेन	फेनिल	भारत	भारतीय
ठण्ड	ठण्डा	जाति	जातीय	माया	मायावी	रंग	रंगीन
काँटा	कँटीला	विदेश	विदेशी	विष	विषैला	श्री	श्रीमान
रोज	रोजाना	भूगोल	भौगोलिक	सुर	सुरीला	विवाह	वैवाहिक
पीड़ा	पीड़ित	पुत्र	पुत्रवान	आदर	आदरणीय	ऋण	ऋणी
आलस्य	आलसी	अंतर	आंतरिक	किताब	किताबी	क्रम	क्रमिक
ईर्ष्या	ईर्ष्यालु	कर्म	कर्मठ	ग्राम	ग्रामीण	घर	घरेलू
करुणा	कारुणिक	कृपा	कृपालु	चतुर	चतुरता	जहर	जहरीला
गुण	गुणी	जल	जलमय	सप्ताह	साप्ताहिक	अनुभव	अनुभवी
जीव	जैविक	तट	तटस्थ	ओज	ओजस्वी	कल्पना	काल्पनिक
तर्क	तार्किक	धर्म	धार्मिक	कुल	कुलीन	गाँव	गँवार
नमक	नमकीन	पत्थर	पथरीला	चमक	चमकीला	चाचा	चचेरा
पल्लव	पल्लवित	पान	पनवाड़ी	दीन	दीनता	नगर	नागरिक
मुख	मुखर	मिठास	मीठा	नागपुर	नागपुरी	परिवार	पारिवारिक
मास	मासिक	मद	मादक	पुष्प	पुष्पित	पिता	पैतृक
रक्त	रक्तिम	रस	रसीला	फ्रांस	फ्रांसीसी	बाहर	बाहरी

शब्द	विशेषण	शब्द	विशेषण	शब्द	विशेषण	शब्द	विशेषण
भय	भयभीत	मधु	मधुर	गाना	गायक	बेचना	बिकाऊ
मौन	मौनी	मन	मानसिक	भागना	भगोड़ा	वन्द	वन्दनीय
मानव	मानवीय	रक्षा	रक्षक	चलना	चलती	घूमना	घुमक्कड़
रघु	राघव	रोग	रोगी	चलना	चालू	मरना	मरियल
वर्ष	वार्षिक	शक्ति	शक्तिशाली	भूलना	भुलक्कड़	पीछे	पिछला
श्रम	श्रमिक	अंत	अंतिम	भीतर	भीतरी	नीचे	निम्न
कागज	कागजी	मर्म	मार्मिक	अणु	आणविक	अधिकार	आधिकारिक
शब्द	शाब्दिक	अज्ञान	अज्ञानी	अनुभव	अनुभवी	अन्याय	अन्यायी
गुलाब	गुलाबी	प्रकृति	प्राकृतिक	अपमान	अपमानित	अभ्यास	अभ्यासी
परिचय	परिचित	पूजा	पुजारी	अवश्य	आवश्यक	आदि	आदिम
रोग	रोगी	ग्राम	ग्रामीण	आयु	आयुष्मान्	उदय	उदित
सुगंध	सुगंधित	मैं	मेरा	उपज	उपजाऊ	एकता	एक
जो	जैसा	आप	आप-सा	अंत	अंतिम	कुल	कुलीन
तुम	तुम्हारा	कौन	कैसा	खर्च	खर्चीला	खून	खूनी
वह	वैसा	पढ़ना	पढ़ाकू	गुण	गुणी		

श्रुतिसम भिन्नार्थक शब्द

शब्द	अर्थ	शब्द	अर्थ	शब्द	अर्थ	शब्द	अर्थ
आदि	आरम्भ	आदी	अभ्यस्त	बन्द	खुला नहीं	बद	बुरा
कुल	वंश	कूल	किनारा	पथ	रास्ता	पथ्य	रोगी का भोजन
अरि	शत्रु	अरी	सम्बोधन	पुर	नगर	पूर	बाढ़
अगम	दुर्गम	आगम	शास्त्र	भवन	महल	भुवन	संसार
अयश	अपकीर्ति	अयस्क	लोहा	लक्ष्य	उद्देश्य	लक्ष	लाख
अपेक्षा	चाहना, तुलना में	उपेक्षा	निरादर	सर	तालाब	शर	बाण
अनिल	हवा	अनल	आग	सर्ग	अध्याय	स्वर्ग	एक लोक
अवधि	काल, समय	अवधी	अवध की भाषा	कर्म	कार्य	क्रम	सिलसिला
आयात	बाहर से आना	आयत	एक आकृति	चिता	शव जलाने के लिए लकड़ियों का ढेर	चीता	बाघ
चिर	पुराना	चीर	कपड़ा	शव	लाश	शब	रात
तनु	पतला	तनू	पुत्र, गाय	शस्त्र	हथियार	शास्त्र	ग्रन्थ
तरंग	लहर	तुरंग	घोड़ा	श्रवण	सुनना	श्रमण	बौद्ध संन्यासी
दारा	स्त्री	द्वार	दरवाजा	मत	विचार	मत्त	मस्त
दूत	संदेशवाहक	द्यूत	जुआ	शोक	दुःख	शौक	चाव
जलद	बादल	जलज	कमल	ग्रह	नक्षत्र	गृह	घर
प्रदीप	दीपक	प्रतीप	उल्टा	कपट	धोखा	कपाट	दरवाजा
प्रसाद	कृपा	प्रासाद	महल	उपयुक्त	ठीक	उपर्युक्त	ऊपर कहा गया
पास	निकट	पाश	बन्धन	सुत	बेटा	सूत	धागा
द्विप	हाथी	द्वीप	टापू	शूर	वीर	सूर	अंधा
देव	देवता	दैव	भाग्य	श्याम	कृष्ण	शाम	संध्या
नीर	जल	नीड़	घोंसला	दिन	वार	दीन	गरीब
पवन	वायु	पावन	पवित्र	कटिबद्ध	तैयार रहना	करबद्ध	हाथ जोड़ना

अनेकार्थक शब्द

शब्द	विभिन्न अर्थ
अंक	संख्या, गोद
अक्षर	वर्ण, ईश्वर
पानी	जल, प्रतिष्ठा
अचल	पर्वत, स्थिर
आम	फल, सामान्य
अंबर	वस्त्र, आकाश
अवस्था	आयु, दशा
उत्तर	दिशा, जबाव
विधि	तरीका, भाग्य
कर	हाथ, टैक्स
कनक	सोना, धतुरा
गुरु	श्रेष्ठ, शिक्षक
हान	भारी हथौड़ा, बादल
जड़	मूर्ख, मूल
कल	मशीन, आनेवाला कल, चैन
सुर	देवता, स्वर

शब्द	विभिन्न अर्थ
द्विज	पक्षी, ब्राह्मण
तीर	किनारा, बाण
प्रकृति	स्वभाव, कुदरत
पत्र	चिट्ठी, पत्र
पद	पैर, उपाधि
फल	परिणाम, फल
तनु	पतला, कोमल
वर्ण	रंग, जाति
हल	समाधान, खेत जोतने का साधन
अशोक	राजा, वृक्ष
आभीर	अहीर, एक राग
एकाक्ष	काना, कौआ
खल	दुष्ट, खलिहान
घट	घड़ा, हृदय
जलज	कमल, मछली
हेम	सोना, जल

सामान्य अशुद्धियाँ

अशुद्ध	शुद्ध	अशुद्ध	शुद्ध
दुनियां	दुनिया	श्रीमति	श्रीमती
सामिग्री	सामग्री	वापिस	वापस
प्रदर्शिनी	प्रदर्शनी	द्वारिका	द्वारका
ऊत्थान	उत्थान	दुसरा	दूसरा
प्रशाद	प्रसाद	अमावश्या	अमावस्या
बसंत	वसंत	बर्ष	वर्ष
विना	बिना	बन	वन
दाइत्व	दायित्व	सम्वाद	संवाद
कुन्डली	कुण्डली	मॉसिक	मानसिक
कन्ठ	कण्ठ	अगामी	आगामी
सप्ताहिक	साप्ताहिक	संसारिक	सांसारिक
आधीन	अधीन	हस्ताक्षेप	हस्तक्षेप
बरात	बारात	क्षत्रीय	क्षत्रिय
तिथी	तिथि	कालीदास	कालिदास
पुर्ती	पूर्ति	अतिथी	अतिथि
नीती	नीति	ग्रहणी	गृहिणी
क्यूँ	क्यों	साधू	साधु
वधु	वधू	रेणू	रेणु
नुपुर	नूपुर	निर्वान	निर्वाण
जादु	जादू	द्रश्य	दृश्य

अशुद्ध	शुद्ध	अशुद्ध	शुद्ध
अनुग्रहीत	अनुगृहीत	बृज	ब्रज
बनस्पति	वनस्पति	श्राप	शाप
सैना	सेना	सेनिक	सैनिक
इतिहासिक	ऐतिहासिक	प्रथक	पृथक
सम्पति	सम्पत्ति	कृतघन	कृतघ्न
बिमारी	बीमारी	व्यक्तिक	वैयक्तिक
वितीत	व्यतीत	निस्वार्थ	निःस्वार्थ
परिस्थित	परिस्थिति	रचियता	रचयिता
मैथिलिशरण	मैथिलीशरण	आर्शिवाद	आशीर्वाद
निरिक्षण	निरीक्षण	पत्नि	पत्नी
शताब्दि	शताब्दी	लड़ायी	लड़ाई
स्थाई	स्थायी	लिखायी	लिखाई
अलोकिक	अलौकिक	कृप्या	कृपया
गंवार	गँवार	असोक	अशोक
दुस्कर	दुष्कर	मूल्यावान	मूल्यवान्
नवम्	नवम	क्षात्र	छात्र
छमा	क्षमा	प्रन्तु	परन्तु
प्रीक्षा	परीक्षा	मरयादा	मर्यादा
दुदर्शा	दुर्दशा	विषेश	विशेष
उज्वल	उज्ज्वल	आल्हाद	आहलाद्

अशुद्ध	शुद्ध	अशुद्ध	शुद्ध
महत्व	महत्त्व	उपलक्ष	उपलक्ष्य
लीये	लिये	पिओ	पियो
हुये	हुए	कवित्री	कवयित्री
प्रमात्मा	परमात्मा	घनिष्ट	घनिष्ठ
यथेष्ठ	यथेष्ट	पियास	प्यास
व्यस्क	वयस्क	त्यौहार	त्योहार
मुसलिम	मुस्लिम	ऐनक	ऐनक
नोकरी	नौकरी	कल्यान	कल्याण
पाणी	पानी	आसा	आशा
हृदय	हृदय	घ्रणा	घृणा
श्रंगार	शृंगार	हिन्दुस्थान	हिन्दुस्तान
प्रशन	प्रश्न	ग्यान	ज्ञान
अन्धेरा	अँधेरा	पेड	पेड़
महयान्ह्न	मध्यान्ह	मेंहदी	मेहंदी
शमशान	श्मशान	चिन्ह	चिह्न
कुंज	कुब्ज	ग्रहस्थ	गृहस्थ
अजोध्या	अयोध्या	अनधिकार	अनाधिकार
अनिष्ठा	अनिष्ट	अनुकुल	अनुकूल
अनुसंगिक	आनुषंगिक	अनुशरण	अनुसरण
अभिसेक	अभिषेक	अरमाण	अरमान
अहिल्या	अहल्या	आदरनीय	आदरणीय
आविस्कार	आविष्कार	उँचाई	ऊँचाई
उत्तरदाई	उत्तरदायी	उपर	ऊपर
उपरोक्त	उपर्युक्त	उश्रृंखल	उच्छृंखल
कलस	कलश	कल्यान	कल्याण
गनित	गणित	जबाब	जवाब
तत्व	तत्त्व	तलाब	तालाब
तिरष्कार	तिरस्कार	त्रिवार्षिक	त्रैवार्षिक
दिपिका	दीपिका	देहिक	दैहिक
द्वन्द	द्वन्द्व	नरायन	नारायण
निरव	नीरव	निरोग	नीरोग
पुष्टी	पुष्टि	पुस्प	पुष्प
पेत्रिक	पैतृक	प्रनय	प्रणय

अशुद्ध	शुद्ध	अशुद्ध	शुद्ध
प्रनाम	प्रणाम	प्रयाप्त	पर्याप्त
प्रसंशा	प्रशंसा	प्रांगन	प्रांगण
प्रान	प्राण	पृष्ट	पृष्ठ
ब्रत	व्रत	भगीरथी	भागीरथी
भरथ	भरत	भष्म	भस्म
मंत्रीमंडल	मंत्रिमण्डल	रसायण	रसायन
राज्यमहल	राजमहल	रामायन	रामायण
वनोवास	वनवास	वानी	वाणी
वाल्मीकी	वाल्मीकि	वास्प	वाष्प
व्योहार	व्यवहार	सन्यासी	संन्यासी
सम्राज	साम्राज्य	सविनयपूर्वक	सविनय
सिंदुर	सिंदूर	स्त्रवण	श्रवण
हरीश्चन्द्र	हरिश्चन्द्र	हिन्दु	हिन्दू
हिन्दूस्तान	हिन्दुस्तान	बुद्धिवान	बुद्धिमान्
भाग्यमान	भाग्यवान	विद्वान	विद्वान्
श्रीमान	श्रीमान्	आंख	आँख
ऊंट	ऊँट	कंगना	कँगना
गॅंगा	गंगा	गांधी	गाँधी
जांच	जाँच	तांगा	ताँगा
दांत	दाँत	मंहगा	महँगा
मांस	माँस	मुंह	मुँह
सांप	साँप	सांस	साँस
हुँकार	हुंकार	निर्पेक्ष	निरपेक्ष
भाष्कर	भास्कर	सन्मुख	सम्मुख
माताहीन	मातृहीन	विद्यार्थि	विद्यार्थी
गुणि	गुणी	द्वैवाषिक	द्विवार्षिक
पूज्यनीय	पूजनीय	अकाश	आकाश
इद	ईद	इसलाम	इस्लाम
ऐैसा	ऐसा	दोसरा	दूसरा
पुत्रि	पुत्री	प्रस्तूत	प्रस्तुत
हरयाली	हरियाली	दिवाली	दीवाली
राष्ट्रिय	राष्ट्रीय	एकहरा	इकहरा
एतबार	इतबार		

वाक्यगत अशुद्धियाँ

अशुद्ध	शुद्ध
हम अच्छी भाषण दिए थे।	हमने अच्छा भाषण दिया था।
आप खाए कि नहीं?	आपने खाया कि नहीं?
वह मुझे देखा तो घबरा गया।	उसने मुझे देखा तो घबरा गया।
मैं किताब पढ़ा हूँ।	मैंने किताब पढ़ी है।
मैं सारी पुस्तक पढ़ डाली।	मैंने सारी पुस्तक पढ़ डाली।
सीता भात खायी।	सीता ने भात खाया।

अशुद्ध	शुद्ध
राम रोटी खाया।	राम ने रोटी खायी।
लड़की ने दही गिरा दी।	लड़की ने दही गिरा दिया।
शुद्ध गाय की घी दो।	गाय का शुद्ध घी दो।
तुम, मैं और वह चलेगा।	तुम, वह और मैं चलूँगा।
राम और सीता आयी थी।	राम और सीता आए थे।
भाई-बहन जा रही हैं।	भाई-बहन जा रहे हैं।

अशुद्ध	शुद्ध
वह लड़की को बुलाओ।	उस लड़की को बुलाओ।
मेरे लिए पढ़ता हूँ।	अपने लिए पढ़ता हूँ।
सीता राम की आज्ञाकारी पत्नी थी।	सीता राम की आज्ञाकारिणी पत्नी थीं।
देरी न करना।	देर न करना।
उसे मृत्युदण्ड की सजा मिली।	उसे मृत्युदण्ड मिला।
हमारे शिक्षक प्रश्न पूछते हैं।	हमारे शिक्षक प्रश्न करते हैं।
कै बजे? तीन बजा।	कितना बजा? तीन बजे।
उसका प्राण उड़ गया।	उसके प्राण उड़ गये।
मैंने आँख से देखा।	मैंने आँखों से देखा।
अपन को पढ़ना है।	मुझे पढ़ना है।
पुस्तक फट गया।	पुस्तक फट गई है।
घोड़ी तेज दौड़ता है।	घोड़ी तेज दौड़ती है।
मेरा प्रणम स्वीकार करो।	मेरा प्रणाम स्वीकार करो।
दो बालक खेलता है।	दो बालक खेलते हैं।

अशुद्ध	शुद्ध
ये सब मेरा पुस्तक है।	ये सब मेरी पुस्तकें हैं।
सूरज पूरब में उगते हैं।	सूरज पूर्व में उगता है।
वह लौट आए।	वे लौट आए।
वहाँ अनेकों लोग थे।	वहाँ अनेक लोग थे।
मेरे को मत मारो।	मुझे मत मारो।
मोहन ने पत्र को पढ़ा।	मोहन ने पत्र पढ़ा।
पुस्तक पर नहीं लिखो।	पुस्तक पर मत लिखो।
वह सज्जन पुरुष है।	वह सज्जन है।
आप हमारे घर आओ।	आप हमारे घर आइए।
हम आपसे कुछ कहे थे।	हमने आपसे कुछ कहा था।
मकान की दायीं ओर सड़क है।	मकान के दायीं ओर सड़क है।
पिताजी घर नहीं हैं।	पिताजी घर पर नहीं हैं।
घर पर सब कुशल हैं।	घर में सब कुशल हैं।
उसे भारी दुःख हुआ।	उसे बहुत दुःख हुआ।
सड़क में मत खेलो।	सड़क पर मत खेलो।

मुहावरे तथा लोकोक्तियाँ

- अँगूठी का नगीना–अत्यन्त महत्त्वपूर्ण।
- अंधा दरबार–न्यायहीन स्थान।
- अंधेर नगरी–न्याय का अभाव।
- अक्ल का दुश्मन–मूर्ख।
- अक्ल का दुम–मूर्ख।
- आँख का तारा–अतिप्रिय।
- ईद का चाँद–बहुत दिनों के बाद दिखाई देना।
- कछुआ चाल–धीमी गति।
- काला नाग–दुष्ट आदमी।
- किताबी कीड़ा–सदैव कुछ-न-कुछ पढ़ना।
- किस्मत का मारा–भाग्य का मन्द।
- कोल्हू का बैल–बहुत कठिन परिश्रम करनेवाला।
- कोड़ी का तीन–तुच्छ।
- खाली हाथ–पैसे का अभाव।
- गाजर-मूली–अशक्त।
- गुलर का फूल–दुर्लभ वस्तु।
- गोबर-गणेश–निरामूर्ख।
- घर का उजाला–कुल-दीपक।
- घड़ियाली आँसू–बनावटी शोक।
- चलता-पुरजा–चालाक।
- चाँद का टुकड़ा–परम सुन्दर वस्तु या व्यक्ति।
- चाँदी का जूता–रिश्वत।
- चार दिन की चाँदनी–थोड़े समय का सुख।
- जलती आँख–क्रोधाभिभूत।
- जीभ का पतला–लालची।
- टेढ़ी खीर–विकट काम।
- ठिकाने की बात–न्यायसंगत बात।
- अढ़ाई दिन की हुकूमत–थोड़े समय का ऐश्वर्य।
- तकदीर का सिकन्दर–भाग्य का बलवान्।
- थाली का बैंगन–मत बदलते रहना।
- दाँत कटी रोटी–घनिष्ठता।
- दाहिना हाथ–सहायक।
- दिल का बादशाह–बहुत बड़ा उदार।
- दूध का दूध और पानी का पानी–उचित न्याय।
- दूध का धोआ–निर्दोष।
- दो दिन का मेहमान–बहुत थोड़े समय ठहरने वाला।
- धरती का फूल–ऐसा व्यक्ति जो हाल में अमीर हुआ है।
- धोबी का कुत्ता–निकम्मा।
- नसीब का मारा–बुरे दिन देखनेवाला।
- निन्यानबे का फेरा–धन बढ़ाने की चिन्ता।
- पत्थर का कलेजा–हर दुःख सहने की शक्ति।
- पत्थर की लकीर–चिरस्थायी सदा सत्य।
- फूलों की सेज–आनन्ददायक कार्य।
- बगुला-भगत–कपटी व्यक्ति।

- बच्चों का खेल–साधारण काम।
- बलि का बकरा–निःसहाय व्यक्ति।
- बरसाती बादल–अस्थायी।
- बात का पक्का–सत्यवादी।
- बायें हाथ का खेल–सरल काम।
- बिन बादल बरसात–असमय लाभ।
- बे-पेंदी का लोटा–बे ठिकाने का आदमी।
- भागीरथ प्रयत्न–अत्यधिक परिश्रम।
- भीष्म प्रतिज्ञा–दृढ़ संकल्प।
- मक्खी चूस–कंजूस।
- मिट्टी के मोल–बहुत सस्ता।
- मोटा असामी–मूर्ख मालदार।
- राम कहानी–आत्मवृतान्त।
- लँगोटिया यार– बचपन का मित्र।
- हवाई महल–कोरी कल्पना।
- आँख लगना–नींद आना।
- आँख खुलना–होश में आना।
- आँखें दिखाना–क्रोध से घूरना।
- आँसू पोंछना–धैर्य बँधाना।
- अन्धे की लकड़ी–एकमात्र सहारा।
- कान भरना–चुगली करना।
- कान पर जूँ न रेंगना–कोई असर न होना।
- नाक कटना–प्रतिष्ठा खत्म होना।
- नाक रगड़ना–दीनता दिखाना।
- नाकों चने चबवाना–खूब सताना।
- मुँह की खाना–बुरी तरह हारना।
- आस्तीन का साँप–विश्वासघाती मित्र।
- कन्धे से कन्धा मिलाना–पूरा सहयोग करना।
- ईंट से ईंट बजाना–पूरी तरह नष्ट कर देना।
- नौ दो ग्यारह होना–भाग जाना।
- दाँत खट्टे करना–बुरी तरह हराना।
- हाथ मलना–पछताना।
- खून का प्यासा–जानी दुश्मन।
- घी के दिए जलाना–खुशी मनाना।
- चार चाँद लगाना–प्रतिष्ठा बढ़ाना।
- तीन तेरह होना–अलग-अलग होना।
- पानी फेर देना–नाश कर देना।
- गाल बजाना–डींगे मारना।
- जान से हाथ धो बैठना–मारा जाना।
- पानी-पानी होना–बहुत लज्जित होना।
- फूला न समाना–बहुत प्रसन्न होना।
- अपना उल्लू सीधा करना–अपना मतलब निकालना।
- आँखें चुरा लेना–अनदेखा कर देना।
- अन्धे की लाठी–एकमात्र सहारा।
- आसमान पर चढ़ना–बहुत अभिमान करना।
- आँखें खुलना–होश आना।
- चोरी और सीना जोरी–दोषी होकर धमकाना।
- आग में घी डालना–क्रोध को भड़काना।
- अँगुली पर नचाना– अच्छी तरह वश में करना।
- एक आँख से देखना–समान दृष्टि से देखना।
- एक ही थैले के चट्टे-बट्टे–एक जैसे।
- ओखली में सिर देना–जान-बूझकर आपत्ति मोल लेना।
- कलेजा मुँह को आना–बहुत दुःखी होना।
- कफन बाँधकर चलना–मौत से न घबराना।
- काँटे बिछाना–बाधा डालना।
- कलेजा ठण्डा होना–सन्तोष होना।
- कमर कसना–तैयार होना।
- खून खौलना–जोश में आना।
- खाक छानना–मारे-मारे फिरना।
- गागर में सागर भरना–थोड़े शब्दों में बहुत कुछ कह देना।
- घाव पर नमक छिड़कना–दुखी को अधिक दुखी करना।
- घी के दिए जलाना–खुशी मनाना।
- घोड़े बेचकर सोना–गहरी नींद में सोना।
- चल बसना–परलोक सिधारना।
- छठी का दूध याद आना–भारी संकट में पड़ना।
- छाती पर साँप लोटना–बहुत ईर्ष्या होना।
- जमीन पर पैर न रखना–अधिक घमण्ड होना।
- झक मारना–व्यर्थ समय खोना।
- टेढ़ी खीर–कठिन काम।
- डींग मारना–अपनी झूठी प्रशंसा करना।
- डूब मरना–बहुत लज्जित होना।
- तलवे चाटना–चापलूसी करना।
- ताक में रहना–मौका ढूँढ़ते रहना।
- दंग रह जाना–आश्चर्य में पड़ जाना।
- दाल न गलना–वश न चलना।
- दाल में काला होना–संदेह होना।
- पीठ दिखाना–हारकर भागना।
- मुँह तोड़ उत्तर देना–खरा उत्तर देना।

वस्तुनिष्ठ प्रश्न

अभ्यास-1

निर्देशः *नीचे प्रत्येक शुद्ध शब्द की वर्तनी के लिए चार विकल्प दिए गए हैं। आपको सही विकल्प का चयन करना है।*

1. A. ऋषि B. ऋषी C. रिषी D. ऋसि
2. A. विषेसन B. विशेषण C. विसेशन D. विशेशन
3. A. दुशासन B. दुसाशन C. दूशाषण D. दुःशासन
4. A. संस्कृति B. संसकृति C. संष्कृति D. संस्कृती
5. A. दूनियां B. दुनियां C. दुनिया D. दूनिआ
6. A. टिपनी B. टिप्पणि C. टिप्पणी D. टिप्पनी
7. A. शाषण B. साशन C. शासन D. शाशन
8. A. किसमस B. किरसमस C. क्रिसमृस D. कृसमस
9. A. अनुग्रहित B. अनुग्रहीत C. अनुगृहीत D. अनुग्रहित
10. A. पराकम B. प्राक्रम C. पराक्रम D. प्राकर्म
11. A. नायका B. नाइका C. नाइक D. नायिका
12. A. समरिधी B. समद्धी C. समृद्धि D. समरिद्धि
13. A. युधिष्ठर B. यूधिष्ठर C. युधिष्ठिर D. युधिष्टर
14. A. वाल्मीकि B. बाल्मीकि C. बालमीकि D. बाल्मिक
15. A. परलोकिक B. प्रलौकिक C. पारलौकिक D. परलौकिक्
16. A. त्रितीय B. तर्तीय C. तृतीय D. तिरतीय
17. A. व्योहार B. व्यौहार C. व्यवहार D. ब्यवहार
18. A. अहिल्या B. अहल्या C. अहिलया D. अहीलया
19. A. आदरनीय B. आदरणीय C. आदरनीया D. आदरणीया
20. A. आर्द B. आद्र C. आर्द्र D. आर्दृ
21. A. आधीन B. अधिन C. अधीन D. अधीम
22. A. आविस्कार B. आविष्कार C. आवीस्कार D. आविश्कार
23. A. आसा B. आषा C. आशा D. अशा
24. A. उज्वल B. उजज्ज्वल C. उजज्वल D. उज्ज्वल
25. A. उन्नती B. उन्नित C. उन्नति D. उन्नती
26. A. कलस B. कलष C. कलश D. कलशा
27. A. गनीत B. गनित C. गणीत D. गणित
28. A. तलाव B. तालाव C. तलाब D. तालाब
29. A. दुष्ट B. दूष्ट C. दुस्त D. दुश्त
30. A. निरोग B. निररोग C. नीरोग D. नीरोगी

उत्तरमाला

1. A	2. B	3. D	4. A	5. C
6. C	7. C	8. C	9. C	10. C
11. D	12. C	13. C	14. A	15. C
16. C	17. C	18. B	19. B	20. C
21. C	22. B	23. C	24. D	25. C
26. C	27. D	28. D	29. A	30. C

अभ्यास-2

निर्देशः *नीचे कुछ शब्द दिए गए हैं। प्रत्येक के पर्यायवाची के चार विकल्प दिए गए हैं। इनमें से एक विकल्प सही पर्यायवाची है, उसका चयन कीजिए :*

1. **अग्नि**
   A. अनिल B. अनल C. गर्म D. ताप
2. **अमृत**
   A. पीयूष B. गरल C. सरस D. जीवनदायनी

3. आँख

A. लोचन B. आस्थि
C. वदन D. जलज

4. आकाश

A. अनन्त B. पाताल
C. वितल D. तल

5. कपड़ा

A. परिधान B. पटिका
C. पीताम्बर D. लँहगा

6. कमल

A. सरोज B. सरोवर
C. पंक D. पुष्प

7. गंगा

A. पाताल नदी B. हिमनदी
C. भागीरथ D. त्रिपथगा

8. चाँद

A. मयंक B. भानु
C. दिनकर D. रवि

9. नदी

A. सरिता B. प्रवाह
C. धारा D. जलधर

10. पर्वत

A. पत्थर B. चट्टान
C. शिखर D. मेरू

11. पवन

A. अनिल B. अनल
C. अग D. विहग

12. पति

A. साजन B. प्रिया
C. भार्या D. दारा

13. पानी

A. मही B. मेदिनी
C. अम्बु D. तरणी

14. पुत्र

A. आत्मज B. तनया
C. सुंता D. आत्मजा

15. पुत्री

A. सुता B. सुत
C. आत्मज D. नन्दन

16. फूल

A. बहार B. मधु
C. माधव D. सुमन

17. वृक्ष

A. विटप B. अम्र
C. प्रसून D. रसा

18. बादल

A. अज B. व्यामोह
C. नीरद D. मधुप

19. बिजली

A. चंचला B. खटका
C. त्रास D. संत्रास

20. माता

A. धात्री B. धरणी
C. धरित्री D. श्यामा

21. घोषणा

A. आवाज B. पुकारना
C. ऐलान D. ललकारना

22. उत्कर्ष

A. आकर्षण B. विकर्षण
C. उन्नति D. निष्कर्ष

23. उदय

A. अन्त B. विकास
C. प्रगट D. व्यस्त

24. दक्ष

A. निपुण B. समर्थ
C. कर्मठ D. मेहनती

25. संवाद

A. विवाद B. झगड़ा
C. सम्बोधन D. वार्तालाप

उत्तरमाला

1. B	**2.** A	**3.** A	**4.** A	**5.** A
6. A	**7.** D	**8.** A	**9.** A	**10.** D
11. A	**12.** A	**13.** C	**14.** A	**15.** A
16. D	**17.** A	**18.** C	**19.** A	**20.** A
21. C	**22.** C	**23.** C	**24.** A	**25.** D

अभ्यास-3

निर्देशः *नीचे चार-चार शब्दों के समूह दिए गए हैं। प्रत्येक समूह में एक शब्द बेमेल है तथा शेष तीन शब्द पर्यायवाची हैं, आपको उस शब्द का चयन करना है, जो बेमेल है :*

1. A. तम B. अंधकार
C. तिमिर D. अंश

2. A. अनल B. आग
C. दहन D. तमिस्त्रा

3. A. अतुल B. अद्वितीय
C. अनुपम D. शुष्मा

4. A. अहं B. अहंकार
C. दर्प D. निराला

5. A. पता B. खोज
C. जाँच D. शोध

6. A. गरल B. पीयूष
C. सुधा D. सोम

7. A. कानन B. जंगल
C. पादप D. वन

8. A. अश्व B. गज
C. घोड़ा D. तुरंग

9. A. दानव B. मानव
C. दैत्य D. राक्षस

10. A. आँख B. चक्षु
C. नयन D. मुख

11. A. अन्तरिक्ष B. वसुन्धरा
C. आसमान D. गगन

12. A. इच्छा B. अभिलाषा
C. कामना D. प्रयोजन

13. A. कपड़ा B. चीर
C. वसन D. पोशाक

14. A. अब्ज B. कमल
C. राजीव D. आम्र

15. A. कोयल B. पिक
C. काग D. वनप्रिय

16. A. गंगा B. देवनदी
C. गोदावरी D. भागीरथी

17. A. गणेश B. एकदन्त
C. देवराज D. गणपति

18. A. घर B. निलय
C. निकेतन D. झोपड़ी

19. A. चाँद B. हिमांशु
C. विनायक D. सुधांशु

20. A. नदी B. तरणी
C. तटिनी D. सरिता

21. A. पक्षी B. चिड़िया
C. सुमन D. विहग

22. A. पवन B. अचला
C. वात D. वायु

23. A. समीर B. पृथ्वी
C. भू D. भूमि

24. A. पानी B. समीर
C. अम्बु D. जल

25. A. पुत्र B. तनया
C. तनय D. सुत

26. A. पुत्र B. तनया
C. सुता D. कन्या

27. A. गृहिणी B. आदमी
C. पुरुष D. नर

28. A. मधु B. फूल
C. पुष्प D. सुमन

29. A. माधव B. तरु
C. पेड़ D. वृक्ष

30. A. माता B. अम्बु
C. अम्मा D. जननी

उत्तरमाला

1. D	2. D	3. D	4. D	5. A
6. A	7. C	8. B	9. B	10. D
11. B	12. D	13. D	14. D	15. C
16. C	17. C	18. D	19. C	20. B
21. C	22. B	23. A	24. B	25. B
26. A	27. A	28. A	29. A	30. B

अभ्यास-4

निर्देशः ***गहरे काले शब्द*** *के विलोम शब्द का चयन कीजिएः*

1. उसे हर काम में **सफलता** मिल रही है।
A. असफलता B. सफल
C. कुशलता D. निपुणता

2. कभी किसी की **निन्दा** नहीं करनी चाहिए।
A. गुणगान B. स्तुति
C. प्रशंसा D. यशोगान

3. आलस्य व्यक्ति का सबसे बड़ा **दुश्मन** है।
A. शत्रु B. घातक
C. मित्र D. सहायक

4. वे बुढ़ापे से **दुखी** हैं।
A. अप्रसन्न B. सुखी
C. खुश D. नाराज

5. यहाँ उसकी **चतुराई** नहीं चली।
A. चालाकी B. बहादुरी
C. निपुणता D. मूर्खता

6. शहद की **मिठास** कम नहीं होती।
A. मीठा B. तीखा
C. कडुवा D. खट्टा

7. साहसी के **साहस** को देखकर मैं चकित रह गया।
A. हिम्मत B. बहादुरी
C. निडर D. भय

8. फिल्मोत्सव में सर्वश्रेष्ठ **अभिनेता** को पुरस्कार प्रदान किया गया।
A. हीरोइन B. नेत्री
C. मीनाक्षी D. अभिनेत्री

9. नाटक में नायक और **नायिका** की भूमिका महत्वपूर्ण होती है:
A. हीरो B. नायक
C. नेत्र D. नेता

10. कवि-सम्मेलन में एक कवि और एक **कवयित्री** को आमंत्रित किया गया था।
A. लेखक B. सम्पादक
C. नेता D. कवि

11. विद्यालय के वार्षिकोत्सव के लिए नेता और एक **नेत्री** को आमंत्रित किया गया।
A. अभिनेता B. विद्वान्
C. विदुषी D. नेता

12. मोहन बहुत **चतुर** है।
A. निपुण B. तेज
C. सुस्त D. मूर्ख

13. सोहन अब पूर्ण **स्वस्थ** है।
A. प्रसन्न B. खुश
C. अस्वस्थ D. अप्रसन्न

14. पक्षी **आकाश** में उड़ते हैं :
A. गगन B. नम
C. धरती D. पाताल

15. वह विद्यालय में देर से आया और **अनुपस्थित** हो गया।
A. पूर्व B. उपस्थित
C. प्रवेश D. समयपूर्व

16. **बालक** चाँद की ओर देख रहा है।
A. बालिका B. लड़का
C. बच्चा D. बच्ची

17. मैं उसके विचार से बिल्कुल **सहमत** नहीं हूँ।
A. समर्थन B. सहमति
C. असहमत D. प्रशंसक

18. उसकी हालत **अधिक** खराब है।
A. बहुत B. कम
C. ठीक D. कुशल

19. **धर्म** की सर्वत्र विजय होती है:
A. अधर्म B. ज्ञान
C. भक्ति D. ईमानदारी

20. अच्छे चरित्र के बिना जीवन **निरर्थक** है:
A. व्यर्थ B. अर्थपूर्ण
C. सार्थक D. कुशल

21. **ईमानदारी** बड़ी दुर्लभ वस्तु है:
A. सच्चाई B. भलाई
C. बेइमानी D. परोपकारी

22. एवरेस्ट संसार का सबसे **ऊँचा** पर्वत है:
A. नीचा B. वितल
C. पाताल D. मध्यम

23. वह विश्वास के **योग्य** नहीं है:
A. काबिल B. विश्वासी
C. अयोग्य D. बेकार

24. क्या वह इतना **मूर्ख** है?
A. चालाक B. विद्वान्
C. बुद्धिमान D. धूर्त

25. कितना सुहावना **दृश्य** है!
A. अदृश्य B. दर्शनीय
C. सुन्दर D. व्यर्थ

उत्तरमाला

1. A	**2.** C	**3.** C	**4.** B	**5.** D
6. C	**7.** D	**8.** D	**9.** B	**10.** D
11. D	**12.** D	**13.** C	**14.** D	**15.** B
16. A	**17.** C	**18.** B	**19.** A	**20.** C
21. C	**22.** A	**23.** C	**24.** C	**25.** A

अभ्यास-5

निर्देशः नीचे प्रत्येक **काले गहरे शब्द** के चार विलोम दिए गए हैं। इनमें सही विलोम का चयन कीजिए :

1. अग्नि
A. आग B. अनल
C. दहन D. जल

2. अग्रज
A. अनुज B. भ्राता
C. भाई D. अम्बा

3. अच्छा
A. बुरा B. खराब
C. गंदा D. भ्रष्ट

4. अंत
A. प्रारम्भ B. समाप्त
C. शेष D. अल्प

5. अचल
A. विचल B. वितल
C. सजल D. चल

6. अति
A. अधिक B. बहुत
C. अल्प D. कम

7. अत्यधिक
A. अल्प B. अधिक
C. स्वल्प D. न्यूनतम

8. अंधकार
A. अंधेरा B. प्रकाश
C. रात्रि D. दिन

9. अतिवृष्टि
A. अनावृष्टि B. वृष्टि
C. वर्षा D. वर्षण

10. अनाथ
A. नाथ B. स्वामी
C. मासिक D. सनाथ

11. अनुकूल
A. मनोकूल B. प्रतिकूल
C. अनुकरण D. मनस्वी

12. अनुराग
A. राग B. विराग
C. विग्रह D. स्नेह

13. अन्त
A. श्री गणेश B. आदि
C. शुरुआत D. समाप्त

14. अपना
A. अपनत्व B. पराया
C. मित्र D. शत्रु

15. अपमान
A. मान B. सम्मान
C. वर्तमान D. स्वाभिमान

16. अपेक्षा
A. इच्छा B. स्वेच्छा
C. प्रविच्छा D. उपेक्षा

17. अमर
A. मर्त्य B. मृत्यु
C. सुधा D. गरल

18. अल्पायु
A. चिरायु B. उमरदराज
C. नश्वर D. सनातन

19. अस्त
A. उदय B. विकास
C. निर्माण D. सृष्टि

20. आकर्षण
A. प्रतिकर्षण B. विकर्षण
C. सम्मोहन D. विरत

21. आकाश
A. गगन B. नभ
C. वसुन्धरा D. पाताल

22. आगे
A. पीछे B. पूर्व
C. पृष्ट D. पृष्ठ

23. आजाद
A. स्वतंत्र B. स्वतंत्रता
C. परतंत्र D. गुलाम

24. आदान
A. आयात B. निर्यात
C. प्रदान D. निदान

25. आधुनिक
A. अर्वाचीन B. नूतन
C. प्राचीन D. वर्तमान

उत्तरमाला

1. D	**2.** A	**3.** A	**4.** A	**5.** D
6. D	**7.** C	**8.** B	**9.** A	**10.** D
11. B	**12.** B	**13.** A	**14.** B	**15.** B
16. D	**17.** A	**18.** A	**19.** A	**20.** B
21. D	**22.** A	**23.** D	**24.** C	**25.** C

अभ्यास-6

निर्देशः *नीचे कुछ शब्द दिए गए हैं प्रत्येक शब्द के चार वैकल्पिक अर्थ दिए गए हैं। सही अर्थ का चयन कीजिए :*

1. सुरक्षित
A. कुशल B. घटना
C. दुर्घटना D. बचाव

2. प्रतिभाशाली
A. सज्जन B. कुशाग्र
C. विद्वान् D. वैभवशाली

3. आत्मसमर्पण
A. अपने आप को सौंपना B. समर्पण
C. अर्पण D. त्यागज

4. सिद्धहस्त
A. निपुण B. कर्मठ
C. मेहनती D. परिश्रमी

5. सुशोभित
A. मजेदार B. सुस्वागतम्
C. अच्छा D. शोभा पाना

6. स्वादिष्ट
A. मजेदार B. बेकार
C. मीठा D. तीखा

7. **स्वावलम्बी**
A. निर्भर B. परालंबी
C. आत्मनिर्भर D. अतिथि

8. **उपकरण**
A. साधन B. युक्ति
C. यंत्र D. मशीन

9. **कीमत**
A. क्रय B. विक्रय
C. मूल्य D. बिक्री

10. **संगठन**
A. एकता B. अनेकता
C. समूह D. संस्था

11. **विपत्ति**
A. दुख B. विपदा
C. मुसीबत D. सुख

12. **तृण**
A. तिनका B. धूल
C. धूप D. लकड़ी

13. **आश्चर्य**
A. निरीक्षण B. दृष्टिगोचर
C. हैरानी D. थकावट

14. **हार्दिक**
A. हृदय से B. शरीर से
C. मन से D. मस्तिष्क से

15. **नियति**
A. भाग्य B. किनारा
C. समय D. पवित्र

16. **सुगन्धित**
A. दुर्गन्ध B. खुशबू वाला
C. फूल D. कमल

17. **उत्साह**
A. होश B. हवास
C. जोश D. हिम्मत

18. **सहयोग**
A. मिलन सार B. मेहनती
C. परोपकारी D. आपसी सहायता

19. **मुसीबत**
A. विपत्ति B. सुशोभित
C. सहायता D. मदद

20. **निरक्षर**
A. साक्षर B. दर्शनीय
C. पठनीय D. अनपढ़

21. **उपवन**
A. वन B. तीर
C. जंगल D. बाग

22. **मेघ**
A. बादल B. पंकज
C. राजीव D. मेघनाद

23. **आधुनिक**
A. प्राचीन B. पुरातन
C. भूतकाल D. आज का

24. **तीर**
A. वाण B. धनुष
C. किनारा D. नदी

25. **परीक्षण**
A. जाँच B. पड़ताल
C. परीक्षा D. इम्तहान

26. **अभिवादन**
A. नमस्ते B. प्रणाम
C. बधाई D. शुभकामना

27. **सर्वत्र**
A. नश्वर B. सजीव
C. ईश्वर D. सभी जगह

28. **हलवाहा**
A. चरवाहा B. किसान
C. मजदूर D. हल चलाने वाला

29. **शिखर**
A. पर्वत B. पहाड़
C. टीला D. चोटी

30. **भयानक**
A. डरावना B. भयभीत
C. डरना D. खूँखार

उत्तरमाला

1. D	2. B	3. A	4. A	5. D
6. A	7. C	8. C	9. C	10. A
11. C	12. A	13. C	14. A	15. A
16. B	17. C	18. D	19. A	20. D
21. D	22. A	23. D	24. A	25. A
26. B	27. D	28. D	29. D	30. A

अभ्यास-7

निर्देशः *नीचे कुछ शब्द दिए जा रहे हैं। प्रत्येक शब्द के* **उपसर्ग** *के सन्दर्भ में चार विकल्प दिए गए हैं। आपको सही विकल्प का चयन करना है :*

1. अलबत्ता
A. अ B. अल
C. लब D. त्ता

2. अलगरज
A. अल B. लग
C. गर D. रज

3. कमसिन

A. क B. कम

C. सि D. सिन

4. अनमोल

A. अ B. अन

C. मो D. मोल

5. अनजान

A. अ B. अन

C. जा D. जान

6. अनपढ़

A. अ B. पढ़

C. प D. अन

7. अधखिला

A. अ B. अध

C. ला D. खिला

8. अधजला

A. अ B. ज

C. अध D. ला

9. अधपका

A. अ B. अध

C. पका D. का

10. अघखिला

A. अ B. अघ

C. खिला D. ला

11. उन्नीस

A. उन B. उन्

C. नीस D. स

12. उनसठ

A. उ B. उन

C. सठ D. ठ

13. दुकाल

A. द B. दुक

C. दु D. काल

14. दुबला

A. दब B. दुब

C. ला D. दु

15. निकम्मा

A. नि B. निक

C. कम्मा D. मा

16. निर्लज्ज

A. निर B. निल

C. नि D. लज्ज

17. बिनब्याहा

A. बि B. बिन

C. ब्याहा D. हा

18. भरपेट

A. भर B. पेट

C. पे D. ट

19. भरपाई

A. भ B. र

C. पा D. भर

20. कुपात्र

A. कु B. कुप

C. पा D. पात्र

21. सुजान

A. सु B. सुज

C. सुजा D. जान

22. गैर कानूनी

A. गै B. गैर

C. कानु D. नुनी

23. गैरसरकारी

A. गैर B. सर

C. का D. कारी

24. अपमान

A. अ B. अप

C. मा D. मान

25. अनुशासन

A. अ B. शासन

C. सन D. अनु

26. अविनीत

A. अवि B. अ

C. नी D. नीत

27. अभिमान

A. अभि B. अ

C. मा D. मान

28. अभियान

A. अ B. मान

C. यान D. अभि

29. अध्ययन

A. अध् B. अधि

C. यन D. न

30. निश्चल

A. नि B. निर

C. निस D. चल

उत्तरमाला

1. B	2. A	3. B	4. B	5. B
6. D	7. B	8. C	9. B	10. B
11. A	12. B	13. C	14. D	15. B
16. A	17. B	18. A	19. D	20. A
21. A	22. B	23. A	24. B	25. D
26. B	27. A	28. D	29. B	30. A

अभ्यास-8

निर्देशः *निम्नलिखित शब्दों में प्रयुक्त प्रत्यय सम्बन्धी चार विकल्प दिए गए हैं, सही विकल्प का चयन कीजिए :*

1. भलाई
A. ई B. लाई
C. आई D. भला

2. चतुराई
A. चतु B. रा
C. ई D. आई

3. भूखा
A. भू B. भूख
C. खा D. आ

4. भिड़न्त
A. भिड् B. भि
C. न्त D. अन्त

5. प्यासा
A. आस B. सा
C. आसा D. सा

6. बिकाऊ
A. बिक B. काऊ
C. आऊ D. ऊ

7. तैराक
A. तै B. तैर
C. राक D. आक

8. सन्नाटा
A. सन् B. सन्ना
C. नाटा D. आटा

9. लोहार
A. लोह B. आरा
C. आरी D. आर

10. मिलान
A. आना B. आने
C. आनी D. आन

11. चढ़ाव
A. चढ़ B. चढ़ा
C. आव D. व

12. लगाव
A. लग B. अव
C. आव D. गाव

13. लिखावट
A. लिख B. लिखा
C. वट D. आवट

14. मिलावट
A. मिल B. वट
C. आवट D. ट

15. मिठास
A. मिठ B. ठास
C. आस D. स

16. चिकनाहट
A. चिक B. नाह्ट
C. हट D. आहट

17. सड़ियल
A. सड़ B. यल
C. ड़ियल D. इयल

18. मरियल
A. मर B. यल
C. मरि D. इयल

19. गड़रिया
A. गड़ B. इया
C. रिया D. या

20. सजीला
A. ईला B. इला
C. ला D. स

21. लुटेरा
A. लुट B. एरा
C. ऐरा D. रा

22. लठैत
A. ए B. ऐ
C. ऐत D. त

23. भगोड़ा
A. ओ B. ओड़ा
C. ड़ा D. भगो

24. खपत
A. ख B. प
C. त D. पत

25. जीवट
A. व B. अट
C. जीव D. जी

उत्तरमाला

1. C	**2.** D	**3.** D	**4.** D	**5.** D
6. C	**7.** D	**8.** D	**9.** D	**10.** D
11. C	**12.** C	**13.** D	**14.** C	**15.** C
16. D	**17.** D	**18.** D	**19.** B	**20.** A
21. B	**22.** C	**23.** B	**24.** C	**25.** B

अभ्यास-9

निर्देशः *नीचे कुछ मुहावरे दिए गए हैं। प्रत्येक के अर्थ के लिए चार विकल्प दिए गए हैं। आपको सही विकल्प का चयन करना है :*

1. अक्ल पर पत्थर पड़ना
A. बुद्धि काम न करना B. दुविधा होना
C. संकट में होना D. परेशान होना

2. अपना उल्लू सीधा करना
A. अवसर देखना B. काम निकालना
C. मतलब साधना D. मूर्ख बनाना

3. अपने मुँह मियाँ-मिट्ठू बनना
A. मिठाई खाना B. प्रशंसा करना
C. निंदा करना D. अपनी प्रशंसा स्वयं करना

4. अपने पाँव पर आप कुल्हाड़ी मारना
A. हानि पहुँचाना B. खेद होना
C. अपना पैर काटना D. अपनी हानि स्वयं करना

5. आँखें चुरा लेना
A. भाग जाना B. छिप जाना
C. अनदेखा करना D. मिल जाना

6. अक्ल का दुश्मन
A. मित्र होना B. शत्रु होना
C. महामूर्ख D. महाविद्वान्

7. अंधे की लाठी
A. एक मात्र सहारा B. मित्र होना
C. शत्रु होना D. दुख पहुँचाना

8. आकाश-पाताल एक करना
A. भाग-दौड़ करना B. परेशान होना
C. थक जाना D. कठिन परिश्रम करना

9. घड़ों पानी पड़ना
A. लज्जित होना B. तुच्छ समझना
C. लाभ होना D. थकावट

10. अगर-मगर करना
A. नुकसान करना B. बहाने बनाना
C. बदनाम करना D. कपट करना

11. मुँह की खाना
A. गिर जाना B. हार जाना
C. भाग जाना D. व्यर्थ होना

12. आस्तीन का साँप होना
A. शत्रु B. मित्र
C. कपटी मित्र D. दयालु

13. एक आँख से देखना
A. बुरा व्यवहार B. समान व्यवहार
C. कपट करना D. लज्जित होना

14. बाल-बाँका न होना
A. घायल होना B. साफ बच जाना
C. क्रोधित होना D. स्वस्थ होना

15. दाँतों तले उँगली दबाना
A. उँगली काटना B. चिंतित हो जाना
C. चकित रह जाना D. प्रसन्न हो जाना

16. जान के लाले पड़ना
A. मरने का खतरा होना B. भाग जाना
C. हार जाना D. मुश्किल में पड़ना

17. बोली मारना
A. ताना देना B. सताना
C. मजाक करना D. याद दिलाना

18. अंधों में काना राजा
A. मूर्खों में अल्पज्ञ को विद्वान् माना जाना
B. सबको मूर्ख समझना
C. अत्यधिक महत्त्वपूर्ण
D. काना राजा

19. अक्ल के घोड़े दौड़ाना
A. बुद्धि लड़ाना
B. कल्पना करना
C. तरह-तरह के उपाय सोचना
D. ज्ञान-प्राप्त करना

20. पानी उतर जाना
A. शर्म करना B. लज्जित न होना
C. भाग जाना D. इज्जत करना

21. तीन-पाँच करना
A. तितर-बितर करना
B. वचन देकर फिर जाना
C. घुमा-फिरा कर बातें करना
D. परेशान करना

22. हथियार डाल देना
A. हार जाना B. जीत जाना
C. धोखा देना D. विजय होना

23. आँख खुलना
A. होश में आना B. अत्यन्त प्यार होना
C. उल्टा काम करना D. क्रोध करना

24. कमर सीधी करना
A. थक जाना B. थकावट दूर करना
C. काम करना D. परिश्रम करना

25. पगड़ी रखना
A. चैन की सांस लेना B. अपमान करना
C. दया की भीख माँगना D. अपमान होना

26. लोहा मानना
A. संघर्ष करना B. विजय होना
C. श्रेष्ठता स्वीकार करना D. खुशामद करना

27. काठ मार जाना
A. दुःखी होना B. चुप होना
C. सफल होना D. मर जाना

28. चाँद पर थूकना

A. अपमान करना

B. बढ़कर बातें करना

C. महान पुरुष पर लांछन लगाना

D. महत्त्वाकांक्षी होना

29. उगल देना

A. अपराध स्वीकार कर लेना

B. सच बोलना

C. उल्टी करना

D. अनपच होना

30. हाथ मलना

A. पश्चाताप करना B. सर्दी मिटाना

C. दुख करना D. तैयार होना

उत्तरमाला

1. A	**2.** C	**3.** D	**4.** D	**5.** C
6. C	**7.** A	**8.** D	**9.** A	**10.** B
11. B	**12.** C	**13.** B	**14.** B	**15.** C
16. D	**17.** A	**18.** A	**19.** A	**20.** B
21. C	**22.** A	**23.** A	**24.** B	**25.** C
26. C	**27.** B	**28.** C	**29.** A	**30.** A

अभ्यास-10

निर्देशः *नीचे कुछ वाक्य खण्ड दिए गए हैं, पूरे वाक्य खण्ड के लिए एक शब्द का चयन कीजिए।*

1. जिसका आदि न हो

A. अनंत B. अमर

C. शाश्वत D. अनादि

2. जो कुछ न जानता हो

A. मूर्ख B. महामूर्ख

C. ज्ञानी D. अज्ञ

3. जो अनुकरण करने योग्य हो

A. अनुकरणीय B. अद्वितीय

C. आदरणीय D. अगम

4. जिसका अंत न हो

A. अनंत B. अनादि

C. आदि D. परलोक

5. जो कभी न मरे

A. मर्त्य B. मुर्त्त

C. अमुर्त्त D. अमर

6. जिसके समान दूसरा न हो

A. अनुकूल B. प्रतिकूल

C. कृतज्ञ D. अद्वितीय

7. जो कम बोलता हो

A. मृदुभाषी B. वाचाल

C. अल्पभाषी D. अल्पज्ञ

8. जिसका इलाज न हो

A. मरणशील B. अमरत्व

C. बिमारी D. लाइलाज

9. जिस का विश्वास न किया जा सके

A. विश्वसनीय B. अविश्वसनीय

C. विश्वासी D. धूर्त्त

10. जिसका कोई नाथ न हो

A. सनाथ B. स्वामी

C. नाथ D. अनाथ

11. कम जानने वाला

A. अल्पज्ञ B. अज्ञ

C. विद् D. विद्वान

12. जहाँ जाना संभव न हो

A. दुर्गम B. अगम

C. तल D. वितल

13. कम खाने वाला

A. बहुभोजी B. पेटु

C. कंजूस D. अल्पाहारी

14. जो बात पहले कभी न हुई हो

A. भूतपूर्व B. अभूतपूर्व

C. प्राचीन D. अर्वाचीन

15. जिस स्त्री के सन्तान न हों

A. बाँझ B. कुलटा

C. पतिता D. विधवा

16. जो कहा न जा सके

A. अकथनीय B. अकथ्य

C. करणीय D. सम्भव

17. एहसान न मानने वाला

A. कृतज्ञ B. कृतघ्न

C. आस्तिक D. विश्वासी

18. जिसने देश के साथ विश्वासघात किया हो

A. विश्वासघाती B. द्रोही

C. आतंकवादी D. देश द्रोही

19. जिसने राष्ट्र के हित में अपना जीवन बलिदान कर दिया हो

A. देशभक्त B. शहीद

C. राष्ट्रभूत D. भारतपुत्र

20. वह जमीन जिसमें कुछ भी पैदा न हो

A. ऊसर B. बंजर

C. उर्वर D. पथरीला

21. वह वस्तु जिसकी चाह हो

A. श्रेष्ठ B. आवश्यक

C. इच्छित D. अभीष्ट

22. दूसरों के पीछे चलने वाला
A. अनुयायी B. अनुज
C. अनुचर D. अनुकरणीय

23. जो पहले न पढ़ा हो
A. पठित B. अपठित
C. पठनीय D. अपठनीय

24. जिसके आर-पार दिखाई देता हो
A. अपारदर्शी B. गम्य
C. अगम्य D. पारदर्शी

25. आज्ञा पालन करने वाला
A. शिष्य B. शिष्या
C. अनुचर D. आज्ञाकारी

26. काम से जी चुराने वाला
A. कामचोर B. आलसी
C. कर्मठ D. परिश्रमी

27. प्रतिदिन होने वाला
A. दैनिक B. शाश्वत
C. सनातन D. अमर

28. जिसका कोई अर्थ न हो
A. सार्थक B. निरर्थक
C. आर्थिक D. अनार्थिक

29. उपकार मानने वाला
A. कृतज्ञ B. कृतघ्न
C. विश्वासी D. अनुयायी

30. हाथ से लिखा हुआ
A. पठनीय B. अपठनीय
C. स्पष्ट D. हस्तलिखित

उत्तरमाला

1. D	**2.** D	**3.** A	**4.** A	**5.** D
6. D	**7.** C	**8.** D	**9.** B	**10.** D
11. A	**12.** A	**13.** D	**14.** B	**15.** A
16. A	**17.** B	**18.** D	**19.** B	**20.** A
21. C	**22.** C	**23.** B	**24.** D	**25.** D
26. A	**27.** A	**28.** B	**29.** A	**30.** D

अभ्यास-11

निर्देशः *नीचे कुछ संज्ञा शब्द दिए जा रहे हैं। प्रत्येक के संज्ञा-भेद के लिए चार विकल्प दिए गये है। सही विकल्प का चयन कीजिए :*

1. तुलसीदास
A. जातिवाचक B. भाववाचक
C. व्यक्तिवाचक D. समूहवाचक

2. यमुना
A. व्यक्तिवाचक B. जातिवाचक
C. समूहवाचक D. भाववाचक

3. बच्चा
A. जातिवाचक B. समूहवाचक
C. भाववाचक D. व्यक्तिवाचक

4. मानवता
A. भाववाचक B. जातिवाचक
C. द्रव्यवाचक D. समूहवाचक

5. हिमालय
A. व्यक्तिवाचक B. जातिवाचक
C. भाववाचक D. समूहवाचक

6. भारत
A. जातिवाचक B. भाववाचक
C. व्यक्तिवाचक D. समूहवाचक

7. एशिया
A. व्यक्तिवाचक B. भाववाचक
C. द्रव्यवाचक D. समूहवाचक

8. महाराष्ट्र
A. जातिवाचक B. व्यक्तिवाचक
C. समूहवाचक D. द्रव्यवाचक

9. सूर सागर
A. व्यक्तिवाचक B. भाववाचक
C. द्रव्यवाचक D. समूहवाचक

10. सोमवार
A. जातिवाचक B. व्यक्तिवाचक
C. द्रव्यवाचक D. समूहवाचक

11. खटमल
A. जातिवाचक B. व्यक्तिवाचक
C. द्रव्यवाचक D. समूहवाचक

12. मैना
A. जातिवाचक B. व्यक्तिवाचक
C. द्रव्यवाचक D. समूहवाचक

13. चाँदी
A. द्रव्यवाचक B. समूहवाचक
C. भाववाचक D. व्यक्तिवाचक

14. अच्छाई
A. भाववाचक B. समूहवाचक
C. जातिवाचक D. व्यक्तिवाचक

15. पीतल
A. द्रव्यवाचक B. भाववाचक
C. व्यक्तिवाचक D. जातिवाचक

16. वीरता
A. भाववाचक B. जातिवाचक
C. द्रव्यवाचक D. समूहवाचक

17. रूस
A. जातिवाचक B. व्यक्तिवाचक
C. भाववाचक D. द्रव्यवाचक

18. लम्बाई
A. भाववाचक B. समूहवाचक
C. द्रव्यवाचक D. व्यक्तिवाचक

19. दल
A. जातिवाचक B. व्यक्तिवाचक
C. समूहवाचक D. द्रव्यवाचक

20. मार्च
A. समूहवाचक B. व्यक्तिवाचक
C. द्रव्यवाचक D. जातिवाचक

21. झुण्ड
A. समूहवाचक B. जातिवाचक
C. व्यक्तिवाचक D. द्रव्यवाचक

22. टोली
A. जातिवाचक B. व्यक्तिवाचक
C. समूहवाचक D. द्रव्यवाचक

23. सुभाष चौक
A. जातिवाचक B. समूहवाचक
C. व्यक्तिवाचक D. भाववाचक

24. संघ
A. जातिवाचक B. द्रव्यवाचक
C. समूहवाचक D. भाववाचक

25. गिरोह
A. समूहवाचक B. द्रव्यवाचक
C. जातिवाचक D. भाववाचक

उत्तरमाला

1. C	2. A	3. A	4. A	5. A
6. C	7. A	8. B	9. A	10. B
11. A	12. A	13. A	14. A	15. A
16. A	17. B	18. A	19. C	20. B
21. A	22. C	23. C	24. C	25. A

अभ्यास-12

निर्देश: *नीचे दिए गए वाक्य में रिक्त स्थान है। प्रत्येक वाक्य के नीचे कारक चिह्न दिए गए हैं। रिक्त स्थान की पूर्ति के लिए उपयुक्त कारक चिह्न का चयन कीजिए :*

1. निम्नलिखित शब्दों........अर्थ बताइए
A. का B. के
C. से D. पर

2. सरकार मुझे नौकरी........मत निकालिए
A. पर B. में
C. से D. को

3. इस कथन........पुष्टि कीजिए
A. को B. से
C. की D. ने

4. छात्र-छात्राएँ राष्ट्र........सम्पत्ति और उसके भावी कर्णधार होते हैं
A. के B. की
C. को D. में

5. प्रत्येक प्रश्न........चार सम्भावित उत्तर दिए गए हैं
A. के लिए B. में
C. के D. से

6. माता बच्चे........पढ़ाती है
A. को B. के
C. की D. से

7. गुरुजी........सबसे छोटे लड़के को एक नारंगी दी
A. ने B. को
C. से D. के लिए

8. मोहन सोहन से मिलने........गया है
A. से B. के
C. को D. के लिए

9. उसने कलम........लिखा
A. के B. में
C. पर D. से

10. मैं ड्राइवर........गाड़ी चलवाता हूँ
A. के B. पर
C. में D. से

11. शिक्षक छात्रों........पुस्तक पढ़वाते हैं
A. के लिए B. मैं
C. पर D. से

12. मैंने दाढ़ी........उसे मुसलमान समझ लिया
A. से B. के
C. को D. के लिए

13. श्याम अपने भाई हरि........आम लाया है
A. के B. के लिए
C. का D. पर

14. मोहन घर........आता है
A. में B. पर
C. से D. का

15. उसे पाँच दिनों........मूर्च्छा आया करती है
A. पर B. से
C. के D. को

16. मेधावी छात्र परीक्षा........चोरी नहीं करते
A. में B. पर
C. से D. के लिए

उत्तरमाला

1. A	2. C	3. C	4. B	5. C
6. A	7. A	8. D	9. D	10. D
11. D	12. A	13. B	14. C	15. B
16. D				

गद्यांश (अपठित-बोध)

गद्यांश 1

यदि हम निरन्तर प्रयत्न करेंगे तो निश्चय ही अपने सभी लक्ष्यों को प्राप्त कर लेंगे, किन्तु प्रायः देखा जाता है कि अधिक आशावादी लोग थोड़ा सा प्रयत्न करके अधिक फल की कामना करने लगते हैं और मनोवांछित फल प्राप्त न होने पर निराश हो जाते हैं। अतः जीवन में सफलता प्राप्त करने के लिए परिस्थितियों के समक्ष घुटने न टेकें, बल्कि दृढ़ता से उनका मुकाबला करें। याद रखें, जितना कठोर हमारा परिश्रम होगा उसका फल भी उतना ही मीठा होगा।

उपर्युक्त गद्यांश को ध्यानपूर्वक पढ़ें और निम्न प्रश्नों के उत्तर के लिए सही विकल्प को चुनें:

1. फल न मिलने पर कौन निराश हो जाते हैं?
   A. आशावादी लोग B. कम आशावादी लोग
   C. अधिक आशावादी लोग D. निराशावादी लोग
2. लक्ष्य प्राप्ति के लिए क्या किया जाना चाहिए?
   A. फल की कामना B. हिम्मत से मुकाबला
   C. निरन्तर प्रयत्न D. परिस्थितियों से मुकाबला
3. आशावादी शब्द का विलोम शब्द है:
   A. निराश B. निराशावादी
   B. दुखी D. अप्रसन्न
4. मनोवांछित शब्द का क्या अर्थ है?
   A. इच्छित B. परीक्षित
   C. लाभदायक D. मन को खुश करने वाले
5. परिश्रम शब्द का अर्थ है:
   A. साहस B. हिम्मत
   C. काम D. कठिन मेहनत

गद्यांश 2

पन्द्रह अगस्त 1947 को हमारा देश स्वतंत्र हुआ। स्वतन्त्रता प्राप्ति के बाद विश्व के दूसरे देशों के साथ भारत के राजनयिक एवं सांस्कृतिक सम्बन्ध जुड़े। पर्यटकों के साथ-साथ राजनीतिज्ञों और साहित्यकारों को भी विदेश यात्रा के पर्याप्त अवसर मिले। विभिन्न प्रकार की छात्रवृत्तियों के माध्यम से बहुत से लोग विदेशों में पढ़ने गए। बहुत से लोगों ने विदेशों में उपलब्ध आजीविका के अवसरों का लाभ उठाया। इन सबके परिणामस्वरूप प्रचुर मात्रा में यात्रावृत्तांत लिखे गए। विदेश-विषयक यात्रावृतांत्तों में रूस और स्वदेश-विषयक यात्रावृतांत्तों में लेखकों की दृष्टि कश्मीर से कन्याकुमारी तक व्याप्त हुई।

उपर्युक्त गद्यांश को ध्यानपूर्वक पढ़ें और निम्नलिखित प्रश्नों के उत्तर के लिए सही विकल्प को चुनें:

1. भारत कब स्वतंत्र हुआ?
   A. 15 अगस्त 1947 B. 15 अगस्त 1946
   C. 15 अगस्त 1948 D. 15 अगस्त 1949
2. स्वतंत्र भारत के अन्य देशों के साथ किस प्रकार के संबंध जुड़े?
   A. राजनीतिक
   B. राजनयिक
   C. धार्मिक
   D. राजनयिक एवं सांस्कृतिक
3. आजीविका का क्या अर्थ है?
   A. उपार्जन B. वेतन
   C. मेहनत D. रोजगार
4. यात्रा-वृत्तांत का क्या अर्थ है?
   A. भ्रमण B. पर्यटन
   C. सफरनामा D. विदेशभ्रमण
5. स्वतंत्र का विलोम शब्द है:
   A. परतंत्र B. आजाद
   C. गुलामी D. मुक्ति

गद्यांश 3

युवा वर्ग का मस्तिष्क नई-नई बातों की ओर ज्यादा तेज दौड़ता है। उसमें अन्य वर्ग के व्यक्तियों से अधिक आवेश और शक्ति होती है। इस अवस्था में यदि सही शिक्षा और उचित मार्ग-दर्शन न मिले तो यही शक्ति प्रेरणा और निर्माण के स्थान पर विनाश की ओर ले जाती है। बिगड़ने और बनने की यही आयु होती है। दुर्भाग्य से हमारे देश में शिक्षा पद्धति केवल उपाधि बाँटने का काम ही करती है। एक सम्पूर्ण व्यक्तित्वपूर्ण मनुष्य बनाना आज की शिक्षा पद्धति के लिए मुश्किल है।

उपर्युक्त गद्यांश को ध्यानपूर्वक पढ़ें और निम्नलिखित प्रश्नों के उत्तर के लिए सही विकल्प को चुनें।

1. निर्माण का विलोम शब्द क्या हैं?
   A. रचना B. बनावट
   C. विनाश D. सृजन
2. मार्ग-दर्शन का क्या अर्थ है?
   A. उपाधि B. रास्ता
   C. उद्देश्य D. रास्ता दिखलाना
3. शक्ति विनाश की ओर कब अग्रसर होती है?
   A. अधिक आवेश और शक्ति के अभाव में
   B. सही शिक्षा और उचित मार्ग दर्शन के अभाव में
   C. दुर्भाग्यपूर्ण शिक्षा पद्धति के कारण
   D. इनमें से कोई नहीं
4. हमारे देश की शिक्षा पद्धति क्या कार्य करती है?
   A. मार्ग-दर्शन B. शक्ति प्रेरणा
   C. उपाधि देना D. उपर्युक्त सभी
5. दुर्भाग्य का विपरीत शब्द है:
   A. भाग्य B. सौभाग्य
   C. भाग्यशाली D. भाग्यवान

गद्यांश 4

भिखारी की भाँति गिड़गिड़ाना प्रेम की भाषा नहीं है। यहाँ तक कि मुक्ति के लिए भगवान् की उपासना करना भी अधम उपासना में गिना जाता है। प्रेम कोई पुरस्कार नहीं चाहता। प्रेम सर्वथा प्रेम के लिए ही होता है। भक्त इसलिए प्रेम करता है कि बिना प्रेम किए वह रह ही नहीं सकता। जब तुम किसी मनोहर प्राकृतिक दृश्य को देखकर उस पर मोहित हो जाते हो तो तुम किसी फल की याचना नहीं करते और न वह दृश्य ही तुमसे कुछ माँगता है। फिर भी उस दृश्य का दर्शन तुम्हारे मन को आनंद से भर देता है।

उपर्युक्त गद्यांश को ध्यानपूर्वक पढ़ें और निम्नलिखित प्रश्नों के उत्तर के लिए सही विकल्प का चयन करें:

1. प्रेम का उद्देश्य क्या होता है?
A. मुक्ति B. उपासना
C. भक्ति D. प्रेम

2. मुक्ति का अर्थ है:
A. आजादी B. स्वतंत्रता
C. परतंत्र D. निर्वाण

3. कैसी उपासना अधम मानी गई है?
A. प्रेम की उपासना B. भगवान की उपासना
C. मुक्ति की उपासना D. भक्ति की उपासना

4. मनोहर शब्द हैं:
A. विशेषण B. संज्ञा
C. सर्वनाम D. अव्यव

5. प्राकृतिक शब्द का अर्थ है:
A. ईश्वरीय B. मानव संबंधी
C. प्रकृति संबंधी D. प्रेम संबंधी

गद्यांश 5

कुछ लोग भाग्यवादी होते हैं और सब-कुछ भाग्य के सहारे छोड़कर कर्म से विरत हो जाते हैं। ऐसे लोग समाज के लिए बोझ हैं। वे कभी कोई बड़ा काम नहीं कर पाते। बड़ी-बड़ी खोज, बड़े-बड़े आविष्कार और बड़े-बड़े निर्माण कार्य कर्मशील लोगों के द्वारा ही संभव हो सके हैं। हम अपनी बुद्धि और प्रतिभा तथा कार्य-क्षमता के बल पर सही मार्ग पर चल सकते हैं, किन्तु बिना कठिन श्रम के अपने लक्ष्य तक नहीं पहुँच सकते। कठिन परिश्रम करने के बाद पाई गई सफलता हमारे मन को अलौकिक आनंद से भर देती है। यदि हम अपने कार्य में अपेक्षित श्रम नहीं करते तो हमारा मन ग्लानि का अनुभव करता है।

उपर्युक्त गद्यांश को ध्यानपूर्वक पढ़ें और निम्नलिखित प्रश्नों के उत्तर के लिए सही विकल्प चुनें:

1. "आविष्कार" शब्द का अर्थ है :
A. अनुसंधान B. खोज
C. निर्माण D. विनाश

2. अलौकिक शब्द का क्या अर्थ है?
A. संसारिक B. भौतिक
C. अमानुषी D. प्राकृतिक

3. सफलता का विलोम क्या है?
A. सफल B. असफल
C. सफलतापूर्वक D. असफलता

4. परिश्रम करने और न करने से हमारे जीवन पर क्या प्रभाव पड़ता है?
A. लोग भाग्यवादी बन जाते हैं
B. कर्म से विरत हो जाते हैं
C. मन में ग्लानि का अनुभव होता है
D. इनमें से कोई नहीं

5. किस प्रकार के लोग समाज के लिए बोझ हैं?
A. भाग्यवादी B. कर्मठ
C. परिश्रमी D. प्रतिभाशाली

गद्यांश 6

वैदिक काल से हिमालय के पहाड़ बहुत पवित्र माने जाते हैं। इसमें कोई सन्देह नहीं कि हिमालय के पहाड़ों का दृश्य अति सुन्दर है। उसकी विशालता को देखकर मन में आनन्द और कृतज्ञता की लहर उठती है। ऐसा लगता है कि यह विशाल सृष्टि प्रभु की अनुपम देन है। सारी सृष्टि के प्रति समभाव जाग्रत होता है। वस्तुतः यह दृष्टि कोरी कल्पनात्मक या आध्यात्मिक नहीं है। देखा जाए तो सारे भारत की जलवायु का समतोल करने वाले यह हिमालय के पहाड़ हैं, विशेषकर उत्तरी भारत को वर्षा और पानी देने वाले ये ही हैं। गंगोत्री, यमुनोत्री, बद्री, केदार को तीर्थ माना जाता है, जो व्यर्थ कल्पना नहीं है। उन स्थानों से निकलने वाली पवित्र नदियाँ ही वास्तव में हमारी प्राणदात्री रही हैं।

उपर्युक्त गद्यांश को ध्यानपूर्वक पढ़ें और निम्नलिखित प्रश्नों के उत्तर के लिए सही विकल्प चुनें :

1. हिमालय के पर्वत बहुत पवित्र कब से माने जाते हैं?
A. पाषाण काल से B. वैदिक काल से
C. प्राचीन काल से D. आधुनिक काल से

2. विशालता शब्द है :
A. जातिवाचक B. भाववाचक
C. विशेषण D. सर्वनाम

3. भारत की जलवायु को समतोल कौन करता है?
A. गंगोत्री B. यमुनोत्री
C. केदार D. हिमालय

4. सृष्टि का समानार्थक शब्द है :
A. सृजन B. रचना
C. प्रकृति D. संसार

5. प्राणदात्री का क्या अर्थ है?
A. गंगोत्री
B. यमुनोत्री
C. प्राणसंचार करने वाली
D. समभाव जाग्रत करने वाली

गद्यांश 7

सच्चा मित्र एक शिक्षक की भाँति होता है। जिस प्रकार शिक्षक अपने छात्र को सन्मार्ग की ही ओर अग्रसर करता है, उसी प्रकार एक सच्चा मित्र अपने मित्र को पाप के गर्त में गिरने से बचाता है। मानव-जीवन अधिक रहस्यपूर्ण है। कभी-कभी जीवन में ऐसे अवसर उपस्थित हो जाते हैं, जब मनुष्य की धर्मबुद्धि नष्ट हो जाती है और उसका मन द्रुत गति से पाप की ओर दौड़ता है। ऐसे समय में मित्र का ही उपदेश अधिक कल्याणकारी सिद्ध होता है। मित्र के उपदेश का जितना प्रभाव हृदय पर पड़ता है, उतना और किसी का नहीं पड़ता है।

उपर्युक्त गद्यांश को ध्यानपूर्वक पढ़ें और निम्नलिखित प्रश्नों के उत्तर के लिए सही विकल्प चुनें :

1. सच्चा मित्र किस प्रकार का होता है?

A. विपत्ति में सहायता देने वाला
B. गलत मार्ग पर चलने से रोकने वाला
C. शिक्षक के भाँति
D. धार्मिक गुरु की तरह

2. सन्मार्ग शब्द का विपरीत शब्द है :

A. अग्रसर B. कुमार्ग
C. सुमार्ग D. मार्गदर्शक

3. व्यक्ति को पाप के गर्त्त में गिरने से कौन बचाता है?

A. शिक्षक B. भाई
C. पिता D. सच्चा मित्र

4. मानव पाप की ओर कब दौड़ता है?

A. जब स्वार्थी बन जाता है
B. जब धर्म-बुद्धि नष्ट हो जाती है
C. जब सच्चामित्र साथ छोड़ देता है
D. जब धनवान बन जाता है

5. उपदेश में कौन-सा उपसर्ग है?

A. उ B. उप
C. दे D. देश

गद्यांश 8

सब तरह के भावों को प्रकट करने की योग्यता रखने वाली और निर्दोष होने पर भी यदि कोई भाषा अपना निज का साहित्य नहीं रखती, तो वह रूपवती भिखारिन की तरह कदापि आदरणीय नहीं हो सकती। उनकी शोभा, उसकी बड़ी सम्पन्नता, उसकी मान-मर्यादा उसके साहित्य पर ही अवलम्बित रहती है। उसके विचारों और राजनैतिक स्थितियों का प्रतिबिम्ब देखने को यदि कहीं मिल सकता है, तो उसके ग्रन्थ साहित्य में मिल सकता है। सामाजिक शक्ति या सजीवता, सामाजिक अशक्ति या निर्जीवता और सामाजिक सभ्यता तथा असभ्यता का निर्णायक एकमात्र साहित्य है।

उपर्युक्त गद्यांश को ध्यानपूर्वक पढ़ें और निम्नलिखित प्रश्नों के उत्तर के लिए सही विकल्प चुनें :

1. साहित्य विहीन भाषा किस प्रकार की होती है?

A. आदरणीय B. भिखारिन
C. रूपवती D. रूपवती भिखारिन

2. रूपवती का पुल्लिंग रूप है:

A. रूपवान B. सुन्दर
C. सुन्दरी D. रूपवत

3. भाषा की मान मर्यादा किस पर निर्भर करती है?

A. लिपि पर B. साहित्यकार पर
C. भक्ति पर D. साहित्य पर

4. ''सम्पन्नता'' शब्द का विपरीत शब्द है:

A. गरीबी B. विपन्न
C. अमीर D. विपन्नता

5. राजनैतिक, सामाजिक शक्ति का दर्शन हमें किसमें मिलता है?

A. समाज B. राज्य
C. नेता D. साहित्य

गद्यांश 9

स्वतंत्र भारत का सम्पूर्ण दायित्व आज विद्यार्थियों के ही ऊपर है, क्योंकि आज जो विद्यार्थी हैं, वे ही कल स्वतंत्र भारत के नागरिक होंगे। भारत की उन्नति, उसका उत्थान उन्हीं की उन्नति और उत्थान पर निर्भर करता है। अतः विद्यार्थियों को चाहिए कि वे अपने भावी जीवन का निर्माण बड़ी सतर्कता और सावधानी के साथ करें। उन्हें प्रत्येक क्षण अपने राष्ट्र, अपने समाज, अपने धर्म, अपनी संस्कृति को अपनी आँखों के सामने रखना चाहिए, जिससे उनके जीवन से राष्ट्र को कुछ बल प्राप्त हो सके। जो विद्यार्थी राष्ट्रीय दृष्टिकोण से अपने जीवन का निर्माण नहीं करते, वे राष्ट्र और समाज के लिए भार-स्वरूप हैं।

उपर्युक्त गद्यांश को ध्यानपूर्वक पढ़ें और निम्नलिखित प्रश्नों के उत्तर के लिए सही विकल्प चुनें :

1. भारत की उन्नति किस पर निर्भर करती है?

A. युवाओं पर B. नेताओं पर
C. साहित्यकारों पर D. विद्यार्थियों पर

2. **उन्नति** का समानार्थक शब्द है :

A. पतन B. उत्थान
C. विकास D. उदय

3. **उत्थान** का विपरीत शब्द है :

A. उदय B. पतन
C. पराजय D. हार

4. किसे अपने जीवन का निर्माण सतर्कता और सावधानी से करना चाहिए?

A. युवाओं को B. नेताओं को
C. बच्चों को D. विद्यार्थियों को

5. धर्म, संस्कृति तथा समाज का रक्षक कौन है?

A. नागरिक B. ग्रामीण
C. विद्यार्थी D. युवा

गद्यांश 10

हास्य एक ऐसा माध्यम है, जो नीरस-जीवन को भी सुखद बना देता है। हास्य का जादू इतना प्रभावशाली होता है कि वह छूत के रोग की तरह चारों ओर फैल जाता है। जिसने कभी हँसना नहीं सीखा, सचमुच उसने जीना नहीं सीखा। सामान्यतः मनुष्य को जीवन में इतनी मुसीबतें झेलनी पड़ती हैं कि वह अपने जीवन को पहाड़ समझने लगता है। ऐसे दूभर जीवन को यदि जीने योग्य बनाना हो तो उसके लिए आवश्यक है कि जीवन में हँसने की गुंजाइश हो। हँसी के सहारे मनुष्य अपने कष्टों को भुलाने का प्रयत्न करता है। संघर्ष, तनाव, व्यस्तता, घुटन यदि आज के जीवन की सहज देन हैं, तो इनसे बचने के लिए यह आवश्यक है कि हम हँसना सीखें।

उपर्युक्त गद्यांश को ध्यानपूर्वक पढ़ें और निम्नलिखित प्रश्नों के उत्तर के लिए सही विकल्प चुनें :

1. नीरस जीवन को कौन सुखद बना देता है?

A. संगीत B. गीत
C. आमोद प्रमोद D. हास्य

2. **नीरस** का संधि विच्छेद है :

A. नी + रस B. नि + रस
C. निः + रस D. नीः + रस

3. किसका जीवन व्यर्थ है?

A. जिसने रोना नहीं सीखा
B. जिसने हँसना नहीं सीखा
C. जिसने गाना नहीं सीखा
D. इनमें से कोई नहीं

4. **हँसना** शब्द है :

A. संज्ञा B. विशेषण
C. क्रिया विशेषण D. क्रिया

5. तनाव और घुटन से बचने के लिए क्या करना चाहिए?

A. रोना चाहिए B. गाना चाहिए
C. हँसना चाहिए D. काम करना चाहिए

गद्यांश 11

किसी पुस्तक को पढ़ने में जल्दी नहीं करनी चाहिए, जो कुछ लेखक कहता है, उसे समझने की चेष्टा करनी चाहिए। प्रत्येक शब्द का अर्थ समझने की चेष्टा करनी चाहिए। यदि लेखक योग्य है, तो दूसरी बार वह पुस्तक और अधिक आनन्द देगी और तीसरी बार और अधिक। प्रत्येक बार अध्ययन करने पर आपको नवीन सुन्दर और नए विचार मिलेंगे और उसे आप जितना ही पढ़ेंगे, उतना ही स्नेह करने लगेंगे। सहस्रों व्यक्तियों ने गीता और रामायण तथा कुरान और बाइबिल को बार-बार पढ़ा है। उनका अनुभव है कि प्रत्येक बार उन्हें नई सूझ और नए विचार मिलते गए। कुछ लोग तो इस बात पर गर्व करते हैं कि उन्होंने अमुक पुस्तक को अनेक बार पढ़ा है, उन्हें कंठस्थ हो गई है।

उपर्युक्त गद्यांश को ध्यानपूर्वक पढ़ें और निम्नलिखित प्रश्नों के उत्तर के लिए सही विकल्प चुनें :

1. किसे समझने की चेष्टा करनी चाहिए?

A. पुस्तक B. रामायण
C. महाभारत D. गीता

2. पुस्तक की सजीवता किस पर निर्भर करती है?

A. लेखक B. प्रकाशक
C. पाठक D. चिन्तक

3. **आनन्द** का विपरीत शब्द है :

A. शोक B. दुख
C. संताप D. खुशी

4. नवीन, सुन्दर और नए विचार हमें कहाँ से प्राप्त होता हैं?

A. पुस्तक को बार-बार पढ़कर
B. सुनकर
C. भाषण से
D. अच्छे व्यक्तियों से मिलने पर

5. **कंठस्थ** शब्द का शब्दार्थ है :

A. कंठ में स्थित B. सुंदर कंठ
C. जबानी याद D. पंडित जी

गद्यांश 12

अहिंसा परम धर्म है और हिंसा आपद् धर्म। मनुष्य बराबर अहिंसा की ओर चलना चाहता है, किन्तु परिस्थितियाँ उससे हिंसा कराती है, अर्थात् परमधर्म की रक्षा के लिए आदमी बराबर आपद्धर्म से काम लेता रहा है। भारत अपनी सेनाओं को विघटित कर दे, तब भी उसका अपमान उससे अधिक होने वाला नहीं, जितना नेफा में हुआ। किन्तु परमधर्म पर टिकने की सामर्थ्य अगर भारत में नहीं है, तो आपद्धर्म पर उसे आना चाहिए। व्यवहारतः आपद्धर्म परमधर्म का विरोधी नहीं, उसका रक्षक है।

उपर्युक्त गद्यांश को ध्यानपूर्वक पढ़ें और निम्नलिखित प्रश्नों के उत्तर के लिए सही विकल्प चुनें :

1. **परमधर्म** का विपरीत शब्द है :

A. महान धर्म B. आपद्धर्म
C. सच्चाधर्म D. इनमें से कोई नहीं

2. आपद्धर्म किसे कहा जाता है?

A. अहिंसा B. सत्याग्रह
C. विपत्ति D. हिंसा

3. मानव से हिंसा कौन करवाती है?

A. लोभ B. स्वार्थ
C. द्वेष D. परिस्थितियाँ

4. **सामर्थ्य** का शब्दार्थ है :

A. संघर्ष B. परिश्रम
C. शक्ति D. पराक्रम

5. **परमधर्म** की रक्षा कौन करता है?

A. अहिंसा B. हिंसा
C. आपदधर्म D. युद्ध

गद्यांश 13

वर्तमान काल विज्ञापन का युग माना जाता है। समाचार-पत्रों के अतिरिक्त रेडियो और टेलीविजन भी विज्ञापन के सफल साधन हैं। विज्ञापन का मूल उद्देश्य उत्पादक और भोक्ता में सीधा सम्पर्क स्थापित करना होता है। जितना अधिक विज्ञापन किसी पदार्थ का होगा, उतनी ही उसकी लोकप्रियता बढ़ेगी। इन विज्ञापनों पर धन तो अधिक व्यय होता है, पर इनसे बिक्री बढ़ जाती है। ग्राहक जब इन आकर्षक विज्ञापनों को देखता है तो वह उस वस्तु-विशेष के प्रति आकृष्ट होकर उसे खरीदने को बाध्य हो जाता है।

उपर्युक्त गद्यांश को ध्यानपूर्वक पढ़ें और निम्नलिखित प्रश्नों के उत्तर के लिए सही विकल्प चुनें :

1. वर्तमान को किसका युग माना जाता है?
A. फैशन B. विज्ञापन
C. संगीत D. धन

2. उत्पादक तथा भोक्ता के बीच कौन संबंध स्थापित करता है?
A. टेलीविजन B. समाचार-पत्र
C. रेडियो D. विज्ञापन

3. **वर्तमान** शब्द का विपरीत शब्द है :
A. अर्वाचीन B. आधुनिक
C. आजकल D. प्राचीन

4. **आकर्षक** का शब्दार्थ है :
A. विकर्षक B. सुन्दर
C. मनमोहक D. आश्चर्यजनक

5. भोक्ता किस कारण वस्तुओं को खरीदने के लिए बाध्य हो जाता है?
A. विज्ञापन
B. आकर्षक विज्ञापन
C. लोकप्रियता के कारण
D. आसानी से उपलब्ध होना

गद्यांश 14

लगभग दो सौ वर्ष की गुलामी ने भारत के राष्ट्रीय स्वाभिमान को पैरों से रौंद डाला, हमारी संस्कृति को समाप्त कर दिया, हमारे विश्वासों को हिला दिया और हमारे आत्मविश्वास को चकनाचूर कर दिया, किन्तु अपने इस बूढ़े देश से प्यार करने वाले, इसके एक सामान्य संकेत पर प्राण न्यौछावर करने वाले दीवानों का अभाव न था। एक आवाज उठी और देखते ही देखते राष्ट्र का दबा हुआ आत्माभिमान उन्मत्त हो उठा। इतिहास साक्षी है जाने और अनजाने सहस्त्रों देशभक्त स्वतंत्रता की अनमोल निधि को पाने के लिए शहीद हो गए।

उपर्युक्त गद्यांश को ध्यानपूर्वक पढ़ें और निम्नलिखित प्रश्नों के उत्तर के लिए सही विकल्प चुनें :

1. **स्वाभिमान** का संधि विच्छेद है:
A. स्वा + भिमान B. स्वः + अभिमान
C. स्व + अभिमान D. स्वा + अभिमान

2. भारत का राष्ट्रीय स्वाभिमान किस कारण समाप्त हो गया था?
A. लम्बे गुलामी से B. निरंकुश शासक से
C. स्वार्थी मानव से D. धर्म के विनाश से

3. **आत्मविश्वास** का शब्दार्थ है
A. घमण्ड B. गर्व
C. अपने पर विश्वास D. अभिमान

4. भारत की अनमोल निधि को पाने के लिए कौन शहीद हो गए?
A. देशभक्त B. नेता
C. युवा D. युवती

5. **अनमोल निधि** का शब्दार्थ है:
A. अनन्त खजाना B. अमूल्य खजाना
C. बहुमूल्य D. स्वतंत्रता

गद्यांश 15

दुनिया के विभिन्न देशों के विकास पर विहंगम दृष्टि डालने से यह स्पष्ट हो जाता है कि आज जिस देश ने वैज्ञानिक उपलब्धियों के सहारे अपना औद्योगीकरण कर लिया, उसी को उन्नत देश कहा जाता है। जिस देश में औद्योगीकरण का स्तर नीचा है, वह पिछड़ा हुआ देश कहा जाता है। वैज्ञानिक आविष्कारों और औद्योगीकरण के आधार पर ही किसी देश की प्रगति को आँका जाता रहा है। विज्ञान ने मानव को पूरी तरह बदल दिया है।

उपर्युक्त गद्यांश को ध्यानपूर्वक पढ़ें और निम्नलिखित प्रश्नों के उत्तर के लिए सही विकल्प चुनें :

1. **विहंगम दृष्टि** का क्या अर्थ है?
A. एक झलक B. गहन दृष्टि
C. गहन चिन्तन D. इनमें से कोई नहीं

2. **विकास** का विपरीत शब्द है :
A. उत्थान B. उदय
C. पतन D. विनाश

3. **वैज्ञानिक** शब्द में कौन-सा प्रत्यय हैं?
A. निक B. वै
C. ईक D. इक

4. मानव जीवन को किसने बदल दिया है :
A. विकास B. वैज्ञानिक
C. विज्ञान D. उद्योग

5. किसी भी देश की स्तर को किससे नापा जाता है?
A. उपलब्धियों पर B. औद्योगीकरण से
C. वैज्ञानिकों से D. आविष्कारों से

गद्यांश 16

विश्व का वर्तमान उन्नत रूप मानव-श्रम की ही कहानी कह रहा है। गगन चुंबी अट्टालिकाएँ, लंबी-चौड़ी सड़कें, बड़े-बड़े विशाल नगर आकाश में उड़ते वायुयान तथा मानव-जीवन को सुखी और समृद्ध बनाने में योगदान करने वाले ज्ञान-विज्ञान के अनन्त रूप-ये सभी मनुष्य के श्रम का जयघोष करते हैं। स्पष्ट है कि मनुष्य और उसका शरीर विधाता की अनुपम रचना है जो निश्चय ही महान उद्देश्यों की संपूर्ति के

लिए दिया गया है। इस दुर्लभ तन को यदि हम आलस्य, प्रसाद अथवा घटिया कामों में गँवा देते हैं तो उस विधाता के प्रति अन्याय करते हैं।

उपर्युक्त गद्यांश को ध्यानपूर्वक पढ़ें और निम्नलिखित प्रश्नों के उत्तर के लिए सही विकल्प चुनें :

1. विश्व का वर्तमान रूप किसका उद्योतक है?
   A. चिन्तक का B. नेता का
   C. वैज्ञानिक का D. मानव श्रम
2. **गगन चुंबी अट्टालिकाएँ** का अर्थ है :
   A. आकाश में उड़ने वाला B. आकाश को छूने वाला
   C. बहुमंजिली इमारत D. इनमें से कोई नहीं
3. आकाश का समानार्थक शब्द है :
   A. वसुन्धरा B. धरा
   C. पयोद D. गगन
4. **सुखी** का विपरीत शब्द है :
   A. प्रसन्न B. अप्रसन्न
   C. दुखी D. उदासी
5. विधाता की अनुपम रचना क्या है?
   A. मानव शरीर B. समुद्र
   C. वन D. पृथ्वी

गद्यांश 17

हमारे देश में एक ऐसा भी युग था जब नैतिक और आध्यात्मिक विकास ही जीवन का वास्तविक लक्ष्य माना जाता था। अहिंसा की भावना सर्वोपरि थी। आज पूरा जीवन दर्शन ही बदल गया है। सर्वत्र पैसे की हाय-हाय तथा धन का उपार्जन ही मुख्य ध्येय हो गया है, भले ही धन-उपार्जन के तरीके गलत ही क्यों न हों? इन सबका असर मनुष्य के प्रतिदिन के जीवनं पर पड़ रहा है। समाज का वातावरण दूषित हो गया है—

बाह्य वातावरण तो दूषित है ही, आज सब जानते हैं पर्यावरण की समस्याएँ कितनी चिन्तनीय हो उठी है। इन सबके कारण मानसिक और शारीरिक तनाव-खिंचाव और व्याधियाँ पैदा हो रही हैं।

उपर्युक्त गद्यांश को ध्यानपूर्वक पढ़ें और निम्नलिखित प्रश्नों के उत्तर के लिए सही विकल्प चुनें :

1. भारत का प्राचीन आदर्श था :
   A. सत्य और अहिंसा B. नैतिक और आध्यात्मिक विकास
   C. धन उपार्जन D. इनमें से कोई नहीं
2. **अहिंसा** का विपरीत शब्द है :
   A. हिंसा B. सत्याग्रह
   C. विनम्रता D. नैतिकता
3. जीवन दर्शन क्यों बदल गया है?
   A. हिंसा के कारण B. अहिंसा के कारण
   C. धन लिप्सा के कारण D. आध्यात्मिक विकास के कारण
4. समाज का वातावरण दूषित क्यों हो गया है?
   A. शारीरिक तनाव B. मानसिक व्याधियाँ
   C. पर्यावरण की समस्याएँ D. धन उपार्जन के गलत तरीके
5. **पर्यावरण** का शब्दार्थ है:
   A. जलमंडल B. स्थलमंडल
   C. वायुमंडल D. वातावरण

उत्तरमाला

गद्यांश 1

1. C 2. D 3. B 4. A 5. D

गद्यांश 2

1. A 2. D 3. D 4. C 5. A

गद्यांश 3

1. C 2. D 3. B 4. C 5. B

गद्यांश 4

1. D 2. D 3. C 4. A 5. C

गद्यांश 5

1. B 2. D 3. D 4. C 5. A

गद्यांश 6

1. B 2. B 3. D 4. A 5. C

गद्यांश 7

1. C 2. B 3. D 4. B 5. B

गद्यांश 8

1. D 2. A 3. D 4. D 5. D

गद्यांश 9

1. D 2. B 3. B 4. D 5. C

गद्यांश 10

1. D 2. C 3. B 4. D 5. C

गद्यांश 11

1. A 2. A 3. A 4. A 5. C

गद्यांश 12

1. B 2. D 3. D 4. C 5. C

गद्यांश 13

1. B 2. D 3. D 4. C 5. B

गद्यांश 14

1. C 2. A 3. C 4. A 5. B

गद्यांश 15

1. A 2. D 3. C 4. C 5. B

गद्यांश 16

1. D 2. C 3. D 4. C 5. A

गद्यांश 17

1. B 2. A 3. C 4. D 5. D

●●●

English Language

1

Comprehension Passages

ENGLISH LANGUAGE COMPREHENSION

The objective of language comprehension test is to ascertain the ability of the candidates to understand the passage properly.

Therefore candidates are required to take notice of the following points:

1. Read the full passage very attentively and intelligently.
2. Try to comprehend the gist of it.
3. Make a mental note of all the important details and points given in the passage.
4. Read the passage for the second time in case you have not been able to understand it satisfactorily.
5. Divide the time proportionately for all the passages.
6. Answer the questions on the basis of facts, as given in the paragraph.
7. Don't waste much time in answering the questions of any one passage.
8. Check all the answers once again, very carefully, to see whether any question is left unanswered by mistake.

MODEL QUESTIONS (FOR PRACTICE)

Directions: *Each of the following passages is followed by five questions. Read the passage carefully and then answer the questions that follow each. For each question, four probable answers A, B, C and D are given. Only one out of these is correct. Choose the correct answer.*

PASSAGE-1

The use of words like 'welcome', 'thank you', 'please', etc., at the right moment reflects a polite nature. The civic sense also lies within the scope of good manners. We should not shout or talk loudly in public places like hospitals and libraries and create disturbance. We should not cheat people or make fun of them. Cleanliness is also necessary. We must not throw the waste on roads and make use of dustbins. We should not harm the public property as it belongs to all of us. While in a queue, discipline should be maintained. We must give fair chance to others.

1. Expressions like 'welcome' 'thank you' and 'please' reflect
A. happiness B. discipline
C. civic sense D. polite nature

2. While in a library, we should
A. respect others B. avoid arguments
C. talk in low tone D. be courteous

3. A public property belongs to
A. nobody B. all of us
C. government D. one who maintains it

4. Discipline is
A. the rule of proper conduct or action
B. the rule of road sense
C. making use of dustbins
D. forming a queue

5. The most appropriate title for this passage would be
A. Polite Nature B. Courtesy
C. Good Manners D. Civic Sense

PASSAGE-2

There is an old proverb 'Early to bed and early to rise makes a man healthy and wise.' I am in the habit of getting up early in the morning and have formed the habit of taking long morning walks in the past two years. It is a light exercise and best for physical fitness. The morning air which is fresh and pure is beneficial for the lungs. The early rays of the rising sun are good for healthy skin. 'Health is wealth' and doctors also recommend morning walk to their patients for gaining sound health and freshness of energy.

1. What is good for lungs?
A. Sunrays B. Fresh air
C. Sound sleep D. Light exercise

2. What is a light exercise?
A. Early to bed B. Early to rise
C. Morning walk D. Gaining sound health

3. What is good for skin?
A. Fresh air B. Morning air
C. Morning walk D. Rising sun's rays

4. What is best for physical fitness?
A. Light exercise B. Long morning walk
C. Early to rise D. Fresh and pure air

5. Long morning walk
A. bring sound sleep
B. ensures physical fitness
C. ensures healthy skin
D. keeps healthy, wealthy and wise

PASSAGE-3

Mahatma Gandhi lived a splendid long life and has set great moral standards before us. He showed to the world the true way to peace. He wished to see India prosper but he became a martyr for the noble cause of Hindu-Muslim unity at the time of partition when a religious fanatic, Nathuram Godse, shot him dead on January 30, 1948. His last words were 'Hey Ram'. He lived and died for his country and countryman.

1. Mahatma Gandhi showed the world the true way to
A. prosperity B. love
C. truth D. peace

2. Mahatma Gandhi became a martyr for the noble cause of
A. truth B. non-violence
C. freedom of India D. Hindu-Muslim unity

3. Mahatma Gandhi was shot dead
A. before India achieved independence
B. by a mad man
C. by an intolerant religious person
D. by a non-religious person

4. Mahatma Gandhi set great moral standards. It means
A. he was a great religious teacher
B. he was a great moralist
C. he made India morally stronger
D. moral was everything to him

5. Gandhiji lived and died for his country and countryman. It means
A. he was born in India and died in India
B. he was a patriot
C. he was a great moralist
D. he sacrified his life for India and her people

PASSAGE-4

On one hot day a crow felt very thirsty. He flew from one place to another in search of water. After long hours of labour he found a pitcher. Eagerly, he perched on the mouth of the pitcher. He found that the water was at the bottom of the vessel. He tried his best to dip his beak but did not succeed. He did not know what to do. Suddenly some pebbles lying nearby gave him an idea. One by one he dropped the pebbles with his beak into the pitcher. The level of water slowly came up to the mouth of the pitcher. The crow then drank the water and quenched his thirst.

1. The crow found a pitcher
A. as it flew
B. after many hours of labour
C. full of water
D. which was empty

2. What is the moral of the passage?
A. No pains, no gains
B. God helps those who help themselves
C. Necessity is the mother of invention
D. Try and try again, you will succeed at last

3. The crow flew from place to place
A. in search of pitcher B. in search of pebbles
C. in search of water D. in search of a vessel

4. The pitcher, the crow found
A. was full of water
B. was dry
C. had little water in the bottom
D. had water up to its mouth

5. As the crow dropped pebbles into the pitcher, what happend?
A. The pitcher broke down
B. The water leaked one of the pitcher
C. The level of water into the pitcher rose up slowly
D. Water level immediately rose to the mouth of the pitcher

PASSAGE-5

Once upon a time a crane and a fox lived in a forest. They were good friend. One day the fox invited the crane to a feast. He made a tasty food and served it before the crane on a plate. The crane could not eat anything because of the long beak. But the fox licked all his food. The crane felt insulted. He decided to teach the fox a lesson. Next day he invited the fox. He prepared the same tasty food and placed it in front of the fox inside a narrow glass. The crane ate easily while the fox looked on. Now, it was the fox's turn to remain hungry.

1. What is the moral of the passage?
A. Beware of the wicked
B. One good turn deserves another
C. Be contented with what you have
D. Tit for tat

2. The crane could not eat tasty food because the
A. food was served in a shallow plate
B. food was very hot
C. food was served in a long jar
D. crane was not hungry

3. The fox had to remain hungry because
A. the food served was not enough in quantity
B. the food was served inside a narrow glass
C. the food served was not tasty
D. the food was all liquid

4. Why did the crane feel insulted?
A. Because he was invited to feast but he could not eat anything
B. Because the food was served in a shallow plate and he could not eat
C. Because the food was too hot
D. Because the fox gulped all the food quickly

5. The crane successfully taught a lesson to the fox when he invited the fox to a feast and served the food
A. in a narrow glass B. in a large plate
C. in a broken plate D. in a long jar

PASSAGE-6

The family set down at the table and began to talk about the summer holidays. They had to decide a place to visit during the vacation. Should they go to their village or to a hill station? The parents preferred the village while the children wished to go the hill station. After few moments of discussion the elders decided to visit both the places. First they shall go to the village for a week and then stay at the hill station for the remaining days. For the first time the family shall be together during the holidays. The children were happy with the holiday plan.

1. The purpose for which the family set down at the table was
- A. to decide a place to visit during the vacation
- B. to educate the children how to carry articles during a visit to a hill station
- C. to decide the date when they should start their journey
- D. to tell the children that they will visit a hill station during this vacation

2. The final plan was to visit
- A. their village
- B. a hill station
- C. their village as well as a hill station
- D. their home town

3. The final decision was made by
- A. the boys B. the girls
- C. the women D. the elders

4. They decided first to go to their village and stay there for
- A. a day B. a week
- C. ten days D. a fortnight

5. Why were children happy?
- A. Because a hill station was included in their holiday plan
- B. Because a visit to their village was excluded from their holiday plan
- C. Because their choice prevailed
- D. Because they were going all alone to the hill station

PASSAGE-7

Once Govind intended to go on pilgrimage with his family. He asked Mirind to accompany. But for his trade's reason, he did not go with him. So Govind thought it safe to leave the box of his jewellery with him, as it was dangerous to leave it in a lone house or take it on the journey. So he went to him with the box. He took him to a lonely place under a tree and handed it over to him. He told Mirind, "Keep it safe with you. I shall return from the journey after six month then I shall take it back from you." Mirind said, "Don't worry, I shall keep it as safe as own."

1. Govind intended to go
- A. for a business trip
- B. to a hill station
- C. on a long journey to a sacred place
- D. to his home town for a long period

2. Why did Govind leave his box of jewellery with Mirind?
- A. Because it was not safe to take the box with him on a long journey
- B. Because Mirind was his fast friend
- C. Because the box was very heavy
- D. Because his house was unsafe

3. Why did Govind take Mirind to a lonely place?
- A. To tell him that the box contained valuable jewellery
- B. So that no third person could see box
- C. To show him what was within the box
- D. To tell him that the box will remain with him

4. Where did Govind hand over the box of jewellery to Mirind?
- A. At Mirind's house
- B. At his own house
- C. In a lonely place
- D. In a lonely place under a tree

5. It was not safe to leave the box in a lone house. Here the word 'lone house' means
- A. a house in a deserted place
- B. a house where none lives
- C. a house without door and lock
- D. a house near the forest

PASSAGE-8

Zahir-ud-din Babar was the first Mughal emperor of India. A descendent of Timur on father's side and Changez Khan on his mother's side, Babar was a brave warrior. After defeating Ibrahim Lodhi in the First Battle of Panipat in 1526 he entered Delhi and soon gained control over Agra. After many more battles with Rajputs he extended his empire over Punjab, Uttar Pradesh and north Bihar. He died at a young age of 48 years in 1530 at his capital Agra without getting much time to consolidate his victories.

1. Zahir-ud-din Babar was the first
- A. Muslim ruler of India B. Mughal ruler of India
- C. Afghan ruler of India D. Turk ruler of India

2. Babar was born in the years
- A. 1480 B. 1482
- C. 1492 D. 1962

3. Babar first occupied
- A. Punjab B. Agra
- C. Delhi D. Panipat

4. Babar was a brave warrior. Here brave warrior means
- A. courageous soldier B. a kind hearted soldier
- C. a clever fighter D. a victorious general

5. Babar extended his empire over Punjab and Uttar Pradesh after many more battles with the
- A. Afghans B. Rajputs
- C. Mughals D. Lodhies

PASSAGE-9

Our National Flag is tricolour. It has three equal horizontal strips. The strip at the top is saffron, in the middle is white and at the bottom is green. The ratio of width to length of the flag is 2 : 3. In the centre of the white strip is a wheel in navy blue. The wheel represents the *chakra.* Its design is similar to the wheel which appears on the abacus of the Sarnath Lion Capital of Ashoka. Its diameter approximates to the width of the white strip. The wheel has 24 spokes. It was adopted by Constituent Assembly on July 22, 1947. We love our national flag. We respect it. We are ready to sacrifice our life to protect its honour. It represents the nation. So it is a symbol of national honour.

1. In our national flag the wheel is located in the centre of

A. saffron strip B. white strip
C. green strip D. blue strip

2. In our national flag which of the strips is at the bottom in our national flag

A. blue C. saffron
B. white D. green

3. Why do we love our national flag?

A. Because it is tricolour
B. Because it has three strips
C. Because it has a wheel at the centre
D. Because it is a symbol of national honour

4. Our national flag was approved by

A. President
B. Lok Sabha
C. Parliament
D. Constituent Assembly

5. The diameter approximates to the width of the white strip. Here the word 'approximates' means

A. is more or less equal
B. is exactly equal
C. is not equal
D. is related

PASSAGE-10

Distance in large cities are long. All the people do not have their own means of transport. They have to depend upon the state or private buses. The number of bus users is very large. Every bus stop is, therefore, crowded. The number of buses is not adequate. Thus people suffer the torture of long wait at the bus stop. Some bus stops are quite orderly. People form queues and get into the buses turn by turn. However, often this order is forgotten and confusion spreads when the bus comes and the law of jungle prevails.

1. Why are the bus stops crowded?

A. Because they are small is size
B. Because the number of passengers is very large
C. Because they are situated at some busy centre
D. Because people do not form queues

2. Long wait at the bus stop is the result of

A. over-crowding in the buses
B. late running of buses
C. shortage of buses
D. slow speed of buses

3. Some bus stops are quite orderly where

A. there is no crowd
B. the number of buses is adequate
C. people do not have to wait for long
D. people form queues and enter the buses one by one

4. Most of the people who travel by buses are

A. non-working
B. do not have their own vehicles
C. have to go a long distance
D. live in large cities

5. What happens when people do not have their own transport?

A. They have to wait for a bus at a bus stop
B. They have to depend upon the state or private buses
C. They have to travel long distances
D. They form queues and get into buses one by one

ANSWERS

Passage	1	2	3	4	5
Passage 1.	D	C	B	A	C
Passage 2.	B	C	D	B	B
Passage 3.	D	D	C	B	D
Passage 4.	B	C	C	C	C
Passage 5.	D	A	B	B	A
Passage 6.	A	C	D	B	A
Passage 7.	C	A	B	D	B
Passage 8.	B	B	C	A	B
Passage 9.	B	D	D	D	A
Passage 10.	B	C	D	B	B

●●●

English Grammar

PARTS OF SPEECH

Part of speech	Definition or Function	Examples
Noun	Name of a person, place, animal, quality or thing	Ram, boy, dog pen, sun, Delhi, truth, honesty
Pronoun	Used in place of a noun	I, you, he she, they
Articles & Determiners	Points out indefinite and definite nouns	a, an, the, few, some
Adjective	Describes a noun or pronoun	big, honest, wooden valuable, quiet, deep, soft, narrow
Adverb	Describes a verb, an adjective or another adverb	silently, widely, softly, quietly, very, carefully
Verb	Tells about action or state of something or someone	is, am, was, have, do, like, walk, work, make, throw, tell
Conjuction	Joins words, clauses or sentences	and, but, when, yet, while, else
Preposition	Links a noun or pronoun to another word	at, to, after, on for, under, over, with
Interjection	Expresses sudden feelings or emotions	Ah!, Alas!, oh!, ouch!, hi!, well!, Hurrah!

NOUNS

A word which denotes a person, a thing, an animal or a place is said to be a noun.

There are two noun numbers in English — the *Singular* and the *Plural*.

Singular Numbers : A noun that denotes one person or one thing, is said to be in the Singular number. For example — book, pencil, bird, dog, hen etc. are in singular number.

Plural Number : A noun that denotes more than one person or one thing is said to be in plural number. For example — boys, pens, lions, girls, men etc. are in plural number.

REMEMBER

Singular	*Plural*	*Singular*	*Plural*
Cat	Cats	Book	Books
Pen	Pens	Room	Rooms
Tree	Trees	Bus	Buses
Bush	Bushes	Box	Boxes
Glass	Glasses	Dish	Dishes
Judge	Judges	Tax	Taxes
Watch	Watches	Calf	Calves
Thief	Thieves	Knife	Knives
Scarf	Scarves	Wife	Wives
Leaf	Leaves	Wolf	Wolves
Half	Halves	Monarch	Monarchs
Roof	Roofs	Hoof	Hoofs
Gulf	Gulfs	Staff	Staffs
Radio	Radios	Bamboo	Bamboos
Folio	Folios	Hero	Heroes
Volcano	Volcanoes	Mango	Mangoes
Potato	Potatoes	Photo	Photos
Piano	Pianos	Baby	Babies
Fly	Flies	Country	Countries
Lady	Ladies	Boy	Boys
Monkey	Monkeys	Ox	Oxen
Child	Children	Man	Men
Woman	Women	Tooth	Teeth
Axis	Axes	Basis	Bases
Foot	Feet	Goose	Geese
Englishman	Englishmen	Radius	Radii
Vertex	Vertices	Stimulus	Stimuli

1. Note the plurals of the following nouns:

Singular	*Plural*	*Singular*	*Plural*
copy	copies	cry	cries
baby	babies	duty	duties
body	bodies	country	countries
family	families	diary	diaries
fly	flies	fairy	fairies
city	cities	spy	spies
army	armies	storey	storeys
bay	bays	monkey	monkeys

2. The following nouns do not undergo any change in plural form, in general.

Singular	*Plural*	*Singular*	*Plural*
deer	deer	sheep	sheep
thousand	thousand	pair	pair
hundred	hundred	score	score
dozen	dozen	gross	gross

Note: We can write—

(*a*) thousands of men; (*b*) two pairs of shoes; (*c*) dozens of mangoes; (*d*) scores of people etc. But—
(*a*) two thousand rupees; (*b*) three hundred men; (*c*) five dozen eggs, etc.

3. The following nouns are usually used in plural forms. They take a plural verb after them—

eatables	fetters	surroundings
riches	alms	spectacles
trousers	pants	scissors
premises	thanks	annals
congratulations	goods	shorts
tongs	pains	arms
breeches	(for troubles)	

4. The following are the nouns which are plural in appearance but are usually used in singular number. They are followed by a singular verb—

news	politics	physics
mathematics	economics	ethics
politics	classics	gallows
statistics	athletics	innings
mechanics	summons	mumps

5. Collective nouns often used as plurals—

public	police	cattle
audience	clergy	folk
people	poultry	nation
elite	gentry	glitterati

6. The nouns that are usually used in singular forms—

advice	hair	rice
fuel	alphabet	machinery
offspring	issue	furniture
mischief	stationery	luggage
bedding	information	abuse

7. Material nouns are always used in singular number—

gold	copper	milk
water	silk	wool

Note: They may be used in plural with a different meaning. copper coins (coppers), chains or fetters (irons), cans made of tin (tins).

GENDERS

The difference in sex is denoted by Gender in grammar. The various genders are as follows :

1. **Masculine Gender :** A noun that denotes a male is said to be of the masculine gender, as man, uncle, ox, boy etc.
2. **Feminine Gender :** A noun that denotes a female is said to be of feminine gender, as woman, aunt, princess, cow etc.
3. **Common Gender :** Nouns which denote both males and females are said to be of the common gender, as friend, cousin, person, parent, baby etc.
4. **Neuter Gender :** A noun that denotes the name of object without life is said to be of neuter gender, as file, table, pencil.

REMEMBER

Masculine	*Feminine*
Boy	Girl
Son	Daughter
Brother	Sister
Murderer	Murderess
Sorcerer	Sorceress
Son-in-law	Daughter-in-law
Father-in-law	Mother-in-law
Man-servant	Maid-servant
Land-lord	Land-lady
Bachelor	Maid
Gentleman	Lady
Monk	Nun
Earl	Countess
Lad	Lass
Sir	Madam
Duke	Dutchess
Emperor	Empress
Milk-man	Milk-maid
Pea-cock	Pea-hen
Step-father	Step-mother
Hero	Heroine
Viceroy	Vicerine
Mr.	Mrs.
Governor	Governess
Master	Mistress
Wizard	Witch
Heir	Heiress
Host	Hostess
Lion	Lioness
Mayor	Mayoress
Actor	Actress
Buck	Doe
Colt	Filly
Dog	Bitch
Horse	Mare
Count	Countess
Hunter	Huntress
Prince	Princess
Abbot	Abbess
God	Goddess
Author	Authoress
Ox	Cow
Widower	Widow
Grand-father	Grand-mother
He-goat	She-goat
Milk-man	Milk-woman
Bridegroom	Bride
Tiger	Tigress
Priest	Priestess
Poet	Poetess
Shepherd	Shepherdess
Nephew	Niece
Stag	Hind

PRONOUNS

The repetition of a noun in a sentence or a set of sentences is really boring. So, instead of repeating the noun, we can use a word (for that noun) called the pronoun.
"A pronoun is a word that we use instead of a noun".

Example:
This is *Sachin. He* plays cricket.
Note: *He* is the pronoun used in place of *Sachin.*

Kinds of Pronouns

1. **Personal pronouns :** A pronoun which is used instead of the name of a person is known as a 'Personal Pronoun'. A list of the 'Personal pronouns' is listed below :

   I, my, mine, me, we (First Person)
   You, your, yours (Second Person)
   He, his, him, she, her, hers, it, its, they, their, theirs, them (Third Person)

2. **Demonstrative, Indefinite and Distributive Pronouns :**

   (a) Demonstrative Pronouns : Pronouns used to point out the objects to which they refer are called Demonstrative Pronouns.

   Examples :
   (i) *This* is a present from my uncle.
   (ii) *These* are merely excuses.
   (iii) Bembay mangoes are better than *those* of Bangaluru.

   (b) Indefinite Pronouns : All pronouns which refer to persons or things in a general way and do not refer to any particular person or thing are called Indefinite Pronouns.

   Examples :
   (i) *Somebody* has stolen my watch.
   (ii) *Few* escaped unhurt.
   (iii) Did you ask *anybody* to come?

   (c) Distributive Pronouns : Each, either, neither are called distributive pronouns because they refer to persons or things one at a time. For this reason they are always singular and followed by the verb in singular.

   Examples :
   (i) *Each* of the men received a reward.
   (ii) *These* men received *each* a reward.
   (iii) *Either* of you can go.

3. **Relative Pronouns :** A relative pronoun refers or relates to some noun going before, which is called its Antecedent.

   Examples :
   (i) I met Hari *who* used to live here.
   (ii) I have found the pen *which* I had lost.
   (iii) Here is the book *that* you lent me.

4. **Interrogative Pronouns :** These pronouns, are used for asking questions.

   Examples :
   (i) *Whose* book is this?
   (ii) *What* will all the neighbours say?
   (iii) *Which* do you prefer, tea or coffee?

   Note : Interrogative pronouns can also be used in asking indirect questions. Consider the following examples :
   (i) I asked *who* was speaking.
   (ii) Tell me *what* you have done.
   (iii) Say *which* you would like best.

Behaviour of the Pronouns

1. If three pronouns are used together in the same sentence they are arranged in the following order :

2	+	3	+	1
↓		↓		↓
Second Person		Third Person		First Person

   Examples :
   I, you and he must help *that* poor man. (Incorrect)
   You, he and I must help *that* poor man. Correct)

2. When two or more singular nouns are joined by and, the pronoun used for them should be plural.

   Examples :
   Mohan and Sohan are friends. *They* play football. *They* live at Lajpat Nagar.

3. But if these nouns joined by and refer to the same person or thing, the pronoun used should be singular.

   Examples :
   (i) Delhi, the beautiful city and the capital of India, is famous for *its* historical monuments.
   (ii) The manager and owner of the firm expressed *his* views on the demands of the workers.

4. When two nouns are used with as well as, the pronoun agrees with the first subject.

   Examples :
   (a) Mohan as well as his friends is doing *his* work.
   (b) The students as well as their teachers are doing *their* work.

5. When two singular nouns joined by 'and' are preceded by *each* or *every,* the pronoun used must be singular and should agree in gender with the second noun.

   Examples :
   (a) Every man and every woman will do *her* best for the nation.
   (b) Each boy and each girl went to *her* house.

6. When two nouns are joined by using 'with', the pronoun agrees with the noun coming before 'with'.

   Examples :
   (a) The boy with *his* parents has gone to see a movie.
   (b) The children with *their* parents have gone to picnic.

7. When two different nouns are joined by either......... or; neither ......,... nor, the pronoun is used according to the number and gender of the second noun.

Examples :

(a) Either your sister or you have done *your* work.

(b) Neither the students nor the teacher was in *his* class.

8. The pronoun coming after '*than*' must be in the same case as that coming before '*than*'.

Examples :

(a) She plays better than *me*. (Incorrect)
She plays better than *I*. (Correct)

(b) His elder brother is more intelligent than *him*. (Incorrect)
His elder brother is more intelligent than *he*. (Correct)

9. 'Many a' always takes a singular pronoun and singular verb.

Example :
Many a soldier has met *his* death in the battle field.

10. 'Who', 'Whose', 'Whom' are used only for persons.

Examples :

(a) *Who* is knocking at the door?

(b) *Whose* pen is this?

(c) *What* do you want?

11. 'Which' is used for things.

Example : *Which* game do you like?

MULTIPLE CHOICE QUESTIONS

Directions: *In the following questions choose the correct options to fill the blanks.*

1. The place was so dirty that ..... wished to run away from there.
A. everybody B. anybody
C. few D. some

2. ..... was there to help me.
A. Somebody B. Anything
C. Anybody D. Nobody

3. Is there .... to eat?
A. some B. something
C. any D. few

4. ..... of the students were making a great noise.
A. Anyone B. Somebody
C. Many D. Nobody

5. ..... of the students can solve this sum.
A. Someone B. Anybody
C. Somebody D. None

6. ...... of us should try our best to make India a heaven.
A. Any B. Somebody
C. Anybody D. All

7. ...... of us do not know the real meaning of our lives.
A. Any B. Something
C. Several D. Many

8. My .... black.
A. hairs are B. hair is
C. hairs shall D. hair will

9. She saw two .... on the last Sunday.
A. thiefs B. theifs
C. thieves D. theives

10. My sister is a ....
A. bacheloress B. bachelor
C. unmaried D. spinster

11. One is supposed to do ....
A. our duty B. their duty
C. one's duty D. his duty

12. Take anything .... you want.
A. that B. which
C. than D. then

13. I cannot tolerate ....
A. separated you B. your separation
C. separation from you D. you separated

14. He is .... faithful partner.
A. Yours B. You
C. Your D. Your's

15. Ajay is more smart than ....
A. her B. hers
C. herself D. she

16. Vivek works harder than ....
A. me B. I
C. her D. his

17. They should help ....
A. the poor people B. the poor
C. the poor persons D. the poor peoples

18. .... are mad.
A. All his sons B. His all sons
C. Sons all his D. All sons his

19. The poor fellow .... to fate.
A. resigned B. resigned himself
C. resigned itself D. resigned themselves

20. Nobody will help you but ....
A. I B. me
C. ours D. his

21. It is a good chance, You must avail .... this opportunity.
A. of B. yourself of
C. for D. from

22. The person who is elected .... my relative.
A. is B. he is
C. his D. him

23. He made ....
A. yours mention B. mention of you
C. mention for you D. mention about you

24. .... I know, he is quite faithful.
A. As far as B. So far as
C. So far this D. So far so

25. It is a duty of a person to take .... for his family.
A. pain B. pains
C. pain-killers D. pained

26. She does not love .... husband.
A. his B. her
C. its D. their

27. Let .... work together.
A. him and me B. he and I
C. he and him D. I and me

28. Copper, Silver and Gold ....
A. each will do B. either will do
C. any one will do D. any will do

29. Jessica and Roma are very irregular .... habits.
A. in her B. in their
C. in its D. in every

30. One likes to enjoy .... who was a great poet.
A. The sonnets of Shakespeare
B. Shakespeare's sonnets
C. Sonnets
D. Shakespeare

ANSWERS

1	2	3	4	5	6	7	8	9	10
A	D	B	C	D	D	D	B	C	D
11	12	13	14	15	16	17	18	19	20
C	A	C	C	D	B	B	A	B	B
21	22	23	24	25	26	27	28	29	30
B	A	B	A	B	B	A	C	B	A

ARTICLES

The family of the articles has only three members. They are : A, An and The. However, they fall under two groups :
(a) Definite Article *(b)* Indefinite Article

'The' is known as definite article whereas 'a' and 'an' are known as indefinite articles.

Use of the Definite Article 'The'

'The' is used before

1. The superlative degree :
He is the ablest man of the town.
(ablest is a superlative degree)
2. The name of states, countries etc. having a descriptive name :
(i) The J & K is a small state. (J & K is a descriptive name)
(ii) He lives in the U.S.A. (U.S.A. is a descriptive name)
(But the Delhi and the America are wrong because neither Delhi nor America is a descriptive name)
3. The names of the scriptures :
The Gita is a holy book. (Gita is a scripture)
4. Name of newspapers :
The Tribune is published from Chandigarh.
5. Name of rivers, canals, seas, oceans, bays, gulfs, groups of islands etc. :
(i) The Ganga is a holy river.
(ii) The Indian Ocean is the deepest ocean.
(iii) The Persian Gulf is a narrow gulf.
6. The name of famous buildings :
The Taj is one of the best buildings in India.
7. The names of nationals, sects and communities:
(i) The English defeated the Germans in the World War.
(ii) The rich should help the poor.
(iii) The Hindus believe in the caste system.
8. Proper nouns used as common nouns :
(i) Kalidas is the Shakespeare of India.
(ii) Delhi is the London of India.
9. Famous historical events :
The Industrial Revolution changed the face of England.
10. The directions and the celestial bodies:
The sun rises in the east.
11. Titles : Akbar, the Great was loved by his subjects.

Do not use 'the'

1. Before languages :
The English is an international language. (Incorrect)
English is an international language. (Correct)
2. Before the names of games :
The hockey is a popular game. (Incorrect)
Hockey is a popular game. (Correct)

Use of the Indefinite Articles 'A' and 'An'

'A' is used before :

1. All singular common nouns beginning with a consonant :
(i) A boy sings a song.
(ii) A black and a white cow were grazing in the field.
2. If a word begins with a vowel but gives the sound of a consonant, 'a' should be used before it :
(i) He was helped in his work by a European.
(ii) He is a one-eyed man.
(iii) It is a useful work.

'An' is used as follows :

1. All singular common nouns beginning with a vowel (*i.e.*, a, e, i, o, u) :
   (i) He is an artist. (ii) He is an old man. (iii) I intend to buy an umbrella.
2. If a word starts with a consonant but gives the sound of a vowel, "an" should be used before it :
   (i) Brutus is an honourable man.
   (ii) He is an honour to his profession.
   (iii) He is an L.L.B.

Demonstratives, that, these and those

1. The demonstrative adjectives and pronouns are for objects nearby the speaker:
   this (singular) those (plural)
   and for objects far away from the speaker.
   That (singular) those (plural)
2. Demonstratives are the only adjectives that agree in number with their nouns.
   That hat is nice.
   Those hats are nice.
3. When there is the idea of selection, the pronoun "one" (or "ones") often follows the demonstrative.
   I want a book. I'll get this (one).
   If the demonstrative is followed by an adjective, "one"(or "ones") must be used.
   I want a book. I'll get this big one.

MULTIPLE CHOICE QUESTIONS

Directions: *In the following questions choose the correct options to fill the blanks.*

1. .... will have to be paid for this material.
A. Half rupee B. Half a rupee
C. A half rupee D. An half rupee

2. .... is taking keen interest in India.
A. The USA B. USA
C. An USA D. A USA

3. Only .... can save our country.
A. the Hitler B. a Hitler
C. Hitler D. an Hitler

4. I can run for ....
A. hundred mileus B. the hundred miles
C. a hundred miles D. an hundred miles.

5. .... man-eater has been killed.
A. The B. A
C. An D. Either A or B

6. What .... fine idea!
A. the B. an
C. a D. No article

7. .... earth is moving around the sun.
A. An B. A
C. The D. No article

8. This is .... first example while I got.
A. the B. a
C. an D. No article

9. This is .... house which was built during earthquake.
A. a B. an
C. the D. No article

10. .... America is a rich country.
A. The B. An
C. A D. No article

11. .... U.S.A. is a developed country.
A. A B. An
C. The D. No article

12. .... Bible is a holy book.
A. A B. The
C. An D. No article

13. .... rich should help the poor.
A. The B. A
C. An D. No article

14. .... Gold is a costly metal.
A. The B. A
C. An D. No article

15. Kalidas is .... Shakespeare of India.
A. a B. an
C. the D. No article

16. I cannot do .... difficult work.
A. a such B. the such
C. such the D. such a

17. How foolish .... plan it is!
A. a B. an
C. the D. No article

18. An ink is .... useful article.
A. an B. a
C. the D. No article

19. There are .... husband and wife.
A. a B. an
C. the D. No article

20. He is learning .... French
A. the B. a
C. an D. No article

ANSWERS

1	2	3	4	5	6	7	8	9	10
B	A	B	C	D	C	C	A	C	D
11	**12**	**13**	**14**	**15**	**16**	**17**	**18**	**19**	**20**
C	B	A	D	C	D	A	B	D	D

ADJECTIVES & ADVERBS

An Adjective is a word which adds something to the meaning of a noun or a pronoun.

Mridula is an *intelligent* girl. He has a *black* goat.
He is a *brilliant* student. She is a *clever* girl.
It is a *beautiful* picture.

In the sentences given above, the words in italics are adjectives.

An Adverb is a word which qualifies the meaning of a Verb, an Adjective or another Adverb.

(*i*) He talks *slowly*.
(*ii*) He is a *very* good student.
(*iii*) He talks *very* slowly.

In sentence (*i*), *slowly* qualifies the verb *talks*.
In sentence (*ii*), *very* qualifies the adjective *good*.
In sentence (*iii*), *very* qualifies the adverb *slowly*.

Adjectives have three degrees of comparison :

1. **Positive Degree :** It expresses the common form of an adjective.

   Example :

   Ram is a *tall* boy.

   In the above sentence *tall* is an adjective and expresses the common form.

2. **Comparative Degree :** It expresses the more of the same form.

   Example :

   Ram is *taller* than Mahesh.

   In the above sentence *taller* is an adjective that expresses the more of the common form of the adjective *tall*.

   "When and How to Use" Comparative Degree?

   (a) Comparative Degree is used when two persons or two groups of persons or things are compared.

   Examples :

   (a) He is *wiser* than his younger brother.
   (b) This glass is *cleaner* than the other.

   (b) When two different qualities in the same person are compared, more is used instead of 'er' to form the comparative. The formula used in this case should be :

   More + Positive Degree

   She is *fairer* than polite. (Incorrect)
   She is *more fair* than polite. (Correct)

   (c) When selection of one out of two persons or things is meant, the degree of comparison is followed by of and *the* is used before it.

   Example :

   Zia is abler of *the* two sisters.

   (d) If two comparatives are used in the same sentence to impress upon an idea, both should be preceded by the definite article.

   Examples :

   (i) The higher you go, the cooler it is.
   (ii) The more we get, the more we desire.

   (e) When one person or thing is compared with another of the same kind, other is used after the comparative degree. In such sentences other is normally preceded by any or all.

   Examples :

   (i) Kalidas is greater than any dramatist. (Incorrect)
   Kalidas is greater than any other dramatist. (Correct)
   (ii) Lead is heavier than all metals. (Incorrect)
   Lead is heavier than all other metals. (Correct)

   (f) Senior, junior, superior, inferior, prior, anterior (earlier than) and posterior (later than) are always followed by 'to'.

   Examples :

   (i) Ram is senior *to* Mohan by three years.
   (ii) That pen is inferior *to* that.
   (iii) He is junior *to* me in rank.
   (iv) This event was posterior *to* that.

   Note: Never use *than* after the above mentioned adjectives.

Important Information

(a) 'Preferable' is also used as an adjective of the comparative degree. As such, it is always followed by *to* and not *a*.

Death is preferable than dishonour. (Incorrect)
Death is preferable *to* dishonour. (Correct)

(b) To intensify the Degree of comparison, we use *far* or *much* before the comparative.

Examples :

(i) This book is *far* better than that.
(ii) His performance was *much* better than Mohan's.

Warning : Always avoid the use of double comparatives.

Don't say : Ram is more cleverer than his younger brother.

Say: Ram is cleverer than his younger brother.

3. **Superlative Degree :** It expresses the most of the common form of an adjective.

   Example :

   He is the ablest man of the town.

How and when to use the Superlative Degree?

(a) The Superlative Degree is used when more than two persons or things are compared.

(b) The Superlative Degree is generally preceded by 'the' and followed by 'of' in most of the cases or otherwise.

(c) When an adjective of the superlative degree is preceded by a Possessive Adjective or a Noun in the Possessive case, 'the' should not be used before it.

Example :

Which is Kalidas' best play?

It will be a blunder to use 'the' before the Superlative Degree in such cases.

Don't say : Which is Kalidas' the best play.

(d) To intensify the degree of comparison, *by far* is used before the superlative degree.

Example :

India is *by far* the most beautiful country of the world.

Note: Always avoid the use of double superlatives.

Don't say : He is the most strongest boy in the class.

Say : He is the strongest boy in the class.

Use of some Important Adjectives

1. (a) **'Some'** is used as follows :

(i) With countable nouns where it means— a little, a small quantity.

(ii) In a question which shows some request.

Examples :

(i) There is some water in the bottle.

(ii) Some of the students were absent yesterday.

(iii) Will you have some milk?

(iv) Will you buy some fruit for me?

(b) **'Any'** is used as follows :

(i) In negative sentences.

(ii) In interrogative sentences.

(iii) After 'Hardly', 'Scarcely' and 'Barely'.

(iv) After 'If'.

Examples :

(i). There is not any sugar in the pot.

(ii) We haven't any rice in the house.

(iii) I have hardly any money.

(iv) There are scarcely any plants in this field.

(v) If there is any danger, blow the whistle.

2. (a) **Older :** Older (and oldest) are used for persons animals and things. But 'Older' and 'Oldest' refer to the persons who do not belong to the same family.

Examples :

(i) Radha is older than Shyama.

(ii) John is the oldest member of the staff.

'Older' and 'Oldest' refer to the persons who do not belong to the same family.

(b) **Elder** (and **eldest**) are used in respect of the members of the same family like sons, daughters, brothers, sisters.

Examples :

(i) My elder sister is a lecturer.

(ii) Meenakshi is the eldest of the three sisters.

Note :

(i) 'Elder' is not followed by 'than'.

(ii) 'Elder' and 'Eldest' cannot be used for things.

3. (a) **'Few'** is negative and is the opposite of 'Many'. It means 'not many'.

(b) **'A few'** is positive and means 'some at least'. It is the opposite of 'None'.

(c) **'The few'** means 'minority' and suggests 'whether there is'.

Examples :

(i) We have few holidays in school.

(ii) Only a few boys will fail in the examination.

(iii) The few poems that he wrote are very popular.

4. (a) **Further** means 'something additional'.

(b) **Farther** means 'a greater distance'.

Examples :

(i) Further discussion will be held in the office of the principal.

(ii) Amritsar is farther from Delhi than Ambala.

5. (a) **Little** is negative. It means, 'not much', or 'hardly any'.

(b) **A little** is positive. It means 'some quantity'.

(c) **The little** denotes quantity. It means, 'not much but all that is, or whatever quantity there is'.

Examples :

(i) There is little hope of his success.

(ii) He knows a little of everything.

(iii) I have spent the little money I had.

(iv) The little knowledge of shoe-making proved very useful to me.

6. (a) **'Much'** expresses 'quantity'.

(b) **'Many'** expresses 'number'.

(c) **'Many a'**—'Singular noun' and 'Singular verb' are used with 'many a'.

Examples :

(i) There is not *much* water in the jug.

(ii) *Many* boys are absent today.

(iii) *Many* a battle has been fought on the soil of India.

7. (a) **'Less'** denotes 'in a small degree'.

(b) **'Fewer'** denotes 'number'.

Examples :

(i) He devotes less time to his studies.

(ii) There are no fewer than ten chairs in this room.

8. (a) **'Each'** is used for a single number of 'two persons' or 'things'.

(b) **'Every'** is used for a single number of 'many persons' or 'things'.

Examples :

(i) Each boy must take part in games.

(ii) There are only two poets. Each poet recited his poem.

(iii) Every man dies in this world.

(iv) Every man is expected to do his duty.

9. (a) **'Either'** means one of the two or both.

(b) **'Neither'** is negative of the either.

Examples :

(i) You may buy either of these two chairs.

(ii) Neither of them could speak on the stage.

10. (a) **'Later'** expresses 'late in time'.

(b) **'Latter'** means 'second in position or order'.

Examples :

(i) My father reached later than I expected.

(ii) The latter position was better than the former.

Use of some Important Adverbs

1. (a) Also, too, enough:
   - (i) He taught English. Also, he edited the school magazine
   - (ii) He is a writer and also he is a painter.
   - (iii) He is too obstinate to listen to any reason.
   - (iv) This is too difficult a piece for the junior students.
   - (v) Sarla was kind enough to help the poor.
   - (vi) He is brave enough to help the truth.

   Note: 'Too' is used in a negative sense, but enough is used in a positive sense.

   (b) Fairly and rather: Both suggest the meaning 'moderately'. But, mainly 'fairly' is used with the words that denote a positive meaning and rather is used with the words that denote a negative meaning:
   - (i) Rita did fairly well in that competition, but her performance was rather poor in sports.
   - (ii) Mona is fairly rich, but she is rather stingy.

   Note: 'Rather' can also be used in a positive sense.
   - (i) This is a rather interesting job.
   - (ii) That boy is rather smart.

   (c) Hardly, barely, scarcely: These words mostly convey the negative suggestions and are almost similar.
   - (i) I have hardly any strength now.
   - (ii) There was barely any supply to the township,
   - (iii) There were scarcely a hundred guests present.

   Note: With slight variance in the meaning, the words given above convey the idea of 'very little', 'not enough', 'lack of quantity and number'.

   (d) Yet, Still: These adverbs can often be used to connect the sentence units:
   - (i) He has been defeated many times in the contest; still he wants to be a competitor.
   - (ii) Mona was sick; yet she went on doing her work.

   (e) Alone:
   - (i) He alone (none else) is capable of handling that fire,
   - (ii) He hunted all alone in the forest. (not in any company)

Special Note:

(a) Apart from their conventional positions the adverbs might be used in different positions with different meanings and angles.
- (i) He had only four books.
- (ii) John only contacted his friend in need.
- (iii) He greeted me only.
- (iv) Only he greeted me there.

(b) Inversion: Some adverbs can be inverted *i.e.* placed in the beginning of the sentence and then be followed by an interrogative form. The most common of these adverb are: so, seldom, never, nowhere, under no circumstances, hardly, scarcely etc.
- (i) So big was the bus that it could not enter the narrow lane.
- (ii) Hardly had he reached the station when he received the message.

MULTIPLE CHOICE QUESTIONS

Directions: *In the following questions choose the correct options to fill the blanks.*

1. The girl whom you met is the .... sister of Ravi.
A. eldest B. elder
C. older D. oldest

2. The historical place is ....
A. seeing worth B. worthy of seeing
C. worth seeing D. worthy seeing

3. These flowers smell ....
A. sweet B. sweetly
C. more sweetly D. sweetest

4. .... aspirant cannot pass the entrance examination.
A. Each B. Every
C. All D. No

5. Harivansh Rai .... second Shakespeare.
A. is a B. is
C. is the D. is an

6. .... student in the class got prizes.
A. Each and every B. Every and each
C. Every D. Never

7. It is .... picture than the one we saw last Monday.
A. interesting B. much interesting
C. more interesting D. most interesting

8. She is clever ....
A. that her mother is B. as her mother is
C. to her mother is D. than her mother is

9. They will get ....
A. Red, green and black paper
B. Red, green black paper
C. Red and green and black paper
D. Red green black paper

10. Health is .... wealth.
A. preferable to B. more preferable than
C. more preferable to D. most preferable then

11. .... water that was in the jug evaporated.
A. Little B. The little
C. Small D. A small

12. He has not sung .... songs.
A. much B. most
C. more D. many

13. Srishti has searched .... office.
A. whole the B. the whole
C. a whole D. some whole

14. Premchand was .... best and .... famous writer.
A. a, the most B. the, a most
C. the, more D. the, the most

15. William Shakespeare is famous as ....

A. a poet and a dramatist
B. a poet and dramatist
C. the poet and the dramatist
D. a poet and the dramatist

16. What does .... leader suggest?

A. other B. another
C. others D. anothers

17. He .... money.

A. has few B. have few
C. has little D. have little

18. The .... boys are rewarded.

A. first two B. two first
C. firsts two D. two's first

19. He is .... brave.

A. stronger than
B. stronger then
C. more strong then
D. more strong than

20. No sooner said ....

A. so done B. and done
C. then done D. but done

21. She returned .... than I had thought.

A. quickly B. more quicker
C. more quickly D. quicker

22. He is .... foolish person.

A. rather the B. a rather
C. rather a D. rather

23. This pen .... rupees.

A. costs twenty B. twenty costs only
C. costs only twenty D. only costs twenty

24. It is .... pride.

A. nothing else but B. nothing else than
C. else nothing than D. but

25. This tea is .... to drink.

A. too hot B. very hot
C. enough hot D. much hot

ANSWERS

1	2	3	4	5	6	7	8	9	10
A	C	A	B	A	C	C	C	A	A
11	**12**	**13**	**14**	**15**	**16**	**17**	**18**	**19**	**20**
B	D	B	D	B	B	C	A	D	C
21	**22**	**23**	**24**	**25**					
C	C	C	A	A					

DETERMINERS

Determiners are actually Adjectives. They are always followed by nouns.

Determiners are of the following kinds:

1. **Demonstrative Determiners :** this, that, these, those
2. **Possessive Determiners :** my, our, your, his, her, its, their
3. **Quantitative Determiners :** some, any, much, enough, sufficient, whole, a little, the little, little, all, both
4. **Numerical Determiners:** a few, some, few, the few, any, several, many, no, etc.

   One, two, three ... (Cardinals)

   First, second, third ... (Ordinals)
5. **Distributive Determiners:** either, neither
6. **Articles: Indefinite:** a, an, **Definite:** the

MULTIPLE CHOICE QUESTIONS

Directions: *In the following questions choose the correct options to fill the blanks.*

1. Give me .... rice.

A. some B. few
C. a few D. any

2. ...... sheep grazing on the slope of the hill had gone away.

A. Any B. The few
C. This D. Much

3. Have you got .... magazines to read?

A. all B. much
C. some D. little

4. I have .... money that I want to spend on shares.

A. any B. much
C. less D. some

5. There is .... owl on the branch of the tree.

A. a B. the
C. an D. some

6. My brother is .... MBA.

A. a B. an
C. the D. any

7. Have you got .... cheese?

A. some B. many
C. a few D. few

8. No, I have not got .... cheese.

A. many B. few
C. any D. some

9. There is only .... milk left in the bottle.
A. enough B. few
C. much D. a little

10. There is .... hope of his recovery.
A. any B. little
C. many D. few

11. .... dogs were barking at the strangers.
A. Some B. Any
C. Much D. Less

12. The girl bought her father .... juice.
A. few B. some
C. any D. many

13. You should take .... honey everyday.
A. any B. many
C. a little D. a few

14. .... boy was punished by the teacher.
A. Either B. All
C. Any D. Many

15. .... girl was asked to join the army.
A. None B. Neither
C. All D. Any

16. .... water in the jug has been drunk by Mohan.
A. The little B. The few
C. A few D. Few

17. I shall play .... piano at the party.
A. some B. any
C. the D. few

18. .... labourers were found dead in the mine.
A. Any B. Fewer
C. Many D. Less

19. Could I borrow .... umbrella?
A. our B. your
C. yours D. my

20. My brother is standing in the .... row.
A. any B. many
C. some D. first

ANSWERS

1	2	3	4	5	6	7	8	9	10
A	B	C	D	C	B	A	C	D	B
11	**12**	**13**	**14**	**15**	**16**	**17**	**18**	**19**	**20**
A	B	C	A	B	A	C	C	B	D

THE VERB

A Verb is a word that tells something about the action or state of or happenning to a person or thing.

A Verb tells the following:

1. What a person or thing does.
Sachin goes to school daily.
The bell *rang* loudly.
Many birds fly in the sky.
She *sang* a song.

2. What a person or thing is.
India *is* the biggest democracy in the world.
Ram Mehar *is* very rich.
They *are* happy.

3. What is done to a person or thing.
You *are liked* by all.
Two thieves *were arrested.*
Four students *were punished* by the teacher.

4. What happens to a person or thing.
His maternal uncle *died* last week.
Two ships *sank* yesterday.
Leaves *turn* yellow in autumn.

5. What a person or thing has, had, and so on.
I *have* a new car.
He *had* a scooter last year.
He *has* several cows and goats.

It goes without saying that a verb is the most important part of a sentence. No sentence is complete without a Verb.

Important Information

1. If two or more singular nouns are joined by 'and' the verb used will be plural.
   Example:
   (i) He and I were going to the market.
   (ii) Ram and Mohan are friends.
2. If two singular nouns joined by 'and' points out to the same thing or person, the verb used must be singular.
   Example:
   (i) Rice and curry is the favourite food of the Punjabis.
   (ii) The Collector and District Magistrate is away.
3. In case two subjects are joined by 'as well as' the verb agrees with the first subject.
   Example :
   (i) Kanta as well as her children is playing.
   (ii) Children as well as their mother are playing.
   In the case of first sentence the verb (is) agrees with Kanta and in the case of second sentence the verb (are) agrees with the children.
4. 'Neither', 'Either', 'Every', 'Each', 'Everyone', and 'Many a' are followed by a singular verb.
   Example :
   (i) Either of the plans is to be adopted.
   (ii) Neither of the two brothers is sure to pass.
   (iii) Every student is expected to be obedient.
   (iv) Everyone of them desires this.
   (v) Many a person is drowned in the sea.

5. If two subjects are joined by 'Either .... or' / 'Neither .... nor', the verb agrees with the subject near to it.

Example :

(i) Either my brother or I am to do this work.

(ii) Neither he nor they are prepared to do this work.

6. 'A great many' is always followed by a 'plural noun' and a 'plural verb'. For example :

A great many students have been declared successful.

7. Similarly if two subjects are joined by 'with', 'together with', 'no less than', in addition to 'and not', etc. the verb agrees with the first subject.

Example :

(i) The boy with his parents has arrived.

(ii) He, no less than I, is to blame.

8. Nouns, plural in form, but singular in meaning, take a singular verb.

Example :

This news was broadcast from television yesterday.

MULTIPLE CHOICE QUESTIONS

Directions: *In the following questions choose the correct options to fill the blanks.*

1. The bus with all its passengers .... lost.
A. were B. was
C. are D. would

2. You as well as I .... responsible for this work.
A. am B. are
C. was D. is

3. Raghava like all his companions .... a spoiled child.
A. are B. were
C. is D. will be

4. Pen and ink .... required for me.
A. are B. were
C. is D. has required

5. Every girl and every boy .... attended the seminar.
A. have B. has
C. is D. are

6. Not only she but all her sisters ...... been married.
A. has B. have
C. is D. are

7. There .... nothing but miseries in life.
A. is B. are
C. were D. will be

8. Neither prose nor poem .... given.
A. were B. was
C. has D. have

9. Either he or I .... wrong.
A. is B. are
C. am D. were

10. Either Sulekha or Rekha .... coming here.
A. are B. is
C. were D. have

11. .... the child or his parents to blame?
A. Is B. Are
C. Were D. Has

12. You and I .... neighbours.
A. am B. are
C. was D. has

13. The house with all its belongings ..... sold away.
A. were B. are
C. was D. must

14. Either water or juice .... required.
A. is B. are
C. were D. has

15. There were not as many tables as .... required.
A. was B. were
C. is D. are

16. They each .... a book.
A. have B. are
C. has D. is

17. He and I .... class friends.
A. is B. am
C. was D. are

18. She as well as I .... guilty.
A. is B. are
C. am D. must be

19. Purushottam .... not read more on this chapter.
A. needs
B. has been need
C. need
D. had been need

20. He came .... to his aunt.
A. run B. running
C. to run D. in run

ANSWERS

1	2	3	4	5	6	7	8	9	10
B	B	C	C	B	B	A	B	C	B
11	12	13	14	15	16	17	18	19	20
A	B	C	A	B	A	D	A	C	B

CONJUNCTIONS

A conjunction is a word which connects words, clauses or sentences.

Look at the following sentences.

(i) He bought apples *and* mangoes.

(ii) God made the country *and* man made the town.

(iii) The door was open *but* there was no one in the house.

(iv) He knows that I am here *and* that I want to see him.

In the sentence (i), *and* connects two words—*apples* and *mangoes.*

In the sentence (ii), *and* connects two sentences—*God made the country* and *man made the town.*

In the sentence (iii), *but* connects two sentences— *The door was open* and *there was no one in the house.*

In the sentence (iv), *and* connects two clauses—*that I am here* and *that I want to see him.*

The main coordinating conjunctions are:

and, but, for, or, nor, also, either ..... or, neither ..... nor.

There are some conjunctions which are used in pairs. They are:

either .... or, ... neither .... nor, both .... and, though .... yet, whether .... or, not only .... but also.

Example: *Either* take it *or* leave it.

It is *neither* useful *nor* ornamental.

They *both* like *and* respect me.

Though he is suffering from high fever, *yet* he does not cry.

He does not care *whether* you go *or* stay.

He is *not only* doltish, *but also* obstinate.

The conjunctions which are used in pairs in this way, are called correlative conjunctions, or merely correlatives.

Use of Important Conjunctions

1. **As soon as :** As soon as denotes simultaneous time.
   Example : As soon as he saw his enemy, he took to his heels.
2. **No sooner .... than :**
   (a) 'No sooner' is always followed by 'than'.
   (b) Please remember that 'No sooner' is always followed by do/does/did. As such only first form of the verb should be used after the subject.
   Example :
   No sooner did he see his enemy than he took to his heels.
3. **Hardly :** Hardly is followed by when.
   Examples :
   (i) Hardly had I left the house when it started raining.
   (ii) We had hardly come into the room when his father began chastising him.
   Note :
   A. Hardly is never followed by than.
   B. 'Scarcely' can also be used in the sense and manner of 'Hardly'.
4. **Lest :** Lest is used in the sense of so that .... not. It is always followed by should. Lest is negative in sense. Hence 'not' should never be used with it.
   Example :
   Work hard lest you should fail.
   Note : 'Lest' is always followed by 'should' and not 'may'.
5. **Unless :** Unless expresses condition. It is also used in the negative sense. Use of 'not' is not allowed with unless because unless is already in the negative sense.
   Example :
   Unless you labour hard you will not pass.
6. **Until :** 'Until' expresses time. It means 'till not'.
   Example : Wait here until I return.
   Note : Until is in the negative sense. So 'not' should not be used with it. Example :
   Wait here until I do not return. (Incorrect)
   Wait here until I return. (Correct)
7. **As well as :** When two subjects are joined by 'as well as', the verb always agrees with the first subject.
   Examples :
   (i) The teacher as well as students is playing.
   (ii) Students as well as the teacher are playing.
   Note : 'Both' and 'as well as' cannot be used together in the same sentence.
   Examples :
   Both Sita as well as Kanta are beautiful. (Incorrect)
   Sita as well as Kanta is beautiful. (Correct)
   Both Sita and Kanta are beautiful. (Correct)
8. **As if :** 'As if' is used in the sense of pretension. While using 'as if' in a sentence, we should see that even the third person singular subject gets 'were'.
   Example : He talks as if he were mad.
9. **Till :** Till expresses time. Till is always used in the affirmative.
   Example :
   We did not come back till sunset.
10. **Rather than :** 'Rather than' is used in the sense of 'preference'. 'Rather' is always followed by 'than'.
    Example :
    I would rather die than submit.
11. **As long as/so long as :** Both express time during which an action or event takes place.
    Example :
    As long as there is life, there is hope.
12. **However :** It is both a subordinate and co-ordinate clause.
    Examples :
    (a) Mala worked hard, she however, failed.
    (b) However hard he may work, he cannot pass.
13. **Such as :** 'Such as' gives us the sense of 'like'. Such is always followed by 'as'.
    Example :
    Life is such a puzzle as cannot be solved.

MULTIPLE CHOICE QUESTIONS

Directions: *In the following questions choose the correct options to fill the blanks.*

1. Neither he .... his friend is good.
A. or B. and
C. but D. nor

2. The officer asked the peon .... why he was late.
A. that B. if
C. but D. No word needed

3. Both Ajay .... Vijay are intelligent.
A. or B. nor
C. and D. No word needed

4. No Sooner did the thief see the public .... he ran away.
A. then B. and
C. but D. than

5. Abhinav .... his brothers was going to Mumbai.
A. but
B. yet
C. No word needed
D. together with

6. He behaves .... he were the captain of the team.
A. as if B. as
C. No word needed D. that

7. Either Rupali .... Sonali is going to attend the meeting.
A. and B. but
C. nor D. or

8. Neither Nirmal .... Ashwinee is going to listen the speech.
A. and B. but
C. nor D. or

9. Ravi .... Prakash are going to Kolkata.
A. or B. nor
C. but D. and

10. Rice .... curry is my usual breakfast.
A. and B. but
C. then D. than

11. Hardly had he left .... his brother came.
A. then B. than
C. when D. that

12. I would rather have a copy .... a book.
A. then B. than
C. when D. that

13. He is no other .... my friend.
A. then B. than
C. when D. but

14. He saw a snake ....he awoke.
A. then B. when
C. than D. No word needed

15. Ten years have passed .... my grandmother died.
A. since B. when
C. then D. than

16. She is .... good .... bad.
A. either, not B. neither, or
C. neither, nor D. neither, than

17. The cellphone is both cheap .... best.
A. than B. and
C. then D. or

18. No sooner did the rogue see the police .... he disappeared.
A. then B. than
C. so D. because

19. Srishti will go .... Sanju goes.
A. if B. than
C. then D. although

20. She is wise .... timid.
A. and B. yet
C. but D. however

21. Make hay .... the sun shines.
A. though B. while
C. after D. before

22. He is so weak .... he cannot walk.
A. but B. that
C. then D. so

23. Although he is rich, ... he is unhappy.
A. but B. yet
C. so D. still

24. Wait here .... I come back.
A. till B. until
C. before D. after

25. He is my friend .... I shall help him.
A. so B. hence
C. that is why D. therefore

26. He must go away .... he will be beaten.
A. otherwise B. and
C. or D. else

27. God loves good men .... good men love God.
A. and B. or
C. that D. those

28. He was late .... he was not punished.
A. but B. yet
C. still D. therefore

29. Walk slowly ...., you may fall.
A. and B. or
C. so D. otherwise

30. Work hard, ... you will fail.
A. and B. or
C. otherwise D. else

ANSWERS

1	2	3	4	5	6	7	8	9	10
D	D	C	D	D	A	D	C	D	A
11	12	13	14	15	16	17	18	19	20
C	B	B	B	A	C	B	B	A	C
21	22	23	24	25	26	27	28	29	30
B	B	B	A	B	C	A	C	D	D

PREPOSITIONS

A *Preposition* is a word which is placed before a noun or a pronoun to show its relation to some other word in the sentence.

1. I saw a goat *in* the field.
2. I am fond *of* hot coffee.

In sentence 1, the word *in* shows the relation between two things—*goat* and *field.*

In sentence 2, the word *of* shows the relation between the attribute expressed by the adjective *found* and *tea.*

The words *in* and *of* are here used as prepositions.

The noun or pronoun which is used with a preposition is called its object. The noun or pronoun is in the objective case. It is governed by the preposition. Now it is absolutely clear that in sentence 1, the noun *field* is in the objective case. The word *field* is governed by the preposition *in.*

A preposition may have two or more objects.

The road runs over *hill* and *plain.*

Here, the words *hill* and *plain* are used as objects.

Use of Important Prepositions

1. Among, Between

'**Among**' is used for more than two persons or things; '**Between**' is used only for two.

Examples :

(i) Distribute these sweets *among* the poor students of the class.

(ii) Distribute these books *between* Ram and Shyam.

2. Among, In

'**Among**' is used before collective plural nouns. '**In**' is used before collective singular nouns.

Examples :

(i) I found him standing *among* the crowd.

(ii) I saw him in the crowd.

3. Beside, Besides

'**Beside**' means 'by the side of'. '**Besides**' means 'in addition to'.

Examples :

(i) The daughter was sitting *beside* her mother.

(ii) *Besides* his relatives, he invited his friends also.

4. In, Within

'**In**' means at the expiry of a period of time in future, '**Within**' means before the expiry of a period of time in any tense.

Examples :

(i) She will return *in* a week.

(ii) I shall finish my work *within* a weak.

5. On, Upon

'**On**' is used for things at rest; '**Upon**' is used for things in motion.

Examples :

(i) He is sitting *on* the floor.

(ii) The dog sprang *upon* the table.

6. By, With

'**By**' denotes the agent or doer, '**With**' denotes the instrument with which anything is done.

Examples :

(i) The bird was killed *by* the hunter with an arrow.

(ii) He beat the dog *with* a stick.

(iii) I shall reach here *by* five o'clock.

7. After, In

'**After**' means at the end of a period of time in the past. '**In**' means at the end of a period of time in future.

Examples :

(i) I shall return your book *in* a week.

(ii) He returned the book *after* a week.

8. For, From, Since

'**For**' is used before a noun denoting a period of time with all the tenses. '**From**' is used before a noun or phrase denoting a point of time, it is used in all the tenses. '**Since**' is used before a noun or phrase denoting some point of time and is always produced by a verb in the perfect continuous tense or third form of a verb.

Examples :

(i) We have been playing cards *for* two hours.

(ii) She stayed with her uncle *from* the 15th of March to the 15th of May.

(iii) I have been reading this book *since* morning.

9. Above, Over

'**Above**' means 'higher from', **Over** is used in the following four senses :

(i) In the sense of 'above' :
At noon, the sun is *over* our heads.

(ii) In the sense of 'beyond' :
I cannot get *over* my disappointment.

(iii) In the sense of 'Superiority' :
God *over* all blesses for ever more.

(iv) In the sense of 'Conclusion' :
It is all *over* with me.

10. At, Towards

'**At**' denotes the idea of aim, '**Towards**' denotes the idea of destination.

Examples :

(i) He threw the stone *at* the cat.

(ii) He went *towards* the house.

11. At, In, On

'At' is used as follows :

(i) '**At**' is used with small towns and villages. **Examples:**

(a) He was born *at* Sonepat.

(b) He lives *at* village Bangra. (Bangra is a village)

(ii) '**At**' is used before a noun denoting a definite point of time.

Example :

He called on me *at* 9 p.m. yesterday.

'In' is used as follows :

(iii) '**In**' is used with the names of big cities, provinces and countries.

Examples :

(a) His father lives *in* England.

(b) His younger brother lives *in* Calcutta.

(iv) '**In**' is used before the names of months and years.

Example :

His elder sister was born *in* 1972 *in* the month of May.

'**On**' is used with dates and names of days. **Examples:**

(a) I joined college *on* the 26th April.

(b) He will leave for Kolkata *on* Wednesday next.

Important Information

1. '**In**' is also used in the following phrases :
   In the morning; In the evening, In winter, In summer.
2. '**In**' also denotes a place inside anything.
   He travelled *in* a crowded bus.
3. '**At**' is used in the following phrases :
   At home, *At* the station, *At* work, *At* play.

12. Below, Beneath

Below means 'of lower level in position, dignity and expectation' etc. *Beneath* means 'under'.

Examples :

(i) It is *below* my dignity to talk to her.

(ii) They rested *beneath* the shade of a tree.

13. In, Into, To

'**In**' expresses Rest or Motion inside anything. '**Into**' expresses Motion towards the inside of anything or change from one medium to another. '**To**' denotes motion from one place to another.

Examples :

(i) The boys are *in* the room.

(ii) Translate this passage from English *into* Hindi.

(iii) Every morning he goes *to* the temple.

14. Till, By, Of, Off

- 'Till' means upto or not earlier than.
- 'By' means not later than.
- 'Of' shows cause, source, separation, quality, contents, possession, apposition, point of reference, space in time etc.
- 'Off' shows separation at a near distance, and detached condition.

Consider the following examples:

(i) I shall work *till* 5 a.m.

(ii) Madhu died *of* cancer.

(iii) The nib *of* the pen is made *of* gold.

(iv) He presented me a bottle *of* perfume.

(v) Our principal is a man *of* principle.

(vi) He lived in the house *of* his friend.

(vii) *By* this time tomorrow, I'll have finished my job.

(viii) My house is *off* the road.

(ix) The book fell *off* the table.

MULTIPLE CHOICE QUESTIONS

Directions: *Tick the correct preposition for the blank in each of the following sentences.*

1. He applied ...... the manager.
A. for B. to
C. with D. by

2. Trust ...... God and do the right.
A. in B. for
C. to D. with

3. She is worthy ...... a prize.
A. with B. for
C. to D. of

4. Mr. Gomes has no taste ...... music.
A. of B. for
C. with D. to

5. You are hard ...... hearing.
A. at B. of
C. with D. for

6. He is sure ...... his success
A. for B. with
C. on D. of

7. Preeti was warned ...... the danger ahead.
A. for B. at
C. of D. about

8. I am thankful ...... you for a good advice.
A. for B. with
C. to D. of

9. Deepak would not surrender ...... the police.
A. with B. to
C. for D. on

10. The small plant in your lawn is very sensitive ...... touch.
A. on B. with
C. to D. about

11. Divya was sure to succeed ..... the examination.
A. for B. in
C. to D. with

12. Geeta was jealous ...... Ravina's beauty.
A. to B. with
C. for D. of

13. He was ignorant ..... what was happening there.
A. for B. of
C. to D. with

14. Your pen is inferior ...... mine.
A. than B. with
C. from D. to

15. Reenu is no match ...... Meenu.
A. to B. for
C. with D. upon

16. It is necessary ...... you to apply for this job.
A. on B. with
C. for D. to

17. Be loyal ...... your country.
A. for B. to
C. on D. with

18. Mukesh is junior ...... me.
A. than B. to
C. from D. of

19. Deepika was innocent ...... the crime.
A. of B. with
C. from D. to

20. I am desirous.... joining the Indian cricket team.
A. for B. of
C. to D. on

ANSWERS

1	2	3	4	5	6	7	8	9	10
B	A	D	B	B	D	D	D	B	D
11	**12**	**13**	**14**	**15**	**16**	**17**	**18**	**19**	**20**
B	D	B	D	B	D	B	B	A	B

SYNONYMS

A synonym is a word which conveys a meaning similar to the given word.

REMEMBER

Words	*Synonyms*
Add	Increase
Adequate	Enough
Adjust	Adapt
All	Aggregate
Allow	Permit
Abode	Dwelling
Apt	Proper
Assess	Appraise
Accuse	Calumniate
Abashed	Timid
Annoy	Displease
Ample	Enough, Sufficient
Amplify	Increase
Apathetic	Unenthusiastic
Accost	Address
Authentic	True
Adjust	Fit
Approve	Assent, Allow, Accept
Adapt	Conform
Adversary	Opponent, Rival, Competitor
Beat	Whack
Benign	Kind
Breeze	Zephyr
Baffle	Puzzle
Booty	Spoil

Words	*Synonyms*
Beauty	Charm
Beast	Animal
Bandit	Robber
Blaze	Shine
Bond	Tie
Bend	Twist
Bate	Diminish
Beg	Plead
Barbaric	Wild, Savage
Bashful	Shy, Reserved
Begin	Start
Blend	Mix, Mingle
Bizarre	Funny
Below	Under
Bedevil	Confuse
Bemoan	Lament
Babble	Nonsense
Blame	Fault
Behaviour	Demeanour
Call	Accost
Copy	Imitate
Close	Shut
Caress	Love
Camp	Stay
Connect	Attach
Cut	Injure, Curtail
Cling	Stick
Conical	Funny
Convey	Carry
Conspicuous	Prominent
Cheerful	Happy, Pleasant

Words	Synonyms
Curtail	Decrease
Cheerless	Sad, Dejected
Curious	Strange
Circumstance	Factor, Situation, Condition
Competent	Capable
Congruent	Overlapping
Cope	Deal, Endure
Confident	Sure
Complex	Intricate
Cajole	Coax, Flatter
Cunning	Crafty
Delectable	Joyful, Delightful
Devilish	Diabolical
Delicate	Soft
Devil	Fiend
Delay	Postpone
Dislike	Repugnance
Destroy	Ruin
Dwell	Live, Dilate
Declare	Pronounce
Drunk	Flushed
Deficient	Lacking
Damn	Condemn, Curse
Decrease	Diminish
Destruction	Devastation
Efficient	Competent
Ethnic	Racial
Enthral	Enslave
Earnest	Serious
Envious	Jealous
Ending	Final
Egg	Incite
Extempore	At once
Extensive	Far-ranging
Extra	Surplus
Existence	Life
Exceed	Overstep
Enormous	Vast
Excessive	Superfluous
Free	Unhindered
Frigid	Cold
Feed	Cater
Fame	Reputation
Frame	Make
First	Initial
Frighten	Terrorise, Intimidate
Fervent	Fervid
Fall	Decline
Feeble	Frail
Fickle	Changeable
Finish	Conclude
Fraud	Deception
Forgiving	Placable

Words	Synonyms
Grow	Develop
Greed	Avidity
Greet	Welcome
Grave	Serious
Group	Constellation
Given	Bestowed
Gratitude	Thankfulness
Have	Possess
Hire	Rent
Hit	Strike
Handsome	Beautiful
Hinder	Prevent
Heap	Pile
Hope	Expect
Hard	Harsh
Help	Aid
Hymn	Song
Henpecked	Enslaved
Hoodwink	Mystify, Cheat
Humble	Polite, Urbane, Modest
Harass	Vex, Trouble
Impart	Instil
Intact	Untouched
Instal	Establish
Indict	Impeach
Imitate	Ape
Instigate	Incite
Initiate	Start, Introduce
Inimical	Unfriendly
Insufferable	Intolerable
Impartiality	Justice
Jolly	Merry
Joyful	Delectable
Join	Conjoin
Kind	Benign
Kill	Murder
Kindred	Similar
Kinship	Relationship
Keen	Sharp
Knowledge	Scholarship
Lazy	Slothful
Large	Substantial, Gargantuan
Listless	Careless, Lackadaisical
Lax	Loose
Little	Small
Lifelike	Realistic
Lofty	High
Lenient	Soft, Gentle
Lacking	Deficient, Wanting
Lessen	Decrease
Middleclass	Bourgeois
Mitigate	Lessen, Abate
Modesty	Humility, Lowliness

Words	Synonyms
Mix	Mingle, Blend
Mixture	Mingling
Mixed	Assorted
Modify	Decrease
Mean	Imply
Multifarious	Varied
Miscarry	Abort
Note	Notice
Noble	Stately
Native	Indigenous
Needful	Necessary
Notify	Declare
Nervous	Shaky, Tremulous, Timid
Natural	Spontaneous
Near	Close
Normal	Natural
Offend	Displease
Oppress	Persecute, Tyrannize
Opponent	Adversary
Obstruct	Hinder, Check
Offence	Fault
Offender	Villain
Overstep	Exceed
Overlapping	Congruent
Occult	Mystic
Profane	Unholy
Patience	Forbearance
Pornographic	Obscene
Plenitude	Abundance
Prominent	Important
Prodigal	Spender
Procrastinate	Postpone
Promote	Develop, Honour
Persecute	Tyrannise
Profess	Claim
Pliant	Flexible
Plebian	Common
Polished	Sophisticated
Quake	Shake
Quit	Leave
Queer	Eccentric
Quell	Suppress
Quantify	Allot
Reply	Answer
Relinquish	Retire
Read	Peruse
Relation	Reference
Render	Do
Remainder	Residuals
Repeat	Reiterate
Repentant	Contrite
Retaliative	Retaliatory
Rumour	Hearsay
Reveal	Divulge

Words	Synonyms
Ritualistic	Ceremonious
Soft	Delicate
Sort	Kind, Choose, Select
Selfish	Egoistic
Sensual	Earthly
Suppress	Quell, Check
Stimulate	Provoke
Tasteless	Insipid
Travel	Journey
True	Authentic, Faithful, Truthful
Turbulence	Turmoil
Tragedy	Calamity
Tasteful	Tasty, Delicious
Touching	Painful
Thankful	Grateful
Tremendous	Great, Huge
Tough	Strong
Terminate	Conclude, End
Theory	Doctrine
Tell	Relate
Tremble	Shake, Shiver
Urge	Spur
Unbeaten	Unsubdued
Use	Utilize, Practise
Underhand	Unfair, Undue
Unfair	Unjust
Unravel	Reveal, Divulge
Unimportant	Common
Unconcerned	Apathetic
Unimitated	Inimitable
Unfortunate	Unlucky
Understand	Perceive, Comprehend
Vain	Proud, Haughty, Conceited, Shameless
Vale	Valley, Dale, Dell
Vice	Fault
Virtue	Quality
Veracity	Reality
Value	Price, Prize
Vex	Tease
Vibrate	Quiver, Shake
Violent	Excessive
Vivid	Clear, Lucid
Victory	Triumph
Vulgar	Indecent
Virtuous	Honest
Variegated	Varied, Multifarious
Well	Good
Yell	Cry, Shout
Yonder	There
Yearn	Wish, Desire
Yoke	Slavery
Zest	Earnestness, Enthusiasm
Zealous	Earnest

ANTONYMS

A antonym is a word which conveys a meaning opposite to the given word.

REMEMBER

Words	*Antonyms*
Abhor	Love
Abnormal	Normal
Able	Unable
Acceptable	Unacceptable
Adequate	Inadequate
Amusing	Boring
Angry	Calm
Apex	Bottom
Attract	Repel
Bad	Good
Barren	Fertile
Beautiful	Ugly
Bitter	Sweet
Brave	Cowardly
Brief	Lengthy
Bright	Dull
Calm	Violent
Careful	Careless
Clear	Vague, Cloudy
Cold	Hot
Cruel	Kind
Dear	Cheap
Deep	Shallow
Difficult	Easy
Direct	Indirect
Dishonest	Honest
Disobey	Obey
Encourage	Discourage
Enormous	Tiny
Excellent	Bad
Expensive	Cheap
Eat	Fast
Fair	Unfair
Fake	Authentic
False	True
Famous	Notorious
Fool	Genius
Generous	Miserly
Genius	Fool
Genuine	Unauthentic
Gigantic	Tiny
Glad	Depressed
Good	Bad
Great	Little
Happy	Sad
Hard	Soft
Hate	Love
Honest	Dishonest
Idle	Busy

Words	*Antonyms*
Immoral	Moral
Include	Exclude
Incorrect	Correct
Intelligent	Unintelligent
Kind	Cruel
Like	Dislike
Long	Short
Lucid	Vague
Major	Minor
Naive	Experienced
Nadir	Apex
Neat	Clumsy
Obedient	Disobedient
Obscure	Clear
Oppose	Support
Optimistic	Pessimistic
Out	In
Patience	Impatience
Peaceful	Belligerent
Pious	Impious
Polite	Impolite
Potent	Impotent
Prominent	Unimportant
Proper	Improper
Pure	Impure
Quick	Slow
Quiet	Disturbance
Real	False, Unreal
Reject	Select, Choose
Reliable	Unreliable
Respect	Disrespect
Right	Wrong
Robust	Feeble, Weak
Sad	Happy
Secret	Open
Sensible	Insensible
Severe	Mild
Sharp	Blunt
Simple	Complex
Sociable	Unsociable
Tall	Short
Tidy	Untidy
Uncanny	Canny
Violent	Calm
Vivid	Vague
Strong	Weak
Big	Small
Easy	Difficult
Fast	Slow
High	Low
Catchy	Unattractive
Ugly	Handsome, Beautiful, Tidy
Tasty	Insipid
Sonorous	Harsh

MULTIPLE CHOICE QUESTIONS

Directions (Qs. 1 to 20): *In the following questions choose the word which best expresses the meaning of the given word.*

1. ABSURD
A. Foolish B. Simple
C. Courageous D. Silly

2. ABANDON
A. Lose B. Profit
C. Vacate D. Foil

3. CAJOLE
A. Pause B. Lenient
C. Blast D. Lure

4. COMBAT
A. Fight B. Conflict
C. Shoot D. Quarrel

5. LAMENT
A. Condone B. Console
C. Complain D. Contribution

6. DEBACLE
A. Disgrace B. Defeat
C. Collapse D. Decline

7. SHIVER
A. Fear B. Tremble
C. Shake D. Ache

8. TORTURE
A. Terror B. Harassment
C. Torment D. Tranquility

9. LAUDABLE
A. Lovable B. Commendable
C. Profitable D. Oblivious

10. FIXED
A. Sterile B. Static
C. Stubborn D. Parennial

11. QUEER
A. Unfamiliar B. Cute
C. Curious D. Strange

12. SUFFICIENT
A. Fit B. Proper
C. Adequate D. Vast

13. GLOSS
A. Brightness B. Soothing
C. Rubbing D. Miracle

14. LONGING
A. Prune B. Apathy
C. Curtail D. Craving

15. JEER
A. Applaud B. Magnanimity
C. Avoid D. Scoff

16. ZENITH
A. Minimum B. Nadir
C. Plant D. Peak

17. GARB
A. Distort B. Dress
C. Trivial D. Rage

18. ABHOR
A. Rude B. Reconcile
C. Crave D. Detest

19. YIELD
A. Shum B. Incisive
C. Retain D. Surrender

20. YOKE
A. Twist B. Release
C. Link D. Extra

Directions (Qs. 21 to 26): *In the following questions choose the word which best expresses the opposite of the given word.*

21. TRAGIC
A. Dramatic B. Strong
C. Gentle D. Comic

22. ORAL
A. Verbal B. Sane
C. Minor D. Written

23. ADMIRE
A. Hate B. Unlike
C. Dislike D. Enough

24. VIOLENT
A. Gentle B. Savage
C. Haughty D. Decline

25. ADVERSITY
A. Windfall B. Inprosperity
C. Prosperity D. Slave

26. GENUINE
A. Spurious B. Obscure
C. Countless D. Apathetic

ANSWERS

1	2	3	4	5	6	7	8	9	10
D	C	D	A	C	C	B	C	B	B
11	**12**	**13**	**14**	**15**	**16**	**17**	**18**	**19**	**20**
D	C	A	D	D	D	B	D	D	C
21	**22**	**23**	**24**	**25**	**26**				
D	D	C	A	C	A				

●●●

3

Sentence Completion

It is such an exercise which starts with the primary schools and continues in the highest level of competitive examinations. One must practise it regularly to score well.

Directions (Qs. 1 to 15): *Pick out the most effective word(s) from the given words to fill in the blanks to make the sentence meaningfully complete.*

1. The student ...... that book from the library to study at home.
A. issued B. borrowed
C. hired D. lent

2. I wish I ...... a king.
A. was B. am
C. should be D. were

3. He ...... to listen to my arguments and walked away.
A. denied B. disliked
C. objected D. refused

4. The flow of blood was so ...... that the patient died.
A. intense B. adequate
C. profuse D. extensive

5. When I met her yesterday, it was the first time I ...... her since Christmas.
A. saw B. have seen
C. had seen D. have been seing

6. Can you pay ...... all these articles?
A. for B. of
C. off D. out

7. I ...... you to be at the party this evening.
A. expect B. hope
C. look forward to D. desire

8. ...... being a handicapped person, he is very cooperative and self-reliant.
A. Because B. Although
C. Since D. Despite

9. The child broke ...... from his mother and ran towards the painting.
A. away B. after
C. down D. with

10. With his ...... income, he finds it difficult to live a comfortable life.
A. brief
B. sufficient
C. meagre
D. huge

11. He could ...... a lot of money in such a short time by using his intelligence and working hard.
A. spend
B. spoil
C. exchange
D. accumulate

12. Though the brothers are twins, they look ......
A. alike B. handsome
C. indifferent D. different

13. Unfavourable weather conditions can ..... illness.
A. cure B. detect
C. treat D. enhance

14. No sooner did the bell ring, ... the actor started singing.
A. when B. than
C. after D. before

15. If I ...... realised it, I would not have acted on his advice.
A. was B. had
C. were D. have

Directions (Qs. 16 to 25): *In each question, an incomplete statement (Stem) followed by four fillers is given. Pick out the best one which can complete the incomplete stem correctly and meaningfully.*

16. Unless you work harder you will fail, means .....
A. if you fail you will work harder.
B. you must at least plan well than you will not fail.
C. hardly you will fail if you do not desire so.
D. if you do not put more efforts, then you will fail.

17. Even if it rains I shall come, means .....
A. if I come it will not rain.
B. if it rains I shall not come.
C. I will certainly come whether it rains or not.
D. whenever there is rain I shall come.

18. Dinesh is as stupid as he is lazy means .....
A. Dinesh is stupid because he is lazy.
B. Dinesh is lazy because he is stupid.
C. Dinesh is either stupid or lazy.
D. Dinesh is equally stupid and lazy.

19. He is so lazy that he .....
A. cannot depend on others for getting his work done.
B. cannot delay the schedule of completing the work.
C. can seldom complete his work on time.
D. dislike to postpone the work that he undertakes to do.

20. He always stammers in public meetings, but his today's speech .....
A. was fairly audible to everyone present in the hall.
B. was not received satisfactorily.
C. could not be understood properly.
D. was free from that defect.

21. In order to raise the company's profit, the employees.....
A. demanded two additional increments.
B. decided to go on paid holidays.
C. requested the management to implement new welfare schemes.
D. offered to work overtime without any compensation.

22. Although, he is reputed for making very candid statements, ...
A. his today's speech was not fairly audible.
B. his promises had always been realistic.
C. his speech was very interesting.
D. his today's statements were very ambiguous.

23. I felt somewhat more relaxed .....
A. but tense as compared to earlier.
B. and tense as compared to earlier.
C. as there was already no tension at all.
D. and tension-free as compared to earlier.

24. With great efforts his son succeeded in convincing him not to donate his entire wealth to an orphanage ....
A. and lead the life of a wealthy merchant.
B. but to a home for the forsaken children.
C. and make an orphan of himself.
D. as the orphanage needed a lot of donations.

25. Even though it is a very large house, ...
A. there is a lot of space available in it for children.
B. there is hardly any space available for children.
C. there is no dearth of space for children.
D. the servants take a long time to clean it.

ANSWERS

1	2	3	4	5	6	7	8	9	10
B	D	D	C	C	A	A	D	A	C
11	**12**	**13**	**14**	**15**	**16**	**17**	**18**	**19**	**20**
D	D	D	B	B	D	C	D	C	D
21	**22**	**23**	**24**	**25**					
D	D	D	C	B					

●●●

4

Spotting Errors

The most common errors in English are of spellings, grammar and usage of words. By regular practice, the errors can be easily spotted and minimised.

MULTIPLE CHOICE QUESTIONS

Directions: *In the following questions some of the sentences have errors and some are correct. Find out which part of a sentence has an error, the number of that part is your answer. If a sentence is free from errors, then your answer is D i.e., No error.*

1. (A) Either Ram or/(B) you is responsible/(C) for this action./(D) No error.

2. (A) The student flatly denied/(B) that he had copied/(C) in the examination hall./(D) No error.

3. (A) By the time you arrive tomorrow/(B) I have finished/(C) my work./(D) No error.

4. (A) The captain with the members of his team/(B) are returning/(C) after a fortnight./(D) No error.

5. (A) After returning from/(B) an all-India tour/(C) I had to describe about it./(D) No error.

6. (A) The teacher asked his students/(B) if they had gone through/(C) either of the three chapters included in the prescribed text./(D) No error.

7. (A) Do you know/(B) how old were you/(C) when you came here?/(D) No error.

8. (A) Beware of/(B) a fair-weather friend/(C) who is neither a friend in need nor a friend indeed./(D) No error.

9. (A) Copernicus proved/(B) that Earth/(C) moves round the Sun./(D) No error.

10. (A) The property/(B) was divided/(C) among the two brothers./(D) No error.

11. (A) I am quite certain/(B) that the lady is not only greedy/(C) but miserly./(D) No error.

12. (A) The brilliant success in the examination/(B) as well as his record in sports/(C) deserves high praise./(D) No error.

13. (A) I cannot find/(B) where has he gone/(C) though I have tried may best./(D) No error.

14. (A) If I was/(B) the Prime Minister of India/(C) I would work wonders/(D) No error.

15. (A) If it weren't/(B) for you,/(C) I wouldn't be alive today./(D) No error.

16. (A) He looked like a lion/(B) baulked from/(C) its prey./(D) No error.

17. (A) Widespread flooding/(B) is affecting/(C) large areas of the villages./(D) No error.

18. (A) If we really set to/(B) we can get the whole house/(C) cleaned in an afternoon./(D) No error.

ANSWERS

1	2	3	4	5	6	7	8	9	10
B	D	B	B	C	C	D	D	B	C
11	**12**	**13**	**14**	**15**	**16**	**17**	**18**	**19**	**20**
C	D	B	A	C	C	C	A	A	C

EXPLANATORY ANSWERS

1. Replace 'is' by 'are'.
2. No error.
3. Replace 'have' by 'would have'.
4. Replace 'are' by 'is'.
5. Replace 'had to describe' by 'described'.
6. Replace 'either' by 'any'.
7. No error.
8. No error.
9. Omit 'that'.
10. Replace 'among' by 'between'.
11. Add 'also'.
12. No error.
13. Replace 'has he' by 'he has'.
14. Replace 'was' by 'were'.
15. Replace 'wouldn't be' by 'would not have been'.
16. Replace 'its' by 'his'.
17. Replace 'areas' by 'area'.
18. Replace 'set to' by 'set on'.

●●●

5

One Word Substitution

There are many single words in English language which can be perfectly used for a number of words. These words help in expressing ideas in a short and correct manner for the right occasion. Such words not only increase the vocabulary but also enable you to economise in the use of words to a great extent.

Multiple Word Expression	*Substitution*
One who always looks towards the bright side of things	Optimist
One who always looks towards the dark side of things	Pessimist
The time when one develops from a child into an adult	Adolescence
The process of growing more plants in order to form a forest.	Afforestation
The science which deals with farming	Agriculture
From some other country or place etc.	Alien
A term, etc. giving more than one meaning	Ambiguous
A vehicle which is used to carry sick persons	Ambulance
An animal which can live both in water and on land	Amphibian
A lawless situation when there is no government	Anarchy
Belonging to the history of thousands of years old	Ancient
Once a year	Annual
A very old object but still valuable	Antique
Words of opposite meanings	Antonyms
Words of similar meanings	Synonyms
Signatures of a famous person	Autograph
A government led by one person with absolute authority	Autocracy
A written work of one's own life history	Autobiography
A person who has never been married	Bachelor
A person usually having no hair on his head	Bald
A place where one can deposit money and get interest	Bank
A person who cuts our hair	Barber
A building/group of buildings where soldiers live	Barracks
A person who makes buns and biscuits	Baker
A person who lives by asking people for food and money without doing any useful job	Beggar
The crime of having married to two persons at the same time	Bigamy
The branch of science which deals with the study of plants	Botany
Able to speak two languages	Bilingual
Able to speak more than two languages	Polyglot
The branch of science which deals with the living organisms	Biology
A powerful snow storm	Blizzard
A great successful book or movie	Blockbuster
A short news on the radio or TV	Bulletin
A system in which the most important works are organised by the government officials	Bureaucracy
A person who has no vision in his eyes	Blind
A page or a series of pages on which the information of days, weeks, months, etc. is given	Calendar
A person who eats human flesh	Cannibal
A complete list of items often arranged alphabetically	Catalogue
A sudden disaster	Catastrophe
A period of 100 years	Century

Multiple Word Expression	*Substitution*
A branch of science which deals with chemicals	Chemistry
A printed leaf usually issued by banks that we sign to carry certain financial deal	Cheque
A person who makes or mends shoes	Cobbler
A group of people who has been chosen by others to make decisions on their own	Committee
A building in which nuns live	Convent
An animal which feeds on other animals	Carnivorous
A person who does criticism	Critic
A person who cannot hear	Deaf
A condition in which one loses a lot of water from one's body because of vomiting, etc.	Dehydration
A system of government in which the people cast their votes to elect their leaders	Democracy
The study of skin problems	Dermatology
A long piece of land covered with sand	Desert
The art of managing relationships between countries	Diplomacy
A piece of information about the words in a book form	Dictionary
A piece of information about the telephone numbers of the people in a book from	Directory
A person in charge of a newspapers, magazine etc.	Editor
A person who thinks he is better than the others	Egoist
To leave your country and settle in some other country	Emigrate
A book or series of books giving almost all knowledge about an area or some persons etc.	Encyclopaedia
Study of insects	Entomology
Time when day and night are of the same duration	Equinox
To sell things out of the country	Export
To purchase things from some other country	Import
A plant or animal no longer in existence	Extinct
A situation when there is a shortage of food for a long period of time	Famine
An amount of money that we pay for some action or services	Fee
Related to women	Feminine
An animal strong and aggressive	Ferocious
A piece of land where plants grow easily from the soil that is favourable to them	Fertile
A work of literature having some imaginary events	Fiction
A large amount of water covering certain area	Flood
A person who sells flowers	Florist
A religious ceremony for burying or cremating a dead person	Funeral
A substance which kills fungus	Fungicide
A person studying or having studied the diseases and the related things of female reproductory system	Gynaecologist
The murder of the person of the same group race or country	Genocide
A substance which kills germs	Germicide
A situation in which many people die because of fire during war	Holocaust
The act of killing a person deliberately	Homicide
A word having the pronunciation as the other one does but it differs in meaning	Homophone
A word having the same spelling as the other one does but it is pronounced in some other way	Homonym
A person who is attracted towards the person of the same sex	Homosexual
Go across and parallel to the ground	Horizontal
A substance which kills the insects	Insecticide
That cannot be corrected	Incorrigible
That cannot be defeated	Invincible
That cannot be eaten	Inedible
That cannot be seen	Invisible
A place in a school or college where books are kept for the benefit of students, teachers etc.	Library
A place in a school or college where scientific experiments are performed	Laboratory

Multiple Word Expression	*Substitution*
An official who is a judge in the lowest court	Magistrate
A piece of music or a book before it is printed	Manuscript
Related to men	Masculine
One who believes in the existence of God	A theist
One who does not believe in the existence of good	An atheist
That can be believed	Credible
That cannot be believed	Incredible
That which dissolves in a solvent	Soluble
That which does not dissolves in a solvent	Insoluble
Hard writing that can be read	Legible
Hard writing that cannot be read	Illegible
A person who does jobs beneficial to mankind	Philanthropist
A person who goes on foot	Pedestrian
A person who fights for his own country	Patriot
An act of killing oneself	Suicide
A woman whose husband is dead	Widow
A man whose wife is dead	Widower
A person who eats vegetarian and non-vegetarian diets	Omnivorous
Something which is everywhere at the same time	Omnipresent
One who knows everything	Omniscient
A child who does not have parents	Orphan
An award etc. given after the death of the person	Posthumous
The place where animals are kept for amusement and to increase the knowledge of the public	Zoo
The science which deals with the study of animals	Zoology

MULTIPLE CHOICE QUESTIONS

Directions: *In questions given below, out of the four alternatives, choose the one which can be substituted for the given words/sentences.*

1. Something that relates to everyone in the world
A. General B. Common
C. Usual D. Universal

2. An expression of mild disapproval
A. Warning B. Denigration
C. Impertinence D. Reproof

3. One who is not easily pleased by anything
A. Maiden B. Medieval
C. Precarious D. Fastidious

4. Murder of a king
A. Infanticide B. Matricide
C. Genocide D. Regicide

5. A remedy for all diseases
A. Stoic B. Marvel
C. Panacea D. Recompense

6. A dramatic performance
A. Mask B. Mosque
C. Masque D. Mascot

7. Study of birds
A. Orology B. Optology
C. Ophthalmology D. Ornithology

8. Ready to believe
A. Credulous B. Credible
C. Creditable D. Incredible

9. Incapable of being seen through
A. Ductile B. Opaque
C. Obsolete D. Potable

10. One who eats everything
A. Omnivorous B. Omniscient
C. Irresistible D. Insolvent

11. A place where bees are kept is called
A. An apiary B. A mole
C. A hive D. A sanctuary

12. One who cannot be corrected
A. Incurable B. Incorrigible
C. Hardened D. Invulnerable

13. One who is in charge of a museum
A. Curator B. Supervisor
C. Caretaker D. Warden

14. Continuing fight between parties, families, clans, etc.
A. Enmity B. Feud
C. Quarrel D. Skirmish

15. A voice loud enough to be heard
A. Audible B. Applaudable
C. Laudable D. Oral

16. A paper written by hand
A. Handicraft B. Manuscript
C. Handiwork D. Thesis

17. Habitually silent or talking little
A. Serville B. Unequivocal
C. Taciturn D. Synoptic

18. To slap with a flat object
A. Chop B. Hew
C. Gnaw D. Swat

19. A person who speaks many languages
A. Linguist B. Monolingual
C. Polyglot D. Bilingual

20. A light sailing-boat built specially for racing
A. Canoe B. Yacht
C. Frigate D. Dinghy

21. A fixed orbit in space in relation to earth
A. Geological B. Geo-synchronous
C. Geo-centric D. Geo-stationary

22. A style in which a writer makes a display of his knowledge
A. Pedantic B. Verbose
C. Pompous D. Ornate

23. A religious discourse
A. Preach B. Stanza
C. Sanctorum D. Sermon

24. A place that provides refuge
A. Asylum B. Sanatorium
C. Shelter D. Orphanage

25. Detailed plan of a journey
A. Travelogue B. Travelkit
C. Schedule D. Itinerary

26. A person who insists on something
A. Disciplinarian B. Stickler
C. Instantaneous D. Boaster

27. A drawing on transparent paper
A. Red print B. Blue print
C. Negative D. Transparency

28. One who believes that all things and events in life are predetermined is a
A. Fatalist B. Puritan
C. Egoist D. Tyrant

29. A school boy who cuts classes frequently is a
A. Defeatist B. Sycophant
C. Truant D. Martinet

30. The act of violating the sanctity of the church is
A. Blasphemy B. Heresy
C. Sacrilege D. Desecration

31. A place where monks live as a secluded community
A. Cathedral B. Diocese
C. Convent D. Monastery

32. One who is fond of fighting
A. Bellicose B. Aggressive
C. Belligerent D. Militant

33. Tending to move away from the centre or axis
A. Centrifugal B. Centripetal
C. Axiomatic D. Awry

34. Words inscribed on tomb
A. Epitome B. Epistle
C. Epilogue D. Epitaph

35. Leave or remove from a place considered dangerous
A. Evade B. Evacuate
C. Avoid D. Exterminate

36. Original inhabitants of a country
A. Abroge B. Aborger
C. Aborgory D. Aborigins

37. Government by the officials
A. Theocracy B. Plutocracy
C. Bureaucracy D. Democracy

38. Incapable of being exhausted
A. Inexhaustible B. Inaexhaustible
C. Exhaustable D. Non-tired

39. A person of good understanding, knowledge and reasoning power
A. Expert B. Intellectual
C. Snob D. Literate

40. One absorbed in his own thoughts and feelings rather than in things outside
A. Scholar B. Recluse
C. Introvert D. Intellectual

ANSWERS

1	2	3	4	5	6	7	8	9	10
D	D	D	D	C	C	D	A	B	A
11	12	13	14	15	16	17	18	19	20
A	B	A	B	A	B	C	D	A	B
21	22	23	24	25	26	27	28	29	30
D	A	D	A	D	B	D	A	C	C
31	32	33	34	35	36	37	38	39	40
D	A	A	D	B	B	C	A	B	C

●●●

6

Spelling Errors

There are thousands of words in English language. It is difficult to remember the spellings and meanings of all at once. Try to learn as many as you can. Use a dictionary regularly.

Directions: *Find the correctly spelt words.*

1. A. Damage B. Dammage C. Damaige D. Dammege
2. A. Efficiant B. Effecient C. Efficient D. Eficient
3. A. Schedule B. Schdule C. Schedale D. Schedeule
4. A. Occurad B. Occurred C. Ocurred D. Occured
5. A. Grieff B. Grief C. Grieef D. Grrief
6. A. Guarantee B. Garuntee C. Guaruntee D. Gaurantee
7. A. Meddicine B. Medicine C. Medicene D. Medicinne
8. A. Benefeted B. Benefitted C. Benifited D. Benefited
9. A. Acommodation B. Acomodation C. Accomodation D. Accommodation
10. A. Querrelsome B. Quarrelsame C. Quarrelsome D. Querralsome
11. A. Sympathetic B. Smypathetic C. Sympothetic D. Sympethetic
12. A. Prograssive B. Progressive C. Progresive D. Prograsive
13. A. Uncivilized B. Uncevilized C. Uncivillized D. Uncevelized
14. A. Extravagant B. Extreragent C. Extreregant D. Extravegent
15. A. Missunderstood B. Miesunderstood C. Misunderstood D. Misunderstod
16. A. Belligerent B. Beligirent C. Belligarant D. Belligerrent
17. A. Astonished B. Astronished C. Astoneshed D. Asstonished
18. A. Sincerely B. Sencerely C. Sincerelly D. Sincerrely
19. A. Rigourous B. Rigerous C. Rigorous D. Regerous
20. A. Satellite B. Sattellite C. Satelite D. Sattelite
21. A. Pesanger B. Passenger C. Pessenger D. Pasanger
22. A. Humurous B. Humorous C. Humoreus D. Humorrous
23. A. Exeggerate B. Exaggerate C. Exadgerate D. Exagerate
24. A. Fariegn B. Forein C. Foriegn D. Foreign
25. A. Excesive B. Excessive C. Exccessive D. Exccesive
26. A. Forcaust B. Forcast C. Forecast D. Forecaste
27. A. Paralleted B. Paralelled C. Parralleled D. Parallelled
28. A. Ocasion B. Occassion C. Occasion D. Ocassion
29. A. Boquet B. Bouquet C. Bouquete D. Bouquette
30. A. Chettering B. Chaterring C. Chattering D. Chatering
31. A. Discourage B. Disscourage C. Discourege D. Discaurage
32. A. Curageous B. Courageous C. Courrageous D. Couregeous
33. A. Abandon B. Abanddon C. Abendon D. Abbandon
34. A. Embarassment B. Emberrassement C. Embarrassment D. Embbaresment
35. A. Eccintric B. Eccentrie C. Eccentric D. Eccintrie
36. A. Occasional B. Occassional C. Occesional D. Occessional
37. A. Querrel B. Querral C. Quarrel D. Quarel
38. A. Contrebution B. Contribution C. Contributtion D. Conterbution

39. A. Desgrace B. Disgrece
C. Disgrice D. Disgrace

40. A. Harassment B. Herassment
C. Harasment D. Harassmient

41. A. Imaginative B. Imeginative
C. Imagenative D. Imaginetive

42. A. Suficient B. Suficiant
C. Sufficient D. Sufficiant

43. A. Adequate B. Edequate
C. Adaquete D. Edaquete

44. A. Exparienced B. Experianced
C. Experienced D. Experrienced

45. A. Flatering B. Fletering
C. Flattering D. Fletaring

46. A. Cuttiveted B. Culltrivated
C. Cultivated D. Caltivated

47. A. Praiceworthy B. Peiseworthy
C. Praiseworthy D. Praisaworthy

48. A. Profesional B. Professionel
C. Professional D. Profissional

49. A. Ameteur B. Amateur
C. Amataur D. Amateor

50. A. Unfevourable B. Unfevaurable
C. Unfavourable D. Unfivourable

ANSWERS

1	2	3	4	5	6	7	8	9	10
A	C	A	B	B	A	B	B	D	C
11	**12**	**13**	**14**	**15**	**16**	**17**	**18**	**19**	**20**
A	B	A	A	C	A	A	A	C	A
21	**22**	**23**	**24**	**25**	**26**	**27**	**28**	**29**	**30**
B	B	B	D	B	C	A	C	B	C
31	**32**	**33**	**34**	**35**	**36**	**37**	**38**	**39**	**40**
A	B	A	C	C	A	C	B	D	A
41	**42**	**43**	**44**	**45**	**46**	**47**	**48**	**49**	**50**
A	C	A	C	A	C	C	C	B	C

●●●

QUANTITATIVE APTITUDE

NUMBER SYSTEM

1. There are four numbers A, B, C and D. Average of the first three *i.e.*, A, B and C is 15 and that of B, C and D is 16. If the last number, *i.e.*, D is 19, then the first number is—

A. 15 B. 16
C. 17 D. 18

2. Of the three numbers, the first is twice the second and thrice the third. If the average of three is 22, the three numbers are—

A. 12, 18, 36
B. 18, 12, 36
C. 36, 12, 18
D. 36, 18, 12

3. If a person is standing on the sixth number in the queue from both the ends, the total persons in the queue are—

A. 9 B. 11
C. 12 D. 13

4. A number 'x' when multiplied by 5 and added to three times its own gives 64, the number is—

A. 8 B. 12
C. 14 D. 18

5. A number which when multiplied by 11 is as much above 180 as it was originally below it. The number is—

A. 25 B. 30
C. 40 D. 45

6. The sum of a number and its reciprocal is thrice the difference of the number and its reciprocal. Find the number.

A. $\sqrt{2}$ B. $\sqrt{3}$
C. $\sqrt{5}$ D. $\sqrt{7}$

7. A boy was asked to find $\frac{7}{9}$ of a fraction. He made a mistake of dividing the fraction by $\frac{7}{9}$ and so got an answer which exceeded the correct answer by $\frac{8}{21}$. Find the correct answer.

A. $\frac{2}{3}$ B. $\frac{5}{7}$
C. $\frac{7}{12}$ D. $\frac{7}{15}$

8. There are 408 boys and 312 girls in a school, which are to be divided into equal sections of either boys or girls alone. Find the maximum number of boys or girls that can be placed in a section. Also find the total number of sections thus formed.

A. 10, 20 B. 24, 30
C. 24, 40 D. 30, 30

9. The sum of all possible two-digit number formed from three different one-digit natural numbers, when divided by the sum of the original three numbers is equal to—

A. 11 B. 18
C. 22 D. 36

10. There are four prime numbers written in ascending order. The product of the first three is 385 and that of the last three is 1001. The last number is—

A. 19 B. 17
C. 13 D. 11

11. If the number 357 ★ 25 ★ is divisible by both 3 and 5, then the missing digits in the unit's place and thousandth place respectively are—

A. 0, 4 B. 5, 4
C. 5, 6 D. 0, 6

12. The difference between two numbers is 1365. When the larger number is divided by the smaller one, the quotient is 6 and the remainder is 15. The smaller number is:

A. 360 B. 295
C. 270 D. 240

13. When a number is divided by 31, the remainder is 29. When the same number is divided by 16, what will be the remainder?

A. 15 B. 13
C. 11 D. Data inadequate

14. In dividing a number by 585, a student applied the method of short division. He divided the number successively by 5, 9 and 13 (factor of 585) and got the remainders 4, 8 and 12. If he had divided the number by 585, the remainder would have been:

A. 584 B. 292
C. 144 D. 24

15. When a number divided by 6 leaves a remainder 3. When the square of the same number is divided by 6, the remainder is:

A. 3 B. 2
C. 1 D. zero

ANSWERS

1	2	3	4	5	6	7	8	9	10
B	D	B	A	B	A	C	B	C	C
11	**12**	**13**	**14**	**15**					
C	C	D	A	A					

EXPLANATORY ANSWERS

1. $\dfrac{A+B+C}{3} = 15,$

or, $A + B + C = 15 \times 3 = 45$ ... (*i*)

$\dfrac{B+C+D}{3} = 16,$

or $B + C + D = 48$ ... (*ii*)

$D = 19$

$\therefore\ B + C + 19 = 48$ or, B +

$C = 48 - 19 = 29$

But, $A + B + C = 45$

Putting the value of $B + C = 29$ in the above equation (*i*), we get $A + 29 = 45$

$\therefore\ A = 45 - 29 = 16.$

2. Let the third number $= x$

$\therefore$ First number $= 3x$

Second number $= \dfrac{3x}{2}$

$\therefore\ \dfrac{1}{3}\left[x + 3x + \dfrac{3x}{2}\right] = 22 \Rightarrow \dfrac{11}{2}x = 66$

$\Rightarrow x = \dfrac{66 \times 2}{11} = 12 =$ Third number,

$12 \times 3 = 36 =$ First number,

$\dfrac{12 \times 3}{2} = 18 =$ Second number.

3. If the person is standing at sixth number in the queue from both sides, that means there are five persons ahead and five persons behind him. Hence, total number of persons in the queue is $5 + 1 + 5 = 11$.

4. $5 \times x + 3x = 64 \quad \Rightarrow 8x = 64$

$\therefore\quad x = \dfrac{64}{8} = 8.$

5. Let the number is x

$\therefore\quad 180 - x = 11x - 180$

$\Rightarrow\quad 180 + 180 = 11x + x$

$\Rightarrow\quad 360 = 12x,$

$\Rightarrow\quad x = \dfrac{360}{12} = 30.$

6. Let the no. $= x$ then its reciprocal $= \dfrac{1}{x}$

By the question, $\left(x + \dfrac{1}{x}\right) = 3\left(x - \dfrac{1}{x}\right)$

$\Rightarrow\quad \dfrac{x^2+1}{x} = \dfrac{3(x^2-1)}{x}$

$\Rightarrow\quad x^2 + 1 = 3x^2 - 3$

$\Rightarrow\quad 3x^2 - x^2 = 3 + 1$

$\therefore\quad x = \sqrt{2}.$

7. Let the required fraction $= x$

then, by the question $x \div \dfrac{7}{9} - x \times \dfrac{7}{9} = \dfrac{8}{21}$

$\Rightarrow\quad x \times \dfrac{9}{7} - \dfrac{7x}{9} = \dfrac{8}{21}$

$\Rightarrow\quad \dfrac{32x}{63} = \dfrac{8}{21}$

$\Rightarrow\quad x = \dfrac{8}{21} \times \dfrac{63}{32} = \dfrac{3}{4}$

Hence, the correct answer $= \dfrac{3}{4} \times \dfrac{7}{9} = \dfrac{7}{12}.$

8.

```
312) 408(1
     312
     ---
      96) 312 (3
          288
          ---
           24) 96 (4
               96
               --
               ×
```

$\therefore$ Maximum number of girls or boys that can be placed in a section = 24 and total number of such

section $= \dfrac{408}{24} + \dfrac{312}{24}$

$= 17 + 13 = 30$

9. Let three different one digit natural numbers be x, y and z.

Then, sum of all possible two digits numbers

$= (10x + y) + (10y + x) + (10x + z)$

$+ (10z + x) + (10y + z) + (10z + y)$

$= 22x + 22y + 22z = 22\,(x + y + z)$

Hence, required number = 22.

10. Let four prime numbers be a, b, c and d respectively.

Now, $\frac{abc}{bcd} = \frac{385}{1001}$

$\Rightarrow \quad \frac{c}{d} = \frac{5}{13}$

Hence, $a = 5$ and $d = 13$

11. 357 ★ 25 ★

For divisible by 5, the last digit must be either 0 or 5.

If last digit is 0, then other required digit will be 2 or 5 or 8

Hence, the numbers are (0, 2) or (0, 5) or (0, 8)

If last digit is 5, then other required digit will be 0 or 3 or 6 or 9

Hence, the numbers are (5, 0) or (5, 3) or (5, 6) or (5, 9)

So, correct option is (c).

12. Here, $(x + 1365) = 6x + 15$

$\Rightarrow 5x = 1350$

$\therefore \; x = \frac{1350}{5} = 270$

Hence, the smaller number = 270.

13. The number = $31x + 29$.

Here, given data is inadequate.

14.

5	a
9	$b - 4$
13	$c - 8$
	$1 - 12$

Now, $c = 13 \times 1 + 12 = 25$

$b = 9c + 8 = 9 \times 25 + 8 = 233$

$a = 5b + 4 = 5 \times 233 + 4$

$= 1165 + 4 = 1169$

$1169 = 585 \times 1 + 584$

Hence, required remainder = 584.

15. The number = $6x + 3$

Now, $(6x + 3)^2 = 36x^2 + 36x + 9$

$= (36x^2 + 36x + 6) + 3$

$= 6(6x^2 + 6x + 1) + 3$

Hence, required remainder = 3.

LCM AND HCF

1. The L.C.M. and H.C.F. of two numbers are 4284 and 32 respectively. If one of the numbers is 204, the other is

A. 672 B. 576
C. 676 D. 572

2. Two numbers are in the ratio of 8 : 15. If their H.C.F. is 4, the numbers are

A. 32 and 60 B. 16 and 30
C. 80 and 150 D. 64 and 120

3. The greatest number that will divide 366, 513 and 324 leaving the same remainder in each case is

A. 21 B. 18
C. 27 D. 42

4. The L.C.M. of two numbers is 45 times their H.C.F. If the sum of the L.C.M. and the H.C.F. of these two numbers is 1150 and one of the numbers is 125, then the other number is

A. 256 B. 225
C. 250 D. 255

5. The H.C.F. and the L.C.M. of two numbers are 50 and 250 respectively. On dividing one of these numbers by 2, 50 is obtained as quotient. The numbrs are

A. 100, 125 B. 80, 100
C. 125, 100 D. 200, 250

6. Three bells ring respectively at an interval of 15 seconds, 20 seconds and 24 seconds. If they ring continuously for 12 minutes then how many times, during this period, will they ring together?

A. 2 times B. 6 times
C. 5 times D. 3 times

7. If the sum of two numbers is 55 and the H.C.F. and L.C.M. of these numbers are 5 and 120 respectively. Find the sum of their reciprocals.

A. $\frac{120}{11}$ B. $\frac{11}{120}$
C. $\frac{601}{55}$ D. $\frac{55}{601}$

8. The LCM of two numbers is 48. The numbers are in the ratio of 2 : 3. The sum of the numbers is

A. 64 B. 40
C. 32 D. 28

9. Find the greatest number that will divide 43, 91 and 183 so as to leave the same remainder in each case.

A. 13 B. 9
C. 7 D. 4

10. The greatest possible length which can be used to measure exactly the length 7m, 3m 85cm, 12m 95 cm is

A. 42 cm B. 35 cm
C. 25 cm D. 15 cm

11. A, B and C start at the same time in the same direction to run around a circular park. A completes a round in 252 seconds, B in 308 seconds and C in 198 seconds, all starting at the same point. After what time will they meet again at the starting point?
A. 46 minutes 12 seconds
B. 45 minutes
C. 42 minutes 36 seconds
D. 26 minutes 18 seconds

12. Which of the following has most numbers of divisors?
A. 182 B. 176
C. 101 D. 99

13. Which is of the following is a co-primes?
A. (23, 92) B. (21, 35)
C. (18, 25) D. (16, 62)

14. Let N be the greatest number that will divide 1305, 4665 and 6905, leaving the same remainder in each case. Then find the sum of the digits in N.
A. 8 B. 6
C. 5 D. 4

15. The greatest number which one dividing 1657 and 2037 leaves remainder 6 and 5 respectively, is:
A. 305 B. 235
C. 127 D. 123

ANSWERS

1	2	3	4	5	6	7	8	9	10
A	A	A	B	A	B	B	B	D	B
11	**12**	**13**	**14**	**15**					
A	B	C	D	C					

EXPLANATORY ANSWERS

1. 1st number × 2nd number = LCM × HCF

$\therefore$ 204 × 2nd number = 4284 × 32

$\therefore$ 2nd number $= \dfrac{4284 \times 32}{204} = 672$

$\therefore$ 2nd number = 672

2. Let the numbers be $8x$ and $15x$

$8x = 2 \times 2 \times 2 \times x$

$15x = 3 \times 5 \times x$

$\therefore$ LCM of $8x$ and $15x = 2 \times 2 \times 2 \times x \times 3 \times 5 = 120x$

Now, 1st number × 2nd number = HCF × LCM

$\Rightarrow 8x \times 15x = 4 \times 120x$

$\Rightarrow 120x^2 = 4 \times 120x$

$\Rightarrow x = 4$

$\therefore$ Numbers are $8 \times 4 = 32$ and $15 \times 4 = 60$

3. Difference between 366 and 513 = 513 − 366 = 147

and difference between 513 and 324 = 513 − 324 = 189

$\therefore$ HCF of 147 and 189

```
147) 189 (1
     147
     × 42) 147 (3
           126
           × 21) 42 (2
                 42
                 ×
```

$\therefore$ The required largest number is 21.

4. LCM of the two numbers = 45 × HCF

and LCM + HCF = 1150

$\Rightarrow$ 45 × HCF + HCF = 1150

$\Rightarrow$ HCF(45 + 1) = 1150

$\Rightarrow$ HCF $= \dfrac{1150}{46} = 25$

$\therefore$ LCM = 45 × 25 = 1125

$\because$ 1st number × 2nd number = LCM × HCF

$\therefore$ 125 × 2nd number = 1125 × 25

$\therefore$ 2nd number $= \dfrac{1125 \times 25}{125} = 225.$

5. According to the condition of the problem, 50 is obtained on dividing one of the numbers by 2

$\therefore$ One of the numbers = 50 × 2 = 100

Now, 1st number × 2nd number = LCM × HCF

$\therefore$ 100 × 2nd number = 250 × 50

$\therefore$ 2nd number $= \dfrac{250 \times 50}{100} = 125$

Hence, numbers are 100 and 125.

6. LCM of 15, 20 and 24

5	15, 20, 24
4	3, 4, 24
3	3, 1, 6
	1, 1, 2

LCM = 5 × 4 × 3 × 2 = 120

$\because$ 12 minutes = 12 × 60 = 720 seconds

$\therefore$ Number of times the bells will ring together during 12 minutes

$= \dfrac{720}{120} = 6$ times.

7. Let the number be x and y.
Then, $x + y = 55$;
$xy = \text{HCF} \times \text{LCM} = 5 \times 120$
$\therefore$ Sum of their reciprocals

$$= \frac{1}{x} + \frac{1}{y} = \frac{x+y}{xy} = \frac{55}{5 \times 120} = \frac{11}{120}.$$

8. Let the two numbers be $2x$ and $3x$;
their LCM = $6x$
Now, $6x = 48$ $\therefore$ $x = 8$
Hence, the numbers are 2×8, 3×8 = 16, 24
Their sum = 16 + 24 = 40.

9.
2240) 3360 (1
2240
1120) 2240 (2
2240
×

1120) 5600 (5
5600
×

Hence, N = HCF of 3360,
2240 and 5600 = 1120
Sum of digits in N = 1 + 1 + 2 + 0 = 4.

10. 7m = 700 cm;
3m 85 = 385 cm;
12m 95cm = 1295 cm

385) 700 (1
385
315) 385 (1
315
70) 315 (4
280
35) 70 (2
70
×

35) 1295 (37
105
245
245
×

Hence, required length = HCF of 700 cm, 385 cm, 1295 cm = 35 cm.

11.

2	252, 308, 198
2	126, 154, 99
3	63, 77, 99
3	21, 77, 33
7	7, 77, 11
11	1, 11, 11
	1, 1, 1

Hence, LCM = $2 \times 2 \times 3 \times 3 \times 7 \times 11 = 2772$
Hence, A, B, C will meet again at the starting point after 2772 sec. = 46 min 12 sec.

12.

Numbers	*Their divisors*
182	→ 1, 2, 7, 13, 14, 26, 91 and 182
176	→ 1, 2, 4, 8, 16, 22, 44, 88 and 176
101	→ 1 and 101
99	→ 1, 3, 9, 11, 33 and 99

Therefore, 176 has the most number of divisors.

13. HCF of 23 and 92 = 23
HCF of 21 and 35 = 7
HCF of 18 and 25 = 1
HCF of 16 and 62 = 2
Hence, 18 and 25 are co-prime numbers.

14. N = HCF of (4665 – 1305), (6905 – 4665) and (6905 – 1305)
= HCF of 3360, 2240 and 5600 = 112
Sum of digit of 1 + 1 + 2 = 4.

15. Required number = HCF of (1657 – 6) and (2037 – 5)
= HCF of 1651 and 2032 = 127.

1651) 2032 (1
1651
381) 1651 (4
1524
127) 381 (3
381
×

AVERAGE

1. One-third of a certain journey was covered at the rate of 25 km per hour, one-fourth at the rate of 30 km per hour and the rest at the 50 km per hour. What is the average speed per hour for whole journey?

A. $33\frac{1}{3}$ kmph B. $44\frac{1}{4}$ kmph
C. $22\frac{1}{2}$ kmph D. 33 kmph

2. A batsman has a certain average of runs for 16 innings. In the 17th innings, he makes a score of 85 runs thereby increasing his average by 3. What is the average after the 17th inning?

A. 33 runs B. 34 runs
C. 37 runs D. 36 runs

3. The average of 6 observations is 12. A new seventh observation is included and the new average is decreased by 1. The seventh observation is

A. 1 B. 3
C. 5 D. 6

4. The average age of 30 students in a class is 12 years. The average age of a group of 5 of the students is 10 years and that of another group of 5 of them is 14 years. The average age of the remaining students is
A. 8 years B. 10 years
C. 12 years D. 14 years

5. Out of the three given numbers, the first number is twice the second and thrice the third. If the average of three numbers is 121, what is the difference between the first and third number?
A. 144 B. 77
C. 99 D. 132

6. If the average marks of three batches of 55, 60 and 45 students is 50, 55 and 60, then average marks of all the students is:
A. 55 B. 54
C. 54.68 D. 55.68

7. The average of 8 numbers is 20. The average of first two numbers is $15\frac{1}{2}$ and that of the next three is $21\frac{1}{3}$. If the sixth number is less than the seventh and eighth numbers by 4 and 7 respectively, then the eighth number is:
A. 27 B. 25
C. 22 D. 18

8. A pupil's marks were wrongly entered as 83 instead of 63. Due to that the average marks for the class got increased by half. What is the number of pupils in the class?
A. 73 B. 40
C. 40 D. 10

9. A cricketer whose bowling average is 12.4 runs per wicket takes 5 wickets for 26 runs and thereby decreases his average by 0.4. The number of wickets taken by him till the last match was:
A. 85 B. 80
C. 72 D. 64

10. The average weight of a class of 24 students is 35 kg. If the weight of the teacher is included, the average rises by 400 g. What is the weight of the teacher?
A. 55 kg B. 53 kg
C. 50 kg D. 45 kg

11. Nine men went to a hotel. Eight of them spent Rs. 3 for each over their meals and the ninth spent Rs. 2 more than the average expenditure of all the nine. What is the total money spent by them?
A. Rs. 29.25 B. Rs. 29.50
C. Rs. 29 D. Rs. 30

12. The average age of 24 students in a class is 10. If the teacher's age is included, the average increases by one. The age of the teacher is
A. 25 B. 30
C. 35 D. 40

13. The average of 5 consecutive even numbers A, B, C, D and E is 34. What is the product of B and D?
A. 1152 B. 1368
C. 1224 D. 1088

14. The average of 50 numbers is 30. If two numbers, 35 and 40 are discarded, then the average of the remaining numbers is nearly:
A. 29.68 B. 29.27
C. 28.78 D. 28.32

15. The average monthly salary of 20 employees of an organisation is Rs. 1500. If the manager's salary is added, then the average salary increases by Rs. 100. Find the manager's monthly salary?
A. Rs. 4800 B. Rs. 3600
C. Rs. 2400 D. Rs. 2000

ANSWERS

1	2	3	4	5	6	7	8	9	10
A	C	C	C	D	C	B	B	A	D
11	**12**	**13**	**14**	**15**					
A	C	A	A	B					

EXPLANATORY ANSWERS

1. Let the total distance covered during journey = 60 km

$\frac{1}{3}$ of the distance covered during journey

$$= 60 \times \frac{1}{3} = 20 \text{ km}$$

$\frac{1}{4}$ of the distance covered during journey

$$= \frac{1}{4} \times 60 = 15 \text{ km}$$

∴ The distance covered during the rest of journey = 60 − (20 + 15) = 25 km

Time taken to cover 20 km at 25 km/h

$= \frac{20}{25}$ hours $= \frac{4}{5}$ hour

Time taken to cover 15 km at 30 km/h

$= \frac{15}{30}$ hours $= \frac{1}{2}$ hour

Time taken to cover 25 km at 50 km/h

$= \frac{25}{50}$ hours $= \frac{1}{2}$ hour

Total time taken $= \frac{4}{5}+\frac{1}{2}+\frac{1}{2}$

$= \frac{9}{5}$ hours

Hence average speed per hour $= 60 \div \frac{9}{5}$

$= \frac{60 \times 5}{9} = \frac{100}{3}$ km/h

$= 33\frac{1}{3}$ km/h

2. Average increase in the score of 17 innings

$= 3$ runs

Total increase in the score of 17 innings

$= 3 \times 17 = 51$ runs

$\therefore$ His average of 16 innings $= 85 - 51$

$= 34$ runs

Hence, average after the 17th innings

$= 34 + 3 = 37$ runs

3. Seventh observation $= (7 \times 11 - 6 \times 12) = 5$

4. Let, the required average age be x

Then, $5 \times 10 + 5 \times 14 + 20 \times x = 30 \times 12$

$\Rightarrow \quad 20x = 360 - 120$

$\Rightarrow \quad 20x = 240$

$\Rightarrow \quad x = 12$

5. Let the three numbers be x, $\frac{x}{2}$ and $\frac{x}{3}$ respectively,

Now, $\frac{1}{3}\left(x+\frac{x}{2}+\frac{x}{3}\right)=121$

$\Rightarrow \frac{11x}{6} = 121 \times 3$

$\therefore \; x = \frac{121 \times 3 \times 6}{11} = 198$

Hence, required difference $= x-\frac{x}{3} = \frac{2x}{3}$

$= \frac{2}{3} \times 198 = 132$

6. Required average Marks

$= \frac{55\times50+60\times55+45\times60}{55+60+45} = \frac{8750}{160} = 54.68$

7. Let the sixth, seventh and eighth numbers are x, $x + 4$ and $x + 7$.

Sum of last three numbers

$= 8 \times 20 - (2 \times \frac{31}{2} + 3 \times \frac{64}{3})$

$\Rightarrow x + x + 4 + x + 7 = 160 - 95$

$\Rightarrow 3x + 11 = 65$

$\Rightarrow 3x = 54 \qquad \therefore x = 18$

New eighth number $= x + 7 = 18 + 7 = 25$

8. Let the total number of pupils in the class be x; then,

$\frac{83-63}{x} = \frac{1}{2} \Rightarrow \frac{20}{x} = \frac{1}{2} \quad \therefore x = 40$

9. Let the number of wickets taken by him be x till the last match.

Then, $\frac{x \times 12.4+26}{x+5} = 12$

$\Rightarrow 12.4x + 26 = 12x + 60$

$\Rightarrow 0.4x = 34 \quad \therefore \; x = \frac{340}{4} = 85$

10. Let the weight of the teacher be x kgs, then

$\frac{24\times35+x}{25} = 35.4$

$\Rightarrow 840 + x = 885 \qquad \therefore \; x = 45$ kgs

12. Age of the teacher $= (25 \times 11 - 24 \times 10)$ years

$= 35$ years

13. Let 5 consecutive even numbers A, B, C, D and E be x, $x + 2$, $x + 4$, $x + 6$ and $x + 8$ respectively.

Now, $\frac{x+x+2+x+4+x+6+x+8}{5} = 34$

$\Rightarrow 5x + 20 = 170$

$\Rightarrow 5x = 150 \qquad \therefore x = 30$

Then, $B = x + 2 = 30 + 2 = 32$;

$D = x + 6 = 30 + 6 = 36$

Hence, their product $= 32 \times 36 = 1152$

14. The average of remaining 48 numbers

$= \frac{50\times30-(35+40)}{48} = \frac{1500-75}{48}$

$= \frac{1425}{48} = 29.68$

15. Let manager's salary be Rs. x, then

$\frac{20\times1500+x}{21} = 1600$

$\Rightarrow 30{,}000 + x = 33600$

$\therefore \; x =$ Rs. 3600

PROBLEMS BASED ON AGES

1. The ratio of ages of A and B is 3 : 11. After 3 years the ratio becomes 1 : 3. What are the ages of A and B?
A. 9 years, 33 years
B. 10 years, 40 years
C. 9 years, 27 years
D. None of these

2. Two years ago, the ratio of Ram's and Mohan's age was 3 : 2 and at present 7 : 5. What are their present ages?
A. 14 years, 10 years B. 15 years, 10 years
C. 13 years, 9 years D. None of these

3. The ages of Samir and Saurabh are in the ratio of 8 : 15 respectively. After 9 years the ratio of their ages will be 11 : 18. What is the difference between their ages in years?
A. 20 years B. 21 years
C. 22 years D. 24 years

4. The present age of father is 34 years more than that of his son. 12 years ago, father's age was 18 times the age of his son. The present age of son in years is:
A. 12 B. 14
C. 16 D. 18

5. A mother is 25 years older than her daughter. Five years ago, the age of the mother was 6 times the age of the daughter. What is the present age of mother?
A. 25 years B. 29 years
C. 32 years D. 35 years

6. The difference between the present ages of P and Q is 4 years. The ratio of their ages after 5 years will be 9 : 8. The present age of P is:
A. 24 years B. 30 years
C. 32 years D. None of these

7. Ten years ago, the age of Divya was half of the age of Namrata. If the ratio of present ages of both is 3 : 4, the sum of their present ages is:
A. 35 years B. 30 years
C. 25 years D. 18 years

8. The ratio between the present ages of A and B is 5 : 3 respectively. The ratio between A's age 4 years ago and B's age 4 years hence is 1 : 1. The ratio between A's age 4 years hence and B's age 4 years ago is:
A. 4 : 1 B. 3 : 1
C. 2 : 1 D. 1 : 3

9. Ram got married 8 years ago. His present age is $\frac{6}{5}$ times his age at the time of marriage. Ram's sister was 10 years younger to him at the time of his marriage. What is the present age of Ram's sister?
A. 40 years B. 38 years
C. 36 years D. 32 years

10. A father said to his son, "I was as old as you are at present at the time of your birth." If the father's age is 38 years now. Five years ago the age of son was:
A. 38 years B. 33 years
C. 19 years D. 14 years

ANSWERS

1	2	3	4	5	6	7	8	9	10
A	A	B	B	D	D	A	B	B	D

EXPLANATORY ANSWERS

1. Let the ages of A and B be $3x$ and $11x$ years; then

$$\frac{3x+3}{11x+3}=\frac{1}{3} \Rightarrow 9x + 9 = 11x + 3$$

$\Rightarrow 2x = 6 \therefore x = 3$

Hence, their present age, $3x = 3 \times 3 = 9$ years; $11x = 11 \times 3 = 33$ years

2. Let the present ages of Ram and Mohan are $7x$ and $5x$ years; then

$$\frac{7x-2}{5x-2}=\frac{3}{2} \Rightarrow 14x - 4 = 15x - 6 \therefore x = 2$$

Hence, their present ages : $7 \times 2 = 14$ years and $5 \times 2 = 10$ years

3. Let the present ages of Samir and Saurabh are $8x$ and $15x$ years respectively; then

$$\frac{8x+9}{15x+9}=\frac{11}{18} \Rightarrow 144x + 162 = 165x + 99$$

$\Rightarrow 21x = 63 \therefore x = 3$

Hence, difference of their ages $= 15x - 8x = 7x = 7 \times 3 = 21$ years

4. Let the present ages of father and his son be $x + 34$ and x years respectively; then
$18(x - 12) = x + 34 - 12$
$\Rightarrow 18x - 216 = x + 22$
$\Rightarrow 17x = 238 \quad \therefore x = 14$
Hence, present age of his son = 14 years

5. Let the present ages of mother and her daughter are $(x + 25)$ and x years respectively; then
$6(x - 5) = x + 25 - 5$
$\Rightarrow 6x - 30 = x + 20$
$\Rightarrow 5x = 50 \quad \therefore x = 10$
Hence, the age of the mother = 10 + 25 = 35 years

6. Let the present ages of P and Q be $(x + 4)$ and x years;
then, $\frac{x+4+5}{x+5} = \frac{9}{8} \Rightarrow 8x + 72 = 9x + 45 \quad \therefore x = 27$
Hence, present age of P = 27 + 4 = 31 years

7. Let the present ages of Divya and Namrata are $3x$ and $4x$ years respectively; then
$\frac{3x-10}{4x-10} = \frac{1}{2}$
$\Rightarrow 6x - 20 = 4x - 10$
$\Rightarrow 2x = 10 \quad \therefore x = 5$
Hence, sum of their ages = $3x + 4x = 7x$ = 7×5 = 35 years

8. Let the present ages of A and B are $5x$ and $3x$ years respectively; then,
$\frac{5x-4}{3x+4} = 1 \quad \Rightarrow 5x - 4 = 3x + 4$
$\Rightarrow 2x = 8 \quad \therefore x = 4$
Hence, their present ages are 20 years and 12 years.
So, required ratio = (20 + 4) : (12 – 4) = 24 : 8 = 3 : 1

9. Let the present age of Ram be x years; then
$\frac{x}{x-8} = \frac{6}{5} \quad \Rightarrow \quad 5x = 6x - 48$
$\therefore \quad x = 48$
Hence, present age of Ram's sister = 48 – 10 = 38 years.

10. Let the age of father was x years at the time of his son's birth, then present age of father and his son will be $2x$ and x years,
Now, $2x = 38 \quad \therefore x = 19$ years
Hence, 5 years ago the age of son was 19 – 5 = 14 years

CHAIN RULE

1. A fort has provision for 50 days. After 15 days a reinforcement of 150 men arrives and the provision now lasts 25 days. How many men were there in the fort?
A. 300 B. 225
C. 275 D. 200

2. In a fort there is provisions for 40 days for 275 persons. If after 16 days 125 persons leave the fort for how many more days the provisions will last?
A. 35 days B. 44 days
C. 45 days D. 53 days

3. 60 men could complete a work in 250 days. They worked together for 200 days. After that the work had to be stopped for 10 days due to bad weather. How many more men should be engaged to complete the work in time?
A. 20 B. 18
C. 15 D. 10

4. A contractor undertook to complete a project in 90 days and employed 60 men on it. After 60 days, he found that $\frac{3}{4}$ of the work has already been completed. How many men can he discharge so that the project may completed exactly on time?
A. 15 B. 20
C. 30 D. 40

5. A flagstaff 17.5 m high casts a shadow of length 40.25 m. The height of the building, which casts a shadow of length 28.75m under similar condition will be:
A. 21.25 m B. 17.5 m
C. 12.5 m D. 10 m

6. If 5 men or 9 women can do a piece of work in 19 days, then 3 men and 6 women will do the same work in how many days?
A. 21 B. 18
C. 15 D. 12

7. A certain number of men can finish a piece of work in 100 days. If there were 10 men less, it will take 10 days more for the work to be finished. How many men were there originally?
A. 110 B. 100
C. 82 D. 75

8. Some persons can do a piece of work in 12 days. Two times the number of such persons will do half of that work in:

A. 12 days B. 3 days
C. 6 days D. 4 days

9. 2 men and 7 boys can do a piece of work in 14 days; 3 men and 8 boys can do the same in 11 days. Then 8 men and 6 boys can do three times of this work in
A. 30 days B. 4 days
C. 21 days D. 18 days

10. If 3 men or 6 boys, working 7 hours a day can do a piece of work in 10 days; how many days will it take to complete a piece of work twice as large with 6 men and 2 boys working together for 8 hours a day?
A. 9 B. $8\frac{1}{2}$
C. $7\frac{1}{2}$ D. $6\frac{1}{2}$

11. If 15 men can do a certain amount of work in 20 days working 8 hours a day, in how many days will 10 men do three times the work working 6 hours a day?
A. 120 days B. 70 days
C. 100 days D. None of these

12. 40 men consume 60 kgs of rice in 15 days, then in how many days will 30 men consume 12 kgs of rice?
A. 9 days B. $6\frac{1}{4}$ days
C. 4 days D. $3\frac{1}{4}$ days

13. 56 men can complete a piece of work in 24 days. In how many days can 42 men complete the same piece of work?
A. 48 B. 32
C. 20 D. 16

14. Running at the same constant rate, 6 identical machines can produce a total of 270 bottles per minute. At this rate, how many bottles could 10 such machines produce in 4 minutes?
A. 1400 B. 1600
C. 1800 D. 2000

15. 400 persons, working 9 hours a day complete $\frac{1}{4}th$ of the work in 10 days. The number of additional persons, working 8 hours a day, required to complete the remaining work in 20 days, is:
A. 275 B. 250
C. 675 D. 200

ANSWERS

1	2	3	4	5	6	7	8	9	10
B	B	C	B	C	C	A	B	C	C
11	**12**	**13**	**14**	**15**					
A	C	B	C	C					

EXPLANATORY ANSWERS

1. Days Men
35↑ x
25 $x+150$↓

$$\Rightarrow \frac{x+150}{x} = \frac{35}{25} \quad \Rightarrow 1 + \frac{150}{x} = \frac{35}{25}$$

$$\Rightarrow \frac{150}{x} = \frac{10}{25}$$

$$\therefore x = \frac{25}{10} \times 150 = 375$$

Required number of men = 375 – 150 = 225

2. Persons Days
275↑ 24
150 x↓

$$\Rightarrow \frac{x}{24} = \frac{275}{150} \quad \therefore \quad x = \frac{275}{150} \times 24 = 44 \text{ days}$$

3. Days Men
50↑ 60
40 x↓

$$\Rightarrow \frac{x}{60} = \frac{50}{40} \quad \therefore \quad x = \frac{50}{40} \times 60 = 75 \text{ men}$$

Hence, number of additional men = 75 – 60
= 15

4. Work Days Men
$\frac{3}{4}$ 60 60
$\frac{1}{4}$↓ 30↑ x↓

$$\Rightarrow \frac{x}{60} = \frac{60}{30} \times \frac{1/4}{3/4}$$

$$\therefore \quad x = \frac{60}{30} \times \frac{1}{3} \times 60 = 40 \text{ days}$$

Hence, number of men to be discharged
$= 60 - 40 = 20$

5.

Shadow (m)	Object (m)
40.25 ↓	17.5 ↓
28.75	x

$$\Rightarrow \frac{x}{17.5} = \frac{28.75}{40.25}$$

$$\therefore x = \frac{28.75 \times 17.5}{40.25} = 12.5 \text{ m}$$

6. 5 men $\equiv$ 9 women

$$\therefore 3 \text{ men} = \frac{9}{5} \times 3 = \frac{27}{5} \text{ women}$$

Hence, 3 men and 6 women $= \frac{27}{5} + 6$

$$= \frac{57}{5} \text{ women}$$

Women	Days
9 ↑	19 ↓
$\frac{57}{5}$	x

$$\Rightarrow \frac{x}{19} = \frac{9 \times 5}{57}$$

$$\therefore x = \frac{9 \times 5}{57} \times 19$$

$= 15$ days

7.

Days	Men
100 ↑	x ↓
110	$x - 10$

$$\Rightarrow \frac{x-10}{x} = \frac{100}{110}$$

$\Rightarrow 110x - 1100 = 100x$

$\Rightarrow 10x = 1100 \quad \therefore x = 110$

Hence, initially the number of men = 110

8.

Work	Persons	Days
1 ↓	x ↑	12 ↓
$\frac{1}{2}$	$2x$	a

$$\Rightarrow \frac{a}{12} = \frac{x}{2x} \times \frac{1}{2} \qquad \therefore \quad a = \frac{1}{4} \times 12 = 3 \text{ days}$$

9. Here, 14×2 men + 14×7 boys $\equiv 11 \times 3$ men + 11×8 boys

$\Rightarrow$ 28 men + 98 boys $\equiv$ 33 men + 88 boys

$\Rightarrow$ 5 men = 10 boys

$\therefore$ 1 man = 2 boys

Then, 2 men and 7 boys $\equiv$ 4 boys + 7 boys
= 11 boys

& also, 8 men and 6 boys $\equiv$ 16 boys + 6 boys
= 22 boys

Work	Boys	Days
1 ↓	11 ↑	14 ↓
3	22	x

$$\Rightarrow \frac{x}{14} = \frac{11}{22} \times \frac{3}{1}$$

$$\therefore \quad x = \frac{1}{2} \times 3 \times 14$$

$= 21$ days

12.

Men	Rice (kgs)	Days
40 ↑	60 ↓	15 ↓
30	12	x

$$\Rightarrow \frac{x}{15} = \frac{12}{60} \times \frac{40}{30}$$

$$\therefore \quad x = \frac{12}{60} \times \frac{40}{30} \times 15 = 4 \text{ days}$$

14.

Machines	Time (minutes)	Bottles
6	1 ↓	270 ↓
10 ↓	4	x

$$\Rightarrow \frac{x}{270} = \frac{4}{1} \times \frac{10}{6}$$

$$\therefore \quad x = \frac{4 \times 10}{6} \times 270$$

$= 1800$ bottles

15.

Work	Hours	Days	Persons
$\frac{1}{4}$ ↓	9 ↑	10 ↑	400 ↓
$\frac{3}{4}$	8	20	x

$$\Rightarrow \frac{x}{400} = \frac{10}{20} \times \frac{9}{8} \times \frac{3/4}{1/4}$$

$$\therefore \quad x = \frac{1}{2} \times \frac{9}{8} \times 3 \times 400 = 675$$

Hence, number of additional persons
$= 675 - 400 = 275$

TIME AND DISTANCE

1. Starting from a point at a speed of 4 km/hr a man reaches at a cerain place and returns back to the point from where he had started journey on bicycle at the speed of 16 km/hr. His average speed during the entire journey will be :
   A. 6.4 km/h B. 8.4 km/h
   C. 5.4 km/h D. 10 km/h
2. A motorist covers a certain distance at a average speed of 48 km/h in 45 minutes. What speed in km/h he must maintain to cover the same distance in 30 minutes?
   A. 66 km/h B. 79 km/h
   C. 80 km/h D. 72 km/h
3. A policeman saw a thief at a distance of 200 m. The policeman and the thief started running at the same time. If the policeman runs at a speed of $4\frac{1}{6}$ m per second and the thief at a speed of $3\frac{1}{3}$ m per second, after what time the policeman will catch the thief?
   A. 12 min B. 10 min
   C. 9 min D. 4 min
4. A monkey wants to climb up a glazed pole. He climbs 12 metres in 1 minute and then he slips back 3 metres in the next minute. If the pole is 63 metre high, how long does he take to climb at the top of the pole?
   A. $11\frac{1}{4}$ min B. $12\frac{1}{2}$ min
   C. $12\frac{3}{4}$ min D. $14\frac{3}{4}$ min
5. The distance between two stations A and B is 300 km. A train leaves the station A with a speed of 40 km/hr. At the same time another train departs from the station B with a speed of 50 km/hr. How much time will these two trains take to cross each other?
   A. 3 hrs 40 min B. 3 hrs 20 min
   C. 2 hrs 20 min D. 3 hrs 45 min
6. Nilesh goes to school from his village at the speed of 4 km/hr and returns from school to village at the speed of 2 km/hr. If he takes 6 hours in all, then what is the distance between the village and the school?
   A. 8 km B. 6 km
   C. 5 km D. 4 km
7. By increasing the speed of the bus by 10 km/hr the time of journey for 72 km is reduced by 36 minutes. What was the original speed of the bus?
   A. 30 km/hr B. 35 km/hr
   C. 40 km/hr D. 45 km/hr
8. A train covers a distance in 50 minutes, if it runs at a speed of 48 km/hr on an average. The speed at which the train must run to reduce the time of journey to 40 minutes will be:
   A. 70 km/hr B. 60 km/hr
   C. 55 km/hr D. 50 km/hr
9. A certain distance is covered by a vehicle at a certain speed. If half of this distance is covered by another vehicle in double the time, the ratio of the speeds of the two vehicles is:
   A. 4 : 1 B. 1 : 4
   C. 2 : 1 D. 1 : 2
10. A is faster than B. A and B each walk 24 km. The sum of their speeds is 7 km/hr and sum of times taken by them is 14 hours. What is the speed of A?
   A. 7 km/hr B. 5 km/hr
   C. 4 km/hr D. 3 km/hr

ANSWERS

1	2	3	4	5	6	7	8	9	10
A	D	D	C	B	A	A	B	A	C

EXPLANATORY ANSWERS

1. Average speed during the entire journey

$$= \frac{2xy}{x+y} = \frac{2\times4\times16}{4+16} = \frac{8\times16}{20} = 6.4 \text{ km/hr.}$$

2. Let required speed be x km/hr; then

$$x \times \frac{1}{2} = 48 \times \frac{3}{4} \quad \therefore\ x = 48 \times \frac{3}{4} \times 2$$

$$= 72 \text{ km/hr}$$

3. Suppose the policeman will catch the thief after t seconds

then, $\left(\frac{25}{6}-\frac{10}{3}\right)t = 200 \Rightarrow \frac{5}{6}t = 200$

$\therefore t = \frac{200 \times 6}{5} = 240$ sec = 4 min.

4. The monkey climbs 12 metres in 1 minute and then he slips back 3 metres in the next minute

$\therefore$ The monkey climbs in the first 2 minutes
= 12 – 3 = 9 metres

$\therefore$ In the first 12 minutes the monkey climbs
= 9 × 6 = 54 metres

Remaining height of the pole to be covered by the monkey = 63 – 54 = 9 metre

$\therefore$ The monkey will climb the height of 9 metres in the 13th minute

$\because$ The monkey climbs 12 metres in 1 minute

$\therefore$ The monkey will climb 9 metres in $\frac{1}{12} \times 9$

$= \frac{3}{4}$ minute

$\therefore$ Time spent in climbing at the top of the pole

$= \left(12+\frac{3}{4}\right)$ minutes $= 12\frac{3}{4}$ minutes

5. The two trains are moving in the opposite directions

$\therefore$ Relative speed = 40 + 50 = 90 km/hr.

$\therefore$ Time taken to cross each other $= \frac{300}{90} = 3\frac{1}{3}$ hours

or, 3 hours 20 minutes.

6. Let x km be the distance between village and the school; then

$\frac{x}{4}+\frac{x}{2}=6 \quad \Rightarrow \frac{3x}{4}=6$

$\therefore x = \frac{6 \times 4}{3} = 8$ km

8. Let x km/hr be the required speed of the train; then

$x \times \frac{40}{60} = 48 \times \frac{50}{60}$

$\therefore x = \frac{48 \times 50}{40} = 60$ km/hr

9. Let x km/hr and t hr be the certain speed and certain time.

Then, ratio of their speeds $= \frac{x}{t}:\frac{x}{2 \times 2t} = 1 : \frac{1}{4} = 4 : 1$

10. Let speeds of A and B are x_1 and x_2 km/hr and times taken by them are t_1 and t_2 hrs, then

$x_1 + x_2 = 7$ km/hr ...(i)

$t_1 + t_2 = 14$ hrs ...(ii)

Now, $\frac{24}{x_1}+\frac{24}{x_2} = 14 \Rightarrow \frac{24(x_1+x_2)}{x_1x_2} = 14$

$\therefore x_1x_2 = \frac{24 \times 7}{14} = 12$

Then, $x_1 - x_2 = \sqrt{(x_1+x_2)^2 - 4x_1x_2}$

$= \sqrt{(7)^2 - 4 \times 12} = 1$ ...(iii)

Solving (*i*) and (*iii*) we get $x_1 = 4$ km/hr

TIME AND WORK

1. A and B working together complete a work in 35 days. If A takes 60 days to complete it, how long would B alone take to complete it?

A. 64 days B. 72 days
C. 81 days D. 84 days

2. A few children working together can do a piece of work in 18 days. If the number of children employed on the work is made double, how long would they take to complete half of the work?

A. $4\frac{1}{2}$ days B. $2\frac{1}{3}$ days
C. $8\frac{3}{4}$ days D. $6\frac{1}{2}$ days

3. 10 men or 18 boys can do a piece of work in 15 days. In how many days would 25 men and 15 boys complete the same work working together?

A. $5\frac{1}{2}$ days B. $4\frac{1}{2}$ days
C. $6\frac{2}{3}$ days D. $2\frac{1}{3}$ days

4. A cistern is filled by a tap in $3\frac{1}{2}$ hours. Due to a leak in the bottom of the cistern, it takes half an hour longer to fill the cistern. If the cistern is full, how long will it take the leak to empty it?

A. 28 hours B. 29 hours
C. $31\frac{1}{3}$ hours D. 38 hours

5. A is twice as good a workman as B and thrice as good a workman as C. If C alone can do a piece of work in 24 days, how long would the three persons take to finish the work working together?

A. $3\frac{3}{11}$ days B. $4\frac{4}{7}$ days

C. $4\frac{4}{11}$ days D. $3\frac{4}{11}$ days

6. If 3 men and 5 women can do a piece of work in 8 days and 2 men and 7 boys can do the same work in 12 days. Find the number of boys, the work done by whom can equate the work done by 10 women.

A. 19 boys B. 21 boys
C. 23 boys D. 15 boys

7. 8 men alone can complete a piece of work in 12 days. 4 women alone can complete the same piece of work in 48 days and 10 children alone can complete the piece of work in 24 days. In how many days can 10 men, 4 women and 10 children together complete the piece of work?

A. 6 B. 8
C. 10 D. 15

8. A works twice as fast as B. If B can complete a piece of work independently in 12 days. Find in how many days A and B together can complete the work?

A. 8 days B. 6 days
C. 4 days D. 18 days

9. A contractor undertook to complete a project in 90 days and employed 60 men on it. After 60 days, he found that $\frac{3}{4}$ of the work has already been completed. How many men can he discharge so that the project may be completed exactly on time?

A. 15 B. 20
C. 30 D. 40

10. A can do a piece of work in 25 days and B can do it in 20 days. They work together for 5 days and then A goes away. In how many days will B finish the remaining work?

A. 33 days B. 20 days
C. 11 days D. 10 days

ANSWERS

1	2	3	4	5	6	7	8	9	10
D	A	B	A	C	B	A	C	B	C

EXPLANATORY ANSWERS

1. (A + B)'s 1 day's work = $\frac{1}{35}$

and also, A's 1 day's work = $\frac{1}{60}$

Hence, B's 1 day's work = $\frac{1}{35}-\frac{1}{60}=\frac{5}{420}=\frac{1}{84}$

So, B will do the whole work in 84 days.

3. 10 men $\equiv$ 18 boys

25 men $\equiv \frac{18}{10}\times 25 = 45$ boys

Hence, 25 men + 15 boys = 45 + 15 = 60 boys

Now, 18 boys can do a piece of work in 15 days.

Hence, 60 boys will do a piece of work in $\frac{15\times 18}{60}=\frac{9}{2}$ days = $4\frac{1}{2}$ days.

4. In 1 hour $\frac{2}{7}$ cistern is filled by the tap.

Hence, in $\frac{1}{2}$ hour $\frac{2}{14}=\frac{1}{7}$ cistern is filled by the tap.

So, $\frac{1}{7}$ cistern is emptied by the leakage in 4 hours.

So, 1 cistern will be emptied by the leakage in 28 hours.

6. Here, (3 men + 5 women) × 8

$\equiv$ (2 men + 7 boys) × 12

$\Rightarrow$ 40 women $\equiv$ 84 boys

$\therefore$ 10 women $\equiv \frac{84}{40}\times 10$ = 21 boys

Hence, work done by 10 women

= work done of 21 boys.

7. B's 1 day's work = $\frac{1}{4}-\frac{1}{12}=\frac{2}{12}=\frac{1}{6}$

Hence, B alone will complete the work in 6 days.

8. Ratio of efficiency of A and B = 2 : 1

Then, ratio of their time taking = 1 : 2

Hence, if B can complete the work in 12 days, then A in 6 days.

Now, (A + B)'s 1 day's work = $\frac{1}{6}+\frac{1}{12}=\frac{3}{12}=\frac{1}{4}$

So, A and B together can complete the work in 4 days.

9. After 60 days remaining work $= 1 - \frac{3}{4} = \frac{1}{4}$

In 60 days $\frac{3}{4}$ work has been done by 60 men

In 30 days $\frac{1}{4}$ work will be done by $60 \times \frac{4}{3} \times \frac{1}{4} \times \frac{60}{30}$

= 40 men.

Hence, required number of men = 60 – 40 = 20 (which are to be discharged).

BOATS AND STREAMS

1. A boat goes 6 km upstream and back to the starting point in 2 hours. If the current of the stream runs at the rate of 4 km/hr, find the speed of the boat in still water.

A. 6 km/hr B. 8 km/hr
C. 10 km/hr D. 12 km/hr

2. A boat covers 24 km upstream and 36 km downstream in 6 hours, while it covers 36 km upstream and 24 km downstream in 6½ horus. Find the speed of the current.

A. 2 km/hr B. 4 km/hr
C. 6 km/hr D. 8 km/hr

3. A man can row 5 km/hr in still water and the speed of the stream is 1.5 km/hr. He takes an hour when he travels upstream to a place and back again to the starting point. How far is the place from the starting point?

A. 2.275 km B. 3.5 km
C. 1.5 km D. None of these

4. The speed of a boat in still water is 6 km/hr and the speed of the stream is 1.5 km/hr. A man rows to a place at a distance of 22.5 km and comes back to the starting point. Find the total time taken by him.

A. 8 hours B. 10 hours
C. 12 hours D. 4 hours

5. A boat covers 20 km downstream and 6 km upstream in 3 hours, while it covers 30 km downstream and 12 km upstream in 5 hours. What is the speed of boat in still water?

A. 6 km/hr B. 8 km/hr
C. 10 km/hr D. 12 km/hr.

6. Samir can travel 12 miles downstream in a certain river in 6 hours less than it takes him to travel the same distance upstream. But when he could double his rowing rate for his 24-mile round trip, the downstream 12 miles would then take only one hour less than the upstream 12 miles. Find the speed of the current in miles/hour.

A. $2\frac{2}{3}$ B. $2\frac{1}{3}$
C. $1\frac{2}{3}$ D. $1\frac{1}{3}$

7. A boat takes 6 hours to travel from place M to N downstream and back from N to M upstream. If the speed of the boat in still water is 4 km/hr; what is the distance between two places?

A. 6 kms B. 8 kms
C. 12 kms D. Data inadequate

8. A man can row upstream at 8 km/hr and downstream at 13 km/hr. The speed of the stream is:

A. 2.5 km/hr B. 4.2 km/hr
C. 5 km/hr D. 10.5 km/hr

9. A man's speed with the current is 15 km/hr and the speed of the current is 2.5 km/hr. The man's speed against the current is:

A. 12.5 km/hr B. 10 km/hr
C. 9 km/hr D. 8.5 km/hr

10. A motorboat, whose speed is 15 km/hr in still water goes 30 km downstream and comes back in a total of 4 hours 30 minutes. What is the speed of the stream (in km/hr)?

A. 10 B. 6
C. 5 D. 4

ANSWERS

1	2	3	4	5	6	7	8	9	10
B	A	A	A	B	B	D	A	B	C

EXPLANATORY ANSWERS

1. Let the speed of a boat in still water = x km/hr; then

$$\frac{6}{x-4}+\frac{6}{x+4}=2 \quad \Rightarrow \quad \frac{2x}{x^2-16}=\frac{1}{3}$$

$\Rightarrow x^2 - 6x - 16 = 0$

$\Rightarrow (x - 8)(x + 2) = 0$

Hence, the speed of the boat = 8 km/hr.

2. Let x km/hr and y km/hr be the speeds of the boat in still water and the speed of the current respectively, then

$$\frac{24}{x-y}+\frac{36}{x+y}=6 \Rightarrow \frac{4}{x-y}+\frac{6}{x+y}=1 \quad ...(i)$$

And, $$\frac{36}{x-y}+\frac{24}{x+y}=\frac{13}{2} \quad ...(ii)$$

Solving these two equations, we get

$x + y = 12;\ x - y = 8$

Hence, $y = \frac{1}{2}(12-8) = 2$ km/hr.

3. Let required distance be x km, then

$$\frac{x}{5-1.5}+\frac{x}{5+1.5}=1 \Rightarrow \frac{x\times 2}{7}+\frac{x\times 2}{13}=1$$

$\Rightarrow\ 40x = 91 \quad \therefore x = 91/40 = 2.275$ km

4. Required time period $= \frac{22.5}{6+1.5}+\frac{22.5}{6-1.5}$

$= \frac{45}{15}+\frac{45}{9} = 8$ hours.

5. Let x km/hr and y km/hr be the speed of boat in still water and speed of current respectively; then

$$\frac{20}{x+y}+\frac{6}{x-y}=3 \quad ...(i)$$

and also, $$\frac{30}{x+y}+\frac{12}{x-y}=5$$

$$\Rightarrow \frac{15}{x+y}+\frac{6}{x-y}=\frac{5}{2} \quad ...(ii)$$

Solving equations *(i)* & *(ii)*, we get $x + y = 10$ and $x - y = 6$

Since, $x = \frac{1}{2}(10 + 6) = 8$ km/hr.

6. Let x km/hr and y km/hr be the speed of rowing in still water and speed of the current respectively; then

$$\frac{12}{x-y}-\frac{12}{x+y}=6 \quad \Rightarrow \quad \frac{24y}{x^2-y^2}=6$$

$\Rightarrow x^2 = y^2 + 4y$ ...(i)

Again, $$\frac{12}{2x-y}-\frac{12}{2x+y}=1$$

$$\Rightarrow \frac{24y}{4x^2-y^2}=1 \quad \Rightarrow x^2=\frac{y^2+24y}{4} \quad ...(ii)$$

From equations (i) and (ii), we get

$$y^2+4y=\frac{y^2+24y}{4} \quad \Rightarrow 3y^2 = 8y$$

$\therefore\ y = \frac{8}{3} = 2\frac{1}{3}$ miles/hr.

8. The speed of the stream $= \frac{1}{2}(13 - 8) = \frac{5}{2}$

$= 2.5$ km/hr.

9. The man's speed in still water

$= 15 - 2.5 = 12.5$ km/hr

Hence, the men's speed against the current

$= 12.5 - 2.5 = 10$ km/hr

10. Let speed of the stream be x km/hr, then

$$\frac{30}{15+x}+\frac{30}{15-x}=4\frac{1}{2} \quad \Rightarrow \quad \frac{30\times 30}{225-x^2}=\frac{9}{2}$$

$$\Rightarrow \frac{200}{225-x^2}=1 \quad \Rightarrow x^2 = 225 - 200$$

$\Rightarrow x^2 = 25 \quad \therefore\ x = 5$ km/hr.

ALLIGATION OR MIXTURE

1. A shopkeeper buys 26 kgs of milk @ Rs. 16 per kg. He also buys from another source an inferior quality of milk @ Rs. 10 per kg. How much quantity of the latter should he buy to mix it with the former so that he can sell the mixture @ Rs. 14 per kg without making any loss?

A. 13 kgs B. 12 kgs

C. 14 kgs D. 16 kgs

2. Two vessels A and B contain mixture of milk and water in the ratio 4 : 1 and 9 : 11 respectively. They are mixed in the ratio of 3 : 2. Find the ratio of milk : water in the resulting mixture.

A. 34 : 16 B. 33 : 17
C. 16 : 34 D. 17 : 33

3. A shopkeeper has 50 kgs of rice. He sells a part of it at 20% profit and the rest at 40% profit. If he gains 25% on the whole, find the quantity of each part.

A. 12.5 kgs and 37.5 kgs
B. 37.5 kgs and 12.5 kgs
C. 23.5 kgs and 21.5 kgs
D. 21.5 kgs and 23.5 kgs

4. A man bought a certain quantity of sugar for Rs. 8000. He sells one-fourth of it at 20% loss. At what per cent profit should he sell the remainder stock so as to make an overall profit of 20%?

A. 20% B. 30%
C. 35% D. 40%

5. Rs. 675 was divided among 75 boys and girls. Each boy gets Rs. 20 whereas a girl gets Rs. 5. Find the number of boys and girls.

A. 20, 55 B. 15, 60
C. 25, 50 D. 30, 45

6. A vessel contains mixture of liquids A and B in the ratio 3 : 2. When 20 litres of the mixture is taken out and replaced by 20 litres of liquid B, the ratio changes to 1 : 4. How many litres of liquid A was there initially present in the vessel?

A. 12 litres B. 18 litres
C. 24 litres D. 22 litres

7. A container is full of milk. One-third of milk is taken out of it and replaced by same quantity of water. Then again one-third of the mixture is taken out of it and replaced by the same quantity of water. The process is repeated 4 times. If 16 litres of milk is left in the container at the end of 4th operation, find the capacity of the container.

A. 76 litres B. 81 litres
C. 82 litres D. 85 litres

8. The cost of type-I rice is Rs. 15 per kg and type-II is Rs. 20 per kg. If both type I and type II are mixed in the ratio of 2 : 3, then find the price per kg of the mixed variety.

A. Rs. 19.50 B. Rs. 19
C. Rs. 18.50 D. Rs. 18

9. In what ratio must a grocer mix two varieties of tea worth Rs. 60 a kg and Rs. 65 a kg so that by selling the mixture at Rs. 68.20 a kg he may gain 10%?

A. 4 : 5 B. 3 : 5
C. 3 : 4 D. 3 : 2

10. A vessel contains 80 litres of milk. 16 litres of milk was taken out of the vessel and replaced by water. Then 16 litres of mixture was withdrawn and again replaced by water. The operation was repeated for third time. How much milk is now left in the vessel?

A. 96.40 litres
B. 50.36 litres
C. 40.96 litres
D. 32.76 litres

ANSWERS

1	2	3	4	5	6	7	8	9	10
A	B	B	B	A	B	B	D	D	C

EXPLANATORY ANSWERS

1.

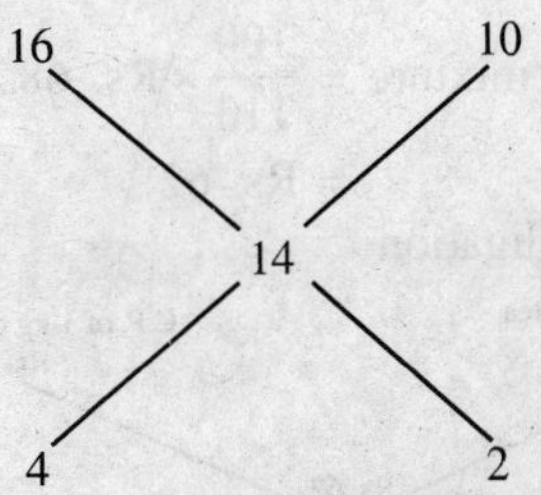

or 2 : 1 $\dfrac{\text{Quantity of milk @ Rs.10 per kg}}{\text{Quantity of milk @ Rs. 16 per kg}} = \dfrac{1}{2}$

So, quantity of milk @ Rs. 10 per kg. $= \dfrac{26}{2} = 13$ kgs.

2. Fraction is *Milk* *Water*

A : $\dfrac{4}{5}$ $\dfrac{1}{5}$

B : $\dfrac{9}{20}$ $\dfrac{11}{20}$

$(3A + 2B) = A$ and $B : \left(\dfrac{12}{5} + \dfrac{9}{10}\right) \left(\dfrac{3}{5} + \dfrac{11}{10}\right)$

$\dfrac{33}{10}$ $\dfrac{17}{10}$

So, Ratio of milk : water in the resulting mixture = 33 : 17.

3.

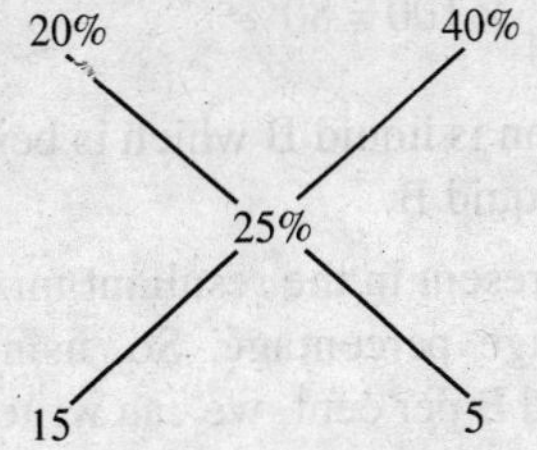

or 3 : 1

Quantity sold at 20% profit = $\frac{3}{3+1} \times 50$

= 37.5 kgs.

Quantity sold at 40% profit = (50 – 37.5)

= 12.5 kgs.

4. Let the remainder stock be sold at x% profit.

– 10   + x

+20

(x–20)   30

$$\frac{x-20}{30} = \frac{1/4}{3/4}$$

or $x - 20 = 30 \times \frac{1}{3}$

or $x = 20 + 10$

x = 30% profit.

5. Average money per head (boy or girl)

= Rs. $\frac{675}{75}$ = Rs. 9

(Boys) Rs. 20   (Girls) Rs. 5

(Average) Rs. 9

4   11

Number of boys = $\frac{4}{4+11} \times 75 = 20$

Number of girls = $\frac{11}{4+11} \times 75 = 55.$

6. % of liquid B initially present in the vessel

$= \frac{2}{3+2} \times 100 = 40\%$

% of liquid B finally present in the vessel

$= \frac{4}{1+4} \times 100 = 80\%$

The second solution is liquid B which is being mixed and it has 100% liquid B.

80% of liquid B present in the resultant mixture may be taken as average percentage. So, using rule of alligation on liquid B per cent, we can write,

40%   100%

80%

20   40

or 1 : 2

The ratio of liquid left in the vessel to liquid B being mixed = 1 : 2

Since the quantity of liquid B being mixed is 20 litres, the quantity of liquid left in the vessel is 10 litres. Therefore, the total quantity of liquid initially present in the vessel

= 10 + 20 = 30 litres

Quantity of liquid A = $\frac{3}{2+3} \times 30$ = 18 litres.

7. Let capacity of the container be x litre; then

$x(1 - 1/3)^4 = 16 \Rightarrow x\left(\frac{2}{3}\right)^4 = 16$

$\Rightarrow x \times \frac{16}{81} = 16 \quad \therefore x = 81$ litres

8. Let the price per kg of mixed variety be Rs. x; then

By the rule of alligation,

cost of 1 kg of cheaper rice Rs. 15   cost of 1 kg of dearer rice Rs. 20

Rs. x (Mean price)

(20 – x)   (x – 15)

Now, $\frac{20-x}{x-15} = \frac{2}{3} \Rightarrow 60 - 3x = 2x - 30$

$\Rightarrow 5x = 90 \quad \therefore x$ = Rs. 18

9. S.P. of 1 kg mixture = Rs. 68.20, Gain % = 10%

Hence, C.P. of 1 kg mixture = $\frac{100}{110} \times$ Rs. 68.20

= Rs. 62

By the rule of alligation

C.P. of 1kg of cheaper tea Rs. 60   C.P. of 1 kg of dearer tea Rs. 65

Rs. 62 (Mean price)

3   2

Hence, required ratio = 3 : 2

10. Amount of milk left = $80\left(1 - \frac{16}{80}\right)^3 = 80\left(\frac{4}{5}\right)^3$

$80 \times \frac{64}{125}$ = 40.96 litres.

PERCENTAGE

1. A student who secures 20% marks in an examination fails by 30 marks. Another student who secures 32% gets 42 marks more than those required to pass. The percentage of marks required to pass is:

A. 20 B. 25
C. 28 D. 30

2. In a college election, a candidate secured 62% of the votes and is elected by a majority of 144 votes. The total number of votes polled is:

A. 600 B. 800
C. 925 D. 1200

3. In an organisation, 40% of the employees are matriculates, 50% of the remaining are graduates and the remaining 180 are postgraduates. How many employees are graduates?

A. 360 B. 240
C. 300 D. 180

4. The population of a village is 4500. $\frac{5}{9}$th of them are males and rest females. If 40% of the males are married, then the percentage of married female is :

A. 35 B. 40
C. 50 D. 60

5. A's income is 10% more than B's. How much per cent is B's income is less than A's?

A. 10% B. 7%
C. $9\frac{1}{11}\%$ D. $6\frac{1}{2}\%$

6. If the price of a television set is increased by 25%, then by what percentage should the new price be reduced to bring the price back to original level?

A. 15% B. 20%
C. 25% D. 30%

7. In an election one of the two candidates gets 40% votes and loses by 100 votes. Total number of votes is :

A. 500 B. 400
C. 600 D. 1000

8. The gross income of a person is Rs. 20000. 10% of his income is exempted from income tax and his net income is Rs. 19100. The rate of income tax is :

A. 3% B. 2%
C. 4% D. 5%

9. The owner of a cell phone shop charges his customer 32% more than the cost price. If a customer paid Rs. 6600 for the cell phone, then what was the cost price of the cell phone?

A. Rs. 5000 B. Rs. 5500
C. Rs. 5800 D. Rs. 6100

10. If the cost of pins reduced by Rs. 4 per dozen, 12 more pins can be purchased for Rs. 48. The cost of pins per dozen after reduction is:

A. Rs. 8 B. Rs. 12
C. Rs. 16 D. Rs. 20

11. In an examination 80% of the students passed in Mathematics and 70% passed in English, while 10% students failed in both the subjects. If 360 students passed in both the subjects, find the total number of students who appeared in the examination.

A. 400 B. 600
C. 630 D. 640

12. Electric tax is increased by 20% and its consumption is decreased by 20%. The change in the expenditure is:

A. 4% decrease B. 4% increase
C. 5% decrease D. 5% increase

13. The selling price of certain commodity was reduced by 25%. As a result of it, the sales increased by 30%. What was the effect of it on cash collected by daily sales?

A. 2.5% decrease B. 2.5% increase
C. 5% decrease D. 5% increase

14. The wheat sold by a grocer contained 10% low quality wheat. What quantity of good quality wheat should be added to 150 kgs of wheat so that the percentage of low quality wheat becomes 5%?

A. 50 kgs B. 85 kgs
C. 135 kgs D. 150 kgs

15. Nilam spends 15% of her monthly income on household expenses. She spends 17% of the monthly income in travelling and 6% on medical expenses and saves the rest Rs. 15,500. What is her monthly income?

A. Rs. 20,000 B. Rs. 25,000
C. Rs. 30,000 D. Rs. 35,000

ANSWERS

1	2	3	4	5	6	7	8	9	10
B	A	D	C	C	B	A	D	A	B
11	**12**	**13**	**14**	**15**					
B	A	A	D	B					

EXPLANATORY ANSWERS

1. 20% of $x + 30 = 32\%$ of $x - 42$

$\Rightarrow$ 12% of $x = 72$

$$\Rightarrow \quad x = \frac{72 \times 100}{12} = 600$$

Pass Mark $= 20\%$ of $600 + 30 = 150$

$$\text{Pass percentage} = \left(\frac{150}{600} \times 100\right)\% = 25\%$$

2. (62% of $x - 38\%$ of x) $= 144$

$$\Rightarrow 24\% \text{ of } x = 144 \quad \Rightarrow x = \frac{144 \times 100}{24} = 600$$

3.
$$\text{Matriculates} = \frac{40}{100}x = \frac{2x}{5}$$

$$\text{Remaining} = \left(x - \frac{2x}{5}\right) = \frac{3x}{5}$$

$$\text{Graduates} = \frac{50}{100} \times \frac{3x}{5} = \frac{3x}{10}$$

$$\text{Remaining} = \frac{3x}{5} - \frac{3x}{10} = \frac{3x}{10}$$

$$\text{Now, } \frac{3x}{10} = 180 \quad \therefore x = \frac{10 \times 180}{3} = 600$$

$$\therefore \text{Graduates} = \frac{3 \times 600}{10} = 180.$$

4. $$\text{Males} = \left(\frac{5}{9} \times 4500\right) = 2500$$

Females $= 2000$

$$\therefore \text{ Married males} = \frac{40}{100} \times 2500 = 1000$$

and married females $= 1000$

$\therefore$ Percentage of married females

$$= \left(\frac{1000}{2000} \times 100\right)\% = 50\%.$$

5. $$\text{Required percentage} = \left[\frac{10}{(100 + 10)} \times 100\right]\% = 9\frac{1}{11}\%.$$

6. $$\text{Required reduction} = \frac{25}{100 + 25} \times 100 = 20\%.$$

7. Out of 100, difference in votes $= (60 - 40) = 20$

20% of $x = 100$

$$\therefore x = \frac{100 \times 100}{20} = 500.$$

8. Gross income $=$ Rs. 20000

Income exempted from income tax $= 10\%$ of gross income

$\therefore$ Income on which income tax is chargeable $= (100 - 10\%) = 90\%$ of gross income

$$= 20000 \times \frac{90}{100} = \text{Rs. } 18000$$

$\therefore$ Total income tax paid on

$=$ Rs. 20000 – Rs. 19100 $=$ Rs. 900

$$\therefore \text{ Rate per cent of income tax} = \frac{900}{18000} \times 100 = 5\%$$

9. Let cost price of the cell phone be Rs. x; then

$$x + \frac{32}{100} \times x = 6600 \quad \Rightarrow \frac{132x}{100} = 6600$$

$$\therefore \; x = \frac{100 \times 6600}{132} = \text{Rs. } 5000.$$

10. Let reduced price by Rs. x per dozen, then

$$\frac{48}{x} - \frac{48}{x+4} = 1 \quad \Rightarrow \quad \frac{48 \times 4}{x^2 + 4x} = 1$$

$\Rightarrow$ $x^2 + 4x - 192 = 0$

$\Rightarrow$ $(x + 16)(x - 12) = 0$

$\therefore$ $x =$ Rs. 12.

11. Here, percentage of students failed in Mathematics and English be 30% and 20% respectively.

Percentage of students failed either one or both subjects $= 30 + 20 - 10 = 40\%$

Hence, percentage of pass students $= 100 - 40 = 60\%$

Now, $60\% = 360$

$$\therefore 100\% = \frac{360}{60} \times 100 = 600.$$

12. Let initially electric tax is Rs. 100 and consumption $=$ 100 units

Decrease in consumption

$= 100 \times 100 - 120 \times 80 =$ Rs. 400

$$\text{Hence, decrease percentage} = \frac{400 \times 100}{100 \times 100} = 4\%.$$

13. Let the selling price of a commodity be Rs. 100 and number of sales $= 100$ units

Decrease in daily cash $= 100 \times 100 - 75 \times 130$

$=$ Rs. 250

$$\text{Hence, decrease percentage} = \frac{250 \times 100}{100 \times 100} = 2.5\,\%.$$

14. Let x kg of good wheat be added; then

$$\frac{10}{100} \times 150 = \frac{5}{100}(150 + x)$$

$\Rightarrow 150 + x = 300 \quad \therefore \; x = 150$ kg.

15. Let her monthly income be Rs. x; then

$$x - \left(\frac{15}{100} \times x + \frac{17}{100} \times x + \frac{6}{100} \times x\right) = 15{,}500$$

$$\Rightarrow x - \frac{38x}{100} = 15500 \quad \Rightarrow \frac{62x}{100} = 15500$$

$$\therefore \; x = \frac{15500 \times 100}{62} = \text{Rs. } 25000.$$

PROFIT AND LOSS

1. Ashok bought 25 kg of rice at the rate of Rs. 6 per kg and 35 kg of rice at the rate of Rs. 7 per kg. He mixed the two and sold the mixture at the rate of Rs. 6.75 per kg. What was his gain or loss in the transaction?
   A. Rs. 16 gain B. Rs. 16 loss
   C. Rs. 10 gain D. None of these
2. Profit after selling a commodity for Rs. 425 is same as loss after selling it for Rs. 355. The cost of the commodity is :
   A. Rs. 285 B. Rs. 390
   C. Rs. 295 D. Rs. 400
3. Ram bought 4 dozen apples at Rs. 12 per dozen and 2 dozen at Rs. 16 per dozen. He sold all of them to earn 20%. At what price per dozen did he sell the apples?
   A. Rs. 14.40 B. Rs. 16.00
   C. Rs. 16.80 D. Rs. 16.20
4. At what price must Kantilal sell a mixture of 80 kg sugar at Rs. 6.75 per kg with 120 kg at Rs. 8 per kg to gain 20%?
   A. Rs. 7.50 per kg B. Rs. 8.20 per kg
   C. Rs. 8.35 per kg D. Rs. 9 per kg
5. A person bought an article and sold it at a loss of 10%. If he had bought it for 20% less and sold it for Rs. 55 more, he would have had a profit of 40%. The C.P. of the article is :
   A. Rs. 200 B. Rs. 225
   C. Rs. 250 D. None of these
6. A dealer sold a machine to a shopkeeper at 20% profit. The shopkeeper sold the machine to a customer so as to get 25% profit for himself. The difference between the selling price of the dealer and that of the shopkeeper was found to be Rs. 129. What is the initial price of the machine?
   A. Rs. 410 B. Rs. 420
   C. Rs. 430 D. Rs. 440
7. A man bought a horse and cart. If he sold the horse at 10% loss and the cart at 20% gain he would not loss anything. If he sold the horse at 5% loss and the cart at 5% gain he would lose Rs. 10 in the bargain. What did he pay for each?
   A. Rs. 400, Rs. 200 B. Rs. 300, Rs. 300
   C. Rs. 250, Rs. 350 D. Rs. 350, Rs. 250
8. The marked price of a radio is 20% more than its cost price. If a discount of 10% is given on the marked price, the gain percentage is:
   A. 8 B. 10
   C. 12 D 15
9. A dishonest dealer sells his goods at the cost price and still earns a profit of 60% by underweight. What weight does he use for a kg?
   A. 625 gms B. 750 gms
   C. 800 gms D. 850 gms
10. A man sells two horses for Rs. 990 each. On one he gains 10% and the other he loses 10%. What is his total percentage of gain or loss in the transaction?
    A. 1% gain B. 1% loss
    C. 2% gain D. 2% loss

ANSWERS

1	2	3	4	5	6	7	8	9	10
C	B	B	D	C	C	A	A	A	B

EXPLANATORY ANSWERS

1. C.P. of 60 kg mixture $=$ Rs. $(25 \times 6 + 35 \times 7)$
   $=$ Rs. 395
   S.P. of 60 kg mixtire $=$ Rs. (60×6.75)
   $=$ Rs. 405
   $\therefore$ Gain $=$ Rs. $(405 - 395)$
   $=$ Rs. 10
2. Let C.P. $=$ Rs. x
   Then, $425 - x = x - 355 \Rightarrow 2x = 780$
   $\therefore$ $x =$ Rs. 390
3. C.P. of 6 dozen apples $=$ Rs. $(12 \times 4 + 16 \times 2)$
   $=$ Rs. 80
   $\therefore$ S.P. $=$ Rs. $\left(\frac{120}{100} \times 80\right)$
   $=$ Rs. 96
   $\therefore$ S.P. per dozen $=$ Rs. $\left(\frac{96}{6}\right) =$ Rs. 16

4. C.P. of 1 kg sugar $= \frac{80 \times 6.75 + 120 \times 8}{200}$

$= \text{Rs. } 7.50$

$\therefore$ S.P. of 1 kg $=$ Rs. $\left(\frac{120}{100} \times 7.50\right)$

$= \text{Rs. 9 per kg}$

5. Let, C.P. = Rs. x,

then, S.P. $= \frac{90}{100} \times x = \text{Rs. } \frac{9x}{10}$

Now, when C.P. = Rs. $\frac{80x}{100} = \text{Rs. } \frac{4x}{5}$;

then, S.P. $= \frac{140}{100} \times \frac{4x}{5} = \text{Rs. } \frac{28x}{25}$

But, $\frac{28x}{25} - \frac{9x}{10} = 55 \Rightarrow \frac{11x}{50} = 55$

$\therefore \quad x = \text{Rs. } 250$

6. Let the initial price = Rs. x; then C.P. for dealer

$= \frac{120}{100} \times x = \text{Rs. } \frac{6x}{5}$

Again, C.P. for shopkeeper $= \frac{125}{100} \times \frac{6x}{5}$

$= \text{Rs. } \frac{3x}{2}$

Now, $\frac{3x}{2} - \frac{6x}{5} = 129 \Rightarrow \frac{3x}{10} = 129$

$\therefore x = \frac{10 \times 129}{3} = \text{Rs. } 430$

7. Here, 10% C.P. of horse = 20% C.P. of cart; Hence, C.P. of horse = 2 × C.P. of cart;

Let C.P. of cart and horse be Rs. x and Rs. $2x$ respectively; then,

$\frac{5}{100} \times 2x - \frac{5}{100} \times x = 10 \Rightarrow \frac{1}{20}x = 10$

$\therefore x = 200$

Hence, C.P. of a cart = Rs. 200 and C.P. of a horse

$= 2 \times 200 = \text{Rs. } 400$

8. Let C.P. be Rs. 100; then marked price

= Rs. 120

Since, S.P. $= \frac{90}{100} \times 120 = \text{Rs. } 108$

$\therefore$ Profit = 108 – 100 = Rs. 8, Hence, gain = 8%.

9. Required weight $= \frac{100}{160} \times 1000 = 625$ gms.

10. Here, loss % $= \left(\frac{10}{10}\right)^2 = 1\%$.

SIMPLE INTEREST

1. A lent a sum of Rs. 1250 to B at a certain rate of interest for 3 years and a sum of Rs. 1500 to C at the same rate of interest for 2 years. If he was paid total Rs. 258.75 as interest in both cases, find the rate of interest at which money was lent by him.

A. $4\frac{1}{6}\%$ B. $6\frac{1}{4}\%$
C. $2\frac{1}{7}\%$ D. $3\frac{5}{6}\%$

2. A invested Rs. 5000 at a certain rate of simple interest and Rs. 4000 for the same period at 1% higher rate of interest. If the interest in both cases is same, the former rate of interest is :

A. 3% B. 4%
C. 6% D. 5%

3. If a certain sum of money at simple interest amounts to Rs. 1900 in 3 years and to Rs. 2050 in 5 years, the rate per cent per annum is :

A. 4½% B. 3½%
C. 2½% D. 5¼%

4. A certain sum of money lent out on simple interest amounts to Rs. 1760 in 2 years and to Rs. 2000 in 5 years. Find the sum.

A. Rs. 1650 B. Rs. 1500
C. Rs. 1580 D. Rs. 1600

5. Out of the sum of Rs. 1550, a part was lent out at 5% p.a. simple interest and the remaining at 8% p.a. simple interest. If the total interest in both cases after 3 years is Rs. 300, the sum of money lent out at 8% p.a. simple interest was:

A. Rs. 760 B. Rs. 775
C. Rs. 750 D. Rs. 780

6. If simple interest on a certain sum of money for 4 years at 5% p.a. is same as the simple interest on Rs. 840 for 10 years at the rate of 4% p.a., the sum of money is:

A. Rs. 1780 B. Rs. 1660
C. Rs. 1680 D. Rs. 1620

7. What equal instalment of annual payment will discharge a debt which is due as Rs. 848 at the end of 4 years at 4% per annum simple interest?

A. Rs. 200 B. Rs. 212
C. Rs. 225 D. Rs. 250

8. Madhavi lent Rs. 5000 to Kamla for 5 years and Rs. 3000 to Vimla for 4 years. Find the rate of interest, if Madhavi gets an interest of Rs. 600 in the end.
A. 1.62% B. 2.5%
C. 3% D. 4%

9. A sum of money doubles itself in 7 years at simple interest. In how many years it will become four fold?
A. 10 years B. 14 years
C. 21 years D. 35 years

10. An amount doubles itself at the end of 8 years with a certain rate of simple interest. What will be the total simple interest on Rs. 8000 at that rate at the end of 4 years?
A. Rs. 2000 B. Rs. 4000
C. Rs. 6000 D. None of these

ANSWERS

1	2	3	4	5	6	7	8	9	10
D	B	A	D	C	C	A	A	C	B

EXPLANATORY ANSWERS

1. $\frac{1250 \times R \times 3}{100} + \frac{1500 \times R \times 2}{100} = 258.75$

$\Rightarrow 6750\ R = 25875$

$\therefore \quad R = \frac{25875}{6750} = \frac{23}{6} = 3\frac{5}{6}\%$

2. Here, $\frac{5000 \times R \times T}{100} = \frac{4000 \times (R+1) \times T}{100}$

$\Rightarrow 5R = 4R + 4 \quad \therefore\ R = 4\%$

3. Simple interest for 2 years
= Rs. 2050 – Rs. 1900 = Rs. 150

$\therefore$ Simple interest for 1 year = Rs. $\frac{150}{2}$ = Rs. 75

Since simple interest for 3 years = Rs. 75 × 3
= Rs. 225

$\therefore$ Principal = Rs. 1900 – Rs. 225 = Rs. 1675

Hence, Rate = $\frac{75 \times 100}{1675 \times 1}$ = 4½%

4. Interest for 3 years = Rs. 2000 – Rs. 1760
= Rs. 240

$\therefore$ Interest for 1 year = Rs. $\frac{240}{3}$ = Rs. 80

And interest for 2 years = Rs. 80 × 2 = Rs. 160
$\therefore$ Principal = Rs. 1760 – Rs. 160 = Rs. 1600

5. Let Rs. x and Rs $(1550 - x)$ were lent out at 8% and 5% respectively; then

$\frac{x \times 8 \times 3}{100} + \frac{(1550 - x) \times 5 \times 3}{100} = 300$

$\Rightarrow 24x + 23250 - 15x = 30000$

$\Rightarrow 9x = 6750 \quad \therefore\ x = \frac{6750}{9}$ = Rs. 750

6. Here, $\frac{P \times 5 \times 4}{100} = \frac{840 \times 4 \times 10}{100} \Rightarrow 5P = 8400$

$\therefore\ P = \frac{8400}{5}$ = Rs. 1680

7. Let equal instalment be Rs. x; then

$x + \frac{x \times 4 \times 3}{100} + x + \frac{x \times 4 \times 2}{100} + x + \frac{x \times 4 \times 1}{100} + x = 848$

$\Rightarrow 4x + \frac{24x}{100} = 848 \quad \Rightarrow \frac{106x}{25} = 848$

$\therefore\ x = \frac{848 \times 25}{106}$ = Rs. 200

8. $\frac{5000 \times R \times 5}{100} + \frac{3000 \times R \times 4}{100} = 600$

$\Rightarrow \quad 250\ R + 120\ R = 600$

$\Rightarrow \quad 370R = 600$

$\therefore \quad R = \frac{600}{370} = 1.62\%$

9. Let principal be Rs. x; then amount = Rs. $2x$, Hence, I = $2x - x$ = Rs. x.

$R = \frac{x \times 100}{x \times 7} = \frac{100}{7}\%$ p.a.

Now, amount = Rs. $4x$; then I = $4x - x$ = Rs. $3x$

Hence, $T = \frac{3x \times 100}{x \times \frac{100}{7}} = \frac{3 \times 100 \times 7}{100} = 21$ years

10. Let principal = Rs. x; then amount = Rs. $2x$; I = $2x - x$ = Rs. x

$R = \frac{x \times 100}{x \times 8} = \frac{25}{2}\%$

Again, $I = \frac{8000 \times 25 \times 4}{100 \times 2}$ = Rs. 4000

COMPOUND INTEREST

1. The compound interest on a certain sum of money invested for 3 years at 5% per annum is Rs. 1891.50. What will be the simple interest on the same sum at the same rate for 2 years?

A. Rs. 1700 B. Rs. 1200
C. Rs. 1500 D. Rs. 2100

2. A sum of money lent out at a certain rate of simple interest amounts to Rs. 6600 in 2 years and to Rs. 6900 in 3 years. What will be the compound interest on the same sum of money if lent out at the same rate for 2 years?

A. Rs. 605 B. Rs. 715
C. Rs. 615 D. Rs. 595

3. A man deposits Rs. 1200 in a bank on the 1st day of each year. If the bank pays 5% per annum compound interest on deposited sum of money, what will be the amount to his credit on the 10th day of the second year?

A. Rs. 2560 B. Rs. 2460
C. Rs. 2370 D. Rs. 2860

4. If the difference between compound and simple interest on a certain sum of money for 3 years at 5% per annum is Rs. 244, the sum is :

A. Rs. 40000 B. Rs. 25000
C. Rs. 30000 D. Rs. 32000

5. A man purchased a sewing machine for Rs. 5000. If due to sustained use value of this sewing machine depreciates by 6% annually, find its value after 3 years.

A. Rs. 3775.67 B. Rs. 4152.92
C. Rs. 4250.25 D. Rs. 4356.25

6. Find the sum on which the difference between compound and simple interest for 3 years at 10% per annum will be Rs. 868.

A. Rs. 29500 B. Rs. 27625
C. Rs. 28500 D. Rs. 28000

7. Samir invested Rs. 15000 at the rate of interest 10% p.a. for 1 year. If the interest compound six months. What amount will Samir get at the end of the year?

A. Rs. 16,500 B. Rs. 16525.50
C. Rs. 16537.50 D. Rs. 18,150

8. The compound interest on a certain sum for 2 years at 10% per annum is Rs. 525. The simple interest on the same sum for double the time at half the rate per cent per annum is:

A. Rs. 800 B. Rs. 600
C. Rs. 500 D. Rs. 400

9. The least number of complete years in which a sum of money put at 20% compound interest will be more than doubled is:

A. 6 B. 5
C. 4 D. 3

10. On a sum of money, the simple interest for 2 years is Rs. 660, while the compound interest is Rs. 696.30, the rate of interest being the same in both cases. Find the rate of interest.

A. Rs. 12% B. 11%
C. 10% D. 9%

ANSWERS

1	2	3	4	5	6	7	8	9	10
B	C	B	D	B	D	C	C	C	B

EXPLANATORY ANSWERS

1. Here, $1891.50 = P\left[\left(1+\frac{5}{100}\right)^3 - 1\right]$

$\Rightarrow \quad 1891.50 = P\left[\left(\frac{21}{20}\right)^3 - 1\right]$

$\Rightarrow \quad 1891.50 = P\left(\frac{1261}{8000}\right)$

$\therefore P = \frac{1891.50 \times 8000}{1261} = \text{Rs. } 12000$

Now, $\text{S.I.} = \frac{12000 \times 5 \times 2}{100} = \text{Rs. } 1200$

2. Here, 1 year's S.I. = Rs. 6900 – Rs. 6600 = Rs. 300

$\therefore$ 2 year's S.I. = 300 × 2 = Rs. 600

$\therefore$ Principal = Rs. 6600 – Rs. 600 = Rs. 6000

Hence, $\text{Rate} = \frac{600 \times 100}{6000 \times 2} = 5\%$

$\therefore$ $$\text{C.I.} = 6000\left[\left(1+\frac{5}{100}\right)^2 - 1\right]$$

$$= 6000\left[\left(\frac{21}{20}\right)^2 - 1\right] = \frac{6000 \times 41}{400} = \text{Rs. } 615$$

3. Required amount $= 1200\left(1+\frac{5}{100}\right) + 1200$

$= 1200 \times \frac{21}{20} + 1200 = 1260 + 1200 = $ Rs. 2460

4. Here, $P\left[\left(1+\frac{5}{100}\right)^3 - 1\right] - \frac{P \times 5 \times 3}{100} = 244$

$\Rightarrow P \times \frac{1261}{8000} - \frac{3P}{20} = 244 \Rightarrow P \times \frac{61}{8000} = 244$

$\therefore P = \frac{244 \times 8000}{61} = $ Rs. 32000

5. Here, value of the machine after 3 years

$= 5000\left(1-\frac{6}{100}\right)^3 = 5000 \times \frac{47}{50} \times \frac{47}{50} \times \frac{47}{50}$

= Rs. 4152.92.

6. Here, $P\left[\left(1+\frac{10}{100}\right)^3 - 1\right] - \frac{P \times 10 \times 3}{100} = 868$

$\Rightarrow P \times \frac{331}{1000} - \frac{3P}{10} = 868$

$\Rightarrow P \times \frac{31}{1000} = 868 \quad \therefore P = \frac{868 \times 1000}{31}$

= Rs. 28000

7. $A = 15000\left(1+\frac{5}{100}\right)^2 = 15000 \times \frac{441}{400}$

= Rs. 16537.50

8. Here, $P\left[\left(1+\frac{10}{100}\right)^2 - 1\right] = 525$

$\Rightarrow P\left[\frac{121}{100} - 1\right] = 525 \Rightarrow P \times \frac{21}{100} = 525$

$\therefore P = \frac{525 \times 100}{21} = $ Rs. 2500

Hence, required S.I. $= \frac{2500 \times 5 \times 4}{100} = $ Rs. 500

9. Here, $P\left(1+\frac{20}{100}\right)^n > 2P \Rightarrow \left(\frac{6}{5}\right)^n > 2$

Hence, if $n = 4$ then, $\left(\frac{6}{5}\right)^4 = \frac{1296}{625} > 2$

So, $n = 4$ years

10. Here, S.I. for 1 year = Rs. 330
Since, simple interest of Rs. 330 for 1 year
= 696.30 − 660 = Rs. 36.30

Hence, required rate $= \frac{36.30 \times 100}{330 \times 1} = \frac{3630}{330} = 11\%$

AREA AND PERIMETER

1. If side of a square is reduced by 50%, its area will be reduced by

A. 50% B. 75%
C. 80% D. 60%

2. If each side of a square is doubled, its area will become

A. double B. four times
C. three times D. eight times

3. Three sides of a triangle are in the ratio of 17 : 15 : 8. If the perimeter of this triangle is 40 m, find its area

A. 50 sq. m. B. 49 sq. m.
C. 60 sq. m. D. 69 sq. m.

4. If the length of a rectangle is increased by 20% and width is decreased by 15%, then its area

A. decreases by 4% B. increases by 2%
C. decreases by 2% D. increases by 3%

5. If the length of a rectangle is increased by 20%, then by how much per cent its breadth must be decreased so as to keep its area unaltered?

A. 25% B. $8\frac{1}{3}\%$
C. $16\frac{2}{3}\%$ D. 20%

6. The ratio of length and breadth of a rectangular plot is 71 : 61 respectively. The area of the plot is 17324 m^2. What is perimeter of the plot?

A. 264 m B. 284 m
C. 528 m D. 614 m

7. If the length and breadth of a rectangular field are increased, the area increases by 50%. If the increase in length was 20%, by what percentage was the breadth increased?

A. 20% B. 25%
C. 30% D. 40%

8. The length and breadth of a varandah is 40 m and 15 m respectively. How many stone slabs of size 6 decimetre × 5 decimetre each are needed in flooring it:
A. 1000 B. 2000
C. 3000 D. 4000

9. The circumference of a circular plot is 396 m. What is the area of the circular plot?
A. 9,446 m^2 B. 9,856 m^2
C. 12,474 m^2 D. 18,634 m^2

10. If the sides of an equilateral triangle are increased by 20%, 30% and 50% respectively to form a new triangle, the increase in the perimeter of the equilateral triangle is:
A. 25% B. $33\frac{1}{3}\%$
C. 50% D. 100%

ANSWERS

1	2	3	4	5	6	7	8	9	10
B	B	C	B	C	C	B	B	C	B

EXPLANATORY ANSWERS

1. Area of the square = x^2 sq. m.

Side of the new square = $x - 50\%$ of $x = \frac{x}{2}$ m

$\therefore$ Area of the new square = $\left(\frac{x}{2}\right)^2 = \frac{x^2}{4}$ sq. m.

$\therefore$ Reduction in area of the square = $x^2 - \frac{x^2}{4}$

$= \frac{3x^2}{4}$ sq. m.

$\therefore$ Percentage reduction = $\frac{3x^2/4}{x^2} \times 100 = 75\%$

2. Area of the square = x^2 sq. m
Now, area of the new square = $(2x)^2 = 4x^2$ sq. m
Hence, it is clear that if side of a square is doubled, its area becomes four times.

3. Suppose sides of the triangle are $17x$ m, $15x$ m and $8x$ metres

$\therefore$ Perimeter = $17x + 15x + 8x = 40x$

Now, $40x = 40$

$\Rightarrow$ $x = 1$ m

Therefore, the sides are $17 \times 1 = 17$ m, $15 \times 1 = 15$ m and $8 \times 1 = 8$ m

$\because$ $(17)^2 = (15)^2 + (8)^2$,

i.e., it is a right angled triangle

$\therefore$ Area of the right angled triangle

$= \frac{1}{2} \times 8 \times 15 = 60$ sq.m.

4. Area of the rectangle = xy sq. metre

Area of the new rectangle = $\frac{120}{100} x \times \frac{85}{100} y$

$= 1.020\, xy$ sq. metre

$\therefore$ Increase in the area = $1.02\, xy - xy = .02\, xy$ sq. m.

$\therefore$ Percentage increase = $\frac{.02xy}{xy} \times 100 = 2\%$

5. Area of the rectangle = xy
On reducing the breadth by A% and increasing the length by 20%

Length of the new rectangle = $\frac{120x}{100} x = 1.2x$

Breadth of the new rectangle = $y - A\%$ of $y = y\left(1 - \frac{A}{100}\right)$

$\therefore$ Area of the new rectangle = $1.2x \times y\left(1 - \frac{A}{100}\right)$

Now, $xy = 1.2\, xy\left(1 - \frac{A}{100}\right) \Rightarrow 1 = 1.2\frac{(100 - A)}{100}$

$\Rightarrow$ $1.2\, A = 120 - 100$

$\therefore$ $A = \frac{20}{1.2} = 16\frac{2}{3}\%$

6. Let length and breadth of a rectangle be $71x$ and $61x$ m; then

$71x \times 61x = 17324 \Rightarrow x^2 = \frac{17324}{71 \times 61} = 4$

$\therefore$ $x = 2$

Hence, length = $71 \times 2 = 142$ m; breadth $= 61 \times 2 = 122$ m

Since, perimeter = $2(142 + 122) = 2 \times 264 = 528$ m

7. Here, $20 + x + \frac{20 \times x}{100} = 50 \Rightarrow x + \frac{x}{5} = 30$

$\Rightarrow \frac{6x}{5} = 30$ $\therefore x = \frac{5 \times 30}{6} = 25$

Hence, breadth was increased by 25%

8. Required number of stone slabs = $\frac{40 \times 15}{\frac{6}{10} \times \frac{5}{10}}$

$= \frac{40 \times 15 \times 100}{6 \times 5} = 2000$

VOLUME AND SURFACE AREA

1. If a solid sphere of 3 cm radius is melted and recast into a right circular cone whose base radius is same as that of the sphere, the height of the cone will be

A. 8 cm B. 12 cm
C. 6 cm D. 5 cm

2. Diameter of a roller is 2.4 m and it is 1.68 m long. If it takes 1000 complete revolutions once over to level a field, the area of the field is

A. 12672 sq. m B. 12671 sq. m
C. 12762 sq. m D. 11768 sq. m

3. If each edge of a cube is increased by 10%, then by how much per cent will the surface area of this cube be increased?

A. 21% B. 18%
C. 15% D. 20%

4. Height and base radius of a solid cylinder are 14 m and 4 m respectively. It is melted and recast into a solid cone of the same base radius as that of the cylinder, what will be the height of the cone?

A. 21 m B. 42 m
C. 48 m D. 54 m

5. A room is in the form of a cube of side 10 m. How many bales of cotton can be kept in it if each bale covers 5 cu m space?

A. 100 B. 175
C. 200 D. 225

6. Three cubes having side 2 cm, 3 cm and 4 cm respectively are melted together to form a new cube. The side of the new cube will be

A. 3.526 cm B. 4.628 cm
C. 4.626 cm D. 4.528 cm

7. If base diameter of a cylinder is increased by 50%, then by how much per cent its height must be decreased so as to keep its volume unaltered?

A. 45.56% B. 55.56%
C. 50.16% D. 62.33%

8. The surface area of a cube is 600 sq. m. Its diagonal is

A. $10\sqrt{3}$ cm B. $5\sqrt{3}$ cm
C. $4\sqrt{2}$ cm D. $10\sqrt{2}$ cm

9. The base diameter of a conical tomb is 28 m and its slant height is 50 m. Find the cost of white washing its curved surface at the rate of 80 paise per sq. m?

A. Rs. 1860 B. Rs. 1760
C. Rs. 1950 D. Rs. 1875

10. The volume of a cuboid is 1120 cu cm and its height is 5 cm while the length and the breadth of the cuboid are in the ratio 8 : 7. The length of this cylinder exceeds the breadth by

A. 4 cm B. 2 cm
C. 7 cm D. 5 cm

ANSWERS

1	2	3	4	5	6	7	8	9	10
B	A	A	B	C	C	B	A	B	B

EXPLANATORY ANSWERS

1. Volume of the cone = Volume of the sphere

$\therefore \quad \frac{1}{3}\pi(3)^2 \times h = \frac{4}{3}\pi \times 3^3 \Rightarrow h = 12$ cm

Hence, height of the cone = 12 cm.

2. Surface area of the roller = $2\pi rh$

$= 2 \times \frac{22}{7} \times 1.2 \times 1.68 = 12.672$ sq. m

In one complete revolution, the roller covers 12.672 sq. m.

$\therefore$ It will cover in 1000 revolutions

= 12.672 × 1000 = 12672 sq. m

Hence, area of the field = 12672 sq. m.

3. Percentage increase in the surface area of the cube

$= \left(x + y + \frac{xy}{100}\right)\%$

$= \left(10 + 10 + \frac{10 \times 10}{100}\right)\% = 21\%.$

4. Here,

volume of the cone = Volume of the cylinder

$\Rightarrow \quad \frac{1}{3}\pi r^2 \times \text{height} = \pi r^2 \times 14$

$\therefore$ Height = 14 × 3 = 42 m

Thus, height of the cone = 42 m.

5. Volume of the cubical room = $(10)^3$
$= 1000$ cu m

Number of cotton bales which can be placed in the room

$$= \frac{\text{Volume of the room}}{\text{Volume of each cotton bale}} = \frac{1000}{5} = 200.$$

6. Volume of the new cube = $2^3 + 3^3 + 4^3$
$= 8 + 27 + 64 = 99$cu cm

$\therefore$ Side of the new cube = $\sqrt[3]{99} = 4.626$ cm.

7. Change in the volume of the cylinder

$$= \left(x+y+(-z)+\frac{xy+y(-z)+(-zx)}{100}+\frac{xy(-z)}{100^2}\right)\%$$

Since volume of the cylinder remains unchanged.

$\therefore$ Change = 0%

Now, $\left(50+50+(-z)+\frac{50\times50-50z-50z}{100}+\frac{50\times50\times(-z)}{100^2}\right)=0$

$\therefore\ 100 - z + 25 - z - .25z = 0$

$\Rightarrow 2.25z = 125 \Rightarrow z = \frac{125}{2.25} = 55.56$

$\therefore$ Height of the cylinder should be decreased by 55.56%.

8. Here, $6 \times (\text{side})^2 = 600$

$\Rightarrow$ $\text{side}^2 = 100$

$\Rightarrow$ side $= \sqrt{100} = 10$ cm

$\therefore$ Diagonal of the cube= $\sqrt{3}\times$side

$= \sqrt{3}\times10$

$= 10\sqrt{3}$ cm.

9. Area of the curved surface of the cone

$= \frac{22}{7}\times\frac{28}{2}\times50 = 2200$ sq. m.

$\therefore$ Cost of white washing at 80 paise per sq. m

$= 2200\times\frac{80}{100}$ = Rs. 1760.

10. Suppose the length and the breadth of the cuboid are $8x$ cm and $7x$ cm

$\therefore$ Here, $8x \times 7x \times 5 = 1120$

$\Rightarrow x^2 = \frac{1120}{280} = 4 = (2)^2 \Rightarrow x = 2$

$\therefore$ Length of the cuboid $= 8 \times 2 = 16$ cm

Breadth of the cuboid $= 7 \times 2 = 14$ cm

Hence, it is clear that length of the cuboid exceeds the breadth by 2 cm.

SERIES

Directions (Qs. 1 to 7) : *In the following number series, one of the numbers does not fit into the series. Find the wrong number.*

1. 2, 5, 10, 18, 26, 37, 50
A. 2 B. 5
C. 37 D. 18

2. 3 , 18, 38, 78, 123, 178, 243
A. 123 B. 178
C. 3 D. 38

3. 380, 188, 92, 48, 20, 8, 2
A. 188 B. 92
C. 48 D. 20

4. 5, 11, 23, 47, 96, 191, 383
A. 11 B. 23
C. 47 D. 96

5. 89, 78, 86, 80, 85, 82, 83
A. 78 B. 86
C. 80 D. 85

6. 58, 57, 54, 50, 42, 33, 32
A. 57 B. 54
C. 50 D. 32

7. 2, 20, 27, 44, 64
A. 27 B. 8
C. 20 D. 44

Directions (Qs. 8 to 10) : *Complete the following series.*

8. 1 4 9 16 25 36 49 ....
A. 54 B. 56
C. 64 D. 81

9. 11 13 17 19 23 29 31 37 41 ....
A. 43 B. 47
C. 53 D. 51

10. 3 7 6 5 9 3 12 1 15 ....
A. 18 B. 13
C. –1 D. 3

ANSWERS

1	2	3	4	5	6	7	8	9	10
D	C	C	D	A	C	C	C	A	C

EXPLANATORY ANSWERS

1. 2 5 10 18 26 37 50

↓ ↓ ↓ ↓ ↓ ↓ ↓

1^2+1 2^2+1 3^2+1 4^2+1 5^2+1 6^2+1 7^2+1

Wrong no. = 18, Correct no. = 17.

2. Only 3 is a prime number.

3. Wrong no. = 48, Correct no. = 44

Each term will be four more than two times the next term.

4. 5 11 23 47 [96] 191 383

+6 +12 +24 +48 +96 +192

Wrong no. = 96, Correct no. = 95.

5. If 87 is written in place of 78 then tens digit of each term will be 8.

6. 58 57 54 [50] 42 33 22

−1 −3 −5 −7 −9 −11

Wrong no. = 50, Correct no. = 49.

7. 2 [20] 27 44 64

+11 +14 +17 +20

Wrong no. = 20, Correct no. = 13.

8. Numbers are $1^2, 2^2, 3^2, 4^2, 5^2, 6^2, 7^2$.

So, the next number is $8^2 = 64$.

9. Numbers are all primes. The next prime is 43.

10. There are two series, beginning respectively with 3 and 7. In one 3 is added and in another 2 is subtracted. The next number is $1 - 2 = -1$.

APPROXIMATE VALUES

1. $85432 \div 2106 + 59.5614 = ?$

(*a*) 100 (*b*) 60

(*c*) 80 (*d*) 140

2. $\sqrt{67621} = ?$

(*a*) 320 (*b*) 260

(*c*) 200 (*d*) 280

3. 9.7 % of 5011 + 55.03 % of 4991

(*a*) 5500 (*b*) 7200

(*c*) 6000 (*d*) 4200

4. $730 \times 199 = ?$

(*a*) 350000 (*b*) 335000

(*c*) 300000 (*d*) 34600

5. $.0144 \times 0.36 = ?$

(*a*) 0.5 (*b*) 0.005

(*c*) 0.05 (*d*) 0.005

6. 31% of 1508 + 26% of 2018

(*a*) 1500 (*b*) 2000

(*c*) 1000 (*d*) 1200

7. $3015 + 13594 + 3738 = ?$

(*a*) 40000 (*b*) 36000

(*c*) 42000 (*d*) 46000

8. $6012 \times 119 = ?$

(*a*) 560000 (*b*) 448000

(*c*) 900000 (*d*) 720000

9. $2712.1563 \div 1805.4018 + 3.4982 = ?$

(*a*) 9 (*b*) 8

(*c*) 4 (*d*) 5

10. $4182.365 \div 20.886 = ?$

(*a*) 300 (*b*) 200

(*c*) 150 (*d*) 250

ANSWERS

1	2	3	4	5	6	7	8	9	10
A	B	D	A	B	C	A	D	D	B

EXPLANATORY ANSWERS

1. $85432 \div 2106 + 60 = 40 + 60 = 100$
Therefore, (B) is the correct answer.

2. $\sqrt{67621} = \sqrt{67600} = 260$
Therefore, (B) is the correct answer.

3. 29.7 % of 5011 + 55.03 % of 4991
= 30 % of 5000 + 55 % of 5000

$= \frac{30}{100} \times 5000 + \frac{55}{100} \times 5000$

$= 1500 + 2750 = 4250 \Rightarrow 4200$
Therefore, (D) is the correct answer.

4. $1730 \times 199 = 1730 \times 200$
$= 346000 \Rightarrow 350000$
Therefore, (B) is the correct answer.

5. $0.0144 \times 0.36 = 0.0140 \times 0.36 = .005040$
$\Rightarrow .005$
Therefore, (B) is the correct answer.

6. 31% of 1508 + 26% of 2018
= 30% of 1500 + 25% × 2000

$= \frac{30}{100} \times 1500 + \frac{25}{100} \times 2000$

$= 450 + 500 = 950 \Rightarrow 1000$
Therefore, (C) is the correct answer.

7. $23015 + 13594 + 3738$
$= 23000 + 13600 + 3700$
$= 40300 \Rightarrow 40000$
Therefore, (A) is the correct answer.

8. $6012 \times 119 = 6000 \times 120 = 720000$
Therefore, (D) is the correct answer.

9. $2712.1563 \div 1805.4018 + 3.4982$
$= 2700 \div 1800 + 3.5 = 1.5 + 3.5 = 5$
Therefore, (D) is the correct answer.

10. $4182.365 \div 20.886 = 4200 \div 21 = 200$
Therefore, (B) is the correct answer.

REASONING ABILITY

SERIES

Directions : *In each of the following series determine the order of the letters. Then from the given options select the one which will complete the given series.*

1. BMK, DLM, FKO, HJQ, ?

A. JIR B. JIT
C. JHS D. JIS

2. A, CD, FGH, ?

A. IJKL B. KLMN
C. JKLM D. LMNO

3. BXJ, ETL, HPN, KLP, ?

A. PHR B. NIR
C. NHR D. MHR

4. PUF, QVG, RWH, ?

A. SXI B. SYZ
C. SXJ D. SVI

5. DEF, HIJ, MNO, ?

A. RTV B. STU
C. PTU D. SRU

Directions : *Which of the following groups of letters will complete the given series?*

6. ab---b-bbaa-

A. babba B. abaab
C. abbab D. baaab

7. aa-ab--aaa-a

A. baaa B. abab
C. aaab D. aabb

8. -baa-aab-a-a

A. baab B. abab
C. aaba D. aabb

9. -a cca-ccca-acccc-aaa

A. ccaa B. acca
C. caac D. caaa

10. c-bbb--abbbb-abbb-

A. abccb B. bacbb
C. aabcb D. abacb

Directions : *In the following questions, select the number(s) from the given options for completing the given series.*

11. 3, 9, 27, 81, 243, ?

A. 486 B. 729
C. 972 D. 359

12. 1, 6, 12, 19, 27, ?

A. 38 B. 35
C. 36 D. 54

13. 2, 6, 14, 30, 62, ?

A. 126 B. 128
C. 120 D. 130

14. 8, 48, 16, 96, 32, ?

A. 192 B. 150
C. 64 D. 288

15. 2, 8, 14, 24, 34, 48, ?

A. 66 B. 62
C. 58 D. 64

Directions : *In the given series find the number which is wrong.*

16. 5, 25, 120, 625, 3125, 15625

A. 15625 B. 625
C. 120 D. 5

17. 4, 8, 11, 22, 18, 36, 24, 50

A. 8 B. 22
C. 36 D. 24

18. 2, 4, 12, 24, 72, 142, 432

A. 432 B. 12
C. 142 D. 72

19. 2, 3, 4, 4, 6, 8, 9, 12, 16

A. 3 B. 9
C. 6 D. 12

20. 97, 91, 86, 83, 79, 77, 76, 76

A. 86 B. 76
C. 91 D. 83

ANSWERS

1	2	3	4	5	6	7	8	9	10
D	C	C	A	B	D	C	B	D	A
11	**12**	**13**	**14**	**15**	**16**	**17**	**18**	**19**	**20**
B	C	A	A	B	C	D	C	B	D

EXPLANATORY ANSWERS

1. The letters in one group correspond to the letters in the next group in the manner +2, –1, +2 respectively.

BMK DLM FKO HJQ JIS

+2 +2 +2 +2

–1 –1 –1 –1

+2 +2 +2 +2

2. The letters are in natural sequence and from one group to the next one letter is dropped. Also the number of letters in groups is increased by one.

A CD FGH JKLM

↓ ↓ ↓

B E I

3. The letters in one group correspond to the letters in the next group in the manner +3, – 4, +2 respectively, *i.e.*,

BXJ ETL HPN KLP NHR

+3 +3 +3 +3

–4 –4 –4 –4

+2 +2 +2 +2

4. The three letters in each group are moved one step forward.

PUF QVG RWH SXI

+1 +1 +1

+1 +1 +1

+1 +1 +1

5. The letters are in natural order. The number of letters dropped in between the groups is increased by one at each step.

DEF HIJ MNO STU

↓ ↓ ↓

G KL PQR

6. The series is abbaab, abbaab

7. The series is aaaaba, aaaaba

8. The series is aba, aba, aba, aba

9. The series is c,a,cc,aa, ccc, aaa, cccc, aaaa

10. The series is cabbbb, cabbbb, cabbbb

11. The numbers in the series are multiplied by 3 to get the next numbers.

12. The difference between the numbers in the series increases by 1, after beginning from 5, *i.e.*,

1 6 12 19 27 36

+5 +6 +7 +8 +9

13. The difference between the numbers in the series doubles each time, after beginning from 4, *i.e.*,

2 6 14 30 62 126

+4 +8 +16 +32 +64

14. *Explanation I* : The sequence in the series is × 6, ÷ 3 which is repeated.

8 48 16 96 32 192

× 6 ÷ 3 × 6 ÷ 3 × 6

Explanation II : There are two alternate series and the numbers are multiplied by 2.

× 2 × 2

8 48 16 96 32 192

× 2 × 2

Series I : 8, 16, 32

Series II : 48, 96, 192

15. The sequence in the series is :

2 8 14 24 34 48 62

+6 +6 +10 +10 +14 +14

The difference increases by 4 at alternate step.

16. The numbers in the series are multiplied by 5 to get the next number.

∴ 125 should be in place of 120.

17. Two numbers form a pair. The first number increases by 7 for the next pair and the second number is the double of first number.

4 8 11 22 18 36 25 50

× 2 × 2 × 2 × 2

+7 +7 +7

∴ 25 should be in place of 24.

18. There are two alternate series and in each series, the numbers are multiplied by 6 to get the next number.

× 6 × 6 × 6

2 4 12 24 72 144 432

× 6 × 6

∴ 144 should be in place of 142.

19. There are three alternate series and in each series, the numbers are multiplied by 2 to get the next number.

× 2 × 2

2 3 4 4 6 8 8 12 16

× 2 × 2

× 2 × 2

Series I : 2, 4, 8

Series II : 3, 6, 12

Series III : 4, 8, 16

∴ 8 should be in place of 9.

20. The difference between the consecutive numbers in the series decreases by 1 at each step.

97 91 86 82 79 77 76 76

–6 –5 –4 –3 –2 –1 –0

∴ 82 should be in place of 83.

ANALOGIES OR RELATIONSHIPS

Directions : *In the questions given below establish the relationship between the two words. Then from the given options select one which has the same relationship as of the given two words.*

1. ADULT : BABY : : FLOWER : ?
A. Seed B. Bud
C. Fruit D. Butterfly

2. WRITER : READER : : PRODUCER : ?
A. Creator B. Contractor
C. Creature D. Consumer

3. ENTRANCE : EXIT : : LOYALTY : ?
A. Treachery B. Patriotism
C. Fidelity D. Reward

4. MOTHER : MATERNAL : : FATHER : ?
A. Eternal B. Detrimental
C. Paternal D. Formidable

Directions : *In the questions given below one term is missing. Based on the relationship of the two given words find the missing term from the given options.*

5. GFC : CFG : : RPJ : ?
A. JRP B. JPR
C. PJR D. RJP

6. BCF : DEG : : MNQ : ?
A. OPR B. PQS
C. OPP D. QRT

7. NATION : ANITNO : : HUNGRY : ?
A. HNUGRY B. UNHGYR
C. YRNGUH D. UHGNYR

8. SSTU : MMNO : : AABC : ?
A. GGHH B. IJKK
C. XXYZ D. NOOP

ANSWERS

1	2	3	4	5	6	7	8
B	D	A	C	B	A	D	C

EXPLANATORY ANSWERS

1. The youngone of an adult is a baby and that of a flower is a bud.

2. A writer aims to please the readers by his writings, a producer aims to please the consumers by his products.

3. The related words are opposites.

4. Relations on the mother's side are maternal and on the father's side paternal.

5. The letters of the first group are reversed.

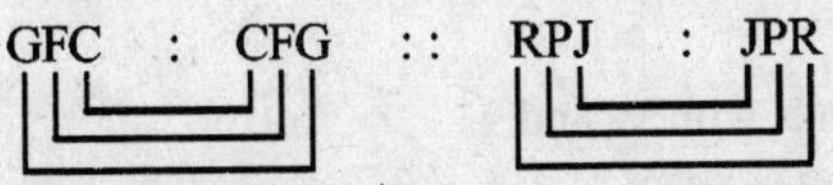

6. The three letters are moved 2, 2 and 1 steps forward respectively.

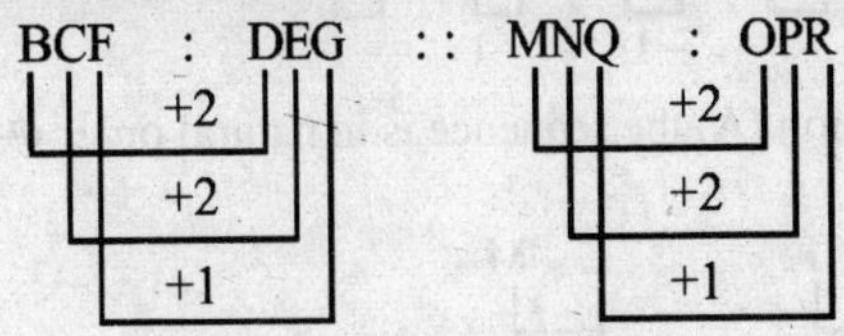

7. The word is divided in sections of two letters and the letters are reversed.

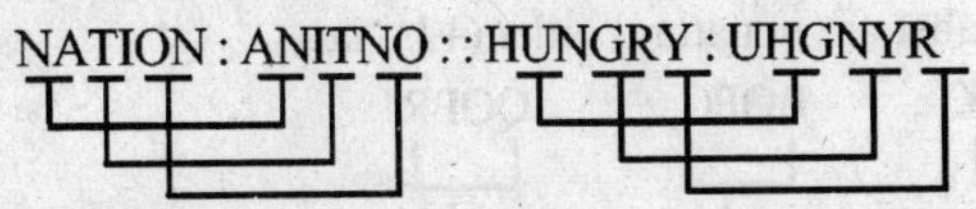

8. The first letter in each group is repeated and followed by two consecutive letters.

ODD ONE OUT

Directions : *Three of the following four in each question are alike in a certain way and so form a group. Select the group of letters that does not belong to that group.*

1. A. ACE B. LOR
C. GIK D. VXZ

2. A. TSR B. LKJ
C. PQO D. HGF

3. A. EF LM B. KJ SR
C. XW HG D. ED YX

4. A. JOPK B. BOPC
   C. QOPR D. TOPS

5. A. DfH B. MoQ
   C. UwY D. lnO

6. A. JKkL B. OPpQ
   C. DEEf D. VWwX

7. A. BdfH B. FHJL
   C. RTvX D. uVwX

8. A. DFHEG B. TWXUV
   C. OQSPR D. JLNKM

9. A. FEUV B. DCXW
   C. BAZY D. HGTS

10. A. UTSR B. XYZW
    C. ONML D. IHGF

ANSWERS

1	2	3	4	5	6	7	8	9	10
B	C	A	D	D	C	D	B	A	B

EXPLANATORY ANSWERS

1. The sequence in each group is +2. Only option B has sequence in +3, *i.e.,*

ABCDE (+2 +2) LMNOPQR (+3 +3)

GHIJK (+2 +2) VWXYZ (+2 +2)

2. The sequence of alphabet in each group is in reverse order. Only option C has sequence in disturbed order.

3. Two consecutive alphabet in each group are in reverse sequence (–1), *i.e.,*

KJ SR; XW HG; ED YX

–1 –1 –1 –1 –1 –1

Only in option (A) the sequence is in natural order (+1), *i.e.,*

EF LM

+1 +1

4. In each group, letters 'OP' are common. The two corner alphabet are in natural order (+1); *i.e.,*

JOPK ; BOPC ; QOPR

+1 +1 +1

Only in option (D) they are in reverse order (–1); *i.e.,*

TOPS

–1

5. In other groups, only the alphabet in the centre is of lower case. In this option letter 'L' on the left is also in lower case.

6. In other groups, the third letter which is a repeat of the second alphabet is in lower case.

7. In each group, the sequence of the alphabet, irrespective of the case, is +2; *i.e.,*

B D f H ; F H J L ; R T v X

+2 +2 +2 +2 +2+2 +2 +2 +2

Only in option (D) the sequence is in natural order (+1), *i.e.,*

u V w X

+1 +1 +1

8. In each group; the alphabet at positions-first, fourth, second, fifth and third, form a natural sequence.

In option (B), the alphabet at positions first, fourth, fifth, second and third, form the natural sequence.

9. In each group, two alphabets in the corner and two alphabets in the centre correspond to their reverse order positioned alphabet. *i.e.,*

natural order → A B C D E F G H I J K L M

reverse order → Z Y X W V U T S R Q P O N

natural order → N O P Q R S T U V W X Y Z

reverse order → M L K J I H G F E D C B A

As such—

D corresponds with W and

C corresponds with X.

B corresponds with Y and

A corresponds with Z.

H corresponds with S and

G corresponds with T.

Similarly,

F should correspond with U and

E should correspond with V;

i.e. letters 'UV' should be written as 'VU'

10. In each group, the alphabet are in reverse order.

In option (B), the order is disturbed.

7

CODING AND DECODING

Directions : *In the following questions select the right option which indicates the correct code for the word or letter given in the question.*

1. If CHAIR is coded as FKDLU then RAID is coded as:

A. ULGD B. ULKG
C. ULDG D. UDLG

2. If CONDEMN is coded as CNODMEN, then TEACHER is coded as :

A. TEACHER B. TAEECHR
C. TCAEEHR D. TAECEHR

3. In a code language COME is written as XLNV and ABLE as ZYOV. How will MOLLY be written in that code?

A. NLOBO B. NLBOO
C. LNOOB D. NLOOB

4. In a certain code PROFESSION is written as EFORPNOISS. In the same code DICTIONARY will be written as :

A. YRANOITCID B. ITCIDYRANO
C. ITCIDYRNAO D. ITCDIYARNO

5. JUNE is coded as NXPF, how will STAY be coded in the same manner?

A. WWCZ B. WVCZ
C. WWDB D. VWZC

Directions : *In the following questions study the coded patterns and then select the right option from the given alternatives.*

6. In a certain language, (a) 'go ju mi' stands for 'plenty of money'; (b) pao ju go nei vu' for 'money creates lots of problems'; (c) 'kol vu nei' for 'problems create tension'; and (d) 'sol tun ju haw' for 'still money is needed'. Which of the following words stand for 'money'?

A. nei B. ju
C. haw D. go

7. In a certain language, (a) 'FOR' stands for 'old is gold'; (b) 'ROT' stands for 'gold is pure'; (c) 'ROM' stands for 'gold is costly'. How will 'pure old gold is costly' be written?

A. TFROM B. FOTRM
C. FTORM D. TOMRF

8. In a certain code '415' means 'milk is hot'; '18' means 'hot soup'; and '895' means 'soup is tasty'. What number will indicate the word 'tasty'?

A. 9 B. 8
C. 5 D. 4

9. In a certain code '643' means 'she is beautiful', '593' means 'he is handsome', and '567' means 'handsome meets beautiful'. What number will indicate the word 'meets'?

A. 5 B. 3
C. 7 D. 6

10. In a certain code language, (a) 'dugo hui mul zo' stands for 'work is very hard'; (b) 'hui dugo ba ki' for 'Bingo is very smart'; (c) 'nano mul dugo' for 'cake is hard', and (d) 'mul ki qu' for 'smart and hard'. Which of the following words stand for 'Bingo'?

A. jalu B. dugo
C. ki D. ba

ANSWERS

1	2	3	4	5	6	7	8	9	10
D	D	D	B	A	B	A	A	C	D

EXPLANATORY ANSWERS

2. In this word, the second and third letters interchange their places and the fifth and sixth letters do the same. Other letters retain their position.

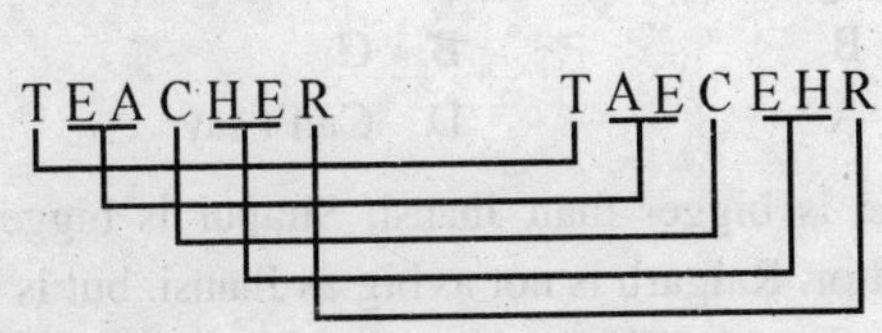

3. The letters of the word are coded by their represented letters in the reverse series.

C O M E → letters in natural series
X L N V → letters in reverse series
↓ ↓ ↓ ↓
3rd15th13th5th → position of letters
A B L E → letters in natural series
Z Y O V → letters in reverse series
↓ ↓ ↓ ↓
1st 2nd12th 5th → position of letters

Similarly,

M O L L Y → letters in natural series
N L O O B → letters in reverse series
↓ ↓ ↓ ↓ ↓
13th 15th 12th 12th 25th → position of letters

4. The word is divided into two equal parts and the letters of each part are written backwards.

PROFE SSION → EFORP NOISS

Similarly,

DICTI ONARY → ITCID YRANO

5. The word is coded by moving the letters +4, +3, +2, and +1 steps respectively.

JUNE → NXPF (+4, +3, +2, +1)

Similarly,

STAY → WWCZ (+4, +3, +2, +1)

6. *Code* — *Sentence*

1. go *ju* mi — plenty of *money*
2. pao *ju* go nei vu — *money* creates lots of problems
3. kol vu nei — problems create tension
4. sol tun *ju* haw — still *money* is needed

In 1st, 2nd and 4th codes and their sentences the word 'ju' is repeated and so is 'money'.

8. *Code* — *Sentence*

1. 415 — milk is hot
2. 18 — hot soup
3. 895 — soup is *tasty*

From 3rd code and its sentence neither number '9' is repeated nor the word 'tasty'.

9. *Code* — *Sentence*

1. 643 — she is beautiful
2. 593 — he is handsome
3. 567 — handsome *meets* beautiful

From 3rd code and its sentence, neither number '7' nor the word 'meets' is repeated.

10. *Code* — *Sentence*

1. *dugo hui* mul zo — work *is very* hard
2. *hui dugo* **ba** *ki* — **Bingo** *is very smart*
3. nano mul *dugo* — cake is *hard*
4. mul *ki* qu — *smart* and hard

From 2nd code and its sentence, neither 'ba' nor 'Bingo' is repeated.
(Words repeated are in italics)

STATEMENT ANALYSIS

1. Among five friends, A is heavier than B; C is lighter than D; B is lighter than D but heavier than E. Who among them is the heaviest?

A. B B. C
C. A D. Can't say

2. Pune is bigger than Jhansi, Sitapur is bigger than Chittor. Raigarh is not as big as Jhansi, but is bigger than Sitapur. Chittor is not as big as Sitapur. Which is the smallest?

A. Jhansi B. Pune
C. Chittor D. Sitapur

3. Ajay works more than Ram. Alok works as much as Raju. Pankaj works less than Alok. Ram works more than Alok. Who works the most of all?

A. Ajay B. Ram
C. Alok D. Raju

4. Vipul is taller than Hans. Hans is taller than Anand. Alok is taller than Ashok. Ashok is taller than Hans. Who among them is the tallest?

A. Vipul
B. Alok
C. Ashok
D. Cannot be determined

5. Pramod is taller than Gopal. Gopal is shorter than Madhu. To find out who among them is the tallest, which of the following further informations is necessary?

A. Madhu is taller than Gopal.
B. Madhu is shorter than Pramod's brother
C. Pramod is taller than Madhu.
D. Pramod is taller than Madhu's brother.

6. Among five friends P, Q, R, S and T, who is the youngest? To arrive at the answer which of the following information given in the statements (*a*) and (*b*) is sufficient?

(*a*) R is younger than P and T.
(*b*) S is younger than Q.

A. Only (*a*) alone is sufficient
B. Either (*a*) or (*b*) is sufficient
C. Both (*a*) and (*b*) together are needed
D. Both (*a*) and (*b*) together are not sufficient

7. Sushma is richer than Rashmi whereas Anand is richer than Priya. Arun is as rich as Rashmi. Shoba is richer than Sushma.

Which of the following statements is correct according to the above propositions?

A. Rashmi is poorer than Priya.
B. Priya is richer than Arun
C. Arun is poorer than Sushma.
D. Anand is richer than Rashmi

8. A is elder to B while C and D are elder to E who lies between A and B. If C be elder to B, which one of the following statements is necessarily true?

A. E is elder to B
B. A is elder to C
C. C is elder to D
D. D is elder to C

9. Vikram is taller than Rajan but shorter than Annie. Jamal is taller than Annie. Sita is taller than Vikram. Rajan is shorter than Sita. Who is the shortest of all in the group?

A. Sita
B. Rajan
C. Vikram
D. Cannot be determined

10. Suresh is as much older than Kamal as he is younger than Prabodh. Navin is as old as Kamal. Which of the following statements is wrong?

A. Suresh is older than Navin
B. Kamal is younger than Suresh
C. Prabodh is not the oldest
D. Navin is younger than Prabodh

ANSWERS

1	2	3	4	5	6	7	8	9	10
D	C	A	D	C	D	C	A	B	C

EXPLANATORY ANSWERS

1. The five friends in descending order of weight are : A/D, B/C, E or A/D, B, C/E. Either A or D is the heaviest.

2. The order of cities in descending order of size is : Pune, Jhansi, Raigarh, Sitapur, Chittor.

3. On the basis of doing work, the descending order will be : Ajay, Ram, Alok/Raju, Pankaj.

4. On the basis of height, the descending order will be Vipul/Alok, Ashok, Hans, Anand. Either Vipul or Alok is the tallest.

5. According to the information both Pramod and Madhu are taller than Gopal. Option (c) decides who is the tallest.

6. Statements are not inter-related.

7. On the basis of wealth, the descending order will be :

1. Shobha, Sushma, Rashmi/Arun
2. Anand, *and* Priya

(The two statements are not inter-related.)

8. The order in descending seniority will be : A/C/D, E, B.

9. On the basis of height the descending order will be :

Jamal/Sita, Annie, Vikram, Rajan.

or

Jamal, Sita/Annie, Vikram, Rajan.

10. On the basis of age the descending order will be : Prabodh, Suresh, Kamal/Navin.

PLACE ARRANGEMENT

Directions: *In the following questions, understand the arrangement pattern and then select the right answer from the given options :*

1. Five boys are sitting in a row. Raghu is not adjacent to Shyam or Amit. Ajay is not adjacent to Shyam. Raghu is adjacent to Mayank. If Mayank is at the middle in the row, then Ajay is adjacent to whom out of the following?

A. Amit B. Raghu
C. Mayank D. Shyam

2. Mini is to the right of Rajni but to the left of Ananta. Saya is to the right of Mini but to the left of Jaya. Who is on the extreme left if all the girls are facing North?

A. Jaya B. Mini
C. Rajni D. Saya

3. Kittu is in-between Mohan and Sohan. Raju is to the left of Sohan and Shyam is to the right of Mohan. If all of the friends are sitting facing South, then who is on their extreme right?

A. Mohan B. Sohan
C. Kittu D. Shyam

4. A, B, C, D and E are running one behind the other. C is not near E and A is not near D. B is next to A and E is not near D. Who is in the middle?

A. B B. E
C. A D. Cannot be said

5. O, P, Q, R, S and T are standing on a bench according to their height. P is taller than O but shorter than S. Only S is taller than T. R is shorter than P but taller than Q. Who is the shortest?

A. O B. Q
C. P D. Cannot be said

ANSWERS

1	2	3	4	5
B	C	D	A	D

EXPLANATORY ANSWERS

1. The order of sitting is :
Amit, Shyam, Mayank, Ajay, Raghu
or
Ajay, Raghu, Mayank, Amit, Shyam

2. The order in which the girls are positioned is :
Rajni, Mini, Ananta, Saya, Jaya
or
Saya, Jaya, Ananta
or
Saya, Ananta, Jaya

3. The order of sitting while facing South is:
Shyam, Mohan, Kittu, Sohan, Raju.

4. The positions while running behind the other is :

E
A
B
C
D

or

E
A
B
D
C

5. In descending order of height, the standing positions are :

S
T
P
R
O
Q

or

S
T
P
R
Q
O

Either O or Q is the shortest. The information given is not enough to clarify the answer.

DIRECTION SENSE

Directions : *In the following questions, select the right answer from the given options to depict the correct direction/distance.*

1. Kittu walks towards East and then towards South. After walking some distance he turns towards West and then turns to his left. In which direction is he walking now?

A. North B. South
C. East D. West

2. A person is driving towards West. What sequence of directions should he follow so that he is driving towards South?
A. left, right, right
B. right, right, left
C. left, left, left
D. right, right, right

3. Richa drives 8 km to the South, turns left and drives 5 km. Again, she turns left and drives 8 km. How far is she from her starting point?
A. 3 km B. 5 km
C. 8 km D. 13 km

4. Dingi runs 40 km towards North then turns right and runs 50 km. He turns right and runs 30 km, and once again turns right and runs 50 km. How far is he from his starting point?
A. 90 km B. 50 km
C. 10 km D. 5 km

5. Debu walks towards East then towards North and turning 45° right walks for a while and lastly turns towards left. In which direction is he walking now?
A. North B. East
C. South-East D. North-West

ANSWERS

1	2	3	4	5
B	D	B	C	D

EXPLANATORY ANSWERS

1. 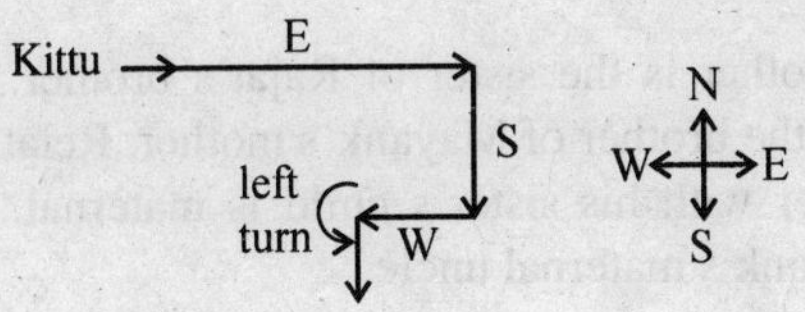

2. 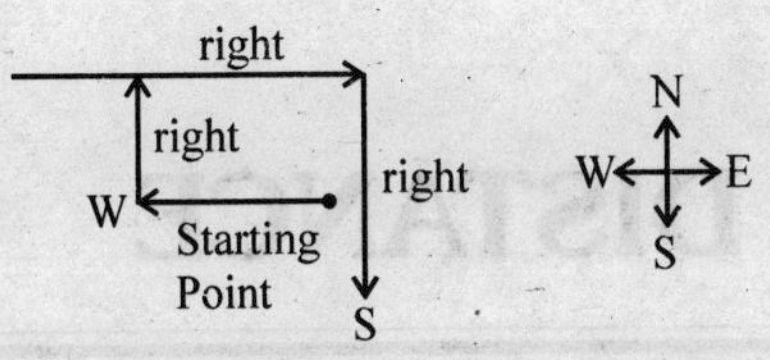

3. 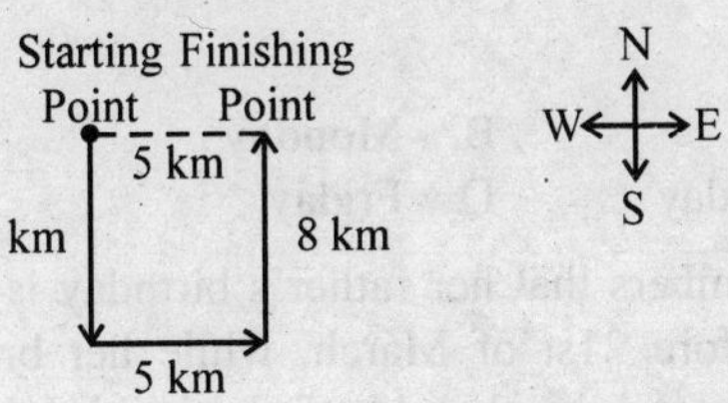

4. 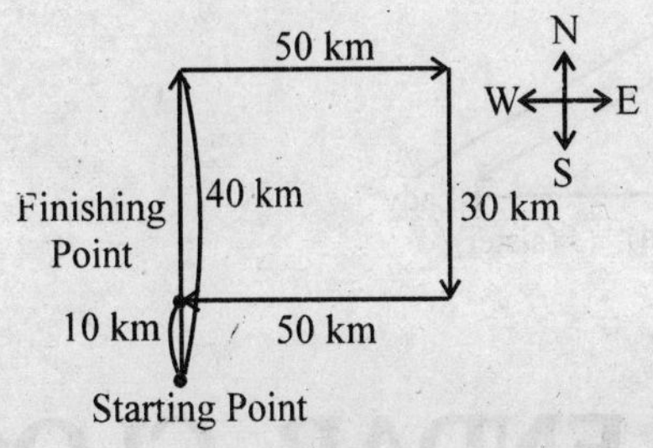

5. 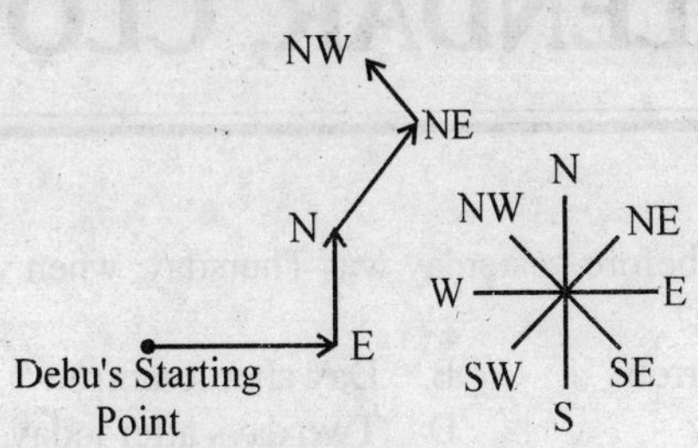

BLOOD RELATIONSHIPS

Directions : *In each of the following questions keenly study the relationship mentioned between the persons, and then from the given options select the right relationship as the answer.*

1. 'A' is the father of 'B' and 'C'. 'B' is the son of 'A' but 'C' is not the son of 'A'. What is 'C's' relation with 'A'?
A. Daughter B. Son
C. Niece D. Nephew

2. A lady said, "The person standing there is my grandfather's only son's daughter". How is the lady related to the standing person?
A. Sister B. Mother
C. Aunt D. Cousin

3. Ravi is the brother of Amit's son's son. What is Amit's relation to Ravi?
A. Cousin B. Father
C. Grandfather D. Son

4. Mayank said, "My mother is the sister of Rajat's brother." What is Rajat's relation with Mayank?
   A. Cousin B. Maternal uncle
   C. Uncle D. Brother-in-law

5. Introducing Lily, Raghav said, "Her father is my mother's only son". How is Lily related to Raghav?
   A. Aunt B. Daughter
   C. Mother D. Sister

ANSWERS

1	2	3	4	5
A	A	C	B	B

EXPLANATORY ANSWERS

1.
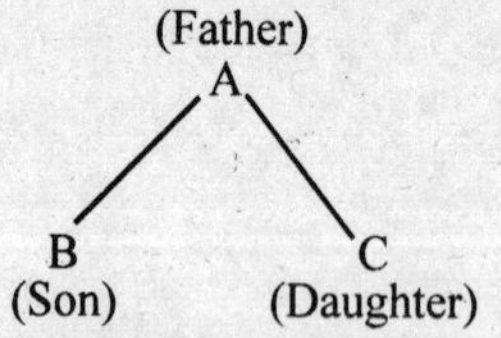

'C' is not the son of 'A', but 'A' is the father of 'C'. So, 'C' is the daughter of 'A'.

2.
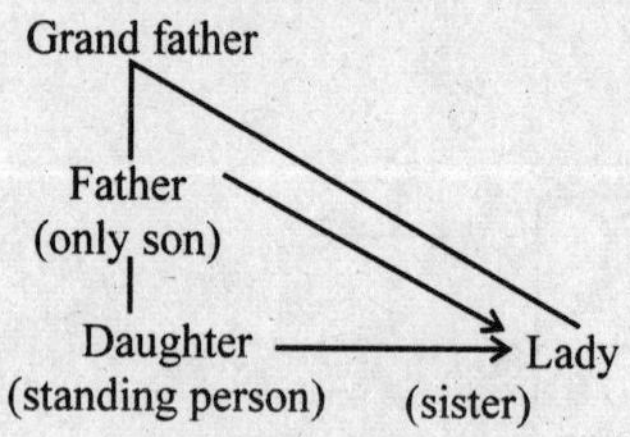

Lady's grandfather's son is lady's father and father's daughter will only be lady's sister.

4.
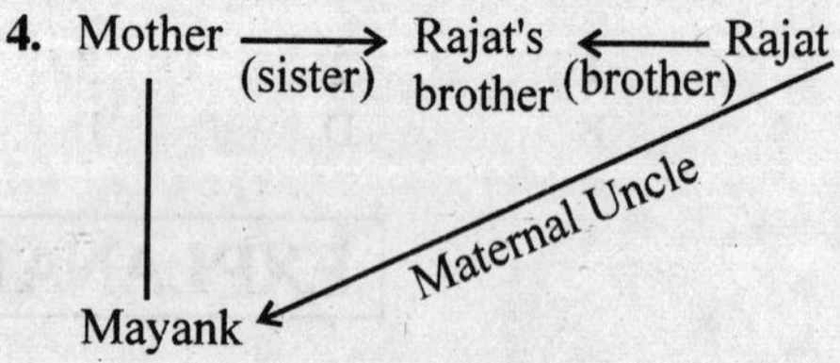

Mayank's mother is the sister of Rajat's brother. So Rajat is also the brother of Mayank's mother. Relation of the brother with his sister's child is maternal. So Rajat is Mayank's maternal uncle.

CALENDAR, CLOCK, TIME, DISTANCE

1. If the day before yesterday was Thursday, when will Sunday be?
   A. Tomorrow B. Day after tomorrow
   C. Today D. Two days after today

2. There are twenty people working in an office. The first group of five works between 8:00 A.M. and 2:00 PM. The second group of ten works between 10:00 AM to 4:00 PM. And the third group of five works between 12 noon to 6:00 PM. There are three computers in the office which all the employees frequently use. During which of the following hours the computers are likely to be used most?
   A. 1:00 PM - 3:00 PM
   B. 12 noon - 2:00 PM
   C. 2:00 PM - 4:00 PM
   D. 10:00 AM - 12 noon

3. If the seventh day of a month is three (3) days earlier than Friday, what day will it be on the nineteenth day of the month?
   A. Sunday B. Monday
   C. Wednesday D. Friday

4. Radha remembers that her father's birthday is after 16th but before 21st of March, while her brother Mangesh remembers that his father's birthday is before 22nd but after 19th of March. On which date is the birthday of their father?
   A. 19th
   B. 20th
   C. 21st
   D. Cannot be determined

5. A man is three (3) years older than his wife and four (4) times as old as his son. If the son attains an age of fifteen (15) years after three (3) years, what is the present age of the mother?
   A. 45 years B. 51 years
   C. 48 years D. 60 years

6. A clock is so placed that at 12 noon its minute hand points towards north-east. In which direction does its

hour hand point at 1.30 P.M.?

A. East B. West
C. North D. South

7. If in the above question clock is turned through an angle of 135° in an anticlockwise direction, in which direction will its minute hand point at 8.45 P.M.?

A. East B. West
C. North D. South

8. A couple married in 1980 had two children, one in 1982 and the other in 1984. Their combined ages will equal the years of the marriage in?

A. 1986 B. 1985
C. 1987 D. 1988

9. Manoj left home for the bus stop 15 minutes earlier than the usual time. It takes 10 minutes to reach the stop. He reached the stop at 8.40 a.m. What time does he usually leave home for the bus stop?

A. 8.30 a.m. B. 8.55 a.m.
C. 8.45 p.m. D. None of these

10. Mamuni went to the movies nine days ago. She goes to the movies only on Thursday. What day of the week is today?

A. Sunday B. Tuesday
C. Thursday D. Saturday

11. If Thursday was the day after the day before yesterday five days ago, what is the least number of days ago when Sunday was three days before the day after tomorrow?

A. Two days ago B. Three days ago
C. Four days ago D. Five days ago

12. 1.12.91 is the first Sunday. Which is the fourth Tuesday of December 91?

A. 31.12.91 B. 24.12.91
C. 17.12.91 D. 26.12.91

13. If the third day of a month is Monday, which of the following will be the fifth day from 21st of that month?

A. Tuesday B. Monday
C. Wednesday D. Thursday

14. Keshav runs a factory in three shifts of eight hours each with 210 employees. In each shift minimum of 80 employees are required to run the factory effectively. No employee can be allowed to work for more than 16 hours a day. At least how many employees will be required to work for 16 hours every day?

A. 30 B. 60
C. Data inadequate D. None of these

15. If 15 horses eat 15 bags of gram in 15 days, in how many days will one horse eat one bag of grain?

A. 15 days B. 1/15 days
C. 1 day D. 30 days

16. A century leap year is divisible by :

A. 4 B. 16
C. 40 D. 400

17. If the fifth day of a month is Friday, which of the following will be the Seventh day from 10th of that month?

A. Tuesday B. Monday
C. Wednesday D. Thursday

18. Day after tomorrow is my birthday. On the same day next week falls 'Holi'. Today is Monday. What will be the day after 'Holi'?

A. Wednesday B. Thursday
C. Friday D. Saturday

19. A clock shows the time as 3 : 30 p.m. If the minute hand gains 2 minutes every hour, how many minutes will the clock gain by 4 a.m.?

A. 23 Minutes B. 24 Minutes
C. 25 Minutes D. 26 Minutes

20. Two brothers were expected to return home on the same day. Rajat returned 3 days earlier but Rohit returned 4 days later. If Rajat returned on Thursday, what was the expected day when both the brothers were to return home and when did Rohit Return?

A. Wednesday, Sunday
B. Thursday, Monday
C. Sunday, Thursday
D. Monday, Friday

ANSWERS

1	2	3	4	5	6	7	8	9	10
A	B	A	B	A	A	D	A	D	D
11	**12**	**13**	**14**	**15**	**16**	**17**	**18**	**19**	**20**
A	B	C	D	A	D	C	B	C	C

EXPLANATORY ANSWERS

1. Thursday —Day-before-yesterday
Friday —Yesterday
Saturday —Today
Sunday — Tomorrow

2. 1. 5 people work between 8 a.m. to 2 p.m.

2. 10 people work between 10 a.m. to 4 p.m.

3. 5 people work between 12 noon to 6 p.m.

So, computers are used most between 12 noon to 2 p.m.

3. 7th day is 3 days earlier than Friday so, 10th day is Friday, so also is 17th.

∴ 19th day will be 2nd day ahead of Friday, *i.e.,* Sunday.

4. Father's birthday

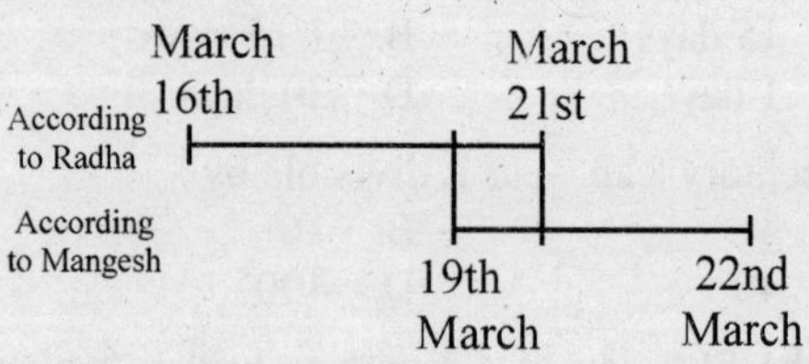

∴ Their father's birthday is on 20th March.

5. Present age of son is 15 – 3 = 12 years. Age of the man is 4 times the age of son, *i.e.*,

12 × 4 = 48 years

Man is 3 years elder to his wife/son's mother.

So Age of the mother is 48 – 3 = 45 years

6.

At 12 noon

At 1.30 p.m. the hour hand will point towards East.

7.

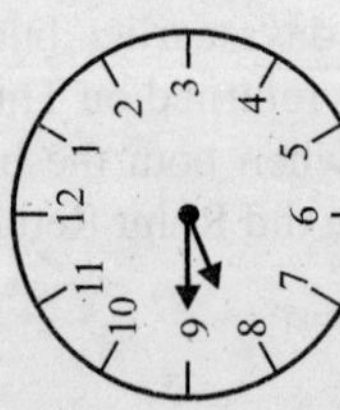

After rotating the clock in earlier question, its minute hand will point towards South at 8:45 p.m.

8. 1982 — 2 years later — 1st child

1984 — 4 years later — 2nd child

Total age of children — 2 years.

1985 — 5 years later — Total age of children: 4 years.

1986 — 6 years later — Total age of children : 6 years.

9. Manoj reached the bus stop at 8.40 a.m. He left his home at 8:40 – 10 minutes = 8:30 a.m. He left 15 minutes earlier than usual, so his actual time of leaving home is 8:30 am + 15 minutes = 8:45 a.m.

10. Mamuni goes to the movies on Thursday, so nine days ago was Thursday.

∴ Two days ago was also Thursday. So, today is Saturday.

11. Day after the day-before-yesterday five days ago is the 6th day which is Thursday. And so, the 3rd day will be Sunday. Three days before the day-after-tomorrow is Yesterday which is the 1st day of the five days. So, two days ago was Sunday.

12. First Sunday is on 1st December

First Tuesday is on 3rd December

3 weeks later, Fourth Tuesday will be on 3 + (7 × 3) = 24th December.

13. 3rd day of the month is Monday

5th day from 21st is 26th

26 – 3 = 23 days

23 days later, 23/7 leaves 2 days.

So, two days ahead of Monday will be Wednesday.

14. 80 employees are required for double shift.

15. 15 horses eat 15 bags of grain in 15 days

15 horses eat 1 bag of grain in 1 day

1 horse eats 1 bag of grain in 15 days

16. A leap year is divisible by 4 and a century leap year is divisible by 400.

17. Seventh day from 10th is 17th.

5th day is Friday. Next Friday is on 12th, 17 – 12 = 5, 5 days ahead of Friday will be Wednesday. So, 17th is Wednesday.

18. Today is Monday

Day-after-tomorrow is Wednesday

Next week 'Holi' is also on Wednesday

So, Day after Holi is Thursday.

19. Hours between 3:30 p.m. and 4 a.m. are — 12½ hours. Number of minutes gained will be 12½ × 2 = 25 minutes.

20. Rajat returned on Thursday. 3 days later was the day of expected return, *i.e.,* Sunday. Rohit returned 4 days after Sunday, *i.e.,* Thursday.

ROWS AND RANKS

1. In a row of trees, one tree is fifth from either end of the row. How many trees are in the row?

A. 11 B. 8
C. 10 D. 9

2. Jaya ranks 5th in a class of 53. What is her rank from the bottom in the class?

A. 49th B. 48th
C. 47th D. 50th

3. Mohan ranks twenty-first in a class of sixty-five students. What will be his (Mohan's) rank if the lowest candidate is assigned rank 1?

A. 44th B. 45th
C. 46th D. Data inadequate

4. If Rahul finds that he is 12th from the right in a line of boys and 4th from the left, how many boys should be added to the line such that there are 28 boys in the line?

A. 12 B. 14
C. 20 D. 13

5. In a row of boys, Rajan is tenth from the right and Suraj is tenth from the left. When Rajan and Suraj interchange their positions, Suraj will be twenty-seventh from the left. Which of the following will be Rajan's position from the right?

A. Tenth B. Twenty-sixth
C. Twenty-ninth D. None of these

6. Mahesh and Suresh are ranked 11th and 12th respectively from the top in a class of 41 students. What will be their respective ranks from the bottom?

A. 32nd and 33rd B. 29th and 30th
C. 30th and 31st D. 31st and 30th

7. Uma ranked 8th from the top and 37th from bottom in a class. How many students are there in the class?

A. 47 B. 46
C. 45 D. None of these

8. In a queue, Sadiq is 14th from the front and Joseph is 17th from the end, while Jane is in between Sadiq and Joseph. If Sadiq be ahead of Joseph and there be 48 persons in the queue, how many persons are there between Sadiq and Jane?

A. 5 B. 6
C. 7 D. 8

9. Rohan ranked eleventh from the top and twenty-seventh from the bottom among the students who passed the annual examination in a class. If the number of students who failed in the examination was 12, how many students appeared for the examination?

A. 48
B. 49
C. 50
D. Cannot be determined

10. Some boys are sitting in a row. P is sitting fourteenth from the left and Q is seventh from the right. If there are four boys between P and Q, how many boys are there in the row?

A. 19 B. 21
C. 25 D. 23

ANSWERS

1	2	3	4	5	6	7	8	9	10
D	A	B	D	D	D	D	C	B	C

EXPLANATORY ANSWERS

1.

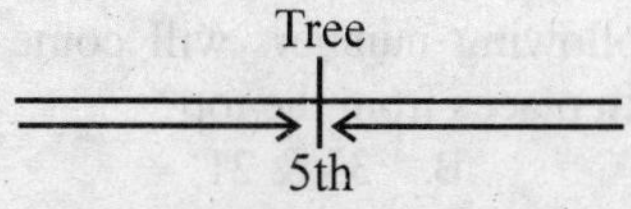

Total number of trees in the row are :
(5 + 5) –1 =9

2.

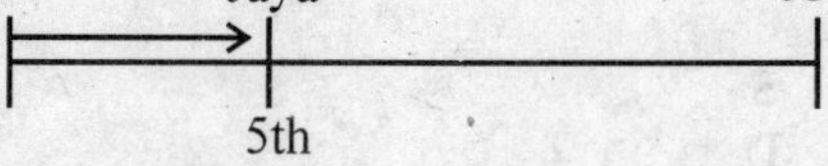

Jaya's rank from the bottom is :
(53 – 5) +1 = 49th.

3.

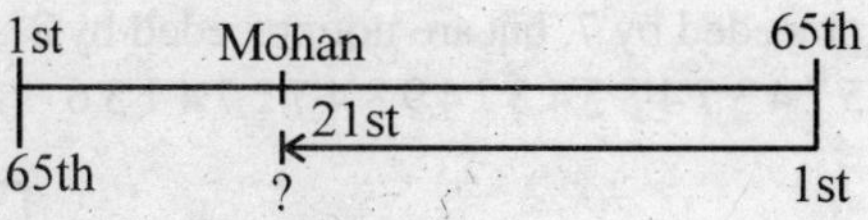

Note : Mohan's rank from the last or the question asked means the same.

Mohan's rank is (65 – 21) +1 = 45th

4.

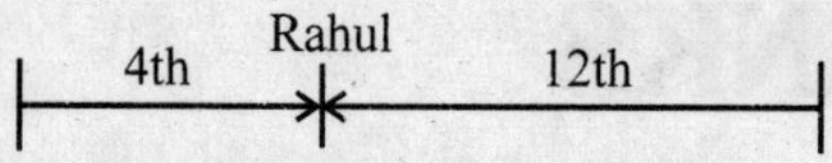

The number of boys in the line are :
(4 + 12) – 1 = 15
To make a line of 28 boys, (28 –15) *i.e.* 13 more boys are needed.

5.

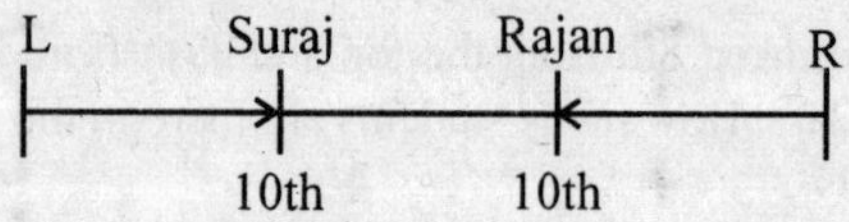

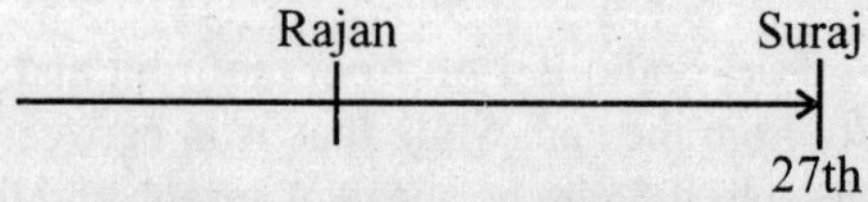

As the position of boys is equal from both ends, Rajan will also be 27th from the right after changing positions.

6.

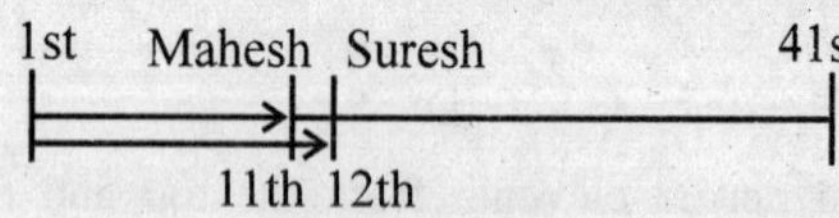

Mahesh's position from bottom is :
(41 – 11) + 1 = 31st
Suresh's position from bottom is :
(41 – 12) +1 = 30th

7.

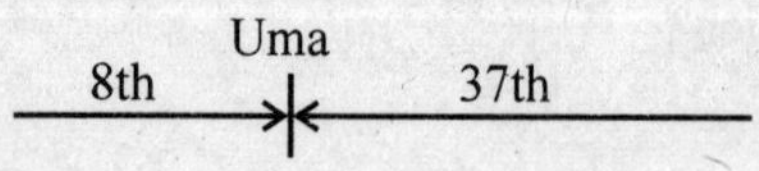

Total number of students in the class are :
(8 + 37) – 1 = 44

8.

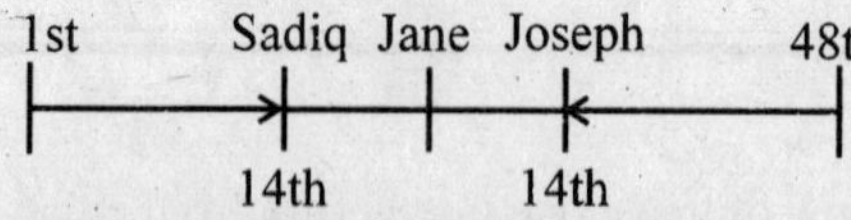

Sadiq's position from last is :
(48 – 14) + 1 = 35th
Number of persons between Sadiq and Joseph are (35 – 17) – 1 = 17
Jane is in-between Sadiq and Joseph *i.e.,* she's at 9th position from both the boys.
∴ there are 8 persons between Sadiq and Jane.
Note : (8 + 8) – 1 = 17

9.

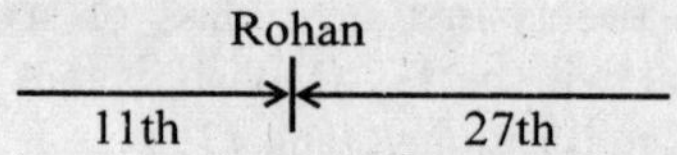

Number of students who passed the examination (11+ 27) – 1 = 37
Those who failed = 12
Total number of students who appeared in the examination = 37 + 12 = 49.

10.

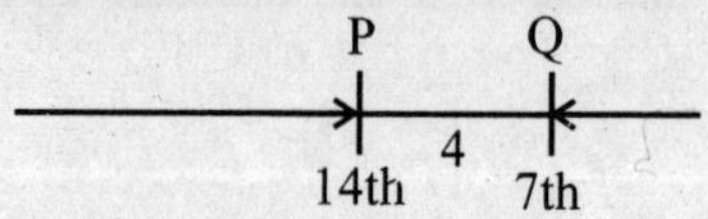

The number of boys in the row are :
(14 + 4 + 7) = 25

NUMBER PROBLEMS

1. How many 6's are there in the following series of numbers which are preceded by 7 but not immediately followed by 9?
6 7 9 5 6 9 7 6 8 7 6 7 8 6 9 4 6 7 7 6 9 5 7 6 3

A. One B. Two
C. Three D. Four

2. In a chess tournament each of six players will play every other player exactly once. How many matches will be played during the tournament?

A. 12 B. 15
C. 30 D. 36

3. How many 4's are there in the following series which are preceded by 7, but are not preceded by 8?
3 4 5 7 4 3 7 4 8 5 4 3 7 4 9 8 4 7 2 7 4 1 3 6

A. 1 B. 2
C. 3 D. 4

4. How many even numbers are there in the following series of numbers, each of which is immediately preceded by an odd number, but not immediately followed by an even number?
5 3 4 8 9 7 1 6 5 3 2 9 8 4 3 5

A. Nil B. 1
C. 2 D. 3

5. If all the numbers from 1 to 51 which are exactly divisible by 3 are arranged in descending order, which of the following numbers will come at the seventh and tenth places from the top?

A. 33 & 27 B. 33 & 21
C. 21 & 30 D. 33 & 24

ANSWERS

1	2	3	4	5
C	B	D	C	D

EXPLANATORY ANSWERS

1. 6795697687678694677695763
(768 — 1, 767 — 2, 763 — 3)

2. When all the players have to play with each other then the method of calculating the number of matches to be played is $\frac{n(n-1)'}{2}$ where *'n'* is the number of players playing the match. So, the number of matches played will be :
$(6 \times 5) \div 2 = 30 \div 2 = 15$

3. 345743748543749847274136
(74 — 1, 74 — 2, 74 — 3, 74 — 4)

4. 5348971653298435
(165 — 1, 329 — 2)

5. The numbers divisible by 3 in descending order are :
51, 48, 45, 42, 39, 36, 33, 30 (7th), 27, 24 (10th), 21, 18, 15, 12, 9, 6, 3.

SYMBOL SUBSTITUTION

1. If "+" means "–"; "–" means "×"; "×"means "÷" and "÷" means "+", then
$15 \times 5 \div 10 + 5 - 3 = ?$
A. 9.5 B. 0
C. – 2 D. 24

2. If "+" means "–"; "–" means "×"; "×"means "÷" and "÷" means "+", then
$15 \times 3 \div 15 + 5 - 2 = ?$
A. 0 B. 10
C. 20 D. 6

3. If "+" means "÷"; "×" means "–"; "÷"means "+" and "–" means "×", then
$16 \div 8 \times 6 - 2 + 12 = ?$
A. 22 B. 24
C. 23 D. 20

4. If "+" means "×"; "–" means "÷"; "÷"means "+" and "×" means "–", then what will be the value of $20 \div 40 - 4 \times 5 + 6 = ?$
A. 60 B. 1.67
C. 150 D. 0

5. If "+" means "×"; "–" means "÷"; "×"means "–" and "÷" means "+", then
$5 + 8 - 4 \times 2 \div 9 = ?$
A. 15 B. 13
C. 17 D. 11

ANSWERS

1	2	3	4	5
C	B	C	D	C

EXPLANATORY ANSWERS

1. $15 \div 5 + 10 - 5 \times 3$
$3 + 10 - 15 = -2$

2. $15 \div 3 + 15 - 5 \times 2$
$5 + 15 - 10 = 10$

3. $16 + 8 - 6 \times 2 \div 12$
$16 + 8 - 1 = 23$

4. $20 + 40 \div 4 - 5 \times 6$
$20 + 10 - 30 = 0$

5. $5 \times 8 \div 4 - 2 + 9$
$10 - 2 + 9 = 17$

MISSING NUMBERS

Directions: *In each question given below which one number can be placed at the sign of interrogation?*

1.

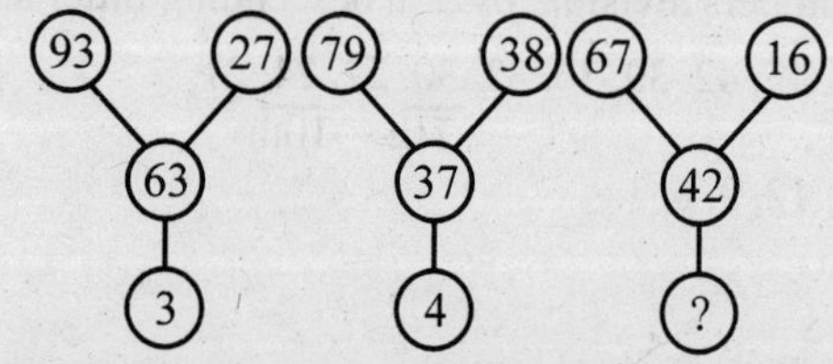

A. 5 B. 6
C. 8 D. 9

2.

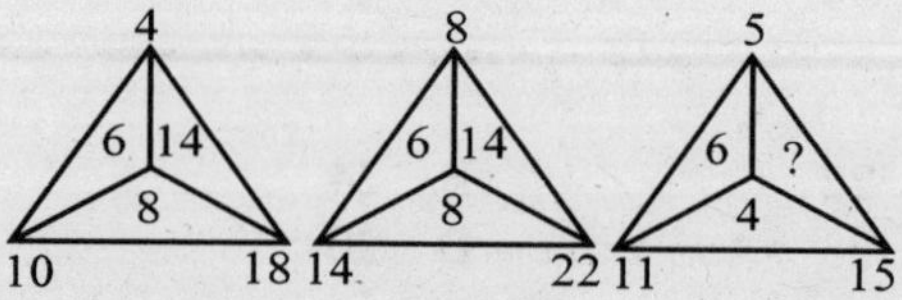

A. 8 B. 14
C. 10 D. 6

3.

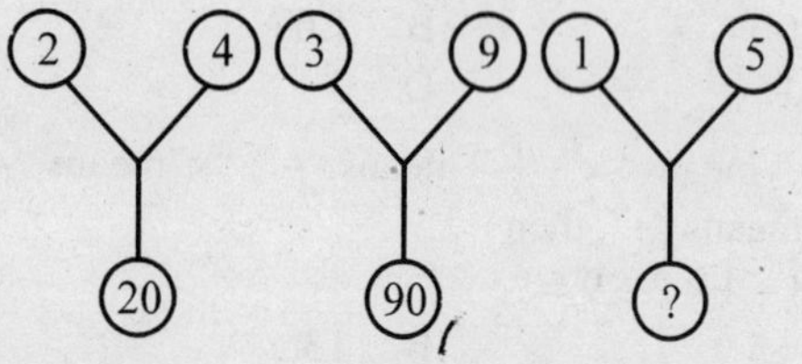

A. 20 B. 25
C. 26 D. 75

4.

27	22	50
13	12	26
9	2	?

A. 12 B. 39
C. 18 D. 24

5.

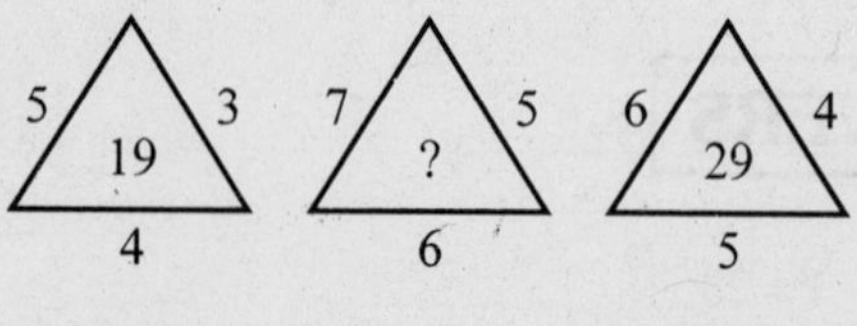

A. 25 B. 47
C. 37 D. 41

6.

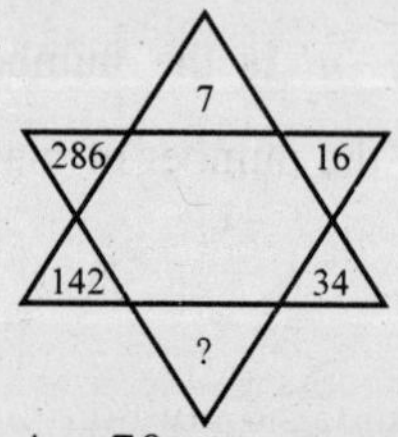

A. 70 B. 68
C. 56 D. 92

7.

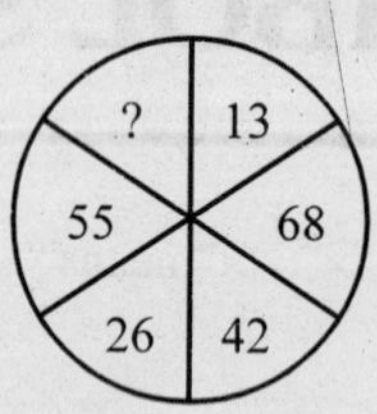

A. 41 B. 37
C. 29 D. 25

8.

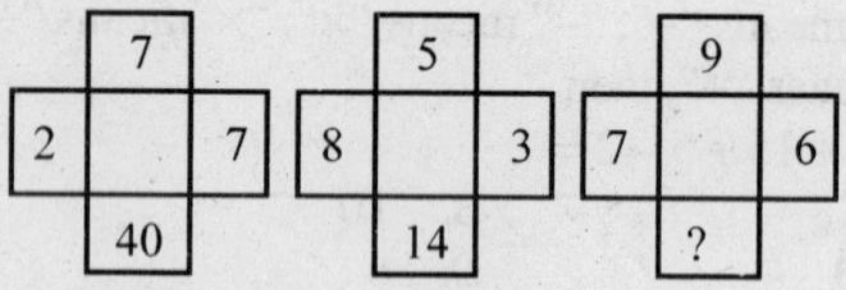

A. 72 B. 68
C. 82 D. 96

9.

42	(21)	22
78	(?)	84
162	(18)	99

A. 12 B. 13
C. 60 D. 72

10.

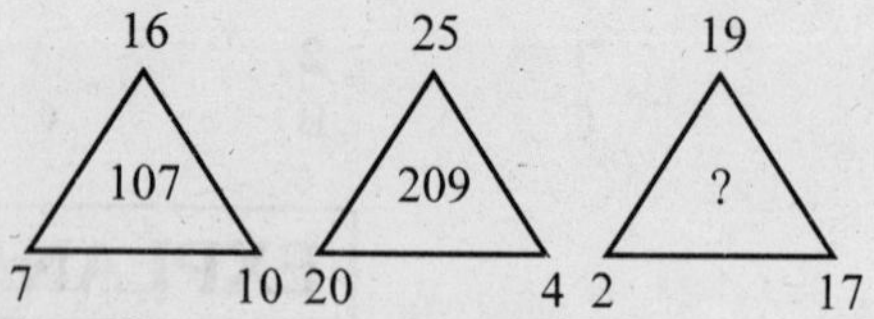

A. 68 B. 93
C. 175 D. 217

ANSWERS

1	2	3	4	5	6	7	8	9	10
D	C	C	A	D	A	C	B	B	A

EXPLANATORY ANSWERS

1. The sum of numbers on right and centre subtracted from the number on the left gives the number at the bottom, *i.e.*,

$93 - (27 + 63) = 3$

$79 - (38 + 37) = 4$

Similarly,
$67 - (16 + 42) = 9$

2. The number inside each triangle is the difference of the numbers at its base *i.e.*
$10 - 4 = 6$, $18 - 4 = 14$ and $18 - 10 = 8$
$14 - 8 = 6$, $22 - 8 = 14$ and $22 - 14 = 8$, similarly
$11 - 5 = 6$, $15 - 5 = 10$ and $15 - 11 = 4$.

3. The sum of squares of two numbers at the top gives the third number below, *i.e.*,
$2^2 + 4^2 = 20$
$3^2 + 9^2 = 90$, similarly
$1^2 + 5^2 = 26$

4. The sum of numbers in 1st and 2nd column plus 1 is the number in the 3rd column, *i.e.*,
$27 + 22 + 1 = 50$
$13 + 12 + 1 = 26$, similarly
$9 + 2 + 1 = 12$

5. The product of numbers on either side of the triangle plus the number at the base is the number inside the triangle, *i.e.*,
$(5 \times 3) + 4 = 19$
$(6 \times 4) + 5 = 29$, similarly
$(7 \times 5) + 6 = 41$

6. Clockwise starting from number 7, the next number is obtained by doubling the number and adding 2, *i.e.*,
$(7 \times 2) + 2 = 16$
$(16 \times 2) + 2 = 34 \ldots$, similarly
$(34 \times 2) + 2 = 70$
$(70 \times 2) + 2 = 142$
$(142 \times 2) + 2 = 286$

7. The difference between the numbers in opposite sectors is 13, *i.e.*,
$26 - 13 = 13$
$68 - 55 = 13$, similarly
The missing number is $42 - 13 = 29$
($42 + 13 = 55$ is not given as option)

8. The number at the bottom is obtained by subtracting the sum of two numbers in the centre grid line from the square of the number at the top, *i.e.*,
$7^2 - (2 + 7) = 40$
$5^2 - (8 + 3) = 14$, similarly
$9^2 - (7 + 6) = 68$

9. The number inside the brackets is obtained by multiplying the number on the left by 2 and then dividing the product by the sum of digits of number on the right, *i.e.*,
$(42 \times 2) \div (2 + 2) = 21$
$(162 \times 2) \div (9 + 9) = 18$, similarly
$(78 \times 2) \div (8 + 4) = 13$

10. Subtracting the sum of squares of two numbers at the base from the square of number at the apex gives the number inside the triangle, *i.e.*,
$16^2 - (7^2 + 10^2) = 107$
$25^2 - (20^2 + 4^2) = 209$, similarly
$19^2 - (2^2 + 17^2) = 68$

ALPHABET PROBLEMS

Directions : *The following questions are based on alphabet series in natural or reverse order and the combinations that can be made by changing the position of alphabet in given words.*

1. Which alphabet comes immediately before the sixth alphabet from the left extreme in alphabetical series?
A. U   B. E
C. F   D. V

2. Which letter is midway between G and S?
A. L   B. N
C. M   D. No letter

3. Which letter should be ninth letter to the left of ninth letter from the right if the first half of the alphabet is reversed?
A. I   B. D
C. F   D. E

4. If the alphabet is in reverse order, which letter will be eighth letter to the left of the seventh letter counting from the right end?
A. O   B. P
C. N   D. Q

5. What will be the fifth letter to the right of the thirteenth letter from the right?
A. R   B. S
C. I   D. O

ANSWERS

1	2	3	4	5
B	C	D	A	B

EXPLANATORY ANSWERS

1. 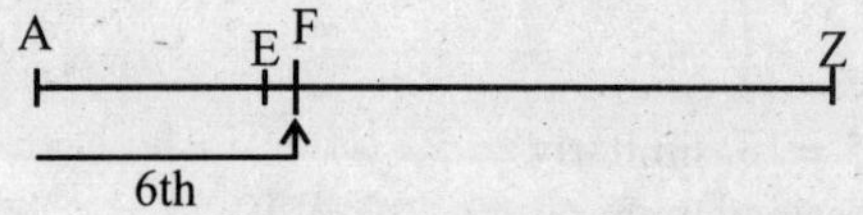

Sixth letter from left is 'F' and letter immediately before 'F' is 'E'.

2. 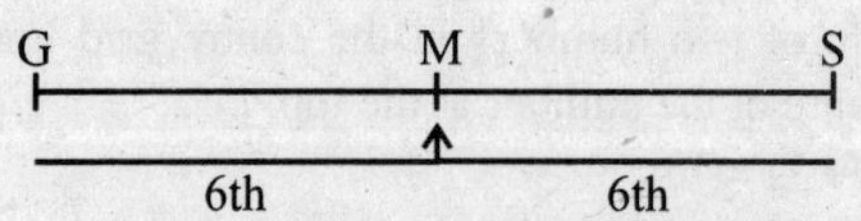

'M' is midway between G and S.

3. MLKJIHGFEDCBANOPQRSTUVWXYZ

9th 9th

4. ZYXWVUTSRQPONMLKJIHGFEDCBA

8th 7th

5. 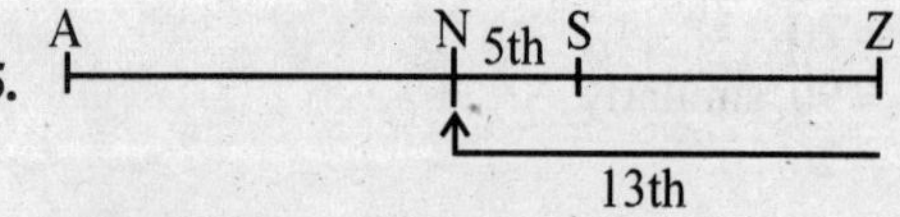

13th letter from right is 'N' and 5th letter to the right of 'N' is 'S'.

NON-VERBAL SERIES

Directions (Q. 1–10) : *In each of the following questions which one of the five answer figures given below should come after the problem figures if the sequence are continued?*

Problem Figures **Answer Figures**

1. 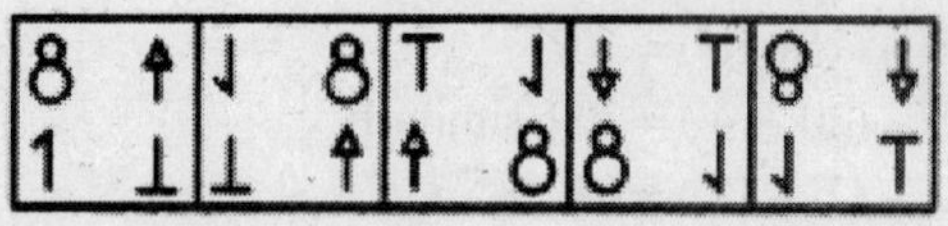 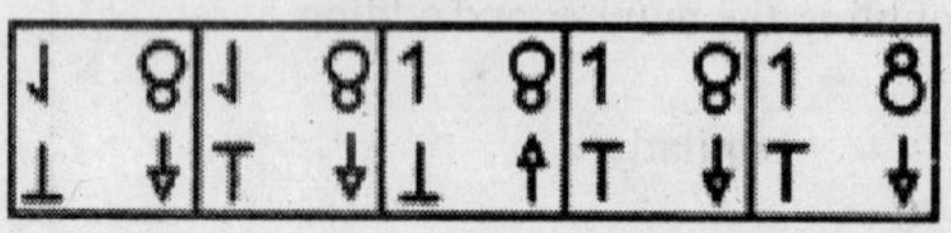

(a) (b) (c) (d) (e)

2.  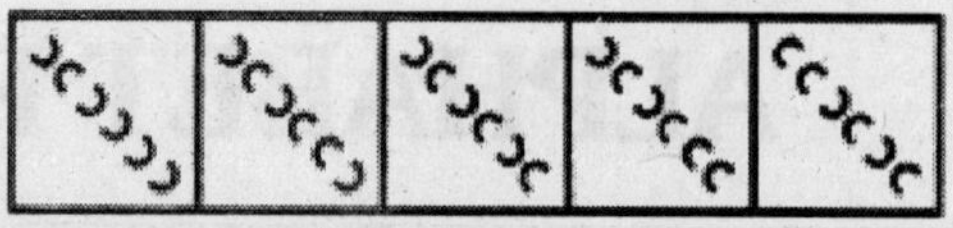

(a) (b) (c) (d) (e)

3. 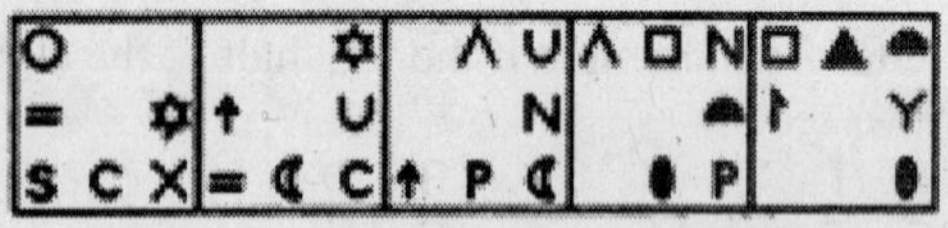 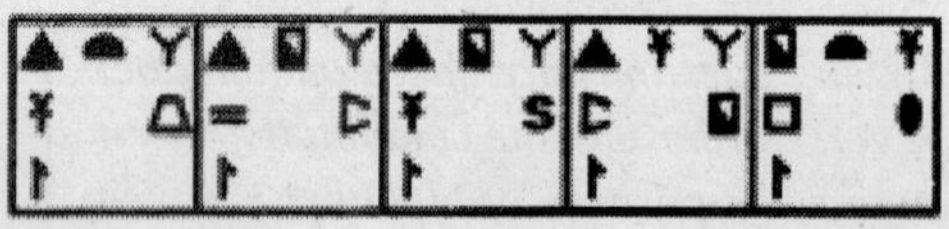

(a) (b) (c) (d) (e)

4.  

(a) (b) (c) (d) (e)

5.  

(a) (b) (c) (d) (e)

6.  

(a) (b) (c) (d) (e)

7. 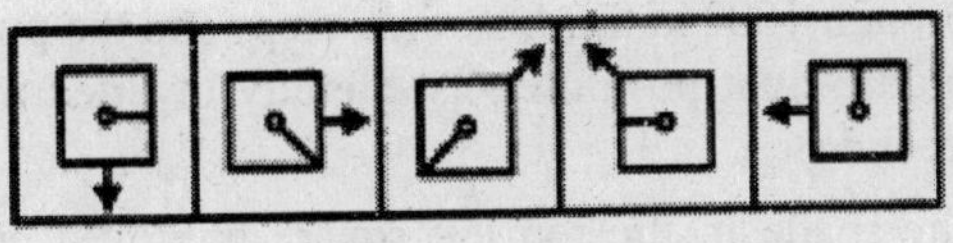

(a) (b) (c) (d) (e)

Problem Figures **Answer Figures**

8. 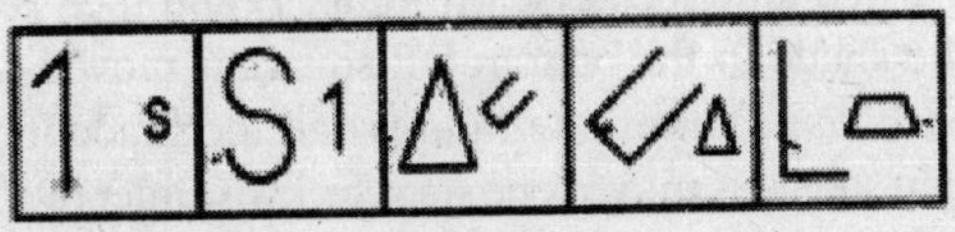

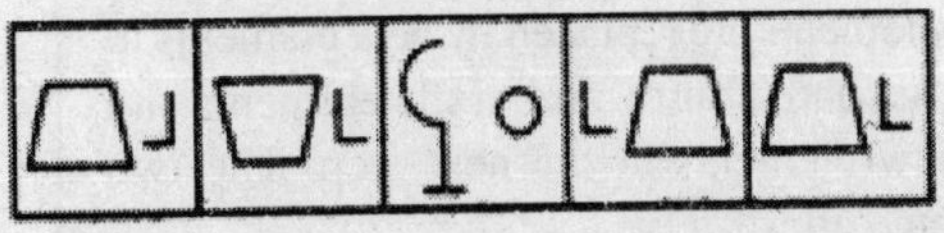

(a) (b) (c) (d) (e)

9. 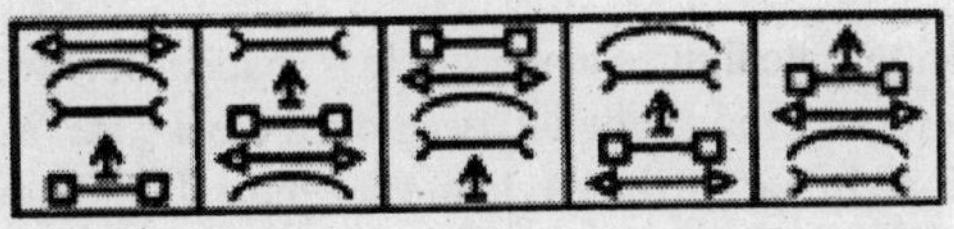

(a) (b) (c) (d) (e)

10. 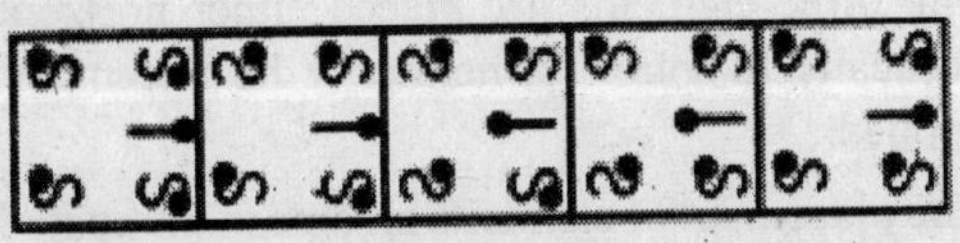

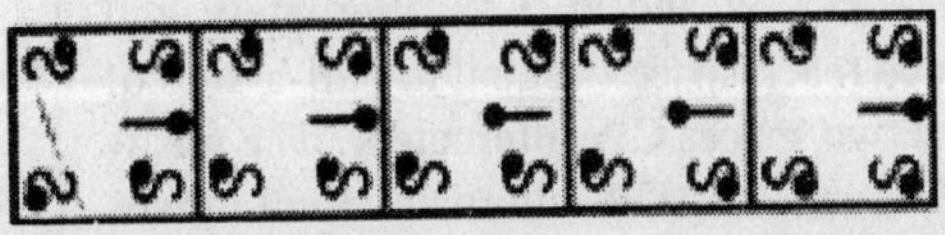

(a) (b) (c) (d) (e)

Directions (Q. 11-20) : *In each of these questions, a series begins with an unmarked figure on the extreme left in the row of figures. One and only one of the five lettered figures in the series does not fit into the series. The two unmarked figures, one on the extreme left and the other on the extreme right fit into the series. Take as many aspects into account as possible of the figures in the series and find out the one and only of the five marked figures which does not fit into the series. The letter of that figure is the answer.*

11. 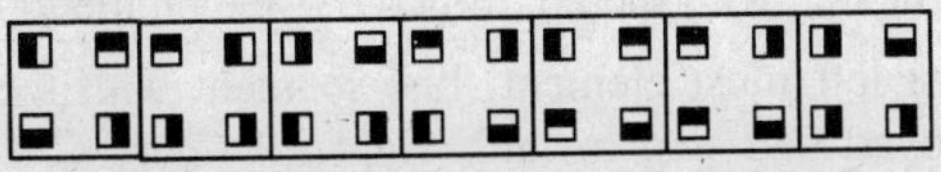

(a) (b) (c) (d) (e)

12. 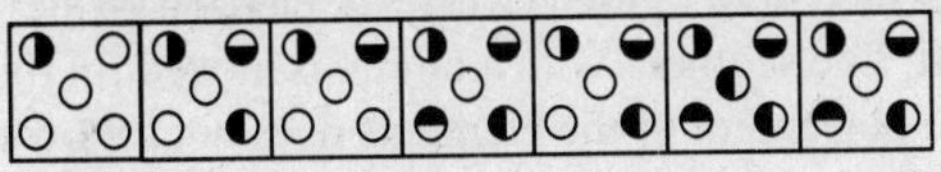

(a) (b) (c) (d) (e)

13. 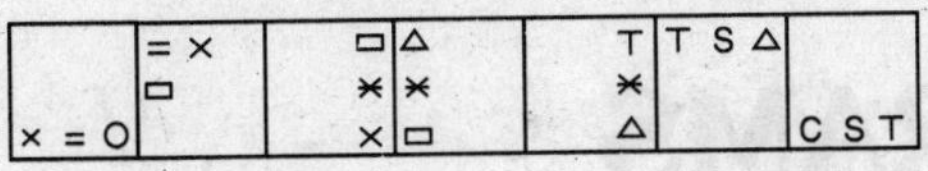

(a) (b) (c) (d) (e)

14. 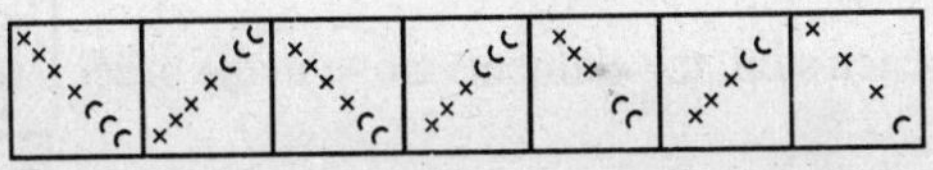

(a) (b) (c) (d) (e)

15. 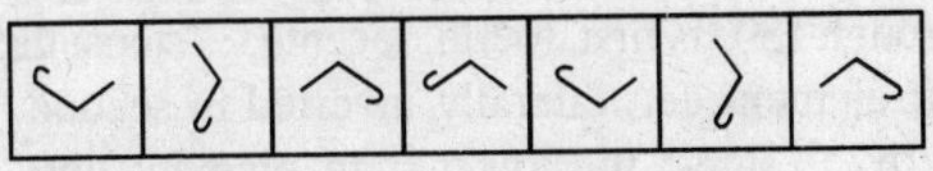

(a) (b) (c) (d) (e)

16. 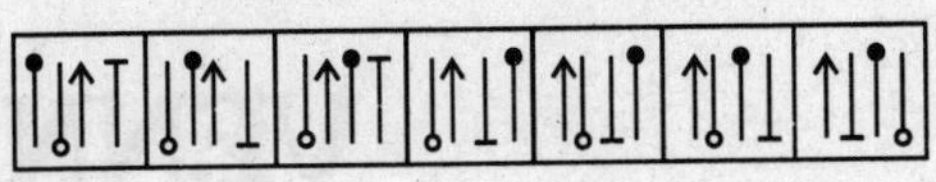

(a) (b) (c) (d) (e)

ANSWERS

1	2	3	4	5	6	7	8	9	10
D	C	D	A	C	E	C	E	C	B
11	**12**	**13**	**14**	**15**	**16**				
A	E	A	C	C	E				

EXPLANATORY ANSWERS

1. In each step, all the elements move to the adjacent corner (of the square boundary) in a CW direction and the element that reaches the upper-left corner gets vertically inverted.

2. We can label the arcs as shown . The arcs get inverted in the sequence (1 & 2), (3, 4 & 5), (6 & 1), (2, 3 & 4), (5 & 6), ...

3. All the elements move half-a-side of the square boundary in ACW direction in each step. Also, first, third and fifth elements are replaced by new elements in one step and second, fourth and sixth elements are replaced by new elements in the next step. The two steps are repeated alternately.

4. In each step, the dot moves one space CW and the arrow moves two spaces CW.

5. One arc and four arcs get inverted alternately.

6. The number of parts increases by one along with the number of sides in the figure.

7. The pin rotates 45°CW and 90°CW alternately and moves one space (each space is equal to half-a-side of the square) and two spaces CW alternately. The arrow rotates 90°ACW and 45°ACW alternately and moves two spaces and one space.

8. In one step, the two elements interchange positions and the smaller element gets enlarged while the larger element gets reduced in size. In the next step, the smaller element is replaced by a new small element and the larger element is replaced by a new large element.

9. In each step, the elements move in the order .

10. The upper-left element gets laterally inverted in first, third, fifth. .... steps; the upper-right element gets rotated through 180° is first, fourth, seventh,.... steps; the lower-left element gets laterally inverted in second, fourth, sixth, ... steps; the lower-right element gets rotated through 180° in third, sixth,... steps and the pin at the middle-right position gets laterally inverted in every second step.

11. The shade in the top left square is moved one step clockwise till figure B and then reversed, the process is repeated. The shade in the top right square is moved one step anticlockwise till figure D and then reversed. The shade in the bottom left square is moved one step clockwise in alternate figures and the shade in bottom right square is moved one step clockwise after two figures. In figure 'A' the rule is isolated by the shade in the bottom left square.

12. In alternate figures a new circle is shaded clockwise. The pattern of the shade is also moved clockwise. In figure 'E' right half of the circle in the centre should have been shaded.

13. The three elements are placed either horizontally or vertically. In option 'A' neither of the placements can be applied.

14. The placement of elements is same in alternate figures. The number and type of elements is same in two subsequent figures. In this manner, figure 'C' should have four crosses and two C shapes.

15. *(c)* : The element is moved one step anticlockwise and the arc at one end is turned outside and inside alternately. In figure 'C' the element should be on the right side with the arc turned outside on the top side.

16. The left most element, line segment with the dot is moved one step towards right till figure C where it reaches the extreme right position. This process is repeated from figure D where the element on the extreme left, line segment with a circle, is moved. In figure 'E' the placement of the elements does not follow the rule of the series.

VENN DIAGRAMS

1. What is the number which is common to only two geometrical figures?

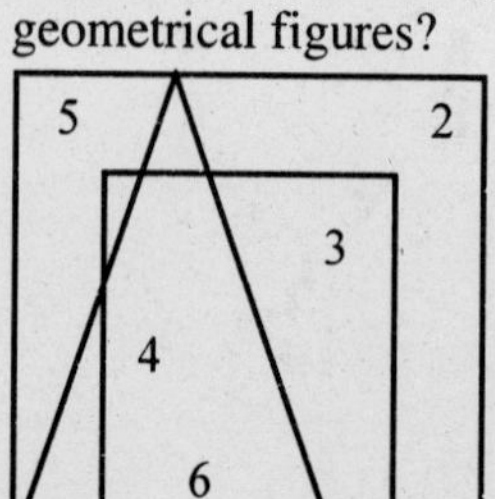

A. 4 B. 3
C. 5 D. 2

Directions (Qs. 2 and 3) : *In the following diagram, rectangle represents Hindi Announcers, circle represents English Announcers, square represents French Announcers, and triangle represents German Announcers.*

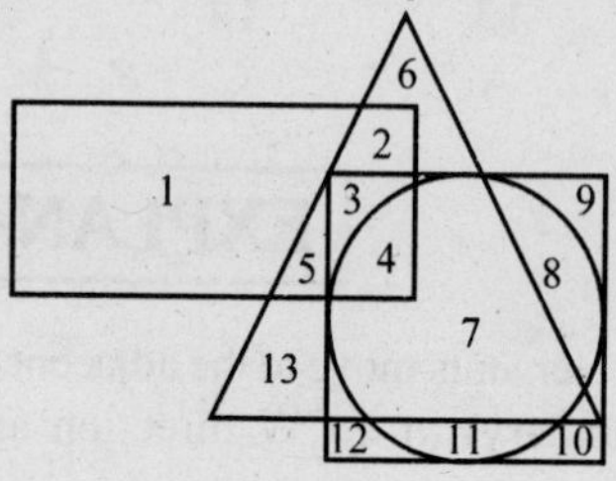

2. Which area represents those announcers who can present programmes in Hindi, French and German only?

A. 1 B. 2
C. 3 D. 4

3 Which area represents those announcers who can present programmes in French and English only?

A. 7 B. 9
C. 11 D. 13

Directions (Qs. 4 and 5) : *Study the diagram to answer these questions.*

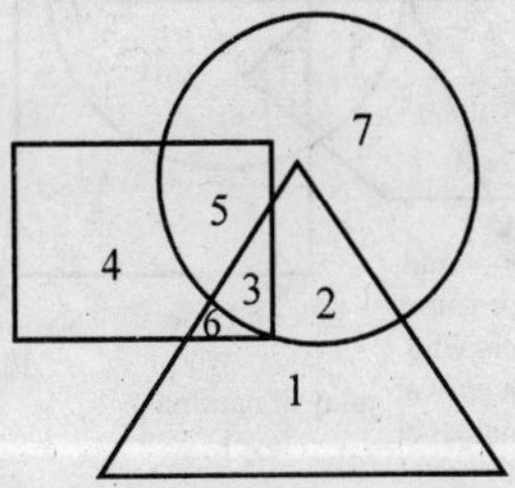

4. Which number is in all the geometrical figures?

A. 5 B. 6
C. 2 D. 3

5. Number 6 is in :

A. Rectangle and triangle
B. Circle and traingle
C. Rectangle and circle
D. Rectangle only

Directions (Qs. 6 to 9) : *In the following diagram*

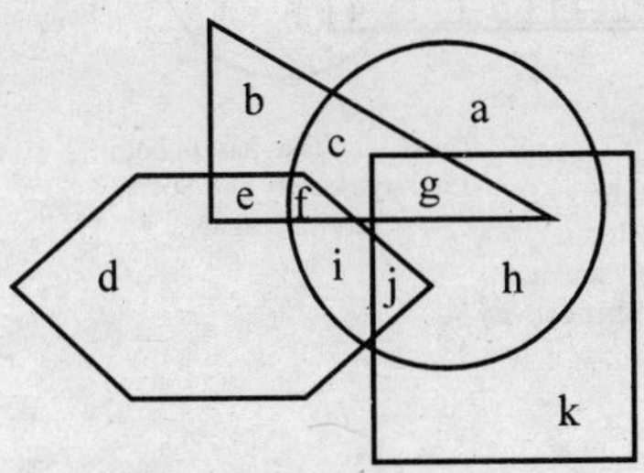

The Circle represents players
The Triangle represents outdoor games
The Hexagon represents indoor games and
The Square represents national level players
Study the diagram and answer the questions given below :

6. The letter in the section representing the players who play indoor games at national level is :

A. f B. i
C. j D. g

7. The letter representing the section of outdoor as well as indoor game players who do not play at the national level is :

A. c B. f
C. e D. i

8. The section representing national level players who do not play either outdoor or indoor games but still come under the category of players is :

A. k B. g
C. c D. h

9. Persons who play outdoor games but do not come under the category of players are represented in the section marked :

A. b B. c
C. a D. d

Directions (Qs. 10 to 13) : *Study the diagram given below.*

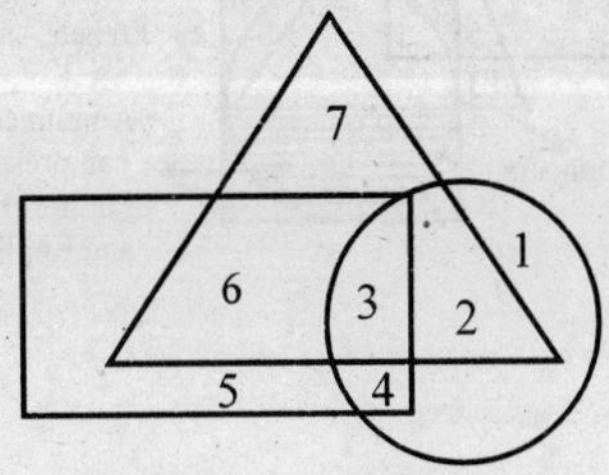

A college provides three different activities, students union represented by triangle, literary society represented by rectangle and social service league represented by circle.

10. Those who take part in both literary society and social service league but not in students union are represented by :

A. 3 & 4 B. 5 & 6
C. 5 & 1 D. 4

11. Those who take part in students union but not in social service league are represented by:

A. 2 & 7 B. 6 & 7
C. 6 D. 7

12. Those students who are members of literary society only and not of any other activity are represented by:

A. 2 B. 5
C. 3 & 4 D. 3

13. Those students who are members of all three groups are represented by :

A. 2 B. 3
C. 4 D. 6

ANSWERS

1	2	3	4	5	6	7	8	9	10
B	C	C	D	A	C	B	D	A	D
11	**12**	**13**							
B	B	B							

EXPLANATORY ANSWERS

1.

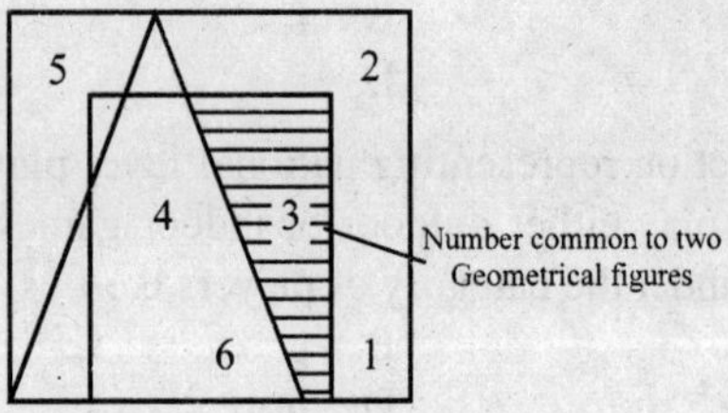

Note : Numbers 4 and 6 are common to all three geometrical figures.

Qs. 2 and 3.

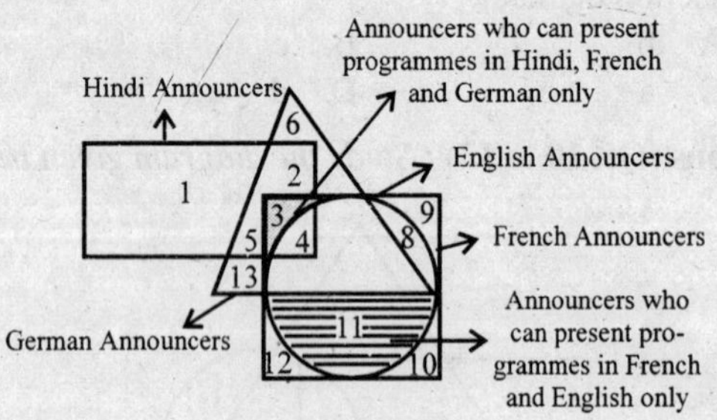

Qs. 4 and 5.

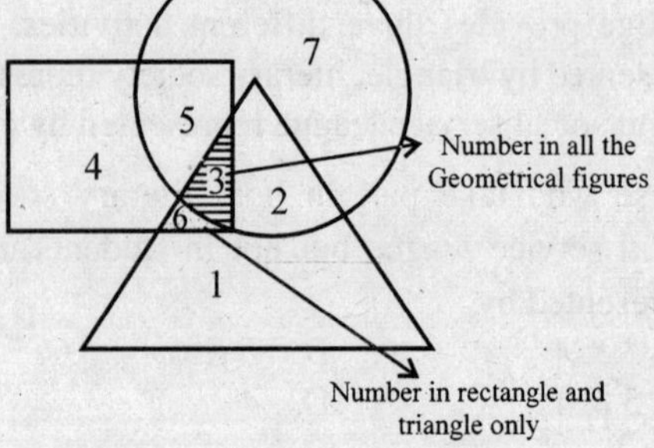

Qs. 6 to 9.

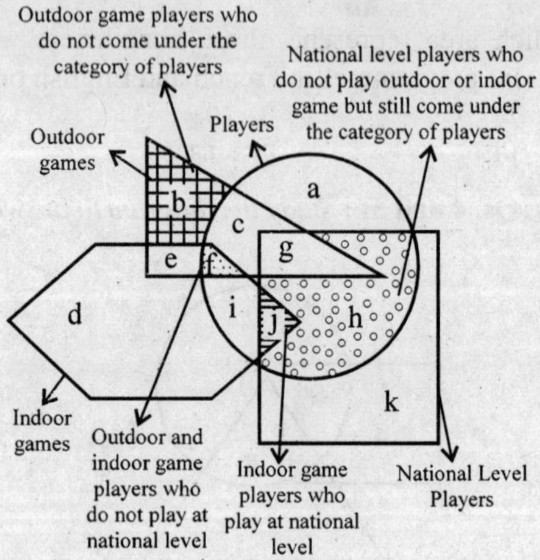

Qs. 10 to 13.

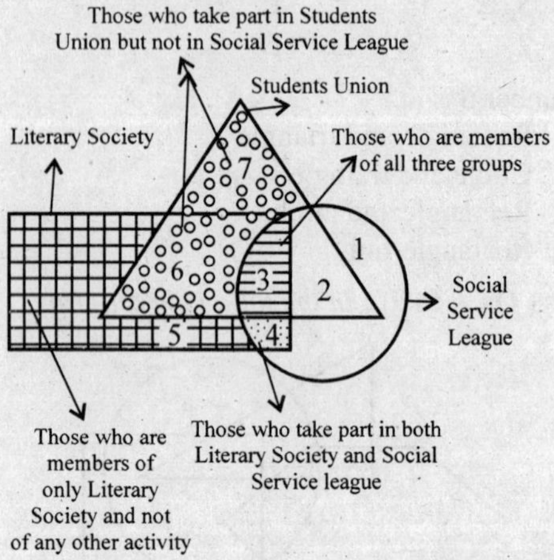

HARYANA

General Knowledge & Awareness

Multiple Choice Questions

1. During the ancient age, modern Haryana state was known as:
(*a*) Brahmavarta (*b*) Brahmarshi region
(*c*) Uttravedi of Brahma (*d*) All of the above

2. Who of the following rulers of Bharata vamsha (descendants of Bharata, according to Rigveda, who were a group of people who lived in the north-west of India) started his campaign from Haryana for establishing his authority in various other Kingdoms of the time?
(*a*) Sudas (*b*) Arjuna
(*c*) Bharata (*d*) Bhishma

3. The famous war of Mahabharata was fought at which of the following places in Haryana?
(*a*) Panipat (*b*) Kurukshetra
(*c*) Jhajjhar (*d*) Ballabh Garh

4. During Mughals, Janapadas of this state were replaced by
(*a*) Gana Sangha (*b*) Gana System
(*c*) Khaps (*d*) Panchayata

5. The territory of modern Haryana was included in which of the following Mahajanapadas of Buddha period?
(*a*) Kuru and Panchala (*b*) Kosala and Vajji
(*c*) Sursena and Avanti (*d*) Asmaka and Vatsa

6. At which of the following places in the state, capital of the Agreyagana was situated?
(*a*) Rewari (*b*) Sirsa
(*c*) Hansi (*d*) Agroha

7. Mahamud Gaznavi attacked on Thanesar in:
(*a*) 1013 AD (*b*) 1014 AD
(*c*) 1016 AD (*d*) 1017 AD

8. Thanesar (now in Haryana) was the capital of which of the following famous rulers of ancient India?
(*a*) Harsha Vardhan
(*b*) Ashoka
(*c*) Chandragupta Vikramaditya
(*d*) Kanishka

9. During the 12th century A.D. who of the following rulers of Chauhan dynasty defeated Tomars of Haryana?
(*a*) Vigraha Raja VI (*b*) Vigrah Raja II
(*c*) Arno Raja (*d*) Prithvi Raj Chauhan

10. When did Sultan Balban of Ghulam dynasty attacked on Mevas of Haryana with a view to establish his authority on Mevas?
(*a*) 1260 AD (*b*) 1265 AD
(*c*) 1266 AD (*d*) 1267 AD

11. Feroz Tughlaq of Tughlaq dynasty built which of the following cities in Haryana?
(*a*) Tohana (*b*) Hansi
(*c*) Siwani (*d*) Fatehabad

12. Timur made an attack on which of the following cities of Haryana?
(*a*) Sirsa (*b*) Fatehabad
(*c*) Hissar (*d*) All of the above

13. The famous battle of 1526 between Babur and Ibrahim Lodi was fought at which of the following places of Haryana?
(*a*) Panipat (*b*) Kurukshetra
(*c*) Tawaru (*d*) Jind

14. Who was the King of Rewari during the reign of famous Mughal Emperor Akbar?
(*a*) Tularam (*b*) Karna Singh
(*c*) Hemachandra (Hemu) (*d*) Phool Singh

15. The famous second battle of Panipat between Akbar and Hemachandra (Hemu) was fought in:
(*a*) 1550 AD (*b*) 1552 AD
(*c*) 1554 AD (*d*) 1556 AD

16. Which of the following famous battle was fought in the state of Haryana between the Marathas and Ahmadshah Abdali?
(*a*) The third battle of Panipat
(*b*) The second battle of Panipat
(*c*) The first battle of Panipat
(*d*) None of these

17. George Thomas built his capital at which of the following places of the state?
(*a*) Raniya (*b*) Tohana
(*c*) The fort of Hansi (*d*) Behram Pur

18. In 1802 AD George Thomas died at which of the following places in Haryana?
(*a*) Mahendragarh (*b*) Behram Pur
(*c*) Narnaul (*d*) Bawal

19. During 1809-10 AD, entire territories of Haryana was under the control of:
(*a*) Marathas (*b*) Satnamies
(*c*) Mughals (*d*) Britishers

20. Modern Haryana state was built on:
(*a*) 1 November, 1966 (*b*) 5 January, 1967
(*c*) 1 November, 1958 (*d*) 15 August, 1947

21. Evidences of Early-Harappan, Mature Harappan and Late Harappan culture have been found at which of the following places in Haryana?
(*a*) Banawali (*b*) Sosawal
(*c*) Mirzapur (*d*) All of the above

22. The period of Aryans of Kuru Vamsha, centuries before the Mahabharata period was marked with the beginning of which of the following ages?
(*a*) Cultivation Age (*b*) Copper Age
(*c*) Iron Age (*d*) Metal Age

23. The essence of the philosophy of Bhagvad Gita preached by Lord Krishna to Arjuna, a noted Commander of the Mahabharata War in the form of a dialogue between the two was delivered at which of the following places of Haryana?
(*a*) Rewari (*b*) Pehwa
(*c*) Kurukshetra (*d*) Panipat

24. During Youdheya period, Haryana was known as:
(*a*) Youdheya confederacy (*b*) Bahudhanyaka region
(*c*) Matsya region (*d*) Gana region

25. The famous pilgrim Hiuen Tsang in his book Si-Yo-ki, has described the prosperity of which of the following cities of Haryana?
(*a*) Sthaneshwar (Thanesmar)
(*b*) Panipat
(*c*) Rohtak
(*d*) Ambala

26. Which of the following treatise provide valuable information about the advancement of trade, art and culture in Haryana during the reign of Tomar Kings?
(*a*) Tahkik-i-Hind (*b*) Harsh Charita
(*c*) Kadambari (*d*) Yashastilak Champu

27. Who was the ruler of the Tawaroo pargana during the invasion of Babur in 1526-27?
(*a*) Hasan Khan (*b*) Mohan Singh Mandhar
(*c*) Faizal Khan (*d*) Jalal Khan

28. During the period of Babur, the Rajput King Mohan Singh Mandhar had its kingdom in Haryana at:
(*a*) Mandhar Pargana of Kaithal
(*b*) Tawaroo
(*c*) Jind
(*d*) Panipat

29. During 1756-57, Haryana was under the control of:
(*a*) Mughals (*b*) Sikhs
(*c*) Marathas (*d*) Satnamies

30. While returning back to his homeland, Ahmad Shah Abdali put the northern part of Haryana (Ambala, Jind, Kurukshetra and Karnal Districts) under the charge of:
(*a*) Mughals
(*b*) Sikhs
(*c*) Jain Khan, the Governor of Sarhind
(*d*) Gen Khan the Governor of Durrani

31. In the sepoy mutiny that broke out in 1857 at Meerut, majority of soldiers who took part in the revolt hailed from which of the following districts of Haryana?
(*a*) Gurugram (*b*) Rohtak
(*c*) Hissar (*d*) All of these

32. Who of the following great warriors of Haryana was the Naib Kotwal of Meerut at the time of Sepoy mutiny:
(*a*) Abdus Samad Khan (*b*) Vikram Singh
(*c*) Rao Krishna Gopal (*d*) Rameshwar Dayal

33. In the battle (for the freedom of India) fought at the village Naseebpur situated near Narnaul, Britishers destroyed which of the following three powers?
(*a*) Rewari, Jhajjhar and Jodhpur
(*b*) Gurugram, Rewari and Jodhpur
(*c*) Jind, Jagadari and Pehwa
(*d*) Panipat, Jhajjhar and Tawaroo

34. In the first Freedom struggle, who of the following Kings of Ballabhgarh led the revolutionary army in Delhi?
(*a*) Raja Karn Singh (*b*) Raja Nahan Singh
(*c*) Raja Suraj Bhan (*d*) Raja Satyapal

35. Which of the following provinces of Haryana extended valuable cooperation to the British army in the revolt of 1857?
(*a*) Bahadurgarh (*b*) Tawaroo
(*c*) Jhajjhar (*d*) Jind

36. In the second Calcutta session of the Indian National Congress held in the year 1886, Haryana was represented by:
(*a*) Pandit Deen Dayal Sharma
(*b*) Lala Murlidhar
(*c*) Bal Mukund Gupta
(*d*) All of these

37. Lala Lajpat Rai had selected which of the following places situated in Haryana as his political and social work-field?
(*a*) Hissar (*b*) Sonipat
(*c*) Gurugram (*d*) Nooh

38. In the fourth session of the Indian National Congress held in 1888 at Allahabad who of the following national leaders represented Hissar?
(*a*) Lala Sultan Singh (*b*) Baldeo Singh
(*c*) Lala Lajpat Rai (*d*) Baini Singh

39. On 8 April, 1919, Gandhiji was arrested from which of the following places of Haryana?
(*a*) Kaithal (*b*) Palwal
(*c*) Gohana (*d*) Ambala

40. When was a conference held at Rohtak presided by Pt. Rambhaj Dutta in which a decision was taken to implement the Non-cooperation movement launched by Gandhiji?
(*a*) January, 1919 (*b*) November, 1919
(*c*) November, 1920 (*d*) September, 1921

41. In the annual session of Congress held at Nagpur, Haryana was represented by :
(*a*) Sardar Buta Singh (*b*) Lala Ugrasen
(*c*) Babu Shyam Lal (*d*) Pt. Neki Ram Sharma

42. On the appeal of Punjab Pradesh Congress, Independence Day was celebrated in entire Haryana on:
(*a*) 12 January, 1932 (*b*) 10 December, 1932
(*c*) 15 August, 1935 (*d*) 26 January, 1932

43. On which day was the Golden Jubilee of Congress celebrated in Haryana?
(*a*) 18 August, 1930 (*b*) 30 January, 1935
(*c*) 28 December, 1935 (*d*) 10 December, 1936

44. Who of the following was the great hero of Haryana who as a member of the INA hoisted the tricoloured flag for the first time on the land of Manipur?
(*a*) Major Pratap Singh (*b*) Major Suraj Mal
(*c*) Darbara Singh (*d*) Bhajan Lal

45. Chaudhary Chhotu Ram started a vigorous campaigns to popularize the Unionist Party in Haryana. In Haryana state this Party was called as:
(*a*) Zamindara League (*b*) Zamindari System
(*c*) Hindu-Muslim (*d*) None of these

46. Publication of which of the following weekly magazine was started by Chaudhary Chhotu Ram in 1916 from Rohtak?
(*a*) Hindu Gazette (*b*) Sikh Gazette
(*c*) Jat Gazette (*d*) None of the above

47. Chaudhary Chhotu Ram alongwith Shri Fazali Hussain set up the Unionist Party in Punjab in:
(*a*) 1919 (*b*) 1921
(*c*) 1922 (*d*) 1923

48. With a view to keep a control on the political activities in Patiala, Jind and Nabha states, a law was enforced in Samvat 1988 Vikrami. What was that law termed as:
(*a*) Hidayat Samvat (*b*) Hizri Samvat
(*c*) Vikram Samvat (*d*) Saka Samvat

49. In 1938, Jind Prajamandal was set up at Sangrur, the capital of Jind by:
(*a*) Rajendra Kumar Jain (*b*) Sadhu Ram
(*c*) Hansraj Rahbar (*d*) Nand Kishore

50. Gandhji was arrested from Palwal on:
(*a*) 5 January, 1919 (*b*) 8 May, 1920
(*c*) 8 April, 1919 (*d*) 17 April, 1921

51. Pt. Deen Dayal Sharma who made a very important contribution in popularizing Sanatan Dharma in whole of the Northern India, hailed from which of the following places of Haryana?
(*a*) Jhajjhar (*b*) Kaithal
(*c*) Hissar (*d*) Jind

52. In the Lahore Session of the Congress in 1892, Hissar was represented by:
(*a*) Balmukund Gupta (*b*) Lala Murlidhar
(*c*) Lala Lajpat Rai (*d*) Pt. Deen Dayal Sharma

53. When was Lala Lajpat Rai and Sardar Ajit Singh were arrested by the British Government and sent to Mandley Jail?
(*a*) In 1907 (*b*) In 1895
(*c*) In 1902 (*d*) In 1896

54. Mahatma Gandhi accompanied with Muhammad Ali and Shaukat Ali arrived Rohtak on:
(*a*) 10 January, 1919 (*b*) 8 October, 1920
(*c*) 1 October, 1920 (*d*) 18 March, 1920

55. The Divisional Political Conference of Ambala Division which was attended by Mahatma Gandhi alongwith Ali brothers, was held at Bhiwani in:
(*a*) March, 1918 (*b*) June, 1920
(*c*) October, 1919 (*d*) October, 1920

56. Even after India became free in 1947, Haryana remained a part of which of the following Indian Provinces?
(*a*) Delhi (*b*) Punjab
(*c*) Uttra Pradesh (*d*) Rajasthan

57. The state Restructuring Commission set up in 1955 by the Government of India had recommended to include which of the following two places in the state of Haryana?
(*a*) Mahendragarh and Jind (*b*) Patiala and Hissar
(*c*) Panipat and Kaithal (*d*) Rohtak and Gurugram

58. The tourist place called 'Tiliyar' is situated in which of the following districts of Haryana?
(*a*) Jind (*b*) Mahendragarh
(*c*) Rohtak (*d*) Kaithal

59. Who was the first Governor of Haryana?
(*a*) Shri Satyapal (*b*) Shri Dharmvir
(*c*) Shri Devilal (*d*) Shri Bansilal

60. Name of the first Non-Congress Chief Minister of Haryana who assumed this office on 24 March, 1967.
(*a*) Chaudhary Bhajan Lal (*b*) Devi Lal
(*c*) Bansi Lal (*d*) Rao Virendra Singh

61. Which of the following Rivers flow from the adjoining areas of Eastern Haryana and Uttar Pradesh?
(*a*) Ganga (*b*) Saraswati
(*c*) Ghaghghar (*d*) Yamuna

62. The main land of Haryana state stretches from 27° 39° N to 30° 55° N latitudes in the North-West of India. It stretches from .... E to .... E longitudes.
(*a*) 74° 28° E to 77° 36° E (*b*) 65° 33° E to 77° 28° E
(*c*) 50° 28° E to 64° 36° E (*d*) 84° 42° E to 89° 41° E

63. Which of the following states is located to the North of Haryana?
(*a*) Uttar Pradesh (*b*) Punjab
(*c*) Himachal Pradesh (*d*) Rajasthan

64. Which of the following states is located to the west of Haryana?
(*a*) Punjab (*b*) Rajasthan
(*c*) Uttar Pradesh (*d*) Himachal Pradesh

65. What is the area of the state of Haryana?
(*a*) 36,154 Sq. km. (*b*) 44,212 Sq. km.
(*c*) 49,105 Sq. km. (*d*) 51,206 Sq. km.

66. Which of the following state is not larger than Haryana by area?
(*a*) Meghalaya (*b*) Bihar
(*c*) Himachal Pradesh (*d*) Punjab

67. Dabwali is a subdivision of which district?
(*a*) Sirsa (*b*) Hissar
(*c*) Rohtak (*d*) Jhajjar

68. The mainland of Haryana is located at the height of .... from the sea level.
(*a*) 700 to 900 ft. (*b*) 750 to 880 ft.
(*c*) 800 to 1000 ft. (*d*) 900 to 1100 ft.

69. Shivalik range is located in which part of Haryana?
(*a*) North-West (*b*) North-East
(*c*) South-West (*d*) South-East

70. Which of the following rivers originate from Shivalik range to flow through the mainland of Haryana?
(*a*) Ghaghghar (*b*) Markanda
(*c*) Tangri (*d*) All of these

71. Which of the following natural parts of Haryana is the largest?
(*a*) the hilly region of the Shivalik
(*b*) the desert of Haryana
(*c*) the mainland of Haryana
(*d*) the dry plains of Aravali range

72. The famous Bibipur and Najafgarh lakes are located in which natural part of Haryana?
(*a*) The Plain
(*b*) The desert
(*c*) Hilly region of the Shivalik
(*d*) The dry plain of Aravali range

73. Which of the following cities of Haryana is not the part of National Capital Region?
(*a*) Sonipat (*b*) Faridabad
(*c*) Hisar (*d*) Gurugram

74. Which part of Haryana experiences maximum rainfall?
(*a*) South-Western Part (*b*) North-Eastern Part
(*c*) North-Western Part (*d*) South-Eastern Part

75. Which of the following parts of Haryana experiences minimum annual rainfall?
(*a*) North-Eastern Part (*b*) South-Eastern Part
(*c*) North-Western Part (*d*) South-Western Part

76. Which type of soil is found on Morney hills of the state?
(*a*) Sandy Soil (*b*) Brownish Soil
(*c*) Laterite Soil (*d*) Sandy Clayee Soil

77. Generally, which type of soil is found in the plains of Haryana?
(*a*) Fertile Soil of Yellow brownish colour
(*b*) Laterite Soil
(*c*) Sandy Soil
(*d*) Sandy Clayee Soil

78. In which of the following districts of Haryana, red chestnut soil is found?
(*a*) Rohtak (*b*) Sirsa
(*c*) Yamuna Nagar (*d*) Bhivani

79. Which of the following rivers of the state of Haryana joins Markanda river near Mulana?
(*a*) Sahibi (*b*) Tangri
(*c*) Krishnawati (*d*) Dohan

80. Which of the following is the oldest and the most important canal of Haryana?
(*a*) Gurugram Canal (*b*) Bhiwani Canal
(*c*) Bhakra Canal (*d*) Western Yamuna Canal

81. Which of the following canals originates from the Yamuna river near Tazewala situated on the Jagadhari-Pona road?
(*a*) Bhakra Canal
(*b*) Western and Eastern Yamuna Canal
(*c*) Jawahar Lal Nehru Canal
(*d*) None of these

82. Jawahar Lal Nehru canal of Haryana originates from:
(*a*) Bhakra Canal (*b*) Bhiwani Canal
(*c*) Gurugram Canal (*d*) Yamuna Canal

83. Which of the following lakes is located in Haryana?
(*a*) Damdama Lake (*b*) Kotla Lake
(*c*) Khalilpur Lake (*d*) All of these

84. Which of the following lakes is situated in Farrukh Nagar block of the state?
(*a*) Sultanpur lake (*b*) Damdama lake
(*c*) Khalilpur lake (*d*) Kotla lake

85. The famous Badkal lake is situated in which of the following districts of Haryana?
(*a*) Gurugram (*b*) Bhivani
(*c*) Faridabad (*d*) Rohtak

86. Which of the following canals of Haryana originates from Yamuna river at Okhla in Delhi?
(*a*) Bhakra Canal (*b*) Gurugram Canal
(*c*) Eastern Yamuna Canal (*d*) None of these

87. Bhakra Canal provides water for irrigation in which of the following districts of Haryana?
(*a*) Sirsa (*b*) Hissar
(*c*) Rohtak (*d*) All of these

88. Which of the following districts of the state gets water for irrigation from Jawahar Lal Nehru Canal?
(*a*) Sirsa (*b*) Rohtak
(*c*) Mahendragarh (*d*) Jind

89. Bhiwani canal originates from which of the following canals?
(*a*) Bhakra Canal (*b*) Gurugram Canal
(*c*) Western Yamuna Canal (*d*) Eastern Yamuna Canal

90. When was the famous Badkal lake of Haryana built?
(*a*) In 1940 (*b*) In 1950
(*c*) In 1974 (*d*) In 1947

91. The famous tourist place 'Tajewala Headworks' is situated in which of the following districts of Haryana?
(*a*) Rohtak (*b*) Faridabad
(*c*) Gurugram (*d*) Yamuna Nagar

92. Haryana has been divided into:
(*a*) 6 Divisions (*b*) 5 Sub Divisions
(*c*) 4 Divisions (*d*) 8 Divisions

93. How many total sub-divisions exist in Haryana state till January, 2026?
(*a*) 60 Sub-Divisions (*b*) 65 Sub-Divisions
(*c*) 68 Sub-Divisions (*d*) 80 Sub-Divisions

94. How many total Tehsils exist in Haryana till January, 2026?
(*a*) 94 (*b*) 68
(*c*) 70 (*d*) 85

95. How many total sub-Tehsils exist in Haryana till January, 2026?
(*a*) 30 (*b*) 31
(*c*) 49 (*d*) 40

96. How many total Blocks exist in Haryana till January, 2026?
(*a*) 95 (*b*) 143
(*c*) 115 (*d*) 119

97. Total number of populated villages in Haryana is:
(*a*) 4,390 (*b*) 4,950
(*c*) 5,845 (*d*) 6,841

98. According to the Census of 2011, the total population of Haryana is:
(*a*) 2,53,51,462 (*b*) 2,40,55,400
(*c*) 2,25,83,912 (*d*) 2,20,45,657

99. Salarganj Gate is situated near which of the following town of Haryana?
(*a*) Rohtak (*b*) Hissar
(*c*) Panipat (*d*) Ambala

100. In terms of area the largest district of Haryana is:
(*a*) Rohtak (*b*) Sirsa
(*c*) Panipat (*d*) Ambala

101. Which of the following minerals is found in abundance in Mahendragarh district of Haryana?
(*a*) Lime stone (*b*) China clay
(*c*) Copper (*d*) All of these

102. At which of the following places in district Rewari, Slate-stone is found in abundance?
(*a*) Kund (*b*) Baval
(*c*) Kusal (*d*) Khol

103. Consider the following statements:
1. Nada Sahib Gurudwara is situated in Ambala.
2. Nada Sahib Gurudwara is situated on the bank of river Ghaggar.

Which of the above statements is/are correct?
(*a*) 2 only (*b*) Both 1 and 2
(*c*) Neither 1 nor 2 (*d*) 1 only

104. At which of the following places in district Bhiwani Granite stones are found?
(*a*) Village Nigana Kalan (*b*) Delheri
(*c*) Riwasa (*d*) All of these

105. When was Shri Krishna Museum established in Kurukshetra?
(*a*) 1987 (*b*) 1970
(*c*) 1989 (*d*) 1995

106. What is the area of the total forest land in Haryana?
(*a*) 1,428 Sq. km. (*b*) 1,614.26 Sq. km.
(*c*) 1,852 Sq. km. (*d*) 1,812 Sq. km.

107. During which of the following years, a comprehensive afforestation scheme 'Greening of Haryana' was started?
(*a*) 1982 - 83 (*b*) 1983 - 86
(*c*) 1989 - 90 (*d*) 1994 - 95

108. Haryana has announced its new Industrial Policy in ....
(*a*) 1995 (*b*) 2011
(*c*) 2005 (*d*) 2002

109. With the aid of the European Union "Haryana Community Development Scheme" (Haryana Samudayiki) was introduced in Haryana in:
(*a*) 1992 - 93 (*b*) 1994 95
(*c*) 1996 - 97 (*d*) 1998 - 99

110. Basai wetland is located in which district of Haryana?
(*a*) Gurugram (*b*) Jhajjar
(*c*) Faridabad (*d*) Kurukshetra

111. As per census 2011, literacy of Haryana is:
(*a*) 80.40% (*b*) 65.72%
(*c*) 75.6% (*d*) 68.85%

112. Which of the following tourist place is situated on Samauli Road Panipat?
(*a*) Jyotisar (*b*) Kala Amb
(*c*) Damdama Lake (*d*) King Fisher

113. Which of the following minerals is found in districts Hissar and Karnal?
(*a*) Pig Iron (*b*) Mica
(*c*) Nitre (*d*) Marble

114. Which of the following minerals is found in Rohtak district?
(*a*) Lime (*b*) Copper
(*c*) Manganese (*d*) Mica

115. Which of the following trees are found in abundance in Jind district of Haryana?
(*a*) Rosewood tree (Sesam) (*b*) Acacia tree (Kikar)
(*c*) Safeda (*d*) All of these

116. In the Agricultural University, Hissar 'research on Paddy' was started in:
(*a*) 1966 (*b*) 1970
(*c*) 1974 (*d*) 1989

117. Where is National Cancer Institute situated?
(*a*) Sampla (*b*) Meham
(*c*) Kalanaur (*d*) Badsa

118. Which of the following districts of Haryana is pre-eminent in the production of mushroom (Khumbhi) in India?
(*a*) Ambala (*b*) Sirsa
(*c*) Sonepat (*d*) Yamuna Nagar

119. Which of the following is a major crop produced in Rohtak district of Haryana?
(*a*) Pearl Millet (*b*) Great Millet
(*c*) Sugar cane (*d*) All of these

120. Sugar Mill is located at which of the following places in Kurukshetra?
(*a*) Pehwa (*b*) Shahabad Markanda
(*c*) Ladawa (*d*) Babain

121. Which of the following districts of Haryana is called "a big bowl of paddy" as it has gained world fame in the production of Basmati rice?
(*a*) Hissar (*b*) Kurukshetra
(*c*) Karnal (*d*) Jind

122. Navagrah temple in Haryana is located at ....
(*a*) Kurukshetra (*b*) Kaithal
(*c*) Gurugram (*d*) Faridabad

123. The total installed capacity of energy available to the state till 2024-25 is ....
(*a*) 8,575 MW (*b*) 8,200 MW
(*c*) 16019.16 MW (*d*) 9,510 MW

124. What was the quantum of production of horticulture crops in Haryana during 2024-25?
(*a*) 4.20 Lakh M.T. (*b*) 9.02 Lakh M.T.
(*c*) 6.15 Lakh M.T. (*d*) 5 .25 Lakh M.T.

125. In which of the following districts of Haryana, with a view to check the soil erosion in Shivalik areas, coordinated water flow Development Project is being implemented?
(*a*) Ambala (*b*) Panchkula
(*c*) Yamuna Nagar (*d*) All of these

126. Indira Gandhi Super Thermal Power Project is situated in which district of Haryana?
(*a*) Sirsa (*b*) Hisar
(*c*) Jind (*d*) Jhajjar

127. In the Ambala district of Haryana, canal irrigation system was made available after completion of which of the following irrigation project?
(*a*) Nangal Lift Irrigation Project
(*b*) Hathni Reservoir Barrage Project
(*c*) Jawahar Lal Nehru Irrigation Project
(*d*) Sewani Lift Irrigation Project

128. Which of the following system of irrigation is used in the sandy plains of Haryana?
(*a*) Canal
(*b*) Well
(*c*) With the help of Tubewell-Fountain irrigation
(*d*) Rain water

129. Water from western Yamuna Canal is used for irrigation in which of the following districts of Haryana?
(*a*) Karnal (*b*) Sonepat
(*c*) Rohtak (*d*) All of these

130. Besides Gurugram, in which of the following districts of Haryana water from Gurgaon canal is used for irrigation?
(*a*) Panipat (*b*) Faridabad
(*c*) Sonepat (*d*) Kaithal

131. Hathni Reservoir Barrage Project is related with which of the following districts of Haryana?
(*a*) Yamuna Nagar (*b*) Gurugram
(*c*) Rohtak (*d*) Faridabad

132. Which of the following irrigation projects was launched in Mahendragarh district of Haryana with a view to bring improvement in the field of agriculture?
(*a*) Loharu Lift Irrigation Project
(*b*) Western Yamuna Nagar Scheme
(*c*) J.L.N. Lift Irrigation Project
(*d*) Hathni Reservoir Barrage Project

133. When water was released for the first time from J.L.N. Lift Irrigation Project launched in Mahendragarh district of Haryana?
(*a*) In 1976 (*b*) In 1980
(*c*) In 1982 (*d*) In 1995

134. Which of the following irrigation projects provided irrigation facilities in Swarup Kalauda, Khurl Kalan, Bhikhewala, Kharadwala, Nehra, Fuliya kalan etc. villages of the state?
(*a*) Jhajjhar Lift Irrigation Project
(*b*) Nakhana Irrigation Project
(*c*) Nangal Lift Irrigation Project
(*d*) Jawahar Lal Nehru Lift Irrigation Project

135. Which of the following irrigation schemes was launched for providing irrigation facility in Ahriwal region of Haryana?
(*a*) Rewari Lift Irrigation Scheme
(*b*) Hathni Reservoir Barrage Irrigation Scheme
(*c*) Mewat Lift Irrigation Scheme
(*d*) Bhakra Canal Irrigation Scheme

136. The largest Animal Farm of Haryana is situated at which of the following places?
(*a*) Rohtak (*b*) Hissar
(*c*) Panch Kula (*d*) Jind

137. Which of the following breeds of the Buffalo of Haryana is famous in entire India?
(*a*) Murra (*b*) Tura
(*c*) Puspa (*d*) Chassa

138. At which of the following places of Haryana cooperative milk plant has been set up?
(*a*) Ambala (*b*) Bhivani
(*c*) Jind (*d*) All of the above

139. In the Thanesar town of district Kurukshetra, the building for Pouttry disease diagnosis Laboratory was built in:
(*a*) 1980 – 81 (*b*) 1984 – 85
(*c*) 1988 – 89 (*d*) 1995 – 96

140. Besides Nilokheri in Haryana, at which of the following places of the state, training in poultry is imparted?
(*a*) Ambala (*b*) Karnal
(*c*) Hissar (*d*) Kaithal

141. Consider the following statements:

1. Rohtak has a Police Commissionerate located there.
2. Sonipat has a Police Commissionerate located there.

Which of the above statements is/are correct?

(*a*) 2 only (*b*) Both 1 and 2
(*c*) Neither 1 nor 2 (*d*) 1 only

142. Intensive Animal Development project in district Bhivani was launched in:

(*a*) 1966 (*b*) 1970
(*c*) 1972 (*d*) 1978

143. At which place in district Mahendragarh a Semen Bank is located and a liquid Nitrogen Plant has been set-up?

(*a*) Ateli (*b*) Narnaul
(*c*) Nangal Chaudhary (*d*) Mahendragarh

144. In district Bhiwani of Haryana, for diagnosing the diseases in animals the District Village Development Body set up the "Animal Disease Diagnosis Laboratory" in:

(*a*) 1978 (*b*) 1980
(*c*) 1984 (*d*) 1990

145. Haryana gets an average rainfall of ....

(*a*) 100 cms. (*b*) 85 cms.
(*c*) 75 cms. (*d*) 45 cms.

146. The ancient town 'Bery' is situated in which of the following districts of Haryana?

(*a*) Jhajjar (*b*) Yamuna Nagar
(*c*) Karnal (*d*) Kurukshetra

147. Where in Haryana, the National Institute of Fashion Technology is located?

(*a*) Panipat (*b*) Ambala
(*c*) Panchkula (*d*) Kurukshetra

148. The products manufactured by the industrial units of district Yamuna Nagar are exported to which of the following countries?

(*a*) Dubai (*b*) Germany
(*c*) South Africa (*d*) All of the above

149. Saraswati Sugar Mill is located in which of the following districts of Haryana?

(*a*) Rohtak (*b*) Panipat
(*c*) Yamuna Nagar (*d*) Faridabad

150. In Yamuna Nagar, Yanuma Gases Limited was set up in:

(*a*) 1973 (*b*) 1975
(*c*) 1980 (*d*) 1981

151. Yamuna Gases Limited operating in Yamuna Nagar attained a leading position in the production of gases in the year:

(*a*) 1969 (*b*) 1973
(*c*) 1972 (*d*) 1975

152. Bharat Starch Chemical Ltd. was established in Yamuna Nagar in:

(*a*) 1929 (*b*) 1932
(*c*) 1938 (*d*) 1948

153. Before 1947, the Timber Market of Yamuna Nagar was known as:

(*a*) Abdullapur Mandi
(*b*) Sadapur Mandi
(*c*) Yamuna Nagar Mandi
(*d*) Yamuna Pur Mandi

154. Charkhi Dadri was carved out from which district?

(*a*) Bhiwani (*b*) Hissar
(*c*) Sirsa (*d*) Rewari

155. "Bhiwani Textile Mill" in Haryana was established in:

(*a*) 1930 (*b*) 1937
(*c*) 1942 (*d*) 1950

156. In Haryana, where the Vulture Conservation Centre is located?

(*a*) Pinjore (*b*) Jind
(*c*) Mahendragarh (*d*) Ambala

157. The Sahibi river does not flow in which of the following district?

(*a*) Rewari (*b*) Jhajjar
(*c*) Gurugram (*d*) Rohtak

158. Consider the following statements in respect of National Security Guards (NSG):

1. Operational Headquarter of NSG is in Manesar.
2. NSG comes under the control of Union Ministry of Home Affairs.

Which of the above statements is/are correct?

(*a*) 2 only (*b*) Both 1 and 2
(*c*) Neither 1 nor 2 (*d*) 1 only

159. Indian Cement Corporation, A Government of India undertaking, took possession of the factory located at Charkhi-Dadri of Haryana on:

(*a*) 5 April, 1980 (*b*) 23 June, 1981
(*c*) 10 June, 1984 (*d*) 23 June, 1988

160. National Beekeeping and Honey Mission (NBHM) Scheme was started in which year in Haryana?

(*a*) 2017 (*b*) 2018
(*c*) 2019 (*d*) 2020

161. Captive Electricity Plant has been set up in which of the following districts of Haryana?

(*a*) Panipat (*b*) Hissar
(*c*) Rohtak (*d*) Karnal

162. At Baholi of district Panipat which of the following factories has been set up?

(*a*) Cloth Factory
(*b*) Agricultural Implements Factory
(*c*) Oil Refinery
(*d*) Slippers Factory

163. 'Ammonia Plant' has been installed in which of the following districts of Haryana?

(*a*) Panipat (*b*) Kaithal
(*c*) Gurugram (*d*) Karnal

164. District Mahanderagarh ranks first in the state of Haryana in the production of:

(*a*) Rice (*b*) Utensils
(*c*) Mustard (*d*) Bicycle

165. According to the 2011 census sex ratio in the state is ....

(*a*) 787 (*b*) 879
(*c*) 987 (*d*) 973

166. Which of the following industries in Rewari district of Haryana is famous all over India?

(*a*) Shoe Sole Industry
(*b*) Brass Utensil Industry
(*c*) Hero Honda Motor Cycle Factory
(*d*) All of these

167. In addition to Bicycle Factory, which of the following other factories are located in Jind district of Haryana?

(*a*) Utensil Factory (*b*) Textile Factory
(*c*) Sugar Factory (*d*) Leather Shoe Factory

168. According to the 2011 census population density in the state is ....

(*a*) 573 (*b*) 752
(*c*) 482 (*d*) 531

169. Total covered area of the Shri Krishna Museum is:

(*a*) 8764 sq.m. (*b*) 8885 sq.m.
(*c*) 8129 sq.m. (*d*) 8649 sq.m.

170. Which of the following articles manufactured in Karnal district are exported to foreign countries also?

(*a*) Liberty Shoes (*b*) Paint
(*c*) Wooden Furnitures (*d*) Steel Furniture

171. Shahabad Cooperative Sugar Mill in district Kurukshetra was established in:

(*a*) 1976 – 77 (*b*) 1984 – 85
(*c*) 1991 – 92 (*d*) 1994 – 95

172. Which of the following factories have been set up in Faridabad District of Haryana?

(*a*) Tractor Factory (*b*) Refrigerator Factory
(*c*) Rubber Tyre Factory (*d*) All of these

173. In which year the strength of Haryana Assembly was raised to 90?

(*a*) 1977 (*b*) 1967
(*c*) 1971 (*d*) 1985

174. At which of the following places in Haryana Maruti Cars are manufactured?

(*a*) Gurugram (*b*) Ambala
(*c*) Faridabad (*d*) Hissar

175. Which among the following is the highly populated district, as per the 2011 census?

(*a*) Rohtak (*b*) Karnal
(*c*) Gurugram (*d*) Faridabad

176. During which of the following years Government of Haryana decided to confer honour on Freedom Fighters?

(*a*) 1980 (*b*) 1981
(*c*) 1985 (*d*) 1997

177. Which of the following districts of Haryana does not share its boundary with any other state of India?

(*a*) Charkhi Dadri (*b*) Palwal
(*c*) Gurugram (*d*) Jind

178. Skylark Tourist Complex is located at ....

(*a*) Faridabad (*b*) Panipat
(*c*) Karnal (*d*) Rohtak

179. Scheme of granting cash amount, amount payable annually and cash in lieu of land to the soldiers awarded with 'Yuddha Sewa Medal' was discontinued in 1988. This scheme was launched again by the Government of Bansi Lal in:

(*a*) April 1995 (*b*) April 1997
(*c*) April 1996 (*d*) April 1998

180. Chaudhary Devi Lal University in Haryana is located at:

(*a*) Hissar (*b*) Karnal
(*c*) Sirsa (*d*) Panipat

181. Who among the following was not the chief minister of Haryana?

(*a*) Babu Parmanand (*b*) B.D. Gupta
(*c*) Devi Lal (*d*) Hukum Singh

182. National Dairy Research Institute is located at ....

(*a*) Karnal (*b*) Hissar
(*c*) Sirsa (*d*) Rohtak

183. Who was the first governor of Haryana?

(*a*) R.S. Narula (*b*) G.D. Tapse
(*c*) Dharamvir (*d*) B.D. Sharma

184. Hostel for the boys of Scheduled Castes who are engaged in unclean occupation is located at:

(*a*) Karnal (*b*) Faridabad
(*c*) Ambala (*d*) All of these

185. Hostel for the boys of exempted castes is located at :

(*a*) Rohtak (*b*) Jind
(*c*) Faridabad (*d*) Gurugram

186. Legal provisions for ban on liquor were enforced in Haryana on:

(*a*) 1 December, 1991 (*b*) 1 June, 1993
(*c*) 1 July, 1996 (*d*) 1 May, 1997

187. Ban on the sale of liquor was lifted by the state government on:

(*a*) 1 May, 1996 (*b*) 1 May, 1997
(*c*) 1 February, 1996 (*d*) 1 April, 1998

188. Which of the following Child Development Projects is related with the State of Haryana?

(*a*) Coordinated Child Development Project
(*b*) Child Health Project
(*c*) Infant Nutrition Programme
(*d*) Helpless Child Development Project

189. Which of the following schemes are being run for the welfare of the girls belonging to poor families?

(*a*) Paraya Dhan Parayee Beti
(*b*) Apni Beti Paraya Dhan
(*c*) Apni Beti Apna Dhan
(*d*) None of these

190. The total length of National Highway in Haryana till December, 2025 is:
(*a*) 1900 kms. (*b*) 1503 kms.
(*c*) 1800 kms. (*d*) 3414 kms.

191. Each and every village of the State of Haryana became electrified on:
(*a*) 10 June, 1966 (*b*) 25 March, 1971
(*c*) 15 April, 1968 (*d*) 29 November, 1970

192. Aruna is the ancient name of which river?
(*a*) Markanda (*b*) Sahibi
(*c*) Ghaggar (*d*) Yamuna

193. Red Soil is found in ....
(*a*) Rohtak (*b*) Sirsa
(*c*) Karnal (*d*) Bihwani

194. With a view to bring improvement in the availability of electricity in Southern Haryana, a new 50 km long single circuit line has been laid from :
(*a*) Gurugram to Badshahpur
(*b*) Badshahpur to Rewari
(*c*) Faridabad to Rewari
(*d*) Jind to Kaithal

195. Which one of the following pairs is not correctly matched?
(*a*) Surajkund Lake – Kurukshetra
(*b*) Tilyaar Lake – Rohtak
(*c*) Damdama Lake – Gurugram
(*d*) Badkhal Lake – Faridabad

196. Sultanpur Lake is located in which district?
(*a*) Bhiwani (*b*) Mahendragarh
(*c*) Gurugram (*d*) Rewari

197. According to the demands made by farmers, which of the following systems for electricity on the basis of the depth of tubewells has been adopted in the entire state?
(*a*) Stove System
(*b*) Electricity Measurement System
(*c*) Test System
(*d*) None of these

198. Thermal Power Station is located at which of the following places in Haryana?
(*a*) Hissar (*b*) Kaithal
(*c*) Jind (*d*) Faridabad

199. At which of the following places, the Power Plant of 432 MW based on Gas has been installed by NTPC in Haryana?
(*a*) Gurugram (*b*) Faridabad
(*c*) Panipat (*d*) Karnal

200. What is the total length of road in Haryana till December, 2025?
(*a*) 33,817 km (*b*) 24,065 km
(*c*) 25,074 km (*d*) 40,760 km

201. The strength of Legislative Assembly of Haryana is ....
(*a*) 102 (*b*) 110
(*c*) 75 (*d*) 90

202. Where is Nahar Wildlife Sanctuary is situated?
(*a*) Ambala (*b*) Sonipat
(*c*) Rewari (*d*) Yamunanagar

203. When the Public Transport in Haryana was brought under the possession of the Government?
(*a*) In 1972 (*b*) In 1976
(*c*) In 1980 (*d*) In 1985

204. 'Rao Tej Singh Pond' is located in:
(*a*) Panipat (*b*) Sonipat
(*c*) Palwal (*d*) Rewari

205. The Magazine of Haryana Sahitya Academy is:
(*a*) Harigandha (*b*) Haryana Samvad
(*c*) Haryana Sandesh (*d*) Panchajanya

206. While travelling on the National Highway from Delhi to Ferozepur, which of the following important town of Haryana comes on the way:
(*a*) Rohtak (*b*) Sirsa
(*c*) Hissar (*d*) All of these

207. Manu Bhaker of Haryana is related with which sports?
(*a*) Badminton (*b*) Boxing
(*c*) Shooting (*d*) Wrestling

208. Which of the following tourist places is situated at Bahadurgarh in Haryana?
(*a*) Dairango Tourist Place (*b*) Gureya
(*c*) Jal Tarang (*d*) Tiliyar

209. In Haryana, in addition to Hissar, Karnal, Bhiwani, Narnaul and Jind, at which of the following airports metalled run-way has been built?
(*a*) Panipat (*b*) Pinjore
(*c*) Faridabad (*d*) Rewari

210. Where is Tilyar lake is situated?
(*a*) Rohtak (*b*) Gurugram
(*c*) Jind (*d*) Faridabad

211. At which of the following places in Haryana, Heavy Vehicle Driving Training Institute is located?
(*a*) Murthal (*b*) Charkhi-Dadri
(*c*) Ambala (*d*) Tawaroo

212. In Shivalik hills near Pinjore-Kalka in Haryana, utensils have been found which pertain to which of the following ages?
(*a*) Stone Age (*b*) Later Vedic Age
(*c*) Harappan Age (*d*) Early Vedic Age

213. In the treatise named "Avanti Sunderi Katha" Vaivast Manu who is known as the father of human beings is said to be the resident of which of the following places?
(*a*) Panipat (*b*) Rohtak
(*c*) Sthaneshwar (*d*) Panchkula

214. Evidences found from the excavations done at Banwali, Siswal, Kunal, Mirzapur, Daulatpur and Bhagawanpura in the state of Haryana revealed links dating back to:

(*a*) Early Harappan Culture
(*b*) Mature Harappan Culture
(*c*) Late Harappan Culture
(*d*) All of the above phases

215. Who of the following started archaeological survey in Haryana for the first time?
(*a*) Sir John (*b*) Alexander Kaningham
(*c*) Lord Munro (*d*) John Marshall

216. Archaeological Survey in Haryana started in:
(*a*) 1862 (*b*) 1892
(*c*) 1900 (*d*) 1905

217. Under the supervision of Dr. Suraj Bhan, excavations at which of the following places of Haryana brought out very valuable historical evidences?
(*a*) Mithathal (*b*) Dadri
(*c*) Ailanabad (*d*) Safidon

218. From which of the following sites of Haryana, evidences have been found for the first time regarding co-existence of the people of Late Harappan culture and Painted Grey Ware (PGW) culture?
(*a*) Narnaul (*b*) Bhagwanpura
(*c*) Sirsa (*d*) Mahendragarh

219. A great mound pertaining to Harappan culture is situated at which of the following places in district Jind of Haryana?
(*a*) Safidon (*b*) Uchana
(*c*) Narwana (*d*) Rakhigarhi

220. Remains of a Stupa have been found at Chaneti which is situated three kilometers east of Jagadhari. Height of this Stupa is 8 m. Its periphery is:
(*a*) 20 m (*b*) 30 m
(*c*) 45 m (*d*) 50 m

221. Consider the following statements:
1. Sonipat and Jhajjar share border with Delhi.
2. Rohtak does not share border with Delhi.
Which of the above statements is/are correct?
(*a*) 2 only (*b*) Both 1 and 2
(*c*) Neither 1 nor 2 (*d*) 1 only

222. A battle axe type Gold Coin which pertains to the age of Samudra Gupta has been found at which of the following places in Haryana?
(*a*) Kosali (*b*) Rohana
(*c*) Mithathal (*d*) Raniya

223. Which of the following areas of Haryana was under the control of Yudheyas during the 3rd century A.D.?
(*a*) Panipat (*b*) Rohtak
(*c*) Hissar (*d*) Ambala

224. The Gold Coin obtained from Jagadhari pertains to which of the following emperors of the ancient India?
(*a*) Kanishka (*b*) Kumar Gupta
(*c*) Pushyamitra Sunga (*d*) Samudragupta

225. From which of the following places in Haryana, copper coin of the age of Harsha Vardhan has been found which contains an account of Pushyabhuti dynasty of Thanesar?
(*a*) Sonepat (*b*) Sirsa
(*c*) Gurugram (*d*) Kaithal

226. At which of the following places located in district Hissar of Haryana excavations was done by Shri H.L. Srivastava of Archaeo-logical Survey of India?
(*a*) Uklana (*b*) Fatehabad
(*c*) Agroha (*d*) Adampur

227. What is the total number of Primary and Pre Primary Schools in Haryana till 2024-25?
(*a*) 9,870 (*b*) 9,399
(*c*) 11,582 (*d*) 8,780

228. What is the total number of Middle Schools in Haryana till 2024-25?
(*a*) 6,215 (*b*) 2,312
(*c*) 5,528 (*d*) 3,850

229. In Haryana 'Brahma Sarovar' is located in:
(*a*) Palwal (*b*) Kurukshetra
(*c*) Panipat (*d*) Sonipat

230. 'Uchana' is located in:
(*a*) Jind (*b*) Karnal
(*c*) Rohtak (*d*) Faridabad

231. The tenure of nagarpalika, municipality or municipal corporation in Haryana is ....
(*a*) 3 years (*b*) 1 year
(*c*) 4 years (*d*) 5 years

232. What is the area of Sirsa district?
(*a*) 4,277 sq.km (*b*) 5,780 sq.km
(*c*) 3,760 sq.km (*d*) 2,765 sq.km

233. What is the total number of literate people in Haryana?
(*a*) 1,66,25,728 (*b*) 1,65,98,988
(*c*) 1,78,10,882 (*d*) 1,32,58,652

234. The historical monument known as the corridor Chhatta of Rai Mukund Das (Birbal Ka Chhatta) is in:
(*a*) Panipat (*b*) Karnal
(*c*) Kaithal (*d*) Narnaul

235. Navodaya Vidyalaya is situated at which of the following places in the state?
(*a*) Titaram (Kurukshetra) (*b*) Odha (Sirsa)
(*c*) Deorala (Bhiwani) (*d*) All of these

236. During which of the following years Government of Haryana introduced 10+2+3 system of Education in Haryana?
(*a*) 1980 - 81 (*b*) 1976 - 77
(*c*) 1988 - 89 (*d*) 1985 - 86

237. M.D. University is located in which of the following towns of Haryana?
(*a*) Rohtak (*b*) Hissar
(*c*) Faridabad (*d*) Rewari

238. Chaudhary Charan Singh Agricultural University is located in which of the following towns of the state?
(*a*) Jind (*b*) Gurugram
(*c*) Hissar (*d*) Kurukshetra

239. In order to promote Punjabi language in Haryana it has been made the .... language of the state.
(*a*) First (*b*) Second
(*c*) Third (*d*) Fourth

240. Chaudhary Devilal University is located in which of the following towns of Haryana?
(*a*) Kurukshetra (*b*) Hissar
(*c*) Rohtak (*d*) Sirsa

241. In order to give promotion to sports in Haryana, the State Government has launched which of the following important schemes?
(*a*) Providing Grant in aid to the Sports Institutions
(*b*) Training Scheme
(*c*) Sports Stadium
(*d*) All of the above

242. In order to impart training to the players through modern and scientific methods, at which of the following places of Haryana a sports hostel has been set up?
(*a*) Gurugram (*b*) Rohtak
(*c*) Faridabad (*d*) Panipat

243. A sports school is situated at Rai in Sonepat district of Haryana. What is the name of this sports school?
(*a*) Jawahar Lal Nehru Sports School
(*b*) Indira Gandhi Sports School
(*c*) Moti Lal Nehru Sports School
(*d*) Rajiv Gandhi Sports School

244. Kamla Nehru School situated in the premises of Moti Lal Nehru Sports School at Rai in Sonepat district was established in
(*a*) 1970 (*b*) 1974
(*c*) 1982 (*d*) 1986

245. Haryana Shehari Vikas Pradhikaran (HSVP), formerly Haryana Urban Development Authority (HUDA) was constituted in ....
(*a*) 1977 (*b*) 1972
(*c*) 1970 (*d*) 1966

246. Who has variously been described as Plato of Jat Tribes?
(*a*) Suraj Mal (*b*) Churaman
(*c*) Raja Ram Bhajja (*d*) None of these

247. Khoria dance is famous in ....
(*a*) Eastern Haryana (*b*) Western Haryana
(*c*) Central Haryana (*d*) Northern Haryana

248. Which player of Haryana won gold medal in Tokyo Olympics 2020?
(*a*) Bajarang Punia (*b*) Neeraj Chopra
(*c*) Ravi Kumar (*d*) Vijendra Singh

249. The Haryana Shawl is known as ....
(*a*) Phulkari (*b*) Ghagra
(*c*) Iungis (*d*) Bagh

250. The famous story writer of Hindi Shri Vishvambhar Nath Kaushik was born in Haryana at
(*a*) Ambala Cantt (*b*) Sirsa
(*c*) Panchkula (*d*) Rohtak

251. Famous writer of Haryana Pt. Neki Ram Sharma had brought out which of the following papers from Bhiwani?
(*a*) Samvahak (*b*) Sandesh
(*c*) Nivaran (*d*) Vani

252. Who of the following players of Indian Cricket hails from Haryana?
(*a*) Kapil Dev (*b*) Sunil Gavaskar
(*c*) Ajay Jadeja (*d*) Azharuddin

253. The Cricket Test Match in which Kapil Dev of Haryana took 432nd wicket to make a record of taking maximum number of wickets was held on
(*a*) 10 January, 1992 (*b*) 8 December, 1996
(*c*) 8 February, 1994 (*d*) 12 August, 1997

254. Kapil Dev announced to abandon the international cricket on
(*a*) 6 November, 1993 (*b*) 2 November, 1994
(*c*) 18 November, 1997 (*d*) 15 November, 1998

255. Who of the following players of Haryana is not related with Gymnastic?
(*a*) Sunita Sharma (*b*) Sandhya
(*c*) Nirmala Guliya (*d*) Geeta Jutshi

256. Who of the following first ever poet is considered a native poet of Haryana?
(*a*) Goswami Tulsi Das (*b*) Kabir Das
(*c*) Kavi Chandbardai (*d*) Rahim Das

257. Who of the following Muslim Saints of Haryana had made significant contributions in the development of Hindi literature?
(*a*) Shekh-U-Alishaha Kalander
(*b*) Saint Sadullah
(*c*) Shekh Bahauddin Chishti
(*d*) All of these

258. Who of the following first ever poet is not related with Haryana?
(*a*) Virbhan (*b*) Mahatma Haridas
(*c*) Banarsi Das (*d*) Narottam Das

259. Haryana got the status of a full state on
(*a*) 1 November, 1964 (*b*) 10 December, 1965
(*c*) 1 November, 1966 (*d*) 15 June, 1968

260. The capital city of Haryana is
(*a*) Chandigarh (*b*) Rohtak
(*c*) Karnal (*d*) Yamuna Nagar

261. With a view to administrative convenience, Haryana has been divided into
(*a*) Three Divisions (*b*) Six Divisions
(*c*) Five Divisions (*d*) Four Divisions

262. The number of Districts in Haryana till January, 2026 is:
(*a*) 16 (*b*) 17
(*c*) 18 (*d*) 23

263. The tourist place called Oasis is situated at which of the following places in Haryana?
(*a*) Faridabad (*b*) Bhiwani
(*c*) Uchchhana (*d*) Rewari

264. Which of the following famous tourist place of Haryana is located at a distance of about 20 kms from Delhi?
(*a*) Suraj Kund (*b*) Red Robin
(*c*) Paracot (*d*) Damdama Lake

265. In vast rocky areas extended to the west of Faridabad by the Delhi-Mathura National Highway which of the following tourist place is situated?
(*a*) Damdama Lake (*b*) Badkhal Lake
(*c*) King Fisher (*d*) Dabchik

266. Between the hills of Arawali on Delhi-Alwar road which of the following famous tourist place of Haryana is located?
(*a*) Shama (*b*) Blue-ze
(*c*) Sohana (*d*) Dairangon

267. Who had discovered the Sultanpur Bird Sanctuary of Haryana situated on Gurugram Farrukh Nagar road?
(*a*) Peter Jackson (*b*) Thomar Roe
(*c*) Sir John Marshall (*d*) Robin Hood

268. On the Gurugram-Farrukhabad road which of the following tourist places of Haryana is situated?
(*a*) Dab-bich
(*b*) Sultanpur Bird Sanctuary
(*c*) Oasis
(*d*) Red Robin

269. The Turban worn by male in Haryana is called
(*a*) Khandwa (*b*) Paggada
(*c*) Toda (*d*) Pagari

270. The tourist centre called 'Shama' is situated at which of the following towns of Haryana?
(*a*) Faridabad (*b*) Kaithal
(*c*) Gurugram (*d*) Jind

271. In Haryana, the skirt worn by females from waist to ankle which is without any gusset and made of hand-spun coarse cloth knitted by using four blue and four red threads is called
(*a*) Dharna (*b*) Khara
(*c*) Thara (*d*) Kachara

272. Which of the following ornaments used in the state is not worn around neck?
(*a*) Hansla (*b*) Fool
(*c*) Galshree (*d*) Batan

273. Which of the following ornaments is worn on face and head on the ladies of the state?
(*a*) Singar Patti (*b*) Tagga
(*c*) Bessar (*d*) All of these

274. Which of the following ornaments used in the state is not worn on nose?
(*a*) Nath (*b*) Purli
(*c*) Dhede (*d*) Kokka

275. Which of the following ornaments used in the state is not worn on hands?
(*a*) Pauhchi (*b*) Kandulla
(*c*) Pachhelli (*d*) Bankri

276. According to the augury, which of the following is considered a good omen in the state of Haryana?
(*a*) A pitcher full of water
(*b*) To have a view of a deer
(*c*) A sweeper with a broom in hand
(*d*) All of the above

277. According to the augury, which of the following is considered a bad omen in the state of the Haryana?
(*a*) Empty pitcher
(*b*) To have a view of grass
(*c*) To experience an itching sensation in feet
(*d*) Meeting with a water carrier carrying water.

278. Which of the traditional ornaments is worn by males in Haryana?
(*a*) Goph (*b*) Tagari
(*c*) Nada (*d*) Kadi

279. At which of the following places of religious importance, lakhs of people from all over India go for a religious ritual on the occurrence of solar eclipse?
(*a*) Gurugram (*b*) Kurukshetra
(*c*) Jagadhari (*d*) None of these

280. At Islampur in the district Gurugram, which of the following festivals (Mela) is organised on the ninth day of Bhado (the sixth month of the year according to the Hindu calendar)?
(*a*) Guga Naumi (*b*) Nag Pooja
(*c*) Yamuna Snan (*d*) Shiv Mela

281. In the months of Chait and Aashadh (respectively the opening and the fourth month of the year according to the Hindu caldendar) in district Gurugram of Haryana on every Monday and Tuesday which of the following famous festivals (Melas) is organised?
(*a*) Buddho Mata Ka Mela
(*b*) Shivji Ka Mela
(*c*) Shitla Mata Ka Mela
(*d*) Baba Buddha Ka Mela

282. In which of the following districts of Haryana famous festivals of Ramsarai and Bhuteshwar are organised?
(*a*) Faridabad (*b*) Jind
(*c*) Rohtak (*d*) Jhajjhar

283. In the monastery at Asthal Bohar in Rohtak district of Haryana which of the following festivals (Melas) is organised during the months of February and March?
(*a*) Baba Mastnath Ka Mela
(*b*) Kapal Mochan Ka Mela
(*c*) Devi Mela
(*d*) Pathari Mata Ka Mela

284. Which of the following festivals (Melas) is organised on Kartik-Purnima at Bilaspur situated near Jagadhari?
(*a*) Aadi Badri Mela (*b*) Mela Kali Mai
(*c*) Kapal Mochan Mela (*d*) Panchmukhi Mela

285. At Lakhan Majra in Rohtak district "Gurudwara of Manji Sahib" is situated. Here which of the following festivals (Melas) is organised?
(*a*) Festival of Satya Teej
(*b*) Festival of Mohola Halla
(*c*) Bawan Dwadashi
(*d*) Maanu Mela

286. At Pathri in district Sonepat, on every Wednesday in the months of Chait and Aashadh, which of the following festivals (Melas) is organised?
(*a*) Mata Ka Mela (*b*) Shiva Mela
(*c*) Dehati Mela (*d*) Pathri Mata Ka Mela

287. At Kharak Ramji situated in district Jind, which of the following festivals (Melas) is organised on the day of Holi?
(*a*) Mata Ka Mela
(*b*) Nag Devata Ka Mela
(*c*) Baba Bhalu Nath Ka Mela
(*d*) Mela Sachcha Sauda

288. At Dubaldhan Majra in Rohtak district which of the following festivals (Melas) is organised in the months of February-March?
(*a*) Mela Mata (*b*) Mela Devi
(*c*) Mela Shyamji (*d*) Mela Baba Buddha

289. At Khori in the Gurugram district which of the following festivals (Melas) is organised during the months of April-May?
(*a*) Shah Chokha Khori Mela
(*b*) Shiva Ka Mela
(*c*) Nagpooja Ka Mela
(*d*) Baba Mast Nath Ka Mela

290. At which of the following places in district Sonepat, festival (Mela) of Dera Nagn Balaknath is organised during the months of February-March?
(*a*) Bega (Tehsil Sonepat)
(*b*) Mehripur (Tehsil Sonepat)
(*c*) Rabhara (Tehsil Gohana)
(*d*) Chulkana (Tehsil Sonepat)

291. Which of the following festivals (Melas) is oraganised at Khubadu situated in district Sonepat during the months of February-March?
(*a*) Satakumbha Mela (*b*) Mela Baba Shamakshah
(*c*) Mela Sanjhi (*d*) Devi Mela

292. Which amongst the following is the State Tree of Haryana?
(*a*) Sacred Fig (*b*) Mango Tree
(*c*) Sal Tree (*d*) Banyan Tree

293. At which of the following places in Haryana festival (Mela) of Baba Khedewala is organised on the day of Raksha Bandhan?
(*a*) Naurangabad (*b*) Kaharak Kalan
(*c*) Riwasa (*d*) Tosham

294. On which of the following occasions in the state of Haryana auspicious "Piliya" folk song is sung?
(*a*) In the months of July-August
(*b*) On the occasion of the birth of a male child in the family
(*c*) On the occasion of marriage ceremony
(*d*) In the months of February-March

295. On which of the following occasions, in the state of Haryana folk songs are sung?
(*a*) On the occasion of the birth of a male child in the family
(*b*) In the months of July-August
(*c*) On the occasion of a festival
(*d*) On all of the above occasions

296. In the state, males perform which of the following dances in open field at moon-lit night on flute, scooped gourd (Tumbi), etc.?
(*a*) Dhamal Dance (*b*) Manjeera Dance
(*c*) Loor Dance (*d*) Damru Dance

297. Which of the following dance performances is famous in Mewat area of Haryana which is accompanied with beating huge kettle drum, tambourine and cymbals?
(*a*) Ghora Dance (*b*) Dhamal Dance
(*c*) Manjeera Dance (*d*) Chhathi Dance

298. In Bagar area of Haryana which of the following dance performances is famous that is performed during the festival of Holi?
(*a*) Damru Dance (*b*) Manjeera Dance
(*c*) Ghora Dance (*d*) Loor Dance

299. The Ghora folk dance popular in Haryana is generally performed on which of the following occasions?
(*a*) On the occasion of marriage
(*b*) In the month of February-March
(*c*) On the occasion of birth of a male child in the family
(*d*) In the Month of July-August

300. In Haryana, which of the following dances is performed after the worship of Guggapir in the month of August-September?
(*a*) Dhamal Dance (*b*) Chchari Dance
(*c*) Loor Dance (*d*) Damru Dance

301. Which of the following folk dances is performed by women in the state?
(*a*) Teej Dance (*b*) Dhamal Dance
(*c*) Damru Dance (*d*) Khodiya Dance

302. Which dance is performed by males among the following folk dances practised in the state?
(*a*) Chhatthi dance (*b*) Teej dance
(*c*) Damru dance (*d*) Khodia dance

303. Which of the following folk dances is performed by men and women both in the state?
(*a*) Teej Dance (*b*) Loor Dance
(*c*) Khodiya Dance (*d*) Fag Dance

304. Which of the following Gurudwaras is situated near Pratap Gate in Kaithal town of Haryana?
(*a*) Gurudwara Neem Sahib
(*b*) Gurudwara Nauvi Patshahi
(*c*) Ragdhaar Gurudwara
(*d*) Gurudwara Chhathi Patshahi

305. Gurudwara Manji Sahib is situated in which of the following towns of Haryana?
(*a*) Karnal (*b*) Panipat
(*c*) Kaithal (*d*) Ambala

306. Which place in Haryana is called as "Chhoti Kashi" due to presence of "Navagraha Kunds"?
(*a*) Narnaul (*b*) Kaithal
(*c*) Gurugram (*d*) Kurukshetra

307. At a few distance from Kaithal in Haryana the grave of which of the following great men is situated where every year next dayof Dushera a large festival is organised?
(*a*) Baba Kali Kamli Wale
(*b*) Baba Haridas
(*c*) Baba Ladana
(*d*) Baba Ramdas

308. Which of the following famous places of pilgrimage is situated near Thanesar City Station in district Kurukshetra of Haryana?
(*a*) Brahma Sarovar (*b*) Hatakeshwar
(*c*) Dhosi (*d*) Pundarik Sarovar

309. Which of the following places of pilgrimage is situated on the Kurukshetra-Pehwa road near Kurukshetra Railway Station which is considered as the permanent abode of Lord Vishnu?
(*a*) Brahma Sarovar (*b*) Kaleshwar Tirth
(*c*) Sannihit Sarovar (*d*) Markanday Tirth

310. At which place of piligrimage in Kurukshetra district Shri Krishna had preached Arjuna?
(*a*) Brahm Sarovar (*b*) Kamal Nabh Tirth
(*c*) Prachi Tirth (*d*) Jyotishwar Sarovar

311. When did Maharaja Darbhanga build metalled platform around the Akshya Vat located near the Jyotishwar Sarovar situated in district Kurukshetra?
(*a*) In 1924 (*b*) In 1930
(*c*) In 1932 (*d*) In 1949

312. Who had built the Krishna-Arjuna Rath (Chariot) and the temple of Shankaracharya near the Jyotishwar Sarovar situated in district Kurukshetra?
(*a*) Maharaja Darbhanga
(*b*) Shankaracharya of Kam Koti Peeth
(*c*) King of Kashmir
(*d*) Swami Vishuddhananda Maharaj

313. What is the total length of Jyotishwar Sarovar situated in district Kurukshetra?
(*a*) 1000 ft. (*b*) 1500 ft.
(*c*) 2000 ft. (*d*) 2500 ft.

314. Who was the founder of "Baba Kali Kamli Wale Ka Dera" situated in district Kurukshetra?
(*a*) Swami Ram Tirth
(*b*) Shri Swami Vishuddhananda Maharaja
(*c*) Shankaracharya of Kamkoti Peeth
(*d*) Swami Parmananda Maharaj

315. Gaudiya Math (monastery) related with the period of Bhakti movement in India, is situated in which of the following districts of Haryana?
(*a*) Ambala (*b*) Jind
(*c*) Kurukshetra (*d*) Mahendragarh

316. At which of the following places in district Kurukshetra Baba Laxman Giri Maharaj went into eternal trance?
(*a*) Ban Ganga (*b*) Prachi Tirth
(*c*) Gaudiya Math (*d*) Balmiki Aashram

317. Raj Ghat Gurudwara is situated at which of the following places in Haryana?
(*a*) Kurukshetra (*b*) Yamuna Nagar
(*c*) Kaithal (*d*) Bhiwani

318. Which of the following places of pilgrimage is not situated in district Kurukshetra of Haryana?
(*a*) Kalkeshwar Tirth
(*b*) Prachi Tirth
(*c*) Dhosi Tirth
(*d*) Kuber Tirth

319. Which of the following places of pilgrimage is situated at a distance of 1 km. to the North-West of Kurukshetra University in district Kurukshetra of Haryana?
(*a*) Markandya Tirth
(*b*) Narakatari (Anrak Tirth)
(*c*) Prachi Tirth
(*d*) Kuber Tirth

320. Which of the following important places of pilgrimage is situated at a distance of 25 km to the west of Thanesar in Haryana that is given the same importance by the people of Haryana and adjoining areas as is given to Gaya by the people of Eastern region of India?
(*a*) Pehova (*b*) Panchavati
(*c*) Safeedon (*d*) Pandu-Pindara

321. In which district of Haryana the 'National Institute of Animal Genetics' is located?
(*a*) Hisar (*b*) Yamunanagar
(*c*) Karnal (*d*) Rohtak

322. A place of pilgrimage known as "Panchavati" is situated at which of the following districts of Haryana?
(*a*) Ambala (*b*) Jind
(*c*) Kurukshetra (*d*) Palwal

323. Which of the following is an ancient place of pilgrimage located by Jind-Gohana Road near Jind where a fair is organised every year on Somawati Amavasya?
(*a*) Pandu-Pindara
(*b*) Safeedon
(*c*) Hans Daihar
(*d*) None of the above

324. Temple of Sthaneshwar Mahadeva situated at a distance of a few kilometres from Thanesar was built by which of the following kings prior to Harshavardhan?
(*a*) Pushyabhuti (*b*) Adityavardhan
(*c*) Narvardhan (*d*) Prabhakarvardhan

325. Mahmud Ghaznavi during his return course to Ghazni took away with him from Haryana to Ghazni, statue of which of the ancient temple located in Haryana?
(*a*) Dukh Bhanjaneshwar Temple (Kuruk-shetra)
(*b*) Lord Shiva Temple (Narnaul)
(*c*) Sarveshwar Mahadeva Temple (Kuruk-shetra)
(*d*) Sthaneshwar Mahadeva Temple (Thanesar)

326. Sthaneshwar Temple of Haryana was reconstructed by
(*a*) Maratha Sadashiva Rao
(*b*) Chandra Gupta Vikramaditya
(*c*) Harshavardhan
(*d*) Narvardhan

327. Devikoop (Bhadra Kali Temple) is one of the 51 Shakti Peeths (Seats of goddess personifying divine power) of India. This temple is located at which of the following places in the state?
(*a*) Rohtak (*b*) Kurukshetra
(*c*) Panipat (*d*) Thanesar

328. Which of the following temples is situated near Sannihit Sarovar in Kurukshetra?
(*a*) Narayana Temple
(*b*) Laxmi Narayan Temple
(*c*) Dukh Bhanjaneshwar Temple
(*d*) Birla Mandir

329. Which of the following temples of Kurukshetra was built by the perfect Saint of Giri Sect Baba Shiv Giri Maharaj?
(*a*) Sarveshwar Mahadeva Temple
(*b*) Narayana Temple
(*c*) Laxmi Narayan Temple
(*d*) Dukh Bhanajaneshwar Temple

330. Who had built the famous 'Sarveshwar Mahadeva Temple' of Kurukshetra?
(*a*) Baba Shravan Nath (*b*) Baba Shiva Giri
(*c*) Baba Tarak Nath (*d*) Shri Jugal Kishore Birla

331. Birla Temple situated by the Kurukshetra-Pehova road was built by Shri Jugal Kishore Birla in
(*a*) 1950 (*b*) 1955
(*c*) 1965 (*d*) 1978

332. "Gyarah Rudri Shiva Temple" is situated in which of the following towns of Haryana?
(*a*) Jind (*b*) Panipat
(*c*) Hissar (*d*) Kaithal

333. Maratha General Mangal Raghu Nath Ji had built which of the following temples after the third battle of Panipat?
(*a*) Shiva Temple of Devi Pond
(*b*) Hanuman Temple
(*c*) Devi Temple
(*d*) Rudra Temple

334. In Amin village of Kurukshetra district which one of the following ancient temples is situated?
(*a*) Panchvati Temple
(*b*) Shiva Temple
(*c*) Temple of Aditi
(*d*) Temple of Dauji

335. In Vanchari village situated at a distance of 55 km. from Faridabad, which of the following ancient temples is situated?
(*a*) Temple of Dauji
(*b*) Temple of Aditi
(*c*) Panchvati Temple
(*d*) Temple of Chamunda Devi

336. The famous ancient temple of Mata Sheetala Devi is situated at which of the following places in Haryana?
(*a*) Rewari (*b*) Gurugram
(*c*) Narnaul (*d*) Jind

337. Temple of Mata Sheetala Devi situated at Gurugram was built by Maharaja of Bharatpur in
(*a*) 1620 (*b*) 1645
(*c*) 1648 (*d*) 1650

338. The ancient Shiva temple where the grave of Baba Thandipuri is also located, is situated at which of the following places?
(*a*) Pundrik Tirth (*b*) Gurugram
(*c*) Hissar (*d*) Rohtak

339. Which of the following ancient temples is situated at village Beri of district Jhajjar in Haryana?
(*a*) Old Shiva-Parvati Temple
(*b*) Temple of Mata Sheetala Devi
(*c*) Lal Rudhmal Temple
(*d*) Temple of Dauji

340. The height of the Shivalaya located in Rudhmal temple at village Beri in district Jhajjar of Haryana is
(*a*) 116 ft. (*b*) 122 ft.
(*c*) 132 ft. (*d*) 140 ft.

341. The Shivalaya located in Rudhmal temple at village Beri in district Jhajjar of Haryana was built in
(*a*) 1842 (*b*) 1850
(*c*) 1892 (*d*) 1899

342. The Shivalaya located in Rudhmal temple at village Beri in district Jhajjar was resurrected for the first time in
(*a*) 1943 (*b*) 1945
(*c*) 1950 (*d*) 1953

343. The temple of Chamunda Devi situated at Narnaul was built and resurrected by
(*a*) Raja Parikshit (*b*) Raja Dilip
(*c*) Raja Noorkaran (*d*) Pandavas

344. Chisti sect was established in Haryana by
(*a*) Boo Alishah Kalandar
(*b*) Shekh Farid (Farid-ud-din-Shakarganj)
(*c*) Altaf Hussain
(*d*) Ibrahim Abidullah

345. The eminent saint of Chisti sect Boo Alishah Kalandar made which of the following places the centre of his meditation?
(*a*) Panipat (*b*) Rohtak
(*c*) Sonepat (*d*) Gurugram

346. Dargah of Sufi Saint Altaf Hussain Hali is situated at which of the following places in Haryana?
(*a*) Jhajjhar (*b*) Rewari
(*c*) Panipat (*d*) Rohtak

347. Regarding which of the following Dargahs (tombs of saints which are pilgrimage spots and places of worship) situated at Panipat is believed that bowing heads by believers accomplishes their attending in celebration of Urs of Khwaza of Ajmer?
(*a*) Dargah of Khwaza Shamshuddin Makhdoom Zalaluddin
(*b*) Dargah of Shekh Usman Jindapeer
(*c*) Dargah of Gauss Alishah
(*d*) Dargah of Boo Alishah Kalandar

348. Dargah of which of the following famous saints is situated at village Dharsun which is at a distance of about 10 kms from Narnaul?
(*a*) Hazarat Shah Kalmuddin Hamzapeer Hussain
(*b*) Meer Shah (Baba Shah Khan)
(*c*) Sheikh Nijamuddin
(*d*) Sheikh Junaid

349. At Fatehabad in the courtyard of the tomb of which of the following Sufi saints inscription of Mughal emperor Humayun is engraved on a stone?
(*a*) Mir Taki Khan
(*b*) Mir Junaidi
(*c*) Sheikh Nizamuddin
(*d*) Mir Shah (Baba Shah Khan)

350. Which of the following tombs situated in Haryana has been declared a monument of National importance under the Archaeological Site and Remnant Act, 1958?
(*a*) Sheikh Chehli
(*b*) Boo Alishah Kalandar
(*c*) Sheikh Farid (Farid-ud-din-Shakarganj)
(*d*) Peer Jamal

351. Tomb of Baba Shah Kamal is situated at which of the following places in Haryana?
(*a*) Gohan (*b*) Fatehabad
(*c*) Kaithal (*d*) Rohtak

352. At which one of the following places in the state, tombs of four Sufi-saints (Kutub Sheikh Jamaluddin Ahmad, Kutub Maulana, Basohddin Sufi Qutubuddin Mannawar, Qutub Nuruddin) are located?
(*a*) Karnal (*b*) Hissar
(*c*) Palwal (*d*) Hansi

353. The tomb of who of the following Sufi-saints is situated between Shahabad and Ambala where watch is offered after a desire is fulfilled?
(*a*) Peer Nagauji (*b*) Hamja Peer
(*c*) Peer Naugaja (*d*) Ibrahim Abidullah

354. Which of the following mosques in Rohtak which was previously a temple was turned into a mosque during the reign of Aurangzeb?
(*a*) Qazi Ki Masjid (*b*) Dini Masjid
(*c*) Lal Masjid (*d*) None of these

355. The Lal Masjid situated in Rohtak was built by famous trader Haji Aashiq Ali in
(*a*) 1930 (*b*) 1931
(*c*) 1935 (*d*) 1939

356. Mosque at Sarai Alawardi village in district Gurugram was built during the reign of
(*a*) Babur (*b*) Jahangir
(*c*) Shahjahan (*d*) Alauddin Khilji

357. Which of the following ancient historical Mosques is situated at village Dujana, situated at a distance of 22 km by Jhajjhar road from Rohtak?
(*a*) Lal Masjid (*b*) Qaji Ki Masjid
(*c*) Karim Ji Ki Masjid (*d*) Jama Masjid

358. The famous historic Lal Masjid at Rewari was built during the reign of which of the following Mughal Emperors?
(*a*) Babur (*b*) Humayun
(*c*) Akbar (*d*) Jahangir

359. In addition to Narnaul, Panipat and Ambala, Sufi-saints made which of the following towns of Haryana as a centre of Sufi-sect?
(*a*) Kaithal (*b*) Thanesar
(*c*) Karnal (*d*) Sonepat

360. The majority of Sufi-saints who lived in Haryana for propagating sufi cult belonged to which of the following sects?
(*a*) Chisti (*b*) Nakshbandi
(*c*) Kadari (*d*) All of the above

361. Tomb of famous Sufi-saint Sheikh Chehli which is called as the Tajmahal of Haryana is situated at
(*a*) Hissar (*b*) Fatehabad
(*c*) Thanesar (*d*) Panipat

362. Tomb of which of the following saints is situated at Kalyana village of Charkhi Dadri district where fair is organised on every Wednesday?
(*a*) Peer Mubarak Shah
(*b*) Sheikh Usman Jindapeer
(*c*) Sheikh Nizamuddin
(*d*) Muhammad Afzal

363. Tomb of Meeran Sahib is situated in which of the following towns of Haryana?
(*a*) Ambala (*b*) Panipat
(*c*) Karnal (*d*) Kaithal

364. Where did Lord Krishna delivered his inspirational messages to Arjuna which have been described in "Gita" as a dialogue between the two?
(*a*) Panipat (*b*) Kurukshetra
(*c*) Hodal (*d*) Thanesar

365. Which of the following towns of Haryana was the capital of Shrikantha Janapada during ancient times?
(*a*) Thanesar (*b*) Chandigarh
(*c*) Rohtak (*d*) Gurugram

366. The detailed description of which of the following ancient cities of Haryana is given in the account presented by Chinese pilgrim Huen Tsang?
(*a*) Rohtak (*b*) Ambala
(*c*) Thaneshwar (*d*) Bhiwani

367. Thaneshwar City of this state was at the pinnacle of its glory during
(*a*) Vardhan period (*b*) Gupta period
(*c*) Sunga period (*d*) Maurya period

368. The famous battle between the armies of Babur and Ibrahim Lodi in 1526 was fought at which of the following places in Haryana?
(*a*) Jhajjhar (*b*) Kurukshetra
(*c*) Rohtak (*d*) Panipat

369. Panipat town was given the status of District on
(*a*) 1 January, 1988 (*b*) 1 November, 1989
(*c*) 1 December, 1990 (*d*) 17 June, 1980

370. Rewari district was formed on
(*a*) 10 June, 1977 (*b*) 5 February, 1979
(*c*) 1 November, 1989 (*d*) 17 June, 1980

371. Hissar is the birth place of which of the following famous kings?
(*a*) Shershah Suri (*b*) Akbar
(*c*) Muhammad Tughlaq (*d*) Feroz Tughlaq

372. In which of the following towns has the largest cattle farm of Haryana?
(*a*) Narnaul (*b*) Hissar
(*c*) Panipat (*d*) Karnal

373. In 1354, who of the following famous ruler of the medieval India built the town of Hissar as a fort?
(*a*) Muhammad Tughlaq (*b*) Balban
(*c*) Feroz Tughlaq (*d*) Alauddin Khilji

374. During ancient times, Mahendragarh town of this state was known as
(*a*) Janauva (*b*) Karnpur
(*c*) Mahipgarh (*d*) Kanaud

375. Name the last king of Ballabhgarh who died as a martyr during freedom struggle of 1857.
(*a*) Nahar Singh (*b*) Vijay Singh
(*c*) Pratap Singh (*d*) Mahar Singh

376. Ballabhgarh town is included in which of the following districts of Haryana?
(*a*) Rohtak (*b*) Faridabad
(*c*) Gurugram (*d*) Karnal

377. Narwana Tehsil is situated in which of the following Districts of the state?
(*a*) Sirsa (*b*) Bhiwani
(*c*) Jind (*d*) Fatehabad

378. Grave of the famous Sultana Raziya of Ghulam dynasty is located in which of the following districts of the state?
(*a*) Kaithal (*b*) Gurugram
(*c*) Ambala (*d*) Faridabad

379. Which of the following towns of Haryana is termed as 'a big bowl of paddy' and 'Paris of Haryana'?
(*a*) Rohtak (*b*) Sonepat
(*c*) Faridabad (*d*) Karnal

380. In 1607, Faridabad town was built by
(*a*) Feroz Shah (*b*) Mubarakshah
(*c*) Baba Farid (*d*) Mansub Ali

381. During the Mahabharata period Sirsa was known as
(*a*) Shishira (*b*) Shairishkam
(*c*) Saurish (*d*) Sirisa

382. During ancient times, Gohana town of the state was known as
(*a*) Gawabh Bhawana (*b*) Gadhana
(*c*) Gapat Zamana (*d*) None of these

383. During ancient times, Bahadurgarh town of the state was known as
(*a*) Bahawalgarh (*b*) Shafirabad
(*c*) Sharfabad (*d*) Balramgarh

384. Britishers confiscated Bahadurgarh from Scindia King and handed it as a Jaghir to the brother of Nawab of Jhajjhar in
(*a*) 1800 AD (*b*) 1801 AD
(*c*) 1805 AD (*d*) 1803 AD

385. Which of the following towns of the state was built by a Rajput named Amba in the 14th century?
(*a*) Jhajjhar (*b*) Rohtak
(*c*) Ambala (*d*) Bhiwani

386. Abdur Rahman Khan who sacrificed his life during freedom struggle, hailed from which of the following towns of Haryana?
(*a*) Kurukshetra (*b*) Jhajjhar
(*c*) Farrukh Nagar (*d*) Rewari

387. Farrukh Nagar was built by which of the following Biloch rulers?
(*a*) Dalel Khan (Faujdar Khan)
(*b*) Shaffuddin Khan
(*c*) Badar Khan
(*d*) Jamaluddin Khan

388. Biloch ruler Dalel Khan (Faujdar Khan) built the town of Farrukh Nagar in the name of which of the following Emperors?
(*a*) Fakhruddin Ahmad (*b*) Farukh Ali
(*c*) Ferozshah Tughlaq (*d*) Farrukh Siyar

389. Great epic Mahabharata was composed by Maharshi Ved Vyas in which of the following towns of Haryana?
(*a*) Panipat (*b*) Rewari
(*c*) Kurukshetra (*d*) Hissar

390. Rise of Vardhan dynasty took place in which of the following towns of Haryana?
(a) Thanesar (Sthaneshwar)
(b) Rohtak
(c) Panipat
(d) Kurukshetra

391. In 1556, the famous battle between the forces of Akbar and Hemchandra (Hemu) of Rewari was fought at which of the following places in Haryana?
(a) Rewari (b) Jind
(c) Kurukshetra (d) Panipat

392. In 1761 the third battle of Panipat was fought between the forces of
(a) Babur and Ibrahim Lodi
(b) Akbar and Hemchandra (Hemu)
(c) Afghans and Marathas
(d) Britishers and Sikhs

393. The town of Panipat was under which of the following districts of Haryana till 31 October, 1989?
(a) Rewari (b) Ambala
(c) Karnal (d) Hissar

394. Which of the following districts of the state was included under Gurugram and Mahendragarh districts before 1989?
(a) Mahendragarh (b) Faridabad
(c) Jind (d) Rewari

395. Jind was given the status of district in
(a) 1966 (b) 1972
(c) 1968 (d) 1975

396. Which of the following districts of Haryana has its headquarters at Narnaul?
(a) Hissar (b) Faridabad
(c) Mahendragarh (d) Karnal

397. Who amongst the following did not play for Haryana in Ranji Trophy?
(a) Kapil Dev (b) Rajinder Goel
(c) Sarkar Talwar (d) Maninder Singh

398. When Hansi came into existence as the 23rd districts of Haryana?
(a) 2024 (b) 2023
(c) 2025 (d) 2022

399. During Mahabharat period, which of the following places was given by Raja Yudhishthir to his Guru Dronacharya as a gift?
(a) Gurugram village (b) Kaithal
(c) Hodal (d) Sirsa

400. Who was the Collector of Gurugram during the freedom struggle of 1857?
(a) Henry (b) Sir Helley
(c) John Marshall (d) Shri Ford

401. In 1858, which of the following districts of Haryana was included in Punjab?
(a) Faridabad (b) Gurugram
(c) Hissar (d) Mahendragarh

402. When Faridabad came into existence as the 12th district of Haryana?
(a) 15 August, 1970 (b) 02 August, 1979
(c) 26 January, 1979 (d) 8 March, 1982

403. Bahadurgarh town is included in which of the following districts of Haryana?
(a) Jhajjar (b) Karnal
(c) Yamun Nagar (d) Faridabad

404. The historical town Gohana is included in which of the following districts of Haryana?
(a) Panipat (b) Sirsa
(c) Sonepat (d) Rewari

405. In which year 'Sirsa' became a district?
(a) 1980 (b) 1975
(c) 1990 (d) 1995

406. Hodal Sub-division is located in which district of Haryana?
(a) Rohtak (b) Sonepat
(c) Palwal (d) Panipat

407. Tosham town of district Bhiwani was given the status of Sub-Division on
(a) 27 April, 1993 (b) 10 June, 1995
(c) 5 March, 1997 (d) 27 April, 1998

408. Which of the following famous temples is situated at historical town "Sadhaura" of district Yamuna Nagar?
(a) Manokamna Temple (b) Gagarwala Temple
(c) Toranwala Temple (d) All of these

409. In which of the following historical towns of Yamuna Nagar district, the Gurudwara of Buddhushah is situated which had helped Guru Govind Singh in the battle of Bhagani?
(a) Sadhaura (b) Radaur
(c) Bilaspur (d) Chhachhrauli

410. In ancient times Bahadurgarh town of Haryana was called as
(a) Charkhabad (b) Hasinpur
(c) Sharfabad (d) Betawabad

411. The historical town of Maham is situated in which of the following districts of the state?
(a) Bhiwani (b) Rohtak
(c) Yamuna Nagar (d) Jhajjhar

412. Maham town situated in district Rohtak was rebuilt by a person called Peshora of Kayastha (Baniya) Community in
(a) 1266 (b) 1295
(c) 1298 (d) 1299

413. Ailanabad town situated in district Sirsa was earlier known as
(a) Ailisabad (b) Chavipur
(c) Kalisabad (d) Khariyal

414. What was the earlier name of the historical town 'Raniyan' situated in district Sirsa?
(a) Rajabpur (b) Sajupur
(c) Rajipur (d) Ratipur

415. Which of the following towns situated in district Ambala was built by the King of Sirmour (Himachal Pradesh) Raja Laxmi Narayan?
(*a*) Barara (*b*) Mulana
(*c*) Narayangarh (*d*) Raipur Rani

416. By excavations done in which of the following historical towns of Sonepat district, earthen utensils belonging to Mahabharata period have been found?
(*a*) Rai (*b*) Kheri Gujjar
(*c*) Gankaur (*d*) Gohana

417. Mythological village Aadi Badri is situated in which of the following districts of Haryana?
(*a*) Yamuna Nagar (*b*) Bhiwani
(*c*) Sirsa (*d*) Rewari

418. Which of the following historical villages situated in district Yamuna Nagar is associated with King Santanu of the Mahabharata period?
(*a*) Chhachhrauli (*b*) Aadi Badri
(*c*) Basantar (*d*) None of these

419. At which of the following places Mazaar of Altaf Hussain Hali is located?
(*a*) Sonepat (*b*) Gurugram
(*c*) Panipat (*d*) Jind

420. Which of the following places was made a powerful centre of Afghan chiefs by Ahmadshah Abdali before the third battle of Panipat?
(*a*) Gharauda (*b*) Nilpe Khedi
(*c*) Asangh (*d*) Kunjpura

ANSWERS

1 (*d*)	**2** (*a*)	**3** (*b*)	**4** (*c*)	**5** (*a*)	**6** (*d*)	**7** (*b*)	**8** (*a*)	**9** (*c*)	**10** (*b*)
11 (*d*)	**12** (*d*)	**13** (*a*)	**14** (*c*)	**15** (*d*)	**16** (*a*)	**17** (*c*)	**18** (*b*)	**19** (*d*)	**20** (*a*)
21 (*d*)	**22** (*a*)	**23** (*c*)	**24** (*b*)	**25** (*a*)	**26** (*d*)	**27** (*d*)	**28** (*a*)	**29** (*c*)	**30** (*c*)
31 (*d*)	**32** (*c*)	**33** (*a*)	**34** (*b*)	**35** (*d*)	**36** (*d*)	**37** (*a*)	**38** (*c*)	**39** (*b*)	**40** (*c*)
41 (*d*)	**42** (*a*)	**43** (*c*)	**44** (*b*)	**45** (*a*)	**46** (*c*)	**47** (*d*)	**48** (*a*)	**49** (*c*)	**50** (*c*)
51 (*a*)	**52** (*c*)	**53** (*a*)	**54** (*b*)	**55** (*d*)	**56** (*b*)	**57** (*a*)	**58** (*c*)	**59** (*b*)	**60** (*d*)
61 (*d*)	**62** (*a*)	**63** (*c*)	**64** (*a*)	**65** (*b*)	**66** (*a*)	**67** (*a*)	**68** (*a*)	**69** (*b*)	**70** (*d*)
71 (*c*)	**72** (*a*)	**73** (*c*)	**74** (*b*)	**75** (*d*)	**76** (*c*)	**77** (*a*)	**78** (*c*)	**79** (*b*)	**80** (*d*)
81 (*b*)	**82** (*a*)	**83** (*d*)	**84** (*a*)	**85** (*c*)	**86** (*b*)	**87** (*d*)	**88** (*c*)	**89** (*a*)	**90** (*d*)
91 (*d*)	**92** (*a*)	**93** (*d*)	**94** (*a*)	**95** (*c*)	**96** (*b*)	**97** (*d*)	**98** (*a*)	**99** (*c*)	**100** (*b*)
101 (*d*)	**102** (*a*)	**103** (*a*)	**104** (*d*)	**105** (*a*)	**106** (*b*)	**107** (*c*)	**108** (*b*)	**109** (*d*)	**110** (*a*)
111 (*c*)	**112** (*b*)	**113** (*c*)	**114** (*a*)	**115** (*d*)	**116** (*b*)	**117** (*d*)	**118** (*c*)	**119** (*a*)	**120** (*b*)
121 (*c*)	**122** (*b*)	**123** (*c*)	**124** (*b*)	**125** (*d*)	**126** (*d*)	**127** (*a*)	**128** (*c*)	**129** (*d*)	**130** (*b*)
131 (*a*)	**132** (*c*)	**133** (*a*)	**134** (*b*)	**135** (*a*)	**136** (*b*)	**137** (*a*)	**138** (*d*)	**139** (*c*)	**140** (*b*)
141 (*a*)	**142** (*c*)	**143** (*b*)	**144** (*a*)	**145** (*d*)	**146** (*a*)	**147** (*c*)	**148** (*d*)	**149** (*c*)	**150** (*a*)
151 (*d*)	**152** (*c*)	**153** (*a*)	**154** (*a*)	**155** (*b*)	**156** (*a*)	**157** (*d*)	**158** (*b*)	**159** (*b*)	**160** (*d*)
161 (*a*)	**162** (*c*)	**163** (*a*)	**164** (*c*)	**165** (*b*)	**166** (*d*)	**167** (*c*)	**168** (*a*)	**169** (*b*)	**170** (*a*)

171 (*b*)	**172** (*d*)	**173** (*a*)	**174** (*a*)	**175** (*d*)	**176** (*b*)	**177** (*a*)	**178** (*b*)	**179** (*b*)	**180** (*c*)
181 (*a*)	**182** (*a*)	**183** (*c*)	**184** (*d*)	**185** (*b*)	**186** (*c*)	**187** (*d*)	**188** (*a*)	**189** (*c*)	**190** (*d*)
191 (*d*)	**192** (*a*)	**193** (*b*)	**194** (*b*)	**195** (*a*)	**196** (*c*)	**197** (*a*)	**198** (*d*)	**199** (*b*)	**200** (*a*)
201 (*d*)	**202** (*c*)	**203** (*a*)	**204** (*d*)	**205** (*a*)	**206** (*d*)	**207** (*c*)	**208** (*b*)	**209** (*b*)	**210** (*a*)
211 (*a*)	**212** (*a*)	**213** (*c*)	**214** (*d*)	**215** (*b*)	**216** (*a*)	**217** (*a*)	**218** (*b*)	**219** (*d*)	**220** (*a*)
221 (*b*)	**222** (*c*)	**223** (*b*)	**224** (*d*)	**225** (*a*)	**226** (*c*)	**227** (*a*)	**228** (*c*)	**229** (*b*)	**230** (*a*)
231 (*d*)	**232** (*a*)	**233** (*b*)	**234** (*a*)	**235** (*d*)	**236** (*d*)	**237** (*a*)	**238** (*c*)	**239** (*b*)	**240** (*d*)
241 (*d*)	**242** (*a*)	**243** (*c*)	**244** (*b*)	**245** (*a*)	**246** (*a*)	**247** (*c*)	**248** (*b*)	**249** (*a*)	**250** (*a*)
251 (*b*)	**252** (*a*)	**253** (*c*)	**254** (*b*)	**255** (*d*)	**256** (*c*)	**257** (*d*)	**258** (*d*)	**259** (*c*)	**260** (*a*)
261 (*b*)	**262** (*d*)	**263** (*c*)	**264** (*a*)	**265** (*b*)	**266** (*c*)	**267** (*a*)	**268** (*b*)	**269** (*a*)	**270** (*c*)
271 (*b*)	**272** (*b*)	**273** (*d*)	**274** (*c*)	**275** (*d*)	**276** (*d*)	**277** (*a*)	**278** (*a*)	**279** (*b*)	**280** (*a*)
281 (*c*)	**282** (*b*)	**283** (*a*)	**284** (*c*)	**285** (*b*)	**286** (*d*)	**287** (*c*)	**288** (*c*)	**289** (*a*)	**290** (*c*)
291 (*b*)	**292** (*a*)	**293** (*a*)	**294** (*b*)	**295** (*d*)	**296** (*a*)	**297** (*c*)	**298** (*d*)	**299** (*a*)	**300** (*b*)
301 (*a*)	**302** (*c*)	**303** (*d*)	**304** (*a*)	**305** (*c*)	**306** (*b*)	**307** (*c*)	**308** (*a*)	**309** (*c*)	**310** (*d*)
311 (*a*)	**312** (*b*)	**313** (*a*)	**314** (*b*)	**315** (*c*)	**316** (*d*)	**317** (*a*)	**318** (*c*)	**319** (*b*)	**320** (*a*)
321 (*c*)	**322** (*d*)	**323** (*a*)	**324** (*a*)	**325** (*d*)	**326** (*a*)	**327** (*b*)	**328** (*d*)	**329** (*c*)	**330** (*a*)
331 (*b*)	**332** (*d*)	**333** (*a*)	**334** (*c*)	**335** (*a*)	**336** (*b*)	**337** (*d*)	**338** (*a*)	**339** (*c*)	**340** (*a*)
341 (*c*)	**342** (*d*)	**343** (*c*)	**344** (*b*)	**345** (*a*)	**346** (*c*)	**347** (*d*)	**348** (*a*)	**349** (*d*)	**350** (*a*)
351 (*c*)	**352** (*d*)	**353** (*c*)	**354** (*b*)	**355** (*d*)	**356** (*d*)	**357** (*b*)	**358** (*c*)	**359** (*b*)	**360** (*d*)
361 (*c*)	**362** (*a*)	**363** (*c*)	**364** (*b*)	**365** (*a*)	**366** (*c*)	**367** (*a*)	**368** (*d*)	**369** (*b*)	**370** (*c*)
371 (*a*)	**372** (*b*)	**373** (*c*)	**374** (*d*)	**375** (*a*)	**376** (*b*)	**377** (*c*)	**378** (*a*)	**379** (*d*)	**380** (*c*)
381 (*b*)	**382** (*a*)	**383** (*c*)	**384** (*d*)	**385** (*c*)	**386** (*b*)	**387** (*a*)	**388** (*d*)	**389** (*c*)	**390** (*a*)
391 (*d*)	**392** (*c*)	**393** (*c*)	**394** (*d*)	**395** (*a*)	**396** (*c*)	**397** (*d*)	**398** (*c*)	**399** (*a*)	**400** (*d*)
401 (*b*)	**402** (*b*)	**403** (*a*)	**404** (*c*)	**405** (*b*)	**406** (*c*)	**407** (*a*)	**408** (*d*)	**409** (*a*)	**410** (*c*)
411 (*b*)	**412** (*a*)	**413** (*d*)	**414** (*a*)	**415** (*c*)	**416** (*b*)	**417** (*a*)	**418** (*c*)	**419** (*c*)	**420** (*d*)

❑ ❑ ❑